CENTRAL EUROPEAN JUDGES UNDER THE EUROPEAN INFLUENCE

The onset of the 2004 EU enlargement witnessed a number of predictions being made about the approaches, capacity and ability of Central European judges who were soon to join the Union. Optimistic voices, foreshadowing the deep transformative power that Europe was bound to exercise with respect to the judicial mentality and practice in the new Member States, were intertwined with gloomy pictures of post-Communist limited formalism and mechanical jurisprudence that could not be reformed, which were likely to undermine the very foundations of mutual trust and recognition the judicial system of the Union is built upon.

Ten years later, this volume revisits these predictions and critically assesses the evolution of Central European judicial mentality, institutions and constitutionality under the influence of the EU membership. Comparatively evaluating the situation in a number of Central European Member States in their socio-legal contexts, notably Poland, the Czech Republic, Slovakia, Hungary, Slovenia, Bulgaria and Romania, the volume offers unique insights into the process of (non) Europeanisation of national legal systems and cultures.

Volume 2 in the series EU Law in the Member States

EU Law in the Member States

Located at the cross-section between EU law, comparative law and socio-legal studies, *EU Law in the Member States* explores the interaction of EU law and national legal systems by analysing comparative evidence of the impact landmark EU measures—from CJEU decisions and secondary legislation to soft-law—have had across different Member States. The nature and operation of EU law has traditionally been analysed in a highly 'centralised' way, through the lenses of Brussels and Luxembourg, and in terms of the Treaty and its interpretation by the Court of Justice. Beneath this orthodoxy, however, lies the complex world of the genuine life of EU law in the Member States. Judicial and administrative practices across the Union's 28 Member States considerably qualify and sometimes even challenge the long-standing assumption that doctrines such as the direct effect and supremacy of EU law ensure a uniform and effective application of its provisions.

Each volume brings together leading academics, national experts and practitioners in order to draw conclusions both for EU law generally and the specific area in question on the basis of Member State reports and broader horizontal papers, and will be of interest to generalist EU lawyers and specialists in each field across the Member States. Academic audiences will benefit from the tight integration of national case studies and doctrinal analysis, whilst practitioners and policy makers will find systematically presented comparative evidence and commentary.

Series Editors
Jeremias Prassl
Michal Bobek

Volume 1: *Viking, Laval* and Beyond
Edited by Mark Freedland and Jeremias Prassl

Volume 2: Central European Judges under the European Influence:
The Transformative Power of the EU Revisited
Edited by Michal Bobek

Volume 3: European Air Passenger Rights, Ten Years On
Edited by Jeremias Prassl and Michal Bobek

Central European Judges Under the European Influence

The Transformative Power of the EU Revisited

Edited by Michal Bobek

·HART·
PUBLISHING
OXFORD AND PORTLAND, OREGON
2017

Hart Publishing

An imprint of Bloomsbury Publishing Plc

Hart Publishing Ltd	Bloomsbury Publishing Plc
Kemp House	50 Bedford Square
Chawley Park	London
Cumnor Hill	WC1B 3DP
Oxford OX2 9PH	UK
UK	

www.hartpub.co.uk
www.bloomsbury.com

Published in North America (US and Canada) by
Hart Publishing
c/o International Specialized Book Services
920 NE 58th Avenue, Suite 300
Portland, OR 97213-3786
USA

www.isbs.com

**HART PUBLISHING, the Hart/Stag logo, BLOOMSBURY and the
Diana logo are trademarks of Bloomsbury Publishing Plc**

First published in hardback, 2015
Paperback edition, 2017

© The Editors and Contributors severally 2015

Cover photograph: © Michal Mazanec 2015

British Library Cataloguing-in-Publication Data
A catalogue record for this book is available from the British Library.

ISBN: PB: 978-1-50991-836-2
HB: 978-1-84946-774-2

Typeset by Compuscript Ltd, Shannon
Printed and bound in Great Britain by
Lightning Source UK Ltd

To find out more about our authors and books visit www.hartpublishing.co.uk. Here you will
find extracts, author information, details of forthcoming events and the option to sign up for our
newsletters.

CONTENTS

Part II: Institutions and Procedures

Part III: Constitutional Courts

NOTES ON CONTRIBUTORS

Matej Avbelj is Associate Professor of European Law and Dean at the Graduate School of Government and European Studies, Kranj, Slovenia.

Mátyás Bencze is a former judge, currently Associate Professor of Law at the University of Debrecen, Hungary and research fellow at the Institute for Legal Studies of the Hungarian Academy of Sciences Centre for Social Sciences.

Erhard Blankenburg is Emeritus Professor for Sociology of Law at the Vrije Universiteit Amsterdam.

Michal Bobek is Professor of European Law at the College of Europe, Bruges, and research fellow at the Oxford University Institute of European and Comparative Law.

Jernej Letnar Černič is Assistant Professor of Law, Graduate School of Government and European Studies, Kranj, Slovenia.

Péter Cserne is Senior Lecturer in Law at the University of Hull, United Kingdom.

Aleš Galič is Professor of Civil Procedure and European Civil Procedure, University of Ljubljana.

Tomasz Tadeusz Koncewicz is Professor and Director of the Department of European and Comparative Law at the University of Gdansk and Advocate at the Polish Bar. In 2015–2016, he is Fulbright Visiting Professor at Berkeley Law School.

David Kosař is Assistant Professor at the Law Faculty Masaryk University in Brno.

Alexander Kornezov is legal secretary at the Court of Justice of the EU, and Associate Professor of EU Law at the Law Institute of the Bulgarian Academy of Sciences.

András György Kovács is administrative judge (head of chamber) at the Hungarian Supreme Court.

Zdeněk Kühn is Associate Professor of Jurisprudence at the Charles University Law School and judge at the Supreme Administrative Court of the Czech Republic.

Rafał Mańko is policy analyst (specialising in European private law) at the European Parliamentary Research Service, Brussels, and external fellow at the Centre for the Study of European Contract Law, University of Amsterdam.

Marcin Matczak is Associate Professor at the University of Warsaw and a partner in DZP, one of the biggest Polish law firms.

Hans-W Micklitz is Professor for Economic Law at the European University Institute in Florence.

Nina Półtorak is Professor of Jagiellonian University in Krakow, and judge, Head of the European Law Department at the Supreme Administrative Court of Poland.

Jiří Přibáň is Professor of Law at Cardiff University Law School, United Kingdom.

Marek Safjan is judge at the Court of Justice and former President of the Polish Constitutional Tribunal.

Allan F Tatham is Lecturer in EU Law at the Facultad de Derecho, Universidad CEU San Pablo, Madrid, and former Assistant Professor, Faculty of Law and Political Sciences, Pázmány Péter Catholic University, Budapest, Hungary.

Marton Varju is senior research fellow at the Hungarian Academy of Sciences, Centre for Social Sciences, Budapest.

Boštjan Zalar is senior High Court judge at the Administrative Court of the Republic of Slovenia and Professor at the University of Ljubljana.

Jan Zobec is judge at the Constitutional Court of Republic of Slovenia.

LIST OF ABBREVIATIONS

AB	Alkotmánybíróság (Constitutional Court, Hungary)
ABH	Alkotmánybíróság Határozatai (Collection of Decisions of the Constitutional Court, Hungary)
AG	Advocate General
BVerfG	Bundesverfassungsgericht (Federal Constitutional Court, Germany)
BVerfGE	Entscheidungen des Bundesverfassungsgerichts (Collection of Decisions of the Federal Constitutional Court, Germany)
CCJE	Consultative Council of European Judges
CE	Central Europe
CEE	Central and Eastern Europe
CFI	Court of First Instance
CJEU	Court of Justice of the European Union
CoE	Council of Europe
Convention	European Convention on Human Rights
CSM	Consiglio superiore della magistratura (Superior Council of the Judiciary, Italy)
Curia	Supreme Court of Hungary
ECJ	(European) Court of Justice
ECHR	European Convention on Human Rights
ECLI	European Case Law Identifier
ECR	European Court Reports
ECtHR	European Court of Human Rights
EFTA	European Free Trade Area
ENCJ	European Network of Councils for the Judiciary
EP	European Parliament
EU	European Union
MK	Magyar Közlöny (Official Journal, Hungary)
NS	Nejvyšší soud (Supreme Court, Czech Republic)
NSA	Naczelny Sąd Administracyjny (Supreme Administrative Court, Poland)
NSS	Nejvyšší správní soud (Supreme Administrative Court, Czech Republic)
GC	General Court of the European Union
KS	Konstitutsionen sad (Constitutional Court, Bulgaria)
OJ	Official Journal of the European Union

LB	Legfelsőbb Bíróság (Supreme Court before 01 January 2012, Hungary)
OTK ZU	Orzecznictwo Trybunału Konstytucyjnego Zbiór Urzędowy (Collection of Decisions of the Constitutional Tribunal, Poland)
TK	Trybunał Konstytucyjny (Constitutional Tribunal, Poland)
TEC	Treaty Establishing the European Community
TEU	Treaty on the European Union
TFEU	Treaty on the Functioning of the European Union
SN	Sąd Najwyższy (Supreme Court, Poland)
ÚS	Ústavní soud (Constitutional Court, Czech Republic)
US	Ustavno sodišče (Constitutional Court, Slovenia)
VS	Vrhovno sodišče (Supreme Court, Slovenia)
VAS	Varhoven administrativen sad (the Supreme Administrative Court, Bulgaria)
VfGH	Verfassungsgerichtshof (Constitutional Court, Austria)
VKS	Varhoven kasatsionen sad (Supreme Court of Cassation, Bulgaria)

Prologue: The Westernisation of the East and the Easternisation of the West

HANS-W MICKLITZ

I. Paying Tribute to Eastern Enlargement

When Michal Bobek asked me to write a prologue I was immediately excited to accept.[1] What a wonderful topic and still not really at the forefront of academic research! Not much attention is devoted, in particular by lawyers—although there are exceptions—to the huge transfer of rules from the West to the East.[2] This is different with political scientists.[3] I call it Westernisation of the new Member States and the candidates. Conversely, the retransfer from the East to the West might be called the Easternisation of the West. This book, or perhaps it is much more appropriate to speak of a 'project', is providing a major contribution to the discussion. It is filling a big gap and at the same time it is disclosing how little we know about the mutual process of 'Westernisation' and 'Easternisation'.

The project is focusing on the judges and the judiciaries in the Central and Eastern European (CEE) countries, on the transformative power of the EU, of a supranational body, to change or even to create national democratic institutions. It is not meant to deal with particular branches of the law, constitutional law, administrative law or private law, although the contributions reflect the differences. More importantly, it is not aimed at analysing the interplay and potential differences between the judiciary and the executive. To put it the other way round: It is not looking into the transformation of ministries or executive agencies. The project is 'only' looking into the judiciary in the CEE, not paying attention to the Baltic States or to the Western Balkan. This is already complicated enough.

---

[1] I would like to thank Michal Bobek for enticing me and encouraging me over the last couple of months to write the prologue and my colleague and friend Thomas Roethe for his comments. The responsibility remains mine alone.
[2] N Reich, 'Transformation of Contract Law and Civil Justice in the New EU Member Countries: The Example of the Baltic States, Hungary and Poland' in F Cafaggi (ed), *The Institutional Framework of European Private Law* (Oxford University Press, 2006) 271; See also Tartu Conference on Recent Development in European Private Law, *Juridica International*, Law Review University of Tartu, 2008.
[3] B Laszlo and G McDermott, 'Governance of Transnational Regulatory Integration and Development' in B Laszlo and G McDermott (eds), *Levelling Playing Fields: Transnational Regulatory Integration and Institutional Change in Emerging Markets* (Oxford University Press, 2014).

My reading and my understanding of the various contributions, however, is slightly different. They report on processes for which the CEE countries are serving as a paradigmatic example. They speak of judges and courts, but the stories told are stories on the society, on us as citizens, on identities, on cultures and traditions, on the transformation of political and legal systems; they report on the making and the transformation of democracies, of markets, of persons, more specifically on transformations of Constitutions, of our legal orders, of the transformation of administrative law, of private law, of our democratic institutions, of ministries, agencies and of peoples. It is in this sense that I would like the learned reader to understand my 'prologue'. Michal Bobek encouraged me to write as a 'Wessi' (ie a 'West German', or, more broadly, a person from the pre-1989 West) on the 'Ossi' (ie an 'East German', or, more broadly, a person from the former East). This means looking at the transformative power of the EU through western eyes. My prologue is therefore by definition 'subjective'. I do not claim to provide hard evidence for each and every argument I am presenting. An 'Ossi' would have certainly written a very different prologue in tone and substance.

I accept being treated as a 'Wessi', although a first question, related to the project, is whether we are life long 'Wessis' and 'Ossis'. How could those 'Ossi' be categorised, who moved from the East to the West and made their career in the West—which happens quite often—or from the West to the East—which happens less often. Let us recall that most of what has been written on the CEE countries is flowing from the pen of East European academics, who moved to the West or spent at least many years in the West. Be that as it may—this little hint might suffice for demonstrating how unsafe and unstable the ground is, on which these categorisations are standing.

II. The Wessi Discovering the East

I moved to Berlin in 1990. These were the times of euphoria and disenchantment, the dream of Berlin becoming a world city and then the reality shock. German unification brought together two worlds. The wall was down but the border remained visible and sensible. I am a Wessi. I grew up in West Germany, though my parents and grandparents had come from Poland and the Czech Republic. I felt an affinity towards the East, which, translated into the mind of an academic, meant that I felt tempted to discover an under-researched social and legal world. It is easy to argue that access to the East before the fall of the wall was difficult for a Wessi. The truth of the matter is that there was also a long lasting disinterest. The wall in the back offered the opportunity to look to the west without any risk, whilst freeing from the need to look (research) to the east. After 1989 it was not only technically possible—the borders were open—but it was socially and politically unavoidable to embark onto the unknown journey into the Eastern reality, into countries 'in transition', countries that were supposed to achieve three things at once: the building of a democratic Constitution; the building of a capitalist market (it became possible to use that word without being blamed for being a communist who would be recommended to move to the other side of the wall);[4] and the building of an open civil society.[5]

A. My/Our Approach to Undertaking Research

Together with my colleague and friend Thomas Roethe,[6] a sociologist, we started empirical studies first in Wessi–Ossi-Land (Germany),[7] then in the CEE countries[8] and not only there. Later we included the Western Balkan[9] and the Baltic States.[10] All this was possible not only thanks to the generous support from various funding organisations (foundations, governments, the European Commission), but, most of all, due to the readiness and the eagerness of the citizens in what later became the new Member States to speak to us Wessis, to accept that the interview was recorded and subject to analysis.

The approach chosen was socio-legal, via qualitative interviews, via reconstructing cases and litigation in the CEE countries. The 'consumer' formed the focus of our interest. At first hand this sounds narrow, but in socio-legal research it opens pathways to the society and the economy. We studied the transformation of the citizen from an object of a socialist state to an autonomous self-responsible consumer in the western capitalist meaning. By the same token, we implicitly studied the transformation of a planned economy to a market economy, more explicitly the role of the European Union and the Member States in the transformation; the huge transfer of rules from the West to the East; the impact of these new rules on the old and more and more the practical importance of these rules; their application through the competent enforcement authorities or through newly established dispute settlement fora for products and types of litigation, which did not exist before.

---

[4] This was a wide spread argument in West Germany before the fall of the Berlin Wall, in particular during the rise of the leftist movement in the late 1960s until the 1980s.

[5] First version H-W Micklitz, 'Divergente Ausgangsbedingungen des Verbraucherrechts in West und Ost' in H-W Micklitz (ed), *Rechtseinheit oder Rechtsvielfalt in Europa?* (Nomos, 1996) 3–22; for a more developed version, H-W Micklitz, 'Verbraucherschutz West versus Ost—Kompatibilisierungsmöglichkeiten in der Europäischen Gemeinschaft—Einige Vorüberlegungen' in H Heiss (ed), *Brückenschlag zwischen den Rechtskulturen des Ostseeraums* (Mohr Siebeck, 2001) 137–82.

[6] T Roethe, *Arbeiten wie bei Honecker, Leben wie bei Kohl* (Eichborn, 1994) and *Der Verbraucher—Rechtssoziologische Betrachtungen* (Nomos, 2014).

[7] H-W Micklitz, C Rößler and T Roethe, *Irreführende/unlautere Werbung und kollektiver Schadensersatz—Eine Pilotstudie im Land Brandenburg*, Manuscript (1993) unpublished, on file with author.

[8] H-W Micklitz, 'Rechtseinheit oder Rechtsvielfalt in Europa?—Zur Rolle und Funktion des Verbraucherrechts in den MOE-Staaten und in der EG' (Band 1 der Schriftenreihe des Instituts für Europäisches Wirtschafts- und Verbraucherrecht 1996).

[9] M Karanikic, H-W Micklitz, and N Reich, *Modernising Consumer Law—The Experience of the Western Balkan* (Nomos, 2012).

[10] H-W Micklitz and T Roethe, 'Produktsicherheit und Marktüberwachung im Ostseeraum—Rechtsrahmen und Vollzugspraxis' (VIEW Schriftenreihe, Band 26, 2008).

When products are scarce, when an order takes 10 years to be executed, the world's best remedies and guarantees remain law in the books.[11] A complaint culture existed during communist times but the addressee of the complaint was the communist party as the ultimate authority.[12] New institutions thus had to be built, which had to handle the complaints, the competent staff had to be recruited and trained. This holds true for each and every institution involved in rule application in democratic societies, consumer organisations, consumer agencies and dispute settlement bodies, each burdened with their particular legacy.[13] Consumer organisations should in theory grow out of the middle of society. In the CEE countries, however, they were often initiated by the respective state and sponsored to a greater or more often lesser extent by it. The European Commission and western development aid agencies were particularly committed to building Non-Governmental Organisations in all fields of the new societies, all in all with little success. Active statutory consumer agencies left little room for the development of consumer organisations—out of the civil society. The statutory agencies were looking after the interests of the new consumers, not only the collective interests but in the best communist tradition also after the individual interests. The strong involvement of statutory agencies in the enforcement of individual rights, *in concreto* the intervention of statutory bodies in bilateral contractual relations to the benefit of consumers, irritated me strongly. Why could statutory agencies play such a prominent role after the break down of communism? The ministries and socialist institutions, from which the statutory agencies emanated, were established already in the 1970s to exercise and monitor the quality of consumer products in particular those which were meant to be exported from the East to the West. In a market society there is no room for quality control at least in principle, setting health and safety issues aside.[14] Quality is subject to competition and not to statutory regulation. To some extent, these institutions were no longer needed. They found, however, in the emerging consumer policy—emerging as it was strongly promoted by the EU—a new field of activity that helped them to survive. And courts? Courts were not really on the agenda for civil litigation between private parties, certainly not with regard to business-to-consumer litigation. Here conflicts were left to dispute settlement bodies outside courts, either originating from socialist times or newly established under pressure from the European Union. This brings me to the prominent role of the EU.

---

[11] This was the fatal destiny of the new *Zivilgesetzbuch* of the GDR, the German Democratic Republic. The book contained wonderful rules on guarantees and remedies, like so many other East German laws and regulations in the field of consumer protection, but they were all largely useless in practice.

[12] I Markovits, *Gerechtigkeit in Lüritz: Eine Ostdeutsche Rechtsgeschichte* (CH Beck, 2006).

[13] A Barkadjivea et al, 'Europeanization of Private Law in Central and Eastern Europe Countries (CEECS)', Preliminary Findings and Research Agenda (EUI Working Papers Law No 2010/15).

[14] See on the path dependency of institutions, A Bakardijeva-Engelbrekt, 'The Impact of EU Enlargement on Private Law Governance in Central and Eastern Europe: The Case of Consumer Protection' in F Cafaggi and H Muir-Watt (eds), *Making European Private Law: Governance Design* (Edward Elgar, 2009) 98.

B. On the Role of the European Union

The EU and the European Commission were omnipresent. European Regulations and European Directives had to be implemented. Whole ministries were transformed in law-writing and law-making institutions, which were rubber stamped by national parliaments. What else could they do? After having applied for EU accession, the candidate countries had to obey by the European rules, they had to accept what the European Union imposed on them. There was no leeway for negotiations. It was a take it or leave it situation, just like a consumer has to accept the standard terms from the seller if he wants to have the products. Whole countries had to accept rules that were elaborated in a different context, in an EU of six, 9, 12 or 15 Member States, for countries with a relatively homogeneous economy and society.[15]

It suffices to study the export of consumer legislation from the West to the East to understand the overall implications for the envisaged and expected transformation of the legal and political systems. Politics, the old Member States and the European Commission, were full of 'good will'. The new Member States should enjoy the same standard of protection as their Western counterparts. There was no reflection on whether and to what extent the recipient countries, the new Member States and the remaining candidates were able to digest the huge transfer of legal rules. There was no discussion on 'legal transplants',[16] no discussion on legal cultures and traditions, no reference and reflection to the colonial past where Western European States had transferred their legal systems to South America, to Africa and to Asia. This is not to say that both events can be put on an equal footing. The new Member States applied to the European Union, whereas the colonies were conquered.[17] The foundational concept of 'Integration through Law', of building Europe through law, was simply extended towards the East. The common European legal culture, revitalised after the Second World War, to merge together the six legal orders of the founding members should now encompass 28 legal orders. The old Member States of the West were certainly driven by best intentions, by the political will of 'this time we get it right'.[18]

In the accession process, the European Commission was entirely focused on receiving progress reports, progress meant implementation of this and that set

---

[15] R Knieper, 'Möglichkeiten und Grenzen der Verpflanzbarkeit von Recht' (2008) 72 *Rabels Zeitschrift* 88.

[16] There is an abundant literature on legal transplants. For a comprehensive discussion of the different positions V Perju, 'Constitutional Transplants, Borrowing and Migration' in M Rosenfeld and A Sajó (eds), *The Oxford Handbook of Comparative Constitutional Law* (Oxford University Press, 2013) 1304.

[17] T Duve, 'Von der Europäischen Rechtsgeschichte zu einer Rechtsgeschichte Europas in global-historischer Perspektive', Max Planck Institute for European Legal History research paper series, No 2012/01, shortened version in English published in European Legal History Global Perspectives Max Planck Institute for European Legal History, research paper series No 2013/06.

[18] K Nicolaidis, 'The Idea of European Democracy' in J Dickson and P Eleftheriadis (eds), *The Philosophical Foundations of European Union Law* (Oxford University Press, 2012) 247, 255.

of EU rules into the national law. How these laws could be implemented and by whom was largely set apart, maybe with the exception of EU and development aid agencies (eg USAID (United States Agency for International Development), GIZ (*Deutsche Gesellschaft für Internationale Zusammenarbeit*)) sponsored training programmes. It was left to the candidate states to provide for the necessary institutional infrastructure, for building competent agencies, which follow the rule of the law and not politically motivated decisions by the political party, for having an independent and competent judiciary, able to handle and interpret the national and the implemented EU law. Only in the united Germany, judges and legal academics were dismissed before they were allowed to re-apply for their former position. Only few succeeded. No similar cleansing can be reported from any other new Member State. Here the institutions (ministries and agencies), the executive and the courts, the administrative agents and the judges, were treated as if they have always been competent, or as if they have learned quasi overnight how to apply and how to enforce the law matching the requirements of a Western democratic society.[19] It is true the Member States and the European Commission were gradually realising the policy deficit. There is little that can be done politically through the EU and/or the old Member States to cope with institutional deficits in the design, equipment and expertise of ministries, agencies and courts in the new Member States. All that remains is the infringement procedure. This looks different with regards to the still remaining candidates, in particular from the Western Balkan, which have to demonstrate that competent institutions are available which are able to enforce the (EU) law.

C. On the Relevance of the Old Times

Is all this still relevant 25 years after the fall of the Berlin Wall, in the year 2015? I am deeply convinced that it indeed is. We cannot understand the transformative power of the EU, its strengths and its weaknesses, its ambiguities, if we do not look deeper into the impact the EU had on democratic institutions, on substantive law, on the courts and the executive. There is even more. We can learn to understand the opportunities and the limits of a European integration process, which is so much relying on law, on legal systems and on the judiciary which is one of the key actors—outside the executive—in charge of holding the two legal systems, the national and the European, together. Furthermore, within the national domain, it must also ensure the compatibility of the national–national (the unaffected national law) and the national–Europeanised (the national law which has been subject to Europeanisation). This is even more so as the enlargement process has not yet come to an end. There are still candidates from the Western Balkan, the unsolved application of Turkey to become a member, and the wish of Georgia and the Ukraine to join the EU.

---

[19] In the research referred to in nn 3–8, we put particular emphasis on interviewing administrative agents and agencies, on learning and trying to understand.

III. A Wessi's View 25 Years Later

With the mandate I got, I feel encouraged to refer to my research and my observations. When we dive deeper into what unites and what separates us, the West and the East, we cannot look into the legal systems alone. That is why I take the freedom to start with more general observations which reach beyond law and legal institutions, although our laws are part of these external values of the law. All this just serves the purpose of underpinning the importance of the 'project' on the transformative power of the EU, on the need to understand the foundations of the law, in the West and in the East, in a Europe composed of West and East, of old and new Member States, of old democracies (or younger Western democracies established after the Second World War) and of new democracies, the former socialist countries.

A. The Broader Picture

I was in Berlin in order to join the big party on the 9 November 2014. Until today I can discover quite easily where the person I am talking to is coming from, whether he or she is a 'Wessi' or an 'Ossi'. How? I do not really know, but a lot has to do with politics, when it comes to hot political issues, subject to controversy in the German society. Can this experience be generalised, not turned upside down within united Germany, but in the relationship between the Western Europeans and the Eastern Europeans, who do not like to be called Easterners? They speak of themselves as coming from the 'Middle' of Europe and the 'East'—Middle and Eastern European countries.

Do Ossis, broadly understood as all those being born and/or living on the other side of the Berlin Wall in the CEE countries, share the same feeling? Do they, or shall I say do 'you' realise immediately whether 'you' are talking to somebody from a former socialist country or somebody from an older capitalist country? I deliberately do not mean the degree to which houses are refurbished or streets are redone. I mean how people talk and speak to each other and to you, with what sentiment, with what kind of rationality on politics, on migration, on EU enlargement, on the Euro-crisis? These are difficult and sensitive issues in light of the still relatively newly gained national identity. Why do we know so little about our neighbours in the East? The EU and more specifically the European Commission is not investing into—what I would call—sociological or in my field socio-legal research. We are overwhelmed with statistics, but we have to rely on anecdotal evidence, poetry or newspapers if we want to get a deeper insight into our societies.[20]

---

[20] I have not given up to convincing my colleague Thomas Roethe to write a book on East and West Germany, 25 years after or so, an update on his book on '*Leben wie bei Kohl und Arbeiten wie Honecker*' (n 6).

Let us assume for a moment that there are such differences, let us say that a German is able to identify that his conversation partner is coming from Poland, after a couple of sentences, or that the Pole can easily realise that he is speaking and talking to a German. Is this only a matter of generation—are 'Besser-Wessis' (this term has been coined in East Germany referring to the Wessis who know everything better)—vanishing away? Is the alienation between West and East decreasing and dissolving with the older (my) generations dying out? *Wächst hier zusammen, was zusammen gehört?*—to use the words of Willi Brandt on his speech at the Rathaus Schöneberg?[21] Again can this be generalised? Are we able to develop in Europe, perhaps not a common language, although we have English as *lingua franca*, but a common identity, a common society and a common European culture, a legal culture? I think yes and no. I do not follow P Legrand[22] in his analysis that European legal cultures are not converging. I do believe that there is room for a shared European legal culture, even for a shared European identity, maybe even for a shared European society. However at the same time, each of us, each nation has its own deeply engrained habits and patterns, which are also reflected in law.[23] But can we stop here? Is there a common culture which all Europeans share, wherever they come from? Or will there be an overarching common European legal culture with persisting differences in reading, understanding and processing these normative settings due to long surviving habits and patterns of meaning, which may resist the unification of Western and Eastern thinking?

The divide between Eastern and Western Europe is not a product of the Second World War alone. For the sake of the argument, however, let us look into the cultural impact of the cleavage between the two worlds. The old post war elite in the West invested tremendously into re-vitalising the culture heritage of old Europe, for example Roman law.[24] There is much debate on whether there is such a thing

---

[21] ['Her is growing together something which belongs together (the two parts of Germany)']. Although it seems as if he has not used these words and that they were only put into his mouth afterwards, see online at <www.faz.net/aktuell/politik/25-jahre-mauerfall/willy-brandts-zitat-zum-mauerfall-ist-wesentlich-aelter-13204476-p2.html>.

[22] 'European Legal Systems are not Converging' (1996) 52 *International and Comparative Law Quarterly* 45.

[23] H-W Micklitz, 'The (Un)-Systematics of (private) Law as an Element of European Legal Culture' in G Helleringer and K Purnhagen (eds), *Towards a European Legal Culture* (Beck/Hart Publishing/Nomos, 2014) 81–115.

[24] F Wieacker, *Voraussetzungen europäischer Rechtskultur* (Verlag Göttinger Tageblatt, 1985) in English translated by E Bodenheimer and published as 'Foundations of European Legal Culture' (1990) 38 *American Journal of Comparative law* 1; F Wieacker belonged to the founding fathers of the European legal culture, in the words of K Tuori:

[T]he exiles and the outcasts, those who were driven from their posts (Fritz Schulz, Fritz Pringsheim, Paul Koschacker) and the collaborators and bystanders, who either thrived in the new circumstances under the Nazis or managed to remain outside controversies (Franz Wieacker and Helmut Coing).

In K Tuori, Reinventing the Foundations of European Legal Culture 1934–1964, ERC Start Grant 2013–2018; see <http://blogs.helsinki.fi/found-law/researchers/kaius-tuori>; same author, *Lawyers and Savages: Ancient History and Legal Realism in the Making of Legal Anthropology* (Routledge, 2014).

as a Western European legal culture, whether it ever existed. Speaking for myself, I felt deeply European when I returned from a longer overseas trip to good old Europe. Does this feeling encompass the CEE countries? I do not know. I have not really had the chance for such a self-test.

But what about the East Europeans, all those who share a common communist heritage? Do they share a feeling of commonality, having suffered from the same tort, is there a common denominator, which could be broken down to the legal system, legal traditions, values, principles or the like, on the role and use of the law?[25] Is there a cultural clash between East and West? The new Member States were keen to insist on the particularities of their countries, they were keen to negotiate individually with the European Commission, instead of trying to build collective bargaining power. The European Commission, however, did not shy away from its one-size fits all approach. Did this help to escape the common communist heritage and even the pre-war diversities between these countries? But where is the law, where is the judiciary and where is the project? Are these questions and observations relevant for the Westernisation of the East and the Easternisation of the West?

B. On Westernisation

Has the Westernisation of former socialist countries, Westernisation being understood as transformation of the society, transformation of the legal order, been a 'success'? What does 'success' mean, for a legal order and for legal institutions? A merger of the old legal system with the new one, a successful transplant? A convergence of the old with the new legal system? From our own research in consumer law, we often came to the conclusion that the westernised imposed consumer law is standing apart from the old (instead of system codifications).[26] However, I wonder whether such a discourse is not overtly simplistic and misleading. Is it not here that we have to give up the language of Wessi versus Ossi, West versus East or East versus West? Can it not be that some CEE countries are much closer to the Western legal order than others? Can it not be that some Western Member States and some Eastern Member States have more in common than they have with their Western, respectively Eastern counterparts? I will deliberately abstain from mentioning countries as this might be too sensitive.

C. On Easternisation

If any, there has been research on the Westernisation, on the impact of the EU enlargement on the Eastern legal systems and societies. However, the opposite perspective, the Easternisation of the Western legal systems is still mainly a black spot.

---

[25] J Roth, *Radetzkymarsch* (first published 1932) shows the differences in the Austria Empire.

[26] After decades of discussion, The Czech Republic and Hungary have revised their civil codes—see L Tichy, 'Tschechisches ZGB' (2014) *Zeitschrift für Europaisches Privatrecht* 467.

Here are very uncomfortable questions calling for answers. In consumer law they are all crystallised. Eastern European countries have started to adopt consumer law since the 1980s, meaning long before the fall of the Berlin Wall. The certainly more modest but nevertheless existent consumer society yielded the need for the adoption of appropriate rules, for instance in the field of consumer guarantees.[27] The following situation thus emerged: On the one hand there was the old socialist consumer law, on the other the Western welfare-state consumer law and in the middle so to say the EU consumer law. The deeper question is what they have in common, the socialist consumer law and the welfare-state consumer law and where and how the EU consumer law, with its shift from consumer *protection* law to consumer law (without protection) could and should be located.[28] Is there a common authoritarian element which unites the three different legal orders? To what extent has the Eastern socialist thinking influenced the Western welfare-state consumer law? The question can easily be generalised. The West has imposed via the EU some 80,000 pages of Western based EU law to the East. This does not mean, however, that there is no backflow. The mechanism via which the backflow is organised and is becoming visible and subject to research is the preliminary reference procedure. This allows Eastern European courts to refer questions to the European Court of Justice (ECJ) that emerge in the context of their own legal order and in the way the EU law has been implemented into their national legal systems.

D. East/West Exchange in the Preliminary Reference Procedure

By its request for a preliminary ruling in *Macinsky*,[29] the Okresný súd Prešov (Prešov District Court, Slovakia) sought guidance as to whether the Slovak rules allowing a creditor to obtain payment of a debt by means of an out-of-court procedure whereby its secured interest over the debtor's assets is enforced ('the procedure at issue') are compatible with, inter alia, Directive 93/13/EEC on unfair terms in consumer contracts. The details of the case are of no relevance in the context. What matters, however, is that Advocate-General Wahl is heavily struggling with understanding the Slovak procedural rules which form the background to the case. He writes:

> I must confess that I have not fully understood how it is that, under Slovak procedural law, the Okresný súd Prešov remains seised, given the fact that the auction will no longer go ahead and regardless of the risk that Dražby might resume the procedure at issue.[30]

---

[27] G Howells and H-W Micklitz, *Report on Consumer Sales and Associated Guarantees in T en CEECS* (Consumer Institutions and Consumer Policy Programme (CICPP), Louvain-la-Neuve, Centre de Droit de la Consommation 1999).

[28] H-W Micklitz, 'The Expulsion of the Concept of Protection from the Consumer Law and the Return of Social Elements in the Civil Law—A Bittersweet Polemic' (2012) EUI Working Paper 2012/03, also in (2012) 35 *Journal of Consumer Policy* 283.

[29] Case C-482/12 *Peter Macinský Eva Macinská v Getfin sro Financreal sro*, http://eur-lex.europa.eu/legal-content/EN/TXT/HTML/?uri=CELEX:62012CB0482&qid=1436288662632&from=PL.

[30] Opinion of AG N Wahl of 21 November 2013, para 35.

Over the years I have read many opinions and many ECJ judgments, but to my knowledge it is extremely unusual (to say the least) for Advocates-General to openly write 'I do not understand the law of the country where the references are coming from'. Personally I agree with AG Wahl, I share his analysis and his feelings. What is happening when an Advocate-General is asked to write an opinion and does so although he does not understand the law of the Member State? This is by far not the only case, where it is near to impossible to understand the national law.

Invitel[31] belongs to the same category. AG Trstenjak has written a ground breaking opinion on the remedy of injunctions, which was largely approved by the ECJ.[32] However, neither the opinion nor the judgment reveals the particular background of the case, which still bears a socialist flavour. This is true with regard to the substance of the conflict, but even more so with regard to the role of the Hungarian consumer authority which is the driving force behind the litigation and the reference. In short, an innocent Western lawyer will find useful guidance on the autonomous interpretation of what an action for injunction might imply. But he or she will totally miss the particular factual, economic and political background. We, meaning Thomas Roethe, Betül Kas and myself,[33] had to invest considerable energy to re-construct the case and to highlight the interplay between the national and the EU law. It seems as if the opinion and the judgment are hanging in the air, rather disconnected from the Hungarian legal system. This is exactly the situation AG Wahl was struggling with in *Macinsky*.

Let me conclude again with a question: Would the opinion in *Macinsky* or in *Invitel* or in other cases have looked different, if the Advocate-General had come from the referring court with a deeper understanding of the respective Slovak and Hungarian legal order?[34] We do not know whether at least with regard to the judgements of the ECJ, the deficit is remedied in the deliberations where the judges coming from the respective countries could interfere to compensate for the deficient understanding. One might argue that comparable consequences may be observed in references from Western courts. The national court may not find the answer it was looking for or the guidance provided by the ECJ might be of limited value or might clash with national legal conceptions.

However, there remains one key difference—AG Wahl is stating 'in public', meaning everybody can read it—that he does not understand the law of the

[31] Case C-472/10 *Invitel Távközlési* ECLI:EU:C:2012:242.

[32] H-W Micklitz, 'A Common Approach to the Enforcement of Unfair Commercial Practices and Unfair Contract Terms' in *M v Boom*, O Akseli and A Garde (eds), *Experiencing Unfair Commercial Practices: Impact, Enforcement Strategies and National Legal Systems. Markets and the Law* (Ashgate, 2014) 173–202.

[33] B Kas is in the fourth year of her PhD. She will have finished her research by the end of the year. A first result of her findings can be found under the heading of 'A Socio-legal Study on the Operation of Hybrid Collective Remedies in the Area of European Social Regulation' in H-W Micklitz, Y Svetiev and G Comparato (eds), *European Regulatory Private Law—The Paradigm Tested* (EUI-ERC Law 2014/04) 19. The analysis of the *Invitel* case by Thomas Roethe is still unpublished. A draft is on file with the author.

[34] See for instance Opinion of 3 July 2014 in Case C-169/14, *Juan Carlos Sánchez Morcillo, María del Carmen Abril García v Banco Bilbao Vizcaya Argentaria SA,* in which he argues that Spanish law is effective to protect consumers but it seems that here he understood the national procedural system.

referring country. This means there is no communication possible. The whole idea and ideology of a judicial dialogue which is enshrined in the preliminary reference procedure collapses.

E. The Future—Sharing Tacit Knowledge

We all know the phrase of 'tacit knowledge', meaning we all know more than we can express. A mutually shared set of knowledge between the members of a culture being so basic that it hardly could be expressively communicated or even indoctrinated. It appears to be a silently working cognitive structure accompanying actions, considerations, deliberations and declarations summing up to the deeper sediments providing the security of common understanding. The idea of tacit knowledge can be found by E-W Böckenförde. Slightly rephrased for our purposes, Böckenförde maintains that democracies are living from requirements that they themselves cannot establish.[35] Democracies need societies, citizens who create and establish the necessary ethical and moral fundament.

Let me try to explain: Germany was shattered by unconditional surrender and the massive destruction of all former convictions deriving from the Kaiserreich over Weimar Republic to the Third Reich. However it was not re-education, it was not the instalment of democratic institutions, it was not the Marshal Plan *alone*—but *also* the offered convincing 'American, British, French Way of Life' displayed in literature, movies, music and fine arts slowly reaching the survivors and upcoming generations. Alas, all that soft seduction happened under occupation law (*Besatzungsrecht*): It was imposed on the West German citizens. The urgent wish of the Eastern European States to join the EU is of a very different shape. They have freed themselves from communism and positively decided to join the EU. Pride and intransigence enshrined in national identities certainly play a crucial role in what is called European integration. I dare to make a prognosis: In the long run, the 'tacit knowledge' will be shared by all Member States, by all peoples of the EU, by the old and the new Member States, the Western and the Eastern societies, if the EU is morally strong enough to walk again and again the extra mile without giving up the extra practical soft standards of its causative philosophy.

In the context of the 'project' here presented, the EU means first and foremost the European Court of Justice. G Comandé[36] is boldly arguing that the Court of Justice of the European Union (CJEU) is about to establish a European identity and a European society. Provided his analysis is correct, identity building and society-building bottom-down must correlate with the necessary willingness and commitment from the citizens' bottom-up.

---

[35] '*Der frühneuzeitliche Staat lebt von Voraussetzungen, die er selbst nicht garantieren kann*'. E-W Böckenförde, 'Staat, Gesellschaft, Freiheit. Studien zur Staatslehre und zum Verfassungsrecht' (Suhrkamp, 1976) 60, a sentence which later was transferred to democracy as such.

[36] G Comandé, 'The Fifth European Union Freedom, Aggregating Citizenship Around Private Law' in H-W Micklitz (ed), *Constitutionalisation of European Private Law* (Oxford University Press, 2014) 61.

1

Introduction: Revisiting the Transformative Power of Europe

MICHAL BOBEK

I. The Topic

Browsing through texts dealing with the judicial method and mentality in Central and Eastern Europe (CEE) at the onset of the 2004 enlargement of the European Union (EU), one acquired a mixed feeling. The mandatory institutional optimism of the various approximation and pre-accession reports stood in contrast with the rather sceptical tones voiced in some of the scholarly writings. 'We-shall-overcome-with-the-help-from-Europe' rhetoric became intertwined with scary images of CEE post-Communist judges that were depicted as limited formalists who seek refuge in the realms of mechanical jurisprudence and senseless sticking to procedures. Afraid to decide on substance and to pass any controversial judgments, they seek to dispose of cases on obscure points of procedure, in the observance of which they are very meticulous.

Such a description of the 'patient' resulted typically in one of the following two predictions. First, the gloomy one: Because of their ideological and methodological shortcomings, CEE judges would not be able to apply EU law properly. They would not be able to operate within the European legal space. Their world of limited (or formalist, textualist, hyper-positivistic or whatever other label was chosen by the respective author) law stood worlds apart from the mode dynamic and purpose oriented reasoning style required by European law. Second, on the more positive note, it was assumed that under the European lead, the CEE ideology and method was bound to change. CEE judges would have to adapt their approaches and re-adjust their judicial method once their respective states acceded to the European Union. The domestic application of EU law was bound to bring about a change in the judicial style.

Ten years have passed since the 2004 big bang enlargement of the European Union. Ten years may be seen as a relatively short but also as a quite long period of time. The length-related relativity depends on our purpose. On the one hand, for confirming the occurrence and genuine persistence of any lasting changes in institutions, mentality, approaches or ideology, 10 years may be too short. On the other hand, for those who suggest the absence of any such useful change, 10 years might be unbearably long. In any case, it is certainly long enough for observing the absence of any positive change.

With the benefit of hindsight, this volume revisits the (non)transformation of CEE judges and judiciaries under the European influence on the tenth anniversary of the 2004 enlargement. It looks into two key overreaching themes. First, have the judges and judiciaries in the new Member States been able to cope with EU law? Is EU law being applied domestically? Is it being duly incorporated into the reasoning of national judges? Moreover, have the CEE judges been able to effectively join and contribute to the broader discourse in the European legal space? Or have they turned out to be a sort of a black passenger, or a poor relative, who just sits silently in the corner and does not dare to engage?

Second, the broader issue of judicial reform (or the absence thereof) in Central and Eastern Europe is re-opened. What is the state of judicial structures, procedures and culture in CEE after 10 years of membership in what is generally seen as quite a prestigious 'rule of law based club'? It ought to be stressed, however, that the transformation of most CEE judiciaries had not started on 1 May 2004. The process took off already in the early 1990s, with the fall of the Iron Curtain. It was further accelerated with the CEE countries applying for their membership of the EU, as well as by their accession to the Council of Europe and the simultaneous submission to the review by the European Court of Human Rights. It was in fact in the pre-2004 period, when the European Union, sometimes acting alone but frequently operating in synergy with other European or international institutions, applied effective transformative pressure onto the CEE candidate countries. With regard to this latter point therefore, the 'examination period' for judicial transformation in CEE is thus not just the last decade, but in fact the last 25 years since 1989.

II. The Structure

The volume is divided into three parts. The first part deals with judicial reasoning and judicial ideology. A lot has been written in the past about CEE judges being formalists and apparently operating on a different 'wavelength' than their Western counterparts from the other side of the former Iron Curtain. The seven chapters contained in the first part of the volume revisit some of this discussion. In chapter two, *Péter Cserne* provides a fresh and thought-provoking introduction into the normative side of the debates on formalism in CEE. Is CEE formalism really anything special? Or are the formalism accusations so widely used within the region just a variety of ideological and cultural wars? Chapters three and four, authored by *Marcin Matczak, Mátyás Bencze & Zdeněk Kühn* and *Rafał Mańko* respectively, offer a quantitative assessment of the Central European reasoning style. What types of arguments do CEE judges in fact use and how often? How frequently do they work with arguments drawn from EU law? Chapter three provides an across the board study of administrative adjudication in Poland, the Czech Republic and Hungary, whereas chapter four presents a more in-depth study in the specific sector of the adjudication of the Polish Supreme Court on unfair terms in consumer contracts. In chapter five, *Aleš Galič* dissects a tremendously important issue encountered in a number of CEE countries: How distrust into the judiciary and its competence translates into legislation, more specifically the delimitation of the space of permissible judicial discretion. The case study relates primarily to judicial discretion in civil procedure. It has nonetheless much broader implications for the relationship between the legislature, the public and the judiciaries in transforming societies. Chapter six, authored by *Jan Zobec* and *Jernej Letnar Černič*, recounts the story of a failed (or at least considerably 'hibernated') judicial transition. Although their particular focus is on Slovenia, it is no secret that similar patterns at least in relation to some elements addressed in the chapter can be encountered throughout the CEE region. Chapter seven by *Boštjan Zalar* concludes the first part by critically engaging with the arguments, ideas and statements voiced in the first part of the volume. In particular, it offers a more nuanced view of the apparently problematic case of Slovenia.

Part two zooms in on the more direct interactions of CEE countries with the EU level and Europe-induced changes in national institutions, structures and procedures. In chapter eight, *Michal Bobek* and *David Kosař* offer a not entirely optimistic case study of 'institutional export' from the West (or rather from the South) to the East via the European level. They explain why an 'off-the-rack Euro-product' of a Latin-style judicial council that kept being offered or even imposed onto CEE candidate countries in the pre-accession period failed to deliver the goods in the name of which it was put in place. In chapters nine and 10, *Marton Varju & András György Kovács* and *Nina Półtorak* respectively look into Europe-induced changes in the national procedural framework following the 2004 enlargement in Hungary and Poland. The Polish example is perhaps more optimistic in tone than its Hungarian counterpart. Both chapters, however, confirm the fact that on the level of substantive and procedural law, both layers, the European and the national, are clearly engaging, with the former exercising some influence over the latter. In chapters 11 and 12, our attention turns to another type of engagement, this time a direct one—the preliminary rulings procedure. The Bulgarian case study offered by *Alexander Kornezov* in chapter 11 is fascinating: A group of younger, administrative Bulgarian judges, largely hired from outside the ranks of the established Bulgarian career judiciary, is effectively using the preliminary ruling procedure as a tool for their self-empowerment within the national judicial hierarchy. However, as a knowledgeable and seasoned observer of judicial behaviour within the EU, *Erhard Blankenburg* asks in his reply in chapter 12, are the patterns emerging from the Bulgarian case study indeed that new, if compared with judicial behaviour in the former 'Western' countries? Chapter 13 authored by *Matej Avbelj* closes the second part with broader critical reflections on the process of legal and judicial transformation as such. The insightful and sharp questions posed therein are as important as they are vexing, dissecting in some detail the problematic cases of Hungary and Slovenia.

In part three, our attention turns to constitutional courts and the constitutional justice in Central Europe. At a first look, the inclusion of such a relatively 'narrow' topic into this volume might appear surprising. On a closer look, however, constitutional courts and constitutional judges are not only a significant element within the judicial landscape in Central Europe that simply cannot be omitted; their mutation since the 2004 enlargement has also been amidst the most striking ones. In the period after 1989 and before the 2004 enlargement, most of the newly created constitutional courts in CEE became the active agents of societal and legal change: Weeding out old Communist laws, pushing for positive change in legal style and method within their respective jurisdictions. After 2004, their reputation became somewhat more mixed, with more conservative and darker tones appearing. Most recently, the Czech Constitutional Court dared into a territory that no other European court has dared before by declaring a judgment of the Court of Justice *ultra vires*. The Polish Constitutional Tribunal has not gone so far, but appears to have stopped one step short of that mark, by 'just' submitting EU secondary law (a regulation) to a full national constitutional review. In chapters 14, 15 and 16, *Tomasz Tadeusz Koncewicz, Jiří Přibáň*, and *Allan F Tatham* respectively analyse some of these perturbing questions by looking at the Polish Constitutional Tribunal, the Czech Constitutional Court and the Hungarian Constitutional Court in turn. Their visions and the narratives they construe are then supplemented by a critical closing chapter authored by *Marek Safjan*, who, thanks to his eminent experience, is able to take a broader, evolutionary and diachronic look at the constitutional justice in the European legal space.

Finally, the conclusions in chapter 18 revisit the three main topics of the volume in turn: Judicial reasoning and the issue of formalism; structural changes under the European lead in both their quantitative as well as qualitative dimension; and the uneasy position of constitutional courts in the European legal space, in particular of those in Central Europe.

III. The Caveats

Several caveats ought to be made at this stage that should help the reader to understand what she might find in this volume and, perhaps more importantly, what she will not find here. There are three sets of caveats: Methodological, personal and geographical.

A. Methodological

The transversal focus of this volume is on *qualitative* change in judicial techniques, mentality and institutions. The volume is thus not offering a quantitative analysis of national (non-)implementation of EU law since 2004 in the new EU Member States. Furthermore, the volume can also not provide any comprehensive and objective assessment of the success or failure of the process of CEE judicial transformations, although there is naturally no shortage of individual, subjective assessment of either the process or its outcome in some of the chapters that follow.

The reasons for the inability to deliver such objective assessment are multiple. First of all, it is notoriously difficult to evaluate the process of 'Europeanisation', which, to start with, we are not even able to define.[1] Capturing the process or its outcome becomes even more difficult if what is being assessed is not the Europeanisation of individual policies, in law typically represented by a comparative study of the transposition and implementation of a directive or other specific piece of EU legislation, but the Europeanisation of politics or polity,[2] ie institutions, structures and procedures not directly flowing from any one single EU legal source. Against this background, to study the transformation of method, reasoning patterns or legal thinking,[3] and establishing a credible causal link or at least a correlation, becomes, certainly on a larger scale, a mission impossible.

Second, in the particular context of judicial transitions in CEE, 'Europeanisation' of judiciaries was, in a way, a journey into an unknown or even inexistent destination. There is no 'EU' model of judiciary that would encompass all the institutional, structural and procedural elements to which a national judicial system could approximate itself to. For example, there is no EU sample or blueprint on how to structure criminal appeals on the national level, how to flesh out their procedure while respecting all the necessary human rights elements, or how to effectively organise the appellate courts' level in criminal matters in a Member State. For these reasons, in the new Member States or the candidate countries, transforming a judicial system under the 'European' lead effectively meant horizontal 'copying' from another, established Western state, which the transforming country largely chose itself. True, the European Union as well as other international actors actively encouraged this practice by funding various 'twinning' and other programmes, but they could hardly serve as a model themselves.

---

[1] See eg K Featherstone, 'Introduction: In the Name of Europe' in K Featherstone and CM Radaelli (eds), *The Politics of Europeanization* (Oxford University Press, 2003) 12; P Graziano and MP Vink (eds), *Europeanization: New Research Agendas* (Palgrave Macmillan, 2007) 7–12, 36–39; S Saurugger, *Theoretical Approaches to European Integration* (Palgrave Macmillan, 2014) 124–29.

[2] eg TA Börzel and T Risse, 'Conceptualizing Domestic Impact of Europe' in Featherstone and Radaelli (n 1) 71 or U Sedelmeier, 'Europeanization' in E Jones, A Menon, and S Weatherill (eds), *The Oxford Handbook of the European Union* (Oxford University Press, 2012) 833.

[3] Recently see eg U Neergaard et al (eds), *European Legal Method: Paradoxes and Revitalization* (DJØF, 2011) and U Neergaard and R Nielsen (eds), *European Legal Method: In a Multi-Level Legal Order* (DJØF, 2012).

The absence of one clear model for judicial transformations in CEE meant, however, that it is difficult to evaluate the transiting countries as to whether 'they are there', whether they by now have in fact arrived at their desired destination. 'Back to Europe' became the omnipresent slogan in some of the CEE countries, in particular in the course of the 1990s. In terms of judicial organisation and performance, however, back to which concrete 'Europe'? Back to Germany? Sweden? Italy? Finland? Greece? Needless to say that the evaluation of the judicial performance of a particular CEE country might turn out quite differently depending on which of these countries would be taken as a yardstick. Furthermore, trying to overcome the model diversity by construing various model-free rules of law or judicial performance indexes and then quantifying the performance and change in the individual countries on their basis tends to lead to more additional problems than helpful answers.

Also for these reasons, this volume can offer no solid empirical answer whether in the CEE countries, all of them or individually, the judicial transition has been a 'success' or a 'failure'. What the volume nonetheless offers is a unique insight into the qualitative side of the process itself, its shortcomings and its discontents.

B. Personal

Can fish objectively comment on the state of fish? Even more importantly perhaps: Does the fish know that it is a fish? In the study of Central and Eastern Europe, its judicial and other transitions, similar questions relating to the potential introspection bias[4] may be raised with renewed importance. As Hans Micklitz diplomatically noted in his Prologue, the debate on CEE judicial transition tends to be dominated by authors and judges coming from that region. These authors naturally have certain visions of reality within which they operate, formed by their values, ideas and convictions. Are they always able to dissociate these values from their vision of the reality when crossing the borders to the 'West' and seeking to explain the state of affairs back home? This problem might become more acute when dealing with a fairly specific topic relating to a system that is difficult to access for an external observer. To put the same point more bluntly, hardly anybody is able to verify their vision of reality since nobody from the outside world tends to have much idea about what is going on in smaller countries in the East with typically an incomprehensible language. Thus, coming to the international fore, the authors might bring with them not only their undisputed knowledge, but also their normative visions and agendas that colour this knowledge. The bias potential grows even stronger if judges from the CEE region are asked to talk on … CEE judges and judiciaries.

Conscious of such potential one-sidedness, all efforts were made to at least minimise its impact. The debates in this volume and at the conference leading

---

[4] Further eg L Epstein and G King, 'The Rules of Inference' (2002) 69 *University of Chicago Law Review* 1, 93.

to it were conceived of as 'triangular' in nature, involving not only academics coming from the CEE region, but also academics from the 'West', as well as CEE judges. Moreover, within the academic stream, an inter-generational exchange was also stimulated. This volume therefore brings together more established and experienced researchers, who themselves contributed to creating the narratives of CEE judicial function before and around the 2004 Eastern enlargement, with the younger generation that joined the discourse in the past few years. In the end, the diversity in views and opinions between the individual 'representatives' of the various streams might be in itself of highest interest to an attentive reader.

C. Geographical

As the title of this volume already foreshadows, its main focus is on 'Central Europe' (CE), which is defined as including Poland, the Czech Republic, Slovakia, Hungary and Slovenia. Several individual chapters reach beyond this area, providing some insights on 'Central and Eastern Europe' (CEE), which, for the purpose of our discussions, might be seen as encompassing also the three Baltic States (Estonia, Latvia, Lithuania), as well as Bulgaria, Romania and perhaps also Croatia and the countries of Western Balkans. However, since the discussion of the latter countries in this volume is not genuinely representative, the title of the book was advisedly kept as referring to Central Europe. At the same time, however, no attempt was made at unifying the terminology across the volume in this regard. Freedom was left to the individual authors with regard to the geographical area they wish to refer to within their chapters.

Finally, partly out of habit, partly out of convenience, the term of 'new Member States' is being used throughout the volume in order to refer to the new states that joined the European Union in 2004, namely Poland, the Czech Republic, Slovakia, Hungary, Slovenia, Estonia, Latvia and Lithuania. Cyprus and Malta joined also in 2004, but since coming from a different cultural background, and more importantly from outside of the former 'Eastern Bloc', they are not specifically aimed at in this volume. On the other hand, the notion of 'new Member States' as used in this volume includes also Romania and Bulgaria that joined in 2007. The pertinent question naturally remains whether it is still correct to refer to these countries, in particular those from the 2004 enlargement, as 'new' Member States, since it has been 10 years and two further enlargements followed.

IV. Acknowledgements

This volume is the fruit of a conference which was held at the European University Institute in Florence on 12 and 13 May 2014, organised jointly by the Centre for Judicial Cooperation of the European University Institute and the Department of European Legal Studies of the College of Europe. Many thanks are due to both institutions for generously funding the conference, and in particular to Loïc Azoulai, co-director of the Centre for Judicial Cooperation, and Inge Govaere, director of the Department of European Legal Studies. The invaluable organisational assistance of Federica Casarosa, Madalina Moraru and Bart Provoost of the Centre for Judicial Cooperation, as well as the editorial help of Anna Perego, Elizabet Ruiz Cairó and Valérie Hauspie from the College of Europe in preparing this volume are also gratefully acknowledged.

Part I

Judicial Reasoning

2

Formalism in Judicial Reasoning: Is Central and Eastern Europe a Special Case?

PÉTER CSERNE

I. Introduction

In both practitioners' comments and the academic literature on the Europeanisation of Central and Eastern European (CEE) legal cultures, there has been a general understanding and much lament about the persistence of certain features of legal thinking of the socialist era among the judiciary after 1989 and even after 2004. The core claim is that compared to fundamental changes in substantive law, judicial practices resist any rapid change and cultural patterns of the late socialist period still characterise judicial reasoning and style.[1] In particular, the judicial style in CEE is often characterised as formalistic, magisterial, terse and deductive.[2] Post-communist CEE is sometimes called 'the last bastion' of formalism.[3]

This chapter advances two points. The first is a general observation about the difficulties of discussing judicial formalism in CEE. I will suggest that it is symptomatic of CEE political cultures that the debate has been conducted in simplified and misguided terms, and historical and normative claims are often mixed. My first point is preliminary to the second one which concerns the terms and methods that may be useful when pursuing either empirical analysis or normative arguments about judicial formalism in CEE. Current empirical research and quasi-empirical writings on the alleged formalism suffer from conceptual and methodological difficulties.

---

[1] See eg G Ajani, 'By Chance and Prestige: Legal Transplants in Russia and Eastern Europe' (1995) 43 *American Journal of Comparative Law* 93; Z Kühn, 'Worlds Apart: Western and Central European Judicial Culture at the Onset of the European Enlargement' (2004) 52 *American Journal of Comparative Law* 531.

[2] A Fogelklou, 'East European Legal Thinking' (2002) *Riga Graduate School of Law Working Papers* No 4, 8, 20, 21.

[3] Z Kühn, 'Formalism and Anti-Formalism in Judicial Reasoning' in B Melkevik (ed), *Standing Tall. Hommages a Csaba Varga* (Pázmány Press, 2012) 224.

As for the first point, one of the difficulties stems from the extremely simple terms of the debate. Is formalism socialist heritage? Is formalism good or bad? When the question is put as bluntly as this, there is little scope for meaningful discussion. For instance, it is trivial that if there is any single answer to the question about the desirable degree of formalism, it lies between the extreme positions. Upon reflection, judges and commentators also know this. Yet in actual debates the evaluation of this perceived formalism of CEE judiciary easily gets polarised in these terms because historical and normative claims are too easily linked with each other, as well as with practical, reformist or conservative, EU-optimistic or EU-sceptical, agendas. The result is a discourse which falls short of both normative and historical plausibility. The claims of this discourse only make sense if we understand them as symptoms or symbolic battlegrounds. In short, contributors to debates on judicial formalism in CEE tend to produce 'interesting exhibit[s] in the gallery of post-communist legal culture, rather than an accomplished study thereof.'[4]

In other words, the debates on the judiciary in general and formalism in adjudication in particular are embedded in the political culture of the region and are thus expected to reflect patterns of thought characterising it more generally. As the debate about judicial formalism becomes linked to deep rooted and long term, sometimes traumatic issues of national identity, patterns of ideological thinking resurface easily. My claim is that this is symptomatic of unresolved problems of collective (political) identity in the region. Formalism easily becomes a battleground for fierce controversies about collective political identity.

At present, this is not more than speculation: A thorough analysis would require detailed case studies as well as the analytical tools of cultural anthropology, political and social psychology. Perhaps the phenomenon of judicial method becoming a battleground for debates about collective identity is not a distinctive feature of CEE political cultures. Other weak or peripheral legal cultures also face and struggle with issues of national identity and collective inferiority complexes.

It is probably also true that the debate on formalism cannot be entirely separated from controversial political claims. Yet, it seems both practically and academically beneficial at least to try. Therefore, my first point is best seen as an effort to diagnose how discussion on formalism may go astray because of the unreflective mixing of historical and normative arguments, leading to a misperception of formalism as a distinct feature of CEE judiciary.

My second point can be understood as an effort in the direction of separation: It concerns the concepts and methods that may be useful when pursuing empirical or normative arguments about judicial formalism in CEE. In this second part of the chapter I shall advance a conceptual, a methodological and an empirical claim. I look at the terminology and the conceptual foundations of the jurisprudential discourse on formalism and suggest distinguishing several dimensions of formalism. Amidst the terminological confusion surrounding formalism, it is

---

[4] J Komárek, 'The Struggle for Legal Reform after Communism' *LSE Law, Society and Economy Working Papers* 10/2014, 1.

sometimes forgotten that formalism is a ubiquitous feature of judicial reasoning in modern legal systems. Whether we start with a broad understanding of formalism or specify it more narrowly, the term refers to aspects of judicial reasoning or judicial style that can be observed in most modern legal systems. Formalism is a catch-all term for a wide range of features of modern Western law which manifest themselves as continuous variables. These features need to be disaggregated and analysed at a lower level of abstraction. Methodologically, the chapter suggests that a moderate functionalist methodology and reliance on social scientific or more broadly empirical research allows a fruitful analysis of formalism as a feature of judicial style. The empirical claim is that if we follow the above methodology, we are unlikely to find sufficient evidence for characterising CEE judicial reasoning as distinctively formalistic.

II. Two Symptomatic Narratives on Formalism

The formalistic style of CEE adjudication has been widely and controversially discussed in the academic literature and in policy debates about institutional reforms.[5] There are at least three questions at stake in this discussion:

(1) The historical causes or origin of this supposed formalism;
(2) the evaluation of judicial formalism in terms of political and moral principles and values, and finally
(3) the question whether and in what sense formalism can be seen as a distinctive feature of CEE judicial style, in particular a heritage of the socialist era.

The first question concerns, roughly speaking, the causal links between certain explanatory variables and the observed/perceived/supposed style of CEE judicial reasoning in the present. Like with any historical inquiry, the set of potentially relevant causes, conditions and prerequisites is virtually endless and any explanatory attempt faces methodological problems usual in historical analysis.[6] Most of the literature focuses on a limited set of explanatory variables, such as institutional history, political events, political and legal ideas and ideologies, legal education, the *de facto* and ideological role of the judiciary, and focuses on relatively recent periods of the pre-history of the region: The Habsburg monarchy, the interwar period and various stages of the socialist era.

The second issue is clearly normative and reveals serious ambiguity among observers. The evaluation of the perceived formalism of CEE judiciary is ambivalent and as we will see, the views sometimes tend towards extremes. In contrast, the third

---

[5] One of the most detailed and refined contributions to this discussion is Z Kühn, *The Judiciary in Central and Eastern Europe: Mechanical Jurisprudence in Transformation?* (Martinus Nijhoff, 2011).

[6] Two classic examples are the plethora of hypotheses and theories suggested as explaining the fall of the Roman Empire and the rise of Western capitalism.

issue seems to have escaped serious explicit analysis. The distinctiveness thesis has been unquestioned or at least unexamined, formalism being seen as a persistent feature (malaise or virtue) of CEE judiciary, inherited from socialist times.

Although these three questions are distinct, in debates about CEE judiciary they are not always clearly distinguished. In fact, they are interwoven in a complex fashion. In particular, answers to the first (historical) question about the origins of formalism are linked to variables which are themselves associated with strong positive or negative value judgements. These judgements are in turn often made in light of the discussants' more or less informed ideas on the nature of adjudication or their further normative commitments and practical standpoints, for example related to the relations of nation states and the European Union.

The discourse on judicial formalism in CEE is extensive, generally well-informed and self-reflective, although some rather naïve arguments seem to resist criticism, for example when common law judicial reasoning is idealised and suggested as a normative benchmark and antidote to the communist heritage.[7] It is also highly important in practical terms: The self-perception and the legitimacy of the judiciary have obvious consequences for the societies in which it operates. There is often a fluid transition between academic and practical considerations, participants' and observers' perspectives. There is also a gap between top-notch jurisprudential theories and everyday operative theories in the mind of practitioners and other non-specialist participants of academic and semi-academic debates. Furthermore, even sophisticated participants of the discourse have their blind spots. As a consequence, arguments easily get misguided and the discourse on formalism as (good *or* bad) socialist heritage becomes symptomatic rather than therapeutic, and thus ultimately counterproductive. But let's start at the beginning.

For the purpose of making sense of this enormously rich debate, it seems useful to begin with a simple distinction between two ideal types of narrative. Both narratives are concerned with the above three questions (origins, desirability, distinctiveness of formalism). Both purport to explain as well as to evaluate the persistence of a formalistic judicial style in the region.[8] Both narratives are ideological in the sense that they combine historical and normative jurisprudential claims in the service of practical political or legal desiderata. These two narratives are mutually exclusive but not jointly exhaustive. By calling these narratives ideal types, I mean that they are theoretical constructs that can be more or less useful for the understanding of complex social (here, discursive) phenomena. At this stage, they can provide no more than a heuristic for understanding contributions to the debate. Let me briefly characterise the two ideal types in turn.

The first narrative interprets formalism in CEE judiciary mainly as the persistent heritage of communist or socialist legal thought and practice. In particular, it is seen as historically linked to the ideology of socialist normativism, the official judicial doctrine in the Soviet Union starting from the late 1930s and in

---

[7] Some claims in J Zobec and JL Černič's work in this volume (below, ch 6) come close to this view.

[8] Various authors use various terms, referring to mechanical jurisprudence, textualism or hyper-positivism. I will briefly return to the terminological issue below.

its satellites in the post-Stalinist era, characterised by a rigid statist conception of law and formalist theory of adjudication. Sophisticated versions of this narrative acknowledge the different shades and phases of Marxist theory, communist ideology and socialist practice about the judiciary. For instance, they acknowledge that in the post-revolutionary period in the Soviet Union and for a short period after the communist takeover in CEE, that is before the political regime became established and socialist normativism became official dogma, certain anti-formalist ideas about the judiciary had some currency.[9] Yet the first narrative is based on the historico-sociological claim that there is continuity between the past and post-communist present. Formalism is seen as a persistent feature of the judicial style and the general tenor of its evaluation is negative: It is considered and condemned as a sign of limited mind, blind conservatism, incompetence or lack of transparency.[10]

The diagnosis of historical continuity and the critical normative stance are usually combined with a positive appreciation of the educative or transformative effect of EU law and national Constitutional/Supreme Courts on the (ordinary/lower echelons of) judiciary. Thus, as a matter of policy, the formalism-as-bad-heritage narrative leads to a reformist agenda. The implications for institutional reform seem obvious: For a thoroughgoing change to happen, (re-)codification and constitutionalisation should be accompanied by a re-organisation of judicial procedures and practices. This, in turn, may require the training of an entire new generation of judges and other judicial personnel, eventually combined with incentives and sanctions.

As the post-socialist transformation of CEE national legal systems progressed and unfolded over the last 25 years, to a large extent under the influence of the EU, this first narrative has gained a de facto dominance in the discourse. The reformist agenda being the default option, it was resistance to reforms that needed extra arguments and justification. In fact, the dominant first narrative has been continuously countered, challenged or qualified by arguments from a counter-narrative.

This second narrative is generally motivated by the perception of EU law (and other real or imaginary supra-national entities)[11] threatening national legal

---

[9] As an illustrative example, consider Hungary where revolutionary anti-formalism represents a very short episode in the jurisprudential discussion (see SK Túry 'Az érdekkutató jogtudomány mai jelentőségéről és szerepéről' (On the Significance and Role of the Jurisprudence of Interests Today) (1948) 3 *Jogtudományi Közlöny* 450) and the theoretical status of dogmatic formalism turned into orthodoxy soon thereafter. See P Cserne, 'Gazdaság és jog viszonya a marxista jogelméletben és a jog gazdasági elemzésében' (The relation of 'economy' and 'law' in Marxist legal theory and in law and economics) (2004) 45/4 *Világosság* 49, 50–52. Judicial practice of the early 1950s is of course a different matter.

[10] Some variants of this type of narrative also include an apparently contradictory historical claim, according to which in the later period of socialism, legal formalism provided a shelter or safe haven against direct political intervention into judicial proceedings. I discuss this argument below.

[11] See eg B Pokol, 'Globális uralmi rend és állami szuverenitás' (Global order of dominance and state sovereignty) (2014) *Jogelméleti Szemle* 1, 105, online at <http://jesz.ajk.elte.hu/2014_1.pdf>, last accessed 1 December 2014. Pokol argues for the protection of 'constitutional identity' against a creeping conspiracy of global financial powers, international human rights NGOs, the Strasbourg court and the Venice Commission.

systems, various features of which are seen as defensible and worth defending. One of these features can be seen as judicial reasoning. Judicial formalism is then seen as challenged by and resistant to purposive reasoning required by the European Court of Justice (ECJ). Thus, the negative evaluation of the perceived formalism of CEE judiciary is widespread but not uniform. In fact, the alternative narrative interprets judicial formalism as an embodiment of courts' commitment to the rule of law and praises it with national/regional pride. The reason for this pride is that formalism is seen as a distinct, historically rooted feature of CEE judiciary. In the second narrative, the argument then needs to be combined with a historical claim. This can be either that deference to the legislator and respect for the separation of powers is congruent and continuous with socialist judicial ideology and/or self-perception (to that extent and in that respect socialist normativism is seen as defensible) or the somewhat different historical claim according to which judges in CEE learned to resist anti-formalist arguments in the Stalinist period of socialism when judges were required to implement political directives over and above what were seen as legal technicalities. In either way an EU-sceptical normative stance and some historical claims about formalism may lead to the narrative of formalism-as-noble-heritage.

Above, I said that both narratives are ideological in the sense that they subordinate the accuracy of historical or present factual details to practical desiderata. To be sure, historical reconstructions are unavoidably selective; focusing on what is 'relevant', 'significant', 'typical' or 'essential', as opposed to what is 'exceptional' or 'accidental'. Yet, some of the historical claims deployed in these narratives raise obvious concerns of plausibility. When talking about plausibility, it is not the accuracy of one or another factual detail at stake (if there are disagreements at this level, they should ideally be checked and eventually rectified) but higher-level generalisations about the region or certain historical periods that may render the plausibility of these narratives questionable.

Let me just mention an example. Several commentators argued that at least in the consolidated periods of socialism, formalism allowed the judiciary to safeguard its independence and avoid being politically involved, misused and corrupted.[12] It is noteworthy that the two narratives would include this alleged safeguarding function of formalism differently. The first could argue that in a liberal democracy there is no more need for such isolation and thus formalism is at least to this extent outdated. Certain versions of the second narrative could, in contrast, argue that this isolation is a virtuous tradition to be pursued: Resistance is still needed or at least justified but now against claims made and policies imposed by (democratically questionable) supra-national entities.

---

[12] M Bobek, 'On the Application of European Law in (Not Only) the Courts of the New Member States: 'Don't Do as I Say'?' (2007–08) 10 *Cambridge Yearbook of European Legal Studies* 1, 24; Kühn (n 3) 77; R Mańko, 'Weeds in the Gardens of Justice? The Survival of Hyperpositivism in Polish Legal Culture as a Symptom/*Sinthome*' (2013) 7 *Pólemos* 223; M Matczak, M Bencze and Z Kühn, 'Constitutions, EU law and Judicial Strategies in the Czech Republic, Hungary and Poland' (2010) 30 *Journal of Public Policy* 81, 83.

scholarship in the inter-war period it was sometimes claimed that judicial formalism, along with abstract logical thought, are foreign to the Hungarian 'national character'.[18] Anti-formalism and customary law were praised as a quicker and more direct route to justice. Customary law, of course, referred to the uncodified character of private law in Hungary, a kind of anachronism in the mid-twentieth century but arguably a workable solution. In this type of legal thinking, formalism was linked to ideological debates about national character, as well as to anti-formalist tendencies in early twentieth century Continental and Anglo-American legal thought. In these debates 'formalism' was often used as a catch-all phrase, sometimes associated with liberalism and/or legal positivism.[19]

Formalism is linked to the identity and aspirations of societies in other parts of the world as well. For instance, in New Zealand in the 1980s and 1990s there was a vivid discourse within the judicial and academic legal elite about the identity and characteristics of a distinct New Zealand legal method (judicial reasoning). One important line of argument was a criticism of and detachment from what was considered the formalism of English common law adjudication.[20] It seems that the debate has been dominated by a narrative that wanted to leave behind formalism as bad (imperial) heritage in favour of what they considered realism or pragmatism in the service of justice or social values characteristic of New Zealand society. But there has also been a counter-narrative which questioned the upright rejection of 'formalism'. What is interesting is that the debate combines valid normative jurisprudential arguments and vague references to a national legal method, and the ultimate stake is very practical, in terms of judicial self-perception and self-representation in a nation state at the periphery of a loosely connected supranational legal system.

Debates on other, less practical and relatively obscure issues in legal thinking may also implicate collective identity issues. An example would be the debate about the existence or persistence of a socialist 'legal family' and its deletion from a key comparative law textbook.[21]

---

[18] J Szabó, 'Hol az igazság? A bíró lélektani problémái' (Where is justice? Psychological problems of the judge) (1942) 22 *Társadalomtudomány* 1, 11–13.

[19] Generated by Radbruch's claim that positivism made lawyers vulnerable to Nazi law, there is now an enormous and sophisticated literature on the relation between legal formalism and Fascist and Nazi legal ideology. See eg C Joerges and NS Ghaleigh (eds), *Darker Legacies of Law in Europe: The Shadow of National Socialism and Fascism over Europe and its Legal Traditions* (Hart Publishing, 2003). Probably we are not too far away from a similar historical debate on the links between formalism and Soviet-type socialism.

[20] See eg J Smillie, 'Formalism, Fairness and Efficiency: Civil Adjudication in New-Zealand' [1996] *New Zealand Law Review* 254; EW Thomas, 'Fairness and Certainty in Adjudication: Formalism v Substantialism' (1999) 9 *Otago Law Review* 459; J Allan, 'The Invisible Hand in Justice Thomas's Philosophy of Law' [1999] *New Zealand Law Review* 213; J Ewans, 'Questioning the Dogmas of Realism' [2001] *New Zealand Law Review* 145; R Bigwood (ed), *Legal Method in New Zealand; Essays and Commentaries* (Butterworth, 2001). Many thanks to Ben Yong (University of Hull) for drawing my attention to this literature.

[21] R Mańko, 'The Culture of Private Law in Central Europe after Enlargement: A Polish Perspective' (2005) 11 *European Law Journal* 527, 547–48.

In fact, the two patterns of thought (adapting models from Europe/the West/ the centre of the Empire versus pursuing distinct national paths) can generate ideological narratives not only in law but in any domain of life. Law and the judiciary are just domains where the political relevance is relatively uncontroversial but other spheres may become perceived as crucial for collective identity as well.[22]

III. Formalism as a Matter for Legal Scholarship

In subsequent sections of this chapter I shall explain my proposal for discussing formalism in an academic discourse. To wit, one should do more conceptual work on formalism, follow a rigorous methodology, and ultimately deconstruct the distinctiveness-of-formalism thesis, commonly assumed in both ideological narratives. As a result, it might turn out that although judicial reasoning and style are closely linked to the general culture and institutional history of the society in which courts operate, talking about formalism as an overall characteristic of CEE judiciary and focusing on this cultural link *only* is misconceived.[23]

As legal scholarship constantly runs the danger of mixing normative and explanatory perspectives in a non-reflexive manner, invoking terms and *topoi* that do not fit easily into academic discourse, it seems advisable to keep academic and policy-oriented debates relatively separate.

The ideologically charged debates about formalism have a rational core, the role of formalism in adjudication, as discussed in both Continental and Anglo-American legal theory. If we focus on this academic discourse, much of the heat and some of the confusion of the debate will disappear. For instance, if we look at formalism at a lower level of abstraction it may turn out that the discussion concerns, among other things, the reasons for and against rule-based decision making; an issue that can be and indeed has been rigorously and fruitfully, albeit inconclusively, analysed in jurisprudence for more than a century. As it was suggested a few years ago in a slightly different but related context, new EU Member States face legal problems which are quite similar to those elsewhere in the EU.[24]

---

[22] As a non-legal example see the papers in Special Issue: 'Design and Polity Under and After the Ottoman Empire' (2007) 20 *Journal of Design History* 2. See especially A Yagou, 'Metamorphoses of Formalism: National Identity as a Recurrent Theme of Design in Greece' (2007) 20 *Journal of Design History* 145 on the debate about the 'Greekness' of formalism in industrial design as a battleground for ideological debates on national identity in Greece in the early 20th century.

[23] As far as the judiciary and its 'transformation' are concerned from a (committed) participant's perspective, my tentative suggestion would be a generalisation of the suggestions by TT Koncewicz in this volume (below, ch 14), who was talking about a 'comity of circumspect constitutional courts'. The generalisation of his suggestion can be ideally imagined as a forum of reasonable discourse. What this means is in part, a matter for theories of adjudication, in part a matter of practical judgement.

[24] L Vékás, 'Models in Central-Eastern European Codes' in S Grundmann and M Schauer (eds), *The Architecture of European Codes and Contract Law* (Kluwer Law International, 2006) 117. This is a partly factual and partly programmatic (counterfactual) claim.

Any meaningful discussion on formalism presupposes an agreement on what the term means. Previous authors looking at the judiciary in CEE have used a number of terms and when they tried to study the issue thoroughly, introduced various measures of formalism as well. Both terminology and methodology being quite diverse and not always compatible with previous studies of judicial reasoning elsewhere, comparison is difficult. At the semantic level, there is indeed some confusion, for example when 'formalism' is used synonymously with terms like 'passivism', 'hyper-positivism', 'mechanical jurisprudence' or 'textualism'. Most of these terms are value-laden and carry negative connotations.[25] Sometimes they refer to a number of distinct phenomena by the same term.

Yet, academic literature does not provide an easy remedy for this terminological confusion. A cursory overview of the literature suffices to realise that the term is, if not essentially contested, very broadly and vaguely used, on both sides of the Atlantic. Some 25 years after Frederick Schauer's seminal article that had noticed and tried to remedy these conceptual and terminological problems,[26] the conceptual landscape is not much clearer. What seems certain is that the term mostly refers to adjudication, more precisely, certain features of judicial reasoning.[27] In normative theories of adjudication, formalism is related to how judges should justify their decisions.[28] In a later paper, Schauer briefly defined formalism as 'the practice (and perhaps it is not necessarily a vice, as we shall see) of following … the plain meaning of the words of the document in the face of plausible arguments for doing otherwise.'[29]

In most commentators' view there is a real tension between legal certainty or the internal coherence of legal reasoning on the one hand and substantive rightness or external justification on the other. Legal formalism is usually associated with the view that gives (absolute or *prima facie*) priority to the former; anti-formalism (realism or pragmatism) being the opposite view that gives priority to substantive goals.[30]

---

[25] Sometimes 'formalism' is used as a minor insult. See eg Craig's use of the term: 'This is, with respect, legal formalism' in P Craig, 'Pringle: Legal Reasoning, Text, Purpose and Teleology' (2013) 20 *Maastricht Journal of European and Comparative* Law 1, 5.

[26] F Schauer, 'Formalism' (1988) 97 *Yale Law Journal* 509.

[27] For instance, Leiter defines 'formalism [a]s a *theory of adjudication*, a theory about how judges *actually* do decide cases and/or a theory about how they *ought* to decide them.' B Leiter, 'Positivism, Formalism, Realism: Review of Legal Positivism in American Jurisprudence, by Anthony Sebok' (1999) 99 *Columbia Law Review* 1138, 1144.

[28] For a useful overview see WNR Lucy, 'Criticizing and Constructing Accounts of Legal Reasoning' (1994) 14 *Oxford Journal of Legal Studies* 303.

[29] F Schauer, 'Formalism: Legal, Constitutional, Judicial' in GA Caldeira, RD Kelemen and KE Whittington (eds), *The Oxford Handbook of Law and Politics* (Oxford University Press, 2008) 431.

[30] Schauer (n 29) 431:

Perhaps most common is the argument that following the plain meaning of the words might produce outcomes inferior to those reached by making the best all-things-considered decisions in light of current pragmatic realities and in light of changes that have taken place in the relevant world since the words were first written.' (…)'It is sometimes the case that exactly following the words in a constitutional or legal text will look either illogical, or inconsistent with other or larger legal and constitutional values, or obsolete (…), and once again the formalist is inclined to disregard those arguments from other values and adhere closely to the plain meaning, come what may.

In mainstream analytical jurisprudence judicial reasoning is usually called formalistic in a more specific sense: When a court uses exclusively or primarily source-based arguments. In formalist adjudication, the set of reasons available is limited to what Raz would call source-based reasons: Judges should not rely on reasons outside this limited domain of source-based law. When these sources run out, judges may be allowed or required to decide cases in light of certain substantive reasons.[31]

Even without rehearsing the rather well-known arguments about the merits and limits of formalism as a normative theory of adjudication, it seems obvious that formalist, that is source-based decision making is often justifiable. But this statement, at this level of generality, is unlikely to provide much ammunition or satisfaction to those who look at CEE judicial formalism as a source of national pride. Nor should it worry those who see what they call formalism as a bad heritage.

This is partly because

> the argument for formalism is ultimately a contextual and empirical one. The task will always be to decide whether in some decision-making environment, in which decision-makers with certain characteristics make decisions of a certain type, there are likely to be more (or more serious) errors when wise and enlightened decision-makers are prohibited by formalist expectations and incentives from reaching wise decisions than there are when misguided or mistaken decision-makers are freed from formalist restrictions to make what seem to them to be the best moral or political or pragmatic decisions.[32]

The other reason is that what are sometimes referred to by the term 'formalism', are judicial practices that are hardly justifiable in terms of any generally accepted normative theory of adjudication. When the term refers to judicial decision making characterised by a lack of or lacunae in logical reasoning or no reasoning at all (for instance, when a judge makes logical errors or claims that their decision follows 'obviously' from the relevant rules, without providing arguments for their conclusion), this is something distinct from formalism in the above senses of the term. Thus while these practices of faulty reasoning are surely undesirable and deserve the implied negative tone, they are easily distinguished from the above sense of formalism as rule-based reasoning. Ultimately, they amount to nothing more than deception. As Schauer suggests, conceptual clarity requires distinguishing these two senses of the term.[33] Moreover, there is no reason to believe that the practice of deception is specific to CEE. Large portions of doctrinal commentary in most legal cultures are exactly about criticism of faulty, floppy or otherwise deficient judicial reasoning.

---

[31] Positivists like Raz would say that what judges are doing in such cases is not legal reasoning any more but qua adjudication it is nonetheless subject to normative criteria of practical reason, more specifically certain moral reasons. Anti-positivists like Dworkin would agree with the second half of the claim only.

[32] Schauer (n 29) 434.

[33] Schauer (n 29) 429: 'it may be important to distinguish the alleged vice of formalism with the alleged vice of deception, or lack of judicial candor.' Kühn (n 3) 216 also talks about two meanings of formalism in this respect: 'formalistic argumentation actually leading to a formalistic result, and formalism in which formalistic argumentation is used as a veil to get the result which, however, could not be reached through formalistic reasoning.'

To further complicate things, in some cases judges refer to vague and highly general legal standards (principles) in support of their decisions and apply them *contra legem*, that is when there is a conventionally clear statutory provision. As these standards are typically formally valid sources of law, their reasoning is sometimes called formalist in this sense. Yet these standards or principles leave a large margin of discretion to judges, and in some sense (which will be discussed below) they allow for anti-formalism. Moreover, recourse to a principle when closer-to-the-case sources would have been available and determinative for the outcome goes against the very rationale of formalism, as well as against meta-rules of systemic reasoning.

In the sense of strict rule-following by judges, the meaning of formalism seems relatively straight-forward and normative theories of adjudication usually refer to this sense of formalism. Yet the term sometimes refers to a number of other aspects of judicial activity or even more broadly, to other features of legal cultures as well, for example when used in a transactional sense[34] or with reference to a methodology in legal theory.[35] Formalism is in fact a key feature of modern Western legal thinking.[36]

Even if we confine our attention to judicial reasoning, it is difficult to identify a single attribute that makes reasoning formalist. In a recent article, Michal Alberstein distinguishes no less than nine senses ('parameters', 'aspects', 'vectors' or 'dimensions') of legal formalism and 'develops a sensitive multidimensional measure ... to evaluate legal texts by examining various vectors of formalism.'[37] This might seem too much but in fact her study offers useful tools to assess the distinctiveness of formalism in CEE.

---

[34] Whether, for instance, contracts require formalism to be enforceable—this is the sense it is used in K Zweigert and H Kötz, *Introduction to Comparative Law*, 3rd edn (transl Tony Weir) (Oxford University Press, 1998) 71.

[35] Ernest J Weinrib, *The Idea of Private Law*, 2nd edn (Oxford University Press, 2012) xiii–xiv. In Weinrib's terminology, formalism refers to the immanent rationality of law as normative practice, ie the idea that law sets the standards of intelligibility for itself, law is not an instrument for another rationality, in light of which it could be judged a better or worse instrument.

[36] 'The formality of modern law is a constitutive element in its operation, but the 'revolt against formalism' and the charge of mechanical jurisprudence are also as old as the law ... Contemporary decision-making in law combines formalistic with nonformalistic expressions as part of its routine operation ... The tendency to formalism ... is never pure and is part of a complex legal culture that usually combines formalistic elements with nonformalistic ones' M Alberstein, 'Measuring Legal Formalism: Reading Hard Cases with Soft Frames' 57 (2012) *Studies in Law, Politics, and Society* 161, 161–62. Theorists from the common law world have emphasised that formality of law is not necessarily linked to codification but it is closely linked to the authority of law and its interpretation. Robert Summers is probably the scholar in the English speaking world who spent the most effort on understanding and theorising the role of formality in law. See RS Summers, 'The Formal Character of Law' (1992) 51 *Cambridge Law Journal* 242; RS Summers, *Form and Function in a Legal System: A General Study* (Cambridge University Press, 2006). For a balanced appreciation of Summers, see B Bix, 'Form and Formalism: The View from Legal Theory' (2007) 20 *Ratio Iuris* 45.

[37] Alberstein (n 36) 161. The paper refers to eight but actually distinguishes nine measures. As she explains, ibid, at 162:

> Each of these parameters can be used to evaluate the level of formalism in a concrete text. The interplay between diverse evaluations of the same case is a subject for inquiry and contemplation. These parameters can also be redefined as variables for a quantitative content analysis, and legal decisions can be coded accordingly. This will enable an analysis of differences between justices, legal issues, legal jurisdictions, and time frames, as well as the correlation between the various parameters of formalism.

When reading cases, one can identify judicial arguments as exhibiting various degrees of formalism, along the following dimensions:

(1)   With reference to the introduction and framing of the legal question, formalism means that legal decision making is based on formal authorisation;
(2)   with regard to the use of extralegal arguments, formalism refers to judicial decision making which involves the strict application of legal norms without reference to external elements in the legal environment in which decisions are made;
(3)   in a third sense, formalism means that judges apply legal norms without reliance on or reference to any policy argument or legal principle;
(4)   fourth, formalism means that judges apply legal norms without discretion or choice;

Judges are formalist as far as

(5)   they apply legal norms based on the objective determination of facts;
(6)   preserve the traditional doctrinal boundaries in law, for example between public and private law;
(7)   and use professional judicial rhetoric and terminology;
(8)   the eighth dimension refers to the gap between law in the books and law in action: a formalist judge would not reflect on the problematics of implementing the rule and would decide cases in definitive ways without sharing the final operative stage with other institutions;
(9)   last, with respect to judicial stability and institutional deference, a formalist judge would refrain from overturning previous decisions, would reinforce institutional boundaries, and would usually not change the existing legal reality or question its validity.

As Alberstein adds,

> the measure suggested above can be applied to any legal decision-making text, in every legal culture … Since most of the claims and counterclaims of formalism are typical of any modern legal system, it is reasonable to expect that a comparative study will explore the concrete mixture of jurisprudential traditions that characterize each legal culture.[38]

Most of what is conventionally or colloquially called formalism, textualism, hyperpositivism or mechanical jurisprudence, is covered by one or several of the above measures. This suggests a way of measuring the degree of judicial formalism in CEE. More importantly this would allow cross-jurisdictional comparisons, both within and outside the CEE region. As far as I am aware, at present there is little systematic quantitative cross-regional comparison of judicial reasoning available.[39]

---

[38] Alberstein (n 36) 178.
[39] M Matczak, M Bencze and Z Kühn, 'Constitutions, EU law and Judicial Strategies in the Czech Republic, Hungary and Poland' (2010) 30 *Journal of Public Policy* 81 and the chapter by Matzak, Bencze and Kühn in this volume (below, ch 3) are quantitative studies on Poland, Hungary and the Czech Republic with some general claims about older EU Member States. The best known currently available

As long as this is the case, we simply do not have sufficient empirical evidence to support the distinctiveness-of-formalism thesis.

IV. How to Grasp Formalism? A Plea for Moderate Functionalism

One may argue, in response, that judicial formalism is a macro-level manifestation of certain general features of a legal culture, which are not necessarily identifiable at the level of individual decisions or arguments. Therefore, the appropriate way to assess the distinctiveness of CEE judiciary may be to analyse formalism as a matter of style.

The term judicial style lends itself to different interpretations. At first glance, it refers to the way (or form) courts argue for their decisions but also to how they present themselves and are perceived in their roles. Style is in part a matter of the form of (typical) decisions or arguments. In this sense, one could call a certain judicial style formalistic if, when generally accepted judicial conventions or canons would allow non-formalistic reasoning, the judge nonetheless (typically) uses formalistic reasoning. But style may also refer to a number of higher-level ('macro') features of court activity that are not necessarily manifest or identifiable in individual decisions or arguments.

Analysing formalism in terms of judicial style may then have methodological implications. To assess whether a certain national or regional legal culture is formalistic arguably requires a different methodology than counting references to EU law or constitutional principles. Possibly it is not simply the lack of data but the lack of a clear and convincing methodology which hampers collecting and analysing sufficient evidence for or against the distinctiveness-of-formalism thesis. What is then the adequate methodology for grasping judicial formalism?

A significant portion of the studies on CEE judiciary, to the extent they explicitly commit themselves to any methodology, adopt what I call a culturalist comparative perspective. This approach lends itself to different interpretations but there are some typical common features. Cultural comparatists typically point at the mentality, implicit would views and other patterns of a national culture, characteristic for and expressed in legal phenomena in general, and various aspects of the judiciary in particular. They look at CEE judicial style in a holistic fashion, in terms of political and legal culture, *mentalité* and institutional history, and identify formalism as a characteristic feature of CEE legal cultures.

Though informative and worth pursuing, a purely culturalist approach alone is unlikely to produce satisfactory results in analysing judicial style. The reason

comparative study that also includes Poland is based on judicial reasoning in the 1980s and is mainly qualitative: DN MacCormick and RS Summers (eds), *Interpreting Statutes. A Comparative Study* (Dartmouth, 1991).

is, very briefly, that without any functional element, the approach cannot get off the ground. This is because the primary way of understanding human actions or artefacts—and judicial reasoning, either as an activity or its product is (an aggregate of) one of these—is in terms of their purpose or function.

As legal scholars we can rejoice in describing cultural artefacts and practices in all their complexity and uniqueness. At a certain level of description we will find every individual case incomparably unique. It is worth remembering though that by doing this, we cannot avoid generalisation completely, even at the level of description.[40] But the main point is a slightly different one: Culturalist interpretations of law presuppose an element of functionalism, minimally for identifying the practice or artefact to be interpreted. Therefore, an account of judicial reasoning should start with these variables or parameters.

The basic idea of a functional account is that judges are considered as purposeful actors within constraints as well as in strategic interaction with other actors. Their decisions (as activities or as artefacts) should be primarily explained in terms of their motivations, information sets and various constraints.[41] This basic premise of the functional perspective is a common starting point for a number of quite diverse lines of research on judicial behaviour. Some are focusing on judicial preferences and heuristics at the individual level, others more on certain constraints (structural or 'ideological'), still others on explaining and predicting decisions based on patterns of judicial preferences revealed in previous decisions. All in all, this is the perspective shared by most kinds of empirical research on the judiciary.[42] An analysis of common and distinct features of judicial reasoning in CEE would be an instance of this.

This functionalist methodological stance is compatible with and can easily account for the fact that judicial reasoning shows culture-specific, that is, national or regional features. It is a functionalist, rather than a culturalist, perspective that can be expected to provide an explanation (rather than a mere description) of these culture-specific features. It is an empirical matter whether there are such features and whether they appear in terms of preferences, constraints or other variables.

In this sense, I do not suggest rejecting the distinctiveness-of-formalism thesis on methodological grounds before actually conducting the analysis. Rather, I suggest adopting a functionalist approach so that the thesis could be operationalised and assessed empirically. If the analysis has explanatory ambitions, the likely connections of judicial formalism are with other variables of judicial behaviour: Attitudinal, behavioural, institutional and organisatory, such as public confidence in the judiciary and judicial self-confidence, legitimacy and political profile.

---

[40] See F Schauer, *Profiles, Probabilities, and Stereotypes* (Harvard University Press, 2006).

[41] This is based, very broadly, on a rational choice theory of human behaviour, as explained eg in J Elster, *Nuts and Bolts in the Social Sciences* (Cambridge University Press, 1989).

[42] Useful introductions include JA Segal, 'Judicial Behaviour' in Whittington, Kelemen and Caldeira (n 29) 19; PT Spiller and Rafael Gely, 'Strategic Judicial Decision-making' in Whittington, Kelemen and Caldeira (n 29) 33; L Epstein and T Jacobi, 'The Strategic Analysis of Judicial Decisions' (2010) 6 *Annual Review of Law and Social Sciences* 341.

As an empirical hypothesis, I would suggest that if there is a gap between West-ern and Central European judiciaries with respect to their degree of formalism, it is much smaller than the ideological narratives suggest. This hypothesis needs to be tested and such an empirical study requires a separate paper or even a set of papers: A task that is still to be done. Maybe the more interesting differences are not quantitative but qualitative. One could argue that for identifying style, it is not the statistically most frequent type of argument that matters. Yet with adequate specifications and methodology even this could be tested. What none-theless seems to be a fair generalisation is that formalist arguments are part of the canon of acceptable arguments and carry controversial ideological connotations throughout so-called modern legal systems. My present empirical claim is thus a negative one: The studies currently available do not provide sufficient evidence that formalism (in the above mentioned, functionalist sense) is more prevalent in new EU Member States than in old ones.

V. Judicial Formalism in Heterogeneous and Dynamic Legal Cultures

Even before starting such an empirical analysis, there are conceptual reasons and anecdotal empirical arguments that raise doubts whether it is sensible to speak of formalism as a culturally fixed feature of national or regional judicial styles. As Alberstein suggested,[43] judicial reasoning in virtually all modern legal systems shows a mixture of formalist and anti-formalist features. Therefore, the frequency and other patterns of judicial formalism should be analysed in specific contexts.

Characterising CEE judicial culture(s) as formalistic *tout court* is both partial and crude. It is partial because it refers to culture as a 'black box' or self-standing *explanans*. Macro-level comparisons, for example between CEE countries and older EU Member States can be misleading by conveying the false impression that national legal cultures are homogeneous and static, while similarities that go across legal boundaries go unnoticed.

It is crude because there are many finer details and differences internal to a national legal regime that cannot be reasonably called formalist(ic) to the same degree or in the same manner. In fact, the canon of acceptable arguments, and insofar as it reflects this canon, judicial reasoning as well, is context-specific and dynamic. The reasoning of the same court is likely to differ significantly and sys-tematically according to doctrinal areas, hierarchical levels but also in terms of what the court wants to achieve or considers acceptable in particular types of cases. Formalist arguments are always available in the judicial repertoire; their use is a matter of 'judicial strategies'.[44] In consequence, the role of formalism is likely

---

[43] Alberstein (n 36) 162.
[44] A term very aptly coined by Matczak, Bencze and Kühn (n 39).

to differ across legal areas, types of courts and even in whether certain outcomes are likely to be politically or socially important.

National and regional differences in judicial reasoning also raise the question of persistence. While some national differences are likely to persist in the long term, some developments are likely to generate dynamic changes in judicial reasoning. As the role of national legal systems changes, national judicial styles and patterns of justification used in courts are likely to change. These tendencies also weaken the distinctiveness-of-formalism thesis.

First, when new transnational legal areas (for example European market regulation, international trade law, commercial arbitration, international criminal law) emerge they create their own organisational or institutional cultures not closely linked to national laws. As organisational cultures, with their own characteristic attitudes, know-how etc, these develop their own style that is easier to identify and distinguish along functional (in the sense of substantive) rather than national lines. In these legal areas, the degree of formalism is likely to track, at least to some extent, organisational rather than national cultures.

The emergence and extension of EU law could be seen as a prime example for this. EU law is embedded in its own (*sui generis?*) legal culture and developed by an epistemic community partly detached from national or regional legal cultures. Certain features of its style are identifiable as coming from some Member States rather than others. International commercial arbitration is another example for a functionally differentiated legal regime with its own organisational culture, cutting across national borders.[45] The point of these examples is that legal orders or regimes have their own style, historically and personally linked to, but in its operation detached from national cultures. The emergence of these new legal domains with their own styles (organisational cultures) potentially has an impact on domestic methods for handling disputes, patterns of justification and judicial style through various channels of legal emulation.[46]

Another way this transformation occurs is through increased activity of national judges in transnational judicial networks and various forms of judicial mobility. As preliminary research suggests, at least some judicial networks operate as 'educational interlocutors', with an expected impact on the outlook of national

---

[45] As a now classic study by Dezelay and Garth argues, international commercial arbitration has become a central and powerful segment of the global legal market, thanks to an elite group of transnational lawyers who constructed an autonomous legal field. As the authors argue, this has transformed commercial arbitration from an informal, settlement-oriented system to an increasingly formalised and litigious one. Y Dezelay and BG Garth, *Dealing in Virtue: International Commercial Arbitration and the Construction of a Transnational Legal Order* (University of Chicago Press, 1996). While this area of law is seen by some as completely independent of national laws, others argue that such detachment is a utopia. See R Michaels, 'Dreaming Law Without a State: Scholarship on Autonomous International Arbitration as Utopian Literature' (2013) 1 *London Review of International Law* 35.

[46] On legal emulation see eg P Larouche, 'Legal Emulation Between Regulatory Competition and Comparative Law' in P Larouche and P Cserne (eds), *National Legal Systems and Globalization: New Role, Continuing Relevance* (TMC Asser Press & Springer, 2013) 247.

courts.[47] Larger scale individual mobility of career judges which temporarily leads them into other professional milieus (organisational cultures) or bring others, for example international and constitutional court judges, within the ordinary judiciary, may have a similar effect.

More specifically, it is possible to argue that old and new EU Member States face similar difficulties regarding the use of EU law or their self-perception as European judges. EU law challenges systemic coherence, traditional doctrinal patterns and argumentative figures in national legal systems and doctrines, across the Union. It is even arguable but would need to be empirically tested that judges in new Member States have been *nolens volens* more open to EU law, as their legal systems are themselves less stable given the transition period.

VI. Conclusion

The answer to the question in the title of this chapter is a qualified yes. I am *not* claiming that CEE is not a special case. This would indeed be a highly implausible, if not an absurd claim: In human matters every case is special. In this sense, the region is no more or less special than, say, Protestant Northern Europe or Latin America. For certain purposes it makes sense to focus on what is unique and common in the CEE region or in other regions, and how this is reflected in or filtered into judicial culture. What has not been demonstrated and I seriously doubt it can be, is that this distinct feature would be judicial formalism.

The distinctiveness-of-formalism thesis is misguided because it leads to an exclusive focus on the region in isolation. By this we lose sight of (1) the formalism versus anti-formalism debates that have occupied a large part of jurisprudential discussion in the last 120 years; (2) the finer details, such as the intra-regional differences; and (3) recent developments that reduce the significance of topographical or historical differences in judicial style.

I have also argued that the reason why the distinctiveness of formalism is part of judicial self-perception, as well as academic commentary on judicial reasoning, has to do with unresolved issues of collective identity in CEE. The question of judicial formalism is embedded in and sometimes serves as a battlefield of political and ideological controversies. In the region, this may lead to the perception of formalism either as a dangerous heritage of socialist past or a source of national pride. This is itself a generalisation and no individual judge's and scholar's views could be reduced to either of these single narratives. Nor is there anything objectionable about the *transparent* normative use of historical arguments, for example when at

---

[47] M De Visser and M Claes, 'Judicial Networks' in Larouche and Cserne (n 46) 345. The authors argue that apart from opening the horizons of national judges, the networks also have an impact on the work of the European Courts, by critically evaluating and improving their functioning or by orchestrating a 'revolt' of national courts.

the beginning of his monograph, Kühn makes it explicit that his historical analysis of 'mechanical jurisprudence' in CEE is future oriented and should be understood in the context of twenty-first century practical debates on judiciary reforms.[48] It is however a different matter when positions in current policy debates about the CEE judiciary are supported by more or less stylised and simplified historical claims. Analysing CEE judiciary in methodologically sound normative-analytical and/or empirical-functionalist terms has clear advantages not only for scholarship but in terms of the political cultures of the region. Arguably, this is one of the best things legal scholars can do against the region's inferiority complex.

---

[48] Kühn (n 5) xvii–xviii.

3

EU Law and Central European Judges: Administrative Judiciaries in the Czech Republic, Hungary and Poland Ten Years after Accession

MARCIN MATCZAK, MÁTYÁS BENCZE AND ZDENĚK KÜHN*

I. Introduction

In 2010 we published a collaborative article in which we showed how the judiciary in three Central and Eastern European (CEE) countries reacted to the institutional changes that were made in these countries at the end of the 1990s and the beginning of the 2000s.[1] In that article we set out the results of an analysis of over 1000 judgments passed by Polish, Czech and Hungarian administrative courts in the years between 1999 and 2004, particularly the types of arguments or values referred to by the judges in their judgments.

Our analysis led to the conclusion that the respective judiciaries did not change their adjudicating method in the years in question despite significant changes in the legal environment, particularly the new Constitutions of the 1990s, pre-accession commitments and accession itself. One of the features of judicial adjudications in the period in question is an unswerving reliance on formal law values[2]

---

* The authors would like to thank all the participants of the conference 'Central European Judges under the EU Influence: The Transformative Power of Europe Revised on the 10th Anniversary of the Enlargement', Florence, 12–13 May 2014, for their insightful comments to this chapter. Our special thanks go also to the members of our research team for their invaluable assistance in the research: Ágnes Kovács, Krisztina Ficsor, Csaba Gondola, Olga Papp, Zsófia Zsoldics, Bartłomiej Osieka, Szymon Łajszczak, Aleksandra Orzeł, Tomasz Kwiatkowski, Krzysztof Kumala and Bartłomiej Dębski.

[1] M Matczak, M Bencze and Z Kühn, 'Constitutions, EU Law and Judicial Strategies in the Czech Republic, Hungary and Poland' (2010) 30 *Journal of Public Policy* 81.

[2] In this article we use the terms 'value' and 'argument' interchangeably. We understand a law value (eg a EU law value) as a state of affairs stipulated by that law (eg free flow of goods and services) and an argument as an affirmation of the need to implement the state of affairs set out by a judge in a judgment. We deem that for the purpose of our deliberations this interchangeable use of these terms is fully justified and does not give rise to confusion.

such as linguistic interpretation of a legal text and references to earlier judgments. Moreover, judges did not show any increased interest in constitutional values or EU law values despite these values having been introduced to the normative systems of each country by the legislators. Nor did judges show any increased interest in values or arguments such as teleological or functional interpretations.

As we characterised the criticised judicial method as *formalistic adjudication* it is crucial to clarify what we exactly mean by the term 'formalism' and what are the consequences of applying this approach. Formalism is often depicted as the 'most-locally-applicable-rule' approach in deciding a legal case[3] or 'bound' judicial decision making.[4] At the most general level this means that practitioners try to solve a given legal problem by relying only on a limited set of arguments such as the above-mentioned text of the law, earlier cases, accepted legal doctrines and traditional interpretative methods *without taking into consideration the wider social and legal context* of the case. The judge presents the decision as a *simple logical deduction* from the general legal standards, as if no substantive value judgements have been added.[5]

This model represents a kind of judicial self-understanding to remain loyal to traditional legal ideology, which according to many lawyers serves best the idea of the rule of law. The other justifying principle of formalism is the separation of powers which requires a clear differentiation between the competence of the legislator and that of the judge. A judge therefore can back the judgment exclusively by those arguments which come from the legislative bodies or which are at least accepted by them.

For a better understanding of what of formalism, we can contrast it with two other judicial approaches, namely the Dworkinian and the pragmatist model. When applied to the process of adjudication, the Dworkinian approach generally takes into consideration the wider legal context of cases—ie the justifying moral and political principles of law—as well as the text of the law and previous rulings.[6] Pragmatism, on the contrary, does not pay much attention to the

---

[3] F Schauer, 'Formalism' (1988) 97 *Yale Law Journal* 509, 519.

[4] J Wróblewski, *The Judicial Application of Law* (Kluwer Law, 1992).

[5] Martin Stone, for instance, found in legal scholarship at least seven varieties of formalism. See M Stone, 'Formalism' in J Coleman and S Shapiro (eds), *The Oxford Handbook of Jurisprudence and Philosophy of Law* (Oxford University Press, 2002) 166–205, 170. *cf* also R Siltala, *A Theory of Precedent. From Analytical Positivism to a Post-Analytical Philosophy of Law* (Hart Publishing, 2000) 50. Siltala distinguishes five basic modes of formalism: 1) Constitutive formality (the formal relation of legal standard to its source, which gives the standard ideally a binary code valid/non-valid); 2) systemic formality, defined by internal coherence of the legal system and its standards; 3) mandatory formality, which relates to the formal binding force of the source of law (binary code binding/non-binding); 4) structural formality, which relates to the degree of closeness of operative facts of the rule (high degree of formalism relates to concrete clear rule); 5) methodological formality, which places emphasis on a literal reading of the law. Our analysis primarily deals with the last sense of formalism in Siltala's understanding, though it relates to other notions of formalism as well.

[6] R Dworkin, The Moral Reading of the Constitution (1996), online at <www.nybooks.com/articles/archives/1996/mar/21/the-moral-reading-of-the-constitution/?page=1>, last visited 1 December 2014.

underlying moral principles. Pragmatist judges believe it to be more important to adequately reflect social needs underpinning the law, ie the wider social context of the case. Several representatives of the pragmatist approach have a clear concept of the social function of law that adjudication should serve.[7]

Nonetheless, moderate use of the formalist approach has its own advantages. Legal certainty and predictability are core elements of modern law, thus formalist decision making reduces the risks of social actions. This has been perhaps best explained by Max Weber, according to whom:

> [J]uridical formalism enables the legal system to operate like a technically rational machine. Thus it guarantees to individuals and groups within the system a relative maximum of freedom, and greatly increases for them the possibility of predicting the legal consequences of their actions. Procedure becomes a specific type of pacified contest, bound to fixed and inviolable 'rules of games'.[8]

However, excessive formalism makes the law very rigid and inflexible; as a consequence, formalistic adjudication loses its connection to the moral and political values as well as the social needs which the law should otherwise serve.

In order to refine further this general picture we have to introduce a distinction between 'honest' and 'strategic' judicial formalism.[9] The former represents a judicial attitude to remain loyal to the text of the law, to the accepted legal doctrines and to the traditional interpretive methods at any cost. Although this judicial strategy works well in 'easy' or 'routine' cases, in 'hard' cases where the law is uncertain the formalist method simply fails: A judge cannot be bound to the text of the rule as the applicability of the 'most local rule' itself becomes questionable in difficult cases.

If a judge insists on presenting her or his argumentation as a logical deduction and denies that political, moral, social or other choices should be involved in any legal decision making even in hard cases,[10] she or he has to use the other (strategic) version of formalism. Under these circumstances formalism may potentially function to 'camouflage' the hidden agenda of a judge. The judge's decision cannot be deduced from the traditional legal arguments that she or he presents in his or her opinion. The judge may be fully aware of this fact, but the judgment, seemingly, is based on appropriate and relevant legal reasons. As a consequence of applying this strategy the judge cannot be subject to the criticism of taking decisions based on illegitimate reasons.

---

[7] RA Posner, 'Pragmatic Adjudication' (1996) 18 *Cardozo Law Review* 1.

[8] M Weber, *Max Weber on Law in Economy and Society* (ed Max Rheinstein, trans E Shils) (Harvard University Press, 1969).

[9] This distinction is a reflection on our observation that authors do not always recognize that formalist judicial style is not necessarily the same as rule-based decision making. Judges many times only pretend that they decide on the basis of the text of the law; however, in these cases they are merely justifying their decision by the text of the law. For a classical example of ignoring this distinction see HLA Hart, *The Concept of Law* (Oxford University Press, 1994) 124–54.

[10] Schauer (n 3) 511.

Strategic formalism has a detrimental effect on the quality of judicial practice. It prevents the parties and the public audiences from getting to know the real considerations driving the judge in the decision making process. The rule of law requires that judges explain in a plausible way and in a detailed manner *why* they decided a case in a certain way. Even if a court decides a case without delay and society is satisfied with the result, the lack of reflective argumentative judicial style makes the decision hard to understand and ineligible for observance in subsequent cases.[11]

Strategic formalism can be plausibly explained by the public choice theory. In public choice models judges are players in the field of politics.[12] Courts are not only institutions with a special judicial function, but they have their own institutional goals and may try to strengthen their political position. The formalist strategy may be appropriate to depict the court as a neutral law-applier agency which refrains from engaging in discussing topical political issues.

In our previous article we identified the probable other causes of formalist judicial style, among them the communist legacy, particularly in terms of judicial education, a phenomenon known as 'escape into formalism' arising from a huge workload and a lack of appropriate resources, and also the unwillingness to adjudicate based on general standards, arising from concerns over too far-reaching judicial discretion.

On the tenth anniversary of our countries joining the European Union, we have again attempted to analyse how administrative courts in Poland, the Czech Republic and Hungary adjudicate. Applying the same methodology, we analysed approximately 1000 judgments passed by administrative courts in the years between 2005 and 2013. In this chapter we set out the results of the analysis, juxtaposing it with the previous analysis to illustrate how the style of administrative court judges' adjudications has altered over the past 15 years. Our aim is to show how the extensive institutional changes in Central and Eastern Europe at the turn of the century influenced judges' method of adjudicating and, more broadly, their thought processes and how they see their role. Does the judiciary continue to see itself as Montesquieu's 'mouth of the law', bowing down before legal formalism? Or has the enormous load of general rules and standards that accompanied the new Constitutions and European law forced them to play the Dworkinian judge Hercules? We attempt to answer these and other questions in this chapter.

We proceed as follows: In the first part, we discuss the research methodology applied in both the previous and the current analysis of administrative judicature. We then move on to show the results obtained in a manner enabling the 1999–2004 period to be compared with the period 2005–2013. In the third part, we interpret the results obtained, broken down into countries analysed and generally.

---

[11] See also above, ch 2 in this volume.

[12] For an overview of this approach see A Dyevre, 'Unifying the Field of Comparative Judicial Politics: Towards a General Theory of Judicial Behaviour' (2010) 2 *European Political Science Review* 304.

In the conclusion to the chapter we try to explain what we can learn from the CEE judges' behaviour since the turn of the millennium and what lessons can be drawn for the future.

II. Research Methodology

We examined judgments passed in the years 1999 to 2004 and those passed in the years 2005 to 2013 by applying the same methodology, which was based to a great extent on a quantitative analysis of the types of arguments used by judges in their statements of reasons. We assumed that judges could refer in their statements of reasons to four types of arguments, which we have also called values:

1) Internal values of law
2) Values external to law
3) Constitutional values and
4) European law values.

Having read through the statements of reasons we then drew up an Excel spreadsheet showing the number and types of references. We included in the first group of internal law values the traditional legal arguments used by the judiciary, including among others, linguistic interpretations, systemic interpretations, references to previous judgments, references to legal doctrine and the application of well-known legal themes, for example *argumentum a contrario*. We considered references to these values to be typical of the traditional model of legal adjudication in which a judge adjudicates on the basis of relatively clear rules. Reference to the values in this group does not require judicial activism or engagement in non-legal analyses (for example analyses of the political or economic purpose of a given law) or a balancing of rules and standards of a general, ambiguous nature.

In the second group, the group of external law values, we included values any reference to which requires a judge to depart from the traditional adjudication model, in the sense that any reference to these values requires an analysis of the effects of political, economic and social factors on the law. We included in the group of these values, for example arguments over the purpose or function of a law, reference to the public or a private interest, and arguments taking into account the social and economic changes made in the judicial environment that a judge deems important to the adjudication method. Although some of the values included in this second group have a place on the traditional list of legal arguments (for example functional interpretation), we deemed that referring to external values requires greater judicial activism and involves an element of balancing values that are not present in argumentation based on internal law values.

We see the third group, the group of constitutional values, as encompassing any argument based on a Constitution, involving both a general reference to constitutional values, rights and principles, and a precise reference to a specific

constitutional principle, for example the principle of proportionality or the principle of the freedom of enterprise. As references to this group of values are a measure
of something that can be called judges' constitutional awareness, we also included
in this group pro-constitutional interpretations and particularly direct application of the Constitution permitted in some of the countries examined. We treated
references to constitutional values as evidence of adjudication based on standards
and the judge's willingness to depart from his or her traditional role, which was
characteristic of judges in the communist era. Adjudication using the Constitution also goes against the formalistic approach, the features of which include a
conviction that a judge should adjudicate based on the most locally applicable
rule, which is a refinement of a more abstract higher ranking principle or a legal
provision. Consequently, direct application of constitutional principles in legal
formalism terms is at the least undesirable.

The fourth and last group of values covered in a broad sense values of EU law
(primarily, we mean by 'European law' the laws of the EU, but we also refer the
judgements of the European Court of Human Rights (ECtHR) by this term). In this
group we included references to provisions of EU law (for example provisions of
directives), references to EU legal principles (for example some of the fundamental freedoms), and also references to the Court of Justice of the European Union
(CJEU) case law and general references to the idea of European integration. In the
first study (1999–2004), the values in this group were in some ways similar to constitutional values, as judicial references in this period were a sure sign of activism.
Although during the second study references to EU law values were similar in terms
of character to internal values (for example in the case of highly detailed regulations of European tax law), they have to a great extent retained the character of
references to legal principles and often require values to be balanced. This group of
values is essential in assessing how the judicial adjudication method has changed as
a result of EU accession. However, the number of references to the group of external and constitutional values could also be interpreted as a measure of how accession has indirectly affected judicial behaviour in Central and Eastern Europe, which
we will try to show in the part dedicated to interpreting the results of our research.

As in our previous study, we carried out a quantitative analysis of references to
the groups of values described above based on *published* judgments concerning
issues *key to business activity*. We compiled published judgments based on their
nature—important, often precedential, cases, that could therefore be treated as
Dworkinian hard cases. Thus they also comprise an interesting field in which to
analyse the spectrum of judicial argumentation which in such cases should, at
least theoretically, be broader than in standard cases. Judgments published are also
judgments selected for publication by the judiciary itself, so their statements of
reasons were consequently deemed by judges to be worthy of dissemination. This
feature has enabled us to state that these judgments reflect the judiciary's perception of how a case should be properly and correctly adjudicated.

We chose judgments concerning business activity, for example judgments in
cases involving tax (VAT, excise), licences and concessions, the construction
process and highly regulated areas of business activity (pharmaceutical, energy

and telecommunications law) as those in which the effect of European integration and the new, free market economy system introduced by the Constitution can be most clearly seen.

In the results given below, we indicate the number of randomly selected judgments that we examined and various configurations of the number of references and changes to them over time. In particular, we show the number of references to individual groups, the change in number in each year and also the most frequent combination of references per judgment. Consequently, we are able to form several theses as regards changes in the spectrum of values used by judges in administrative case law in the countries examined.

In this article we do not justify our choice of administrative judgments as subject of our study (and not judgments in criminal or civil cases, for instance), we do not discuss the similarities and differences between how the administrative judiciary works in our countries, neither do we discuss the history of institutional changes that were made to them at the turn of the century. We refer readers who are interested in these issues to our previous article[13]—the considerations therein also apply to the current analysis.

III. Research Results

Below we present the main results of our research for all three countries.

Table 1. **References to specific groups of standards in all examined judgments and comparison to the results of the previous analysis—Poland**

All PL (400)				
EU Law Topics	**Constitutional Law Topics**	**Internal Values of Law**	**Values External to Law**	**Total**
105	209	1637	231	2182
4.8%	9.6%	75.0%	10.6%	100.0%

	1999–2004	**2005–2013**	**Change**
EU Law Topics	0.9%	4.8%	433.3%
Constitutional Law Topics	7.4%	9.6%	29.7%
Internal Values of Law	81.5%	75.0%	−8.0%
Values External to Law	10.2%	10.6%	3.9%
	100.0%	100.0%	

[13] Above (n 1).

Table 2. References to specific groups of standards in all examined judgments and comparison to the results of the previous analysis—Hungary

All HU (358)				
EU Law Topics	Constitutional Law Topics	Internal Values of Law	Values External to Law	Total
97	39	799	128	1063
9.1%	3.7%	75.2%	12.0%	100%

	1999–2004	2005–2013	Change
EU Law Topics	0.8%	9.1%	1037.5%
Constitutional Law Topics	2.5%	3.7%	48.0%
Internal Values of Law	87.5%	75.2%	−14.06%
Values External to Law	9.3%	12.0%	29.03%
	100.0%	100.0%	

Table 3. References to specific groups of standards in all examined judgments and comparison to the results of the previous analysis—Czech Republic

All CZ (180)				
EU Law Topics	Constitutional Law Topics	Internal Values of Law	Values External to Law	Total
84	101	852	303	1340
6.3%	7.5%	63.6%	22.6%	100.0%

	1999–2004	2005–2013	Change
EU Law Topics	1.6%	6.3%	293.75%
Constitutional Law Topics	8.0%	7.5%	−6.25%
Internal Values of Law	71.9%	63.6%	−11.54%
Values External to Law	18.6%	22.6%	21.5%
	100.0%	100.0%	

IV. Interpretation of Results

A. Poland

The results of an analysis of Polish court judgments are in keeping with the trends seen in all three countries examined. Since the period from 1999 to 2004 there has been a significant rise in references to EU law arguments (an increase of over 400 per cent) and a rise in references to constitutional arguments (of nearly 30 per cent). These increases were accompanied by a fall in the number of references to internal arguments (of 8 per cent). Such results, according to the assumptions made in the previous study, are clearly signs of deformalisation in the administrative adjudication. We had not encountered this deformalisation in the previous study, therefore the current results seem to confirm our thesis on a delayed impact of the institutional changes in CEE on judicial behaviour.

In comparison to the Czech Republic and Hungary, Polish judges most frequently interpret internal law in accordance with EU law—the pro-European interpretation principle constitutes over 60 per cent of all references to an EU law value applied by Polish judges. This phenomenon may be deemed a sign of judicial maturity in its approach to the use of EU law and a sign that judgments are becoming deformalised, though in the case of Poland this seems to be limited to judgments relating to tax and financial law. As already indicated, as opposed to automatic citation of particular provisions of EU law, interpreting the provisions of domestic law in accordance with EU law is never an action based on simple syllogism and as such is a more complex form of argumentation, characteristic of an informal manner of adjudicating.

An interesting phenomenon that can be seen in citing constitutional values in judgments is that Polish judges generally do not make such analyses *ex officio*. The constitutional deliberations made by judges are usually due to the parties' attorney, who raise arguments of this type in appeals and consequently, as it were, force judges to enhance the spectrum of argumentation applied in a given judgment. A similar practice has been present in both Hungarian and Czech jurisdictions.

The results for Poland should be interpreted in light of a discussion that took place in Poland after the results of the first study for the years 1999 to 2004 were published (2006). The conclusions of the previous study, and therefore the findings regarding far-reaching formalism in administrative court judgments, were fiercely criticised by judges.[14] Administrative court judges questioned both the research methodology and the results themselves, taking the stance that the statements of reasons for court judgments do not require all the arguments used to be cited and

---

[14] This criticism was raised particularly by judge B Gruszczyński, 'Czy formalizm orzeczeń sądów oznacza powierzchowne rozpoznanie sprawy?' [Does the formalism of administrative judiciary's decisions equate to superficial verdicts?] Prawo i Podatki, 2006, nr 4, 23–26.

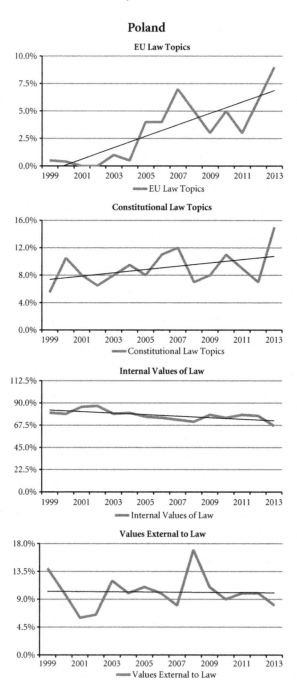

Chart 1: Trends of frequency of references to specific groups of standards between 1999 and 2013

also that, as constitutional values have been taken into consideration by lawmakers while enacting more detailed provisions of law (for example at the statutory level), there is no need to consider them in each judgment that applies the statutory laws. The current study seems, however, to confirm the theory set out in the previous analysis, particularly that regarding the delayed effect of the constitutionalisation and Europeanisation of the law on judges' actions. Moreover, the qualitative analysis of Polish judgments suggests that the Polish judiciary is taking greater care to use deformalised, including constitutional, arguments in judgments passed after 2005 and greater sensitivity to the sub-legal effects of judgments.

We believe that the discussion on the results of the first study on administrative judiciary that appeared in Poland[15] could play an important role in bringing judges' attention to the significance of recognising general principles as a valid source of judicial argumentation. This approach is clearly illustrated by a quotation from a judgment passed in 2009 by judge B Gruszczyński, one of the most active critics of the first study:

> The axiological aspect of the issue examined is also important. The appellant loses the entry made if the court discontinues the proceedings as devoid of purpose … It has been rightly noted in literature that, when a sense of justice deviates far from the desired model and is not built up widely in the minds of doctrinal and judicature representatives but is forged through the daily procedural reality of entities … then an interpretation of provisions that leads to the law colliding with generally accepted values, including justice, should be avoided.[16]

The direct reference to general axiological principles that can be seen in the quoted verdict is hard to reconcile with the previous position represented by the judges, namely that those principles are already present in the detailed legal provisions and as such do not require any direct application by the judges. It is also difficult to regard the approach reflected in the quoted judgment as strongly formalistic and from the perspective of a comprehensive examination of cases it certainly deserves to be praised.

B. Hungary

Since the 1 January 2012 Hungary has had a new Constitution ('Hungarian Fundamental Law') and the structure of its administrative courts has slightly changed since 1 January 2013. They have been unified with the labour courts and have been re-organised at a regional level extracting administrative (and labour) judges from the professional supervision of Division of Civil Cases of the County Courts which

---

[15] D Galligan and M Matczak, *Strategie orzekania sądowego. O wykonywaniu władzy dyskrecjonalnej przez sędziów sądów administracyjnych* (Warszawa, 2005); D Galligan and M Matczak, 'Formalism in Post-Communist Courts. Empirical Study on Judicial Discretion in Polish Administrative Courts Deciding Business Cases' in R Coman and J-M De Waele (eds), *Judicial Reforms in Central and Eastern European Countries* (Vanden Broele, 2007).

[16] Decision of the SN, Case No II GPS 3/09.

they previously were subject to. This shift aimed at supporting the more efficient work of the affected branches of judicial administration (they currently have their own professional leaders who are experts of administrative law; they have trainings and meetings focusing on their own special problems etc). Although these changes may have a significant impact on adjudicative quality and style in the long run, they took place only one year before the end of the examined period. Thus we do not need to take them into consideration in evaluating our research data.

Based on the primary quantitative analysis of our data we can see that EU accession has had a strong direct impact on Hungarian administrative courts, in particular on the administrative division of the *Kúria* (Hungarian Supreme Court or Curia of Hungary). The proportion of references to EU law arguments has increased more than 10 times compared to the proportion of EU law references made by courts in the period of 1999 to 2004. The huge change in quantity can be the sign of change in quality, that is, our data can be interpreted as the first step of the Hungarian judiciary departing from the traditional model of adjudication.

That hypothesis is supported by two other facts. First, we can see a consistent increase in the number of references to EU law topics year by year between 2005 and 2013 (see chart 2 below).

Given the date of the EU accession (2004) these figures can demonstrate that the Hungarian judiciary has learnt to use EU law as a reasoning tool gradually. Step by step acceptance of legal arguments derived from EU law indicates organic, 'bottom-up' development of judicial practice which may result in reflective, well-reasoned decision making in cases where EU related issues emerge.

Second, we are also witnessing a significant increase in the proportion of references to constitutional law arguments (48 per cent) and to values external to law (29 per cent, see chart 2 below). Although references to values internal to law have preserved their prevalence, this dropped more than 30 per cent. Meanwhile, the more frequent use of non-traditional reasons can be interepreted as a new type of judicial thinking which is in line with the values and principles of the legal system of the EU. The new model for how judges see their role seems to be more sensitive to protection of rights than the one that existed before the EU accession.

Before declaring the Europeanisation of the judicial reasoning too soon we have to examine the deeper layers of the collected data. The reference to the category of 'other EU law' is the highest by far amongst all EU law arguments (82.3 per cent). References to particular provisions of EU directives, regulations and CJEU judgments (or references to the 'jurisprudence of CJEU' as such) were included in this category. The character of these 'written' EU law arguments is very similar to the traditional domestic legal rules and judicial practice. In some cases a judge has to deal with 'black letter laws' of the EU that can be considered as the 'most locally applicable rules'. Applying the 'written EU law' is not a significant challenge for a trained judge; it does not require involvement in the discussions concerning legitimate policies, values and interest behind the text of the (EU) law ('unwritten' elements of EU law). Products of EU legislation and CJEU judgments can be used 'mechanically', that is, in a very formalistic manner even when the appropriate

Hungary

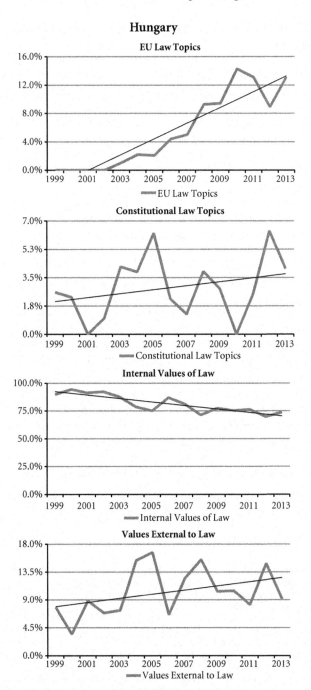

Chart 2: Trends of frequency of references to specific groups of standards between 1999 and 2013

application of the particular EU legal materials demand the opposite (argumentative, reflective and consequence-orientated) judicial style.

Moreover, frequent references to EU law can be used for strategic reasons: The judge tries to present his or her controversial (or arbitrary) decision as a logical deduction from the written law. In doing so they may benefit from the new legal arguments (EU law) at hand.[17] Another point of strategic application of EU law amongst Hungarian judges may be that by using the preliminary ruling procedure an ordinary judge can 'skip' the constitutional review of the *Alkotmánybíróság* (Hungarian Constitutional Court, hereinafter 'AB') which has the competence to review the judgments of ordinary courts since 2012. Ordinary courts may try to strengthen their position against the AB in this way.[18]

There is another reason for strategic use of EU values: According to an earlier study non-traditional arguments in the judge's written opinion do not add any extra value to the line of classical legal reasons in many cases. The new model legal arguments serve as 'ornaments' or 'decorum' in the reasoning of the judgment.[19] EU law values may share this fate also.

Another striking figure is 'zero reference' to the EU law proportionality principle, since this principle is one of the key features of effective judicial review according to EU law and to the jurisprudence of ECtHR.[20] Although judges refer to the proportionality principle in cases without European context in 23.1 per cent of all pro-constitutional arguments, experts warn that Hungarian courts do not use the proportionality test in the way the CJEU or ECtHR use it. Hungarian judges examine only whether the administrative agency exercises its discretional power in a 'reasonable' way and they do not tend to judge the agency's discretional decision on merit. Where judges refer to the proportionality rule in the examined cases, they, predominantly, simply state that the administrative agency took (or did not take) all relevant circumstances of the case into consideration. They seem to ignore the broader policy and governance context of the case when making their decision in questions of proportionality. As Kovács and Varju put it:

> The introduction of [genuine] proportionality to replace unreasonableness as a general principle in determining the intensity of judicial review in Hungarian administrative law

---

[17] I Bartha and M Bencze, 'Az európai jog alkalmazása a magyar bírói ítélkezésben 2004 és 2007 között' [Enforcement of EU law in the Hungarian adjudication between 2004 and 2007] in P Máté (ed), *Európai jog és jogfilozófia*. Konferenciatanulmányok az európai integráció ötvenedik évfordulójának ünnepére (Szent István Társulat, 2008).

[18] Lively debates between the Legfelsőbb Bíróság (Hungarian Supreme Court before the establishment of the Kúria, hereinafter 'LB') and the AB on the question of 'who determines the Hungarian judicial practice ultimately?' have already taken place in the early 1990s in Hungary. See M Szabó, 'Change of Legal Thought in Hungary 1990–2005' in A Jakab, P Takács and AF Tatham (eds), *The Transformation of the Hungarian Legal Order 1985–2005* (Kluwer Law International, 2007) 600–01.

[19] M Bencze, 'Díszítőelem, álcázóháló vagy tartóoszlop? A magyar büntetőbírói gyakorlat viszonya az alkotmányhoz' [Enforcement of the Constitution in the Hungarian adjudication in criminal cases] (2007) *Fundamentum* 3, 5–21.

[20] See also below, ch 9 in this vol.

would require the reassessment of current doctrine and the reconsideration of the role of courts in the scrutiny of administrative discretion.[21]

C. Czech Republic

The Czech Republic presents in some ways a unique case study for the period 2005 to 2013. Prior to 2003 the Czech administrative judiciary had been a plethora of eight regional courts without a high court at the top which would unify their conflicting case law. In 2003 the Czech administrative judicial system was transformed by establishing a new institution of the *Nejvyšší správní soud* (Supreme Administrative Court, hereinafter 'NSS'). In our previous analysis we covered the period until 2004; by then the number of decisions of the NSS in our sample remained very low and did not affect the overall results of our study. Unlike the previous study, the published case law between 2005 and 2013 is dominated by decisions of the NSS (they make approximately nine out of 10 cases in our sample). Our research therefore covers a decisive part of the development of the NSS in its first decade (2003–2013).

In its first few years, the NSS suffered from a flood of cases and many vacancies in the judicial personnel. The NSS started in 2003 with less than half the number of judges sitting in the NSS in 2014 (originally 13 as opposed to 30 today). In the first few months of 2003, judges were not supported by any law clerks. Not surprisingly, many delays and backlogs followed. This had an impact on the quality of the earliest judgments of the NSS. Judgments remained very short, they included just the very basic framework of textual analysis of the law. Purposive argumentation as well as any other argumentation external to law was largely missing.

In around 2006 the situation shifted. That year the NSS moved into a new modern building, judges were equipped with new technologies. The number of judges doubled and reached almost 30, thus making the workload more manageable. Every judge hired a second law clerk. A new comparative law section of the NSS was established, one of its functions preparing comparative analysis for judges when facing cases with EU or foreign law elements. This section is composed of young lawyers, recent law school graduates, fluent in many languages (besides those frequently spoken Polish, Spanish and Italian are also represented here). Interestingly, judges do not hesitate to use the output of the comparative analysis when justifying their verdicts.

The NSS, composed of 30 judges today (2014), is rather small if compared to its European counterparts. It includes both career judges and judges coming from other legal professions (bureaucracy, private firms, academia). The former group now makes up less than half of the NSS. Being composed of judges with different

---

[21] Ibid.

professional backgrounds the NSS is much more diverse than the Czech *Nejvyšší soud* (Czech Supreme Court, hereinafter 'NS').

At the beginning of the twenty-first century it can be said that the Czech judiciary does not use a single style which would unite constitutional, administrative and general judiciary. Even within one single NSS one can find more styles, which do relate to personalities of judges who write the opinion. However, if we shall simplify, the civil and criminal judiciary represented by the NS stays closer to the cognitive and formalistic ideal of legalistic argumentation which used to dominate Czech law until the 1990s. This ideal is linked to openly formalistic and mostly brief opinion, without accepting interpretational alternatives. The disadvantage of this rather conservative style is its limited persuasiveness: the reader does not know how the court addressed the arguments which called for an alternative approach. The decisions retain their legalistic façade, the judge presents his view as if he or she were a 'subsumption' automaton, without showing reasons why they chose one premise over another. The decisive reason of the correctness of judicial interpretation is the hierarchical position of the NS within the judicial system.

In contrast, the development of a different style of the administrative judiciary accelerated after 2004 (the year when we finished our first research). It followed the patterns developed in the 1990s by the *Ústavní soud* (Czech Constitutional Court, hereinafter 'ÚS'). After all, as we mentioned in the first study, it was the ÚS which effectively served as a substitute to the non-existent NSS until 2003, unifying the case law of regional administrative courts. This explains the high percentage of constitutional reasoning in the administrative judiciary of the Czech Republic as early as the late 1990s.

Today the decisions of the NSS and often also regional administrative courts are written in a dialogical and discursive style, their length increasing every year. Judges are often trying hard to deal with all alternatives of the interpretation of a particular legal problem. The nature of reasoning is quite often substantive, it is openly accepted that the law has more than just one possible meaning. Judges are seeking to find all the reasons why the interpretation chosen by the court is the correct one; sometimes judges are so open that they make it explicit that multiple interpretations are possible, and then they give their reasons why the outcome they choose is the best one. Although the rank of the NSS within a judicial hierarchy matters (the court is right because it is final), the NSS tries to legitimise its reasoning by sincere attempts to persuade the readers. The disadvantage of this style is its length and diffuseness.

Both styles, the legalistic style of the NS and dialogical of the NSS do coexist in the same legal culture. That is why it is premature to say which one would prevail in a longer run. It remains to be seen whether a longer decision with more reasons is more persuasive within a civilian legal culture, or whether the judiciary by doing this is not losing part of its (fictitious but publicly important) legitimacy as the institution endowed with knowledge of the 'objective' truth of the law's interpretation.

Against this backdrop one must interpret the changes visible in our sample data since 2007. The average length of the judgment multiplied, say from two or three pages in the 1990s and the early 2000s to 10 or 12 pages in the late 2000s and the early 2010s. The judgment is now supposed to address all arguments presented by all parties to the procedure. It is not just the judge's authority which decides the case. Instead it is the judicial authority combined with the sincere and open dialogue with both parties which together decide the case. If this is true for many decisions dealing with hard cases, it is even more applicable for the decisions of the grand chamber of the NSS, which is supposed to unify the case law of the NSS.[22] As a rule, decisions of the grand chamber are openly dialogical, they deal with all interpretational alternatives and are explicitly based on weighing substantive reasons.

Since the 1990s a rather frequent use of external arguments, especially if compared with Poland and Hungary, has continued. Those arguments are quite often substantive and value-driven. The more visible rise of non-formalist argumentation, as represented in our graphs through 'values external to law', started in 2006 and accelerated since 2007. Unlike the situation until 2006, more recent judgments do approach hard cases in a much more transparent way, using teleological or purposive argumentation routinely. The relatively smaller number of references to legislative history, especially if compared to Poland (a Czech judge is almost three times less likely to refer to legislative history than his Polish counterpart), relates to the fact that Czech *travaux preparatoires* are notorious for being of very poor quality, usually lacking any substantial information. In contrast, the use of purposive argumentation (often called objective teleological argumentation: The law's purpose as envisaged by the interpreter) is now a standard exercise of Czech administrative judges.

EU law arguments come most often from VAT cases, customs law, some areas of environmental law and competition law, which is also the case in the two other countries. Cases where EU law is directly applicable have been decided by the NSS since the end of the first decade of this century, taking into account the delay between facts of the case, subsequent administrative procedure and finally judicial proceedings. It is generally possible to say that the judges of the NSS, supported in their research by the numerous professional staff and comparative apparatus and two law clerks, are inclined to address EU law arguments more often than lower administrative judges. For the latter it is still in some way a luxury for which they often lack time, resources and energy. After all, almost all preliminary references to the Court of Justice were made by the NSS rather than by lower administrative courts. The use of EU law arguments is quite often promoted by the parties to a case. In some other cases the parties try to argue against the use of EU law if the

---

[22] The NSS routinely decides in three judges chambers. The grand chamber is composed of seven judges and is supposed to issue verdicts binding for the entire court if the case law is conflicting or a regular chamber wants to deviate from the earlier case law.

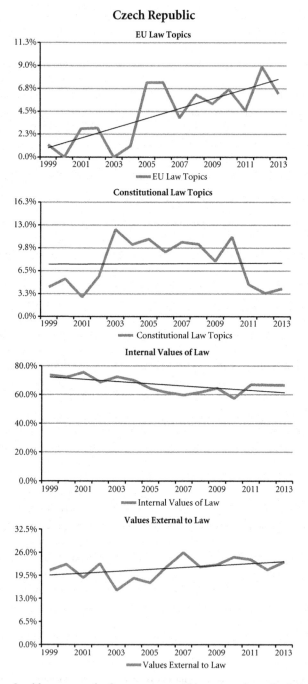

Chart 3: Trends of frequency of references to specific groups of standards between 1999 and 2013

result is likely to be detrimental to them. Often the parties try to set aside EU law by referring to the domestic constitutional law which is allegedly in conflict with EU law (such as the abuse of rights, carousel frauds in VAT etc). And yet in some different cases ignorant parties do not argue by EU law and the judge would invoke the argument on her own motion (typically if the parties' submission brought the general legal argument which has also its EU law underpinning).

Whether or not the use of EU law is a sign of anti-formalism is difficult to say. The use of EU law is in many cases anti-formalistic (if general principles or other open-ended standards of EU law are applied as well as EU law harmonising arguments). However, as already discussed above in relation to Hungary, it can easily become the exercise of overt formalism, especially if judges arbitrarily recite some abstract or unrelated EU rules which then serve as a façade for the result reached in a different way.

Czech judges do tend to quote legal literature much less frequently than the Polish courts but much more frequently than their Hungarian counterparts. Among published cases 3.5 per cent of judgments did refer to scholarly work, whereas in Poland the number is more than three times higher (11.4 per cent). In contrast, Hungarian judges almost never quote legal literature (0.3 per cent). The Czech legal culture historically belongs to the Germanic legal family where the role of legal academia has been always very important (in Germany often referred to as professorial style of law). Thus, the current situation when the Czech judges do not view legal academics as a meaningful support for their task of interpreting the law is part of the continuing failure of the domestic legal academia to provide an impetus to judge-made law.

Recently (say since 2010 or 2011) we can see to some extent a reverse phenomenon and the return to a different style of formalism. Also this is visible in our tables as the rise of values internal to law after 2010. This rise of formalist arguments is not the move back to statutory textualism. Instead, it is accompanied by the rise of the role of the earlier case law (case law formalism).[23] Whereas in the earliest years the judgments seldom referred to precedent as there was literally nothing (we remind our readers that the NSS started to operate in 2003 and the first year it issued few judgments), recently one can hardly find a decision which would not quote at least one precedent. In many judgments the number of cited precedents is much higher, though, and it often happens that the number of cases used and quoted is in two digits. Unlike Hungary, the NSS always gives a proper citation so the reader might find the source of argument. Furthermore, the proper quotation of the arguments used by the NSS makes the judicial argumentation more transparent and open to criticism.

On the other hand, NSS's argumentation is becoming more self-referential and sometimes even sterile because all arguments seem to be embedded in the earlier

---

[23] Signs of case law formalism are also present in Hungary, see Z Ződi, 'Analysis of Citation Patterns of Hungarian Judicial Decisions', online at <http://papers.ssrn.com/sol3/papers.cfm?abstract_id=2410070>, 26.

cases. The law's reason is often lost under the surface of texts separated from their factual environment in the earlier case law. Interestingly, this new wave of formalism sometimes results in counter-textual legal reasoning: In some cases judges refer to the case law related to an earlier version of the text of the law without noticing that the interpreted law itself had been amended. In fact, the way we conducted our research underestimates this new phenomenon as it includes cases which have been meant by their authors as being at least in some way novel. Many other cases which shall have been interpreted in a non-trivial fashion, all things considered, are often decided mechanically, just referring to the earlier case law which however was dealing with a different factual scenario. Such cases would remain unpublished.

D. General Evaluation of the Style of CEE Countries

i. The Direct Impact of EU Accession

The research results set out in the previous section point to several noticeable trends in CEE administrative courts' argumentation. First, an obvious trend is the significant rise in references to EU law arguments, which, in each of the countries examined, was several hundred per cent. This direct effect of the accession is easy to explain—together with the accession, EU law became an element of the internal legal system of Member States and references to this law have over time become similar to references to internal law values. This is particularly true in the case of adjudications relating to customs and tax law, especially in cases involving VAT or excise duty. The impact of the accession is not limited to EU law-related issues but extends into purely domestic cases. In the case of Poland and the Czech Republic, the most frequently (in Hungary the second most frequently) cited argument in the EU law values group is the principle of interpretation of domestic law in accordance with EU law. This type of argument is not a typical internal or 'written' argument that is applied automatically, as it requires from the judge a complex process of argumentation which is unique in each case. The substantial rise in the application of pro-Union interpretations could therefore be regarded as a serious change in the adjudicating culture of judges in CEE. This type of argumentation is structurally different from the arguments used in the past and consequently is something new in judicial practice, which cannot be said of specific EU law regulations being applied in a manner similar to the current application of domestic provisions.

ii. The Indirect Impact of the EU Accession

In addition to the rather obvious direct impact of EU law on the spectrum of arguments used by judges in CEE, our research also shows the occurrence of an indirect impact. First, we observed a significant increase in the number of referred reasons per judgments in comparison to the previously examined period (see table 4 below).

Table 4. Comparison of number of arguments per judgment of the currently examined period to the previous period

Number of arguments per judgment	Poland	Hungary	Czech
1999–2004	3.5	1.92	3.53
2005–2013	5.4	3	7.6
Change	54%	36%	115%

It can be assumed that the more reasons a judge uses in a case, the more persuasive his decision becomes. We believe this is a sign of a greater understanding of the needs of the external stakeholders, like the parties to the case, their representatives and a wider public audience that can better understand the grounds of a particular verdict.

Second, compared to the results of the study carried out for the years 1999 to 2004, there has been a drop in the number of references to internal law arguments together with a change in the frequency of using non-formalistic arguments other than those of the EU law. This specifically applies to constitutional arguments, though to a lesser degree, arguments based on values external to a law, such as the aim or function of laws.

The fall in the number of references to internal arguments, particularly the lower frequency with which linguistic interpretation is used (a 10 to 15 per cent drop, depending on the country), may be an indication of the deformalisation of administrative court judgments. Of course, to a certain extent this change corresponds to the greater number of references to EU law arguments. These references have in many cases, especially in tax cases, replaced references to internal arguments. This is why, in order to show deformalisation tendencies in administrative case law, it is necessary to point out other changes, particularly as regards the frequency of references to constitutional and external arguments.

As indicated in the paper setting out our research for the years 1999 to 2004, constitutional argumentation shows that judges are willing, in a specific judgment, to apply principles of law understood to be general, unspecified standards. This willingness goes against the formalistic approach, which centres on the application of bright-line rules and is adverse to argumentation based on principles and standards thus requiring judges to take important axiological decisions. Under formalism these decisions are reserved for the legislator and it is deemed that the application of principles by a judge leads to a great risk of unbridled decision making discretion.

However, taking into account values such as the aim or function of law shows that judges' awareness goes beyond the letter of the law to cover how application of the law affects society and the economy. In our view, the fact that EU law is clearly rooted in the idea of economic, social and even cultural integration naturally requires that in many cases related to EU law judges have to consider the relationship between the law and society and its development. There is no doubt that a functional and teleological interpretation, based for example on the analysis of the themes in European directives, is a key element in applying European law. Consequently, it may be deemed that acceptance of this by judges leads to greater willingness to apply internal law functionally and teleologically. The application of values external to law is therefore proof of a departure from the formalistic tendencies that decry the use of extra-textual values in judicial argumentation.

In both areas of judicial activity discussed, our research shows that changes have taken place since our study of the years 1999 to 2004. In both Poland and Hungary the increase in the frequency of references to constitutional values is impressive— an almost 50 per cent rise in Hungary and a 30 per cent rise in Poland. Data on the Czech Republic do not support this trend, though it should be noted that in the 1999–2004 results judgments passed by Czech courts were the least formalistic of the three countries examined (and were in direct interactions with the *ÚS* which served as a sort of substitute to the then non-existent high administrative court). Thus it could be said that the willingness to apply the Constitution, promoted by the influential ÚS, has remained stable and at a relatively high level in the Czech Republic.

Among the constitutional references in all the countries examined, at the forefront are references to generally understood constitutional rights and freedoms without them being specified by judges. This may show that the constitutional awareness of the judiciary in administrative courts is relatively low and is limited to an awareness that constitutional rights and freedoms should be taken into account in judgments, though this is not based on an in-depth analysis of the functions and relevance of individual constitutional principles. Hungarian judges are an exception in this respect. In their judgments almost a quarter of all references to the Constitution are references to the proportionality principle. This principle plays a key role in assessing whether it is reasonable for the administration to interfere in the lives of citizens, thus it is also certain that this popularity among administrative court judges should become a model. A similar role in the Czech case is played by the due process clause which guarantees the right to fair trial (Article 36 of the Czech Bill of Rights). This clause serves as a sort of default rule which generates constitutional reasoning if no more clear rights are available. When a Czech lawyer does not have another constitutional provision to use she would simply refer to Article 36. Both the Czech NSS and the ÚS use this fundamental right for both procedural and substantive law errors before the ordinary courts.

Although there has been an increase in the number of references to external values in Hungary and the Czech Republic (a rise of about 20–30 per cent in both countries), no such increase can be seen in Poland. The most popular of the external values are references to the aim and function of the law and also to the legislator's intent. Note should be taken of the occurrence in judicial argumentation of references to a principle that is of key importance for citizens—that of *in dubio pro libertate* (if in doubt, adjudicate in favour of freedom of permitted action), which we found little evidence of in our study of the years 1999 to 2004. Our current research shows that it is becoming increasingly popular to apply this principle in Hungary and in the Czech Republic.

A useful summary of the interpretation of our research results is given in one more table, illustrating the spectrum of values referred to by judges in a single judgment.

Table 5. Combinations of arguments per judgment (proportions of the same combinations as found in the previously examined period are in brackets)

All Poland (400)						
Intern	Const/ Intern	Intern/ Extern	Const/Intern/ Extern	EU/ Intern	Other	Total
165	60	60	45	30	39	399
41.4% (60.8%)	15.0% (10.0%)	15.0% (19.8%)	11.3% (5.6%)	7.5%	9.8%	100%

All Hungary (358)						
Intern	Intern/ Extern	EU/ Intern	Const/ Intern	EU/Intern/ Extern	Other	Total
187	63	50	15	22	21	358
52.2% (82.4%)	17.6% (12.2%)	14.0%	4.2% (3.0%)	6.1%	5.9%	100.0%

All Czech Republic (180)						
Intern	Intern/ Extern	Const/Intern/ Extern	EU/Intern/ Extern	EU/Const/ Intern/Extern	Other	Total
31	77	29	22	18	3	180
17.2% (41.8%)	42.8% (33%)	16.1% (9.4%)	12.2%	10.0%	1.7%	100.0%

This table shows, *inter alia*, how many administrative cases are adjudicated by judges solely on the basis of formalistic (internal) arguments, and in how many cases other values play a part. In our view, a good judgment should be justified using a whole range of interpretations and therefore the cogency of a linguistic interpretation should be supported by a functional, pro-Union and pro-constitutional interpretation. Thus the fall in the number of judgments based solely on internal values should be seen as a positive change in how administrative court judges adjudicate. The table above shows this fall—at present fewer than half of all administrative court judgments are based solely on internal argumentation, which we deem formalistic, while the study of the years 1999 to 2004 indicated that as many as two thirds of judgments did not use any external, constitutional or EU arguments (for example Poland). We regard this change as one of the most noticeable pieces of evidence of the evolution that administrative judgments have undergone in CEE due to the accession of countries in the region to the European Union.

iii. Some Doubts about Deformalisation

We have been witnessing recently a considerable change in the proportion of EU law arguments in judgments delivered by CEE judges. Nonetheless, the higher proportion of using written EU law arguments in reasoning is a natural consequence of the EU accession and it is not necessary a sign of the Europeanisation of the judicial thought. As EU law is being more and more developed the number of its specific and directly applicable norms are increasing. Provisions of EU law therefore, as we indicated above, can also become the 'most locally applicable rules'.[24] In addition, national higher courts gradually build a bunch of precedents around cases related to EU law which can determine the direction of adjudication in future cases and, at the same time, can make judicial practice rigid and inflexible ('case law formalism'). It is a realistic possibility that many judges choose the formalistic way of applying EU law without reflecting the policy considerations, values and purposes behind the text of EU law. Using the text of EU law without accepting the judicial thinking of the Court of Justice and the ECtHR will not serve the purpose of deepening European integration.

Formalistic application of EU law is strengthened by one of the characteristic developments in the past two decades in CEE countries, namely the 'politicisation of adjudication'. This means that courts played the role of the 'arbiter', more and more frequently, in cases having political implications. It is obvious that it is the constitutional courts, in the first place, which represent this type of self-understanding. Nonetheless the effort of the courts to extend their political competence has caused heavy criticism amongst politicians and other stakeholders and statutory restriction of the power of constitutional courts has become a realistic

---

[24] It is worth noting that the question of correct interpretation of EU norms which frequently requires serious effort from the judge (exploring the social backgrounds and complex political aims behind the applicable norm) has to be differentiated from the problem of formalistic application of EU arguments which is also possible (there is no legal system fully protected from formalistic adjudication).

opportunity.[25] Ordinary courts may therefore hope they can avoid that kind of criticism if they show a minimalist approach in deciding issues having any political implications. A law-applier bureaucrat serves better this institutional goal than a Dworkinain 'Hercules' who protects the rights of the individual against state intervention under any circumstances. This sociological explanation also suggests that *under uncertain political circumstances,* particularly in young and relatively weak democracies, courts try to remain strictly minimalist and present a modest, textualist argumentation when discussing cases with political implication. This judicial strategy can support the formalistic judicial style.[26] In summary, although formalist adjudicative strategy has a detrimental effect on the quality of the reasoning it still may have some positive impact on the institutional position of the courts in the political arena.

There is another factor which pushes judges toward treating EU law in a formalistic way. The workload of judges which is commonly considered as a heavy burden on them has not decreased significantly since our previously studied period (1999–2004). It goes without saying that there is a steady and strong pressure on judges from both public audience and courts leaders to resolve legal cases as fast as possible. As the time of finishing cases is a measurable and easily controllable criterion when evaluating judicial activities, judges pay more attention to timeliness than to construing a well-founded and reflective legal reasoning which would otherwise be essential in applying EU law. The reason we can still be optimistic about the future of CEE adjudication is that the increase in the number of EU law arguments was followed by a similar increase in the references to other non-traditional arguments (with the exception of constitutional law arguments in the Czech Republic). These data indicate that judges tend to take into consideration the wider legal (constitutional arguments) and social (values external to law) context of cases before them. This judicial approach necessarily presupposes a certain level of awareness of deeper layers of law even if non-traditional arguments are often invoked first by involved parties and judges only refer to those arguments in their statements of reasons.

iv. Risks of Non-formalism and Strategic Formalism

Examining and evaluating the developments of application of EU law in CEE countries cannot be completed without taking the broader context of enforcement of rule of law into consideration. From this aspect fidelity to traditional legal arguments has its own advantages. In easy cases where the content of the written law is obvious and it is clear what the law requires from the addressees (or where originally unclear law has been interpreted by established case law), it can

---

[25] Á Kovács, 'Szükség van-e alkotmánybíróságra? Instrumentális érvek a törvényhozás bírói kontrollja mellett' [Do we need constitutional courts? An instrumentalist approach to the judicial control of the legislature] (2013) 68 (5) *Jogtudományi Közlöny* 243.

[26] For detailed discussion of this sociological framework see PH Solomon, 'Courts and Judges in Authoritarian Regimes' (2007) 60 *World Politics* 122.

be dangerous to make judicial decisions based on uncertain and vague principles, values or extra-legal factors even if such a decision seems to be right. Some argue that in cases where we would have good reasons to deviate from the plain meaning of the text we should avoid doing this: A fallible human decision maker does better if she or he treats the legal text as a reliable indicator of the intention of legislator.[27]

Spreading of non-formalism and strategic formalism (in the latter case the decision, *per definitionem*, is not driven by the text of the law either) without reasonable constraints certainly threatens the rule of law as it may violate the requirement of transparency and thus, it may expose the adjudication to illegitimate influencing factors (pressure group's interests, political party's intentions etc). In analysing the selected judgments we found some dubious arguments which may disguise the actual reasons behind the judgment.

As for the strategic formalism, we realised that Hungarian judges, unlike their Polish and Czech colleagues, prefer using the token argument of 'judicial practice' without any clarification and without mentioning any concrete previous decision. Furthermore, in certain Hungarian cases we found references to vague categories such as 'the conviction of the court' serving as the basis of the decision without any further specification. These kinds of arguments do not meet the requirement of transparent legal reasoning as neither the affected parties nor the wider public audience are aware of the true reasons behind the decision of the judge.[28] A serious disadvantage of such a style of legal reasoning is that it may weaken the convincing force of the judgments and consequently the public trust in courts as well.

As further evidence of this approach we found reference to the 'legal practice of the administrative agency' in a case where the very practice of the competent administrative agency was questionable. That is a good example of how judges, under the umbrella of a seemingly formalistic argumentation, can defend the so-called state-interest ('raison d'etat') instead of protecting the right of conducting free commercial activities.[29] It is a commonly received view that one of the

---

[27] A Vermeule, *Judging Under Uncertainty: An Institutional Theory of Legal Interpretation* (Harvard University Press, 2006) 63–85.

[28] One telling example from Hungary is the case (BH 2006. 376) where the Customs Authority imposed a relatively high fine on a wine producer who failed to officially report on time that a part of their wine stock was ruined because of a leak in one of his wine tanks. According to the relevant law he should have reported the change 'at the time of the event [of the damage]'. The misfortune occurred at 8am and the producer wanted to report the event at the end of the working day (after the necessary and urgent work, in order to reduce damages to the minimum, was done). LB said that the referred text of the law does not require immediate reporting by the plaintiff, but the court did not explain how it had come to that conclusion. In our opinion, the arguments would have been complete if the court had referred to the proportionality principle since, taking into consideration the special circumstances of the situation, the immediate obligation to report the damage would have put an extreme burden on the wine producer.

[29] This is not to question that the legal practice of a governmental agency has been an established German category which serves here primarily to protect the interests of the parties to administrative proceedings. The corresponding principle prohibits deviating from this practice unless good reasons are offered.

main characteristics of the so-called Socialist legal system is the 'reversed hierarchy of legal norms'. That means that judges and administrators prefer applying the most detailed directives (ordinances, opinions, circular letters etc), even if they did not count as 'hard law'. As a consequence, this 'state-friendly' approach was clearly detectable in two other cases, where the court held the disagreement of two administrative agencies against the business entity.[30]

Non-formalist argumentation also can go against the values of the rule of law. If a judge just refers to a certain constitutional principle or a human right (or as we saw it in one Hungarian case: To the 'the moral judgments of the society') as a reason for his decision and does not put that argument in its proper constitutional context or ignores the particular circumstances of the case when she or he delivers a judgment, he or she may be breaching his or her duty.[31]

The answer to the question of which adjudicative style better serves the enforcement of the rule of law and the interest of the whole political community may depend on the type of cases to be decided. A judge has to have the necessary 'judicial wisdom' to decide when she or he has to apply an innovative, new solution and when she or he has to remain loyal to the text of the law. Although judicial wisdom cannot be acquired from books, there are some institutional solutions which can help judges recognise the broader context of their decisions and also make the process of judicial thinking more reflective. One of these solutions is to have more balanced courts, composed not only of career judges but also of the outsiders to the judiciary, with experience from other fields of life than the judiciary.

V. Conclusions

In our previous study we stated that due to the strong formalist tradition CEE judges may need some time to fully adjust their judicial decision making style to the new legal environment resulting from the EU accession. In this chapter we presented the results of an analysis of more than 900 administrative judicial

---

[30] In one of these cases (BH 2006. 137) the Building Authority gave permission to an entrepreneur to build a factory on its own land. After that the Land Registry Agency imposed a fine on the entrepreneur because he did not ask for a licence to build premises in an agricultural area.

[31] We have a Hungarian example (LB Kfv.II.39.166/2007) for this attitude (this administrative judgment is not one of the examined cases): In the early 1990s a church building was built in the centre of a residential district of a Hungarian town. After its opening, residents were subject every morning—including weekends—to a long-lasting and very loud chiming starting at six o'clock. After some unsuccessful meetings with the representatives of the Catholic Church, the residents brought the case to the competent administrative agency which ordered reasonable decrease in chiming in terms of volume and period. The Church then challenged this decision before the court in 2007. The court quashed the decision of the agency stating that the expression of religious convictions is protected by the constitution and chiming, without any doubt, qualifies as such. The court did not make any effort to explain why residents' right to a healthy environment was irrelevant in that case (ignoring the constitutional context), and also overlooked 'the most locally applicable rule', namely the ministerial decree on protecting citizens from noisy activities (ignoring the particular circumstances of the case).

decisions from three CEE countries, dated from 2005 to 2013. Based on our quantitative analysis we can declare with some certainty that significant changes have occurred in the judicial style of administrative courts since 2005. Our data clearly show that judges of the CEE countries have used more non-formalistic, non-traditional arguments (pro-constitutional, pro-EU reasons and values external to law) in the examined period than they used before EU accession. These findings allowed us to argue that EU accession has had both a direct and indirect influence on judicial behaviour in CEE countries.

This shift is a clear sign of departure from the classical 'French judicial style' to a reasoning which serves as genuine guidance for both the parties and other judges in deciding similar cases. Using non-formalistic arguments in an increasing number does not only result in a change of the 'language of judicial reasoning' but may be an indicator of a change of judicial thinking. The more arguments a judge considers in the reasoning the more the chance of socially sensitive, problem-orientated and open-minded decision making. This kind of judicial thinking is of special importance in administrative cases where there is an asymmetry in strength between the litigating parties.

One of the reasons for this shift is obviously EU accession—together with EU membership, EU law became an element of the internal legal system of Member States and references to this law have over time become similar to references to internal law values.[32] In addition, we have witnessed a process of 'internationalisation of adjudication': over recent decades, judicial associations, as well as formal and informal networks of judges have emerged. CEE judges, therefore, currently have many transborder opportunities to learn something new, educate themselves, take part in conferences and communicate to each other in various ways.

We cannot overestimate the impact of information technology (especially the internet) on everyday judicial work. Numerous professional and open-access databases facilitate the exploration of the relevant case-law, literature or other necessary legal materials when a judge discusses a difficult case. The internet also makes it easier to ask for or give advice.

Besides that we must remember that since the political transition a brand new generation of lawyers (judges) has been coming of age. Many of them speak foreign language(s), took part in the Erasmus program, learnt comparative law at university and are familiar with the jurisprudence of the CJEU, ECtHR and their own national constitutional court, too. Therefore it is no surprise that, in contrast to their predecessors, they are willing to accept non-formalistic arguments in their legal reasoning.

---

[32] However, we were warned by senior judges that similarly significant changes might not occur in 'traditional' fields of the adjudication (civil and criminal cases). The reason for this is that administrative law is the legal branch most exposed to the influence of EU law while other branches of law preserve their own national characteristics.

However we have to be careful in relying on empirical data in evaluating the developments of the adjudicative style in CEE countries. Some findings of the qualitative content analysis have indicated that the spectacular increase in the numbers is neither necessarily in straight correlation with improving the quality of adjudication nor does it mean that CEE judges have developed the same perspective as Western ones of Western judges.

We saw some cases of abuse of non-formalistic arguments: for example, presenting vague categories as decisive reasons is far from transparent legal reasoning. Furthermore, a special version of formalism (strategic formalism) seems to survive or even acquire new forms (case law formalism). This causes problems if judges apply these kinds of formalist strategies systematically in deciding hard cases. Such a problem can be that formalism may strengthen the 'law-applier' mentality which does not take the protection of rights of the plaintiffs seriously. This attitude may lead to the emergence of a non-conscious state-friendly 'default setting' in deciding administrative cases.

In conclusion, despite the above-described signs of deformalisation, the formalism of administrative judiciaries has not fully disappeared, especially in its new form—'case-law formalism'. A possible explanation of its persistence (besides the steady pressure on judges to finish their cases as fast as possible) may be that in young and relatively weak democracies courts try to remain strictly minimalist in discussing cases with political implications and administrative cases often have such implications.

4

The Impact of EU Membership on Private Law Adjudication in Poland: A Case Study of the Polish Supreme Court's Case Law on Unfair Terms in Consumer Contracts

RAFAŁ MAŃKO*

I. Introduction

The tenth anniversary of Poland's membership in the EU, coinciding with the twenty-fifth anniversary of the country's transformation from 'actually existing socialism' to parliamentary democracy and a market economy in 1989, fully justify posing the question of the impact of the case law of the Court of Justice of the European Union (ECJ) upon Polish legal culture, with particular reference to private law adjudication. Indeed, the issue is a pertinent one not only for Central Europe. Addressing the question whether 'the case law of the [ECJ] is accepted and followed by national courts', Michal Bobek remarked that '[t]he frank answer is that no one knows, at least at the overall European level'.[1] Fully conscious that it is only a drop in the ocean, this chapter is an attempt at partly filling that gap.

* The author would like to thank Michal Bobek, Jakub Łakomy, Martijn W Hesselink, Marcin Matczak, Marek Safjan and Boštjan Zalar for their comments on earlier versions of this paper. All errors are exclusively my own. All views presented in the chapter are strictly and exclusively those of the Author and should not be attributed to the European Parliament or any other EU institution, agency or body. Email: r.t.manko@uva.nl.
    [1] M Bobek, 'Of Feasibility and Silent Elephants: The Legitimacy of the Court of Justice through the Eyes of National Courts' in M Adams et al (eds), *Judging Europe's Judges: The Legitimacy of the Case Law of the European Court of Justice* (Hart Publishing, 2013) 208.

With that regard it is noteworthy that it was only in March 2015 that a Polish court[2] submitted a first preliminary reference to the ECJ in the field of substantive private law,[3] which permits the conclusion that formal judicial dialogue in this area between the Polish judiciary and the ECJ is only about to begin. Out of the 79 preliminary references submitted until June 2015 by Polish courts,[4] the vast majority were concerned with public law;[5] nevertheless six (eight per cent of the total) regarded the interpretation of EU civil procedure instruments.[6] As regards the Polish Supreme Court (*Sąd Najwyższy*, 'SN')—the highest judicial authority in private law adjudication in Poland[7]—its Civil Chamber (competent for core areas of private law) has not submitted a single reference to the ECJ. However, the Chamber for Labour, Social Security and Public Matters has submitted five preliminary references[8] and the Criminal Chamber has submitted one.[9]

Given the lack of formalised judicial dialogue between Plac Krasińskich[10] and Plateau de Kirchberg on issues of Europeanised private law, the question arises whether, in spite of that, the ECJ's case law has exerted any influence upon the SN's understanding of national implementing provisions, or not. To address this issue, I resort in this chapter to a case study, narrowing down the scope of enquiry to only one area of European private law, namely the law of unfair terms in consumer contracts. The choice is justified by two main reasons. First of all, prior to the implementation of the Unfair Terms Directive[11] ('the Directive' or 'UTD'), Polish private law virtually did not know a regime of consumer protection against unfair terms,[12] and the whole area of private law in question can be described as

---

[2] Polish procedural laws, in particular the Code of Civil Procedure, do not provide for a rule explicitly allowing a national court to submit a preliminary reference to the ECJ. This is in contrast to most EU Member States (see M Bobek, 'Learning to Talk: Preliminary Rulings, the Courts of the New Member States and the Court of Justice' (2008) 45 *CML Rev* 1611, 1626–27).

[3] Case C-119/15 *Partner*, preliminary reference on third party effects of decisions regarding a term unfair under the Unfair Terms Directive, submitted by the Court of Appeal in Warsaw.

[4] Data according to ECJ search engine at curia.europa.eu (last checked: 3 June 2015).

[5] Especially tax law, social security law and competition law.

[6] The Insolvency Regulation (Case C-444/07 *MG Probud Gdynia* [2010] ECR I-417 and Case C-116/11 *Bank Handlowy and Adamiak* ECLI:EU:C:2012:739), the Taking of Evidence Regulation (Case C-283/09 *Weryński* [2011] ECR I-601), the European Order for Payment Regulation (C-215/11 *Szyrocka* ECLI:EU:C:2012:794) and the Service of Documents Regulation (Case C-325/11 *Alder* ECLI:EU:C:2012:824 and Case C-70/15 *Lebek*. One should also mention Case C-38/13 *Nierodzik* ECLI:EU:C:2014:152 in the field of labour law).

[7] For a brief institutional characterisation of the SN see eg R Mańko, '"War of Courts" as a Clash of Legal Cultures: Rethinking the Conflict Between the Polish Constitutional Tribunal and Supreme Court over "Interpretive Judgments"' in M Hein et al (eds), *Law, Politics and the Constitution: New Perspectives from Legal and Political Theory* (Peter Lang, 2014), 82–83.

[8] Case C-3/14 *Polska Telefonia Cyfrowa* (pending); Case C-633/13 *Polska Izba Informatyki i Telekomunikacji* (radiated); Case C-440/09 *Tomaszewska* [2011] ECR I-1033; C-410/09 *Polska Telefonia Cyfrowa* [2011] ECR I-3853; Case C-375/09 *Tele2 Polska* [2011] ECR I-3055; Case C-99/09 *Polska Telefonia Cyfrowa* [2010] ECR I-6617.

[9] Case C-489/10 *Bonda* ECLI:EU:C:2012:319.

[10] Krasiński Square, the seat of the Polish Supreme Court in Warsaw.

[11] Council Directive 93/13/EEC of 5 April 1993 on unfair terms in consumer contracts (OJ L 95, 21/04/1993, 29–34).

[12] For a broader background see R Mańko, 'The Institutional Implications of the Unfair Terms Directive in Poland' in J Rutgers (ed), *European Contract Law and the Welfare State* (Europa Law Publishers, 2012) 146–49.

being a completely new one, in fact created as a result of Poland's (planned) accession to the EU.[13] Thus, the law of unfair terms was uncharted territory for the Polish judiciary and one could have expected that guidance from the ECJ would be sought.

Second, the rules on unfair terms have been the object of a solid body of domestic case law.[14] In the present analysis, I limit myself to the case law of the SN (amounting to 45 cases as of mid-April 2014), assuming that cases decided either in cassation or in domestic preliminary reference proceedings can be said to represent the most legally complex issues.

The chapter addresses two distinct, but closely inter-connected, research questions. The first one is concerned with the impact of the ECJ's doctrine on unfair terms, that is the substance of its understanding of the Directive. The second one is concerned with the impact of the ECJ's judicial style, characterised by purpose-oriented and extra-textual reasoning upon SN.

Methodologically, the chapter adopts a descriptive, rather than normative approach. It seeks to describe, analyse and explain the practice of the SN with regard to the application of national implementing provisions of the Directive. However, it also takes for granted three fundamental assumptions stemming from EU constitutional law, in light of which the judicial practice of the SN may be evaluated. These assumptions are as follows: First, the duty of the SN to apply national implementing provisions in light of the Directive by virtue of the principle of harmonious interpretation (or indirect effect);[15] second, the binding nature (vis-à-vis the SN) of ECJ case law interpreting the Directive, with the result that the duty of harmonious interpretation includes following ECJ precedent;[16] and

---

[13] R Mańko, 'Resistance Towards the Unfair Terms Directive in Poland: The Interaction between the Consumer Acquis and a Post-Socialist Legal Culture' in J Devenney and M Kenny (eds), *European Consumer Protection: Theory and Practice* (Cambridge University Press, 2012) 415–18.

[14] As of 15 April 2014, the LEX database of Polish law contained as many as 196 cases interpreting Article 385[1] of the Polish Civil Code (*kodeks cywilny*, hereinafter 'kc') alone (that article implements the general prohibition of unfair terms) and 3436 cases interpreting Article 385[3] kc containing the list of unfair terms.

[15] P Craig and G de Búrca, *EU Law: Text, Cases and Materials*, 5th edn (Oxford University Press, 2011) 200–11; Bobek (n 1) 210. The leading cases are Case 14/83 *Von Kolson* [1984] ECR 1891, Case C-106-89 *Marleasing* [1990] ECR I-4135, Case C-397-403/01 *Pfeiffer* [2004] ECR I-8835 and Case C-555/07 *Kücükdeveci* [2010] ECR I-365. The duty of harmonious interpretation was explicitly reiterated by the ECJ with regard to the Unfair Terms Directive in Joined Cases C-240/98 and C-244/98 *Océano* [2000] ECR I-4941. In Polish literature see eg A Wróbel, 'Zasady ogólne (podstawowe) prawa Unii Europejskiej' [The General (Fundamental) Principles of European Union Law] in A Wróbel (ed), *Stosowanie prawa Unii Europejskiej przez sądy* [The Application of European Union Law by Courts] (Zakamycze, 2005) 101–02; A Łazowski, 'Stosowanie prawa UE na płaszczyźnie wewnętrznej państw członkowskich' [The Application of EU Law within the Member States] in MM Kenig-Witkowska (ed), *Prawo instytucjonalne Unii Europejskiej* [The Institutional Law of the European Union] 3rd edn (CH Beck, 2007) 309–15.

[16] Craig and de Búrca (n 15) 475–76. The leading cases are Case 283/81 *CILFIT* [1982] ECR 3415 and Joined Cases C-10/97 and C-22/97 *IN.CO.GE.* [1998] ECR I-06307. In Polish literature see eg A Wróbel, 'Pytania prawne sądów państw członkowskich do Europejskiego Trybunału Sprawiedliwości (Sądu Pierwszej Instancji)' [Preliminary References from Courts of the Member States to the European

third, the duty of the SN, as a court of last instance, to submit a preliminary reference whenever it harbours doubts as to the correct interpretation of the Directive.[17] As will become evident, there are reasons to believe that the judicial practice of the SN regarding the application and interpretation of the national implementing measures of the Directive may fall short at least of the first two of these duties stemming from EU law.

In the chapter I resort both to qualitative and quantitative methods. First of all, I analyse the formal aspects of referring to the Directive and to ECJ case law in the grounds of SN judgments and compare the results with the SN's references to its own case law interpreting the national implementing provisions.[18] Second, I analyse the frequency and types of policy-oriented arguments in the SN case law on unfair terms, and compare the results with a control sample of SN case law in civil cases. As regards qualitative analysis, I focus on a number of selected themes discussed in the SN case law in order to show how its doctrine evolved and whether it was inspired by the Directive and ECJ case law.

The chapter is structured as follows: Section II presents the institutional background focusing on formalism in Polish legal culture, with particular reference to its historical roots and the formalist face of the SN; section III presents the regulatory background, focusing on the Directive and its implementation in Poland; section IV presents the results of a quantitative analysis of SN case law on unfair terms, and section V presents the results of the qualitative analysis. Section VI concludes the chapter.

Court of Justice (Court of First Instance)'] in A Wróbel (ed), *Stosowanie prawa Unii Europejskiej przez sądy* [The Application of European Union Law by Courts] (Zakamycze, 2005) 811–12; M Taborowski, 'Procedura orzeczeń wstępnych' ('The Preliminary Reference Procedure') in A Łazowski (ed), *Unia Europejska: Prawo instytucjonalne i gospodarcze* [European Union: Institutional and Economic Law] (ABC, 2007) 442–43; TT Koncewicz and Z Brodecki in Brodecki (ed), *Europa sędziów* [Judges' Europe] (LexisNexis, 2007) 33–35; Z Brodecki, *Prawo integracji: Konstytucja dla Europy* [Law of Integration: A Constitution for Europe] 4th edn (LexisNexis, 2011) 111–13; K Schmidt, 'Stosowanie prawa Unii Europejskiej przez sędziego polskiego' [Application of European Union Law by Polish Judges] in M Pichlak (ed), *Profesjonalna kultura prawnicza* [Professional Legal Culture] (Scholar, 2012) 178–79. For a somewhat diluted approach to the force of ECJ precedent among Polish scholars see eg R Ostrihansky, 'Współpraca sądów krajowych z TS' [Cooperation of National Courts with the CJ] in Kenig-Witkowska (n 15) 419–21.

[17] Article 267(3) TFUE. See Craig and de Búrca (n 15) 446–47. The leading cases are Case C-393/98 *Gomes Valente* [2001] ECR I-1327; Case C-99/00 *Lyckeskog* [2002] ECR I-4839 and Case C-458/06 *Gourmet Classic* [2008] ECR I-4207. The purpose of this duty is 'to prevent a body of national case law that is not in accordance with EU law from being established in a Member State' (Craig and de Búrca (n 15) 446). Specifically on the duty of the Polish Supreme Court to submit preliminary references see eg Taborowski (n 16) 408–09.

[18] This is done on the assumption that if a court cites an authority, it either actually relied on it as to the substance of its reasoning, or at least refers to it in order to justify an outcome reached otherwise (*cf* M Bobek, *Comparative Reasoning in European Supreme Courts* (Oxford University Press, 2013) 225). Judges, of course, can resort to four scenarios with regard to legal authority, such as ECJ case-law: '(i) not to read and not to quote; (ii) not to read and to quote; (iii) to read and not to quote; (iv) to read and to quote' (ibid, 227).

II. Institutional Background: Formalism in Polish Legal Culture

A. Formalism and Anti-formalism in Legal Culture

Despite differences as to the details both of typology and terminology among various authors,[19] I assume that empirically existing legal cultures can be placed on a continuum running between text-oriented formalism on the one side, to substance-oriented pragmatism or anti-formalism on the other. I also assume that the formalism of a given legal culture is manifested inter alia in the prevailing style of judicial reasoning.[20] Judges in a formalist legal culture will either prefer or even limit themselves to text-oriented arguments (analysing the linguistic aspects of a legal text and its internal structure), whilst judges in a pragmatist or anti-formalist legal culture will display preference for arguments going beyond the mere legal text, looking into the purposes and socio-economic effects of legislation, the underlying public policies, as well as the interests of relevant stakeholders ('policy-oriented arguments').

B. Historical Roots of Polish Formalism

Without much exaggeration one can say that Polish legal culture is a rather formalist one. On an ontological level, the concept of 'limited law' prevails, whereby only texts emanating from the state are considered to be 'the law'.[21] On an epistemological level, legal interpretation is usually reduced to an exegesis of legal texts, coupled with a belief that there exists one correct interpretation of a text, usually the literal one.[22] Systemic and teleological arguments are allowed only if literal interpretation gives rise to totally unacceptable results.[23] Finally, on a pragmatic level the judge is usually viewed as someone performing an automatic act

---

[19] See eg TC Gray, 'Judicial Review and Legal Pragmatism' (2003) 38 *Wake Forest Law Review* 473 ('formalism' vs 'pragmatism'); Z Kühn, *The Judiciary in Central and Eastern Europe: Mechanical Jurisprudence in Transformation?* (Martinus Nijhoff, 2011) 67–87 ('formalism', 'anti-formalism', 'ultra-formalism'). The types of arguments used by courts may also be dubbed as 'formalist'/'anti-formalist'/ 'pragmatist', or 'internal to the law' vs 'external to the law', as in D Galligan and M Matczak, 'Formalism in Post-communist Courts. Empirical Study on Judicial Discretion in Polish Administrative Courts Deciding Business Cases' in R Coman et al (eds), *Judicial Reforms in Central and Eastern European Countries* (Van den Broel, 2007) 236–37.

[20] See eg MW Hesselink, *The New European Legal Culture* (Kluwer, 2001) 9.

[21] See eg E Łętowska, 'The Barriers of Polish Legal Thinking in the Perspective of European Integration' (1997) 1 *Yearbook of Polish Legal Studies* 55, 56.

[22] See eg E Łętowska, 'Kilka uwag o praktyce wykładni' [Some Remarks on the Practice of Interpretation] (2002) 11(1) *Kwartlanik Prawa Prywatnego* 27, 43.

[23] See eg T Stawecki and P Winczorek, *Wstęp do prawoznawstwa* [Introduction to Jurisprudence] 4th edn (CH Beck, 2003) 174–75.

of 'subsumption' of facts under legal rules, rather than a creative agent engaged in the process of making the law.[24]

The preference of the majority of Polish judiciary and legal scholars for a formalist approach to law can be explained by historical reasons.[25] In particular, formalism was the prevailing current of Western European continental legal cultures which moulded Polish legal culture as it emerged after Poland regained independence in 1918.[26] Therefore, it predates the period of actually existing socialism and its origins can be traced to Western European legal cultures. However, it seems that the key to the ongoing prevalence of formalism in Polish legal culture is the socialist period, and not without a paradox. This is because initially, directly after World War II, when the legal texts in force had not yet been adapted to the needs of the new political and socio-economic system, the judiciary, and notably the SN, embarked upon openly political judicial law-making, eagerly using general clauses, such as the 'principles of social life',[27] refusing to apply rules which did not seem fit to the new system or even referring directly to Communist Party documents in the argumentation.[28] However, this mode of legal interpretation was a feature of the Stalinist period.[29] Following the 1956 transformation from totalitarianism to post-totalitarian authoritarianism,[30] the practice of open judicial law-making was criticised and abandoned. The Polish legal community embraced formalism perceiving it as a guarantee of (or substitute for) the rule of law, violated during the Stalinist period.[31] Furthermore, an escape into formalism was one of the ways of securing a greater degree of autonomy of the legal community vis-à-vis the ruling Communist party: By stating that their task consists only of a more or less

---

[24] M Zirk-Sadowski, 'Transformation and Integration of Legal Cultures and Discoursess—Poland' in W Sadurski et al (eds), *Spreading Democracy and the Rule of Law? The Impact of EU Enlargement on the Rule of Law, Democracy and Constitutionalism in Post-Communist Legal Orders* (Springer, 2006) 308–09; T Milej, 'Europejska kultura prawna a kraje Europy Środkowej i Wschodniej' [European Legal Culture and the Countries of Central and Eastern Europe] (2008) 15(1) *Przegląd Legislacyjny* 60, 68–69.

[25] R Mańko, 'Weeds in the Gardens of Justice? The Survival of Hyperpositivism in Polish Legal Culture as a Symptom/Sinthome' (2013) 7(2) *Pólemos: Journal of Law, Literature and Culture* 207, 221–26.

[26] R Mańko, 'The Culture of Private Law in Central Europe After Enlargement: A Polish Perspective' (2005) 11(5) *European Law Journal* 527, 531. *cf* M Bobek, 'Judicial Transformations in Post-Communist Societies: A Study in Institutions, Administrations and Interpretation', *Centre for Advance Study Sofia Working Paper* no 4/2011, 4.

[27] For a discussion see R Mańko, 'Quality of Legislation Following a Transition from Really Existing Socialism to Capitalism: A Case Study of General Clauses in Polish Private Law' in J Rozenfelds et al (eds) *The Quality of Legal Acts and Its Importance in Contemporary Legal Space* (University of Latvia Press, 2012) 543–47.

[28] As in Case C 1208/52 *Zofia W et al v Józef B and Skarb Państwa* (13 December 1952), where the SN stated: 'The *Ideological Declaration* of the PZPR [Polish United Workers' Party] ... states that: "The Party will fight ... for the inculcation and grounding of socialist morality among the masses". The educating role of the courts obliges them to take an active part in this task of the Party.'

[29] Bobek (n 26) 38.

[30] In distinguishing, within Poland's post-War political history, a period of 'totalitarianism' (1944–1956) and 'post-totalitarian authoritarianism' (1956–1989), I follow L Mażewski, *Posttotalitarny autorytaryzm. PRL 1956–1989. Analiza ustrojowo-polityczna* [Post-Totalitarian Authoritarianism, The Polish People's Republic 1956–1989: An Analysis of the Political System] (Arte 2010).

[31] *cf* Kühn (n 19) 116–23, 156–57, 161–63.

mechanical application of legal rules, judges could limit their interaction with the world of politics.[32] Finally, formalism with its vision of a judge as a 'grey mouse', a cog in a broader mechanism, corresponded to the social reality and limited prestige of judges under actually existing socialism.[33]

After the transformation of 1989, formalism was not instantly abandoned, but has remained as a kind of 'legal survival' of the period of actually existing socialism.[34] Actually, it can even be suggested that in the post-socialist period formalism was strengthened, as a result of a misconceived notion of division of powers (legislative versus judiciary) and an exaggerated understanding of judicial independence.[35] Both were downplayed during the socialist period, when the dogma of unity of state power, rather than division of powers, obtained,[36] and when judicial independence was obviously limited in a monoparty authoritarian system.

This does not imply that all Polish judges and courts are formalist, and indeed recent research has detected a trend away from formalism, visible in the rise of policy-oriented arguments during the last decade.[37] Nevertheless, judicial formalism remains a background feature of Polish legal culture which is part of its tradition.[38]

C. Formalism at the *Sąd Najwyższy*

The SN is rather a typical, conservative continental court, much attached to traditional paradigms of textual interpretation. Established in 1917, it will soon have enjoyed a century of uninterrupted existence, save for the period during World War II.[39] Despite the two radical socio-economic transformations experienced by Poland in the twentieth century, surprisingly it even managed to maintain a relatively high continuity of its judicial personnel.[40] The current system of judicial appointments at the SN favours the reproduction of the judicial elite, in that the SN itself screens candidates and forwards the selected ones to the National

---

[32] ibid, 158–59; D Piana, 'The Power Knocks at the Courts' Back Door: Two Waves of Postcommunist Judicial Reforms' (2006) 42(6) *Comparative Political Studies* 816, 820; Bobek (n 26) 38–39; Mańko (n 25) 223. *cf* M Zirk-Sadowski, 'Uczestniczenie prawników w kulturze' [Lawyers' Participation in Culture] (2002) 9 *Państwo i Prawo* 3, 7.

[33] Bobek (n 26) 6; Mańko (n 25) 222.

[34] On formalism ('hyperpositivism') as a legal survival see Mańko (n 25). On legal survivals in general see R Mańko, 'Legal Survivals: A Conceptual Tool for Analysing Post-Transformation Continuity of Legal Culture' in J Pleps (ed), *Tiesību efektivitāte postmodernā sabiedrībā [The Effectiveness of Law in Post-Modern Society]* (LU Akadēmiskais apgāds, 2015) 16–27.

[35] M Bobek, 'The Fortress of Judicial Independence and the Mental Transitions of the Central European Judiciaries' (2008) 14(1) *European Public Law* 99, 101ff.

[36] Bobek (n 26) 4.

[37] See above, ch 3 in this vol.

[38] *cf* Mańko (n 26) 534–36.

[39] D Malec, 'Sąd Najwyższy w latach 1917–1939' [The Supreme Court Between 1917 and 1939] in *Sąd Najwyższy Rzeczypospolitej Polskiej: Historia i współczesność [The Supreme Court of the Republic of Poland: History and the Present Day]* (TNOiK, 2007) 121–89.

[40] See A Bereza, 'Sąd Najwyższy w Polsce Ludowej' [The Supreme Court in People's Poland] in *Sąd Najwyższy* (n 39) 201, 223, 283–85; W Kozielewicz, 'Sąd Najwyższy Rzeczypospolitej Polskiej 1990–2007' [The Supreme Court of the Republic of Poland between 1990 and 2007], in *Sąd Najwyższy* (n 39) 302.

Council of the Judiciary, which makes the final selection and presents it to the President.[41]

As to the prevalent style of judicial reasoning at the SN, it seems to be rather conservatively text-oriented, as it follows from the Court's own *dicta* on methods of legal interpretation. Indeed, the SN has made explicit declarations pledging its allegiance to the idea of primacy of linguistic interpretation over functional:

> According to principles governing the interpretation of legal provisions, as settled in the case-law, linguistic interpretation has a fundamental significance, and only if it fails, leading to results which cannot be reconciled with the reasonable action of the legislator and the purpose, which a given norm is intended to serve, resort is permissible to directives of systemic and functional interpretation.[42]

The SN also makes a sharp distinction between legal interpretation and judicial law-making, as in the following passage:

> There is no doubt that a court within the framework of performing its task of adjudicating interprets legal provisions; however this interpretation may not have a law-making character. In the interpretive process the court must take into account the principle of division and balance between the legislative, executive and judicial powers ...[43]

A departure from this principle, that is 'creative' interpretation, could lead—in the SN's view—to an 'unacceptable interference of the judicial power with the sphere of competences reserved for the legislature.'[44] This traditional approach to judicial ideology in Poland has also been identified in empirical research (based on interviews with judges and questionnaires) performed recently by Urszula Jaremba.[45] Summarising her research, she claimed that Polish civil judges still perceive themselves as '*bouches de la loi*' or '*Subsumptionsautomate*',[46] functioning within a 'realm of a very positivistic, highly formalised and legalistic legal culture.'[47]

III. Regulatory Background: The Unfair Terms Directive and its Implementation in Poland

A. The Directive

The Directive, enacted in 1993, aimed at bringing about minimum harmonisation of national laws on the review of unfair terms in consumer contracts. It contains

---

[41] Mańko (n 7) 82–83.
[42] Case III CZP 75/03 *Krystyna R et al v Urszula S et al* (25 November 2003).
[43] Case I CSK 59/12 *Adam Z v Skarb Państwa* (6 September 2012).
[44] ibid.
[45] U Jaremba, *National Judges as EU Law Judges: The Polish Civil Law System* (Martinus Nijhoff, 2014).
[46] ibid, 97.
[47] ibid, 161.

a general prohibition of unfair terms, which resorts to general clauses ('good faith' and 'significant imbalance'), as well as a list containing examples of unfair terms. The scope of the Directive is limited to non-negotiated terms in consumer contracts only, and the review of unfairness does not extend to the main subject-matter of the contract, or to the balance between the price paid by the consumer and the counter-performance of the trader.

The Directive contains also a number of detailed rules, in particular the requirement of transparency, whereby terms must be written in clear and intelligible language and the corresponding *contra proferentem* rule which obliges courts to seek a consumer-friendly interpretation of vague terms.

Finally, the Directive contains a procedural rule which requires Member States to introduce measures allowing for consumer organisations to seek, by way of an *actio popularis*, the elimination of unfair terms from standard contracts following their *in abstracto* review. The Directive has been hitherto interpreted in 32 ECJ cases.[48]

B. The Polish Implementing Provisions

The Directive was implemented in Poland in 2000, partly in the Civil Code[49] and partly in the Code of Civil Procedure.[50] Without delving into the doctrinal details of the Polish implementing provisions, I will only draw attention to their most problematic aspects.[51] First of all, the general clauses used in the prohibition of unfair terms in the Directive (that is 'good faith' and 'significant imbalance') were replaced by 'good morals' and 'manifest violation of consumer interests'. Second, despite the creation of two parallel procedures for the review of unfair terms, that is an *in concreto* procedure (review of a concrete contract concluded by a specific consumer) and an *in abstracto* procedure (review of a standard contract as such), the legislature failed to specify whether the test of unfairness provided for in the Civil Code is applicable, and if yes, whether directly or *mutatis mutandis*. Third, terms deemed unfair in an *in abstracto* review are to be entered into a publicly available Unfair Terms Register. The Code of Civil Procedure provides that a judgment condemning a term as unfair is to have effects also vis-à-vis third parties. However, the exact scope and extent of third-party effects were not laid down in the Code, giving rise to controversies as to its extent *ratione personae* (only the trader who was party to the *in abstracto* review of proceedings or also other traders), and *ratione materiae* (only the specific term in the specific contract, or also similar terms in similar contracts, or even in different contracts).

---

[48] The most recent ECJ case on the Directive, at the time when this chapter was sent to the press being C-96/14 *Van Hove* (23 April 2015).

[49] Articles 385¹–385³ kc.

[50] Articles 479³⁶–Art 479⁴⁵ of the Polish Code of Civil Procedure (*Kodeks postępowania cywilnego*, 'kpc').

[51] For a more ample treatment see Mańko (n 12) and (n 13).

IV. Quantitative Analysis of *Sąd Najwyższy*'s Case Law on Unfair Terms

A. Introduction

According to my findings, as of mid-April 2014, there were 45 reported decisions[52] of the SN interpreting national measures implementing the Directive,[53] rendered between 16 October 2012 (*Dariusz D v TUiR*) and 6 December 2013 (*Szota v Uniwersytet Śląski*). At the time when the latest of these decisions was rendered, there were 24 decisions of the ECJ interpreting the Directive available, the last of them being *Anuntis Segundamento*,[54] issued on 5 December 2013. Out of these 24 ECJ decisions, only seven were handed down before Poland's accession to

---

[52]   Cases: V CKN 1337/00 *Dariusz D v TUiR* (16.10.2002); III CKN 431/01 *Rafał W v Towarzystwo Ubezpieczeniowe 'D'* (24.9.2003); V CK 277/02 *Grzegorz S v TUiR Warta* (9.10.2003); 19.12.2003, III CZP 95/03 *Powiatowy Rzecznik Praw Konsumentów v Międzynarodowa Korporacja Gospodarcza InCo* (19.12.2003, '*InCo*'); III CZP 110/03 *Re Bank Enforcement Title* (31.3.2003); I CK 472/03 *Krawczyk v BIG Bank Gdański* (6.4.2004); I CK 635/0 *UOKiK v AICE Polska* (8.6.2004); I CK 162/04 *Białas v Bank Handlowy* (6.10.2004); III CZP 76/04 *PZU Życie* (6.1.2005); I CK 509/04 *UOKiK v BIG Bank Gdański* (15.2.2005), I CK 586/04 *UOKiK v Lipiński* (23.3.2005); I CK 690/04 *Damian B v Zakład Ubezpieczeń* (13.5.2005); I CK 832/04 *Krawczyk v Millenium Bank* (13.7.2005); V CSK 90/05 *Krystian B v Towarzystwo Ubezpieczeń A* (26.1.2006); I CK 297/05 *Miejski i Powiatowy Rzecznik Konsumentów v UPC Polska* (3.2.2006); III SK 7/06 *Górnośląski Bank Gospodarczy v UOKiK* (20.6.2006); III SZP 3/06 *Towarzystwo Finansowo-Inwestycyjne v UOKiK* (13.7.2006, '*TFI v UOKiK*'); I CSK 173/06 *UOKiK v Amplico Life* (27.10.2006); III CSK 266/06 *Urszula S v Compensa* (7.12.2006); IV CSK 307/06 *Elżbieta L v Filar* (12.1.2007); III SK 21/06 *UOKiK v Profesja* (19.3.2007); I CSK 27/07 *Centrum Leasingu i Finansów* (19.4.2007); I CSK 484/06 *UOKiK v Regionalna Telewizja Kablowa AutoCom* (25.5.2007, '*UOKiK v AutoCom*'); I CSK 117/07 *Mirosław M v Andrzej Z* (5.6.2007); III CZP 62/07 *Aleksandra W v PZU SA* (29.6.2007); III SK 19/07 *Kowalczuk v Telekomunikacja Polska SA* (11.10.2007, '*Kowalczuk v TPSA*'); I CSK 70/08 *54 Rafał P v Bank A* (3.10.2008); III CZP 80/08 *Lexus v BPET* (7.10.2008); III SK 37/08 *UOKiK v Cardiff Polska* (14.4.2009); I CSK 404/09 *Ćmiela v Tele2* (4.3.2010); III SK 29/09 *In Merito v Polska Telefonia Cyfrowa* (13.5.2010); I CZ 121/09 *Jan C v Polska Telefonia Cyfrowa* (19.5.2010); I CSK 694/09 *MZ v Inter Polska* (13.10.2010); III CZP 119/10 *Makuszewska v Szkoła Wyższa Rzemiosł Artystycznych* (13.1.2011); I CSK 218/10 *Lexus v PKN Orlen SA* (20.1.2011); I CSK 676/10 *UOKiK v Aster* (16.9.2011); I CSK 310/11 *Kuźbińska v Gospodarczy Bank Spółdzielczy* (21.12.2011); I CSK 428/11 *UOKiK v Polska Telewizja Cyfrowa* (13.4.2012); II CSK 515/11 *Zenon K v W* (13.6.2012); I CZ 135/12 *Adam G v Getin Noble Bank* (25.10.2012); I CSK 350/12 *Ewa G v N Bank Polska* (14.12.2012); I CSK 313/12 *Towarzystwo Lexus v Alior Bank* (15.2.2013), I CSK 408/12 *Ewa M-G and Waldemar G*; (21.2.2013); II CSK 708/12 *CW v Towarzystwo Ubezpieczeń* (20.9.2013); I CSK 167/13 *Szota v Uniwersytet Śląski* (6.12.2013). In Poland cases are normally referred to by date and case number, but not by name. However, since this makes it very difficult to refer to case law, whenever the data was available, I indicated the names of cases following more or less the common law style. The most common source of actual names of parties were the publicly available Unfair Terms Register and the decisions of the Consumer Court published in the *Monitor Sądowy i Gospodarczy*.

[53]   These findings are based on an extensive search in the LEX database under those Articles of the Polish Civil Code and Code of Civil Procedure which implement the Directive. Decisions not mentioned under these articles, but referred to in other decisions, were also included in the empirical material.

[54]   Case C-413/12.

the EU,[55] meaning that 17 are available in the Polish language on easily accessible internet portals (EUR-LEX and CURIA), which have interfaces also in the Polish language. Soon after accession, all new ECJ judgments have been made available on CURIA in Polish translation already on the day of the judgment, and many of those concerning the Directive have been accompanied by press releases, also available in Polish.

B. References to Directives and ECJ Case Law

However, in spite of its broad availability, also in the Polish language, the impact of ECJ case law on the case law of the SN has been very limited, as can be seen already in the following table:

Table 1

EU legal source	References in SN case law on unfair terms	
	Number of cases	Frequency (within the pool of 45)
Unfair Terms Directive	8	17.8%
Injunctions Directive	2	4.4%
Unfair Commercial Practices Directive	2	4.4%
Case C-240-244/98 *Océano*	4	8.9%
Case C-478/99 *Commission v Sweden*	1	2.2%

Out of the ECJ's rich case law, only two cases have merited the attention of the SN: *Océano*, cited in four out of 45 decisions, and *Commission v Sweden*, cited in only one decision. The remaining case law has not been referred to even once. The situation is scarcely better with regard to references to EU legislation. The Unfair Terms Directive, which is in the lead, was referred to in less than one in five cases (17.8 per cent), the Injunctions Directive, only in two cases, just as the Unfair Commercial Practices Directive. The Treaty provisions regarding consumer protection as one of the aims of the EU have not been referred to even once. Incidentally, the same can be said about the Polish Constitution's provision on consumer protection,[56] which has not given any visible guidance to the SN.

---

[55] None of which has been published in Polish on the list of 'historical case-law' of the ECJ. See http://curia.europa.eu/jcms/jcms/Jo2_12768/liste-des-57-arrets-de-1954-a-2000 [last accessed: 15/4/2014] and http://curia.europa.eu/jcms/jcms/Jo2_12854/liste-des-79-arrets-de-2001-a-2004 [last accessed: 1 December 2014]. With regard to availability of pre-accession case law *cf* the critical comments of A Łazowski, 'Half Full and Half Empty Glass: The Application of EU Law in Poland (2004–2010)' (2011) 48.2 *CML Rev* 503, 523.

[56] Article 76.

C. References to SN's Own Case Law on Unfair Terms

One could argue that perhaps it is not in the habit of the SN to cite any case law, but that is not the case, as it is most usual for it to cite domestic case law.[57] In the 45 cases of the SN regarding unfair terms, 25 did not contain any references to national case law, whilst 20 did. The amount of references grew over time, which seems to indicate that a stock of case law was being built up.

Table 2

Period	Number of cases	Number of cases with references to ECJ case law		Number of cases with references to SN case law	
2002–2005	13	1	7.7%	0	0%
2006–2009	16	4	25%	11	68.8%
2010–2013	16	0	0%	9	56.3%

If we analyse the references to SN's own case law on the provisions implementing the Unfair Terms Directive, as well as to ECJ case law interpreting that Directive, divided into three four-year periods (2002–2005, 2006–2009 and 2010–2013)[58] we can see that references to SN's own case law appeared only in the second period (references in two out of three cases), and have continued in the third period (references in more than half of cases). This is in contrast to references to ECJ case law. Whereas in the first period only one in 13 cases contained such a reference, this grew to one in four during the 2006–2009 period, but since 2010 there has been no single reference. The SN seems to have created a case law of its own, and is no longer interested in following what the ECJ has to say about unfair terms.

D. Frequency of Policy-oriented Arguments

Owing to the fact that the provisions implementing the Directive are relatively new (since 2000), and their wording, especially with regard to some controversial aspects (for example third-party effects) has been identified as vague and ambiguous (see above section III.B), one might expect a growth of the frequency of policy-oriented arguments in the SN case law on that topic. And indeed, out of the 45 cases under scrutiny, at least one policy-oriented argument occurred in 30 of them (66 per cent), which is significantly higher than the average (43 per cent)

---

[57] Mańko (n 26) 540–41.

[58] I grouped the cases into three four-year periods due to the relatively low number of cases paper year. The first period (2002–2005) covers mainly pre-accession cases (taking into account the time before a case reaches the Supreme Court), whilst the second period (2006–2009) follows directly Poland's accession to the EU.

for the Civil Chamber of the SN.[59] It is interesting to analyse the type of policy-oriented argumentation that appeared.

Table 3

Type of policy-oriented argument	Frequency
Purpose and/or function of legislation (or specific provision)	17
Interests of the parties to the contract and/or consumer interests in general	8
Economic nature of the contract	3
Good and/or bad faith of parties	2
Public policy	2
Purpose and/or function of the term in consideration	2

Among policy-oriented arguments which—as I have pointed out—appeared in two-thirds of the case law, the most popular type of arguments were those pointing to the purpose and/or function of the legislation in question (which appeared in 17 out of 45 cases, that is in 37.7 per cent).[60] Very frequently the SN justified its interpretation by pointing to the purpose of *in abstracto* and/or *in concreto* review, sometimes opposing them (in order to underline the differences), sometimes analysing them together in order to underline their common objective of eliminating unfair terms.

The second most popular type of policy-oriented argument was based on the interests of parties and/or on the interest of consumers in general. Such interest-based arguments occurred in eight out of 45 cases (17.7 per cent).[61] Other types of policy-oriented arguments were less frequent, and included the economic nature

[59] The average was calculated on the basis of two samples of reported case law of the Civil Chamber of the Supreme Court, published in its official reporter (*Orzecznictwo Sądu Najwyższego. Izba Cywilna*, published by LexisNexis) for 2005 and 2013. The samples covered the first 100 reported cases in each year (items 1–100 in the reporter), which constitutes a bit less than half of cases published yearly in the official reporter. The frequency of purely linguistic arguments amounted to 98% in both samples. The frequency of policy-oriented arguments (policies, interests, purposes) amounted to 37% for 2005 and 49% for 2013. When calculating the frequency, I took into account the appearance of at least one policy-oriented argument in each case.

[60] *InCo* (n 52); *PZU Życie* (n 52); *UPC Polska* (n 52); *Górnośląski Bank Gospodarczy* (n 52); *TFI v UOKiK* (2006); *Profesja* (n 52); *Mirosław W v Andrzej Z* (n 52); *Kowalczuk v TPSA* (n 52); *Lexus v BPET* (n 52); *Jan C v Polska Telefonia Cyfrowa* (n 52); *UOKiK v Aster* (n 52); *UOKiK v Polska Telewizja Cyfrowa* (n 52); *Zenon K v W* (n 52); *Adam G v Noble Bank v Ewa G v N Bank Polska* (n 52); *Towarzystwo Lexus v Alior Bank* (n 52); *Szota v Uniwersytet Śląski* (n 52).

[61] *Re Bank Enforcement Title* (n 52); *Profesja* (n 52); *Amplico Life* (n 52); *Centrum Leasingu i Finansów* (n 52); *UOKiK v AutoCom* (n 52); *Mirosław W v Andrzej Z* (n 52); *UOKiK v Cardiff Polska* (n 52); *UOKiK v Polska Telewizja Cyfrowa* (n 52).

of the contract in question (in three cases),[62] the good and/or bad faith of the parties to the contract (in two cases),[63] public policy (of card holder protection and of consumer protection) (two cases),[64] and finally the purpose and/or function of the term under consideration.

Despite a lack of direct influence of ECJ case law, it might as well be that the Court of Justice's method of interpretation, placing a focus on the function and purpose of legislation, rather than on its specific wording, has had a somewhat indirect impact upon the SN. However, there were also cases in which the SN presented its *spécialité de la maison*, that is formalist, text-oriented argumentation, as will become visible in the next section.

V. Qualitative Analysis of SN Case Law on Unfair Terms

A. General Overview of the Case Law

Despite being a court of law, and not of fact, the SN—unlike the ECJ[65]—does not avoid pronouncing itself on the (un)fairness of specific terms. Within the 45 cases handed down until now, the SN has analysed the fairness of terms in 17 of them, mainly concerning insurance contracts,[66] banking contracts,[67] telecommunications services contracts,[68] as well as a timeshare contract,[69] an education services contract,[70] a leasing contract,[71] and a housing development contract.[72]

On numerous occasions the SN has pronounced itself on the meaning of the criteria used in the test of unfairness, that is 'good morals' and 'flagrant violation of consumer interests'. As a rule, it did so without referring to the Directive and its notions of 'good faith' and 'significant imbalance',[73] although there were

---

[62] *Krawczyk v Millenium Bank* (n 52); *MZ v Inter Polska* (n 52); *Ewa M-G and Waldemar G* (n 52).

[63] *Rafał W v Towarzystwo Ubezpieczeniowe 'D'* (n 52); *Krystian B v Towarzystwo Ubezpieczeń A* (n 52).

[64] *UOKiK v BIG Bank* (n 52); *TFI v UOKiK* (n 52).

[65] The ECJ, despite giving some guidance as to the test of unfairness, has ruled only on one kind of term as being unfair—a jurisdiction clause ousting the courts of the consumer's place of residence (Case C-240-244 *Océano*).

[66] *Rafał W v Towarzystwo Ubezpieczeniowe D* (n 52); *UOKiK v Amplico Life* (n 52); *UOKiK v Cardiff Polska* (n 52); *MZ v Inter Polska* (n 52).

[67] *Białas v Bank Handlowy* (n 52); *UOKiK v BIG Bank* (n 52); *Rafał P v Bank A* (n 52); *Kuźbińska et al v Gospodarczy Bank Spółdzielczy* (n 52); *Ewa G v N Bank Polska* (n 52); *Towarzystwo Lexus v Alior Bank* (n 52).

[68] *UOKiK v AutoCom* (n 52); *Kowalczuk v TPSA SA* (n 52); *Ćmiela v Tele2* (n 52).

[69] *UOKiK v Lipiński* (n 52).

[70] *UOKiK v Profesja* (n 52).

[71] *Centrum Leasingu i Finansów* (n 52).

[72] *Zenon K v W* (n 52).

[73] *UOKiK v AICE Polska* (n 52); *Krawczyk v Millenium Bank* (n 52); *UOKiK v Amplico Life* (n 52); *MZ v Inter Polska* (n 52); *Zenon K v W* (n 52).

exceptions.[74] A great deal of attention was devoted by the SN to the third-party effects of judgments declaring, within the framework of *in abstracto* proceedings, a term to be unfair. Other issues analysed by the SN included, inter alia, the notion of the main subject-matter as applicable to specific types of contracts,[75] the applicability of the unfair terms regime to specific types of agreements,[76] the legal value of the list of unfair terms,[77] the *contra proferentem* rule and its effects,[78] as well as the extent of factual circumstances that need to be taken into account within the framework of *in abstracto* review proceedings.[79] The Court also pronounced itself on procedural issues, such as *locus standi* to initiate *in abstracto* review,[80] or the (lack of) *res judicata* applicable to decisions declaring a term not to be unfair.[81]

From a procedural point of view, most of the decisions of the SN were rendered in cassation proceedings (36) or interlocutory appeal proceedings (two), but seven of them[82] in domestic preliminary reference proceedings.[83] It must be noted that such a preliminary reference is admissible only if the court of second instance encounters 'a legal question giving rise to serious doubts'.[84] This does not necessarily mean that those serious doubts required an interpretation of EU law, but this may well have been the case.

B. Test of Unfairness

The criteria of unfairness used in the Unfair Terms Directive—violation of the 'requirement of good faith' causing 'a significant imbalance in the parties' rights and obligations arising under the contract, to the detriment of the consumer'— are notoriously vague. An additional problem arises in connection with the fact

---

[74] *Miejski i Powiatowy Rzecznik Praw Konsumentów v UPC Polska* (n 52) (referring to Directive and to *Océano*).

[75] *Grzegorz S v Warta* (n 52); *Krawczyk v BIG Bank Gdański SA* (n 52); *PZU Życie* (n 52); *Damian B v Zakład Ubezpieczeń* (n 52); *Aleksandra W v PZU SA* (n 52).

[76] *Towarzystwo Lexus v Orlen* (n 52) (promotional schemes at petrol stations); *Urszula S v Compensa* (n 52) (out-of-court settlement between consumer and insurance company).

[77] *Białas v Bank Handlowy* (n 52); *Miejski i Powiatowy Rzecznik Konsumentów v UPC Polska* (n 52); *Kowalczuk v TPSA* (n 52).

[78] *Dariusz D v Towarzystwo Ubezpieczeń i Reasekuracji* (n 52); *Krystian B v Towarzystwo Ubezpieczeń A* (n 52); *Elżbieta L v Korporacja Ubezpieczeniowa Filar* (n 52); *Centrum Leasingu i Finansów* (n 52); *Ewa M-G v Waldemar G* (n 52).

[79] *UOKiK v Profesja Centrum Kształcenia Kadr* (n 52); *Towarzystwo Lexus v BPET* (n 52); *UOKiK v Polska Telewizja Cyfrowa* (n 52); *CW v Towarzystwo Ubezpieczeń E* (n 52); *In Merito v Polska Telefonia Cyfrowa* (n 52).

[80] *Miejski i Powiatowy Rzecznik Konsumentów v UPC Polska* (n 52); *Jan C v Polska Telefonia Cyfrowa* (n 52); *Adam G v Getin Noble Bank* (n 52); *Szota v Uniwersytet Śląski* (n 52).

[81] *UOKiK v Aster* (n 52); *Ewa G v N Bank Polska* (n 52).

[82] *Międzynarodowa Korporacja Gospodarcza InCo* (n 52); *Re Bank Enforcement Title* (n 52); *PZU Życie* (n 52); *TFI v UOKiK* (n 52); *Aleksandra W v PZU* (n 52); *Towarzystwo Lexus v BPET* (n 52); *Makuszewska* (n 52).

[83] Polish Civil Procedure allows, since 1953, for a court of second instance (appellate court) to submit a preliminary reference to the Supreme Court on a point of law (Article 390 kpc).

[84] Article 390 § 1 sentence 1 kpc.

that the Polish implementing provisions resort to different concepts, namely 'good morals' and 'flagrant violation of consumer interests'. A uniform application of the test of unfairness across the EU certainly requires a judicial dialogue between national courts and the ECJ. Indeed, as the latter ruled in *Pénzügyi Lízing*,[85] its jurisdiction extends to the interpretation of the concept of an 'unfair term' and to the criteria that must be applied when examining a particular term, although the decision whether a specific term is unfair is left to national courts. However, the SN has preferred to interpret those criteria on its own, not only refraining from submitting a preliminary reference, but also failing to refer to ECJ case law.

In *UOKiK v AICE Polska* the Court based its interpretation on a linguistic analysis of the national implementing provisions, without any attempt at linking them to the notions found in the Directive. Analysing the two criteria found in the Polish implementing rules (violation of 'good morals' and 'flagrant violation of consumer interests') the SN found that they are independent and must be fulfilled jointly. Commenting on the meaning of 'good morals', the Court failed to refer to the notion of good faith, but held that the essence of good morals is 'respect for other people'. As to the second notion, namely 'consumer interests', the SN ruled that they must be understood broadly, as covering not only economic, but also non-economic interests, such as lack of organisational comfort, loss of time, dishonest treatment, violation of privacy.

In *Krawczyk v Millenium Bank*,[86] once again without any reference to the Directive nor to ECJ case law, the ECJ explained the meaning of the criteria of unfairness, indicating that 'acting against good morals' means the creation of terms which hamper contractual balance, whilst a 'flagrant violation of consumer interests' occurs if there is an unjustified disproportion of rights and duties to the detriment of a consumer within the framework of a specific obligatory relationship. Whereas the latter understanding of 'flagrant violation' brings it into line with the notion of 'significant imbalance', found in the Directive, the explanation of the notion of 'good morals' makes it synonymous to significant imbalance, leading to the merger of the two criteria into a single one.

The equation between the Polish notion of a 'flagrant violation of consumer interests' and the Directive's notion of a 'significant imbalance' was further strengthened in *MiPRK v UPC Polska*,[87] where the Court relied explicitly on the Directive. This time, the Court did not equate the notion of 'good morals' with 'contractual balance' (as in the previous cases), but held that good morals are 'ethical rules concerning honest and loyal conduct in trade'. This arguably brought the Polish 'good morals' closer to 'good faith'.[88]

---

[85] Case C-137/08, [2010] ECR I-10847.
[86] Above (n 52).
[87] ibid.
[88] As the ECJ later held in C-415/11 *Aziz v Catalunyacaixa* ECLI:EU:C:2013:164, the requirement of good faith implies the duty to deal fairly and equitably with the consumer, and a standard term violates good faith if it can be assumed that the consumer would not have accepted it, had he had the possibility of negotiating it.

In *MZ v Inter Polska*,[89] once again without referring to the Directive or to ECJ case law, the SN explained the criteria of unfairness by resorting to its preferred linguistic methods of interpretation. It first noted that the formulation of the general prohibition of unfairness in the Civil Code requires that the criteria of 'violation of good morals' and 'flagrant violation of consumer interests' are separate, and therefore need to be fulfilled jointly. It observed that, as a rule, a flagrant violation of consumer interests is simultaneously *contra bonos mores*, but that need not be the case and must be proven. It pointed out that good morals can mean either 'customary and moral norms, commonly accepted conduct, customary principles of honest behaviour'; or 'traditional elements of ethics, principles of loyalty, respect for other people, as well as behaviour not making use of disinformation, ignorance, credulousness or insufficient information' of the consumer. Characteristically, the SN did not refer to the notion of good faith and its understanding in the Directive. Furthermore, its approach to 'good morals' was very positivistic, in the sense that it attempted at understanding them as a certain set of rules ('customary and moral', 'traditional' 'ethical').

Turning to the second standard in the general prohibition of unfairness, that is a 'flagrant violation of consumer interests', the Court likewise adopted a text-oriented, linguistic approach, holding that:

> Synonymous with the adjective 'flagrant' are the words 'dramatic' and 'screaming'. The adjective 'flagrant' means, in the sense of a negative feature, 'clear', 'uncontested', 'obvious'. In other words, the violation of consumer interests must be characterised by a high level of intensity. The term 'consumer interests' is understood broadly, as encompassing not only economic interests, but also the discomfort resulting from the loss of time, inconvenience, or satisfaction with the conclusion of the contract, etc. Such a broad understanding of consumer interest is reduced in this way that it may not infringe the justified interests of entrepreneurs engaged in an economic activity.[90]

MZ v Inter Polska is yet another example of a case in which the SN approached the criteria of unfairness using linguistic (if not downright dictionary) methods of interpretation, and did not see the need of coordinating its understanding with the notions used in the Directive or the way they are understood in ECJ case law.

The SN's last word, until now, on the understanding of the criteria of unfairness is to be found in *Zenon K et al v W*,[91] a case concerning an *in concreto* review of unfair terms. As usual, without referring to the Directive or to ECJ case law, but relying on its own earlier case law (*AICE Polska* and *Krawczyk v Millenium Bank*) it explained the meaning of the general standards used in the prohibition of unfair terms as follows:

> According to settled-case law [of the SN] it is contrary to [good] morals to introduce into contracts terms hampering contractual balance. A flagrant violation of consumer interests consists in an unjustified disproportion of rights and duties to the consumer's

---

[89] Above (n 52).
[90] ibid.
[91] Above (n 52).

detriment. Both these criteria ought to be fulfilled jointly ... A limitation of the freedom of concluding contracts has an exceptional character, which indicates [the need for] a strict application of the criteria leading to the conclusion that a contract contains prohibited terms.[92]

Once again, the two-prong test of unfairness in the Directive (good faith *and* significant imbalance) have been merged into one, because the notion of 'good morals' has absorbed contractual imbalance. The element of good faith, understood as the duty of the court to have 'particular regard ... to the strength of the bargaining positions of the parties, whether the consumer had an inducement to agree to the term and whether the goods or services were sold or supplied to the special order of the consumer' which 'may be satisfied by the seller or supplier where he deals fairly and equitably with the other party whose legitimate interests he has to take into account',[93] is absent from the test devised by the SN.

The case law of the SN interpreting the criteria of unfairness has developed to a large extent without any reference either to the text of the Directive, or to the ECJ case law interpreting it. There are reasons to believe that this has led to the emergence of a national test of unfairness which is different from the one provided for by EU law. In particular, in the absence of the notion of 'good faith' in the Polish implementing provisions, which was replaced by 'good morals', the SN has displayed a notable tendency towards identifying the latter expression with contractual balance, thereby collapsing two separate criteria (good faith, significant imbalance of rights and duties) into merely one (significant imbalance only). Furthermore, it does not seem from the case law of the SN that it is drawing inspiration from the ECJ's interpretation of the two notions, especially with regard to the understanding of the notion of 'good faith'.

C. Unfairness of Terms Violating Mandatory Rules

A contractual term can violate a mandatory[94] provision of law. Under national law, such a term is invalid, but the question arises whether it can be simultaneously unfair. The issue is addressed neither in the Directive, nor in the Polish Civil Code, and therefore required a creative interpretation from the SN.

The SN first addressed this issue in *UOKiK v BIG Bank Gdański*,[95] where it analysed the fairness of a term which violated a mandatory rule of the Civil Code. The SN held that if a term of contract violates a statutory rule, it is *eo ipso* a violation of good morals, and therefore it must be considered as unfair. This finding was made without any reference to the Directive and its understanding of unfairness.

---

[92] ibid.
[93] Preamble to the Unfair Terms Directive.
[94] A mandatory provision is one which may not be deviated from by agreement of the parties, as opposed to a default provision.
[95] Above (n 52).

The holding of *UOKiK v BIG Bank Gdański* was later confirmed in *UOKiK v AutoCom.*[96] Analysing a number of terms in a telecommunications contract, the SN assumed, without any consideration for EU law, that those which violate mandatory rules of law are automatically to be considered as unfair.

This fairly established line of case law was departed from in *Makuszewska*, a case in which the SN was seised in a domestic preliminary reference procedure.[97] The referring court explicitly asked whether a term in a standard contract, which violates a mandatory rule of private law may also be considered to be unfair. The SN, relying only on domestic legal sources and domestic case law, found that that '[a] term in a standard contract, infringing a mandatory statutory provision, cannot be deemed to be a prohibited contractual term (Article 385^1 § 1 kc)'. Arguably, the exclusion of illegal contractual terms from review as to their fairness leads to the narrowing down on the scope of review in comparison with the Unfair Terms Directive, and thereby leads to a level of consumer protection below that which is provided for by the Directive. Since the lower court obviously harboured doubts as to the interpretation of EU law, a reference to the ECJ would have been an appropriate course of action.

D. Unfair Commercial Practices and Unfair Terms

The relationship between various EU law instruments aiming at the protection of the consumer is not necessary entirely clear. This applies also to the Unfair Commercial Practices Directive ('UCPD') on the one hand, and the Unfair Terms Directive (in this section: 'UTD') on the other, with particular reference to the respective notions of an 'unfair commercial practice' and 'unfair term'. This issue was explored by the SN in *Rafał P v Bank A*,[98] a case concerning *in abstracto* review of a standard credit card contract, which provided in small print for 24 days of credit without interest, although the bank's advertising campaign was based on a slogan claiming '54 days without interest'. The consumer, having reached the SN, explicitly invited it to submit a preliminary reference to the ECJ in order to clarify the relation between the UTD and the UCPD. The SN refused and ruled on the issue by itself instead. Characteristically, the Court limited itself to a narrowly text-oriented and formalist style of reasoning:

> ... [The UCPD] is not applicable to standard contract terms regulated by [the UTD]. This conclusion follows not only from motive 10 in the preamble to [the UCPD], but also from Art 14 and 15 of the [UCPD] which contains a list of directives amended by [the UCPD] ... Unfair commercial practices ... are a distinct category from standard terms ... The present proceedings are concerned with considering whether a standard term is

---

[96] ibid.
[97] In contrast to the *UOKiK v BIG Bank Gdański* and *AutoCom*, which were heard as cassations launched in *in abstracto* review procedures.
[98] Above (n 52).

unfair and not with the question of unfair commercial practices ... which excludes the application of [the UPCD] ... Had the Union legislator envisaged that [the UCPD] ought to be taken into account in the interpretation of [the UTD], the former would contain appropriate amending provisions. There is no solution like that in [the UCPD].[99]

The complex issue, solved by the SN by resorting to purely formalist reasoning, certainly merited submitting a reference to the ECJ, as evidenced by the later case of *Pereničová*,[100] where the Luxembourg judges held that '[a] finding that ... a commercial practice is unfair is one element among others on which the competent court may ... base its assessment of the unfairness of the contractual terms...', although, admittedly, it has 'no direct effect on the assessment' of unfairness.

E. Third-party Effects

A recurring theme in the case law of the SN has been the third-party effects of a judgment, rendered in the procedure of *in abstracto* review of unfair terms. Such a judgment, declaring that a given standard term of contract is unfair, is then entered into the publicly available Unfair Terms Register. The question arises, whether such terms are prohibited only vis-à-vis the trader who was condemned, or vis-a-vis all traders but with regard to similar contracts, or vis-à-vis all traders and in all standard contracts. The views of the SN on the issue underwent a characteristic evolution, from strong third-party effects, whereby a standard term entered into the Unfair Terms Register would be prohibited in all standard contracts of all traders,[101] towards a limited view,[102] whereby the third-party effects are limited to a specific standard contract of a specific trader.[103] In the following paragraphs I will present two cases regarding the issue that merit particular attention: First, the *TFI* ruling in which the SN opted for extremely broad third-party effects, and second *Lexus v BPET* in which the Court overruled *TFI*.

In *TFI v UOKiK* the SN was seised by a preliminary reference explicitly concerning third-party effects of the Unfair Terms Register. The Court answered that terms entered into the Unfair Terms Register are prohibited for all traders and in all standard contracts, and their use constitutes a practice violating the collective interests of consumers. In the grounds of the judgment it added that terms once entered into the Unfair Terms Register are prohibited across the board, in standard contracts used in any sector of the economy. The Court also opined that a term

---

[99] ibid.

[100] Case C-453/10, ECLI:EU:C:2012:144.

[101] *InCo* (n 52); *Górnośląski Bank Gospodaczy* (n 52); *TFI v UOKiK* (n 52); *Mirosław W v Andrzej Z* (n 52).

[102] *Towarzystwo Lexus v BPET* (n 52).

[103] This line of case-law has been upheld since in *In Merito v Polska Telefonia Cyfrowa* (n 52) and *CW v Towarzystwo Ubezpieczeń E* (n 52).

from the Unfair Terms Register, if it appears in a standard contract, is automatically null and void. It is remarkable that the SN relied heavily on ECJ case law on *effet util* and argued that such strong third-party effects are necessary in order to ensure that the purposes of the Unfair Terms Directive and Injunctions Directive are attained.

Nevertheless, the SN's interpretation of the *in abstracto* review of unfairness, adopted in the *TFI* ruling, departs from what the ECJ later explained in *Invitel.*[104] In particular, according to the latter case, a national court performing an *in abstracto* review should evaluate a given term in light of all other terms of the standard contract in question, and against the background of national default rules which would have been applicable in the absence of the contested term. However, the *TFI* understanding does not allow for such an evaluation, since it provides for automatic invalidity of all terms having the same content as a previously condemned unfair term, without the possibility of analysing the context of a different standard contract or the different default rules applicable to different types of contracts in different sectors of the economy.[105]

Lexus v BPET, the case in which *TFI* was overruled, was likewise decided in a domestic preliminary reference procedure: A lower court enquired whether the extended *res judicata* of a decision declaring a term to be unfair under *in abstracto* review, extends also to proceedings between different parties than those who took part in the proceedings in which the unfairness of the term was declared. On the basis of the right to a fair trial,[106] the SN argued that broad third-party effects infringe the rights of those traders, who were not parties to the original *in abstracto* review proceedings, but who nevertheless would have to stop using certain terms in their own standard contracts. Referring to the Directive, the Court pointed out that even if the broad third-party effects would serve to fulfil its objectives, that is also possible without violating the right to a fair trial.

In both cases analysed in this section, despite the obvious connection of the issue of third-party effects with the Directive,[107] neither the SN, nor the lower courts, considered the need of submitting a preliminary reference. In fact, both in *TFI* and *Lexus v BPET*, the SN was seised of the matter in a domestic preliminary reference procedure, which clearly indicates that Polish courts, when faced with a problem with the interpretation of national implementing provisions of an EU directive, feel more comfortable asking their domestic Supreme Court for guidance, than to submit a reference to the ECJ.

---

[104] Case C-472/10, ECLI:EU:C:2012:242.

[105] It remains open whether *TFI* does not provide a higher level of consumer protection than the Directive, and would therefore be compatible with it.

[106] Art 45 of the Polish Constitution.

[107] Which can be seen from the fact that the ECJ accepted and replied to the questions posed in *Invitel*.

VI. Conclusions

The case study has shown that 10 years after Poland's accession to the EU the impact of EU law and specifically ECJ case law upon private law adjudication remains limited. The quantitative analysis revealed that only two of the over two dozen decisions of the ECJ on unfair terms have been referred to by the SN. On top of that, no references have occurred since 2009. A possible explanation for this could be the fact that in the meantime the Polish implementing provisions have been covered by a layer of domestic case law, presumably making it—in the eyes of the SN judges—redundant to follow the developments of ECJ case law any longer. If that were the case, it could be said that national case law has been acting, since 2009, as a screen shielding the SN from the EU origins of the Polish rules on unfair terms. The same could be said about references to the Unfair Terms Directive, which occur only in one out of six decisions of the SN, and for the last time in 2008.[108] Judging from the grounds of SN decisions, the Polish implementing provisions seem to have definitely cut their umbilical cord from EU law.

Another aspect worth underlining is that Polish courts, when harbouring doubts as to the interpretation of national implementing provisions, prefer to submit domestic preliminary references to the SN, rather than seise the ECJ. Indeed, seven of the 45 cases rendered hitherto by the SN reached it in the domestic preliminary reference proceedings. It must be noted that such a preliminary reference is admissible only if the court of second instance encounters 'a legal question giving rise to serious doubts'.[109] This does not necessarily mean that these serious doubts required an interpretation of EU law, but at least in some of these cases this seems to have been the fact. The SN—*ex definitione* a court of last resort under Article 267 TFEU[110]—has not considered it appropriate to refer to the ECJ either, even though at least once it was explicitly urged to do so by a litigant.[111]

It seems to me that at least in some of the cases dealing with unfair terms the SN should have considered whether it actually harboured doubts regarding not only the interpretation of the national implementing provisions, but also the interpretation of the Directive itself. Nevertheless, it did not make any such doubts explicit and consequently did not submit a single preliminary reference to the ECJ. What should be underlined is that the SN did not make any reference to the *CILFIT* criteria. Actually, not a single of the analysed SN decisions devotes a single sentence[112] to persuade the public that the issues at stake were covered by the *acte clair* doctrine.

---

[108]   In *Lexus v BPET* (n 52).
[109]   Article 390 § 1 sentence 1 kpc.
[110]   Taborowski (n 16) 408–09. *cf* Bobek (n 1) 209.
[111]   *Rafał P v Bank A* (n 52).
[112]   *cf* Bobek (n 2) 1631–32.

All in all, in the vast majority of the 45 cases under scrutiny I detected what Bobek called 'silence on the part of national courts' with regard to EU law and ECJ case law. As he points out:

... the fact that national courts do not openly revolt against the guidance given in the case law of the [ECJ] could mean that they agree with it. It can, however, also mean something quite different: that they do not know EU law and case law of the [ECJ] or, more problematically, that they do not care about it, or, in the worst case scenario, that they know it but for whatever reason they do intentionally not care about it.[113]

Which of the four scenarios envisaged by Bobek is applicable to the case study analysed in this chapter? Whilst the first scenario (knowledge and acceptance of ECJ case law, along the lines of 'to read and not to quote'[114] approach) cannot be ruled out *a limine*, it nevertheless seems that rather one of the other three scenarios should be taken into account, perhaps with an emphasis on '"ignorance" and "disregard"'.[115]

Whilst it is difficult to put forward a conclusive explanation of this phenomenon, a number of reasons may be suggested, both for the absence of EU law from the reasoning of the SN, and for the lack of consideration for ECJ case law altogether. First of all, one should take into account the time pressure factor.[116] Despite a case selection mechanism at the SN, litigants still need to wait 10 months for a decision on the merits from the Civil Chamber,[117] and the Chamber decides around 4,500 cases yearly;[118] even if many of them are dismissed as having insufficient legal relevance, such a decision must be justified. Waiting for the ECJ to answer would only prolong proceedings, and judges, working under the pressure of time, are reluctant to take such a step.

Second, the lack of a clear linkage between the national implementing provisions (the EU origin of which is not specified) and the Directive as well as ECJ case law, could be a factor.[119] Not only is the Directive not explicitly mentioned in the Civil Code, but even legal databases containing Polish case law do not refer to EU case law under the relevant articles of the Civil Code and Code of Civil Procedure, making it more difficult for lawyers (representing parties in court) and assistants of SN judges to access it.[120] In fact, Polish civil judges (from the lower courts),

---

[113] Bobek (n 1) 209.

[114] *cf* Bobek (n 18) 227.

[115] Bobek (n 1) 212.

[116] *cf* Michal Bobek, 'Quantity or Quality? Reassessing the Role of Supreme Jurisdictions in Central Europe' (2009) 57(1) *American Journal of Comparative Law* 33.

[117] *Informacja o działalności Sądu Najwyższego w roku 2013* [Information Regarding the Activity of the Supreme Court in the Year 2013] (Sąd Najwyższy, 2014) 171.

[118] ibid, 175.

[119] Polish judges are usually unaware of the directives which the Civil Code transposes into Polish law, as Przemysław Polański points out with regard to Directive 1999/93/EC in his forthcoming *Europejskie prawo handlu elektronicznego. Sposoby regulacji usług społeczeństwa informacyjnego* [European Law of Electronic Commerce: Methods for Regulating Services in an Information Society] (CH Beck, 2014).

[120] I would like to thank Przemysław Polański for his comments regarding this aspect.

asked whether they apply EU law in their everyday practice, usually replied[121] by pointing out that the 'infrequency of the occurrence of EU law is actually one of the biggest problems attached to it', frankly stating that '[s]o far I have not dealt with any EU law issue', or even saying that 'we simply have no time to engage with EU law', with a conclusion that 'the whole issue [of EU law] remains a rather abstract one. It is different; interesting but irrelevant.' Explaining why they do not apply EU law, they pointed to a lack of knowledge and the fact that parties do not raise EU arguments.[122] Whilst these answers were given by lower court civil judges, they may provide an indication as to how SN judges and their assistants might perceive things too.

Third, differences in legal culture between the rather formalist SN and the ECJ, perceived as anti-formalist, could play a role, limiting the willingness of the SN to enter into a dialogue. SN judges, imbued with formalism,[123] may consider the teleological reasoning of the ECJ as illegitimate judicial law-making, violating the (formalist notion of the) rule of law.[124]

Fourth, the ECJ decisions may seem, also due to factors of legal culture differences, of little substantive persuasion to the SN. This may, incidentally, also explain why the SN is reluctant to submit a preliminary reference itself (issues of power and prestige aside): It could simply be concerned about the quality of the ECJ's decision it would receive which, according to certain scholars, are sometimes incomprehensible or insufficiently motivated.[125]

Finally, a reason for not citing the ECJ (and, for that matter, not submitting a preliminary reference) may be connected to SN's concerns over its power and prestige within the national judicial structure. If we keep in mind how jealously the SN has been defending its field of competence vis-a-vis the national constitutional Court,[126] it comes as no surprise that it is not willing to give way to the ECJ, fearing that its position as supreme court of the land could be weakened, should it openly ask the ECJ for guidance or cite its case law as authority. National courts, hitherto using the domestic preliminary reference procedure, could become tempted to bypass Plac Krasińskich and head straight for Plateau de Kirchberg.

---

[121] All quotes in this sentence after Jaremba (n 45) 213.

[122] ibid, 217.

[123] See eg Mańko (n 7) 84–85, 88.

[124] Bobek (n 26) 41 notes (with the *caveat* that '[t]his comparison is, of course, exaggerated') that 'there are ... some striking similarities between the communist/Marxist and Community approaches to legal reasoning, and the requirements of judicial activism placed on national judges ... [B]oth approaches are similar: open-ended clauses take precedence over textual interpretations of the written law ... The only visible difference is that the universal "all-purpose" argument has changed—from the victory of the working class to the full effectiveness of EC law.' In this context it should be borne in mind that the ECJ is perceived negatively by part of the Polish judiciary, as found in a recent empirical study: Certain Polish civil judges of the ordinary courts (anonymously) opined that the ECJ enjoys unchecked power without a democratic mandate and that it is engaged in judicial law-making instead of 'applying' the law (Jaremba (n 45) 280). *cf* P Cserne, 'The Recodification of Private Law in Central and Eastern Europe' in P Larouche and P Cserne (eds), *National Legal Systems and Globalization: New Role, Continuing Relevance* (TMC Asser, 2013) 50–51.

[125] *cf* Bobek (n 2) 1639–40.

[126] Mańko (n 7).

Regardless of the reasons behind these phenomena, EU law is not, at least for the Civil Chamber of the SN, its 'daily bread, in spite of the baker saying it ought to be.'[127] As I indicated in the introduction to this paper, I am not intending to be normative and join the choir of those admonishing the national courts for not being sufficiently Euro-enthusiastic. However, it does seem to me that the practice of the SN, at least with regard the interpretation of the national implementing provisions to the Unfair Terms Directive, could be described as falling somewhat short of the EU law obligations stemming from the principle of harmonious inter- pretation and indirect effect, at least if one adopts the point of view of the ECJ.

---

[127] Bobek (n 1) 213.

5

The Aversion to Judicial Discretion in Civil Procedure in Post-Communist Countries: Can the Influence of EU Law Change it?

I. Introduction

Resentment regarding judicial discretion is not limited to post-communist countries. A distinguished English judge stated already in the eighteenth century:

> The discretion of a judge is the law of tyrants; it is always unknown; it is different in different men; it is casual, and depends on constitution, temper and passion. In the best it is very often caprice, in the worst it is every vice, folly and passion to which human nature is liable.[1]

This quotation is not intended to set the pace for the main message of this chapter. The prevailing views in England have changed since the mid-eighteenth century and judicial discretion, especially concerning case management, has become one of the major tools in the 1998 Civil Procedure Rules after the Woolf Reform.[2] More importantly, the scope of this chapter is narrower than usual treatises on judicial discretion. It concerns only discretion in procedural law and without relating to discretion in judicial decision making on the merits. Moreover, reasons for resentment towards judicial discretion in post-communist countries are more complex than in other countries and should be considered against the background of the

---

[1] Lord Camden CJ, *Hindson v Kersey* (1765). Cited by: N Andrews: 'Judicial Discretion in Common Law Jurisdictions: USA, England, Canada, Australia' in M Storme and B Hess (eds), *The Discretionary Power of the Judge: Limits and Control* (Kluwer, 2003) 119.
[2] See, eg, A Zuckerman, 'Court Control and Party Compliance—The Quest for Effective Litigation Management' in N Trocker and V Varano (eds), *The Reforms of Civil Procedure in Comparative Perspective* (Giappichelli Editore, 2005) 149 ff; N Andrews, *English Civil Procedure, Fundaments of the New Civil Justice System* (Oxford University Press, 2003) 143.

specific conditions which the region endured in the second half of the twentieth century.

Furthermore, discretion in procedural law (in a narrower sense) can be defined as the possibility of a judge to choose between two different courses of action in proceedings which are both equally lawful.[3] However, in this chapter I use the concept of 'judicial discretion' in a much broader sense: Here it covers different methods and procedural tools, which all have in common that they enable greater flexibility in conducting proceedings. This is assessed in light of one of the common features of the worldwide trend in modern civil procedure reform, granting more room to the judge in order to adapt the unfolding of proceedings and its time frame to the characteristics of each particular case.[4] Legislators around the world have realised that if the goal of civil justice is to effectively guarantee the protection of rights in a reasonable time at a reasonable cost (the so-called 'tri-dimensional concept of justice'), this goal cannot be pursued through the same model of procedure rigidly conceived as applicable in every case.[5] Litigation must be tailored to the size and nature of the dispute.[6] The judge should, thus, adopt procedural decisions that she considers best on the basis of fairness and after weighing the facts and circumstances. This is achieved by granting the judge greater powers of discretion (for example regarding case management) or by extending the use of open-ended terms in procedural legislation (open-textured rules and open-ended exceptions; for example 'good faith', 'due diligence', 'good administration of justice', 'prevention of the abuse of rights', 'reasonable' etc).[7] Another legislative method available in order to achieve this goal is to provide for different 'tracks' that will follow the preparatory phase of proceedings, which the judge is free to choose from.[8] General principles, especially proportionality, are promoted, as an overriding guideline not

---

[3] S Shetreet, 'The Discretionary Power of the Judge—General Report; Part II' in Storme and Hess (n 1) 75.

[4] See eg D Chan and PCH Chan, 'Hong Kong Special Administrative Region (China) National Report' in D Maleshin (ed), *Civil Procedure in Cross-cultural Dialogue: Eurasia Context, IAPL World Conference on Civil Procedure* (Statut Moscow, 2012) 173; Andrews (n 2), 36 ff; P Oberhammer, *Schweizerische Zivilprozessordnung—Kurzkommentar* (Helbing Lichtenhahn Verlag, 2010) 215; N Trocker and V Varano, 'Concluding Remarks' in Trocker and Varano (n 2) 247 ff; B Karolczyk, 'Pretrial as a Part of Judicial Case Management in Poland in Comparative Perspective' (2013) 15 *Comparative Law Review* 151, 153.

[5] Trocker and Varano (n 4) 248.

[6] Andrews (n 2) 39.

[7] Trocker and Varano (n 4) 247 ff.

[8] An English judge has a duty to determine to which of the available 'tracks' he will direct the case: the *fast track, small claims track*, or *multiple track*—especially the latter enables the court to tailor the conduct of litigation, depending on the particularities of the case at hand: Andrews (n 2) 39 ff. A similar approach was adopted in Hong Kong (Chan (n 4) 173). Likewise in France (short track—*circuit court*, middle track—*circuit moyen*, long track—*circuit long*): F Ferrand, 'The Respective Role of the Judge and the Parties in the Preparation of the Case in France' in Trocker and Varano (n 2) 18 ff. In Germany the judge decides, at an early stage of proceedings, by discretion, taking into account the peculiarities of each individual case, whether to conduct a written preparatory procedure or schedule an early preparatory oral hearing (paras 275–76 *Zivilprozessordnung*). In Austria (since the 2002 Reform) the role of the preparatory hearing is strengthened and the judge enjoys more flexibility in determining (with the co-operation of the parties) the so-called procedural plan (*Prozessprogramm*) in order to determine the schedule for the unfolding of proceedings.

just for the legislature but for the judge in every individual case as well.[9] Hence, flexibility in proceedings is ensured by allowing the court to exercise discretion pursuant to standards rather than rules.[10] The main restriction on this discretion again relates to standards rather than rules—standards concerning fundamental procedural guarantees, such as the right to be heard, the equality of arms and the right to effective access to court.

In line with this approach, a prominent Slovenian intellectual (and one of the leading dissidents in the period of communist Yugoslavia), Dr France Bučar, observed:

> We degraded judges to mere bureaucrats. A judge must have a personality and be worthy of having confidence in him. But because of the totalitarian past in Slovenia, we thought that every step of the proceedings should be prescribed in detail for the judge to follow. However, if you prescribe their every move, judges will not strive for justice, they will seek only their own protection. Judges need more discretion.[11]

These are powerful words. However, in Slovenia, and possibly in other post-communist countries,[12] very few are willing to support this trend. The dominant perception is exactly the opposite. The perception prevails that judicial discretion inevitably leads to arbitrariness or even judicial abuse, and therefore endangers legal certainty as the fundamental value of decision making.[13] A firm and rigid procedural regime is preferred as an expression of the 'principle of legality'. Procedural rules of an open-textured nature, relying on principles or enabling judicial discretion in the narrower sense are thus often rejected with aversion as being 'unclear', 'too vague', 'unreliable and unpredictable', equated to a 'lottery',[14] and 'jeopardising legal certainty', and therefore open to abuse and arbitrary decision-making.[15] Even if the legislature ultimately adopts procedural instruments that strengthen the judges' powers and promotes the idea of judicial discretion, this will face heavy opposition and criticism.

This chapter, thus, attempts to shed some light on the difficult question of whether the 'transformative power of Europe' has any potential to influence the attitude towards judicial discretion and procedural flexibility in post-communist countries, or at least in Slovenia. Can the ever-expanding European civil procedure and judicial cooperation in civil and commercial matters in the EU *really* change

---

[9] B Hess, 'Juridical Discretion—General Report; Part I' in Storme and Hess (n 1) 48–51.

[10] Karolczyk (n 4) 153.

[11] Cited by Borut Mekina, 'Demontaža države' (2008) 28 *Mladina* 9.

[12] For Poland, see Karolczyk (n 4) 185, for Croatia, A Uzelac, 'Survival of the Third Legal Tradition?' (2010) 49 *Supreme Court Law Review* 377, 390, for the Czech Republic, Z Kühn, 'The Authoritarian Legal Culture at Work: The Passivity of Parties and the Interpretational Statements of Supreme Courts' (2006) 2 *Croatian Yearbook of European Law and Policy* 19.

[13] Compare A Uzelac, 'Accelerating Civil Proceedings in Croatia—A History of Attempts to Improve the Efficiency of Civil Litigation' in RCH van Rhee (ed), *The Law's Delay—Essays on Undue Delay in Civil Litigation* (Intersentia, 2004) 77.

[14] Nevenka Šorli, 'Sodno varstvo—loterija' [Judicial protection—a lottery] (2012) 6 *Pravna praksa* 5.

[15] The Comments concerning the draft of the Civil Procedure Act Amendment, Celje Court of Appeals President's Office, dated 22 June 2007.

the mentality and working methods of judges in post-communist countries? This chapter, which is focused on the case of Slovenia, suggests that it can. However, such a positive expectation cannot be taken for granted and—for reasons that shall be discussed—cannot be expected on a short or medium term. In order to come to this conclusion, the chapter first analyses why judicial discretion was a problem under Communism. The chapter then demonstrates that resentment towards judicial discretion still persists in Slovenia and tries to detect reasons— both within the (insufficiently reformed) judiciary as well as looking at external factors—why this is so. The second part of the chapter argues that European civil procedure is in fact, if a closer look is taken, increasingly fond of procedural flex- ibility and judicial discretion, sometimes perhaps even at the expense of existing substantial differences in quality of the judiciaries among the states in the EU. Finally, an assessment is made as to whether this message was adequately received in the Slovenian judiciary, speculating on the impact beyond Slovenia in other post-communist countries.

II. Can a Diagnosis for Slovenia be Generalised to All Post-Communist Countries?

Many authors contend that there exists a deep continuity in the methods of legal reasoning employed by judges in the post-communist countries originating from the communist era.[16] Hence, in order to understand and analyse the pressing problems of the legal science and legal profession in these countries today, we have to understand their communist predecessors.[17] The accuracy of this finding is not disputed. But these 'communist predecessors' cannot be adequately analysed and understood on the basis of (over)generalisations, independently of also acknowl- edging far-reaching and fundamental differences between the communist regimes of the era. Against this background, it is important to note that at least after the late 1950s Yugoslavia (Slovenia being its most developed federal unit) opted for what could most easily be described as a 'milder version of socialism'. Yugoslavia managed to stay out of the Soviet Bloc and remained open to the Western coun- tries with unrestricted and visa-free travel to these countries for individuals as well. Personal and academic contacts with Western Europe thus remained widely available and exercised on a regular basis. There was no language barrier since at least in the northern parts of Yugoslavia (Slovenia, Croatia), English (and not Russian) was the foreign language taught in primary and secondary schools. The main source of knowledge and professional links in legal academic circles (books,

---

[16] Z Kühn, *The Judiciary in Central and Eastern Europe: Mechanical Jurisprudence in Transformation* (Martinus Nijhoff, 2011) 165–66, Karolczyk (n 4) 185, Uzelac (n 12) 385.
[17] Kühn (n 16) XV and 165.

monographs, commentaries) came from West Germany, Austria and even the USA (which were all freely available in law schools' libraries), whereas there was, at least in Slovenia and Croatia, practically no trace of, for example, Soviet academic writing on civil procedure. Private business, although brutally restricted, was nevertheless allowed to a greater extent and the system of a 'centrally planned state economy' did not apply. The major trading partners of Yugoslavia were (West) Germany and Italy. It is indicative that the Yugoslav Bar Association was the only one from the—then—communist countries that was considered to be sufficiently compatible with the western standards of independence and was therefore accepted into the International Bar Association. Admission to law schools (and to the Bar) was unrestricted and no careful scrutiny of candidate students (concerning their political 'correctness' and even family background) applied, unlike in certain Soviet Bloc countries.[18]

These characteristics inevitably expressed themselves in the regulation and practice of civil procedure as well. Unlike in the Soviet Bloc countries, communist ideological principles and political slogans were left out of the Civil Procedure Act.[19] For example, the principle (and main statutory instruments) of respect for party autonomy was recognised in the law (contrast this with, for example, Hungary, where the public prosecutor had standing to bring lawsuits on behalf of people who were unable or unwilling (!) to do so by themselves).[20] Furthermore, the judge was bound by the relief sought and also could not introduce facts that were not asserted by the parties.[21] Dispositive acts (settlement, acknowledgment of a claim, relinquishment of a claim—all with a *res iudicata* effect) were freely available (contrast this, for example, with communist Hungary or Poland, where the judge could prevent parties from settling the case if he found that this was not 'in the best interest of the parties', or the Soviet Union, where the judge was prohibited from assisting parties to settle).[22] A judgment by default as a typical expression of party autonomy was retained in Yugoslavia, whereas it was mostly abolished in 'Soviet style' civil procedure.[23] The possibility of the intervention of a public prosecutor in civil litigation was much more limited than in the Soviet Bloc jurisdictions, where the 'omnipresence' of a public prosecutor was endemic in civil procedure.[24]

---

[18] S Vacarelu, 'Romanian National Report' in Maleshin (n 4) 303–04.

[19] There was merely one reference to 'socialist morality': Art 3/3 of the CPA-1976.

[20] For Hungary, see I Varga, 'Foreign Influences on Hungarian Civil Procedure' in M Deguchi and M Storme (eds), *The Reception and Transmission of Civil Procedural Law in the Global Society* (Maklu, 2008) 275, 279.

[21] For Romania, compare Vacarelu (n 18) 303, for Hungary, Varga (n 20) 279, for Poland, K Weitz, 'Die Bedeutung der Rezeption für die Entwicklung des polnischen Zivilprozessrechts' (2010) 27 *Ritsumeikan Law Review* 141, 145.

[22] See in detail: M Kengyel, 'Veränderungen des Inhalts der Dispositions- und Verhandlungsmaxime im ungarischen Zivilprozess' (1997) 2 *Zeitschrift für Zivilprozess International: Jahrbuch des Internationalen Zivilprocessrechts* 270, 275.

[23] For Hungary, see Varga (n 20) 279.

[24] Compare eg Vacarelu (n 18) 301–02, Weitz (n 21) 145, Varga (n 20) 279, Kühn (n 16) 43.

In addition, there was no possibility for appeal courts to give binding directions to lower courts (or to take cases therefrom).[25]

Let there be no doubt: Civil justice in socialist Yugoslavia suffered from painful degradation, political interference,[26] unmeritorious promotion criteria and cronyism, ideological burdens, a serious decrease in quality and excessive delays in adjudication (it should be noted that in application substantial differences existed between the autonomous republics of Yugoslavia, which were politically less repressive and economically more developed—foremost Slovenia—and those which were less developed). These distortions of civil justice were nevertheless implemented (or expressed themselves) on a much subtler level than in the countries of the Soviet Bloc. For example, while the principle of respect for party autonomy was (almost) adequately recognised in the written law, practice often tended toward a much more paternalistic approach. This is clearly incompatible with the liberal concept of respect for human freedom—which is inevitably linked to human self-responsibility. This was partly an expression of the ideological view that courts (that is: The state) are omnipotent and have the capacity to produce the one right answer, are able to find the truth to provide for substantive justice and to affirm the 'socialist legality' without any hindrances.[27] Secondly, it was an expression of a certain disrespect for the autonomy of the individual and his ability to be responsible for his acts and omissions. Thirdly, it was an expression of a certain scepticism regarding the Bar as an independent legal profession and lawyers' ability to effectively accomplish their role of protecting the rights of their clients.

So, the 'starting point' at the time of the fall of communism in Slovenia and in the (then) Soviet Bloc countries was not identical. On the one hand, this was, for obvious reasons, an advantage. But on the other hand it was in a certain sense also a disadvantage. Reliance on the better 'starting point' resulted in a kind of self-satisfaction and prompted many to believe that there was no pressing need for serious reform. Perhaps this state of complacency already caused Slovenia, at least in certain aspects, to fall behind certain other former communist countries that were aware that reform, although painful, was urgently needed. Hence, although the title of this chapter contains reference to 'post-communist countries', I wish to resist the temptation to overgeneralise.[28] I am not confident enough that findings based on my knowledge of the country which I know best (Slovenia) are

---

[25] For such instruments (in Hungary) see Varga (n 20) 279.

[26] See, eg, M Dika and A Uzelac, 'Zum Problem des richterlichen Aktivismus in Jugoslawien' [1990] *Zbornik Pravnog fakulteta u Zagrebu* 391, 394.

[27] For such an ideological foundation concerning the doctrine of the primacy of the material truth see S Kamhi, *Građanski sudski postupak* [Civil Procedure] (Sarajevo, 1957) 22–24.

[28] Compare with Uzelac (n 12) 383, who contended—based on the experience of former Yugoslavia—that a wide range of available appeals, an 'endless circle of remittals' resulting in the excessive duration of proceedings, is a common characteristic of the 'socialist legal tradition'. But in response, Vacarelu (n 18) 302, explained that—quite to the contrary—individual appeals were not even admissible in Romania (probably the most repressive country in the Soviet Bloc) and that speedy proceedings were a typical feature of Romanian socialist courts.

immediately 'transferable' to other post-communist countries; this is left for the reader to weigh.

III. Reasons for Resentment with Regard to Judicial Discretion: A Look at the Past

The question of promoting judicial discretion is closely linked to the question of judicial empowerment. The following quotation summarises what this is all about: 'Discretion means choice. Choice means the freedom to select. When this freedom concerns people's rights and duties, discretion in fact means power.'[29]

The objections to greater discretion and the power to adapt the proceedings to the particularities of each case are an expression of a lack of trust in judges and the judiciary in general. At the same time, it is a method of preventing the judiciary from establishing itself as a genuinely independent and important branch of the state power. Constraining judges in the exercise of their functions in a procedural system characterised by strict rigidity is an efficient method of preventing the empowerment of the judiciary. It is thus not surprising that a rigid procedural order that leaves judges no space to adjust the conduct of proceedings to the characteristics of the case at hand was a characteristic feature of the old, socialist civil justice. That was the period when the judiciary was denied the position of an independent branch of state power.[30] In addition, the prestige of judges was deliberately kept rather low. The perception of a judge with a strong personality entrusted with powers to find just (procedural) results for any situation that may appear in the specific case just could not fit well into this concept. True, the judge was supposed to have the dominant role in the courtroom—but not as an expression of judicial empowerment. Rather it was an expression of the paramount importance placed on the 'principle of material truth' as well as an expression of state paternalism. It was a strict procedural formalism that was perceived as a proper method for achieving this paramount goal, rather than broad judicial discretion. In addition, the aversion to judicial discretion was also a consequence of the perception that there should be as many levels of 'control' in the judicial process as possible. Since discretionary decisions are by definition not suitable for a close appellate review, the perception of a strong hierarchical structure of the judiciary and the ideology of a full appellate review of every possible judicial activity was another reason speaking against empowering judges of the first instance court with more discretionary powers.

---

[29] Andrews (n 1) 121.
[30] The principle of the separation of powers did not apply in Socialist Yugoslavia. The judiciary was perceived as merely one of the methods for exercising the sovereign powers of the working class. A typical explanation can be found in L Ude, *Civilno procesno pravo* [Civil Procedure] (ČZ UL Ljubljana, 1988) 28.

Giving judges more power to adjust the conduct of proceedings to the characteristics of each individual case was and still is strongly opposed by a large number
of judges as well. Perhaps this is primarily linked to another problem that was
typical of the judiciary in the former Yugoslavia and still is a persistent problem
in Slovenia today: Evading responsibility for decision making.[31] Logically, a judge
who does not want to bear the responsibility for decision making will not genuinely want to embrace a system where he is expected to rely on principles and
standards rather than detailed rules or where he is entrusted with the power to
choose by his own discretion between different courses of action. This is a sign of
a serious lack of self-confidence (and perhaps a lack of self-esteem) of the judiciary. On the other hand, it can also be an expression of a 'self-defence' instinct
in a political environment, which makes judges politically accountable for their
decisions and where the tenure of the judge is subject to periodic (political) re-
appointment. A judge who was aware of the following 'warning' (made in 1957,
by an author from Bosnia) would prefer very detailed rules (and then apply them
without any creative construction), thus minimising the chance that his decision
will be considered unlawful:

> Every arbitrary departure from the letter and the spirit of the law is an attack on the
> heritage of the peoples' liberation war, on the fundaments of the socialist construction,
> and on the power of the working class. A violation of legality, even if unconscious or well
> intended, is a hostile act directed against the interests of the Yugoslav people and is a
> threat to the existence of the state.[32]

Turning to another point, in certain instances excessive formalism was also a kind
of 'self-defence' mechanism of the judiciary against overburdening. For example,
due to the huge workload, the supreme courts in former Yugoslavia tended to
invoke an overly formalistic and restrictive construction of the formal admissibility criteria[33] (for example regarding the calculation of the value of the claim,
regarding time limits as to when the value of a claim needed to be determined or
regarding the formal criteria necessary for a validly submitted power of attorney,
etc).[34] Such an approach was to a certain extent understandable, as the formal
admissibility criteria were the only tools that the supreme courts could use in order

---

[31] Uzelac (n 12) 383.

[32] Kamhi (n 27) 22–25. It should be stressed that, on the other hand, the textbooks of (Slovenian)
J Juhart, *Civilno procesno pravo* [Civil Procedure] (Univerzitetna Založba Ljubljana, 1961) or (Croatian)
S Zuglia, *Građanski parnički postupak* [Civil Procedure] (Školska knjiga, 1957), even from that early
communist period, are almost free of such communist slogans.

[33] Uzelac (n 12) 383.

[34] For insight into some of the difficulties concerning the formal criteria of the calculation of the
value of a claim as a threshold for admissibility regarding access to the supreme court, see judgments
of the ECtHR in *Dobrić v Serbia*, App no 2611/07 and 15276/07 (ECtHR, 21 June 2011) and *Garzičić v
Montenegro*, App no 17931/07 (ECtHR, 21 September 2010). Also constitutional courts in certain
countries of ex-Yugoslavia prevented the supreme courts from applying an excessively formalistic
approach to the calculation of the amount in controversy (Croatian Constitutional Court Decision No
RH U-III-2646/07 of 18 June 2008, Slovenian US Decision No Up-418/05 of 11 January 2007).

to prevent their overburdening. In the same manner, highly overburdened first instance judges invented very formalistic standards as regards certain procedural requirements in order to dispose of cases without an examination on the merits or—even more often in the time of socialism—to achieve repeated adjournments of hearings.

On the face of it, the reasons stated above might seem to be of merely historical significance. Why would the reasons stated above, linked to the communist era, result in the persistence until today of aversion to judicial discretion and procedural flexibility? Although 'old habits die hard', 20 years after the collapse of communism should be enough. Nevertheless, this aversion remains. In the pages that follow I will try to find explanations for this state of affairs—first in relation to national civil procedure and in the final part in relation to European civil procedure law. But perhaps some lessons might also be learnt from recent heated debates in Slovenia concerning civil procedure law reforms. Thus I start with one example.

IV. Introduction of Sanctions Against Late Submissions of Facts and Evidence Labelled as 'Excessive Formalisation of Procedure'

A. A Look at the Past: Experience from the Communist Yugoslavia

Pursuant to the Yugoslav Civil Procedure Act of 1976, parties were free to submit new facts and evidence until the end of the last session of the main hearing. Such a system did not allow for the proper organisation of the preparatory stage of litigation, structuring of proceedings and early identifying of disputed and relevant issues of the case. It was also not able to prevent the common—however, from the aspect of the efficiency of proceedings, outright fatal—practice that attorneys filed further preparatory briefs, adducing new facts and evidence, as late as during the main hearing.

Both the accentuated responsibility of the judge, on the one hand, and the nonexistence of sanctions against the parties' belated submission of facts, evidence and preparatory briefs were an expression of the paramount importance placed on the 'principle of material truth'. However the experience in Slovenia from the period such a system was in force demonstrates that the high importance assigned to the material truth often led to results exactly the opposite of those it strove to achieve. The procedural system that lacked adequate sanctions against the parties' inactivity and delay caused the goal of substantive justice to fade. The lack of effective tools that would enable the timely gathering of procedural materials resulted in frequent adjournments of hearings, in a 'piecemeal' manner of the presentation of facts and evidence and in culpably delaying a case's progress.[35] It is disastrous, not just from the viewpoint of speed, but as well from the viewpoint of substantive justice, if new arguments and fresh evidence are adduced only at the hearing itself, causing either constant adjournments or that neither the court nor the opponent can adequately reflect on newly submitted arguments. The idea that it is in the interests of justice that evidence in the hands of one party should be disclosed to the other party in a timely fashion, such that both the opposing party as well as the court can properly consider it, found no response.

The paternalistic expectation that the judge is required to supplement any inactivity, incompetence or lack of research and analysis of the case by the attorneys led to results which were disastrous not only from the viewpoint of delay, but also from the very viewpoint of pursuing substantive justice. Since attorneys were aware that any insufficient diligence in preparing the case would need to be rectified by the activism of the judge, they increasingly became completely inactive and negligent in the preparation and conduct of their clients' cases. This system which enabled attorneys to attend court hearings totally unprepared, whereby these hearings were reduced to a mere formality with the exchange of further briefs, followed by another adjournment, inevitably also resulted in the passivisation of judges. It was increasingly common that not only the parties' legal counsel but also judges appeared at hearings with little or no real knowledge of the case and its factual and legal bases. Understandably, when the habit of a lack of diligent preparation for the hearing prevailed, numerous adjournments of hearings were actually preferred by all—attorneys and judges alike.

B. The 2008 Reform and a Severe Criticism Against it

Already the first Slovenian Civil Procedure Act (1999) introduced the rule that the parties may assert new facts and evidence at the first main hearing at the latest, whereas at the latest stages the parties are allowed to present new facts and new evidence only with a proper excuse for the belated submission (Article 286 of the 1999 Civil Procedure Act). Further steps were made through an amendment in 2008.[36] In order to enable the other party's right to be heard and to organise his case, the first party is now obliged, whenever possible, to file new preparatory briefs in sufficient time for them to be served on the other party with adequate time before the main hearing. Furthermore, judges now have the discretionary power to require (and to impose binding time limits) that parties make further submissions and clarifications concerning facts, evidence and legal positions in the set time limit (Article 286a/1 of the 1999 Civil Procedure Act). The judge

---

[35] See, eg N Betetto, 'Ob predlogu novega ZPP' [On the draft of the new civil procedure act] (1995) 341 *Pravna praksa* 10, in general for Yugoslavia, see Uzelac (n 12) 384.

[36] Act Amending the Civil Procedure Act; *Zakon o spremembah in dopolnitvah Zakona o pravdnem postopku (ZPP-D)*, Official Gazette, No 45/2008.

may exercise this discretion already in a written form before the main hearing. The system of procedural sanctions is flexible. The judge is empowered but not obliged to use the described tools and also has discretion to relieve the parties from the sanctions. It is also acknowledged that preclusions restrict parties' right to be heard and thus they should be applied carefully and with a proper balance between competing policies.[37]

The introduction of the judge's power to disregard facts asserted and evidence adduced past the time limits that are imposed, whether by the law itself or set by the court, was soon faced with heavy opposition. The strengthening of procedural obligations, combined with the system of sanctions is often perceived as a formalisation of the procedure and as an expression of an (assumed) trend that a goal of reaching substantive justice is fading.[38] Certain authors even go so far as to suggest that the single paramount principle of civil justice is establishing the truth and that imposing any legal obstacles, which prevent the court from finding the truth, is 'far from being compatible with a contemporary idea of civil justice'.[39] One can only conclude that such views amount to an outright 'resurrection of the idea of material truth' in a manner not different from the one promoted in the early years of firm communist rule. Compare:

> 1957: 'In contrast to a bourgeois state a socialist state is deeply interested in achieving the goal of finding the real truth in every litigation, regardless of how unimportant and minor the dispute seems to be.'[40]

> 2008: '[Time limits for submissions of new facts and evidence] … do not pursue the overriding principle—reaching a decision correct in the factual and legal aspect. Hence any obstacles on the path towards this goal are a step back and not forward.'[41]

Such a simplified view of the goals of civil justice cannot be supported. Intensification of the expectation that the parties shall bring forward facts and means of evidence in a timely manner is not aimed at enabling the judge to 'get rid of the matter easily by means of excessive formalism without deciding it on the merits'. Extended and intensified procedural requirements for the timely submission of facts and means of evidence should primarily be understood as a clear message to the parties (their counsel) that a diligent and active preparation for their case is necessary. This can only be beneficial for the substantive quality of judicial

---

[37] Judgment of the Supreme Court of Slovenia No II Ips 197/2009 of 7 April 2011.

[38] Typically D Wedam Lukić, 'Profesor Stojan Cigoj in civilno procesno pravo' [Professor Stojan Cigoj and law of civil procedure] in M Pavčnik (ed), *Stojan Cigoj: 1920–1989: zbornik razprav* (SAZU, 2009) 64: 'Today, it is increasingly becoming a common view that it is fair if the party loses the case only because she was not diligent enough and had not on time submitted facts and evidence … But justice is not done!'

[39] L Varanelli, 'Sodišče in ocenjevanje dokazov v civilnem postopku' [The court and the assessment of evidence in civil procedure] (2012) 2 *Pravna praksa* 6.

[40] Kamhi (n 27) 23.

[41] M Jelačin, 'Novela ZPP-D, njene skrite pasti in pravne praznine' [The Civil Procedure Act Amendment, its hidden traps and legal loopholes] (2008) 25 *Pravna praksa* 10.

process. But a system of sanctions must be attached to the imposed time limits, otherwise it would remain entirely without effect. In addition, the parties should be well aware of the fact that the judge will not too leniently relieve them from these sanctions.[42] It is however not unrealistic to expect that in most cases time limits and court orders are respected and that the culture of compliance prevails.

It is wrong to perceive the introduction of procedural sanctions against non-compliance with the requirement to put forward facts, evidence and preparatory briefs in a timely fashion as an expression of excessive formalism.[43] Therefore it did not come as a surprise when in 2009 the *Ustavno sodišče Republike Slovenije* (the Constitutional Court of the Republic of Slovenia, hereinafter US) confirmed that it is necessary that the statutory regulation be designed in such a way that it forces—under a threat of adverse consequences—the parties to prepare themselves diligently.[44] Thereby, the responsibility lies with the legislator as well as in every particular case with the judge, when exercising discretion, to find the right balance between ensuring concentration and acceleration of the proceedings, on the one hand, and adequate results on the merits, on the other. It should be noted that the very same US otherwise has little or no understanding for procedural novelties which amount to an excessive formalisation of procedure.[45] The latter shows that a real danger of abuse of procedural instruments leading to a pure formalisation of proceedings without any real benefits of legitimate aims of civil justice truly exists, and that they can put the fairness of the trial in jeopardy. It must, therefore, be constantly and critically assessed whether both the legislature and the judge in every individual case have managed to find a proper balance between the goals of concentration, speed and procedural economy on the one hand, and the goal of achieving justice on merits on the other. Review of the case law of the US shows that an individual assessment must be made in each specific case, since it is not possible to attach the label of a 'mere formalisation of procedure' to every accentuated procedural requirement or every procedural sanction.

---

[42] J Zobec, 'Zloraba procesnih pravic' [Abuse of procedural rights] (2009) 6 *Podjetje in delo* 1369, 1373.

[43] J Zobec, 'Predlagane novosti glede zamudne sodbe in posledic izostanka ter glede vmesne sodbe' [The proposed novelties concerning judgment by default and interim judgment] (2007) 6 *Podjetje in delo* 1045, 1060.

[44] Decision of the US No Up-2443/08 of 7 October 2009.

[45] The US declared unconstitutional the rule that a claim filed by an attorney is immediately stricken out, without the possibility of rectification, if it does not fulfil all formal criteria or if a correct power of attorney is not submitted (Art 108/2 and Art 98/5 CPA); decisions No U-I-200/09-14 of 20 May 2010 and No U-I-74/12-6 of 13 September 2012. It annulled strict procedural sanctions of automatically striking out a claim in cases where the claimant did not attend the main hearing (Decision No U-I-164/09-13 of 4 February 2010) and the sanction of an automatic judgment by default, if it was the defendant who did not attend the main hearing regardless of whether he had previously duly filed a defence plea (Decision No U-I-161/10-12 of 9 December 2010).

C. The Mechanical Application of Principles—Just an Oxymoron?

Many (self-proclaimed) fierce opponents of (assumed) judicial formalism in Slovenia today are often persons who held influential positions (law professors, politicians) within or close to the Communist Party and government structures already during the communist era. It is therefore perhaps not surprising that those who once mechanically applied the rules of law, but now perceive themselves as 'messengers' of anti-formalism, today in the same manner apply principles instead of rules: Making mechanical and simplistic conclusions without trying to understand the purpose of the law and the impact of the advocated decision, not just for the case at hand, but for the future behaviour of the addressees of the law.

Perhaps the polemics regarding the flexibility of a judge in organising the course of litigation tells us that the divide between (assumed) backward formalists and (self-proclaimed) progressive anti-formalists is not always clear. The presented reform is a fine expression of the empowerment of the judiciary and is hence deeply anti-formalist. But in Slovenia this reform (just like the reform concerning the introduction of the leave to appeal system for access to the Supreme Court) was opposed exactly in the name of 'anti-formalism'. The arguments invoked by the opponents of the reform often brought them dangerously close to (or even deeply absorbed into) a 'Soviet-style' understanding of civil procedure. For example, concerning the introduction of the leave to appeal system for access to the Supreme Court, one author fiercely opposed the reform and advocated—in the name of anti-formalism and the quest for justice—unlimited 'control' over appellate courts on the motion not only of the parties but also of public prosecutors(!).[46] Turning to the other example, critics who do not hesitate to label procedural tools aimed at promoting the greater diligence of the parties and their counsel as 'formalism' or (due to sanctions attached to these tools) 'repression' do not realise that they promote a paternalistic approach typical of the communist era. Although they often invoke the argument of proportionality (and constitutional procedural guarantees), they do so in a mechanical and textualist fashion (for example sanction equals repression and repression is disproportionate; or sanction prevents finding the truth and *any* obstacles in the quest for truth are disproportionate and formalistic). They fail to realise that the legislature as well as the judge in every specific case has to seek out the proper balance between the goal of reaching a substantively correct decision, on the one hand, and using the adequate resources and time that can be devoted to that goal, on the other, as well as the proper balance between the burdens of the judge and of the parties.

What is also typical of 'formalists turned anti-formalists' is that they fail to consider what consequences a judicial decision in a case at issue has for the functioning of the justice system in general. For example, the procedural sanction of

---

[46] P Feguš, 'Revizija in zahteva za varstvo zakonitosti kot izredni pravni sredstvi v teoriji in praksi po novi procesni ureditvi' [A final appeal on points of law and a request for the protection of legality in theory and in practice under the new procedural regime] (2009) 47 *Pravna praksa* 6 ff.

debarring late facts and evidence is, if applied in the individual dispute that happens to be before the court, repressive and runs contrary to the goal of reaching adequate results on the merits. But in applying the principle of proportionality the judge should be concerned with the more general consequences that the management of an individual case could have for the system as a whole.[47] The effect of such sanctions from this perspective is predominantly preventive—thus resulting in better, more diligent and timely preparation by all participants in proceedings and it is hence beneficial exactly from the substantive aspect of adjudication.

The new (self-proclaimed) anti-formalists like to present themselves as liberal protectors of human rights and justice itself, while labelling those who advocate the responsibility and activity of parties as 'repressive'. Nevertheless, it might be even easier to claim just the opposite. The concept that a party should not bear responsibility for its actions and decisions is not liberal at all, it is paternalistic. Denial of responsibility is in fact a denial of autonomy and hence freedom. This is often neglected in debates concerning procedural instruments that are based on the expectation that parties (their counsels) will diligently and actively prepare and participate in litigation. In one of the recent heated debates concerning the law of the execution of judgments in civil cases, some authors argued that it is disproportionate if a party suffers substantial negative financial consequences merely because he chose to ignore the pending proceedings and thus did not make use of otherwise easily available defences. They suggested that the only way to ensure proportionality is to require the court to act *ex officio* on behalf of the defaulting party. Again, this is a very simplistic understanding of the principle of proportionality, which brings us dangerously close to the 'Soviet style' civil procedure. It was only in such civil procedure that instruments based on respect for party autonomy, such as a default judgment or payment order, were unavailable. Should we abolish these instruments in the name of anti-formalism and the principle of proportionality? It is wrong to expect that the court should always be there to remedy omissions and a lack of diligent preparation of the litigants in order to achieve adequate results on the merits. It is necessary to strike a proper balance with the goal of promoting the liberal concept that the party must be perceived as a person who has the capacity and hence the responsibility for his own choices.

V. Resentment Regarding Judicial Discretion in Slovenia Today: Why won't it Fade Away?

Many things have already been written as regards what the judiciary itself can do to improve. Primary responsibility rests with the judiciary. Issues like quality control, combined with proper selection criteria and selection procedures; evaluation

---

[47] Zuckerman (n 2) 149.

of the 'output' (not merely in the form of appellate reviews), doing away with false professional solidarity; ensuring that promotion within the judiciary is based on merit-based criteria; promoting an ethic of hard and responsible work, continued judicial training, etc. But in the following part of this chapter I turn to certain other aspects, which—in my opinion—are often neglected in these debates.

A. The Strict Hierarchical Mentality of the Judiciary and the Fear of Overly Interventionist Appellate Courts

In England it has been correctly realised that judicial discretion in first instance court proceedings must inevitably be accompanied by sufficient self-restraint in appellate courts concerning how deep they will review discretionary decisions.[48] After all, it is the first instance judge who is in a better position to assess all the circumstances of a given case. But this finding still has not reached Slovenian appellate courts. Therefore, first instance judges prefer to refrain from using discretionary powers (or if such powers are not yet provided for in the law, oppose their introduction) fearing the risk of having their judgments quashed by higher courts. It is the appellate courts where the bureaucratic fashion of deciding cases *in camera* and excessive formalism are still very much present.[49] Again, this is an expression of a fear of decision making—this time in appellate courts. Appellate courts still tend to find ways to quash judgments and remand cases to the lower courts. And of course, open-textured norms in procedural legislation offer endless chances for appellate courts to replace the understanding of the first instance court with their own, thus enabling a remittal due to a 'violation of process'. A very wide construction of the (constitutional) right to appeal comes in handy for this purpose as well. The problem is linked to the perception that the first instance judge is a kind of 'apprentice', a 'beginner' (which in the Slovenian system of a 'career judiciary' is actually not entirely untrue), who cannot be fully trusted and that therefore close appellate scrutiny of his decisions is inevitable. Such an environment is not suitable for the empowerment of the judiciary—at least not of first instance judges.

B. The Quality of Practising Attorneys (the Bar)?

It is interesting that sharp critics of the state of the judiciary in the post-communist countries focus their attention almost exclusively on judges. Practising attorneys usually escape such (critical) attention. But in my opinion, the Bar bears substantial responsibility for the pressing problems concerning the judiciary in the post-communist states—both in relation to quality as well as the excessive cost and duration of proceedings. In addition, the Bar often blocks attempts at necessary

---

[48] ibid, 151.
[49] Uzelac (n 12) 393.

reform (for example reshaping the system of attorneys' tariffs in order to stimulate focused instead of piecemeal litigation). There is an urgent need to improve not only the level of expertise and diligence but also the perception of how much the Bar should contribute to the effectiveness of proceedings. The accentuated paternalistic activity of the judge in the communist era resulted in a passivisation of legal counsel. This was a quite comfortable position in proceedings. It is thus not surprising that the majority of attorneys today oppose reforms, striving to promote their more active role and greater diligence.

Furthermore there was and to some extent still is a widespread misperception among attorneys that the rule of *iura novit curia* (the court knows the law) means that attorneys are not expected to undertake any legal analysis and legal research and put forward legal arguments or references as to the settled case law at all. Attorneys often invoke demagogic arguments and address demands for them to perform their work diligently and competently and to be active in proceedings as 'repression'. They are not aware that by advocating that the law preserves the systematically built-in expectation that an attorney's negligent and incompetent work will be remedied by the judge, they in fact express great distrust towards the Bar. Precisely the expectation that attorneys should contribute to the quality of civil justice is an expression of trust therein. This expectation enables the Bar to assume its proper role in society. Denying the role the attorney is supposed to play in civil proceedings would in the last instance lead to the position the Bar 'enjoyed' in the communist countries of the Soviet Bloc—that is, first the disappearance of attorneys from the courtroom, then to the disappearance of the Bar itself as an independent profession.

C. Legal Textualism as a 'Shield' Against Destructive Unwarranted Attacks on the Judiciary

The quality of the judiciary in Slovenia (and other post-communist countries as well) is a serious issue and there is a pressing need for improvement. Undoubtedly, there are many things that the judiciary itself can do to improve and it should not perceive judicial independence as immunity from criticism. Judicial independence is not meant to protect the judiciary as a whole and individual judges from accountability. It is hence necessary to constantly raise a critical voice in this regard. But I equally firmly reject the view that due to this quality problem the judiciary in these countries is a 'legitimate target' for destructive, demagogic and populist attacks on the judiciary and judges, undermining their authority and dignity. Neither does it mean that the principle of the division of powers has therefore lost its significance. Acts that would constitute a clear case of contempt of court or would be considered an intolerable political interference in one country should not become legitimate in another country only because the judiciary is not equally fit there. At least unless the quality and integrity of the judiciary has disintegrated to such an extent that one can speak of 'the judiciary', 'a court of law' and 'judges' merely in a formal, but no longer in a substantive sense. I do not think it can be seriously argued that the situation in Slovenia (a country that has been a member of the EU since 2004 and which has since enjoyed relative political, social and—until couple of years ago—also economic stability) has reached that stage. The feedback from the European Court of Human Rights (ECtHR) and from the European Commission (although it shows that the Slovenian justice system suffers from structural deficiencies and is still hampered by excessively long proceedings)[50] does not support such a destructive criticism. The idea that the judicial process and administration of justice in the post-communist countries do not merit being protected from unwarranted attacks has no following in the ECtHR. Commenting on one decision of the Czech Constitutional Court, the ECtHR stated:

> Moreover, the Court cannot but agree with the Constitutional Court that 'the activities of certain politicians referred to by the applicant, be they verbal expressions to the media or other, aimed at creating a negative atmosphere around the legal actions of the applicant or constituting direct attempts to interfere in these proceedings, [were] unacceptable in a system based on the rule of law.'[51]

In a different context, the US recalled that it is always possible to raise a critical, even very critical opinion concerning the conduct and result of a court case in a respectful manner, without jeopardising the dignity and authority of the judge and the judiciary as a whole.[52] If this is true for the parties and their counsel in the course of proceedings, it should equally apply to the way the justice system in general and individual cases in particular are discussed in public—be it by politicians, the media, or members of the legal community such as academics or members of the Bar. The aforementioned refers to a derogatory or outright defamatory style of commenting on pending and lost cases and to symbolic acts of disrespect of the court, such as avoiding attendance at scheduled court hearings without a proper excuse, avoiding the service of judicial documents(!) and even—for purely symbolic purposes—avoiding compliance with a final judgment in a civil case (so that formal enforcement proceedings need to be implemented). Regrettably, it seems that there are already no limits as to how low (both in style and substance) one can afford to go in criticising judges, whereby attacks and smears *ad personam* instead of criticism *ad rem* are becoming increasingly common, just like negative overgeneralisations. Especially politicians should be aware of the fact that they set

---

[50] Assessment of the 2013 national reform programme and stability programme for Slovenia—Commission Staff Working Document, Brussels, 29 May 2013, SWD(2013) 374 final. But compare also: 'Disposition Time for litigious civil and commercial cases in first instance courts in 2010 is still not adequate, being above the EU27 mean, although an improvement compared to the previous years. The Clearance Rate is around 100% which means that the situation is stable.' The functioning of judicial systems and the situation of the economy in the European Union Member States, Strasbourg, 15 January 2013; Report prepared for the European Commission (Directorate General JUSTICE), p 516, available at <http://ec.europa.eu/justice/effective-justice/files/cepej_study_justice_scoreboard_en.pdf> (1 October 2014). See also the 2014 EU Justice Scoreboard <http://ec.europa.eu/justice/effective-justice/files/justice_scoreboard_2014_en.pdf> (1 October 2014).

[51] *Kinsky v Czech Republic*, App no 42856/06 (ECtHR 9 February 2012).

[52] Decision of the US No U-I-145/03 of 23 June 2006.

an example that will probably be followed by the general public. They should as well be aware of the confidence of the public that the courts are the proper forum for solving disputes. The position of the judiciary as one of the fundamental state powers is thereby—probably quite intentionally—undermined, which is especially troublesome as unlike the other two branches of government, the judiciary is much more vulnerable to such attacks.[53] It is a serious defect in the political culture that the courts and judges are not shielded from baseless attacks on their integrity. Perhaps it is not so much the judiciary, but certain politicians in Slovenia who have not sufficiently detached themselves from the methods that plagued the communist era.

I have already mentioned[54] that the resentment against judicial discretion was (inter alia) a kind of self-defence of judges during the old regime. Something similar is happening nowadays as well. It does not come as a surprise that under heavy destructive and contemptuous attacks, often accompanied by barely disguised physical threats, many judges use the 'shield' of the letter of the law and use the 'it is not my fault, the law did not leave me any choice' excuse. In such hostile conditions it cannot realistically be expected that judges would ever dare to use discretion to reach just but sometimes inevitably unpopular results, knowing that these will again stir up demagogic and destructive attacks.[55]

VI. Judicial Discretion in European Civil Procedure Law

The trend of emphasised reliance on judicial discretion and the judge's reliance on general principles is not only characteristic of contemporary reforms of 'national civil procedure'. It is increasingly also characteristic of the 'European Civil Procedure'—a broad EU legislative package of cross-border procedural instruments (rapidly expanding and developing judicial cooperation in civil and commercial matters). It might come as a surprise to promote the European Civil Procedure as an example supporting judicial discretion. The first impression is exactly the opposite. By far the most widely known and widely used and thus practically the most important instrument of judicial cooperation in civil matters is

---

[53] See, eg, *Skałka v Poland*, App no 43425/98 (ECtHR 27 May 2003).

[54] Above in s III of this chapter.

[55] Especially if at the same time political demands are made that judges should be subject to 'swift adoption of *rigid lustration laws* in all Member States which have not yet done so, as well as their thorough implementation.' (European People's Party Resolution on the Situation in Slovenia, adopted 13 November 2013. Available at: www.epp.eu/epp-political-assembly-expresses-concerns-about-situation-slovenia). It should be noted that the demands for 'lustration' today can hardly relate to the judges' activities in the communist era (which can be a legitimate request), since most of the judges who are active today were too young to hold such positions in the communist era.

the Brussels I Regulation (formerly the Brussels Convention).[56] The jurisdictional regime is the very fundament of the European Civil Procedure. And it was precisely the (then) Brussels Convention (and later the Brussels I Regulation) that opted for the clear application of the continental concept of jurisdictional rules, pursuing legal certainty and the predictability (but at the same time rigidity) of the jurisdictional regime. These instruments generally value legal certainty, uniformity and predictability above substantive justice in individual cases.[57] The alternative option—which was rejected—was the common law approach, based on broad jurisdictional norms, but at the same time combined with broad discretional freedom given to the judge to decline jurisdiction over a matter on the basis that there is a more suitable and appropriate forum available to the parties elsewhere. Clearly the *forum non conveniens* doctrine is a prime example of both judicial discretion as well as the goal of striving for just results (concerning jurisdictional issues) in every individual case. This instrument also demonstrates full trust in the individual judge's ability to achieve such results by considering the particulars of every individual case. But the goal of pursuing justice in every individual case by vesting the judge with broad discretion to decline exercise of jurisdiction was sacrificed on the altar of predictability and legal certainty. For this reason Lord Goff observed that:

> A system, developed by distinguished scholars, was embodied in the Brussels Convention, under which jurisdiction is allocated on the basis of well-defined rules. This system achieves its purpose, but at a price. The price is rigidity, and rigidity can be productive of injustice. The judges of this country, ... have to accept the fact that the practical results are from time to time unwelcome.[58]

The approach adopted by the legislature was subsequently also reaffirmed on many occasions by the European Court of Justice (ECJ). Not only did the ECJ extend the prohibition on applying the forum *non conveniens* doctrine in favour of a court in a non-EU Member State.[59] If indications as to judicial empowerment consist in the ability of the court to engage in creative judicial decision making and creative interpretation whereby teleological reasoning is increasingly given prevalence over strict literal interpretation,[60] here again the case law of the ECJ concerning the Brussels I regime would not exactly be an ideal example supporting this finding. There are numerous cases where the ECJ admitted that the (jurisdictional) result achieved might not be just and might not even be in line with the

---

[56] Regulation No 44/2001 of 22 December 2000 on jurisdiction and recognition and enforcement of judgments in civil and commercial matters, OJ L 12/1 (the Brussels Regulation), since 10 January 2015 replaced by the Regulation No 1215/2012 of 12 December 2012 on jurisdiction and the recognition and enforcement of judgments in civil and commercial matters (recast), OJ L 351/1 (the Brussels I—Recast).

[57] See in detail eg Jacco Bomhoff, *Judicial Discretion in European Law on Conflicts of Jurisdiction* (Sdu Publishers, 2005) 26 ff.

[58] *Airbus Industrie GIE v Patel and Others* [1998] 2 All ER 257 (Lord Goff of Chieveley).

[59] Case C-281/02 *Owusu v Jackson* [2005] ECR I-01383.

[60] Kühn (n 16) 200–08.

legislatures' intentions, but nevertheless left no room for creative reasoning and instead relied fully on literal interpretation—often invoking the need to promote legal certainty and predictability.[61]

But in one other aspect the case law of the ECJ relating to the Brussels I Regulation clearly demonstrates the judicial power (although not judicial discretion in the narrower sense). It is generally accepted that the case law of the ECJ forms an integral (built-in) part of the Brussels I regime and it is exactly the jurisprudence of the ECJ that contributed massively to its undisputed success. Actually, the massive corpus of the ECJ's case law concerning the Brussels I regime in itself shows that the idea of 'firm, clear and predictable' rules of jurisdiction is a myth (otherwise it would not be necessary for the ECJ to intervene so often).

The affirmation of judicial discretion (in the broader sense of flexibility) in the European Civil Procedure started with the adoption of so-called 'second generation regulations' (the European enforcement order for uncontested claims,[62] the European order for payment[63] and the European small claims procedure),[64] when the European Civil Procedure slowly started to detach itself from traditional domains of international private law. Certain—although still fragmented—areas of 'pure' civil procedure are now subject to regulation at the EU level. In these procedural instruments the idea of procedural flexibility and judicial discretion (in the broader sense) is deeply rooted (for example concerning conducting a small claims procedure, including fundamental issues such as scheduling an oral hearing, taking evidence, deciding on the reimbursement of costs, etc).[65]

What should also be mentioned in this regard is the growing influence of the Charter of the Fundamental Rights of the European Union[66] (hereinafter the Charter) on the European Civil Procedure (for example relating to excluding legal

---

[61] See Case C-111/09 *Česká—Vienna Insurance Group v Michal Bilas* [2010] ECR1-4545 and Case C-462/06 *Glaxosmithkline, Laboratoires Glaxosmithkline v Jean-Pierre Rouard* [2008] ECR 1-3965, para 33: 'would be difficult to reconcile with the principle of legal certainty, which is one of the objectives of the Regulation and which requires, in particular, that rules of jurisdiction be interpreted in such a way as to be highly predictable...'.

[62] Regulation No 805/2004 of the European Parliament and of the Council of 21 April 2004 creating a European enforcement order for uncontested claims [2004] OJ L 143.

[63] Regulation No 1896/2006 of the European Parliament and of the Council of 12 December 2006 creating a European order for payment procedure [2006] OJ L 399/1.

[64] Regulation No 861/2007 of the European Parliament and of the Council of 11 July 2007 establishing a European small claims procedure [2007] OJ L 199/1.

[65] Just one example: Pursuant to Art 20 of the European Payment Order Regulation (an almost identical provision is also contained in Art 18 of the European Small Claims Regulation), the defendant may apply for an extraordinary review of the European Order for Payment (inter alia) where the defendant was prevented from objecting to the claim ... due to force majeure or extraordinary circumstances without any fault on his part, provided that he acts promptly. Not only a CEE judge would expect more precise grounds for an extraordinary review of a final judicial decision, but foremost would expect at least a specific time limit for filing such a review. But here the European legislature expressed full trust that the judge will reach adequate and just conclusions concerning both the *extraordinary circumstances* that the review can rely on as well as the question whether the application was submitted *promptly*.

[66] OJ 2007 C 303, p 1.

persons from free legal aid,[67] the omission of reasons in a judgment by default,[68] fictitious service upon a defendant whose whereabouts are unknown,[69] the mandatory pre-litigation mediation procedure, and the right to effective judicial protection,[70] methods of fictitious service under national law aimed at avoiding service abroad, and the right to be heard).[71] We are currently in the middle of the process of a genuine 'constitutionalisation of the European Civil Procedure'. In this context, especially the principle of proportionality is increasingly referred to in the case law of the ECJ. It suffices to refer to the judgment in the *Alder* case, where the Court strove to strike a proper balance between the conflicting values in the context of the cross border service of judicial documents: The claimant's right to effective judicial protection, on the one hand, and the defendant's right to be heard, on the other.[72] The application of the test of proportionality certainly does not amount to judicial discretion in the narrower sense.[73] Nevertheless, confidence that the judge will justly apply this test depending on the peculiarities of each individual case relates to the phenomenon of judicial empowerment.

VII. The Impact of the European Civil Procedure on the Legal Method and Mentality of National Judges

At least when it comes to judges, aversion to judicial discretion is to some extent, although not exclusively, a consequence of a lack of knowledge of trends and contemporary reforms in foreign legal systems and in European Civil Procedure Law. An optimistic prognosis is that increased contact with EU law as well as increasing familiarity with the case law of the ECJ and its judicial methods and reasoning will gradually lead to the fading away of resentment regarding judicial discretion in the Slovenian judiciary. But I am not entirely optimistic, for the reasons listed below.

First, one (unfortunate) fact is that many Slovenian judges still perceive EU law as 'foreign law'. And just as they are not very keen on accepting arguments based in comparative law or learning examples from foreign laws (considering it a 'waste of time'), they are not very enthusiastic about the 'EU law argument' either. For example, topics relating to EU law—although heavily promoted by organisers of judicial training programmes—rarely raise much interest in the audience. This is probably

---

[67] Case C-279/09 *DEB v Germany* [2010] ECR I-13849.
[68] Case C-619/10 *Trade Agency Ltd v Seramico Investments Ltd* (CJEU, 6 September 2012).
[69] Case C-292/10 *G v Cornelius de Visser* (CJEU, 15 March 2012).
[70] Case C-317/08 *Rosalba Alassini v Telecom Italia SpA* [2010] ECR I-02213.
[71] Case C-325/11 *Krystyna Alder and Ewald Alder v Sabina Orlowska and Czeslaw Orlowski* (CJEU, 19 December 2012).
[72] ibid.
[73] Hess (n 9) 51.

not for any doctrinal error but for practical reasons, at least when it comes to the European Civil Procedure. Although this field of law is rapidly expanding (and although especially the Brussels I Regulation has a huge significance as regards the effective functioning of the common market), the fact is that an average Slovenian judge still very rarely deals with a case involving a cross-border element, which is a prerequisite for triggering the application of instruments of the European Civil Procedure. For most judges it is almost a 'once in a lifetime' situation. As long as the presence of EU civil procedure does not penetrate into the day-to-day work of judges, the attitude towards it will barely change. Consequently, until this perception of a 'foreign law' prevails, the influence of this law on the legal methods of the Slovenian judiciary will remain low.

Second, as explained above, at least the European Civil Procedure (including the case law of the ECJ relating to it) is not always exactly a prime example of the prevalence of the flexibility and creative interpretation of the law. Furthermore, even if EU legislation does have an influence on national legislation,[74] that does not automatically result in an influence on the legal method of national judges in *applying* legislation. Third, paradoxically, whereas the huge importance attributed to the ECJ's case law in the European Civil Procedure certainly adds to the empowerment and to the esteem of the ECJ, it does not necessarily produce the same effects for judges in national courts. In certain circumstances, it might even be counter-productive since a system has been adopted whereby the national judge is not entitled to solve a hard case involving the construction of EU law by himself, but is expected to submit the question for a preliminary ruling to the ECJ. Although the purpose of this system is clear (effectively to ensure the uniform application and development of EU law; discussion of this issue is not a topic of this chapter), negative practical consequences concerning the awareness of national judges of their great responsibility in the adjudicative process perhaps remain underestimated.[75] It is not ideal for the goal of the empowerment of first instance judges if a mentality prevails whereby it is left for 'some higher instances' (be it on the supranational or national level) to solve hard questions of law. In my experience, when discussing open issues of EU law in training programmes with judges and trying to stimulate creative thinking (hinting at the background and the *ratio* of the rule), the question 'what do you think' is often met with the answer 'if it ever happens, I will ask the European Court of Justice'.

Fourth, and most importantly, the issue of building of mutual trust should be addressed. This is indeed a cornerstone of 'judicial cooperation in civil matters' and a prerequisite for a genuine integration. But the building of mutual trust has thus far not concerned genuine, real trust, but rather a required, imposed trust. The principle of 'blind' mutual trust is inevitably linked to the 'dogma' that

---

[74] Compare E Storskrubb, 'What Changes Will European Harmonization Bring' in J Walker and O Chase (eds), *Common Law, Civil Law and Future of Categories* (Lexis Nexis Canada, 2010) 405.

[75] For an in-depth analysis, see J Komarek, '"In the Court(s) We Trust?" On the Need for Hierarchy and Differentiation in the Preliminary Ruling Procedure' (2007) 32 *EL Rev* 467, chs III and IV.

the judiciaries of individual Member States are all equally fit and trustworthy concerning the expectation that they will correctly apply the law and safeguard fundamental rights. The main objective on the Commission's agenda concerning the European Civil Procedure, is to achieve the genuine 'free movement of judgments', without any hindrances in the form of a review in exequatur proceedings in the country of enforcement.[76] A goal to do away with the *ordre public* (public policy) reservation concerning recognition and enforcement of judgments from other Member States was the main objective of the Commission in promoting the reform of the Brussels I Regulation.[77] Logically, it is difficult to push for the immediate introduction of such a system and at the same time openly admit that there are serious deficiencies in the functioning of civil justice in certain Member States. But the long-term efficiency of the policy of mutual trust would require much more action than the (rapid) drafting of new regulations. As has been stated:

> The European Union should pay much more attention to the quality of the judiciaries than it does at present in order to justify the mutual trust expected from its citizens and courts.[78]

More critical oversight of the national judiciaries by EU institutions would therefore be required in order to achieve that they will gradually be genuinely on a more equal footing as regards quality and integrity. If there occurs a crisis as to the rule of law in one or more Member States, this should be openly admitted and the problem seriously addressed (either by formal or informal means)[79] in order to remedy the shortcomings. Such an approach would perhaps on a short term slow down the pace of adopting new regulations in the field of judicial cooperation in civil matters. But at least in the long term it would serve the idea of genuine European integration for the benefit of its citizens and companies in the field of judicial cooperation much better. Promoting the political agenda of (imposed) mutual trust now often results in unwarranted complacency within certain national judiciaries in the EU. But in order to ensure that a genuine mutual trust grows there

---

[76] Especially the 'second generation regulations' are based on the idea that if some control is still necessary (especially in order to ensure that certain procedural guarantees—'minimum standards'— have been complied with) it is done exclusively in the country of origin. The courts in the country of enforcement cannot re-examine whether the 'certification' in the country of origin was rendered in compliance with the Regulation. The principle of (required) mutual trust and recognition is hence set to a much higher level.

[77] The Commission was not successful in pursuing this goal. Due to a major opposition of (most) Member States, the new (Recast) Brussels I Regulation (Regulation No 1215/2012 of the European Parliament and of the Council of 12 December 2012 on jurisdiction and the recognition and enforcement of judgments in civil and commercial matters (recast), while formally abolishing exequatur procedure, nevertheless retained grounds for non-enforcement, practically in the same manner as the old Regulation.

[78] P Oberhammer, 'Abolition of Exequatur' (2010) 3 *Praxis des Internationalen Privatund Verfahrensrechts* 197, 203.

[79] Concerning legal bases for such oversight (and their possible further elaboration) see C Closa, D Kochenov and JHH Weiler, *Reinforcing Rule of Law Oversight in the European Union*, RSCAS Working paper No 2014/25, electronic copy available at: http://ssrn.com/abstract=2404260 (1 July 2014) 7.

should be greater responsibility of the Member States to ensure the quality of their judiciaries and also a greater degree of their oversight by the EU authorities. This is not to suggest that there has been no such scrutiny (resulting in positive reforms and better performance) in the Member States thus far. Certainly there has been.[80] But much more could—and should—be done. It should also be noted that the shortcomings in functioning of civil justice are not confined to the post-communist EU Member States. After all, the so called 'Italian Torpedo'—which is almost a synonym for the problems arising out of the promotion of full mutual trust although judiciaries in certain Member States are not entirely trustworthy[81]—is not named after a new Member State.

On a more optimistic note, at least since the Stockholm Programme,[82] the Commission emphasised for the first time—more in a retrospective manner but undoubtedly quite necessarily—the questions of quality control, evaluation, scrutiny and the consolidation of what has already been achieved. Practical tools are being implemented in order to achieve that mutual trust will genuinely grow and for the first time the Commission seems to be willing to realistically admit that perhaps mutual trust first has to be established on the ground. In this context, the Commission suggests a new framework to safeguard the rule of law in the European Union.[83] In addition, efforts to highlight judicial training have been strengthened and a forum for discussing EU justice policies and practice is finally becoming relevant.[84] Adequate judicial training is becoming a focal point to enhance mutual

---

[80] See, eg, Assessment of the 2014 national reform programme and stability programme for Slovenia (Commission Staff Working Document); *Accompanying the document:* Recommendation for a Council Recommendation on Slovenia's 2014 national reform programme and delivering a Council opinion on Slovenia's 2014 stability programme (Brussels, 2.6.2014, SWD(2014) 425 final) 31.

[81] Under the Brussels I regime the debtor, having reason to believe that he might be sued in near future and acting in bad faith, could file a negative declaratory action (typically: of noninfringement of a patent—or an action for patent invalidation) in an Italian court (notorious for huge delays), although clearly lacking jurisdiction with a goal to constitute a *lis pendens* and thus prevent the creditor from claiming their own rights (typically: damages for patent infringement), even in a court, designated in a jurisdiction agreement. The latter court had to suspend proceedings until the first court declared that it lacked jurisdiction (which could, even in a straightforward case, take several years in certain Italian courts). The ECJ confirmed that the fact that the duration of proceedings before the courts of the Contracting State in which the court first seised is established is excessively long is not sufficient to derogate from the *lis pendens* rule. The principle of mutual trust must enjoy priority (Case C-116/02, *Gasser v Misat* [2003] ECR I-14693). The recast Brussels I Regulation to a certain degree rectified the problem, although only to the benefit of the court, designated in a jurisdiction agreement. Pursuant to Article 31 paragraph 2 if the court first seised is not the one designated by the parties, that court shall stay the proceedings until the one chosen by the parties declares it has no jurisdiction.

[82] The Stockholm Programme—An open and secure Europe serving and protecting citizens [2009] OJ C 115.

[83] Communication from the Commission to the European Parliament, the Council, the European Economic and Social Committee and the Committee of the Regions: The EU Justice Agenda for 2020—Strengthening Trust, Mobility and Growth within the Union (Strasbourg, 11.3.2014 COM (2014) 144 final).

[84] Resolution of the Council and of the Representatives of the Governments of the Member States meeting within the Council on the training of judges, prosecutors and judicial staff in the EU, 2008, OJ C299/1; Communication from the Commission on the creation of a Forum for discussing EU justice policies and practice, COM (2008) 38, 4 February 2008.

trust.[85] In addition, the 'EU Justice Scoreboard' has been created as an information tool aiming to assist the EU and Member States to achieve more effective justice by providing objective, reliable and comparable data on the quality, independence and efficiency of justice systems in all Member States.[86] These might seem to be minor, insignificant steps, but fostering personal and professional contacts with fellow judges in other EU Member States might actually be the most powerful tool for changing the mentality and working methods of judges.

VIII. Conclusions

Judicial discretion, procedural flexibility in a broader sense and reliance on general and constitutional principles are all linked to the phenomenon of judicial empowerment. It is thus hardly surprising that they were rejected in communism. In this context Slovenia is a special story among Central and Eastern Europe (CEE), since its starting point in the period of transition was considerably better than in countries of the former Soviet bloc. On the other hand, it seems that the country has been sleeping on its laurels after the transition and failed to adequately reform its judiciary. The aversion to judicial discretion amongst Slovenian judges, still very present today, can thus be seen as a legacy of the communist era, at least to a certain extent. However, other contemporary factors leading to this aversion are equally important. Adding to the complexity of the problem, some of these contemporary factors relate to the judiciary itself, whereas others relate to other stakeholders—the Bar, the academia and (equally inadequately reformed) political elites (on both sides of the political spectrum).

Yet another factor relevant for the aversion towards judicial discretion that should not be ignored lies with the recent direction of development of European civil procedure law. European civil procedure in its more recent phases of development is clearly and increasingly fond of judicial discretion and procedural flexibility. The same holds for the growing importance and immediate applicability of constitutional procedural guarantees. This area of EU law with its clear political agenda of judicial integration (in civil and commercial matters) in Europe certainly has the potential of genuine transformative power, helping to build actual mutual trust among Member States. Nevertheless, ignoring existing substantial differences of quality amongst judiciaries in different EU countries and blindly repeating the dogma of mutual trust, does not help to achieve this goal. In fact it can even cause adverse consequences in growing complacency within certain

---

[85] Communication from the Commission to the European Parliament, the Council, the European Economic and Social Committee and the Committee of the Regions: The EU Justice Agenda for 2020—Strengthening Trust, Mobility and Growth within the Union (Strasbourg, 11.3.2014 COM (2014) 144 final).

[86] See http://ec.europa.eu/justice/effective-justice/scoreboard/index_en.htm (1 October 2014).

national judiciaries. Rather, a more critical oversight of national judiciaries in post-communist states by EU institutions is required in order to gradually but genuinely arrive at a more equal standing as regards quality and integrity of the judiciary.

This chapter, thus, answers the question put forward in its title in the positive, although with certain reservations. In the short and medium term, European civil procedure does not seem to be capable of changing the prevailing mentality and working methods of Slovenian judges and, probably, of the similar mentality of judges in other post-communist countries. In the long term, however, provided that the European Commission, as it seems to be the case in the latest developments, ceases to insist on 'blind trust' and finally becomes willing to confront the problem that some Member States' judiciaries are more fit regarding the quality and integrity of the judiciary than others, European civil procedure indeed has the capability and possibility to play an important role in improving the quality of the judiciary in post-communist countries by steering them in the direction of judicial discretion and ability to rely on standards and principles rather than rules.

6

The Remains of the Authoritarian Mentality within the Slovene Judiciary

JAN ZOBEC AND JERNEJ LETNAR ČERNIČ

I. Introduction

The state of mind in the Slovene judiciary 10 years after joining the EU and more than 20 years after the fall of communism and Slovenia's independence is still in transition. During this time, three important legal turning points occurred which were expected to significantly alter the legal culture and mentality of the judiciary.

The first turning point was represented by Slovenia's independence and the constitutional documents on the basis of which Slovenia embarked on its path to a liberal constitutional democracy. A break from the fundamental value concept of the former constitutional regulation occurred, as the *Ustavno sodišče* (Slovenian Constitutional Court, hereinafter 'US') stated in Decision No U-I-109/10. The judiciary became an autonomous and independent branch of power. In contrast with the former system, the independence was not merely declaratory, but constitutional. Thus, institutional guarantees were introduced as well, inter alia by establishing the US as the highest body of the judicial power for the protection of constitutionality and human rights and fundamental freedoms.

In 1994, a second turning point followed with the ratification of the European Convention on Human Rights (ECHR), whereby Slovenia submitted to the jurisdiction of the European Court of Human Rights (ECtHR). Consequently, courts found themselves faced with a new task—during trials, they also had to apply the ECHR, which as a living instrument encompasses much more than just the plain text of the Convention. The case law of the ECtHR began (or should have begun) to permeate the considerations of Slovene constitutional judges, even though problems still persist with execution of ECtHR judgments before lower ordinary courts.

The third turning point occurred on 1 May 2004 when Slovenia joined the EU. The supranational law of the EU, which also includes the (*erga omnes* effective) case law of the Court of Justice in Luxembourg, entered directly into the Slovene legal environment and became an integral part of the Slovene legal order.

Thereby, (at least) formally, the transition from a totalitarian into a liberal democratic society should have been concluded. The transition of the judiciary should have ended with the inclusion of the Slovene judiciary into the so-called Germanic circle of the continental family of legal systems (to which it historically belongs). We question whether this in fact happened. If it did not, why not; how, and in what forms, are the remains of the old mentality reflected; and what kind of influence do they have on the new concept of Slovene law and on the new legal paradigm of the Slovene state and society?

We examine the situation of the judiciary at the time of the fall of communism, which was defined by two characteristics. The first was the preoccupation with the fundamental characteristics of socialist law that was based on an authoritarian and monolithic legal culture. It was expressed already in an affirmative and non-discursive conception of legal studies, and continued with the legal profession conceived in the same manner, offering scientific and professional legitimacy to the ideas of the ideological legislature, and afterwards confirmed by the style in which judgments were written and the conciseness of the legal opinions of the highest courts. The second characteristic (and a consequence of the first one) is the strictly positivistic (textual) approach to the 'application' of law, limited to the application of a simple syllogistic formula. If, as France Bučar, a prominent Slovenian intellectual (and one of the leading dissident in the period of socialism) concludes, lawyers were the first and greatest victims of the division between ethics and positive law in socialism,[1] what then were the judges, whom the law 'liberated' from categorical imperatives?

This chapter will outline some of the most outstanding features of the Slovenian judiciary. Taken together, they indicate serious deficiencies which may contribute to the overwhelming rule of law crisis. Although displayed as a list of detached facts or 'selected issues', all those unpleasant truths about the Slovenian judiciary are not only intertwined and interconnected, but they also hold a common reason. We presuppose that it lies in the legacy of the past and in the lack of the relevant professional (and policy) will of the judicial elites and oligarchies, which master the judiciary, to let necessary changes be brought not only into the judicial system as such but foremost into the mindset of the judiciary. Recruitment of judges certainly plays an important role in this respect. However, it is not a cause in itself. The manner in which judges are recruited is merely a method of how an autopoietic system works and renews itself and tells little or nothing about the substance of the subject. Its corpus regenerates in the same manner as a human body, which is biologically completely restored, by the same genetic programme, in approximately seven years. It becomes materially a completely different, new person, but is essentially still the same (approximately seven years older) person (with the same convictions, values and ideological positions). So far, the situation

---

[1] See F Bučar, 'Pravnik v današnjem času' (uvodno predavanje na 30. Dnevih slovenskih pravnikov) [Lawyer in the Current Times, The Introductory Lecture at 30th Days of Slovene Lawyers] (2004) 36 *Pravna praksa* 5.

of the Slovenian judiciary has been the same. A gradual inflow of new personnel, although better educated, did not alter substantially the governing corporative and authoritarian structured mentality, inherited from the past.

This chapter analyses the present situation in the Slovene judiciary. Since the situation has essentially not changed (despite the inevitable influence of the US, the ECtHR, and the CJEU (Court of Justice of the European Union) on Slovene case law), we assess the possible reasons for the prolonging of the past in the new (democratic and European) context. The following sections attempt to answer if the shortcomings of the Slovene judiciary can be explained by the lack of lustration, the absence of pluralistic legal tradition, the system of advancement of judges, the closed nature of judicial institutions, the presence of a judicial culture of fear and the self-sufficiency of the judiciary, the wider (political) social context or, perhaps, all of these reasons are intertwined.

II. Legal (Dis-)Continuity

Totalitarian systems dehumanise man while hoping to erase all traces of their actions.[2] The contemporaries of totalitarianism naturally do not perceive them as bad, because such comprehension is formulated only *ex post facto*.[3] Hannah Arendt already wrote in her book *The Origins of Totalitarianism* that a 'disturbing factor in the success of totalitarianism is rather the true selflessness of its adherents'.[4] There are two traits that characterise every totalitarianism, as the Spanish philosopher, active between the two world wars, José Ortega y Gasset described in his visionary work *La rebelión de las masas* (The Revolt of the Masses): 'the free expansion of his vital desires, and therefore, of his personality; and his radical ingratitude towards what has made possible the ease of his existence.'[5] The fall of the totalitarian regimes in Central Europe is probably most notably symbolised by the fall of the Berlin Wall and the Velvet Revolution in the former Czechoslovakia,[6] that were gradually followed by the fall of the rest of totalitarianism in Central Europe, including Slovenia.[7] Without the changes that occurred at that time[8]

---

[2] See for example A Vode, *Skriti spomin* [Hidden Memory] (Nova revija, 2006).

[3] See for example L Lisjak Gabrijelčič, *Razumeti totalitarizem: interpretacije totalitarizma pri Hannah Arendt, Slavoju Žižku in Viktorju Blažiču* [Understanding Totalitarianism: Totalitarianism Interpretations by Hannah Arendt, Slavoj Žižek and Viktor Blažič], Diplomska naloga [Thesis for the Bachelor's Degree] (Ljubljana Filozofska fakulteta Univerza v Ljubljani, 2006).

[4] H Arendt, *The Origins of Totalitarianism* (Schocken Books, 2004) 409.

[5] J Ortega y Gasset, *Upor množic* [The Revolt of the Masses] (1929) translated by N Košir (Slovenska matica, 1985) 56.

[6] M Kundera, 'Tragedija Srednje Evrope' [Tragedy of Central Europe] (1984) 30(3) *Nova revija* 3456. See also P Vodopivec, *Srednja Evropa* [Central Europe] (Mladinska knjiga, 1991).

[7] J Letnar Černič, 'Srednja Evropa Václava Havla' [Václav Havel's Central Europe] (2012) *Razpotja Journal*.

[8] ibid.

we would probably still be dreaming of an autonomous and independent state, and consequently of a Constitution.[9]

When there is a change in the nature and quality of the constitutional legal system, it is necessary to clarify whether the existing legal acts may continue to be used also in the new democratic legal system. The issue is all the more pressing in the case of a transition from an undemocratic system that systematically violated human rights into a democratic one. Can legal acts that enabled and facilitated violations of fundamental human rights be used in a democratic legal order?

A. Legal (Dis-)Continuity in the Slovene Constitutional Legal Order

Some states opt for a complete break with the former constitutional system, others choose a gentle transition, while the majority take the middle path. For instance, the Spanish legal order opted for a peaceful transition and most of the legal acts that were in force under the Franco regime remained in force and are still applicable in the democratic legal order. In the Slovene legal order, we decided for the middle way by implementing the principle of legal continuity of the Slovene legal order with the previous totalitarian legal order, except in cases where the previous legal order violated human rights and freedoms.

In recent years, there has been an attempt to create the impression in the Slovene public that the legal quality of the Slovene independent and democratic state is equated with its Yugoslav predecessor. Such a belief is wrong and misguided. The US has repeatedly confirmed that the former state 'did not function as a state governed by law and that within it human rights were grossly violated'.[10] Even more, the Basic Constitutional Charter on the Sovereignty and Independence of the Republic of Slovenia recognised the undemocratic and totalitarian nature of the Yugoslav system. It states in the second indent of its preamble that 'the SFRY does not function as a state governed by law and that within it human rights, national rights, and the rights of the republics and autonomous provinces are grossly violated'.[11] The Slovene state therefore, at least at the constitutional level, does not follow the fundamental guidelines of the previous totalitarian legal order in whatever regard.[12]

---

[9] D Jančar, 'Srednja Evropa med meteorologijo in utopijo. Srednja Evropa' [Central Europe between Meteorology and Utopia. Central Europe] in Vodopivec (n 6) 87–94.

[10] L Šturm, 'Omejitev oblasti' [Restrictions of Power] (1998) *Ljubljana Nova Revija* 23.

[11] Official Gazette RS, No 1I/1991.

[12] See, for instance, L Šturm, 'Pravna država' [State Governed by the Principles of the Rule of Law] in L Šturm (ed), *Komentar Ustave RS—Dopolnitev A* [Commentary on the Constitution of the Republic of Slovenia, Supplement—A] (Brdo pri Kranju Fakulteta za državne in evropske študije, 2011) 16–43.

In the Slovene context, there is no doubt as to what the nature of the former Yugoslav system was. The US stated in one of its earlier decisions that

> the former Yugoslav system ... did not put human rights at the forefront and did not define any clear legal restrictions for the state authorities and their violence. Thus, it made arbitrary government possible...[13]

The former undemocratic system was therefore opposed to the protection of at least the fundamental human rights. Moreover, the undemocratic regime based and kept its power through intimidation of the population and getting them to spy on each other and then collecting such information in files to which access was given only to the privileged few. This regime used methods that were thus contrary to the most basic standards of human rights protection in force in the Slovene constitutional legal order of a democratic state that is party to the ECHR. The division between the undemocratic and democratic systems is well illustrated by the US Judge Lovro Šturm who in his separate opinion in the case No U-I-121/97 stated that everyone who lived in the former regime was 'subject to sustained and systematic threats to human rights and fundamental freedoms'.[14]

The US reached a similar conclusion already in Decision No U-I-69/92 of 10 December 1992. There the US stated that in the previous system we had

> a state whose authorities had after the end of the war carried out mass executions of former military and current political opponents, legally unacceptable trials followed by death penalties, illegal seizure of property, obstruction and liquidation of political parties in violation of its own legal system etc, thus making the injured parties afraid, with good reason, for their lives in case of residing in such a country.[15]

The US has expressed itself even more clearly in the decision regarding Tito Street in which it wrote the following: 'In Slovenia ... the development of democracy and free society based on respect for human dignity began with the break up with the former system'.[16] Slovenia thus separated itself from the previous undemocratic regime. In a certain way, one can understand the nostalgic memories of those who live in a parallel world and want to obscure the historical facts. They wish, as perhaps everybody else does in general, to remember the good things of their youth and forget the bad memories.

One of the recent decisions of the US put again the issue of legal (dis-)continuity with the previous system to the fore. On 14 April 2011, the US rejected a petition of the National Assembly stating that unconstitutional consequences would occur as a result of the dismissal at a referendum of the Act Amending the Protection of Documents and Archives and Archival Institutions Act.[17] Judge Deisinger in his concurring opinion, which was joined by Judges Mozetič

---

[13] No U-I-158/94, dated 9 March 1995, para 13.
[14] Separate opinion of Judge L Šturm, No U-I-121/97 of 23 May 1997, 2.
[15] No U-I-69/92 of 10 December 1992, para 8.
[16] No U-I-109/10 of 3 October 2011, para 18.
[17] No U-II-2/11.

and Zobec, also addresses the issue of legal continuity of the Slovene legal order with the former Yugoslav legal order. The judges have clearly stated that the legal order of the democratic Slovene state cannot be equated with the legal order of the previous totalitarian system. It follows from the concurring opinion that 'there can be no talk of legal continuity with the former SFRY'.[18] The difference in quality between the former and the current system is that the former Yugoslav state 'was not even a "state" or "community" governed by the rule of law'.[19] The judges also stated that 'all regulations and actions of the bodies that were related to violations of human rights were no longer to be used in the Republic of Slovenia. In view of these provisions therefore legal discontinuity existed.'[20] The judges substantiated their position by explaining that in the Slovene legal order legal acts that infringe upon human rights are prohibited.

However, despite the fact that the former system did not act as a legally regulated state, there was no comprehensive cut-off of the new Slovene legal order with the previous undemocratic one. Only a partial cut-off with the previous system was implemented in cases of serious human rights violations and even in these cases the cut-off was very mild. If one asks law school students today which principle is followed by the Slovene legal order, the principle of legal continuity or discontinuity with the previous undemocratic legal order, the answer is ambiguous. In principle in the Slovene legal order, the principle of legal continuity with the previous system is in force. However, on the formal legal level the Slovene legal order does not pursue legal continuity with the former legal order of the Yugoslav federation regarding the general and individual legal acts that violated fundamental human rights and freedoms.

Many are therefore wondering how effectively the Slovene legal order executes the principle of legal discontinuity with the former state in relation to the legal acts that violated human rights. Should the principle of legal discontinuity be applied so that the persons who were unfairly sentenced under the former regime as 'the enemies of the people' must themselves demand annulment of judgments? Or that in the whole 20 years after the alleged cut-off there have not been any criminal proceedings against alleged perpetrators of crimes against humanity on Slovene territory after the Second World War or that a statue of the instigator of the violations of the most fundamental human rights is still standing in the capital city?

Based on the above, it is difficult to defend the view that the principle of discontinuity with the previous system in relation to legal acts that violated human rights has been fully implemented in the Slovene legal order. At the formal legal level, it is possible to agree with the constitutional judges that there can be no talk of legal continuity. However, to enforce the principle of legal discontinuity, its full implementation in practice is needed, which depends on the people who create the Slovene legal order on a day-to-day basis. In any case, the principle of legal

---

[18] ibid, para 4.
[19] ibid.
[20] ibid, para 5 of the decision.

discontinuity should, at least regarding the afore-mentioned legal acts, constitute the foundation of the independent Slovene state which is based on the rule of law.

B. Legal (Dis-)Continuity in Practice

In the Slovene public, there persists a predominant belief that in the Slovene democratic society, human rights are protected only in the formal legal acts and at the rhetorical level, while there is a lack of consistent respect for them in practice, and that the majority of state bodies as well as private individuals apply these according to their particular—private—interests. The activities of the various Ombudsmen in the last decade confirm such an appearance. The protection and exercise of human rights in the Slovene legal order is therefore selective, unequal and inefficient.

Bearers of this protection are, of course, people, and often people coming from different periods. Unfortunately, in Slovenia the following outdated dogma is still valid that similar and comparable human rights violations have not been examined equally. For instance, one issue that has not been properly addressed are crimes against humanity in Slovenia at the end of the Second World War. As many as 130,000 people are estimated to have been summarily executed in Slovenia in the months following the end of the Second World War on 8 May 1945.[21] It is further estimated that around 15,000 of those executed were of Slovenian nationality, others included Croats, Serbs and Germans.[22] The victims were mostly civilians but also members of the Slovenian Home Guards[23] and other political opponents of the resistance movement led by the Slovenian Communist Party. These crimes, carried out by members of the Slovenian section of the Yugoslav Secret Police, were committed mostly in the form of systematic summary executions at hidden locations across Slovenia, predominantly in unpopulated rural areas and in forests.[24] They were part of a systematic plan of the Slovene Communist Party to eliminate their political opponents and their families, civilian or otherwise. It is still unclear whether the order for the liquidation of alleged political opponents and civilians originated from the head of the former Yugoslav Security Police in

---

[21] See P Jamnik, 'Post-World War Two Crimes on the Territory of Slovenia: Police Investigation and Proof Regarding Criminal Offences that do not Fall under the Statute of Limitations' in P Jambrek (ed), *Crimes Committed by Totalitarian Regimes* (Slovenian Presidency of the Council of the European Union, 2008) 207. See also J Dežman, 'Communist Repression and Transitional Justice in Slovenia' in Jambrek, ibid, 204.

[22] J Letnar Černič, 'Responding to Crimes Against Humanity Committed in Slovenia after the Second World War' in D Svoboda, C O'Connor and J Liška (eds), *Crimes of the Communist Regimes: International Conference: An Assessment by Historians and Legal Experts: Proceedings* (Ústav pro studium totalitních režimů, 2011) 313–28.

[23] Slovenian Home Guards movement was established after the Slovene Communist Party monopolised resistance and after it extra-judicially executed hundreds of Catholic members of the resistance struggle against Italian and German forces.

[24] J Pučnik, 'Mass Post-War Killings' in D Jančar (ed), *The Dark Side of the Moon. A Short History of Totalitarianism in Slovenia 1945–1990* (Ljubljana, Nova Revija, 1998) 39.

Belgrade or the Slovenian branch in Ljubljana. The Commission for the Settlement of Hidden Mass Gravesites of the Government of the Republic of Slovenia has indicated that almost 600 hidden mass graves have been found in Slovenia thus far.[25] Its long-term goal is the exhumation and re-burial of victims killed on Slovenian territory.

Most state bodies do not deal with the most serious violations of human rights in the last century. We can look in vain in the reports of the Office of the Ombudsman in the period from 2006 to 2011 for mention of the crimes against humanity, let alone calls for the enforcement of responsibility of perpetrators and the improvement of the situation of the victims of the most serious violations and their relatives.[26] The Slovene judiciary bodies are also silent. The European Court of Human Rights decided in the case of *Janowiec and Others v Russia*[27] that Russian authorities have not done anything to explain the whereabouts of the victims of the Katyn massacre during the war. The ECtHR also confirmed that

> a denial of crimes against humanity ... runs counter to the fundamental values of the Convention and of democracy, namely justice and peace ... and that the same is true of statements pursuing the aim of justifying war crimes ... By acknowledging that the applicants' relatives had been held prisoners in the Soviet camps but declaring that their subsequent fate could not be elucidated, the Russian courts denied the reality of summary executions that had been carried out in the Katyn forest and at other mass murder sites.'[28]

The ECtHR has thus distanced itself considerably from the standpoint of Russian courts. It held that the approach of the latter 'has been contrary to the fundamental values of the Convention and must have exacerbated the applicants' suffering.'[29] The ECtHR concluded 'the applicants were left to bear the brunt of the efforts to uncover any facts relating to the manner in which their relatives died, whereas the Russian authorities demonstrated a flagrant, continuous and callous disregard for their concerns and anxieties.'[30] In the view of the chamber of seven judges, the actions of the Russian authorities attained 'the minimum level of severity to be considered inhumane treatment within the meaning of Article 3 of the Convention.'[31]

---

[25] For a detailed historical account see M Ferenc, *Topografija evidentiranih grobišč'* [*Topography of Recorded Gravesites*], 'Poročilo Komisije Vlade Republike Slovenije za reševanje vprašanj prikritih grobišč 2005–2008* [Report of the Commission for the Settlement of Hidden Mass Gravesites of the Government of the Republic of Slovenia 2005–2008] (Ljubljana, Družina Publishing, 2008); or T Griesser-Pečar, *Razdvojeni narod* [A Torn Nation](Ljubljana, Mladinska knjiga Publishing, 2004).

[26] Office of the Ombudsman, Annual Reports 2006–2011, www.varuh-rs.si/publikacije-gradiva-izjave/letna-porocila/ (last accessed on 5 December 2014).

[27] European Court of Human Rights, Judgment *Janowiec and Others v Russia* of 10 October 2012 (Nos 55508/07 and 29520/09) para 163.

[28] ibid, para 165.

[29] ibid.

[30] ibid, para 166.

[31] ibid.

The case *Janowiec and Others v Russia* thus clearly indicates that the ECHR obliges states, including Slovenia, to investigate how and where the victims of extrajudicial killings were killed, and seek those responsible. The silence of state bodies regarding extrajudicial killings of civilians is an inhumane treatment prohibited by the fundamental principles of modern liberal and democratic societies. The circumstances of wartime and post-war killings in Slovenia remain largely not investigated, and the alleged perpetrators enjoy impunity. The state does not fulfil its obligation under international law to investigate all sites of extrajudicial killings. The bones of the victims continue to remain buried in the forests, caves, and mine shafts. It applies to domestic and European courts, just as it does for each and every one of us, that humanity, compassion and respect for the victims of massive and systematic violations of human rights should play a central role in the adoption of any decision. The suffering of the relatives of the victims in Katyn will not disappear by itself just as the dark chapter in the recent European history will not close by itself. The Katyn victims and victims in similar dark stories, including the Slovene one, are still waiting to be buried properly and to be remembered in a dignified and decent manner.

It is not easy to discuss reconciliation in Slovenia, especially regarding its substance. Interest groups use it easily as a rhetorical stock phrase and abuse it for the realisation of their own private interests. It is even easier for some to put themselves on a moral pedestal, appropriate themselves of the moral authority and wag their finger at their opponents saying, if you do not accept one or other of the interpretations of the recent history, we will never achieve a reconciliation. Such quasi-moral authorities do not care much about reconciliation, let alone about the victims and their relatives on both sides of the ideological divide.

Reconciliation will never be achieved if current opponents keep on stubbornly insisting on their positions without a will and desire to try to understand the feelings and suffering of their brothers and sisters on the opposite, but neighbouring side. The path to a genuine reconciliation is much more difficult than just insisting on opposite positions and avoiding the responsibility for one's own mistakes. Such compassion is hard to attain without sacrificing parts of one's own ideals and compassions, as individual and collective catharses begin at a subconscious level. The feeling of guilt and shame are there at war with the prevailing feelings of oblivion in regard to the worst crimes against humanity. Only after the feelings of shame and guilt evolve, the process of forgiveness slowly begins, and even then not in all situations.

Forgiveness is most easily attained by an open discussion between victims and perpetrators of crimes, where everyone must make an effort to understand the other. Such discussion requires courageous individuals on both sides. It is more difficult to organise the discussions when either the victims or perpetrators are deceased, since their relatives are often (un)intentionally caught in a stranglehold of ideology as well as family stories and myths that prevent them from escaping from an unhappy past. Finding forgiveness is as difficult as being able to regret the crimes committed by an individual or a society as a whole. This is also clear from the proceedings before international criminal courts, where perpetrators rarely confess and regret their crimes.

Of course, perpetrators are never found only on one side of the axis of the society in the recent history, but are located in various degrees at all corners of the society. Maturity that equally condemns the crimes on one or the other side of the society is difficult to achieve. Crimes against humanity and systematic human rights violations are not and never will be dependent on the ideological side. Human rights and the prohibition of crimes against humanity are above such debates and do not depend on the subjective interpretation of the various interest groups.

Reconciliation is possible if every pore, segment, shade and level of the society strives for it and at the same time wants to distance themselves away from the worst events in the Slovene society. However, it is in principle impossible to achieve reconciliation without an unconditional condemnation of crimes of all three totalitarian regimes that have sowed death on Slovene soil. Such recognition is difficult to achieve, in most cases the latter is almost impossible since members of the opposing sides persist in their thinking and do not wish to admit that the other, opposing side is also right in many ways. Each side celebrates their heroism and makes every effort that their own crimes fall into oblivion. The manner of doing this and its dynamics are different. Some conceal hidden burial sites; others forget the controversy of collaboration with the occupying forces. It is, however, common for all sides that they avoid a different and pluralistic discussion with those who disagree. Only a subconscious catharsis of Slovene society can help the society to finally mature.

In addition to a catharsis of the subconscious mind, a pluralistic discussion of the painful and dark sides of the Slovene society is necessary for achieving its maturity. A public debate regarding the crimes committed by totalitarian regimes is crucial for increasing the democratic discourse in Slovene society. Freedom of such discussion must not be constrained from the moral pedestal of one or the other side, often by a self-proclaimed goody-two-shoes. It is necessary to allow a discussion that is critical, sharp, even insulting, because such is required by a democratic society and not least by the ECtHR. The most extreme forms of expression, calling for violence, hatred or intolerance, must of course be rejected. It is however true that the most extreme forms of expression can be prosecuted, but only a discussion giving room to everyone equally will finally eliminate all forms of incitement to intolerance, hatred and discrimination from the sub-layers of society.

A dignified and humane treatment of the dead is, however, of equal importance as the catharsis and a pluralistic discussion. As Boris Pahor said at the Day against Totalitarianism ceremony in Kobarid: 'Let's give a standing ovation to all the dead victims who died for us.'[32] Therefore, the victims of crimes deserve at least that we dignifiedly pay tribute to their memory, and that the state finally digs out their bones and constructs memorial parks and museums in their memory so

---

[32] B Pahor, speech at the ceremony at the Day against Totalitarianism, Kobarid, 30 August 2013.

that something like this will never happen again. Until that happens, the society will continue to be crippled. A state that does not bury their dead and lives on their suffering and bones is not much different from the animal world.

III. The State of the Judiciary During Transition: The Absence of Lustration

Slovenia did embark on the path of liberal constitutional democracy with independence and constitutional acts, but this was only the first, formal, and therefore easiest step toward the final destination. Slovenia belongs to the set of states that have not implemented lustration after the lapse of the Communist rule. Why that did not happen is a matter for political and historical analysis. In general it is however possible to state that the true reason for the absence of lustration lies in the fact that Slovenia, like some other post-communist states, belongs to an evolutionary model of continuity and transformation of the nomenclature into elite groups. It is characteristic of this model that it excludes the possibility of lustration of parts of the old nomenclature.[33]

Nevertheless, with regard to the lustration of judges, a so-called 'Pučnik Amendment'[34] was adopted, which was introduced into the third paragraph of Article 8 of the Judicial Service Act. It determines (as one of the general conditions for election to the function of a judge) that judges who adjudicated or adopted a decision in an investigation or judicial proceedings, in which human rights and fundamental freedoms were violated by a judgment, do not fulfil the conditions for re-election to a judicial function after the expiry of their term in office. This general condition referred only to those judges who at the time when the Judicial Service Act entered into force exercised their function as a judge at regular courts and had the right, before and after the expiry of their term in office, to apply for the position of a judge under the terms of that Act.

One of the characteristics of the socialist judiciary was the existence of a limited term of office of a judge (limited to eight years). At the same time, however, one of the first transitional measures in the judiciary was the introduction of the permanent term of office. The transition to the permanent term of office was, however, not automatic. The judges could only pass from the limited to the permanent term in office after a professional evaluation of their judicial work had been carried out—and which was required by the already established Judicial Council (*Sodni svet*). However, this evaluation was then not conducted by the Personal Council

---

[33] See A Milardović, 'Elite Groups in the Waves of the Democratization and Lustrations' in V Dvořáková and A Milardović (eds), *Lustration and Consolidation of Democracy and the Rule of Law in Central and Eastern Europe* (Political Science Research Centre Zagreb, 2007) 93, 94.

[34] It is named after the proposer of the amendment Jože Pučnik, who is regarded as a key personality for the Slovene independence and the liberation from totalitarian state power.

(*Personalni svet*), which evaluates candidates who apply for the first time for the function of a judge. The evaluation of the judges of courts of first instance was carried out by the competent higher courts, the evaluation of the judges of higher courts by the Supreme Court, and the evaluation of the judges of the Supreme Court by that very same Court in a plenary session.

Therefore, the (still existing) lustration clause is not about the 'cleansing' of unwanted personnel, that is their removal due to their political beliefs, but about their cooperation with, and activities performed, in the framework of communist authorities exercising state power when fundamental human rights and freedoms were violated. In this way, it was not a big surprise that the lustration provision 'survived' constitutional review. All three fundamental prejudices regarding lustration were refuted by the review carried out by the US. It was suggested that first, lustration entails retribution and is applied against political opponents; second that it is a measure of collective, not individual responsibility; and third that the lustration procedure does not meet the conditions of fair and just decision making by an impartial body.[35] However, the constitutional review revealed not only the deficiency of the lustration provision, but also the naivety of the legislature, which again is confirmed when we look at the inception of the lustration provision from the time distance of 20 years. The lustration clause is a naive one since it is redundant, as some of the judges of the US correctly stressed in their separate opinions. 'Lustration' considerations are namely included in every normal evaluation of the work of a particular judge. In any case it should be impossible to overlook, during the evaluation of his or her work, which is the basis for his or her election to a permanent term in office, that a judge, under the communist regime, submitted to political criteria and violated human rights during trials. Such a judge should not be reinstated to the position he or she occupies.

The judicial transition to a liberal democracy based on the rule of law has therefore taken place with the old personnel (trained in socialism). This was, however, no different to the situation of lawyers in general and other legal professions. In this regard, already Bučar noted that

> with their often unnecessary or at least excessive meekness … they themselves have strengthened the totalitarian system, as by their conduct and laxness they were giving it justification of at least acceptability, if not legitimacy, and thus inadvertently confirming that it is right and simultaneously giving it an absolution for its violations of fundamental human rights.[36]

Exactly this is one of the fundamental problems of the post-socialist judiciary. Furthermore, it may not stop at the national level. It may result in the fear of socialist judiciary and its lawyers being nominated as judges at the Strasbourg

---

[35] See V Rakić-Vodinelić, 'An Unsuccessful Attempt of Lustration in Serbia' in Dvořáková and Milardović (n 33) 170, 171.
[36] See Bučar (n 1) 6.

Court. For example, already in 1997, Lord Browne-Wilkinson cautioned against strict observance of the case law of the ECtHR while stating that:

> I have found the jurisprudence of the European Court of Human Rights excellent, but a major change is taking place. We are now seeing a wider range of judges adjudicating such matters, a number of them drawn from jurisdictions 10 years ago not famous for their observance of human rights. It might be dangerous to tie ourselves to that...[37]

In addition, and perhaps most importantly, already more than 20 years ago, Sajo and Losonci found that the introduction of judicial 'self-government' in a situation of transition does not entail anything other than the preservation of the judiciary as it was established by the undemocratic communist authorities.[38] The authoritarian legal culture and the ethics of obedience (which is reflected in submissiveness, political opportunism, political correctness and, consequently, in the judges' self-censorship) were preserved thought patterns of the old regime as a heritage of the totalitarian period and in the collectivist and corporatist mentality. It keeps being preserved as one of the forms of a parallel, covert or deep state, and it feeds and fertilises itself mentally, with values and ideological points of view through the very institutionally closed nature and self-sufficiency. In a normal state with a democratic tradition and legal culture that would have a positive effect—to maintain that which already exists, that is an internally, mentally independent judiciary. However, in states in transition (and Slovenia is, at least regarding the judiciary, still deeply in transition) what is maintained is what already exists, and that, however, is anything but an intellectually autonomous and independent judiciary.[39]

IV. The Remnants of the Old Judiciary Culture

Slovenia's post-socialist judiciary emerged directly from the totalitarian 'actually existing socialism'. It did therefore not inherit the mind and the spirit necessary for judicial independence. The Slovenian judiciary was simply not prepared for the shift from the world of unified power in the hands of toiling people, where the judiciary was not granted the position of an independent branch of government,

---

[37] Other prominent British lawyers have expressed themselves in a similar tone *cf* W Sadurski, 'Partnering with Strasbourg: Constitutionalisation of the European Court of Human Rights, the Accession of Central and East European States to the Council of Europe, and the Idea of Pilot Judgements' (2009) 3 *Human Rights Law Review* 409.

[38] See A Sajo and V Losonci, 'Rule by Law in the East Central Europe: Is the Emperor's New Suit a Straightjacket?' in D Greenberg et al (eds), *Constitutionalism and Democracy—Transitions in the Contemporary World* (Oxford University Press, 1993) 322.

[39] This characteristic of most post-socialist states is confirmed by similar experiences in the Czech Republic, Slovakia, Croatia, Hungary and Bulgaria. See for instance S Spac, *Judicial Development after the Breakdown of Communism in the Czech Republic and Slovakia* (Budapest Central European University, 2013) 24 ff; see A Uzelac, 'Survival of the Third Legal Tradition?' (2010) 49 *Supreme Court Review* 388 ff.

into the normal liberal democracy, based on the rule of law and separation of powers. Communism was not built on one's personality, on a strong, ethically rooted individual, yet it adhered to regulations. Hence also the role of the judges was strictly 'technological'—they were expected to serve the regulation. In doing so, they also protected themselves. Hidden behind the text of the regulations, they felt comfortable, safe and protected.

We may agree with Uzelac who claims that socialist judges are different from their common law counterparts. The latter are characterised by a heroic stance and endeavours to contribute to the legal history with prudent, brave and brilliantly reasoned decisions. Socialist judges are afraid—afraid of responsibilities, afraid of possible retribution. They stay on the sidelines. They want to remain as inconspicuous as possible, even anonymous. Therefore, socialist judges delay adopting a decision. They like resorting to formalisms, allowing them to escape from forming a substantive decision, which entails an escape from authoritative decision making. Bureaucratic, administrative decision making is, of course, not an authoritative decision making. Judges who perceive themselves in such a way see themselves as a mere mechanical extension of real power, such as a policeman or an official behind a counter.[40]

Thus, the issue is a difference in mentality. In the traditional western democracies, foremost in common law systems, the judge is power. In socialism, the judge is (was) more of an official and therefore more susceptible to pleasing the political power than respecting the law. Equally, legal formalism refers more to a blind obedience of power and disrespect for the law, than a blind obedience of the law.[41]

Thus, in times of living socialism, even in those cases when judges departed from a bare legal wording, they did that for the sake of political instruction or foremost due to their 'self-censorship', but typically not for the courage of their convictions. Legal education was perfectly in line with such an approach and so was the practical training during the judicial apprenticeship. Jurists were not raised as persons with deeply anchored legal culture and a broad value rootedness. A jurist, who fit the bill of the communist regime, was the one who could be characterised as a legal technologist, suitable for serving as a tool of leading political elites.[42] Finally, in a nutshell, that suits the general communist position to the law which is ultimately conceived as a tool of a ruling class, that is political elites. Such an understanding still remains in the deep subconscious of the Slovenian judiciary, as will be demonstrated on individual elements in the following sections.

A. Formalism

Excessive positivism, certainly one of the most persistent survivals of the socialist legal tradition, is just an expression of the above-described legal culture. A lot of

---

[40] See Uzelac (n 39) 383.

[41] See Z Kühn, *The Judiciary in Central and Eastern Europe: Mechanical Jurisprudence in Transformation?* (Martinus Nijhoff, 2011) 147.

[42] See F Bučar, 'Demokracija in kriza naših ustavnih institucij' (1998) *Ljubljana Nova revija* 134, 135.

this symptom is present also in the more recent case law of the *Vrhovno sodišče* (Supreme Court, hereinafter 'VS') and higher courts. Just three of the most blatant examples will be offered here.

First, in a 2007 decision,[43] the VS upheld the position of the Administrative Court that the presumption of disloyalty determined in the second paragraph of Article 35 of the Citizenship of the Federal People's Republic of Yugoslavia Act,[44] operating as an obstacle for the restitution of nationalised property to persons of German nationality, also applies to persons who were children at the time of World War II. The assumption can only be successfully challenged by providing evidence of the active loyal behaviour of the children during World War II. Their loyal behaviour is assessed independently from the loyalty of their parents. Such approach would thus mean that also persons who were children at the time of World War II (regardless of their age at that time) would have to prove their active loyal behaviour.[45]

Second, the rejection of the legal remedy requested by the Supreme State Prosecutor only because the judgment under appeal was not properly quoted according to the VS's guidelines may also be seen as extremely formalist. Paradoxically, the VS recognised at the same time that it was quite clear from the very motion of the Supreme State Prosecutor which judgment was being challenged.[46]

The last example of excessive formalism: The Higher Court in Koper[47] found that already before the motion for execution was lodged the real property referred to in the instrument authorising enforcement had been divided into two separate condominium units, one of which was now the debtors' property. It therefore concluded that as the initial real property against which execution was initiated no longer legally exists, the execution against the real property referred to in the instrument authorising enforcement was rendered impossible. It is impossible—and will never be possible—to compulsorily enforce the instrument authorising enforcement of the creditors' claim against a co-owner's share of a part of certain property, as the object of execution ceased to exist due to the conversion of co-ownership into condominium.[48]

Legal formalism makes judicial thinking de-contextual. Social and economic circumstances of the case become excluded from the judge's considerations. Thus, judges cease being able to identify and to sanction abuses of legal concepts. Such legal concepts, or legal transplants, become transferred from normal legal environments where they operate efficiently and for the good of the people, and degenerate in our midst—the body rejects them. At the same time, the unwillingness and disinclination of the courts to sanction and prevent abuses on the basis

---

[43] Judgment X Ips 355/2007 of 13 September 2007.

[44] Official Gazette DFY, No 64/45, and Official Gazette of the FPR of Yugoslavia, No 54/46 et seq.

[45] See the US decision No Up-3451/07 of 12 March 2009, Official Gazette RS, No 25/09.

[46] Decision of the VS, I Ips 15867/2012 of 13 December 2012.

[47] Decision I Ip 273/2011 of 29 August 2011.

[48] See US decision No Up-1268/11 of 19 September 2012, Official Gazette RS, No 79/12.

of general and open general clauses is understandable. It is due to the fear of using judicial discretion, rooted in the fear of real authoritative decision making and responsibility that is associated with such. This in turn drives the legislature to legislating in a particular, casuistic and formalist fashion. As a consequence, however, the legislature exposes itself (instead of the courts) to the dangers and pitfalls associated with this approach. The excessive zeal seeking to prevent abuse may generate an imbalance in the system of procedural rights and excessively limit or even block some of these rights.

Looking from a more distant perspective and after a passage of time, it seems that the Slovene legislature might have tackled the abuse of procedural rights too quickly and without giving it enough thought and consideration. Such casuistic manner of solving the issue has two disadvantages. The first is that the casuistic legislative style is by its very nature less adaptable to concrete life situations. The legislature can never predict exhaustively all the possible life situations. By necessity, it must generalise, find typical characteristics and make equations. This is in the very nature of law. By the same token, however, the new legislation is then also applicable to other situations, where it should not been applied, for instance by simply not taking into account certain positions that are more difficult to predict and that stand out from the average.[49] Due to the lack of importance given to the principles and excessively casuistic rule-making, the legislature is exposed to the danger that individual rules which anticipate situations of abuse are inconsistent with the Constitution (for example, where the courts cannot weigh different constitutionally protected values due to such an approach). This is evidenced by the decisions of the US which annulled several amendments that amounted to an excessive formalisation of procedure and whose objective was to prevent abuse of procedural rights and to make civil proceedings more efficient. It should be taken into consideration that most of these amendments were introduced upon the initiative of the Ministry of Justice or certain judges.[50]

The second weakness is that such a casuistic and formalistic approach of the legislator discourages the courts from employing the general prohibition of abuse of rights provision. It conveys the message that the statute with all its individual rules has already foreseen comprehensively and in advance all forms of abuse (that are relevant according to the legislature), and that therefore the courts must be restrained when directly applying general principles. This only contributes to the consolidation of legal formalism.[51]

---

[49] *cf* R Alexy, *A Theory of Constitutional Rights*, trans J Rivers (Oxford University Press, 2007) 50.

[50] See A Galič, 'A Judge's Power to Disregard Late Facts and Evidence and the Goals of Civil Justice' in V Nekrošius and M Storme (eds), *Recent Trends in Economy and Efficiency of Civil Procedure, Materials of International Conference* (Vilnius University Press, 2013) 103, 104.

[51] ibid, 76 ff and 103 ff.

B. Legal Opinions of Principle—Difficulties with the Harmonisation of Case Law

The core of the new system of appeal to the *Vrhovno sodišče* in civil law and in labour and social dispute proceedings is the 'leave to appeal' system. The system seeks to establish the appeal as a means to achieving goals that are objectively important to the legal order in its entirety. It thereby allows the VS as the highest judicial authority with regard to the interpretation and application of statutes to take a position on significant legal issues. Thus, the appeals system ought to ensure the further evolution of the law through case law. It emphasises and reinforces the responsibility of the VS for harmonisation of case law in the state and thereby for ensuring equality before the law.[52]

With this purpose of the appeal system in mind, the US had no difficulty in finding that the statutory provisions allowing the VS to limit its reasoning to merely general reference to the statutory reasons for dismissing the leave to appeal is not contrary to the Constitution. A requirement to provide reasoning on the merits of orders dismissing leaves to appeal would undermine the purpose of the regulation of appeals to the VS. Consequently, the significance of the VS would be weakened. The VS is, however, important to the development of the law, to protection of the human right to equality before the law, and, in a broader sense, to the foundations of constitutional democracy.[53]

Notwithstanding this, the VS exercises (especially in recent years) its role as the highest court in the legal system particularly by adopting completely abstract legal opinions of principle. The latter are, however, adopted in an authoritarian manner. Legal opinions of principle, which are binding on all the senates of the VS (and are by the same fiat de facto binding on all lower courts), do not originate from concrete cases and from a dialogue with the parties and between the courts of different instances. Pluralism of opinions is not their characteristic feature. The right answer is achieved through a 'one way' process and is backed by threat and force rather than by the persuasive force of arguments. The fact that, unlike before when they were issued in the form of short and simple unequivocal sentences, the opinions are nowadays being extensively reasoned, does not change their basic nature. Such opinions have no connection with the facts of a case which are necessary for the understanding, interpretation and definition of the scope of the legal position contained therein. With such opinions, the VS 'is assuming

[52] *cf* A Galič, 'Za reformo revizije v pravdnem postopku' [In Favour of a Reform of the Appeal to the Supreme Court in the Civil Procedure] (2007) 43 *Pravna praksa* 26.
[53] See Decision No U-I-302/09, Up-1472/09, U-I-139/10, Up-748/10 of 12 May 2011, Official Gazette RS, No 43/2011 and the critique thereof in A Galič, 'Does a Decision of the Supreme Court Leave to Appeal Need to Contain reasons?' in J Adolphsen et al (eds), *Festschrift für Peter Gottwald zum 70. Geburtstag* (CH Beck, 2014) 181 ff.

the position somewhere between the legislature and a legal scholar'.[54] It performs a quasi-legislative function that is very controversial in terms of separation of powers.[55]

The procedure for the adoption of such opinions is also problematic. All the members of the plenary session of the VS decide on the adoption of the proposed opinion. The VS plenary is composed of all VS judges, even those who belong to the section where the proposed opinion will not be used. Thus, for example, a majority that will never use a criminal law opinion can simply outvote the judges of the Criminal Law Section. Such practice is even more controversial as it does not conform to the Rules of Procedure of the Plenary Session of the VS. These provide that in the event that the legal opinion (of principle) does not secure a majority, and there is no counter-proposal made at the plenary session, the President of the VS nominates a judge who prepares a counter-proposal that is in general voted on at the next plenary session. If even then no proposal secures a majority, the President of the VS forms a group with the task of preparing a coordinated proposal of a legal opinion.[56] Since these mechanisms, intended to mitigate the rigidity of the body responsible for the harmonised case law of the Chambers of the VS, are obviously not used in practice, a draft opinion, if it is assumed that it will not secure a majority at the plenary session, is not even placed on the agenda of such a session. It is thus not surprising that no opinions are eventually adopted and that the different sections continue to have different views on the same issues.

Instances in which the VS was unable to harmonise its case law are (or at least were in the past) quite common (for example on the issue of interest rates, or on counting the deadlines during the court vacations). In recent years, the 'dispute' regarding the procedural entitlements of a *procura* representative of a company stands out. Whereas the Commercial Law Section represents the position that the *procura* representative is also entitled to perform procedural acts,[57] the Civil, Social and Labour, and Administrative Law Sections are of the opposite opinion.[58] The attempt to harmonise the interpretation of this controversial statutory provision by a legal opinion (of principle) was unsuccessful. Although the interpretation of the law is a constitutional competence of the courts, headed by the VS, it is understandable (although from a constitutional perspective very controversial) that they, due to the apparent inability to carry out this constitutional task in this case, call for the legislature to resolve the dilemma

> [by] either adopting a clear statutory definition of the notions of legal capacity and legal personality or by a clear statutory provision on the scope of the *procura* power of attorney by which the legislature would have expressly stated whether a *procura* representative

---

[54] *cf* A Galič in L Ude, 'Reforma pravnih sredstev v pravdnem postopku' [Reform of Legal Remedies in the Civil Procedure] (2002) 6–7 *Podjetje in delo* 1584.

[55] M Bobek, 'Quantity or Quality? Reassessing the Role of Supreme Jurisdictions in Central Europe' (2009) 45 *The American Journal of Comparative Law* 33.

[56] Art 25, § 6 of the Rules of Procedure of the VS.

[57] eg III Ips 229/2008 of 13 October 2009.

[58] eg VIII Ips 448/2007 of 20 April 2009 or X Ips 440/2007 of 26 March 2009.

is entitled to perform procedural acts and granting the power of attorney for such acts or not.[59]

Synchronous divergence of the case law of the body whose constitutional duty it is to ensure its harmonisation can have fatal consequences for equality before the law, legal certainty, trust in the law and the functioning of the judiciary as a whole. Finally, the fact that the same chamber of the VS adopted two diametrically opposite legal positions on the same day (23 August 2012) regarding the same legal issue (when the return of property must be exceptionally allowed pursuant to the provisions of the Denationalization Act despite the expiry of the deadline determined in the first paragraph of Article 64 of the Denationalization Act)[60] is very telling with regard to the difficulties the VS has in securing the coherence and the predictability of the case law.

C. The Absence of a Discourse

As in most former socialist states, legal studies in Slovenia were also conceived in an affirmative, apologetic, descriptive and repetitive manner. A good lawyer was the one who has memorised the law. She or he has mastered the simple mental operations of a static interpretation of the law. In contrast, somebody who doubted, thought critically, argued and questioned more than he or she answered would not fall into this category. It was believed that law is the study for those who have difficulty with mathematics.[61]

All this is concisely summarised in the statement of one of our German colleagues: 'Your lawyers know the statutes and regulations, but they do not understand the law.'[62] We may observe a similar situation at the state law examinations. The candidates typically do not have problems with definitions, concepts and demonstrating the capabilities of their memory. Almost all candidates have a well-functioning memory which is what interests the majority of examiners and with which most are content. However, difficulties arise when it is necessary to find a solution to a particular legal issue, when one expects something more from the candidate than just the ability of simple deduction. For example, consider a question regarding the (in)validity of the contract of sale of a body part (for example, a kidney) by which the seller wishes to obtain funds to finance emergency surgery that is vital for the survival of their child (the statute prohibits the sale of human body parts, but allows donations, however only between close relatives and emotionally related persons). The vast majority of candidates state that such a contract

---

[59] See S Ana and K Valant, 'Prokuristova procesnopravna upravičenja' [Procedural Entitlements of the *Procura* Representative] (2011) 23 *Pravna praksa* 8, 9.

[60] See Decisions II Ips 52/2012 and II Ips 181/2012.

[61] *cf* S Rodin, 'Discourse and Authority in European and Post-Communist Legal Culture' (2005) 1 *Croatian Yearbook of European Law* 12; or Kühn (n 39) 133 ff.

[62] See F Emmert, 'Administrative and Court Reform in Central and Eastern Europe' (2003) 3 *European Law Journal* 295.

is invalid and substantiates it by a simple deduction: The general prohibition on the sale of human body parts applies. They do not see a connection between the two contracts, let alone a common basis for both contracts and the purpose of the prohibition on trade with human body parts and the permission of donations.

Also at the judges' schools, the most frequently visited are lectures at which the speakers (usually higher courts' and VS's judges) give concrete answers to participating judges' questions that the latter encountered in open proceedings. Asking for such concrete, casuistic solutions instead for methods and thinking about them is arguably less strenuous and safer at the same time for the participating judges. Incidentally, it is questionable how such public expressions of opinion by judges of higher instances affect their impartiality—but so far that has not disturbed anyone.

D. Reasoning of Judgments (Judicial Opinions)

Another consequence of the legal culture described in this chapter is the impersonal, technically legalistic, cryptic and (therefore) often contradictory writing style in judicial decisions.[63] The style is quite far from the expectation that the reasoning will consolidate the fairness of the trial and render a judgment acceptable also for the party losing the lawsuit.[64] Difficulties with understanding precedents are also very common. A characteristic example of this feature is demonstrated by a recent decision of the US,[65] in which the US found that the VS had violated the prohibition of arbitrary decision making that flows from Article 22 of the Constitution. The VS based its decision on a previous decision of the US, without however comparing the circumstances of the case at issue with those that the US particularly underlined as decisive within the framework of the earlier case and its argumentation. The VS further failed to explain why the facts of the present case required the reference to the previous decision. Finally, the already outlined troubles with unification of the case law, as well as the use of techniques of legal reasoning other than a simple subsumption formula (weighing, analogy, contextual argument),[66] respect for EU law,[67] are still a typical element within the Slovene judiciary.

E. Duration of Proceedings

Slowness and tendency to delay proceedings are both common features of post-communist judiciaries. They are partly due to the incoherent, unpredictable and

---

[63] See US Decision No Up-270/01 of 19 February 2004, and the legal opinion of the plenary session of the VS of 30 June 2004 (published in the publication Pravna mnenja Vrhovnega sodišča RS [Legal Opinions of the Supreme Court], I/2004, 14–17).

[64] See JM Jacob, *Civil Justice in the Age of Human Rights* (Ashgate, 2007) 87, 88.

[65] Decision No Up-545/11, Up-544/11, of 7 June 2012.

[66] See Galič (n 50) 84.

[67] *cf* US Decision No Up-1056/11 of 21 November 2013.

divergent case law, already discussed above. However, they result also from the judges' (bureaucratic) fear of responsibility for making authoritative decisions, which then translates into a fear of failure before courts of higher resort.

Furthermore, there is an abundance of legal remedies, which is based on the assumption that the decisions of the courts (that is the judiciary as a whole) are not to be trusted. This lack of trust into the finality of judicial decisions was enhanced, until recently, by the simple and uncomplicated access to jurisdictions of higher resort. Legal remedies are mostly conceived of as rights. This results in a large number of disputes and, consequently, an over-abundant and (therefore) unclear corpus of case law that is difficult to manage. If we add to this the accelerating growth of the multitude of legal writing—both domestic and foreign, and case law of the ECtHR and the CJEU that is increasingly difficult to manage—the problems further multiply. Increasing production of information is turning already into data-pollution. It, in fact, overturns its goal and the importance that it has for legal certainty and trust in the law. This entails a universal relativisation (that is already otherwise a characteristic of the law), opens up possibilities for manipulation and deception and increases the chances of unpredictability in judicial decision making. Metaphorically speaking, such data-pollution operates as a department store offering a variety of goods: If one searches carefully and patiently through the shelves, everybody eventually finds something useful for themselves—something that will fit their specific legal interests.[68] At the same time, the inconsistent and unpredictable case law functions as a catalyst of disputes. When the outcome of a dispute is uncertain, litigants decide to proceed, even those for whom it should have been clear in advance that the litigation is pointless, just a waste of time and resources, since they will lose the case anyway.

F. Recruitment

The recruitment methods for judges and human resources policy within the judiciary present a special issue.[69] The judges are recruited mainly from the ranks of advisers to the courts—after their laxness and compatibility with the system are tested—while lawyers outside this circle (for example the excellent advisors of the US) are almost systematically refused. A special quality of the candidate that is repeatedly emphasised in the clichés and platitudes of the opinions issued by the judiciary personnel councils is for example that the candidate is 'co-operative and has a sense of teamwork'—which in other words signifies the candidate's overall laxness regarding general and dominant thought patterns, and sensitivity to the ethics of obedience. Kühn's findings made with respect to the Czech judiciary probably also apply to the Slovene situation: The young candidates have

---

[68] M Taruffo and M La Torre, 'Precedent in Italy' in DN MacCormick and RS Summers (eds), *Interpreting Precedents* (Ashgate, 1997) 186.

[69] See M Bobek, 'The Fortress of Judicial Independence and the Mental Transitions of the Central European Judiciaries' (2008) 14 *European Public Law* 1, 15, 16.

an advantage over the older ones with professional experience gained outside the judiciary. But the latter type of candidates tend to be rejected due to fear that those who would come from the outside would introduce something new, untested and not established.[70] There exists, thus, a fear of the new, fresh, competitive. As suggested by Bobek, young, recent graduates entering into the system can be more easily influenced. This ensures inbreeding and a reproduction of the existing mentality. The entire socialisation, acquisition of values and working habits is therefore done exclusively within the judiciary. This creates a special caste, separate from society, thus generating problems with regard to the representativeness and accountability of the judiciary.[71]

Hungary and Croatia have had similar experiences with restrictions and, in terms of recruitment, an incestuous way of selecting new judges. A judiciary that sets out its own rules, is supposed to control itself and is responsible only to itself, has the tendency of leaning towards oligarchisation. Persons who meet the expectations of the traditional post-socialist (judiciary) elites are nominated to important and high positions in the judicial hierarchy. These are most often persons from the depths of the system. What Uzelac notes with regard to Croatian judges holds very much true also for their Slovene counterparts: Those belonging to judicial oligarchy skilfully integrate themselves into structures of political power.[72]

The recent Draft of the Act Amending the Judicial Service Act[73] is unfortunately further heading into this direction. The Judicial Council would get the statutory authority to determine the uniform criteria for selection of candidates for judicial positions, as well as the criteria for the assessment of the quality of judicial work. Among the uniform criteria for selection and promotion of judges and for assessment of their judicial service are (in addition to work skills and expertise) the personality traits and social skills. It follows from the reasoning of the draft act that the personality traits are for example emotional stability, prudence, ability to self-reflect, reliability and responsibility, taking initiative. Social skills encompass communication skills, conflict resolution skills and the ability to work as part of a team. All of the above is supposed to be evaluated by the Judicial Council. However, since these qualities cannot be established or measured to any reasonable degree, the discretion of the Judicial Council and thus its impact on the recruitment of judges will only be further strengthened. In particular, the notion of 'social skills' can be considered very arbitrarily, also as the laxness regarding general social and dominant political currents, which is fundamentally contrary to judicial integrity. The Amendment to the Judicial Service Act will thus further contribute to the oligarchisation of the Slovene judiciary. As the Judicial Council

---

[70] See Kühn (n 41) 171.
[71] See Bobek (n 69) 15, 16.
[72] See Uzelac (n 39) 395. See also Z Fleck, 'Judicial Independence in Its Environment in Hungary' in J Přibáň, PI Roberts and J Young (eds), *Systems of Justice in Transition. Central European Experiences since 1989* (Ashgate, 2003) 129. In this sense also Bobek (n 69) 12 ff.
[73] EVA 2013-2030-0110.

supports it, it seems as though the Judicial Council is entering its own sins into the Act in order to legitimise them.

V. Conclusion

The principal problem facing the Slovene judiciary is a lack of mental and intellectual independence, lack of free, open and courageous legal (as well as democratic) thought and internal autonomy of judges.[74] Lustration, even if carried out, would be able to neither cleanse the Slovene juridical mind (and foolishness) nor to remove the prevailing authoritarian thought patterns of the old regime. Even a gradual influx of new judges does not significantly alter the legacy of the (pre) dominant corporate and authoritative mindset that was inherited from the totalitarian period. The young, although more educated and legally better informed judicial staff, must subordinate themselves and adapt to the system or the system will suck them dry. They will be either forced to leave or to choose the path of lonely travellers. The *forma mentis* of the Slovene judiciary remains always the same. That also explains why the old regime politicians do not need to make an effort to secure their influence over the judiciary and retain it in the long run. That is why the same politicians are such keen supporters of judicial independence.[75]

The only real and effective lustration of the judiciary is a mental lustration— the one carried out by the US, the ECtHR and the CJEU within their respective case law. These judiciary institutions do not lustrate only the Slovene legal order, they also lustrate the constitutional culture in general, especially in the meaning of affirmation of a culture of argumentation and open multilateral legal dialogue.

One can agree with Gray stating that law consists of the rules laid down by judges. Namely, a statute is, for Gray, not a law, but only a source of law, which becomes law only after it has been interpreted and applied by a court.[76] We can therefore repeat the proposition that 'like judiciary, like law', and in particular, 'like judiciary, like degree of legal development and the rule of law'.

Slovenia has the highest number of judges per 100,000 inhabitants in the EU. The judiciary is therefore a large system in a small country in Slovenia. Consequently, the cultural and ideological thought patterns, views on the status and role of a judge in society, the general expectations for the judicial profession within the judiciary, are changing very slowly. The inertia, rigidity and slow responsiveness may be seen already in the fact that it often takes a long time for the judiciary to

---

[74] See Bobek (n 69) 100–27.

[75] Authors elsewhere have arrived at the same conclusions. *cf* PC Magalhaes, 'The Politics of Judicial Reform in Eastern Europe' (1999) 32 *Comparative Politics* 1, 48; see also B Schönfelder, 'Judicial Independence in Bulgaria: A Tale of Splendour and Misery' (2005) 57 *Europe-Asia Studies* 1, 61–92.

[76] See L Fuller, 'Positivism and Fidelity to Law—a Reply to Professor Hart' (1957) 71 *Harvard Law Review* 633.

respond to certain legislative changes, even when they are as fundamental as the change in the concept of damages for non-pecuniary damage.

Nearly 25 years since the judiciary became a sovereign and independent branch of power, the remnants of the old mentality, based on authoritarian culture, the essence of which is obedience to the authority of power, that is political authorities (once the party, but today also influential groups and networks), or the bare text of the statutory norm, remain. Another problem of the Slovene judiciary is that each public criticism of the judiciary is now viewed by the members of the judiciary as an attack on judicial independence and the rule of law. The judiciary accepts with difficulty that the origin of the requirement for trust in the judiciary is in the responsibility of the judiciary towards the people. Trust in the judiciary is thus above all the responsibility of the judiciary. This is a requirement that is first and foremost addressed to judges, who must earn the public's confidence by their scrupulous, committed and highly professional work, which is something that is outwardly reflected by a culture of argumentation and high professional and personal integrity. The legitimacy of the judiciary is thus to be found in a justifiable, not 'forced', trust in the judiciary.

When a sufficient critical mass of judges is assembled, of judges who possess not only opinions, but firm, clear and coherent convictions of what is right, and who in addition have the courage to implement these convictions, then this critical mass will break through the ossified and institutionally closed mental collectivism. Then, we believe, the US will not have to annul so many arbitrary judgments or judgments that violate human rights; there will not be that many contradictory judgments; then Slovenia will no longer hold the record for the longest duration of judicial disputes, the resolution of which is key for the survival of commercial subjects; and then also the legislature will no longer employ ad hoc (and thus often unconstitutional) solutions, because it will trust the judiciary.

We have no idea when this will happen. We do know, however, that for the reorganisation of the Slovene judiciary mental lustration and the lustration of the judicial awareness are much more important than personal lustration. The case law of the US and the case law of the courts from Luxembourg and Strasbourg contribute significantly to this lustration. All of these judicial instances, which lustrate not only the Slovene legal order, but also the constitutional culture of the population, are however characterised by an authoritative legal culture, meaning a culture of argumentation and open multilateral legal discourse.

7

From a Discourse on 'Communist Legacy' Towards Capacity Building to Better Manage the Rule of Law

BOŠTJAN ZALAR

I. Introduction: The 'Communist Legacy' of the Past?

The key topics discussed in this volume are first, whether the use of text-oriented methods of interpretation by judges in Central and East European (CEE) countries still dominates over policy-oriented methods of interpretation as a result of the so-called communist legacy and, second, whether there is a delay in the impact of EU law and case law of the Court of Justice (ECJ) on domestic jurisprudence. In this chapter, I will not suggest that policy-oriented judicial reasoning as flowing from the practice of the ECJ is a template that national courts should follow in every case and that they should follow it without supplementing it with methods of interpretation that are necessary for the effective implementation of human rights. There are several reasons for this rejection. In legal disputes where there is no EU legal dimension involved, national courts are not obliged to follow the methods of interpretation established by the ECJ's case law. Furthermore, in cases where the highest national courts deal with the interpretative questions concerning EU law, the relationships between the highest national courts and the ECJ are governed by the provision of and case law relating to Article 267(3) of the TFEU (Treaty on the Functioning of the European Union) as to when it is necessary to send an order for a preliminary ruling to the ECJ and how to formulate it. In these cases, the roles, competences and positions of the ECJ and national courts in the overall system of the rule of law differ substantially and their methods of interpretation of the law cannot therefore be examined using the same principles. Only in cases where national courts implement EU law, it is necessary that national judges use (not just policy-oriented, but all) methods of interpretation developed by the

ECJ. However, even these methods are to be followed only as a starting point. They should be further adapted by national courts as to provide for the effective implementation of human rights in individual disputes, because the ECJ has not (yet) developed extensive jurisprudence in this particular regard. The latter argument will be supported by concrete examples of cases decided by the ECJ on preliminary rulings in the fields of asylum and immigration.

It is furthermore clear that even legal formalism may sometimes have strong policy-oriented outcomes. For example, in the *Qurbani* case,[1] the referring German court submitted a request for preliminary ruling concerning the interpretation of Article 31 of the Geneva Convention of 28 July 1951 relating to the Status of Refugees. This provision regulates prohibition of criminal penalties for the illegal entry or presence of asylum seekers and refugees in the territory of the EU. The ECJ rejected the jurisdiction in this case. It simply stated that the request for a preliminary ruling contains no mention of any rule of EU law, which would make a *renvoi* to Article 31 of the Geneva Convention, although Article 14(6) of the Directive 2004/83 makes *renvoi* to Article 31 of the Geneva Convention.

Therefore, in terms of the eventual methodological model that CEE judges should follow, the over-simplified suggestion that judges should apply policy-oriented methods of interpretation more often than text-oriented methods of interpretation would not necessarily lead to an improvement in the rule of law.

However, it is probably the case that critical discussions and evaluations of the policy-making functions of the ECJ are much more developed and frequent in relevant (scientific) literature[2] than critical discussions and empirical studies on the excessive text-oriented legal reasoning of national courts in Member States. For this reason, although the question relating to the text-oriented versus policy-oriented methods of interpretation is not sufficiently specific and detailed, it may certainly be deemed appropriate in terms of time and place.

---

[1] Case C-481/13, *Qurbani*, ECLI:EU:C:2014:2101, para 28.

[2] See, for example, for criticism of judicial activism in case of ECJ: KJ Alter, 'The European Legal System and Domestic Policy. Spillover or Backlash?' (2000) 54 *International Organization* 489; SJ Kenney, 'Beyond Principles and Agents: Seeing Courts as Organizations by Comparing Référendaires at the European Court of Justice and Law Clerks at the US Supreme Court' (2000) 33 *Comparative Political Studies* 593; FW Scharpf, 'The Joint-Decision Trap Revisited' (2006) 44 *Journal of Common Market Studies* 548; J-M Josselin and A Marciano, 'How the Court Made a Federation of the EU' (2007) 2 *Review of International Organizations* 59; R Herzog and L Gerken, 'Stop the European Court of Justice: Competences of Member States are being Undermined: The Increasingly Questionable Judgments from Luxembourg Suggest a Need for a Judicial Watchdog' (2008) *Frankfurter Allgemeine Zeitung* No 210, 8.9.2008, 8 (published in German); FW Scharpf, 'Legitimacy in the Multilevel European Policy' (2009) 37 *Leviathan* 244; KJ Alter, 'The European Court's Political Power: Across Time and Space' and same author, 'Law and Politics in Europe and Beyond' in KJ Alter (ed), *The European Court's Political Power* (Oxford University Press, 2009).

II. Is Central and Eastern Europe a Special Case in Judicial Reasoning?

There are two main streams that may be encountered in discussions relating to text-oriented reasoning and formalism.[3] The first stream assumes that judges in CEE countries predominantly use text-oriented methods of interpretation as a result of the political legacy from the past. The second stream casts some doubts over this statement by asking questions like whether and in what sense formalism can be seen as a distinctive feature of the CEE judicial style, what are the causes of this supposed formalism and whether judicial formalism is a good or a bad thing. Some advocates of the second stream also support the need to apply a rigorous scientific methodology and qualitative empirical research approach that would be based on a thorough evaluation of the case law in order to test eventual presumptions on judicial reasoning and ideology. The second stream is sometimes supported by the clear view that formalism, when properly understood, is often unavoidable and in many cases desirable.

In my view, defining formalism in terms of being good or bad must be linked to a differentiation made between easy, standard and complex legal disputes.[4] Furthermore, formalism should be analysed in conjunction with other elements such as behavioural, attitudinal, institutional and organisational factors. As Judge Richard Posner puts in his book *How Judges Think*, judges are 'all-too-human workers, responding as other workers do to the conditions of the labor market in which they work'.[5] Based on my experiences in judiciary during the last 15 years, I can confirm that behavioural, attitudinal, institutional and organisational factors affect also judges in CEE countries. The most powerful example of such organisational or institutional factors that affect the chosen methods of interpretations in each individual case is a bureaucratically imposed administrative workload for judges[6] and non-professionalised practices of performance measurement of judges in many CEE countries.

Within the second stream of arguments, there is a consideration that keeps being raised, namely that new transnational legal areas, such as international trade law, commercial arbitration, international criminal law and judicial networks are likely

---

[3] See above, chs 2–6.

[4] See, for example, N Soininen, 'Easy Cases and Objective Interpretation' in J Husa and M van Hoecke (eds), *Objectivity in Law and Legal Reasoning* (Hart Publishing, 2013).

[5] R Posner, *How Judges Think* (Harvard University Press, 2008) 7; see in particular pt 1, ch 1 (Nine Theories of Judicial Behaviour) and pt 1, ch 2 (the Judge as a Labour Market Participant) of Posner's book.

[6] See for example, B Zalar, 'Administrative Workload for Judges: A Dangerous Approach to Case-Flow Management' in B Zalar (ed), *Five Challenges for European Courts: The Experiences of German and Slovenian Courts* (Supreme Court of the Republic of Slovenia, Slovenian Association of Judges, 2004) 101–84.

to transform national judicial styles.[7] As regards judicial networks, the early contributions of Anne Mary Slaughter have perhaps initiated great expectations concerning the potential transformative power of judicial networks.[8] However, despite very intense judicial networking, such as is present for example in the field of asylum law, the empirical study of Hélène Lambert and Guy S Goodwin-Gill shows different and quite considerable obstacles to these expected developments concerning the potential for transnational cross-fertilisation. Their study of nine European states shows that judges rarely use each other's decisions within the EU although they all apply the same EU law on asylum and the Geneva Convention.[9] Therefore, different sorts of judicial dialogue or networks in specific fields of law have probably very limited transformative powers. However, judicial networks in the field of international law such as asylum law can be developed into a stronger transformative mechanism on the condition that these networks are supported by the institutional actors of the EU. For example, a recent development in the field of asylum where the European Asylum Support Office (EASO) was established by Regulation No 439/2010 and received a mandate to establish and develop training for judges, shows that judicial networks can lead to the development of a core professional training manual for judges, provided they are institutionally supported by the EU and provided that they are sensibly managed in order to preserve judicial independence. This has considerable potential for transformative power in terms of convergence in the implementation of EU law across all Member States of the EU.

On the side of the first stream of arguments, the discussion in the first part of this volume offers a tentative thesis in relation to the case of Slovenia, namely that text-oriented reasoning adopted by Slovenian judges could be associated with the remains of authoritarian mentality. Based on my experiences in administrative law and on my observations collected in various kinds of legal disputes, I agree that the problem of text-oriented reasoning in Slovenia exists. I nonetheless disagree with the argument that this can be simply explained by some kind of 'authoritarian mentality'.[10] It is worth mentioning that the starting point of the aforementioned thesis was a general distinction between the common law and civil law tradition which was centred on a reference to Justice Oliver Wendell Holmes—his famous saying from the nineteenth century that 'the life of the law has not been logic: it has been experience.'[11] With this starting point, Justice Zobec developed the argument that unlike civil law, common law is by its very nature resistant to

---

[7] See above, ch 2.

[8] A-M Slaughter, 'A Typology of Transjudicial Communication' (1994) 29 *University of Richmond Law Review* 99; A-M Slaughter, 'The Real New World Order' (1997) *Foreign Affairs* 183.

[9] GS Goodwin-Gill and H Lambert (eds), *The Limits of Transnational Law: Refugee Law, Policy Harmonization and Judicial Dialogue in the European Union* (Cambridge University Press, 2010).

[10] As an example of authoritarian mentality Justice Zobec and J Letnar Černič (see above, ch 6) give abstract legal opinions that have been adopted by the plenary of the Supreme Court. These opinions are binding on all judges of the Supreme Court, although these opinions do not stem from specific cases.

[11] See the opening sentence of the Holmes's *Common Law* (1881) and his later article, 'The Path of the Law' (1897) 10 *Harvard Law Review* 457.

positivism. Whereas a judge in a common law system is expected to solve a dispute fairly, intelligently and reasonably, the traditional paradigm of judges in the civil law system is a mentally simple subsumption formula, derived from the ideological assumption that the legislature has already solved the dispute on an abstract level.

I do not see the difference between common law and civil law to be so striking. A different understanding of the so called pragmatic legalism of Justice Holmes can be found in Posner's book *How Judges Think* and in the concurring opinion of Justice Brandeis in the *Ashwander* case.[12] Posner indicates that Justice Holmes used the aforementioned expression on law as being a matter of experience in order to

> reject the orthodox notion that judges could decide difficult cases by a process very similar to logical deduction from premises given by authoritative legal texts, or by unquestioned universal principles that inspire and subsume those texts (natural law).[13]

On this occasion, I can even tentatively say that the modern and orthodox judicial practice of legalism, which goes against policy-oriented judicial reasoning in matters pertaining to the judicial review of the constitutionality of legislative acts, has its origins in the common law tradition of the US Supreme Court, specifically in the concurring opinion of Justice Brandeis in the *Ashwander* case. Brandeis argued 'the most important thing we [judges] do is not to do.' This should hold for Justice Brandeis also in cases of constitutional litigation with only two exceptions: privacy and freedom of expression.[14]

However, it would be a mistake to think that Brandeis' judicial approach of 'doing nothing' can only be linked to textual positivism. It may also be associated with the policy-oriented method of interpretation. A good example of this is an interpretation of the ECJ in the case of *Diouf*,[15] which is a very relevant judgment for the further development of the rule of law in the EU. The decision concerned the access to effective judicial protection. Its consequences are not limited just to the field of asylum law. Despite the fact that language of Article 47 of the EU Charter of Fundamental Rights is clear in the sense that it regulates the 'right' to an effective remedy, the ECJ in the *Diouf* judgment transformed it into a general 'principle'.[16]

The consequences of this transformation are substantial, since Article 52(3) of the Charter states that

> the provisions of this Charter which contain principles may be implemented by legislative and executive acts taken by institutions … of the Union, and by acts of Member

---

[12] *Ashwander v Tennessee Valley Authority*, 297 US 288 (1936).

[13] Above (n 5) 232.

[14] S Goldstein, 'The Rule of Law vs The Rule of Judges: A Brandeisian Solution' in S Shetreet and C Forsyth (eds), *The Culture of Judicial Independence* (Martinus Nijhoff Publishers, 2012) 127.

[15] Case C-69/10, *Diouf*, ECLI:EU:C:2011:524.

[16] In paras 28, 35, 48, 50, 69 of the Diouf judgment the ECJ uses the term 'principle'. In contrast to these, in some paras (35, 36 and 64) the ECJ also uses the term 'right' to an effective remedy.

States when they are implementing Union law, in the exercise of their respective powers. They shall be judicially cognisable only in the interpretation of such acts and in the ruling on their legality.[17]

By declaring the right to a judicial remedy to be a 'principle' instead of a 'right', and despite the clear wording of the Charter to the contrary, the ECJ adopted the aforementioned 'doing nothing' approach. The ECJ gave a clear signal to the whole of the European Union in the sense that it will give a considerable freedom of choice to the EU legislator to regulate effective judicial protection specifically in each field of EU law. This interpretation goes against another aspect of the wording of Article 47(1) of the Charter which gives everyone the right to an effective legal remedy in compliance with the conditions laid down 'in this Article' and not in compliance with conditions laid down in secondary law. With such interpretation, which is clearly not based on a text-oriented method but on the policy-oriented method of interpretation, the ECJ precluded any potential positive judicial activism in relation to effective judicial protection, which is one of the paramount components of the rule of law.

This example demonstrates that the judicial approach of 'doing nothing' can also be linked to a policy-oriented method of interpretation and not solely to a text-oriented method of interpretation. In fact, I see the main problem with exaggerated text-oriented methods to be closely related to adjudication on fundamental rights. Namely, in the last 13 years I have actively participated as an invited speaker or trainer at 85 seminars, conferences and training events for judges (and also partly for public prosecutors and other lawyers) at all continents, except Australia. Around 2,400 participants attended those training sessions or conferences (30 per cent of whom were judges or lawyers from Slovenia). Based on this experience, I can say that textual positivism is a problematic issue in cases where judges involved in complex disputes choose not to apply the general principles of constitutional law, international law, EU law and ECtHR (European Court of Human Rights) case law.[18] However, textualism is not exclusive to CEE judges.

This fact can be confirmed by observing the case-law of the ECJ in light of the question as to what interpretative power has been given by the ECJ to the fundamental rights from the primary EU law in comparison to the provisions from the secondary EU law. Is it correct to say that the Charter of Fundamental Rights of the EU (the Charter), being EU primary (and fundamental) law, is placed at the top of the pyramid as regards legal interpretation and argumentation, that is superior to secondary law? No, it is not. Based on the interpretation of the ECJ in

---

[17] Under the Article 51(1) of the Charter rights shall be respected, while principles shall be observed.

[18] This problem has been acknowledged already in 2006 in the Opinion no 9 of the Consultative Council of European Judges (CCJE) for the attention of the Committee of Ministers of the Council of Europe on the role of national judges in ensuring an effective application of international and European law (Strasbourg, 10 November 2006). The opinion was not limited to the situation in the Central and East European countries.

the already mentioned case of *Diouf*,[19] it may be concluded that secondary law will be more important than primary law, even in relation to the right to an effective legal remedy and a fair trial. It is true that in the field of asylum law, the Charter is frequently referred to in the judgments of the ECJ. However, in most cases, mention is only made of the Charter in the part of the judgment where the ECJ states its preliminary observations. Furthermore, in the majority of cases, the Charter is mentioned because the reference to the Charter is made in the preamble of the relevant secondary law. However, apart from that, no special interpretative power is given to the Charter in those cases. Exceptions exist in cases where the ECtHR has previously developed case law on human rights protection on a given legal issue.[20]

The situation in other fields of EU law is similar to that in asylum law.[21] For example, in preliminary rulings concerning detention of illegal immigrants, the Charter is not even mentioned,[22] although all these cases refer to the right to personal freedom in Article 6 of the Charter. The only exception in the field of the detention of illegal immigrants is the case of *Mahdi*. In this case, however, the ECJ used Articles 6 and 47 of the Charter (under point 1 of the operative part of the judgment) only for stating that the detention order must be 'in the form of a written measure that includes the reasons in fact and in law'.[23] For the other two important elements under points 2 and 3 of the operative part of the *Mahdi* judgment, that also relate to judicial supervision, the grounds for detention and the proportionality principle, the ECJ did not make any reference to the Charter. Such weak use of interpretative methods that would aim at effective implementation of human rights in the case law of the ECJ can be partly explained by the different roles that the courts of the Member States and the ECJ play in the protection of human rights. In the aforementioned judgments in the field of asylum and immigration, the ECJ gives clear indications to the national courts that it is the responsibility of the courts of the Member States to establish, in full compliance with their obligations arising from international law and EU law, the grounds on which

---

[19] Above (n 15).

[20] See, for example, Case C-411/10 and C-493/10 *NS and ME* ECLI:EU:C:2011:865; Case C-179/11, *Cimade*, ECLI:EU:C:2012:594; Case C-71/11 and C-99/11, *Y and Z*, ECLI:EU:C:2012:518.

[21] See, for example, cases where the protection of human rights from the Charter played a significant role in the decisions of the CJEU due to the more or less visible influences of the case law of the ECtHR: Case C-400/10 PPU *J McB*, ECLI:EU:C:2010:582; Cases C-92/09 and C-93/09 *Volker und Markus Schecke*, ECLI:EU:C:2010:662; Case C-279/09, *DEB*, ECLI:EU:C:2010:811; Cases C-293/12 and C-594/12 *Digital Rights Ireland Ltd*, ECLI:EU:C:2014:238; Case C-131/12, *Google Spain*, ECLI:EU:C:2014:317.

[22] See Case C-357/09 PPU, *Kadzoev*, ECLI:EU:C:2009:741; Case C-61/11 PPU, *El Dridi*, ECLI:EU:C:2011:268; Case C-329/11, *Achughbabian*, ECLI:EU:C:2011:807; Case C-430/11, *Sagor*, ECLI:EU:C:2012:777; Case C-534/11, *Arslan*, ECLI:EU:C:2013:343; Case C-474/13, *Pham*, ECLI:EU:C:2014:2096; Case C-383/13 PPU, *MG and NR*, ECLI:EU:C:2013:533.

[23] Case C-146/14 PPU *Mahdi*, ECLI:EU:C:2014:1320. In the Case C-383/13 PPU, *MG and NR* (n 22), the ECJ referred to the right to be heard, the right to defence and the right to access to the file, but did not make any reference to the specific provision from the Charter.

an asylum seeker may be detained or kept in detention.[24] It is up to the referring court to examine whether the refusal of the right of residence undermines the right to respect for private and family life from Article 7 of the Charter.[25] It is furthermore the duty of the Member States to interpret and apply EU secondary law in a manner which is consistent with the fundamental rights protected by the EU legal order or with the other general principles of EU law.[26] Equally, when for example a person is refused to cross the border, it is for the referring court to ascertain whether the refusal to grant the claimant the right to bring his claims before the court infringes the rights provided for in Article 47 of the Charter.[27]

Therefore, it is incorrect and particularly risky to state in general terms that policy-oriented methods of interpretation, such as the methods of interpretation frequently employed by the ECJ, as opposed to text-oriented methods of interpretation, are better or worse for the effective judicial protection of human rights. The methods of interpretation are merely tools to be used for proper adjudication and are not goals as such. The goal should be the effective judicial protection of human rights in individual cases.

III. Different (Mis)Conceptions on Judicial Self-Government

Judicial 'self-government' is another theme that often arises in the discussions of CEE judiciaries and their reform. András Sajo and Vera Losonci suggested that the

> introduction of judicial self-government in a situation of transition does not entail anything other than the preservation of the judiciary as it was established by the undemocratic communist authorities.[28]

It is worth comparing this finding with the empirical study of researchers from Bologna University, Carlo Guarnieri and Daniela Piana, who discovered in their empirical analysis that between 1998 and 2007, in spite of the strong pressure exerted by the EU[29] in order to strengthen judicial independence, the rule of law

---

[24] *Arslan* (n 22), para 56.

[25] Case C-256/11, *Dereci* ECLI:EU:C:2011:734, para 72.

[26] *NS and ME* (n 20), paras 77 and 99.

[27] Case C-23/12, *Zakaria* ECLI:EU:C:2013:24, para 40.

[28] A Sajo and AV Losonci, 'Rule by Law in the East Central Europe: Is the Emperor's New Suit a Straightjacket?' in D Greenberg, N Katz, MB Oliviero and SC Wheatley (eds), *Constitutionalism and Democracy—Transition in the Contemporary World* (Oxford University Press, 1993) 322.

[29] In my opinion this includes efforts made by the relevant institutions of the Council of Europe and, among them, special importance must be ascribed to the opinions of the Consultative Council of European Judges for the attention of the Committee of Ministers (eg Opinion no 1 from 2001 on the standards concerning the independence of the judiciary and the irremovability of judges, and Opinion no 10 from 2007 on Councils for Judiciary in the service of society) for the establishment of independent judicial councils in CEE countries as an important feature of judicial self-governance.

index scores in CEE countries remained more or less stagnant.[30] Declines in rule of law scores have been identified in Poland, Hungary and the Czech Republic. Slovenia, Slovakia and Romania had stable rule of law index scores, whereas Estonia and Latvia have improved in this regard, and Bulgaria and Lithuania too, but to a lesser degree. Estonia, which experienced a lower level of judicial independence (which includes the element of self-government of judiciary), has the highest rule of law index score. However, like Estonia, this was also the case with Sweden.[31] In my opinion, this does not mean that the efforts made to strengthen judicial independence are bad for the rule of law. This only means that institutional arrangements put in place for judicial independence should be accompanied by the development of professionalised court management practices such as case-flow management, better human resource management within the judiciary, a knowledge management system and reliable measurement of the performance of courts that would properly address demands for the public accountability of the judiciary.

For example, in their chapter, Justice Zobec and J Letnar Černič[32] referred to several relevant issues in judicial self-government that should be improved. They refer to the so called 'bureaucratic fear' held by Slovenian judges that their judgments will be overturned by a higher court. Indeed, this is an empirically tested problem experienced in the CEE judiciaries that was highlighted in the *Kiev Recommendations on Judicial Independence* from 2008. The authors of these recommendations were the Organization for Security and Cooperation in Europe and the Max Planck Institute's Minerva Research Group. Their findings were especially relevant for CEE because the performance of judges in these countries is evaluated through quantitative indicators, whereas the qualitative indicators are incorrectly measured solely using rates of reversal calculations.[33]

The next important issue relating to (mis)conceptions regarding judicial self-government, which had also been raised by the aforementioned commentators, are critical remarks concerning the judicial human resources policy. I am not sufficiently informed to be able to share the view stated that the main problem with human resources policy in Slovenia is that it serves 'post-socialist (judiciary) elites'. The main problem with human resources mismanagement as I see it, which not only affects the judiciary but the whole public sector, has (probably) its origins in the strong egalitarian syndrome in general in Slovenian society. The problem is that individuals in the public sector compete where they should cooperate. Conversely, the systems for the promotion and selection of experts in the public sector

---

[30] The state of the rule of law in Europe has been assessed through the index provided by the World Government Indicators (WGI) of the World Bank—see C Guarnieri and D Piana, 'Judicial Independence and the Rule of Law: Exploring the European Experience' in S Setreet and C Forsyth (eds), *The Culture of Judicial Independence* (Martinus Nijhoff Publishers, 2012) 118.

[31] ibid, 121–22.

[32] See above, ch 6.

[33] Kiev Recommendations on Judicial Independence, organised by OSCE (Office for Democratic Institutions and Human Rights) and Max Planck Minerva Research Group on Judicial independence, Appendix IX, in Shetreet and Forsyth (n 30) 609, 615.

(including judges) do not support fair competition between the candidates based on meritocratic principles, where open and transparent competition would be required. Furthermore, there are substantial differences in the (mis)conceptions as to what constitutes a (high) quality judiciary, the quality of a particular court and the quality of performance of the judicial service provided by an individual judge. As a result, the relevant actors in the judiciary are unable to properly reward good judicial performances or to sanction or to address problems related to poor judicial performances—except that, in the egalitarian sense, the prevailing perception seems to be that both aforementioned extremes should be forced together as much as possible.

Thus, in Slovenia we have not yet been able to develop the counterpart or the twin principle to judicial independence, which is judicial accountability. This would mean public accountability for the judiciary in the sense that judicial leadership (presidents of courts, personal councils in courts and the Judicial Council) develops a systemic and sustainable model of quality management.[34] As a result, there is generally a low level of trust within Slovenian society, few opportunities and no real prospects for innovative development outside isolated or particular projects.[35]

I believe that the recent developments within the European Network of Councils for the Judiciary (ENCJ) that focus on reconceptualisation of judicial self-government by searching for a better balance between the independence and accountability of the judiciary, represent a good starting point for further systemic developments of the concept of the quality of justice in national judicial systems in Europe.[36] Furthermore, recent developments within the EU Commission and the Council concerning the establishment of some of the indicators for measuring the rule of law could also be promising.[37]

IV. To what Extent Should Empirical Methodology Examine (the Quality of) Judicial Reasoning?

Another element discussed in the chapters relating to judicial reasoning and judicial ideology is empirical evaluation of judicial performance and reasoning. Rafał

---

[34] For the early work on the concept of judicial accountability, see M Cappelletti, 'Who Watches the Watchmen? A Comparative Study on Judicial Responsibility' (1983) 31 *American Journal of Comparative Law* 1.

[35] It needs to be mentioned that, in the recent past, recognition has been made of two specific innovative projects in the Slovenian judiciary by the competition of the European Commission for Efficiency and Justice ('Crystal Scales of Justice'). These were an award presented to the 'Pilot Project on Accelerated Litigation and Court-Annexed Mediation' of the Ljubljana District Court in 2003 and a special mention in 2010 for the 'Automated System for the Enforcement of Authentic Documents' developed by the Supreme Court of the Republic of Slovenia.

[36] See European Network of Councils for the Judiciary, 'Independence and Accountability of the Judiciary', ENCJ Report 2013–2014, ENCJ Project 2013–2014, adopted in Rome on 13 June 2014.

[37] Communication from the Commission to the European Parliament and the Council: A New EU Framework to Strengthen the Rule of Law, Brussels, 19 March 2014 COM (2014) 158 final/2.

Mańko empirically examines the case law of the Polish *Sąd Najwyższy* (SN) in relation to a very specific area of private law—unfair terms in consumer contracts.[38] In case of empirical studies on judicial reasoning, it is of crucial importance that the researcher provides convincing reasons for choosing a particular area of law, together with reasons for selecting a particular methodology in relation to a quantitative and qualitative assessment of the judicial reasoning applied, and that she or he defines clearly research questions.

The question asked by Mańko relates to the impact of ECJ case law on the SN. Among the impact indicators that Mańko uses are the numbers of references to directives and to the case law of the ECJ. No doubt, this is a relevant quantitative indicator of the impact of the ECJ on the SN. It can, nonetheless, provide only a very general picture. In my opinion, quantitative indicators for describing a situation should always be combined with a qualitative assessment on a case-by-case basis. This is because the objective of the empirical analysis is the judicial reasoning in a specific case, and each instance of judicial reasoning depends on the specific factual and legal circumstances at hand. For example, scholars in Europe sometimes join the EU Commission in putting forward an argument concerning the rise in the numbers of cases where the ECJ cites the Charter.[39] However, this may be a misleading observation since a qualitative examination of ECJ judgments in the field of asylum shows that the importance usually ascribed to the text of the Charter or its interpretation in judgments on preliminary rulings is surprisingly insignificant despite the fact that the ECJ cites the Charter with increasing frequency.[40]

Mańko's empirical study does not stop, quite rightly, at examining quantitative indicators only in terms of the number of references to EU secondary law and the case law of the ECJ. His in-depth assessment of judicial reasoning is based on a thorough qualitative analysis of six judgments from the standpoint of a proper application of EU law. However, what would be interesting to know for the purpose of eventual future policy formation within the court management (broadly speaking) is whether the real problem is the non-application of EU law standards as a result of a lack of knowledge, or whether the real problem is excessive text-oriented reasoning, which is alleged to be embedded in the legal tradition of the particular judiciary. I take the view that besides the need to further encourage the development of a qualitative and critical evaluation of judgments on the proper

---

[38] See above, ch 4.

[39] See, for example, Report of the Commission to the European Parliament, the Council, the European Economic and Social Committee and the Committee of the Regions on the Application of the EU Charter of Fundamental Rights (2011 Report, Brussels, 16.4.2012, COM (2012) 169 final); E Guild, S Carrera, L den Hertog and J Parkin, *Implementation of the EU Charter of Fundamental Rights and its Impact on EU Home Affairs Agencies* (Directorate General for Internal Policies, Policy Department, Citizen's Rights and Constitutional Affairs, 2011).

[40] For more on this, see B Zalar, 'Basic Values, Judicial Dialogues and the Rule of Law in the Light of the Charter of Fundamental Rights of the European Union: Judges Playing by the Rules of the Game' (2013) 14 *ERA Forum* 319–33. See also the argument on 'strategic formalism' or the so-called 'pseudo judicial formalism' in the contribution of Matczak, Bencze and Kühn, above ch 3.

application of EU law, commentators should search for further answers concerning the particular attitudes of judges in judicial reasoning, using the empirical method indicated in the conclusion of his chapter. There, Mańko makes reference to the findings of the interviews conducted by Urszula Jaremba on Polish judges concerning the attitudes of Polish (civil) judges towards the application of EU law, but the key question still remains unanswered: Why in certain judgments of the SN is the 'transformative power' of the EU law evident, but not in other, similar cases? Is this perhaps owing to the personal professional interests, knowledge and/ or work ethics of each judge?

A further interesting observation is that a rise in the citations of the SN's own case law coincided with the decline (and eventual disappearance) of references to ECJ case law.[41] Here, one could attempt to defend the SN because, as Gráinne de Búrca discovered, three years after the EU Charter came into force, it is clear that the ECJ is referring even less now to the ECHR than it did before, and even more rarely to the case law of the ECtHR.[42]

The chapter by Marcin Matczak, Matyas Bencze and Zdenek Kühn[43] takes, to some extent, a comparable empirical approach to the chapter of Rafał Mańko. The former is, however, more ambitious since it examines and produces conclusions for administrative case law (900 judgments in complex cases) in business disputes in the period between 2005 and 2013 in three countries: Hungary, the Czech Republic and Poland. The authors wished to check whether their findings from 2010 regarding the delay in the response of judges to the then looming EU accession during the period between 1999 and 2004 still hold true or not. While it seems that the authors attempted avoiding the qualitative assessment of the examined case law for Poland and Hungary, the important part of the evaluation of the case law of the Czech *Nejvyšší správní soud*, taking judgments since 2007 into account, deals with quality assessment, too. The authors are obviously aware of the drawbacks of a purely quantitative analysis since they warn that frequent references to EU law can be a sign of a strategic formalism, which means that judges may attempt to present their controversial (arbitrary) decision as a logical deduction stemming from the written law or that a new type of legal argument serves as 'ornaments' or 'decorum' in the reasoning of the judgment.

---

[41] The research paper of Matczak, Bencze and Kühn confirms this finding for the period after 2010 or 2011 when the so-called new wave of formalism was identified under which the argumentation of Polish Supreme Court is becoming more self-referential.

[42] G de Búrca, 'After the EU Charter of Fundamental Rights: The Court of Justice as a Human Rights Adjudicator?' (2013) New York University School of Law, Public Law & Legal Theory Research Paper Series, Working paper no 13-51, 16. In this context of judicial dialogue between the highest national and European courts, Advocate General Villalón uses Schopenhauer's hedgehog dilemma in order to describe 'a situation in which a group of hedgehogs seek to become close to one another in order to share heat during cold weather, while at the same time having to remain apart, as they cannot avoid hurting one another with their quills' (P Cruz Villalón, 'Rights in Europe: The Crowded House' (2012) Working paper 01/2012, King's College London, Centre of European Law 5.

[43] See above, ch 3.

In my opinion, apart from the methodological issues,[44] the crucial issue in empirical studies relating to judicial reasoning is the extent to which the researchers should carry out only an empirical examination of judgments, or whether this ought to be complemented also by a thorough evaluation of the quality of judgments from the standpoint of a proper application of (European) law. I am convinced that, in examining the excessively text-oriented judicial reasoning of judges in CEE countries, the dual approach is preferable, that is the quantitative approach should be checked by the qualitative one. Furthermore, researchers should compare various sets as much as possible, connecting the evaluation of national courts' cases with for example, a critical assessment of the policy-oriented judicial reasoning of the ECJ. As stated by Andreas Grimmel: 'We cannot judge the judges for the interests we think they might have, or for the non-testable belief in a political judicial activism—at least not in the context of science.' In this context, Grimmel cites A Arnull[45] who claims that 'the allegation of undue activism can only be tested by a close examination of the legal arguments advanced by the Court in support of its decisions'. Grimmel adds that 'integration through law does not depend on the fact that the ECJ developed this or that law in a certain leading case, but how it developed it, and if it is consistent and coherent with the context of European law'.[46]

However, apart from the section of their chapter in which Matczak, Bencze and Kühn open a theoretical debate on the qualitative analysis of judicial reasoning by making a distinction between 'honest and strategic or pseudo judicial formalism', the authors further shift the discussion from the problem of text-oriented judicial reasoning as being considered a problem per se and a legacy of communism to the problem of measuring the rule of law, which requires judges to explain in a plausible and detailed manner why they decided a case in a certain way.

V. Conclusion: Towards Professionalised Quality Management in Judiciaries

At the end of their contribution, Matczak, Bencze and Kühn ask which 'adjudicative style' serves better to enforce the rule of law. They say that this would always

---

[44] As a highly relevant methodological tool for empirical examination of the quality of judicial reasoning I would certainly recommend also the qualitative analyses of judgments and decisions of the ECtHR against particular Contracting State and qualitative analyses of judgments and decisions of the constitutional courts in procedures on constitutional complaints against the judgments of the highest national courts.

[45] Arnull's citation is taken from his book: *The European Union and its Court of Justice* 2nd edn (Oxford University Press, 2006).

[46] A Grimmel, 'Judicial Interpretation or Judicial Activism?: The Legacy of Rationalism in the Studies of the European Court of Justice' (2010) Center for European Studies Working Paper Series 176, Harvard University, 26–27.

depend on the type of case to be decided. I agree that the relevant question is which 'adjudicative style' better serves the rule of law. However, a selection of the methods for the interpretation of law in a particular case is rarely a matter of 'adjudicative style'. It is rather a matter of the independent and correct application of law.[47] Thus, a policy-oriented style of judicial reasoning is not an independent variable. Instead, it is one of the methods of interpretation, the relevance of which depends on the particular circumstances of the case and the jurisdiction in question.

In all the contributions presented in the previous chapters of this volume I was able to find the starting elements in better defining the standards for judicial thinking and reasoning. I would certainly suggest to policy makers within the judiciaries to concentrate on better training—including the methods of interpretation and the principles of application of EU law; better human resource management (this should include a rigorous evaluation of candidates in promotion procedures); improved case-flow (and workload) management—including a balance between the values of timeliness and quality of adjudication; a better system for measuring the performance of judges; further support for judicial networks; better information technology; the importance of having a combination of younger and older judges at the highest judicial levels in CEE countries. Since EU legal developments have already been influenced to some extent by the global concept of the 'multi-door courthouse',[48] where the adjudicative role of the courts is becoming accompanied by a facilitative role (mediation, conciliation and other forms of alternative dispute resolution) and an advisory role (early neutral evaluation) of the courts, which also forms part of modern court management, it remains to be seen as to how researchers in Europe will examine judicial 'reasoning and ideology' or even the 'mentality' of judges in relation to these new and important judicial roles.

[47] In the words of Lord Justice Bingham in the famous Belmarsh case, 'the function of independent judges charged to interpret and apply the law is universally recognized as a cardinal feature of the modern democratic state, a cornerstone of the rule of law' (*A and others v Secretary of State for the Home Department* [2005] 2 WLR 87, p 135, paras 86, 87).

[48] This concept was first articulated in the USA in 1976 by Professor Frank EA Sanders from the Harvard Law School at a conference convened by Chief Justice Warren Burger to address problems faced by judges in the administration of justice (G Kessier and LJ Finkelstein, 'The Evolution of a Multi-Door Courthouse' (1988) 37 *The Catholic University Law Review* 577).

Part II

Institutions and Procedures

8

'Euro-products' and Institutional Reform in Central and Eastern Europe: A Critical Study in Judicial Councils

MICHAL BOBEK AND DAVID KOSAŘ

I. Introduction

Judicial independence appears on most laundry lists of all bodies or institutions engaged with the rule of law.[1] It is considered an unqualified public good. As a result, both European organisations, the European Union as well as the Council of Europe, jointly encouraged legal and judicial reforms in Central and Eastern Europe (CEE), together with other international players. Moreover, the European Union included judicial independence among its core requirements for the accession countries. Thus, institution-building in the area of the judiciary and its administration in the pre-accession CEE countries and in some of the new Member States has been happening under a distinct European influence.

How to achieve judicial independence tends to be frequently reduced, however, to just one aspect: The institutional reform. Furthermore, the institutional reform itself has been typically limited to promoting one particular model of court administration: The Judicial Council model. The model has been suggested as the universal and 'right' solution that should eradicate the vices of previous models, in particular the administration of courts by a Ministry of Justice. The new Judicial Council model ought to enhance judicial independence. It should insulate the judiciary from political tumult. It should also improve the overall performance of judges.

The new model thus came with the promise of an independent, better functioning judiciary. The main argument of this chapter is that in transition countries in the

---

[1] This chapter is a revised version of an article previously published under the title 'Global Solutions, Local Damages: A Critical Study in Judicial Councils in Central and Eastern Europe' (2014) 15(7) *German Law Journal* 171.

CEE, the universally promoted 'Euro-model' of the court administration in the form of a Judicial Council has not lived up to that promise. It did not deliver the goods it was supposed to. Even more: In a number of countries in the region, the situation has been made worse following the establishment of a Judicial Council. The new institution typically halted further reforms of the judiciary and soon negated the values in the name of which it has been put in place. This evolution seriously questions not only the further promotion of the Judicial Council model elsewhere in the world, but also, to some extent, the process of 'Europeanisation' itself.

The argument of this chapter proceeds as follows. Sections II and III critically examine how European and international 'soft standard', which were later pushed onto the CEE transition countries, emerged. Who and how designed these standards? Section IV suggests why in the end the Judicial Council model prevailed over all competing alternatives of court administration in Europe, and why it has been promoted by the European actors. Section V analyses the normative shortcomings of such a 'European' model in terms of democracy and legitimacy. Section VI shows with which incentives and by which actors has the Judicial Council model been in fact imposed onto most of the CEE countries in the course of their transition. Sections VII and VIII stand in contrast to each other: Section VII outlines what outcomes the Judicial Council model was supposed to deliver, while section VIII looks at what it in fact delivered and how it has been operating in the CEE states in reality. Conclusions in section IX are humble. It is suggested that when transforming judiciaries, it is essential to focus first on personal renewal and small scale function-related court reforms than on grand schemes of irreversible and constitutionally entrenched institutional designs. Making a post-totalitarian judiciary a self-administrative body before any genuine internal change and renewal has taken place may result in establishing an institutionally independent judiciary without many individually independent judges in it.[2]

II. How do European Standards of Court Administration Emerge?

Where do European standards with respect to the 'proper' way of administering courts come from? Two questions are essential in this respect: Who drafts these standards and according to what processes? The answer to the former question is straightforward: It is typically judges themselves. The answer to the latter question is more complicated. The processes of creating European or international

---

[2] Contrast Ferejohn who referred to the US judiciary as '[the] system of independent judges within a dependent judiciary': J Ferejohn, 'Independent Judges, Dependent Judiciary: Explaining Judicial Independence' (1999) 72 *Southern California Review* 353, 362. See also above in this volume, chs 6 and 7.

standards of court administration vary from one international organisation to another. Furthermore, the processes tend to be quite opaque, with only limited access to information regarding their rules and design.

Starting with the international level, within the United Nations, it was the General Assembly which adopted already in 1985 the Basic Principles on the Independence of the Judiciary ('UN Basic Principles').[3] While the UN Basic Principles addressed several aspects of court administration in the broader sense, they merely set the goals. The States were left to choose the means how to meet those goals.[4] The 2002 Bangalore Principles of Judicial Conduct ('Bangalore Principles')[5] took a similar approach. These principles explicitly called for enhancing 'institutional independence of the judiciary'.[6] But they stopped short of advocating for a particular model of court administration. They instead zeroed in on six general values which ought to be pursued: independence, impartiality, integrity, propriety, equality, competence and diligence.[7]

The process that led to the drafting of the 2002 Bangalore Principles of Judicial Conduct clearly illuminates the shift towards a greater role of judges in defining standards of court administration. The origin of the Bangalore Principles dates back to the meeting of the Judicial Group on Strengthening Judicial Integrity in Bangalore, India in February 2001 (therefore 'Bangalore Principles'). The meeting united eight chief justices from Asia and Africa. In the meeting, they drafted a code of judicial conduct that was supposed to complement the UN Basic Principles '[i]n light of increasing reports of judicial corruption, and sensing a lack of guidance on measures of judicial accountability'.[8] This code, partly revised, was subsequently adopted by the UN Special Rapporteur Param Cumaraswamy.[9]

The UN thus ex post provided this in fact private initiative with a 'veil of legitimacy' in the form of institutional approval. However, the input from other law professionals than judges, for example from government officials, scholars and other stakeholders, in the drafting process, was minimal. What is even more striking is that despite the clear motivation behind this code, there is not a single mention of the words 'corruption' or 'accountability' in the Bangalore Principles.

---

[3] Adopted at the Seventh UN Congress on the Prevention of Crime and the Treatment of Offenders held in Milan in 1985, endorsed by GA Res 40/32, 29 November 1985, A/RES/40/32 and GA Res 40/146, 13 December 1985, A/RES/40/32.

[4] See eg principle no 10 ('Any method of judicial selection shall safeguard against judicial appointments for improper motives'), or principle no 13 ('Promotion of judges, wherever such a system exists, should be based on objective factors, in particular ability, integrity and experience'), or no 17 ('A charge or complaint made against a judge in his/her judicial and professional capacity shall be processed expeditiously and fairly under an appropriate procedure').

[5] Report of the Special Rapporteur, 10 January 2003, E/CN.4/2003/65 Annex.

[6] The 2002 Bangalore Principles of Judicial Conduct, para 1.5.

[7] Report of the Special Rapporteur (n 5).

[8] L Neudorf, 'Promoting Independent Justice in a Changing World' (2012) 12 *Human Rights Law Review* 107, 112.

[9] Report of the Special Rapporteur (n 5).

Instead, the Bangalore Principles start with a bold paragraph, which, if taken in its fullness, would represent an antithesis to judicial accountability:

> A judge shall exercise the judicial function independently on the basis of the judge's assessment of the facts and in accordance with a conscientious understanding of the law, free of any extraneous influences, inducements, pressures, threats or interference, direct or indirect, from any quarter or for any reason.[10]

In contrast to the UN level, in Europe, the process of standardisation of court administration went much further and deeper. This process can be roughly divided into two periods. The first period spans from the 1950s until the early 1990s. The second period lasts from the early 1990s until today. Until the early 1990s, neither the European Union nor the Council of Europe (CoE) paid significant attention to the models of court administration. The turning point was the adoption of the EU Copenhagen criteria in 1993 and the ensuing EU accession process and its conditionality vis-a-vis the candidate countries.[11] Since then, the EU as well as the CoE considerably increased their resources devoted to setting the standards of court administration. The synergic effect of activities of these two international organisations in turn created strong pressure mainly on the CEE States[12] to put their models of court administration in sync with the promoted European Judicial Council model (JC model).

The CoE gave a preference to the JC model of court administration as early as 1994.[13] On the other hand, in that period, a diversity of models across Europe was still acknowledged. The CoE refrained from proposing to change the alternative systems of court administration that 'in practice work[ed] well'.[14] However, over the years, both the EU and the CoE have abandoned their initial flexibility and became staunch advocates of the JC model. In the 2004 enlargement wave that involved mainly former communist Central European and Baltic States,[15] the European Commission used the so-called 'pre-accession conditionality'[16] to exercise significant pressure on Estonia, Latvia and Slovakia and enticed them to adopt the JC model. In Slovakia, the European Commission succeeded and the Judicial

---

[10] The 2002 Bangalore Principles of Judicial Conduct, para 1.1.

[11] C Parau, 'The Drive for Judicial Supremacy' in A Seibert-Fohr (ed), *Judicial Independence in Transition* (Springer, 2012) 619, 643.

[12] But note that the pushing for one JC Euro-model is by now no longer limited to the CEE. For instance, the Parliamentary Assembly of the CoE has recently criticised Germany for not having a judicial council. See Resolution 1685 (2009), Allegations of politically-motivated abuses of the criminal justice system in CoE member states, adopted 30 September 2009, para 5.4.1. For further details, see also A Seibert-Fohr, 'European Perspective on the Rule of Law and Independent Courts' (2012) 20 *Journal für Rechtspolitik* 161, 166 who argues that the problem of recent documents produced by the CoE is that they have gradually shifted the emphasis from obligations of *results* to obligations of *means*.

[13] Committee of Ministers, Recommendation No R (94) 12, 13 October 1994, printed in: (1994) 37 *Yearbook of the European Convention on Human Rights* 453. Principle I 2 c).

[14] ibid, at para 16 of the Explanatory Memorandum to the Recommendation.

[15] Namely Poland, the Czech Republic, Slovakia, Hungary, Slovenia, Estonia, Latvia, Lithuania. The other two countries which joined the EU also in the 2004 enlargement were Malta and Cyprus.

[16] Further below in this ch, s VI.

Council of the Slovak Republic came into being in 2002. Estonia adopted a somewhat modified Judicial Council 'Euro-model' in the same year. Latvia resisted the pressure and eventually created its judicial council only in 2010.[17] The European Commission went even further in the 2007 enlargement wave and basically required from Romania and Bulgaria to adopt the JC model 'as it is'.[18]

The eventual creation of the Judicial Council 'Euro-model' presents a puzzle. Neither the EU nor the CoE have ever laid down any normative underpinnings of this model. There has never been any process of review or discussion of the model similar to those that apply to adopting EU legislation or to the drafting of an international treaty. Both organisations just internalised the recommendations of various judicial consultative bodies, without much addressing or assessing their content.

The intricate web of different consultative bodies that have played a major role in setting this standard is in itself difficult to disentangle.[19] There is nonetheless one thing that all of these consultative bodies have in common: Judges have a significant and often even a decisive voice therein. For instance, the Consultative Council of European Judges (CCJE), an advisory body of the CoE on issues related to the independence, impartiality and competence of judges, is composed exclusively of judges. Similarly, the Lisbon Network, consultative body of the CoE in the field of judicial education, consists of judges only, namely judges who are directors or deputy directors of national judicial schools. The European Network for Councils for the Judiciary (ENCJ), an independent body, politically and financially supported by the European Commission, which is particularly active in setting the standards of court administration, is open to representatives of other professions, but judges have a majority there too. Even in the Venice Commission, the CoE's advisory body on constitutional matters writ large, whose composition is most diverse, judges have an upper hand.

In other words, judges control virtually all European bodies that deal with issues of court administration. Given the fact that the European standards of court administration are created by judges themselves, it is not surprising that these standards are based on the belief that the rule of law is best served by judicial autonomy.[20] This belief materialises in the vision of a very robust institutional separation of the judiciary from the rest of legal and political institutions within the national state.

---

[17] Generally on the double or even multiple standards in the accession process, see eg D Kochenov, *EU Enlargement and the Failure of Conditionality* (Kluwer Law International, 2008) 264–66, 271–90.

[18] See eg, D Smilov, 'EU Enlargement and the Constitutional Principle of Judicial Independence' in A Czarnota, M Krygier and W Sadurski (eds), *Spreading Democracy and the Rule of Law: The Impact of EU Enlargement on the Rule of Law, Democracy, and Constitutionalism in Post-communist Legal Orders* (Springer, 2006) 313, 323–25; or Parau (n 11).

[19] For a comprehensive overview of these bodies, see D Piana, *Judicial Accountabilities in New Europe: From Rule of Law to Quality of Justice* (Ashgate, 2010) ch 2.

[20] Parau (n 11) 646–47.

III. What was in the Package? The Core Requirements of the Euro-model

Officially, there is no formal document that would define any required 'Euro-model' model of court administration. Therefore, we must excavate the parameters of this model from various documents originating from diverse bodies of the European Union and the Council of Europe, with further impetus coming from the United Nations, the World Bank or other international organisations.

There are five key requirements of the JC Euro-model which may be distilled from the plethora of documents produced by numerous organs and affiliated bodies of the EU and the CoE, and on which there appears to be some consensus in Europe.[21] These are as follows:

(1) A judicial council should have constitutional status;[22]
(2) at least 50 per cent of the members of the judicial council must be judges and these judicial members must be selected by their peers, that is by other judges;[23]
(3) a judicial council ought to be vested with decision-making and not merely advisory powers;[24]
(4) a judicial council should have substantial competences in all matters concerning the career of a judge including selection, appointment, promotion, transfer, dismissal and disciplining;[25] and
(5) a judicial council must be chaired either by the President or Chief Justice of the Highest Court or the neutral head of state.[26]

---

[21] See further also A Seibert-Fohr, 'Judicial Independence in European Union Accessions: The Emergence of a European Basic Principle' (2009) 52 *German Yearbook of International Law* 405 or Piana (n 19).

[22] The European Network of Councils for the Judiciary (ENCJ), Councils for the Judiciary Report 2010–2011, para 1.4; and Opinion no 10 (2007) of the Consultative Council of European Judges (CCJE) to the attention of the Committee of Ministers of the Council of Europe on the Council for the Judiciary at the service of society, Strasbourg, 21–23 November 2007, para 11. See also European Charter on the Statute for Judges, Strasbourg, 8–10 July 1998, para 1.2.

[23] ENCJ, Councils for the Judiciary Report 2010–2011, para 2.1; and CCJE, Opinion no 10 (2007), para 18. See also European Charter on the Statute for Judges, Strasbourg, 8–10 July 1998, para 1.3; Resolution of the ENCJ on 'Self Governance for the Judiciary: Balancing Independence and Accountability' of May 2008 (hereinafter only 'Budapest Resolution'), para 4 (b); and Recommendation CM/Rec (2010) 12 of the Committee of Ministers to Member States on judges: independence, efficiency and responsibilities, adopted by the Committee of Ministers on 17 November 2010, para 27.

[24] ENCJ, Councils for the Judiciary Report 2010–2011, paras 3.4 and 3.13; CCJE, Opinion no 10 (2007), paras 48, 49 and 60. See also European Charter on the Statute for Judges, Strasbourg, 8–10 July 1998, paras 3.1, 4.1 and 7.2; and Recommendation CM/Rec (2010) 12 of the Committee of Ministers to Member States on judges: independence, efficiency and responsibilities, adopted by the Committee of Ministers on 17 November 2010, para 46.

[25] ENCJ, Councils for the Judiciary Report 2010–2011, para 3.1; and CCJE, Opinion no 10 (2007), para 42. See also European Charter on the Statute for Judges, Strasbourg, 8–10 July 1998, para 1.3.

[26] ENCJ, Councils for the Judiciary Report 2010–2011, para 4.1; CCJE, Opinion no 10 (2007), para 33.

This set of five criteria is by no means the definitive or exhaustive list of requirements and recommendations proposed by the EU and the CoE. Many documents produced by these two organisations demanded more stringent criteria as well as additional requirements.[27] The abovementioned set is rather the highest common denominator of what is expected and what the EU and the CoE advocate for.

It is clear that these criteria may not always be framed as 'must requirements'. The documents employ 'should language'. However, the language should not obfuscate the obligatory nature of these requirements for the so-called 'new democracies' in CEE. In fact, most EU and CoE documents use the 'should language' for two reasons. First, the 'should language' carves out exceptions for the so-called 'old democracies' in Europe, which are not willing to modify their current models of court administration. Second, the 'should language' is employed in order to make these documents as inclusive as possible and to speak also to bodies in some European states which represent different styles of court administration, such as the Court Service model,[28] or hybrid models of court administration.[29]

As is apparent from the five requirements listed, the 'self-government' of judges represents a golden thread running through all five criteria.[30] Some documents make this claim more explicit when they stress that the judicial council must 'secure the independence of the judiciary "from every *other* power"', that is from the executive and the legislature (not from the judiciary), and 'ensure effective self-governance'.[31]

Interestingly, the JC Euro-model completely overlooks the threats from within the judiciary and does not stipulate any checks against the capture of this model by a narrow group of judicial leadership. More specifically, court presidents and vice presidents are not precluded from becoming members of the judicial council and no maximum ratio of these judicial officials among judicial members of the judicial council is generally set.[32] Similarly, any rule ensuring the representation

---

[27] For instance, some documents preclude the participation of the Minister of Justice in the judicial council or require judicial councils to have budgetary powers, oversee judicial training, process complaints from the users of courts, comment on bills affecting the judiciary or propose new legislation. See eg ENCJ, Councils for the Judiciary Report 2010–2011, paras 3.5–3.9 and 3.14–3.18; or CCJE, Opinion no 10 (2007), paras 65–90.

[28] The Court Service model is sometimes referred to as a 'Northern European Model' of judicial council—see eg W Voermans and P Albers, 'Councils for the Judiciary in EU Countries, European Council for the Efficiency of Justice' (2003) CEPEJ. We reject this label as unhelpful and misleading; see also N Garoupa and T Ginsburg, 'Guarding the Guardians: Judicial Councils and Judicial Independence' (2009) 57 *American Journal of Comparative Law* 103, fn 20 at 109.

[29] These different models are described immediately below in the following section.

[30] It could be suggested that the term 'self-government model' should be used instead of the 'judicial council model'. In our opinion, however, the term 'judicial council model' captures better the nature of the institutional design in question of which the judicial self-government is an important but not the sole component. Furthermore, the 'judicial council model' is also the term under which the model has been promoted and marketed in the CEE.

[31] ENCJ Councils for the Judiciary Report 2010–2011, para 1.4. Emphasis added.

[32] CCJE, Opinion no 10 (2007), para 26. Contrast, however, ENCJ, Councils for the Judiciary Report 2010–2011, para 2; European Charter on the Statute for Judges, Strasbourg, 8–10 July 1998, para 1.3; 'Budapest Resolution', para 4 (b); and Recommendation CM/Rec (2010)12, para 27. Similarly, the JC Euro-model does not set any limit on the number of senior judges of appellate and top courts.

of all echelons of the judiciary in the judicial council is missing. This omission means that there are no check and balances between the judicial leadership and regular judges. Internal independence of an individual judge vis-a-vis the judicial leadership who may decide through the JC Euro-model on their careers is thus left unprotected.

IV. What was not Included? Competing Models of Court Administration

In order to see the specific features of the promoted JC Euro-model of court administration more clearly, it is helpful to juxtapose this model with its alternatives. This short detour should also save us from a common vice in the scholarship on judicial systems, namely that scholars tend to compare only countries *with* judicial councils and debates therein and ignore countries *without* judicial councils and debates therein.[33] We will start with the models of court administration present in Europe and then locate the JC model among these alternatives.

There are broadly speaking five models of court administration in use in Europe:[34]

(1) The Ministry of Justice model;
(2) the judicial council model;
(3) the courts service model;
(4) hybrid models; and
(5) the socialist model.

The Ministry of Justice model is the oldest one. In this model, the Ministry of Justice plays a key role in both the appointment and promotion of judges and in the administration of courts and court management. This model is in place in Germany, Austria, the Czech Republic, Finland and other countries. One caveat must be added here. It is misleading to claim that judges themselves play no role in the appointment and promotion of judges or in the administration of courts and court management in this model and that the national Ministry of Justice controls all these processes unilaterally. In the ministerial model, it is also other bodies, such as the legislature, the President of a given country, judicial boards, and the ombudsman or professional organisations, which often play a significant role or at least have their say as well. Moreover, a crucial role in these systems is in fact played

---

[33] A rare exception is the synthesis report on states without judicial councils compiled by Lord Thomas. See *Councils for the Judiciary: States without a High Council* (preliminary report), CCJE (2007) 4, Strasbourg, 19 March 2007.

[34] Different classifications are equally plausible. Our classification relies on N Picardi, 'La Ministère de la Justice et les autres modèles d'administration de la justice en Europe' in P Abravanel et al (eds), *L'indipendenza della giustizia, oggi. Judicial independence, today: liber amicorum in onore di Giovanni E Longo* (Dott A Giuffre Editore, 1999).

by presidents of appellate and supreme courts, who are consulted regarding judicial promotion, appointments and other key issues. Some of the appointments or promotions cannot even be carried out without their consent. Thus, albeit called the 'Ministry of Justice model', it does not mean that all is run exclusively by the executive. The strong criticism one may encounter with respect to this model in a number of international documents and/or academic writings and which the proponents of the judicial council model often criticise with fervour is rather a parody of the Minister of Justice model that no longer exists in Europe.[35]

The judicial council model is a model where an independent intermediary organisation is positioned between the judiciary and the politically responsible administrators in the executive or the parliament. The judicial council is given significant powers primarily in appointing and promoting judges and/or in exercising disciplinary powers vis-a-vis judges. While judicial councils may also play a role in the areas of administration, court management and budgeting of the courts, these powers are only secondary to their competences relating to judges and personnel generally. Belgium, Bulgaria, France, Hungary (until 2011), Italy, Lithuania, the Netherlands, Poland, Portugal, Romania, Slovakia, Slovenia and Spain can be said to belong to this group. However, as will be shown below, not all of these judicial councils meet the criteria of the JC 'Euro-model'.[36]

In contrast, in the court service model, the primary function of an independent intermediary organisation is in the area of administration (supervision of judicial registry offices, case loads and case stocks, flow rates, the promotion of legal uniformity, quality care etc), court management (housing, automation, recruitment, training, etc) and the budgeting of the courts. In contrast to judicial councils, the court services have a limited role in the appointment and promotion of judges and do not exercise disciplinary powers vis-a-vis judges. These powers are sometimes vested in independent organs such as judicial appointment commissions that operate separately from the court service. Denmark, Ireland, Norway and Sweden are examples of countries that have adopted the court service model.

By hybrid models we mean any model that combines various components of the previous three models in such a way that it is significantly distinct from each of them. Hybrid models operate in England and Wales, Estonia, Hungary (since 2011), Iceland, Switzerland and in European micro-states. These models are so specific that one cannot generalise about them in order to create one clear box. They include judicial appointment commissions that deal only with the selection of judges up to a certain tier of the judicial system, whereas the rest of the court administration is vested in another organ (England and Wales); countries where the judicial council coexists with another strong nationwide body responsible

---

[35] What many critics attacked in the CEE was in fact the 'state administration of courts', which was based on the socialist model (which is discussed immediately below in this section) rather than the current Ministry of Justice model.

[36] Moreover, the classification of several judicial councils is open to debate. For instance, one may reasonably claim that the Dutch judicial council is in fact closer to the Court Service model.

for court administration (Hungary since 2011); countries where the Minister of Justice shares power with judges of the Supreme Court (Cyprus); federal countries where the court administration varies from one state to another (Switzerland); and micro-states that have peculiar systems of court administration tailored to their specific needs (Lichtenstein and Luxembourg).

Finally, the socialist model of court administration concentrated the power over judges and the judicial system in general in three institutions—the General Prosecutor (procurator), the Supreme Court and court presidents—which are then, however, themselves controlled by the communist Party. In fact therefore, it is the Party controlling the courts through these institutions. Specific features of this model varied from one communist country to another and changed with time. The following mechanisms were nonetheless quite common: The relocation and demotion of judges without a decision of the disciplinary court; arbitrary assignment of cases by court presidents; the reassignment at will of judges within their courts or deciding on salary bonuses of judges; the power of the Supreme Court to remove any case from the lower courts and decide it itself.[37] Apart from these mechanisms available within the judiciary, judges were subject to frequent retention reviews, the Communist Party had a residual power to dismiss judges who did not exercise judicial office in line with the Party policies and the General Prosecutor had the right to ask for the review of any judicial decision, including those that had already became final. The pure socialist model of court administration no longer exists in Europe.[38] However, it is important to mention this model[39] in the European context, as some of the post-communist countries in CEE have still not got rid of all features of the socialist model. Even more importantly, in a number of these countries, the legacy of the omnipotent Supreme Court and court presidents is lasting until today.

A quick glance at the models of court administration in Europe suggests that a great number of current EU Member States have opted for the judicial council model. This does not, however, mean that all of them would have indeed taken on board and introduced the promoted JC Euro-model outlined above and

---

[37] For descriptions of the office of the Procurator and its functions in English, see eg GB Smith, *The Soviet Procuracy and the Supervision of Administration* (Sijthoff and Noordhoff, 1978); or GG Morgan, *Soviet Administrative Legality: The Role of Attorney General's Office* (Stanford University Press, 1962). A comparative East/West assessment is offered in M Cappelletti and JA Jolowicz (eds), *Public Interest Parties and the Active Role of the Judge in Civil Litigation* (Giuffrè/Oceana, 1975).

[38] Only the Belarusian model of court administration gets close. On the state of the Belarusian judiciary, see A Vashkevich, 'Judicial Independence in the Republic of Belarus', in Seibert-Fohr (n 11) 1065, 1068–71, 1101–03, 1109–10, 1115–18. However, the socialist model is still alive outside Europe, for instance in China; see eg Peter H Solomon, 'Authoritarian Legality and Informal Practices: Judges, Lawyers and the State in Russia and China' (2010) 43 *Communist and Post-communist Studies* 351; Xin He, 'Black Hole of Responsibility: The Adjudication Committee's Role in a Chinese Court' (2012) 46 *Law & Society Review* 681.

[39] Alternatively, we may perceive the socialist model of the administration of courts as a perverse version of the classic Ministry of Justice model. However, the merging of these two models into one would ignore important differences between them.

advocated by the EU and the CoE. The composition and competences as well as the power of judicial councils varies considerably even among European countries that established some sort of judicial council and could thus be said to represent the judicial council model.[40] Many of these judicial councils do not even meet the criteria of the Euro-model we identified above. For instance, French, Dutch and Portuguese judges are in the minority on the judicial councils in their countries. In Spain judicial members of the judicial council are not selected by their peers. In Belgium, Poland and Slovenia, judicial councils do not play any role in disciplining judges. Finally, the Hungarian Judicial Council met the requirements of the EU/CoE Judicial Council Model only until Orbán's government passed the 2011 judicial reform that took many powers from the Hungarian High Council for the Judiciary (*Magyar Köztársaság Bíróságai*) and transferred them to the newly established National Judicial Office.[41]

Therefore, the JC Euro-model is in fact only a subset of judicial councils that exist in Europe. The key feature that distinguishes the promoted Euro-model from its competing alternatives, including other types of judicial councils, is that it centralises competences affecting virtually *all* matters of the career of judges at one place and grants control over this body to the judges. The Euro-model is built on the premise that judges are reliable, solid actors, who know their business and are able to administer it. It is therefore considered wise to insulate the judiciary from the democratic process.

If we compare the Euro-model with the existing judicial councils in the EU Member States, it is evident that the Euro-model had been heavily inspired by the Italian judicial council rather than one of France, Spain or Portugal. In the latter countries, the national Ministries of Justice have preserved some influence over judicial recruitment.[42] Given the prominent position of Italians in the relevant Pan-European bodies, the preference for absolute judicial autonomy does not come as a surprise.

V. One Size Fits All? A Critique of Euro-models

Based on the previous three subsections, we can start pinpointing some of the deficits of the Euro-model of court administration. Five points of critique will be raised in this section, largely from a normative point of view. Some of these points of critique will be elaborated further on in the ensuing sections of this chapter from an empirical point of view.

---

[40] For a helpful taxonomy of judicial councils, see Garoupa and Ginsburg (n 28) 122.

[41] The Hungarian model of court administration after the 2011 judicial reforms thus belongs to the category of 'hybrid models'.

[42] Parau (n 11) 643–44. See also T Renoux (ed), *Les Conseils superieurs de la magistrature en Europe* (La documentation francaise, 1999); or J-F Weber, 'Conseil supérieur de la magistrature (CSM)' in T Renoux (ed), *La Justice en France* (La documentation française, 2013) 219, 221–22.

First and foremost, the major objection to the Euro-model of court administration is that it suffers from the *lack of democratic legitimacy*. It disempowers elected branches of the government and transfers virtually all personal competences over judicial career to the judiciary.[43]

Moreover, the lack of output (content) legitimacy of the JC Euro-model can certainly not be substituted by its input (process) derived legitimacy.[44] As has already been suggested,[45] the process of setting the standards of a Euro-model of court administration is opaque. It side-steps democratic process and relies exclusively on a narrow group of judges and high-ranking officials of international and supranational bodies. The drafting process of reports of these bodies lacks openness and transparency. Other stakeholders can rarely comment on or influence the wording of the proposed standards.

Even if one were to assume that such standards were to be drafted by judges only, the lack of input legitimacy is further exacerbated by the *problem of representation*. It has two dimensions: State-internal and trans-European. With respect to the former, it is questionable how far the judicial members of the current European or international consultative bodies really represent the national judiciaries as a whole and not rather the particular interests of a narrow group of court presidents and senior judges. One might even suggest, with a certain degree of simplification, that a narrow coterie of judicial officials meets a few times a year in a closed session and once in a while announces a standard that defines the desired contours of their own power.

With respect to the latter, there is the trans-European representativeness problem within the consultative and advisory judicial bodies. How far and how strongly are the various judicial and legal cultures present within Europe indeed represented? To put it differently, why is it that the JC Euro-model so closely resembles the Italian model of judicial council? How was it possible that the Italian model found such widespread support among judges from other European states, and became in fact translated into a 'Euro-model'? True, the Italian *Consiglio superiore della magistratura* (CSM) is considered a success in Italy and is one of the oldest judicial councils in Europe. It might therefore, arguably, enjoy a privileged status based on its seniority. However, the Italian CSM has also been repeatedly criticised for corporativism, a lack of judicial accountability and suboptimal efficiency, to say the least.[46]

---

[43] To paraphrase Roberto Unger, one of the little secrets of the Euro-model is its discomfort with democracy. See R Unger, *What Should Legal Analysis Become* (Verso, 1998) 72–73 or J Waldron, 'Dirty Little Secret' (1998) 98 *Columbia Law Review* 510.

[44] For the discussion of this traditional distinction, see eg FW Scharpf, *Governing in Europe: Effective or Democratic* (Oxford University Press, 1999) 6–30 or FW Scharpf, 'Legitimacy in the Multilevel European Polity' (2009) 1 *European Political Science Review* 173.

[45] Above, s II of this ch.

[46] See eg C Guarnieri and P Pederzoli, *The Power of Judges: A Comparative Study of Courts and Democracy* (Oxford University Press, 2002) 54–59 and 174–77; ML Volcansek, 'Judicial Selection in Italy: A Civil Service Model with Partisan Results' in K Malleson and PR Russell (eds), *Appointing Judges in an Age of Judicial Power: Critical Perspectives from around the World* (University of Toronto Press, 2006) 159.

Moreover, there were other templates to choose from that range from a different model of judicial council such as the one in place in France to the Court Service model or the well-functioning German Ministry of Justice model.[47] One must thus search for additional explanations. As one commentator suggested, the success of CSM as a European model

> is also the result of the international presence and activism of the Consiglio superiore della magistratura and its members (it is not by chance that the ENCJ was formally established at the General Assembly of 20–21 May 2004 in Rome, and that [its] first President was Italian).[48]

Second, the Euro-model ignores the worldwide rise of power of courts, which calls for greater accountability of judges, and not really for their increased insulation behind the veil of a self-administering judicial council. Furthermore, while *l'esprit de corps* and ethical standards may be higher in established democracies, it is not necessarily so in developing or transforming countries. Leaving the judiciary unchecked by external actors in the latter countries might easily lead to corruption and judicial accountability avoidance.[49]

Third, even if we assume that the judiciary should even under such conditions be granted further autonomy, the Euro-model is not really able to deliver it with respect to individual judicial decision making. It neglects the internal threats coming from within the judiciary. The Euro-model shields the judiciary from external influence, but it pays little attention to the improper pressure on individual judges exercised by senior judges and court presidents. It is important to remember that the judiciary is not 'it' but 'they'.[50] The Euro-model empowers only a narrow group of judges who in turn may favour their allies and shape the judiciary according to their views.[51] They may even use their newly accrued power to settle the score with their competitors, critics or opponents *within* the judiciary.

This is a significant failure of the JC Euro-model, which is embedded in its institutional design. The omission of the JC Euro-model we identified above[52] ought to be recalled at this stage: Court presidents and vice-presidents are generally not precluded from becoming members of the judicial council. There is typically no set maximum number of these judicial officials among members of the judicial council. Similarly, the JC Euro-model does not set any limit on the number of

---

[47] See above s IV of this ch.

[48] S Benvenuti, 'The French and the Italian High Councils for the Judiciary: Observations Drawn from the Analysis of their Staff and Activity (1947–2011)', paper presented at 2012 IPSA World Congress, 8–12 July 2012, at 2 (on file with authors).

[49] On judicial accountability avoidance and other negative accountability phenomena, see D Kosař, 'The Least Accountable Branch' (2013) 11 *International Journal of Constitutional Law* 234, 259–60.

[50] A Vermeule, 'The Judiciary Is A They, Not An It: Interpretive Theory and the Fallacy Of Division' (2009) 14 *Journal of Contemporary Legal Issues* 549.

[51] See B Pokol, 'Judicial Power and Democratization in Eastern Europe' in *Proceedings of the Conference 'Europeanisations and Democratisation: The Southern European Experience and the Perspective for the New Member States of the Enlarged Europe* (2005) 165, 182 and 188.

[52] Above, s III in this ch.

senior judges of appellate and top courts that can sit in the judicial council. Thus, the judicial council need not be representative of all echelons of the judicial hierarchy. This means that lower court judges may also elect appellate judges or court presidents as their representatives in the judicial council.

As a result, court presidents may have a majority on the judicial council. The model previously advocated as 'self-governance' of judges may quickly become nothing else than unbounded administration by senior judicial officials. This is particularly troubling in the CEE region, where court presidents have strong powers within their courts (the meso-level).[53] If they are allowed to combine their powers at the meso-level with additional powers at the meta-level (within the judicial council), they accumulate considerable power within the judicial system.

One might even wonder, with tongue-in-cheek, whether the silence of the JC Euro-model regarding the selection of the representatives of the judiciary was not intentional. The Euro standards were created under the auspices of various consultative bodies of the EU and the CoE. In these bodies, national judiciaries are usually represented by the Supreme Court president or prominent appellate judges. This narrow group of court presidents and senior judges would hardly be inclined to share or even to yield their own extant powers. When they advocated the transfer of the competences from the Ministry of Justice to the judiciary, what they likely had in mind was in fact the transfer of this power to *them* acting as the judicial council. That might explain why the Euro-model leaves such great latitude regarding the electoral laws of the judicial members of the judicial councils. Put differently, the silence of the JC Euro-model on the eligibility of court presidents to become members of the judicial council and on the ratio of senior judges on the judicial council is its critical component.[54] Without it, there might have been far less support for the JC Euro-model among judicial officials in power.[55]

Fourth, it is confusing or even suspicious that international and supranational bodies in which representatives of established democracies still have a major say advocate for the model of court administration that most established democracies themselves have been either reluctant to introduce so far or outright rejected. Thus, the already outlined lack of democratic legitimacy was further multiplied. Not only was the way in which such recommendations have been adopted at the international/European forum and their content highly problematic. In those established countries, where democratic control of the incoming international standards was possible, they were not taken on board. Thus, such standards could

---

[53] Piana (n 19) 43–44; Solomon (n 38) 354; M Bobek, 'The Administration of Courts in the Czech Republic: In Search of a Constitutional Balance' (2010) 16 *European Public Law* 251, 253–54; or Kosař (n 49) 249–50.

[54] We will explain how this electoral law, or its deficiencies, can influence the functioning of the judicial council in s VIII, where we discuss the Slovak case study. The mode of selection of judicial members had great consequences also on the operation of the Hungarian judicial council (before Orbán's 2011 judicial reform)—see Pokol (n 51) 188–89.

[55] See the Slovak case study discussed in s VIII below. For a more detailed analysis, see D Kosař, *Perils of Judicial Self-Government* (Cambridge University Press, forthcoming 2015).

not have gained any further or substitute legitimacy through the national levels, by being embraced in established democracies and thus providing certain 'leading by example' for the transforming countries.

Fifth, the Euro-model is portrayed as an 'off-the-rack' product that will produce the promised results in any environment. It does not take into account the specifics of each judicial system, its vices and virtues, the legal culture the relevant judiciary is embedded in and its historical legacies and path-dependency. In this sense, the Euro-model is unhistorical.

However, in reply to such normative critique, a realist (or a cynic, depending on the individual definition of optimism) might suggest that in 'going European' and projecting their own ideas and wishes onto the international forum, judges of the last few decades in fact just started copying the behaviour of national executives. The executive 'escape' from the national parliamentary control towards the international or the European level is by now a well-known phenomenon in post-World War II Europe and beyond.[56] In Europe and in particular within the European Union, it just reached quantitatively new dimensions. National governments, which are facing unpopular but necessary measures to be taken on the national level, which would be either harmful to their reputation or could not be even pushed through the national parliament, take these issues to the European or international level. There they find sympathetic colleagues from other national administrations, frequently facing a similar set of problems in their respective countries. After reaching a mutually beneficial agreement and adopting a new treaty or a new EU measure, they return to the national constituency with the impenetrable argument 'Brussels wills it' in case of a EU measure and with reference to 'our international obligations' with respect to international treaties.

Thus, is there anything that surprising or strange with judges starting to copy the same behaviour as the national administrations? Both of them are at odds with democracy and accountability, the national governments perhaps less than judges. This development may not necessarily mean that judges would immediately become an 'international priesthood' which would seek to 'impose upon our free and independent citizens supra-national values that contradict their own'.[57] On the international level, judges meet in public. The outcomes of the meetings are known and published. At the same time, however, there is indeed a qualitative leap: Judges became an internationally organised force.[58]

---

[56] Traditionally, governments do not have a strong record for willingly keeping the national parliaments informed about international affairs. Even if they inform national parliaments, the parliamentary control tends to be carried out only ex post and limited to the (non)ratification of treaties negotiated by the executive. Within the EU context, see eg A Maurer and W Wessels (eds), *National Parliaments on their Ways to Europe: Losers or Latecomers?* (Nomos, 2001) or J Fitzmaurice, 'National Parliamentary Control of EU Policy in the Three New Member States' (1996) 19 *West European Politics* 88.

[57] A Scalia, 'Commentary' (1995–1996) 40 *St Louis University Law Journal* 1119, 1122.

[58] The buzzword of the last 10 years or so in Europe is 'judicial networks'—see recently eg M Claes and M de Visser, 'Are You Networked Yet? On Dialogues in European Judicial Networks' (2012) 8 *Utrecht Law Review* 100.

VI. Promoting the Euro-model
in the New Europe

The story of the importation of the judicial council Euro-model of court administration into the new Member States is one of indirect, diagonal law exportation
through 'Europe'. The JC model has been exported through the European institutions and marketed as the 'Euro-solution' for the judicial reform across the CEE.
The puzzling question is how was it possible that a model of a strong and insulated
judicial council, which might be said to generate certainly less than optimal results
in terms of judicial performance in the countries of its origin,[59] has been able to
become the dominant and in fact the 'Euro-model' pushed forward and advocated
by the European institutions?

There are several factors which were crucial in this marketing success: Structural
as well as circumstantial. *Structurally* speaking, genuine reform and transformation
is a lengthy and tiresome process. It is therefore not much favoured by national or
international political actors, who wish for visible and quick solutions. What tends
to be preferred is the establishment of a new, grand institution than the reform of
the old one(s). In terms of a judicial reform, a new national council of the judiciary
as the symbol of a new era might certainly be politically more visible and internationally better to check as a sign of 'progress' than the tedious small scale work on
the ground, such as for instance issues of work management, auxiliary court staff,
systems of random case assignment, publicly accessible online search engines of
national case law, reasonable judicial performance evaluation etc.

This is not to suggest that these two issues (macro and micro scale reform) are
not connected. What is rather suggested is that once the 'grand design' in the form
of a new umbrella institution of a judicial council has been created, the appropriate box on the international compliance sheet has been ticked off. This invariably
meant, in terms of judicial reform in the CEE, that once a new judicial council
based on the best Euro-standards has been established, the 'mission accomplished'
flag was hung. Attention has quickly moved to other policy areas and other institutions. However, as evidenced in a number of countries in the CEE, the real
problems were just about to start.

Structural preference for institutional novelty to the detriment of genuine
internal reform met with ideal *circumstantial* conditions, both external as well as
internal. Internally, those in favour of a partial or full self-administration of the
judiciary by the fiat of a judicial council tend to be judges themselves, in particular
senior judges. Their suggestion would often be supported by non-governmental
organisations as well as parts of legal scholarship. To be sure, politicians and
administrators tend not to welcome the idea of a self-administering judiciary.
However, in systems of transition, their voices tend to be weakened, especially if

---

[59] See eg the critical voices on the state and performance of the Italian CSM quoted (n 46).

external pressure is being put on them. The pressure was particularly strong in the EU pre-accession stage. Potential national political disagreement was considerably weakened by the EU conditionality and the 'alliance of interests' in favour of the establishment of robust judicial councils was the strongest. The national judicial, non-governmental and academic demands were boosted by external support: Governmental as well as non-governmental.

On the governmental level, both the CoE as well as the EU were, in terms of standards, suggesting the introduction of the judicial council Euro-model as the model for the transition countries in the CEE.[60] This overall and general 'soft' suggestion as to the best practice started becoming a de facto requirement with respect to the CEE candidate countries for EU membership. In 1993, in the so-called Copenhagen criteria,[61] the EU set a number of conditions a candidate country must fulfil in order to become a new Member State of the EU. The first of the criteria required that the candidate country has achieved stability of institutions guaranteeing democracy, the rule of law, human rights and respect for and protection of minorities.[62]

The Copenhagen criteria were later fleshed out in Agenda 2000.[63] Therein, the European Commission announced that it would report regularly to the European Council on progress made by each of the candidate CEE countries in preparations for membership and that it would submit its first Report at the end of 1998. Requirements as to the quality of the judicial system in the candidate countries were included under the heading 'democracy and the rule of law'. One of the clearly stated requirements included in the Commission's regular monitoring reports was the 'independence and self-government of the judiciary'.[64]

The message sent from the European institutions in this respect was quite clear: If you wish to join the 'Euro club', you ought to introduce (at least some features of) self-government of the judiciary.[65] This external pressure and conditionality was also amplified by a further set of transnational actors, which could be perhaps

---

[60] In detail above, s II.

[61] European Council in Copenhagen 21–22 June 1993, Conclusions of the Presidency (SN 180/1/93 REV 1) 13.

[62] Generally see eg Kochenov (n 17) or K Inglis, 'EU Enlargement: Membership Conditions Applied to Future and Potential Member States' in Steven Blockmans and Adam Lazowski (eds), *The European Union and its Neighbours: Legal Appraisal of the EU's Policies of Stabilisation, Partnership and Integration* (TMC Asser Press, 2006).

[63] Agenda 2000—Vol. I: For a stronger and wider Union (COM/97/2000 final) and Vol II: The challenge of enlargement (COM/97/2000 final).

[64] See eg European Commission's Regular Report On Czech Republic's Progress Towards Accession—the 2001 report published on 13 November 2001 as SEC (2001) 1746, 18–20 or the 2002 report published on 9 October 2002, document no SEC (2002) 1402, 22–24.

[65] ie mostly in the period before the EU Accession. The two new Member States which joined the EU in 2007, Romania and Bulgaria, represent in this respect a special case of de facto extending the pre-accession conditionality to the period after the Accession. However, also in these countries, the EU's input has been crucial. *cf* eg D Bozhilova, 'Measuring Success and Failure of EU-Europeanization in the Eastern Enlargement: Judicial Reform in Bulgaria' (2007) 9 *European Journal of Legal Reform* 285. See also Parau (n 11) 655.

aptly labelled as the international 'rule-of-law-industry'. They transnational actors would include a heterogeneous set of non-governmental organisations, development agencies and international scholars who would invariably also push for the establishment of judicial self-administration in the form of a judicial council. A notable example from this set of actors with respect to the EU candidate countries in late 1990 and early 2000 would for instance represent the Open Society Institute. It compiled a series of comparative reports on the state of judiciary in CEE that, among other things, reprimanded those countries who would not have adopted self-administration of courts.[66]

However, while it is open to debate which of the two factors, external or internal, played the key role in a given CEE country, it is clear that some domestic actors greeted the JC Euro-model with open arms. External pressure met with partial internal demand. Several scholars have even suggested that domestic judicial institutions, rather than supranational influences, have been the major factor in judicial policymaking and agenda-setting in this region. For instance, Daniela Piana argues in her book dealing with judicial governance in five post-communist countries in CEE (Bulgaria, the Czech Republic, Hungary, Poland and Romania) that those actors (the Ministry of Justice or the Judicial Council) who emerged as winners from the first transitional wave of reforms were better placed in the second pre-accession wave. They accordingly exploited the opportunities provided by the looming EU accession to entrench existing domestic allocations of powers.[67] These winners used their leverage from the first transition wave to increase their own powers or at least to prevent the transferral of significant powers to other organs. Cristina Parau puts forth a different argument,[68] but she also posits that the supranational origin of the JC Euro-model does not adequately explain the success of this design template. She argues that an equally important but far less observable cause for their success was the 'dormancy' of the CEE parliaments. In particular, it was the puzzling lack of resistance by the majority of elected representatives to their own correlative disempowerment.[69]

Against such supranational as well as domestic demand for a new institution for the judiciary, the Latin-styled Judicial Council model clearly emerged as 'the'

---

[66] *cf* Open Society Institute comprehensive report *Judicial Independence* (Central European University Press, 2001), accessible online at <www.opensocietyfoundations.org/reports/monitoring-eu-accession-process-judicial-independence>, for instance with respect to the Czech Republic (Judicial Independence in the Czech Republic), at 112–13 and 127–28.

[67] Piana (n 19) 162–63.

[68] Parau (n 11).

[69] In Slovakia, which is covered neither by Piana's nor Parau's research and which we discuss in more detail below (s VIII), the internal factors prevailed too. The major rationale for the introduction of the JC Euro-model in Slovakia was 'anti-Mečiarism'. The period of 'mečiarism' refers to years between 1992 and 1998, when Vladimír Mečiar was the Prime Minister of Slovakia. Mečiar was known for his autocratic style of government. In 1998, after the democratic centrist coalition won the general elections, it wanted to ensure that 'Mečiar-style interferences' with the judiciary could not be repeated. In order to prevent these interferences, the centrist coalition founded a new institution—the Judicial Council of the Slovak Republic that meets all the criteria of the Euro-model.

model for the CEE countries. The imposition of this model through the European institutions yet again confirms the fact that, as in the business, the product which in the end sells is not necessarily the best one in terms of quality, but the product which has good marketing. In contrast to other models of judicial administration,[70] the advantage of the Latin-styled judicial council model is the fact that it presents an advanced structure with dedicated force to the entertaining of 'foreign relations' within the national judicial council structures. The model is thus much better able to 'reproduce' itself internationally. In the words of the already introduced marketing parallel, there is an in-house (international) 'sales department'. One may only contrast this with the (Germanic) Ministry of Justice model or the much more restrained and pragmatic quality-oriented court services model in the north of Europe, which do not dispose of means and tools for self-propagation on the international level. In other words, such models are arguably more concerned with internal quality and efficiency than with entertaining flamboyant external relations.[71]

Thus, in contrast to the complex variety of national models of administration of judiciary extant across Europe, the Latin-style judicial council model provided an ideal off-the-rack and ready-made product available at the right place in the right time. Apart from this, the model was also alluring in its seemingly elegant simplicity: A clear cut new institution will be introduced whose task it to redress the deficiencies of the previous model. Before entering into the discussion of the genuine life and sociological impact of judicial councils in CEE, a glance at the (normative) promise of what the model was supposed to deliver in the first place is nonetheless necessary.

VII. What was the Euro-model Supposed to Deliver?

If we want to identify the goals the JC Euro-model was supposed to achieve, we must search again through the documents of the Council of Europe and the European Union. Two caveats must be added at the very beginning. First, it goes without saying that goals set by 'founding fathers' and advocates of the JC Euro-model may somewhat differ from the actual effects of this model. Some sort of standard functional deviation is thus inevitable, certainly in the short or mid-term. It is clear, however, that if the ensuing reality of a model denies its founding values and promises completely, one can hardly talk of any permissible deviation or modification. Second, in our search for the effects of the introduction of the Euro-model, we focus only on institutional and personal consequences for the judiciary and

---

[70] Outlined above, s IV of this chapter.
[71] Above (n 48).

judges. We thus leave aside the potential impact of this model on various values external to the judiciary such as 'the rule of law, civil liberties, individual freedoms [and] basic human rights'.[72] This is intentional: Important as these values are, they are also either contested terms and/or so vague that they are in practice impossible to measure to any reasonable degree.[73]

We can therefore narrow down the question to be answered in this section as follows: Which values or characteristics of the judiciary was the introduction of the Euro-model supposed to enhance? There is one particular value which stands out in the policy documents produced under the auspices of the CoE and the EU: Judicial independence. In fact, virtually all the documents of these two bodies claim that the JC model improves judicial independence.[74] Unfortunately, none of these documents spell out what they mean by judicial independence. They usually acknowledge the difference between the independence of individual judges and the independence of the judiciary and claim that judicial councils enhance both of these facets of judicial independence.[75] It would appear nonetheless that the documents clearly prioritise the latter aspect: The autonomy of the judiciary.[76]

Other potential values or goals of the JC model are mentioned far less frequently. As early as 1994, the CoE stressed the importance of the efficiency of judges.[77] Later on, both the CoE and the EU contended that the JC model improves the efficiency of the judiciary.[78] In fact, speeding up judicial procedures and reducing workloads became a mantra of the EU Accession Reports. Eventually, the quality of justice was added as a separate value, which the JC model is also supposed to deliver.[79]

---

[72] See eg ENCJ Councils for the Judiciary Report 2010–2011, § 1.2 in fine.

[73] See eg T Ginsburg, 'Pitfalls of Measuring the Rule of Law' (2011) 3 *Hague Journal on the Rule of Law* 269 or J Waldron, 'Is the Rule of Law an Essentially Contested Concept?' (2002) 21 *Law and Philosophy* 137 (regarding the rule of law). These challenges apply, mutatis mutandis, to other values mentioned in the ENCJ Report.

[74] See ENCJ, Councils for the Judiciary Report 2010–2011, para 1.7; CCJE, Opinion no 10 (2007), para 8; Budapest Resolution, para 1; European Charter on the Statute for Judges, para 1.3; and Recommendation CM/Rec (2010)12 of the Committee of Ministers to member states on judges: independence, efficiency and responsibilities, adopted by the Committee of Ministers on 17 November 2010, para 26.

[75] See CCJE, Opinion no 10 (2007), para 8; or Recommendation CM/Rec (2010) 12 of the Committee of Ministers to member states on judges: independence, efficiency and responsibilities, adopted by the Committee of Ministers on 17 November 2010, para 26.

[76] See eg ENCJ, Councils for the Judiciary Report 2010–2011, para 2.2; CCJE, Opinion no 10 (2007), paras 12–13; or Recommendation CM/Rec (2010) 12 of the Committee of Ministers to member states on judges: independence, efficiency and responsibilities, adopted by the Committee of Ministers on 17 November 2010, para 4.

[77] See Committee of Ministers, Recommendation No R (94) 12, 13 October 1994, printed in (1994) 37 *Yearbook of the European Convention on Human Rights* 453.

[78] See Budapest Resolution, para 1; ENCJ, Councils for the Judiciary Report 2010–2011, para 1.7; CCJE, Opinion no 10 (2007), para 10; or Recommendation CM/Rec (2010) 12 of the Committee of Ministers to member states on judges: independence, efficiency and responsibilities, adopted by the Committee of Ministers on 17 November 2010, para 26.

[79] See ENCJ, Councils for the Judiciary Report 2010–2011, para 1.7; CCJE, Opinion no 10 (2007), para 10.

Surprisingly, much less attention has been paid, until very recently, to other generally acceptable values such as transparency, participation and accountability. During the accession process, the European Commission was mostly preoccupied with judicial independence and the efficiency of the judiciary and side-lined transparency mechanisms.[80] So was the CoE.[81] Recently, both of these international organisations have stressed the importance of transparency in their documents on judicial councils.[82] They nonetheless still tend to focus on the transparency of the judicial council itself and not on the transparency of the judiciary.[83] Participation has undergone similar development. The EU and the CoE, after initial reluctance, relaxed their position on the composition of the judicial council and accepted the parity between judges and non-judges.[84]

What is most striking, given the well-known problems of venality of CEE judiciaries and their low ethical standards, is how little attention the EU and the CoE paid to judicial accountability. The relevant policy documents that define the JC Euro-model do not mention this value at all, despite the fact that judicial accountability has gradually emerged as the second most important goal of judicial councils in the scholarly literature (competing with judicial independence).[85] The relevant policy documents focus on (limited) accountability of the judicial council instead of accountability of the judiciary and/or individual judges,[86] or make clear that 'the accountability of the judiciary can in no way call into question the independence of the judge when making judicial decisions'.[87]

The fact that not a single document of the consultative organs of the CoE and the EU produced over the years sets standards regarding how judicial councils and self-administrating judiciaries ought to address corruption of judges is also quite telling. All in all, the values promoted and goals set deeply reflect the way in which the standards were created: By (senior) judges and for (largely also senior) judges. Thus, great attention is being paid to institutional and power-enhancing elements,

---

[80] *cf* in particular the pre-Accession Reports with respect to the individual CEE countries, put together by the European Commission (n 64).

[81] See eg Committee of Ministers, Recommendation No R (94) 12, 13 October 1994, printed in (1994) 37 *Yearbook of the European Convention on Human Rights* 453; or European Charter on the Statute for Judges, Strasbourg, 8–10 July 1998 (which do not mention transparency at all).

[82] See eg ENCJ, Councils for the Judiciary Report 2010-2011, paras 1.7 and 7.2; or Budapest Resolution, in fine.

[83] See CCJE, Opinion no 10 (2007), Part VI; or ENCJ, Councils for the Judiciary Report 2010–2011, para 2.5.

[84] Compare the most recent documents (eg ENCJ, Councils for the Judiciary Report 2010–2011, para 2.2; or Recommendation CM/Rec (2010) 12 of the Committee of Ministers to member states on judges: independence, efficiency and responsibilities, adopted by the Committee of Ministers on 17 November 2010, para 27) that accept 'only' 50% of judicial members in the judicial council with older documents that claim that 'a substantial majority of the members should be judges' (eg CCJE, Opinion no 10 (2007), para 18).

[85] See Garoupa and Ginsburg (n 28) 110.

[86] See CCJE, Opinion no 10 (2007), Part VI. But *cf* ENCJ, Councils for the Judiciary Report 2010–2011, para 2.2.

[87] Budapest Resolution, para 10.

whereas somewhat meagre attention has been paid to the less comfortable but for the functional judiciary extremely important 'house-keeping' elements.

In sum, the declared 'general mission'[88] of the JC Euro-model has been to safeguard and enhance judicial independence, which was primary viewed in its macro- or institutional dimension. Besides judicial independence, the Euro-model was also supposed to, according to its 'founding fathers', deliver the following 'goods': (1) To increase the efficiency of the judicial system; (2) to enhance the quality of justice; (3) to depoliticise the judiciary; and, according to most recent documents, also (4) to increase the transparency of the judicial system.

VIII. What did the Euro-model in Fact Deliver?

Stated in a nutshell, the constitutional independence of the judicial power in the form of a judicial council might work in the case of mature political environments, where decent ethical standards extant and embedded in the judiciary guarantee that the elected or appointed judges-administrators will put the common good before their own. However, the same constitutional insulation of the judicial power in countries *in transition* in the new Member States or candidate countries has been either awkward or had outright negative consequences for judicial independence and for the state and reform of judiciaries in general in these countries.

Judicial self-administration in the form of a judicial council is based on the (in general understandable) assumption that the more senior members of the profession have more experience. They should thus be better administrators. The institutional design of the judicial councils is such as to bring the more senior members of the judiciary to the fore; either directly, making some senior judges *ex lege* members of the JC (chief justice, presidents of other supreme courts etc), or indirectly, by election.

However, in transitional societies, which experience value discontinuity, there always is an inherent discrepancy between experience and values. Those with experience will typically adhere to the old system and other values. Senior judges will be inherited from the communist regime. Given the lack of purges within the judiciary and the shortage of judges after the fall of communist regimes, the number of judges from the communist era is particularly high at the higher echelons of the CEE judiciaries. One may speak of an 'inverse pyramid'. As Zdeněk Kühn put it, 'the higher one goes in the structure of the judiciary, the higher the percentage of ex-communists'.[89]

Once a national self-administrative body of the judiciary is established quite soon after the regime change, it is precisely the communist-grown judges who,

---

[88] CCJE, Opinion no 10 (2007), title of Part II.

[89] Z Kühn, 'The Democratization and Modernization of Post-communist Judiciaries' in A Febbrajo and W Sadurski (eds), *Central and Eastern Europe After Transition* (Ashgate, 2010) 177, 181.

because of their standing and seniority, will be given the key positions in the new institutional set-up. In the practice in the CEE countries which introduced the JC Euro-model,[90] this scenario kept repeating itself. Judicial councils and the self-administration of the judiciary came simply too early, before much or genuine structural reform and above all the (natural) renewal of judges could take place. Once established, the senior (Communism-inherited) judicial cadres took over, either halting or sometimes even reversing the reforms already carried out. However, this time around, the political process cannot say much in this respect, because the show is run by a constitutionally entrenched judicial council.

The fact that the Euro-model for the creation of the 'right' form of a judicial council came with just the institutional skeleton and little or no internal judicial virtues, was understandable and to a certain degree predictable. Law importation is typically limited to the importation of the structure, hardly to simultaneous importation of its internal culture and conventions.[91] What is being exported is the institutional exoskeleton, not the flesh which in the end indeed forms the genuine life of the institution. There was, however, a further problem with the skeleton itself: The institutional structure created and recommended[92] has in fact no genuine equal in the national states themselves.

How could a model be so strongly recommended if it in fact had no genuine parallel in reality? The point to remember in this respect is the way in which the recommended Euro-model was created, described in the previous sections of this chapter: It was by national judges meeting in various European and national fora and conjuring a model which they themselves would like. Such a model, apart from the obvious normative problems associated with its creation,[93] is also flawed from a *functional* point of view. The end product is in fact a mélange of judicial wishes 'this is the way we would love to have it, if ever anybody in our national state agreed to it'. However, the model itself was never genuinely tested in any real legal environment.

Said as a metaphor, all this resembles the situation in which a curious tourist from Eastern Europe visits a shop in, say, Munich and wishes to buy a pair of shoes. She has heard a lot positive about the quality of German products and thus is

---

[90] Note that not all CEE countries adopted the JC Euro-model. For instance, the Czech Republic retained its Ministry of Justice model. However, the Czech Republic is not alone. Some countries that introduced the judicial council model did not opt for the JC Euro-model. For instance, Poland never transferred virtually all powers regarding the career of judges to its National Council of the Judiciary (NCJ) and, moreover, in 2007 it banned court presidents from membership in the NCJ—see A Bodnar and L Bojarski, 'Judicial Independence in Poland' in Seibert-Fohr (n 11) 667, 669–79. Estonia also preferred the cooperative model of court administration, where judicial councils share many powers with the Ministry of Justice—see T Ligi, 'Judicial Independence in Estonia' in Seibert-Fohr (n 11) 741–55. In contrast, Slovak, Romanian, Bulgarian and Hungarian (until Orban's judicial reforms in 2011) judicial councils are examples of the JC Euro-model.

[91] Further see M Bobek, *Comparative Reasoning in European Supreme Courts* (Oxford University Press, 2013) 255.

[92] See in particular the judicial council model envisaged by ENCJ, Councils for the Judiciary Report 2010–2011; and CCJE, Opinion no 10 (2007).

[93] Above s V.

ready to invest a bit more money in order to obtain the real German '*Qualität*'. However, only after having brought the new shiny shoes home, she discovers the little label well hidden on the inside of the shoe stating 'Made in China'. After wearing the shoes for about a week, an unpleasant rash starts spreading around her heels. Enquiring with the producer of the shoes as to the genuine nature and composition of the product, she discovers that what she bought is in fact a series of experimental design with new types of untested dyestuff and materials used.

The same metaphor applies to the type of exportation of the JC Euro-model to the CEE countries. A model being marketed under the patronage of European institutions with a political sticker 'Made in Europe' should more correctly bear the title 'Made in Latin Europe', or rather, with tongue in cheek: 'Health Warning: Untested—Made by Judges for Judges'.

All of the abovementioned factors account for the emergence of façades of judicial independence with respect to the newly established judicial councils in transition countries in the CEE. Unfortunately, there might also be more pathological developments within a new judicial council in which senior judicial cadres coming from the communist period are given the chief say. This may even amount to certain 'hijacking' of the new institution by the communist-era judicial elites, and sealing it off behind a veil of judicial independence.

The Slovak National Judicial Council might be a sad example at hand in this respect.[94] In 2001, Slovakia opted for the JC Euro-model following the fall of the autocratic Mečiar's government. The Judicial Council of the Slovak Republic ('JCSR') is a body with constitutional standing.[95] It is composed of 18 members: Eight judges are elected from within the judiciary, three members are elected by the Slovak Parliament, three members are appointed by the President of the Slovak Republic and three members are appointed by the Government. The last (or, more precisely, the first) member of the JCSR, which is at the same time *ex lege* its chairman, is the President of the Slovak *Najvyšší súd* (Supreme Court, hereinafter NS). In practice, professional judges were always in the majority in the JCSR. The 'first' JCSR (2002–2007) was composed of 12 judges and six non-judges. The 'second' JCSR (2008–2013) even consists of 16 judges and two non-judges.[96] This shows how important it is to decide who selects judicial members of the judicial council and how the electoral law to the judicial council is designed.[97]

The importation of this new Euro-model has nonetheless not been matched by any visible rise in efficiency of the judiciary or the quality of justice. Depoliticisation

---

[94] We do not intend to provide a deep level empirical study of the impact of the JCSR on the Slovak judiciary—for such a thorough study see Kosař (n 55). However, we believe that the ensuing snapshot at what has been happening after the introduction of the JCSR clearly support the main arguments of our article.

[95] Art 141a of the Constitution of the Slovak Republic and related legislation, especially zákon č 185/2002 Z z, o Súdnej rade Slovenskej republiky [Law no 185/2002 Coll, on the Judicial Council of the Slovak Republic].

[96] Nominally at least 9 members must be judges; in practice, however, even the other institutions appoint judges as members of the JCSR.

[97] Above s V.

of the Slovak judiciary was also rather wishful thinking. Every election of the JCSR's chairman led to protracted constitutional litigation that attracted comments from all segments of the Slovak political scene. The new regime also allowed judges to become ministers without losing judicial office. Mr Štefan Harabin exploited this option in 2006, when he became the Minister of Justice. In 2007, judges avowedly called for and accepted nominations to the JCSR from politicians. The election of the new president of the NS in 2008–2009 became a political theatre. However, the politicisation of the judiciary reached its apex in 2010, when centrist parties won the parliamentary elections. The new government had little understanding for Harabin's methods and the war between the Minister of Justice, Mrs Lucia Žitňanská, and Mr Harabin, broke out. Not a single week passed without ferocious attacks waged by Harabin,[98] especially when Žitňanská announced her judicial reform that was supposed to reduce the influence of the president of the NS and the JCSR on the Slovak judiciary. On the other hand, Harabin's critics have been also very vocal. But all sides had one thing in common—they wanted to get as much support as possible from their political allies. In any case, the JCSR gradually brought the judiciary to the forefront of Slovak politics rather than insulating it from political tumult.

Similarly, the JCSR did little for enhancing transparency of the Slovak judiciary.[99] Appointment as well as promotion of judges remained as opaque as under the Ministry of Justice model. It became perhaps even more nepotistic than before. The access to judicial decisions did not improve until the Ministry of Justice, not the JCSR, started to publish online all decisions of district and regional courts in civil and commercial law cases in 2006 and passed through the law that required online publication of all judgments of Slovak courts in 2011.[100] To the contrary, the JCSR rather hindered transparency. The JCSR has been accused of *per rollam* voting,[101] secretiveness, and holding its meetings in awkward locations that dissuaded the public and journalists from attending them.

The introduction the JCSR had even more negative effects on the public confidence in the Slovak judiciary. To be fair, the situation was far from being bright in 2002, when the JCSR started to operate. The results of the 2002 Transparency International poll speak for themselves: 60 per cent of respondents stated that

---

[98] See G Woratsch, 'Zpráva o stavu slovenské justice—fenomén Štefan Harabin' [Report on the State of the Slovak Judiciary—the Štefan Harabin Phenomenon], Pecs, 23 April 2011 (hereinafter the 'Woratsch Report').

[99] See eg J Dubovcová, 'Umožňuje súčasný stav súdnictva zneužívanie disciplinárneho konania voči sudcom, zneužívanie výberových konaní a dáva výkonnej moci oprávnenie zasiahnuť do súdnej moci?' [Does the Current State of the Judiciary Enable the Misuse of Disciplinary Proceedings Against Judges, Misuse of Public Procurement, and Gives the Executive the Right to Interfere with the Judicial Power?] in Transparency International Slovensko (ed), *Výzvy slovenského súdnictva a možnosti zlepšenia existujúceho stavu* (Transparency International Slovensko, 2010) 50, 53–56; L Bojarski and W Stemker Köster, *The Slovak Judiciary: Its Current State and Challenges* (Open Society Foundation, 2011) 94 and 107–09; or the Woratsch Report (n 98).

[100] See Art 82a of Law No 757/2004 Z z, on Courts, as amended by Law No 33/2011 Z z and Law No 467/2011 Z z.

[101] Voting done by the so called 'per rollam' (by letter) means that it is a voting without calling a meeting (eg by correspondence), which meant that nobody could attend the JCSR's meetings.

corruption at courts and *prokuratura* existed and was widespread; 25 per cent of respondents stated that corruption at courts and *prokuratura* existed but they did not know how widespread it was; and only 1 per cent stated that corruption at courts and *prokuratura* did not exist.[102] At that time, it was generally thought that the judiciary reached its bottom during Mečiar's rule and that the situation could not get any worse.

However, after a decade of the functioning of JCSR, the confidence in the judiciary reached its lowest ebb ever in the Slovak history. The 2011 poll of the Institute for Public Affairs, which provided separate results for three categories of respondents—lay people, legal experts and judges—shows the deleterious impact of the JC Euro-model. As to lay people, 35 per cent of respondents trusted the NS of Slovakia and only 26 per cent of respondents trusted the judiciary as a whole,[103] whereas 59 per cent did not trust the NS and 70 per cent did not trust the judiciary.[104] The judiciary ranked last among all public institutions. The view of experts was similar regarding the judiciary, but it differed significantly as to the NS. While 21 per cent of experts trusted the judiciary, only 10 per cent trusted the NS. The level of distrust vis-a-vis the judiciary was very high (79 per cent), but the distrust of the NS reached an astonishing number (86 per cent).[105] What is most shocking is the view of judges themselves. Only 68 per cent of respondent judges trusted the judiciary, whereas 32 per cent indicated that they did not trust the Slovak courts.[106] The results of the poll regarding the NS are even more revealing. As many as 54 per cent of judges in the survey responded that they did not trust the NS, while only 46 per cent indicated that they trusted the NS.[107] This meant that judges themselves considered the NS the least trustworthy institution in Slovakia.

One thing has, however, changed. Before the introduction of the self-administration of the judiciary and the judicial council, one of the most frequently heard arguments was that the undue influence that the executive has over the judiciary must be misused in influencing decision making of the courts and the individual judges. Judicial self-administration was thus presented as a way of protecting judicial independence and as preventing politicians from putting pressure on judges. However, even with self-administration and the shielding of judges from political pressures, the instances of influencing of judges and their individual decision making still flourished and perhaps even increased in the period from 2002

---

[102] K Staroňová, 'Projekt "Súdny manažment" ako protikorupčný nástroj' [The 'Judicial Management' Project as Tool of Fight Against the Corruption] in E Sičáková-Beblavá and M Beblavý (eds), *Jedenásť statočných: prípadové studie protikorupčných nástrojov na Slovensku* (2008) 215, 217 (quoting the Transparency International Slovakia poll from 2004).

[103] Note that the Constitutional Court of Slovakia is not considered to be a part of the system of general courts in Slovakia and thus it was not covered by this question.

[104] Institute for Public Affairs (IVO), 'Slovenská justícia očami verejnosti, odborníkov a sudcov' [The Slovak Judiciary through the Eyes of the Public, Experts, and Judges] (2011), at 1. Note that the remaining responses (up to 100%) were 'I do not know'.

[105] ibid, at 2.

[106] ibid, at 2.

[107] ibid, at 2.

to 2009. The only difference was that before it could at least be maintained that these things were carried out by the corrupt political elite and because of system deficiencies. Now it was plainly the judges themselves who were to blame.

Moreover, in 2009, with the election of Mr Štefan Harabin to the presidency of the JCSR, the idea of judicial self-administration has lost any remaining credit in the Slovak society. So also did the idea that a judicial council of the Euro-model sort would be able to guarantee even a basic degree of judicial independence. Already the advent of Harabin to the head of the JCSR is quite telling: Harabin, after being appointed as the Minister of Justice in 2006, publicly announced steps which would be aimed at limiting the 'undue power' of the self-administration of the judges. However, later in 2008, when the position of President of the NS (and, by virtue of that position, also chairman of the JCSR) fell vacant, his policy changed. In early 2009, the Slovak government and parliament approved bills submitted by the Minister of Justice, Harabin. They carried out a series of amendments which broadened the scope of the self-administrative powers of the (already strong) JCSR, adding most significantly some budgetary and inspection powers. By this legislative change, the last remaining important competences of the Ministry of Justice were placed in the hands of the JCSR. In June 2009, the Minister of Justice, Harabin, sent the list of his preferred candidates to the JCSR, which exercised pressure on the electors. According to the 2011 Woratsch report, due to this pressure several of his allies, many of whom were court presidents, became members of the JCSR.[108] Given this orchestrated support, Harabin, while still the Minister of Justice, was elected unanimously by the JCSR to the position of the President of the NS and therefore also to the position of the chairman of the JCSR.

Since then, media allegations have included instances of corruption, nepotism and incompetence, the abuse of the powers of the NS president and the misuse of the JCSR's disciplinary powers against Harabin's critics.[109] Harabin was particularly eager to silence his critics at the NS. He himself initiated 12 disciplinary motions against NS judges in 2009 and 2010. The JCSR chaired by Harabin triggered one more motion.[110] Several lower court judges who dared to criticise Harabin also faced disciplinary trial, as a result of which they were often suspended and their salaries were significantly reduced during this interim period.[111]

In sum, the Slovak Judicial Council, created following the best practices of the Euro-model, has turned gradually into a 'mafia-like' structure of intra-judicial oppression, run in the name of 'judicial independence' by judges who started their judicial careers in the communist period. Whereas before one might have nourished the perhaps somewhat idealistic hope that one day there would be enough political will to do something with the administration of justice, the hopes for a new reform of a stillborn model, which has meanwhile acquired a constitutional status, are now close to zero.

---

[108] The Woratsch Report (n 98) 105.
[109] See Bojarski and Köster (n 99); Dubovcová (n 99) 54–56; or the Woratsch Report (n 98).
[110] Some of these cases are reported in Bojarski and Köster (n 99) 102–05.
[111] Dubovcová (n 99) 54–55.

Similar negative examples from other countries in the New Europe that established strong judicial councils, such as Hungary,[112] Bulgaria[113] or Romania,[114] keep telling a similar story: Granting extensive self-administration powers to the judiciary before its genuine internal reform is dangerous. In a better scenario, the new institution will be, for a few years or decades to come, a somewhat empty shell. In the worst case scenario, which appears to be unfortunately more frequent, behaviour and patterns start emerging which are very distant from anything the model was supposed to deliver: Judicial independence in the form of individual judicial independence and impartiality is not only unprotected, it may even be suppressed by judicial bosses. To speak of efficiency, quality, and/or transparency, that is of other values apart from the judicial independence the system promised to deliver, would amount to idealism bordering on naivety.

Conversely, there is the example of the Czech Republic. Castigated in a number of international reports,[115] the Czech Republic was considered, in terms of institutional reform of the judiciary, the 'black sheep' of the CEE region. By a historical accident rather than by a premeditated design, no judicial council was ever established in the Czech Republic, in spite of the EU pre-accession pressure. However, over the years, the post-communist Ministry of Justice model started evolving gradually: More and more powers have been de facto shared between the Ministry and court presidents.[116] Today, the Czech judiciary, in particular through the court presidents, have a considerable say in the administration of courts. However, the power is shared between the Ministry and the presidents of courts. The system has thus been generating a different balance, which is perhaps more sound than judicial unilateralism and isolation in a judicial council: Mutual checks and balances between the executive (controlled by the Parliament) and senior members of the judiciary.

In face of the above outlined questionable if not outright negative experience with judicial councils, what one may see today in CEE are somewhat extreme political reactions and measures being taken against judicial councils and judicial bosses running them. A number of these measures are plainly inappropriate and extreme, being later censured by European institutions and/or the international community: The recent evolution in Hungary and the 2011 Hungarian constitutional reform is a case in point here.[117] Some of the measures taken by the new

---

[112] Pokol (n 51) or Z Fleck, 'Judicial Independence and its Environment in Hungary' in J Přibáň, P Roberts and J Young (eds), *Systems of Justice in Transition: Central European Experiences since 1989* (Ashgate, 2003) 12.

[113] See eg Smilov (n 18) 313.

[114] Parau (n 11); R Coman and C Dallara, 'Judicial Independence in Romania' in Seibert-Fohr (n 11).

[115] Examples above, nn 64 and 66.

[116] For detailed discussion see Bobek (n 53).

[117] For an overview, see eg: A Jakab, 'On the Legitimacy of a New Constitution. Remarks on the Occasion of the New Hungarian Basic Law of 2011' in MA Jovanović and Đ Pavićević (eds), *Crisis and Quality of Democracy in Eastern Europe* (Eleven Publishing, 2012) 61 or L Salamon, 'Debates Surrounding the Concepts of the New Constitution' (2011) 3 *Hungarian Review* 1522. See also ch 13 further in this volume.

Hungarian constitutional majority included radical reforms of the Hungarian judicial council and the judiciary as such.[118] In spite of some of these measures being extreme, they should be read and understood in their context, which is not that dissimilar to other countries in the CEE.[119] Politicians, lawyers as well as the general public became increasingly frustrated with the judicial (non)performance in the institutional context of judicial brotherhoods or even mafia-like structures declaring themselves to be untouchable due to their 'constitutionally guaranteed' institutional independence.

Extreme problems may unfortunately generate extreme reactions. However, before censoring or praising either side, it is always essential to acquaint oneself with the genuine state of affairs on the ground. With respect to the judiciary and its (non)reform, it would certainly be useful for a number of international academics, who tend to publicly censure reform proposals on the paper, to have a closer look at the genuine state of a number of judiciaries in the CEE. They could perhaps try to get a case through the judicial system there. They could also acquaint themselves with persons and the style in which the institutions they are about to fervently advocate are in fact run. This is in no way a defence of highly problematic and often populist measures recently taken by a number of the CEE governments with respect to judges and the judiciary. It is rather a classical reminder that in any comparative study, understanding the context matters considerably.

Finally, it should also be born in mind that with respect to already 'hijacked' judicial councils in Slovakia as well as other CEE countries, time becomes of the essence. Judicial councils in these countries were given considerable personal powers as well, relating to (non)promotion, salaries and discipline of judges. Thus, potential dissenters within the judiciary are gradually weeded out (in disciplinary proceedings, by non-promotion, various other tools of oppression) and no potential dissenters are by definition allowed to enter the judiciary. The judicial councils, or rather that is to say the judicial bosses running them, control the appointment of new judges as well. Personal control is translated into a full 'inbreeding' of the existent structures: Sub-optimal judges choose docile and sub-optimal judicial trainees as their offspring. In the even least inventive scenario, judicial offices become de facto hereditary, with nepotistic family appointments of new judges becoming the rule.

This evolution and this reality gives the final blow to suggestions that condemning judicial councils as an unsuitable institutional design for countries in transition some ten or fifteen years after their establishment in these countries is premature and too rushed. True, no institution is perfect in its beginnings. Its positive elements may show only with time, once the environment and the people in it

---

[118] Including the lowering of the compulsory retirement age for judges, which has been subsequently declared unconstitutional by the Hungarian Constitutional Court (Decision 33/2012. (VII. 17.) AB, published also in the Magyar Közlöny 2012/95). The new law was also declared to be in violation of EU law in Case C-286/12, *Commission v Hungary*, ECLI: ECLI:EU:C:2012:687.

[119] And clearly voiced in a number of other chs in this volume—see in particular chs 6 and 13.

have matured as well. However, such pious wishes are off the point once the entire institution of the judicial council has not only been hijacked (which could indeed be just temporal), but the hijackers were also given the power to replicate themselves, thus being able to ensure their own continuation. One can always hope for positive changes in the future. These have, however, due to flawed institutional design, been delayed for years or, more realistically, for decades.

IX. Conclusions

The establishment of judicial councils in the new Member States and further EU candidate countries under the European lead can be seen as a case study for the process of Europeanisation of national institutions. The authors of this chapter are certainly in favour of European and international standards and the exchange of best practices. However, this chapter unfortunately provided a strong example of a case against European standards and best practices.

The case study has shown that if unconstrained by a democratic process, negotiation and compromise-making with other branches of the government, the judiciary might be tempted to promote constitutionally separate, even insulated models of judicial administration. Such models strongly favour institutional independence of judges (or rather judicial leadership and the court presidents in particular), to the detriment of individual judicial independence and impartiality of judges. If politically unchecked, judicial wishes adopted on a European level are then put into various non-binding instruments, which are then de facto imposed onto (yet) politically less stable systems. The effects might be problematic if not outright tragic.

To be precise, there is no problem with judges meeting on the international level and making recommendations, devising best practices etc. Quite to the contrary, it is the people with expertise who should devise expert solutions. Such outcomes must be, however, made subject to democratic discussion and critical scrutiny by other actors on the international level itself, or, failing to do so, on the national level. Democratic parliamentary scrutiny might be available in only some environments (such as within the European Union, with a directly elected European Parliament). However, at least executive scrutiny should be possible. In particular, national government representatives should be granted the voice in these matters so that they can critically examine the proposals adopted by judges in the transnational networks.

Such critical review at different levels ought to be available under normal circumstances. The particular setting of the JC Euro-model exportation to the CEE countries in the EU pre-accession period however demonstrated that sometimes such scrutiny may get lost in the cracks of multi-layered international environments. In the old Member States, where such recommendations were indeed just recommendations, that is international soft law, no one cared much, because this was something primarily concerned with the reforms in the 'East'. No one seriously thought of imposing these standards on the old Member States, being well aware of the strong political resistance. Such neglect might, however, eventually backfire onto the old Member States, as they are now being pushed by the international organisations to adopt the same model as well.[120] In the new Member States, with political processes weakened, there was not much serious democratic discussion, which would not be quickly overridden by the all-powerful argument 'Europe wills it'. Thus, as this case study furthermore demonstrated, the label 'soft law' or 'recommendations only' might be quite misleading with respect to a number of instruments adopted on the international or European level. As far as their capacity permits, other branches of government, national or supranational, would be well-advised to monitor soft law production very closely. The 'soft' rules might become 'hard' rules quite quickly.

Finally, in view of the evidence emerging from the CEE countries, it is suggested that the Euro JC model is an unsuitable institutional design for countries in transition. Judicial councils should cease to be promoted as 'the solution' to judicial reform in Europe and beyond. If adopting grand new institutions is not the best way forward for a judiciary in transition, what is? With respect to *transition* countries, we believe that cultural change and personal renewal must precede steps towards more 'macro' constitutional independence for the judiciary as such. The 'micro' independence, that is the independence and impartiality of individual judges, must be established and guaranteed first, before any grand and irreversible steps towards more 'macro' constitutional independence of the judicial power as such are taken. But this can in fact be achieved without a judicial council, or even, with tongue-in-cheek, *especially* if there is no judicial council, as the example of a number of other European countries daily demonstrates. Equally, the discussed 'black sheep' of the CEE transition region, the Czech Republic, might be now and also certainly in the nearest future with respect to individual judicial independence and performance much better off than Slovakia, the exemplary pupil of the JC Euro-model. Both countries, however, started from very similar settings with their negotiated break-up in 1993.

Put differently, the JC model is unsuitable for countries in transition, where internal ethical culture and a strong sense of judicial duty are still lacking. On the other hand, a 'do as you please' tactic is perhaps not helpful either. What we suggest is, in the first years and decade or two of transition, to divert the effort from the large-scale institutional design to smaller scale reforms, in particular by putting emphasis on enhancing efficiency and transparency within the judiciary and on writ-small mechanisms. These steps may include, among other things, open and transparent procedures for appointment and promotion of judges within the existing system of judicial appointments; openness to middle and senior level judicial appointments to the candidates from outside the professional judiciary;

---

[120] For instance, Germany has been recently criticised by the CoE for not having a judicial council (n 12).

education and formation of judges, including foreign languages and international experience; expanding auxiliary judicial staff in courts, thus de-burdening judges from administrative duties; professionalism in case and court management; publication of all judicial decisions online; uploading biographies of judges on the website of the relevant courts; providing real-time information about how each case file is handled; strictly random case assignment; and so on.

Among all the avenues of smaller scale reforms mentioned, one clearly stands out in terms of importance: The issue of open, transparent and competitive access to the judicial profession. If a transition country is able to establish and maintain it, half the battle for judicial reform has already been won.[121] Unfortunately, the JC model as practised in the CEE countries as well as in a number of Latin countries of its origin has precisely the opposite the tendency: Corporativism, mental closure, and even favouritism and nepotism in selection of new judges, if done only by the judges themselves. Any judicial body selected in this way, its quality and performance, will be by default always highly questionable, to say at least.

On a deeper level, it is apparent that our yardsticks for a successful judicial transformation are more rooted in the focus on the quintessential nature of judging: an independent and impartial decision in an individual case, delivered in a speedy way and of a reasonable quality. For that, individual guarantees on a micro-level are essential, together with strong individual judges. Unfortunately, what the Euro-model of judicial councils brings about in transition countries is strong institutional independence of the sum of judges, or rather the complete lack of control of few senior judicial officials, but little of individual judicial independence and courage.

---

[121] Also with regard to the application of EU law on the national level, as the intriguing Bulgarian case study demonstrates, presented below in ch 11 of this volume.

9

The Impossibility of Being a National and a European Judge at the Same Time: Doctrinal Rifts Between Hungarian and EU Administrative Law

MARTON VARJU AND ANDRÁS GYÖRGY KOVÁCS

I. Introduction

This chapter examines how doctrinal rifts between EU and domestic administrative law have affected the ability of Hungarian courts to fulfil their obligations under EU law as courts of the European Union. Specifically, it will look at the dilemma faced by Hungarian administrative courts of being required to observe domestic legal doctrine regulating their jurisdiction in the judicial review of administrative action and the conflicting doctrines of EU law governing the participation of national courts in the effective legal enforcement of EU law at the national level. Hungarian courts—confronted with conflicting loyalties—may find it impossible to deliver administrative justice which is constitutional under domestic law and which complies with EU obligations at the same time. This jeopardises not only the success of legal integration in the EU and the domestic reception of EU law, but also the protection offered in domestic and EU administrative law to individuals under the rule of law and under the right to effective judicial protection. It represents a further problem that the potential solutions available in the domestic jurisprudence may leave both EU and domestic legal doctrine unsatisfied making judicial review in Hungary susceptible to challenges from both domestic and EU constitutional law.

Ten years after the 2004 enlargement, the jurisdiction available to Hungarian courts in the judicial review of administrative action under national and EU law is still exercised in parallel dimensions. In the two domains, the jurisprudence of Hungarian courts uses different principles and the boundaries of their jurisdiction seem to be defined differently. In particular, while Hungarian law keeps the judicial supervision of administrative discretion within rather narrow doctrinal bounds, the review of legality on the basis of the proportionality principle of administrative conduct falling under the scope of EU law allows for a more robust judicial intervention. As a result, although Hungarian courts have acknowledged their obligations in the application and enforcement of EU law, they seem unable to integrate fully in administrative law domestic and European legal doctrine and reconcile their differences. This is not unheard of in other national administrative laws in Europe. Other Member States have also experienced the division on administrative law into separate domains where European and domestic law is applied depending on the circumstances of individual cases.[1]

The root of the problem is that Hungarian courts, administrative courts in particular, operate within a fairly strict domestically determined constitutional framework affecting doctrine in administrative law. Hungarian administrative courts are not provided with jurisdiction to examine the substance of administrative decisions, it is doctrinally excluded for them to supervise the choices made by public authorities under the powers available to them in legislation unless they are manifestly unreasonable (and defy the rules of logic), and they may interfere with the assessment of evidence and the facts of the case as established by the public authority when they are vitiated by obvious errors. In their supervision of the legality of administrative decisions, they are excluded from considering the suitability of administrative action and the availability of more appropriate alternatives. In this light, it is particularly problematic for them to accommodate the principle of proportionality and the principle (right) to effective judicial protection, as they follow from the jurisprudence of the Court of Justice. They are unable to ignore in the judicial review of administrative discretion the constitutionally informed doctrinal position that public authorities may enjoy no substantive discretion offering genuine choices between alternative decisional routes in delivering their decisions, although there are clear circumstances when substantive administrative discretion is made available to national authorities under EU law. The changes required from EU law, if they were implemented with due regard to domestic doctrine, would affect the position of Hungarian administrative courts under the domestic system of separation of powers, alter their role in the existing domestic systems of legal accountability, and it would modify the legitimacy of their decisions delivered in judicial review. In assessing the reaction of Hungarian courts to these challenges, we must revert back to the most significant theories of legal integration in the EU and examine whether their contrasting explanations of national court behaviour would cover the judicial responses to the doctrinal impasses of legal integration.

---

[1] See in this regard ML Fernandez Esteban, 'National Judges and Community Law: The Paradox of the Two Paradigms of Law' (1997) 4 *Maastricht Journal of European and Comparative Law* 143; J Bell, 'Mechanisms for Cross-fertilization of Administrative Law in Europe' in J Beatson and T Tridimas (eds), *New Directions in European Public Law* (Hart Publishing, 2000); C Hilson, 'The Europeanization of English Administrative Law: Judicial Review and Convergence' (2003) 9 *European Public Law* 125.

The dilemmas faced by Hungarian administrative courts reveal that the transformative impact of EU law has its legal limitations. Because national legal doctrine represents impediments to legal integration in Europe, effective transformation may require bottom-up rather than top-down approaches. It cannot be ignored that the constitutional position for refusing judicially engineered change in domestic administrative doctrine as ordered by EU law is—in formal terms—legitimate and rational. Matters such as the separation of powers and judicial involvement in matters of government, warrant domestic resistance and they should require the involvement of decision makers having legitimacy different from courts. Also, preserving complex domestic legal doctrine against the functional, effectiveness-based agendas of EU law seems compatible with the mandate of domestic courts under national law. Furthermore, because of the constitutional weight of the affected domestic doctrines, the accommodation of European administrative law requirements should assume a domestically initiated and coordinated reconsideration of judicial review and accountability at the national level. Enabling domestic courts to fulfil the task of acting as genuine agents of European Union law should be part of this process and the European involvement of Hungarian courts should be assessed from the perspective reinforcing administrative accountability in Hungary.

In this chapter, we will first look at the different theories of judicially driven legal integration in the European Union and consider whether they provide an apt description of potential judicial behaviour in circumstances, such as those faced by Hungarian administrative courts. Then we continue with an overview of the legal and doctrinal basis of judicial review in Hungary paying particular attention to those elements which have proved to be most problematic in light of the obligations of national courts following from EU law. This is followed by a short account of the applicable requirements of EU public law and the reception of those requirements by Hungarian courts. This will enable the discussion on the doctrinal gap between EU and Hungarian administrative law and on the potential solutions offered both at the EU and the national level.

II. Theories of Legal Integration and National Court's Dilemmas

Basic structural accounts of legal integration in the European Union regard the position and roles of national courts as fairly straightforwardly determined in the decentralised judicial system established for the legal enforcement of EU policies at the national level. They tell the tale that national courts were invited to act as the courts of the European Union by interpreting and enforcing EU law within their own jurisdiction and, with this, to secure the legitimacy—which is measured in the success of its outputs—and the effectiveness of the EU polity. By reinforcing

Member State compliance with EU policies, the participation of national courts in the EU framework gave a very concrete shape to the foundational principles of solidarity and equality among the Member States in the EU polity and it also gave concrete legal effect to the principle of loyalty of the Member States to the Union.[2] National courts are, therefore, positioned as crucial actors in the EU judicial system which are equipped with rights and burdened with obligations concerning the uniform and effective enforcement of EU law.

These discussions reveal, however, only very little of Member State courts' perspectives and motivations, and they seem to ignore the practical and doctrinal dilemmas faced by national courts proceeding under their EU and national mandate. Imagining national courts in the EU judicial system through the expansive matrix of the integrative (gravitational) principles of the EU legal order governing the enforcement of EU policies (for example direct effect, duty of interpretation, supremacy etc) does not unveil the finer details, the controversies and the dilemmas of national courts acting as the courts of the Union. It ignores the relevance of national factors in legal integration in Europe, in particular, that the reception of EU legal doctrine requires some form of legal grafting in domestic law and the operation of the relevant EU principles assumes some form of doctrinal incorporation by national courts, which latter could involve national courts determining the foundations and the limits of their obligations.[3] Because of the predominant perspective of top-down accounts of legal integration, they overlook the circumstances in which for domestic courts it may be impossible to act as a national and a European judge at the same time.

The theories of European legal integration—following Karen Alter's categorisation—can be grouped into four dominant groups. The legalist theory suggests that the internal dynamic expansion of EU law—as generated by its inherent legal logic—is responsible for national courts feeling compelled to follow the integrative legal doctrine developed in the jurisprudence of the Court of Justice.[4] More controversially, the theory continues that national courts have become partners in the enforcement of the integrationalist and functionalist legal doctrine of the Court of Justice because they were 'convinced' by the legal arguments supporting it and because they found their own institutional importance in the Member State concerned through the application of EU law.[5] In this context, where the compelling nature of legal doctrine and its clear logic could secure the loyalty of national courts, individual judgments disobeying or departing from EU law should be interpreted as caused by misinformation and incompetence, which in

---

[2] M Klamert, *The Principle of Loyalty in EU Law* (Oxford University Press, 2013) 37.

[3] In the case of Hungary, see M Varju and F Fazekas, 'The Reception of European Union Law in Hungary' (2011) 48 *CML Rev* 851 and M Varju, 'The Judicial Reception of EU Law' in M Varju and E Varnay (eds), *The Law of the European Union in Hungary* (HVG-Orac, 2014).

[4] K Alter, 'Explaining National Court Acceptance of European Court Jurisprudence: A Critical Evaluation of Theories of Legal Integration' in AM Slaughter, A Stone Sweet and JHH Weiler (eds), *The European Court and National Courts—Doctrine and Jurisprudence* (Hart Publishing, 1998) 227–51, 230.

[5] ibid.

all instances can be corrected by pointing out to national courts the correct legal solution.[6]

The perhaps least substantiated neo-realist explanation suggests that the relevant legal decisions at the EU level and before national courts are 'shaped by national interest calculations', which proposition is based on the rather broad assumption that national governments can influence court behaviour and jurisprudence.[7] The EU legal system creating individual incentives for actors at EU and Member State level is the core explanation arising from neo-functionalist theories, which hold that national legal actors have a direct—financial, professional (prestige), or political—stake in applying EU legal doctrine.[8] For national courts, this means, in particular, gaining powers in judicial review which powers have not been made available to them under national law.[9]

Alter's inter-court competition theory, which follows from discourses on bureaucratic politics, is based on the assumption that national courts as bureaucratic actors have their own identifiable interests which they pursue within the bounds imposed on them by politics and law.[10] According to her, EU legal doctrine is used in the bureaucratic struggles between the different layers within the national judiciary and between the judiciary and the political bodies at state level, which presumption entails that the judicial reception and application of EU law in the Member States is only an inadvertent consequence of bureaucratic politics.[11] The conduct of national courts is governed by their own institutional interests and by their bases of institutional support, and the most significant bureaucratic factor influencing national court behaviour is the competition between the different, often contradicting interests of higher and lower courts, which sees higher and lower courts interacting in the application of EU law like members of a complicated—if not troubled—nuclear family.[12]

Although the different theories of legal integration have provided detailed insights into national court behaviour, they—because of the perspective taken—neglect explaining the potential impediments at the Member State level to national courts applying EU law and observing their EU legal obligations. They also neglect taking into account the different domestic experiences with the reception of EU legal doctrine. As it will be shown below, the judicial reception of EU law in Hungary was characterised by reserved professionalism and the making of studious efforts to avoid failure. It was a task which needed to be performed on the basis of legal obligations laid down in EU and domestic law, and it presented national courts—the Curia, that is the Supreme Court of Hungary, in particular—with the technical task of micro-managing the application and interpretation of EU law

---

[6] ibid.
[7] ibid, 234.
[8] ibid, 238–39.
[9] ibid.
[10] ibid, 241–42.
[11] ibid.
[12] ibid.

(for example clarifying the misinterpretation of EU law by lower courts, correcting wrong early judicial practice or managing the influx of litigation based on EU law). Keeping (restoring) the professional image of the Hungarian judiciary (saving face for the Hungarian judiciary) was of paramount importance. Considerable emphasis was placed on the training, supervising and aiding of judges in order to ensure that the work will be done and will be done correctly even in unfavourable circumstances (for example, language barriers, unfamiliar legal culture, lack of adequate resources).[13]

The measured implementation of reception obligations under EU law signals that Hungarian courts were reluctant to abandon in the reception process national legal doctrine and to revisit their commitment to the constitutional settlement reflected therein. They were rather cautious about overstepping the boundaries of their jurisdiction under domestic law and they were careful with applying EU legal principles (for example proportionality) which would extend their jurisdiction. While this gain could be interpreted in legalist terms, the resulting dilemma of choosing between competing obligations and the resulting doctrinal and legal split in domestic administrative law escapes the confines of the legalist and the other previously mentioned theories. This is even more evident when we consider that the solution to this problem seems to lie in voluntary bottom-up adjustment initiated at the national level which needs to be carried out in the framework of a comprehensive reassessment of the functions of administrative justice in Hungary. This latter possibility has received only very limited attention in the dominant theoretical discourses.

III. Judicial Review in Hungary and its Doctrinal Basis

The dilemmas faced by Hungarian administrative courts under pressure from their EU obligations originate from the markedly confined position of judicial review and administrative justice—as a matter of doctrine and practice—in domestic law. When proceeding in judicial review, courts are invited to ensure the control of the legality of administrative decisions and thus they form an integral part of the system giving effect to the separation of powers doctrine recognised in the Hungarian Constitution. Administrative courts and administrative justice are given a special constitutional position as expressed in Article XXVIII paragraph 7 of the Chapter of the Hungarian Fundamental Law on 'Freedom and responsibility'. It holds—providing a direct constitutional foundation for the judicial control of the administration—that every person has a right to legal redress against judicial and administrative decisions which violate his or her rights or legitimate interests.

---

[13] For an overview of training and learning opportunities available to judges in Hungary, see AF Tatham, 'The Impact of Training and Language Competence on Judicial Application of EU Law in Hungary' (2012) 18 *European Law Journal* 577.

Although its direct constitutional relevance makes the jurisdiction available in judicial review stand out from the general powers exercised by Hungarian courts, the actual institutional system of administrative justice in Hungary holds no particularities. It is operated by ordinary courts on three distinct layers of jurisdiction. General first instance jurisdiction in administrative cases is exercised by the 20 administrative courts which are distinct from ordinary civil and criminal courts only in their institutional organisation. Appeal to appeal courts is allowed only in a restricted group of cases where the administrative decisions under challenge are reached in a single instance procedure before public authorities. Against the first instance and the appeal court judgments, extraordinary appeal on questions of law may be submitted to the Curia which will be examined by specialist judicial chambers designated within the administrative and employment law division. As a special statutory obligation, the Curia is also endowed with the general task of monitoring the practice of lower courts based on its express constitutional responsibility for maintaining the uniformity of judicial practice in Hungary.

In the Hungarian administrative system, the statutory regulation of administrative procedure[14] recognises that redress against first instance administrative decisions should be made available in the form of an appeal within the administration, which could then be challenged in judicial review before administrative courts in a single instance process. As an exception from the norm, there is the previously mentioned special group of administrative cases decided by certain central administrative agencies where appeal is not provided against first instance administrative decisions (competition decisions of the Hungarian Competition Authority, decisions of the Hungarian National Bank on banking supervision, decisions of the Hungarian Public Procurement Authority, decisions of the National Media and Infocommunications Authority, or the decisions of the Hungarian Energy and Public Utility Regulatory Authority). In these cases, because no appeal is afforded, the first instance court proceeding in judicial review is given jurisdiction to reform the administrative decision challenged. Its judgment can be appealed before the Budapest Metropolitan Court which is a regional court located in Budapest with appeal jurisdiction reserved for such matters. The appeal judgment of the Budapest Metropolitan Court may be challenged in extraordinary appeal before the Curia.

In order to cement its constitutional position, the Fundamental Law contains further key provisions relevant for judicial review. Article XXIV paragraph 1 of the Chapter on 'Freedom and responsibility' holds that every person has the right to have his or her case decided by administrative authorities in a reasonable time in an impartial and fair procedure. This also includes the obligation of public authorities to provide reasons for their decisions, as determined in statute. This constitutional provision, which also appears in the Act on Administrative Procedures as

---

[14] Act 2004:CXL on the general rules of administrative procedures and services rendered by the administration.

the right to fair (good) administration,[15] indicates the potential heads of review of administrative action by administrative courts. It must be distinguished from the separate constitutional right to a fair judicial process. The right to a fair judicial process is regulated by Article XXVIII paragraph 1 of the Fundamental Law as the right to have criminal charges against a person or civil rights and obligations determined within a reasonable period of time in a fair and open trial by an independent and impartial court established by law. Although it has not been tested, fair trial rights are not applicable to administrative procedures, therefore public authorities need not observe the constitutional requirement of independence and they only have to meet the lower threshold impartiality requirement of the right to fair administration.

The key doctrinal boundary for the jurisdiction available in judicial review is the prohibition for courts to substitute the assessment of the public authority on matters of substance with their own. The relevant legal principle holds that administrative decisions may only be subject to the supervisory jurisdiction exercised by courts in judicial review when they are vitiated by illegality. The dividing line between the review of legality and the review of the merits of the case is, however, not always clear in Hungarian law. For instance, it may be particularly difficult to distinguish questions of legality (rationality and reasonableness) and expediency, which could both be addressed in appeal but not in judicial review. In such instances, administrative courts proceeding in the judicial review of administrative decisions—often based on the use of discretionary powers—must avoid overstepping the bounds of their jurisdiction and touching upon the merits of the reviewed decision by way of extending their examination to matter of expediency.

A related further significant doctrinal boundary laid down in Hungarian judicial practice concerns the constitutional limit (prohibition) on courts to interfere in judicial review with matters decided within the discretion available to public authorities. As it follows from the relevant statutory provisions and as acknowledged by courts, discretionary decisions by public authorities will be lawful when the public authority has managed to establish the facts of the case adequately, it has observed the relevant procedural requirements, it has taken into account in the use of discretionary powers transparent and relevant considerations, and the administrative decision delivered is reasonable as indicated in the reasons provided by the public authority.[16] This is based on the understanding in Hungarian administrative law that the discretionary powers available to public authorities always follow from a direct authorisation based on legislation. Most frequently, these are legislative provisions which enable a choice for administrative authorities between different decisional routes under the same factual circumstances. The exclusion of other legitimate forms of discretionary powers in Hungarian administrative law is a requirement under the rule of law. It holds among others that discretionary powers must be strictly regulated in legislation, legislation must

---

[15] Act 2004:CXL, Art 4(1).
[16] Code on Civil Procedure, Art 339/B.

spell out the boundaries of the discretion available, and that it must indicate the considerations which need to be taken into account by public authorities acting under discretionary powers.[17] The rule of law also prohibits that legally unlimited discretion is made available for administrative bodies and that broad discretionary powers are available outside instances when it is absolutely necessary.[18]

Based on these requirements, the use of discretionary powers by public authorities is guided as a norm by considerations laid down in legislation as relevant. These usually follow from terms used in legislative provisions qualifying the use of powers made available, for instance, terms like 'rational', 'guilty', 'unfair' or 'relevant'. They enable that public authorities use their powers subject to the regulatory principles and objectives of the relevant piece of legislation. In case legislation does not identify the considerations relevant for the use of discretionary powers, public authorities remain bound by the fundamental rules of logic and their decisions must be reasonable ('*okszerű*'). In other words, in Hungarian doctrine the use of discretionary powers will be lawful when public authorities decide according to the relevant legislative provisions and their decision is the most appropriate in the particular circumstances of the given case. This necessarily determines the scope and the intensity of the judicial review exercised by administrative courts. Their supervisory jurisdiction will be limited to examining whether the relevant considerations have been observed, and whether the administrative decision is logical and reasonable. Apart from reconsidering whether the assessment of evidence was devoid of mistakes, they are prevented from engaging in any form of reassessment of the administrative decision.

In Hungarian administrative law, we must distinguish between the discretion available to public authorities to decide cases and the discretion enjoyed by them in the assessment of evidence. This latter refers to the statutory power of public authorities to choose on the basis of the same evidence submitted between different routes in the determination of the facts of the case. Allowed nearly complete freedom in the assessment of evidence, which is only constrained by the boundaries determined in the law of evidence,[19] public authorities examine every piece of evidence individually and in relation with each other, and make their assessment within their own discretion. The use of the discretionary powers to assess evidence by the public authority, as in case of the discretion available to decide the case, must comply with the requirements of rationality, in other words, it must be reasonable. The discretionary assessment of evidence is not available to public

---

[17] These decisional alternatives may follow from the framework character of regulation, from the use of inadequately determined legal concepts, or from direct legislative authorisation.

[18] Hungarian legal terminology uses the term 'discretion' ('*diszkrecionális*') specifically to describe the rare instances where the decisional liberty of administrative bodies is legally unlimited. Having the ability to make discretionary decisions denotes the possibility granted in legislation for public authorities to make contradicting decisions under similar factual circumstances without jeopardising the substantive lawfulness of their decisions whatever they may be.

[19] This also follows from the fact that the relevant legal provisions do not include the term 'free' before the word 'discretion' ('*meggyőződés*') as in Art 206(1) of the Code on Civil Procedure, applicable to courts, and in Art 50(6) in Act 2004:CXL, applicable to public authorities.

authorities in every instance. They may not be provided with alternative routes in the assessment of evidence and they may be bound to establish a certain fact on the basis of a certain piece of evidence.[20]

The doctrinal position of the judicial control of substantive administrative discretion could be summarised as follows. Judicial review is available in case the administrative decision brought within discretionary powers contradicts the file (that is, it is based on an error in the assessment of facts/evidence) or it is (manifestly) unreasonable.[21] Unreasonableness as a cause of illegality refers to the use of administrative discretion in breach of the rules of logic. This must be distinguished from matters of expediency. Expediency, which can be examined in applications for appeal and not for judicial review, allows considering whether alternative decisional routes could have been followed under the discretionary powers available. As opposed to unreasonableness, it enables the public authority or court proceeding in appeal to examine whether more reasonable, more optimal or better administrative decisions than those challenged were available, and to disagree with the particular use of the powers available. It would be incompatible with the constitutional position of judicial review to include—as under expediency—the assessment of the administrative decision from a perspective or with a weight which is different from that selected by the public authority.

These doctrinal boundaries of the jurisdiction available in judicial review appear to be difficult to reconcile with the requirements imposed on national courts exercising the supervisory jurisdiction under the principle of proportionality, as they follow from the jurisprudence of the Court of Justice and the European Court of Human Rights in Strasbourg. Even if we accept that judicial review under proportionality and reasonableness may indeed lead to similar standards but different intensity of judicial review,[22] Hungarian administrative law does not seem to offer the sliding scale which would enable reasonableness to operate as a functional equivalent of proportionality. It must not be ignored that Hungarian administrative law does not accept that substantive discretion would be available to public authorities under domestic law, and, therefore, the doctrinal boundaries developed for judicial review having this in mind may not be able to react appropriately to circumstances when domestic public authorities are given substantive discretion by EU law and EU legal doctrine requires Hungarian courts to assess the

---

[20] When pieces of evidence contradict each other, public authorities must follow the statutory provisions of the law of evidence, for instance, the legal provisions on the burden of proof and the weight of evidence. In case the contradiction remains unresolved, the public authority may assess the evidence within its discretion.

[21] Manifest unreasonableness is interpreted as the logical inconsistency of the decision having an impact on its substance or merits. This implies that the application for judicial review, after establishing the manifest unreasonableness of the administrative decision, must be able to demonstrate what would have constituted a reasonable decision. This then could be acknowledged by the court when reforming the administrative decision, provided that it is endowed with such jurisdiction. For the legal test, see Decision 3085/2013 of the Hungarian Constitutional Court.

[22] See, inter alia, M Bobek, 'Reasonableness in Administrative Law: A Comparable Reflection on Functional Equivalence' in G Sartor et al (eds), *Reasonableness and Law* (Springer, 2009).

suitability and proportionality of the resulting administrative decisions. Crucial from the perspective of individuals, owing to the different doctrinal bases Hungarian courts—bound by EU and domestic law—are required to exercise their jurisdiction in judicial review differently (exercise different jurisdictions for judicial review) when proceeding under Hungarian and under European law. While altering the judicial understanding of judicial review is not excluded, it must be kept in mind that the doctrines governing the scope and the intensity of judicial review are based on the constitutional positioning of judicial review and also on the restraints following therefrom on the jurisdiction available to courts. It is a different question, however, that the current jurisdictional bounds for judicial review could be maintained considering that the parallel application of different systems of judicial review violates legal certainty and formal equality—also protected under the Fundamental Law. This has implications beyond the impact of EU law as the reduced scope and intensity of judicial review—coupled with restrictive standing conditions—could jeopardise the very right providing the constitutional basis of judicial review, the right to the effective judicial control of the administration.[23]

IV. Judicial Review and EU Requirements

The jurisdiction exercised by national courts in judicial review—when proceeding under the scope of EU law—is subjected to the general requirement addressed to national courts in Article 19(1) TEU (Treaty on European Union) laying down the general clause of effective legal protection. This, together with the corresponding principle of/right to effective judicial review/protection before domestic courts developed by the Court of Justice,[24] covers the procedural and the substantive, remedial components of national judicial systems including the scope and intensity of judicial review. Based on broader considerations of effective compliance with EU policies and supporting the principles (for example supremacy, direct effect) responsible for effective legal compliance at national level, it requires that effective legal redress is available before Member State courts for the protection of rights derived from EU law.

The relevant EU jurisprudence recognises concrete requirements flowing from the right to effective judicial protection. These detailed requirements could affect 'an individual's standing and legal interest in bringing proceedings'

---

[23] The requirement of an effective judicial review of administrative action also follows from EU law, especially from the law on regulated markets affecting judicial review against national regulatory agencies. See P Larouche and X Taton, *Enforcement and Judicial Review of Decisions of National Regulatory Authorities* (Cerre (Centre on Regulation on Europe) Study, Brussels, 2011).

[24] Case 222/84 *Johnston* [1986] ECR 1651 and Case 222/86 *Heylens* [1987] ECR 4097. See also Case C-424/99 *Commission v Austria* [2001] ECR I-9285, where the ECJ held that internal appeal to an administrative authority cannot be regarded as being equivalent to a review by a genuine judicial body.

before national courts, and the national provisions caught under the effective legal protection requirement must meet, within the discretion available to the Member States in this connection,[25] the general principles of equivalence and effectiveness.[26] Regarding the substance of judicial review, EU law demands from national courts to protect legitimate expectations[27] and that they must apply the principle of proportionality when controlling—under the scope of EU law—the decisions of administrative authorities and the sanctions imposed by them.[28] The application of the proportionality principle entails examining, beyond the control of administrative decisions on the basis of the applicable legislative requirements, whether the discretionary choices by public authorities were suitable, necessary and proportionate in the sense that public authorities have struck a fair balance between the relevant competing considerations.[29] The proportionality principle could require courts proceeding in judicial review to examine whether the administrative authority could have reached a more suitable and/ or less restrictive decision.[30] This latter element of the proportionality principle has been characterised as enabling national courts to reach beyond the jurisdiction provided to them in judicial review under national law and interfere with the use of discretionary powers by public authorities beyond the examination of the reasonableness of the administrative decision.[31]

Judicial review before national courts faces further requirements in multi-layered arrangements, namely, in the judicial control of EU Commission investigatory powers available in the enforcement of EU competition law. Interference by EU law with judicial review at the national level was justified by the Court of Justice by identifying the relevant national rules and guarantees as crucial safeguards for the protection of the right to private life in EU competition enforcement procedures.[32] Based on the requirement of the effective supervision (judicial review) by national courts of coercive measures used in EU competition investigations

---

[25] The autonomy of the Member States in regulating national procedures is expressly recognised in connection with the introduction of procedural measures for the protection of legal certainty and regarding the determination of the details of those rules in the context of national procedural law and regarding the determination of the details of those rules in the context of national procedural law, Case C-246/09 *Bulicke* [2010] ECR I-7003, para 36; Case C-63/08 *Pontin* [2009] ECR I-10467, para 48.

[26] Joined Cases C-87/90 to C-89/90 *Verholen* [1991] ECR I-3757, para 24; Case C-13/01 *Safalero* [2003] ECR I-8679, para 50; Case C-12/08 *Mono Car Styling* [2009] ECR I-6653, para 49; Joined Cases C-317/08 to C-320/08 *Alassini* [2010] ECR I-2213, para 48.

[27] Case C-5/89 *Commission v Germany* [1990] ECR I-3437; Case C-24/95 *Alcan Deutschland* [1997] ECR I-1591.

[28] See T Tridimas, *The General Principles of EU Law*, 2nd edn (Oxford University Press, 2006) ch 4.

[29] Inter alia, Case 120/78 *Rewe-Zentral AG v Bundesmonopolverwaltung für Branntwein* [1979] ECR 649.

[30] Inter alia, Case C-112/00 *Schmidberger* [2003] ECR I-5659.

[31] See the discussion in English administrative law, inter alia, J Jowell and A Lester, 'Beyond Wednesbury: Substantive Principles of Administrative Law' [1987] *PL* 368; J Jowell and A Lester, 'Proportionality: Neither Novel Nor Dangerous' in J Jowell and D Oliver (eds), *New Directions in Judicial Review* (Stevens, 1988); I Leigh, 'Taking Rights Proportionately: Judicial Review, the Human Rights Act and Strasbourg' [2002] *PL* 265.

[32] Case C-94/00 *Roquette Frères* [2002] ECR I-9011, paras 30–32 and 34–30.

in the territory of the Member States, the Court of Justice confirmed the obligation of national courts to contribute to the effectiveness of EU competition procedures, and it examined the limitations barring national courts from questioning the necessity of Commission investigations and their lawfulness and the power available to them to ensure that 'the coercive measure envisaged is not arbitrary or disproportionate to the subject-matter of the investigation ordered.'[33]

Concerning the ability of national courts to control the use of coercive powers in investigations conducted by the EU Commission, the Court of Justice distinguished between two scenarios. First, when judicial review is carried out to examine the arbitrariness of investigatory measures, the Court of Justice confirmed the requirement that national courts should control arbitrary coercive measures in EU competition investigations and it discussed how the Commission may facilitate the effectiveness of national judicial control for the protection of the rights of the undertaking concerned.[34] The Court also urged national courts to assume a more autonomous role in applying EU law and to refrain from making preliminary references to the Court of Justice, the latter of which may hinder the effectiveness of the Commission's investigations.[35] Second, regarding the examination by national courts of whether the investigatory measures were disproportionate, the judgment emphasised that judicial review at the national level must extend to the control of proportionality and that the assessment by national courts should extend to a number of factors affecting the lawfulness of the discretionary choices made by the Commission.[36] Accordingly, judicial review must extend to the assessment of the seriousness of the suspected infringement, the nature of the involvement of the undertaking concerned, the importance of the evidence sought, whether the necessity to interfere with the rights of the undertaking concerned is minimal, and whether the interference would be manifestly disproportionate and intolerable.[37]

Overall, under EU law national courts proceeding in judicial review may be required to stretch the boundaries of the jurisdiction available under national law in order to meet the requirement of effective legal protection under Article 19(1) TEU. While it is not excluded that this may be compatible with domestic legal doctrine, the judicial scrutiny demanded, especially under the proportionality principle, could be more intensive than that under the reasonableness test and judicial review could reach much further into the discretion exercised by public authorities than that allowed in domestic law. It is likely that under EU law the jurisdiction exercised by domestic courts could contradict the domestic doctrinal bases of the supervisory jurisdiction available to them in domestic constitutional law for controlling the legality of administrative action.

---

[33] ibid, paras 51–52.
[34] ibid, paras 54–68.
[35] ibid.
[36] ibid, paras 77–80.
[37] ibid.

V. The Reception of EU Law Requirements by Hungarian Administrative Courts

Since 2004, most of the principles governing the application and interpretation of EU law by national courts has been incorporated into Hungarian judicial practice without identifying incompatibilities between EU requirements and domestic doctrine. The execution of the reception process fits particularly well with the legalist theory on European legal integration as Hungarian courts keenly relied on provisions of domestic law and the relevant jurisprudence of the Court of Justice in anchoring the principles of EU law. Regarding reception as a process of meeting legal obligations is reflected particularly clearly in Hungarian courts recognising their tasks and obligations under EU law without opening a dialogue with the Court of Justice and settling most issues within their own jurisdiction. This inward looking process, despite the prospect of doctrinal and legal incompatibilities between EU and domestic law, avoided openly addressing the potential doctrinal crises and assessing the impact of the reception of EU law from the perspective of general domestic constitutional requirements, such as legal certainty or equality before the law.

The reserved technical-legal character of the reception process was made clear by the Curia assuming very early the responsibility for ensuring the development of uniform judicial practices in the application of EU law[38] and for issuing authoritative judgments, which determined the correct interpretation and application of EU law and consolidated the relevant domestic jurisprudence.[39] As a starting point, judicial practice established that EU law forms part of the Hungarian legal order and Hungarian courts are ordinary courts of the European Union.[40] The basis for the justiciability of EU measures was found in the Europe-clause of the Constitution (now Article E of the Fundamental Law), which governs both Hungary's membership of the EU and the applicability of EU law in the Hungarian legal order.[41] The principles of supremacy and direct effect found their way into Hungarian judicial practice with heavy references to the jurisprudence of the Court of Justice.[42] It was accepted that supremacy and direct effect provide the basis for establishing the illegality of administrative measures and lower court judgments under EU law.[43] Hungarian courts have never been hesitant to set aside

---

[38] Case No Kfv.I.35.021/2006/8.

[39] The extremely important PK-KK Joint Opinion 1/2009, discussed in detail below, is a non-binding instrument used by the Curia in the coordination of the reception process.

[40] Case No Kfv.I.35.052/2007/7, Kfv.I.35.055/2007/5, Kfv.I.35.014/2007/4, and BH 2006.35.

[41] Case No EBH 2006.1442.

[42] Cases No Kfv.I.35.052/2007/7, Kfv.I.35.160/2007/4, Kfv.IV.37.757/2009/6, Kfv.I.35.508/2007/6, Kfv.I.35.055/2007/5, Kvf.III.37.043/2007/4, EBH2006.1442 and Kfv.V.35.470/2011/6.

[43] Inter alia, Cases No Kfv.I.35.052/2007/7, Kfv.IV.37.757/2009/6, Kfv.I.35.055/2007/5, Kfv.III.37.043/2007/4, Kfv.I.35.511/2007/7 and Kfv.IV.37.240/2007/11.

domestic legal provisions to give effect to EU measures.[44] Hungarian judicial practice regards supremacy primarily as a principle determining the applicable law before Hungarian courts and setting out the obligations of national courts when applying EU law. Direct effect is applied in the context of enforcing non- or badly implemented directives subject to the restrictions and distinctions established in EU law.[45] The duty of interpretation as an instrument for the enforcement of EU obligations was also recognised.[46]

Judicial practice also took notice of the obligations of national administrative authorities following from EU legal doctrine. The jurisprudence directed national authorities to follow the principles laid down in the judgments in *Constanzo* and *Larsy*.[47] The Curia ruled that public authorities (here, tax authorities) must take account of the relationship between domestic tax legislation and EU law and its consequences on the application of national law, as they follow from the directly relevant jurisprudence of the EU Court.[48] It was also declared by the Curia that examining the compatibility of the application of Hungarian law by public authorities with EU law falls within its jurisdiction in judicial review.[49] Hungarian courts have also recognised that the obligation to set aside domestic measures which are incompatible with EU law is applicable to all legislative, judicial and administrative authorities in the Member States and that the failure of public authorities to observe the compatibility of the applicable domestic legal provisions with EU law undermines the legality of administrative decisions.[50] There have also been a couple of not particularly well-agreed attempts to establish the responsibility of public authorities for ensuring the full force and effect of EU law and for the effective protection of rights derived from EU law.[51]

The principle of loyalty (cooperation) of the Member States, as laid down in Article 4(3) TEU, offered a seminal black letter instrument for the Hungarian judiciary to administer the reception process. It served as the basis for the recognition of legal principles in domestic law, such as the applicability of EU law before domestic courts,[52] the *ex officio* application of EU law in place of domestic law,[53] the legally binding nature and enforceability of decisions addressed to Member States,[54]

---

[44] Inter alia, Cases No Kfv.I.35.160/2007/4, Kfv.IV.37.757/2009/6, Kfv.III.37.043/2007/4, Kvf.I.35.165/2008/7 and Kfv.I.35.344/2008/7.

[45] Cases No EBH2006.1442, Kfv.I.35.165/2008/7, Kfv.III.37.043/2007/4, Kfv.I.35.160/2007/4, Kfv.I.35.165/2008/7 and Mfv.II.10.889/2011/4.

[46] Cases Kfv.I.35.165/2008/7 and Kfv.IV.37.177/2008/4.

[47] Case 103/88 *Costanzo* [1989] ECR 1839, para 31 and C-118/00 *Larsy* [2001] ECR I-5063, paras 43–45 and 51–53.

[48] Cases No Kfv.I.35.312/2007/5, Kfv.I.35.052/2007 and Kfv.I.35.008/2007. Joined Cases C-290 and 333/05 *Nádasdi and Németh* [2006] ECR I-10115.

[49] Case No Kfv.I.35.276/2008/2.

[50] Case No 24.K. 33.917/2008/5 and No 3.K-30698/2006/33.

[51] Case No Kfv.I.35.344/2008/7 and No Kfv.I.35.275/2011/3

[52] Case No EBH 2006.1442 and No 9.K.30 582/2006/4.

[53] Case No 9.K.30 582/2006/4.

[54] Cases No Pf.III.20.255/2009/5 and 11.K. 31.613/2007/3. The court proceeding at first instance relied on the clear and simple formula that decisions are enacted to bind the addressee after being published or communicated to that person, Case No 9.G.40268/2008/10.

the proportionality of Member State action under EU law,[55] the principles of supremacy and direct effect in relation to international treaties concluded by the EU,[56] the basis and conditions of the liability for breaches of EU law,[57] and the requirement for the state not to legislate in contravention of EU law.[58] Most importantly, the *UMTS*[59] judgment of the Budapest Metropolitan Court relied on Article 4(3) TEU to develop a jurisprudential solution which met the requirement of effective judicial protection under EU law but which challenged standing domestic administrative legal doctrine head on. The judgment was the first recognition in the relatively smooth legalistic reception process that there may be irreconcilable rifts between domestic doctrine and EU requirements, which left the question open whether domestic courts are allowed to decide cases in doctrinally questionable ways and that as a matter of Hungarian constitutional law creative judicial solutions expanding jurisdictional boundaries are acceptable responses to the pressures arising from EU law.

The reception of the law on remedies against breaches of EU law entailed further doctrinal and legal uncertainties for Hungarian courts. The traditional legalist reflexes were by-and-large insufficient as the relevant principles of EU law are less certain and less well-rehearsed than those governing the application and enforcement of substantive EU law.[60] Introducing damages liability for legislation violating EU obligations had some interesting twists and turns. While the domestic jurisprudence had included indications that this legislative misconduct by Parliament or other legislative bodies in breach of EU law—in particular the failure to harmonise domestic law with EU law—is, in principle, a potential basis for state liability.[61] The brand new Hungarian Civil Code—intentionally—kept quiet about this form of liability.[62] The ruling of the Court of Justice in *Baradics*[63] dealing with the liability in tort of the Hungarian state for unlawful legislative conduct clarified matters. The receiving judgment by the Budapest Regional Court of Appeal established that the Hungarian state is liable in tort for damages caused by the inadequate implementation of an EU directive and that it was unable in justifying its conduct to establish that the implementing measure was in fact lawful.[64] It was,

---

[55] Case No Pf.III.20.255/2009/5.

[56] Case No 14.K.20.933/2006.6.

[57] Case No 15.G.42.273/2010/11.

[58] Case No ... P. .../2007/12 (the complete case number is not available; the judgment is on file with the authors).

[59] Case No 7.K.30467/2005/45. In the court's view, the principle of loyalty includes the effective protection of rights derived from EU law, enforcing the directly effective provisions of directives against the Member States, interpreting domestic law in the light of EU law, ensuring judicial review on the basis of EU law against administrative decisions, and securing the compatibility of domestic law with EU law.

[60] Case No 24.K.33.917/2008/5; Kfv.I.35.071/2007/7; 5.Pf.20.499/2007/4, 5.Pf.20.700/2007/12 and No 5.Pf.20.700/2007/12.

[61] Cases No 5.Pf.21.533/2011/7 (first instance judgment 15.G.42.273/2010/11) and 5.Pf.21.063/2008/9. See, to the contrary, Case No 9.Pf.20.215/2012/4.

[62] Act 2013:V.

[63] Case C-430/13 *Baradics*, order of 16 January 2014, ECLI:EU:C:2014:32.

[64] 3.Pf.20.182/2014/2. It also declared, as a principle, that under Section 339(1) of the former Civil Code the Hungarian state is responsible for the damages caused to private individuals by the inappropriate implementation of EU directives.

however, vitiated by a number of hiatuses. First, it failed to clarify the relationship between EU law and national law on remedies when it declared that the liability of the state for the breach of EU law follows from the corresponding provision of the (former) Civil Code. In effect, it decided to interpret Hungarian civil law in light of the relevant EU jurisprudence, which led to the unfortunate consequence that the detailed legal tests of the EU case law—for example, the question whether there was a sufficiently serious breach of EU law—were not given adequate recognition.[65] Secondly, using its discretion recognised in the *Baradics* ruling in determining the question of causality, the Hungarian court declined to take into account the few available judgments from the Court of Justice and its assessment of causality might have fallen short of the benchmark of direct causality required by EU doctrine. Finally, it is particularly troubling that while in EU-related litigation the tortious liability of the Hungarian state can now be established, no such remedy seems available under Hungarian law in purely domestic cases.

In the *UMTS* judgment,[66] the Budapest Metropolitan Court proceeding at first instance had to address a deeply rooted incompatibility between the law on national remedies in the EU and the domestic regulation of administrative procedures and remedies. It was decided that the narrow jurisdiction available under domestic law in judicial review of discussion—as we discussed earlier—may not 'necessarily' breach the EU requirement of effective judicial protection demanding a much broader judicial scrutiny of administrative action. The court held that the requirement under EU law that judicial review should cover the formal, procedural and substantive aspects of the administrative decision challenged, simple and complex questions of fact, and evaluations made within administrative discretion could, in principle, be met by Hungarian law. It suggested that Hungarian administrative courts when establishing their jurisdiction in the judicial review of administrative discretion must adopt an 'appropriate interpretation of the law'. This, however, proved to be extremely difficult to achieve for the court delivering the judgment bound by both EU obligations and domestic legal doctrine. In order to conclude that judicial review against all relevant administrative decisions by all relevant parties must be available in the case at hand, the court, as discussed extensively in the judgment, had to carry out a complex and legally controversial juggling exercise. In that, it managed to uphold the applicable substantive legal framework, observe domestic procedural and doctrinal bounds of judicial review, meet the requirement of legal certainty by avoiding the application of different rules to different disputes depending on whether EU law was affected, and to give effect to the right to effective judicial protection as required by EU law. The judgment—an exception in many ways from the standard jurisprudence—seems to have achieved the reception of the relevant EU legal principles by compromising domestic doctrine despite the effort of the court to reconcile its competing obligations under national and EU law.

---

[65] It must be mentioned that criteria similar to those in EU law for sufficiently serious breach are examined in Hungarian law when deciding on the justifiability of the conduct at issue.

[66] Above (n 59).

VI. Doctrinal Rifts Between Domestic and EU Administrative Law

With the exception of individual rulings—such as the *UMTS* decision or the judgment implementing *Baradics*—which indeed attempt to reconcile domestic and EU administrative law, the general silence of the jurisprudence of Hungarian administrative courts integrating the relevant EU legal principles indicates that the potential grave incompatibilities between their competing obligations under EU and domestic law have been swept under the carpet. The performance of Hungarian administrative courts as courts of the European Union will be compromised until the doctrinal rifts between EU and domestic law, which may make accommodating the EU legal obligations affecting the judicial review of administrative decisions in Hungarian legal doctrine impossible, are adequately addressed. Without conscious and informed judicial and legislative intervention at the national level, it is very likely that the law on the judicial supervision of administrative discretion will not be able to meet the requirement of effective legal (judicial) protection as it follows from Article 19(1) TEU and the jurisprudence. This presents a pressing dilemma for national courts which—torn between competing loyalties—need to ensure that their fundamental obligation under domestic and EU law of providing effective legal protection against unlawful administrative action is not frustrated.

The most evident gap between Hungarian legal doctrine and EU law concerns the judicial control of administrative discretion. As discussed earlier, Hungarian courts are afforded jurisdiction to review the reasonableness of discretionary administrative decisions only and their scrutiny is constrained by the prohibition that they must not substitute the assessment of the public authority on the merits of the case with their own. The examination of evidence in judicial review may offer the possibility of a more intrusive judicial scrutiny, however, the jurisdiction available in this regard is subject to the same constitutional limitations. The law specifically excludes that courts examine alternative decisional pathways which may have been available for the public authority, and courts are also prevented from identifying more reasonable decisions for closing the administrative case. These, in principle, fall short of the judicial review of administrative discretion on the basis of the proportionality principle as demanded by EU law, and they exclude national courts, unless there is legal authorisation in national law, to apply that principle in judicial review.

However, with Hungary's commitments under the Council of Europe and the European Union frameworks, domestic administrative courts cannot avoid reviewing the use of discretionary powers by public authorities, affecting Convention rights or under the scope of EU law, by relying on the principle of proportionality. In the cases falling under the scope of application of either EU law or the European Convention, the domestic jurisprudence has recognised the applicability of the proportionality principle and courts have used proportionality in cases which concerned the adequate use of administrative discretion or which examined whether the appropriate sanction/penalty had been applied. In this parallel universe of domestic administrative law, the actual application of the proportionality principle poses limited complications for Hungarian courts, although the quality and transparency of the reasoning provided could improve. For example, in a competition case dealing with the unfair manipulation of consumers, it was examined whether a prohibition of a particular commercial practice could be lawfully imposed for the protection of consumers and whether imposing the obligation of following alternative commercial practices would constitute a disproportionate interference with the freedom of the person concerned to pursue an economic activity. The court proceeding at first instance examined in detail the relevant case-law of the Court of Justice and held with reference to the facts of the case—following a slightly condensed reasoning—that establishing the breach of Hungarian consumer protection law did not constitute a disproportionate restriction of the free circulation of the product in question.[67]

The most problematic consequence of these developments is that separate bodies and distinct modes of judicial review have been created in Hungarian administrative law. Depending on the facts and the circumstances of the case before administrative courts, the legal control of the administration and the effective legal protection of individuals against administrative action attract different judicial treatment, which may be impossible to justify in constitutional and legal terms. Arguably, the doctrinal conflicts between EU and domestic law are the products of the inward looking, legalistic and technical process of incorporating EU law into the domestic legal order and into domestic judicial practice. Although organising the reception of EU law in such a manner can project certainty and assurance that the process is manageable, it has hushed up potential crises of rejection and ignored visible possibilities of incompatibility and non-compliance. Ultimately, in case the legislator and courts do not address the resulting problems and dilemmas as in the *UMTS* judgment, the incomplete reception of EU law will threaten the values of administrative justice and the delivery of administrative justice in Hungary.

As mentioned earlier, the integration of the Hungarian judiciary into the EU judicial system could be described by what in Alter's typology is labelled as the legalist (or 'nuanced' legalist)[68] theory. The judicial reception of the relevant EU principles was based on legal obligations and followed from recognising the compelling character of the Court of Justice's jurisprudence, and most mistakes could be accounted for as caused by misinformation and personal incompetence. It is more uncertain, however, whether the dilemmas faced by Hungarian courts

---

[67] Judgments 2.Kf.27.430/2006/8, 7.K.30.482/2005/10 and reviewed decision of the Competition Authority in Vj-126/2004/39. See also the judgment in the online gambling case, Kfv.III.37.454/2010/5, where the Curia decided, somewhat controversially, the proportionality of the interference with the free movement provisions of the Treaty with reference to the proportionality of the sanctions applied.

[68] Alter (n 4) 231, which does not purport that national judges are convinced by the integrationist principles of the Court of Justice.

following from the doctrinal conflicts between EU and domestic administrative law could be explained by the legalist theory, or by any of the other theories. While seeing these negative legal consequences of EU membership as a matter of institutional and personal unpreparedness to meet EU obligations, which could be corrected by pointing out the right legal solution to national courts, seems acceptable, such hindrances to legal integration are more deeply rooted and they are much more complicated to resolve than basic misapprehensions of EU obligations. There may be a constitutional foundation, such as the principles determining the position of the judiciary with regards the executive and also the legislative, making national courts reluctant to ignore domestic legal doctrine, which is likely to make solutions mediating between EU and national law impossible to implement, as it will be discussed shortly.[69] The inherently top-down structuring of the legalist thesis misses that in such instances careful bottom-up adjustment—preferably within the framework of a comprehensive reassessment of the domestic law on judicial review—is needed. The other, essentially bottom-up oriented theories, because of their orientation, are not particularly useful in responding to this issue.

Nevertheless, judgments like the *UMTS* ruling and the judicial responses to *Urbán*[70] and *Baradics*[71] suggest that the dialogue model—understood in a somewhat altered form than that presented in the literature[72]—could emerge as an attractive legalist explanation for the Europeanisation of judicial review in Hungary. Its core assumption is that in the process the EU and the national courts need and influence each other. On this basis, the model is able to conceptualise the process of Europeanisation as a chain of mutually supporting reactions between EU and national law in which EU law indicates the limitations of legal doctrine (and potential avenues for reform) in the Member States and national law, as part of reacting to those indications, brings light to the doctrinal limitations in national law of national courts acting as courts of the European Union. This is consistent with the central idea that the reception of EU law depends by and large on the ability of the national legal order to reconsider national legal doctrine in the course of national legal dialogues and/or processes.[73] As indicated by the Hungarian experience, this entails that the necessary changes to meet the requirements related to the effective judicial enforcement of EU law must come from within the national legal order.

The weight of the problem caused by doctrinal incompatibility is clearly represented by the recent judgment of the Court of Justice in *Urbán*, which caused considerable headaches in much different ways both to the Court of Justice and

---

[69] Incompetence, misinformation and complacency, as potential causes for the inadequacy of legal integration, do not recognise that national courts being torn between their competing (legitimate obligations) in EU and national law could also be the source of the unsuccessful incorporation of EU law into domestic judicial practice.

[70] Case C-210/10 *Urbán*, judgment of 9 February 2012, nyr.

[71] Above (n 63).

[72] Alter (n 4) 232 and the literature cited.

[73] ibid, 233.

to Hungarian courts. Following the judgment of the Court of Justice in the case, which was rather limited in its appreciation of its potential local impact, Hungarian courts were confronted with a genuine difficulty with reconciling their obligation to review administrative sanctions on the basis of the proportionality principle, as it follows from EU law and from national statutory provisions implementing the corresponding requirements of EU law, and the doctrinal prohibitions in domestic law which exclude substituting the assessment of the public authority regarding the severity of the penalty with that of the court and which prevent courts from reassessing the weight of the breach of law as determined by the public authority. The root of the conflict was that in domestic doctrine the judicial review of administrative penalties imposed under discretionary powers may only take place with reference to the statutory framework for imposing the penalty and not on the basis of a broader examination of suitability and necessity. Domestic courts would examine the statutory maximum and minimum amounts of penalties and they would volunteer to re-examine the assessment of the public authority only in exceptional circumstances, for instance, when the maximum penalty was imposed for insignificant breaches of formal legal requirements by individuals.

Urbán was a relatively insignificant transport administration case—one of the many tachometer cases before Hungarian courts—where a fine of 100.000 HUF was challenged by the transport undertaking arguing that considering the weight of its unlawful conduct (out of 15 tachometer disks one failed to indicate the arrival position of the speedometer) the sum of the penalty was excessive. The applicant raised this submission despite the fine having been imposed on the basis of objective legislative provisions which did not allow public authorities to depart in the circumstances of individual cases from the sum specified therein. The Hajdú-Bihar County Court seeing the potential conflict between national and EU law turned to the Court of Justice for a preliminary ruling asking whether the objective imposition of fines contravened the EU requirement on the proportionality of penalties imposed under the scope of EU law. In response, the Court of Justice ruled that while an objective (strict) system of fines (a 'strict system of liability') is prima facie compatible with EU law, the imposition of the fine in the particular case was indeed disproportionate.[74] It argued, among others, that 'the amount of that fine is almost equivalent to the average monthly net income of an employee in Hungary. Consequently, the severity of the penalty appears, in the main proceedings, to be disproportionate to the infringement committed.'[75]

---

[74] ibid, para 52. See the note by A Vincze, 'Objektív felelősség és az arányosság elve—Az Európai Bíróság ítélete a C-210/10. sz. Urbán Márton kontra Vám- és Pénzügyőrség Észak-alföldi Regionális Parancsnoksága ügyben' [Objective responsibility and the principle of proportionality—the judgment of the European Court of Justice in Case C-210/10 Márton Urbán v Vám- és Pénzügyőrség Észak-alföldi Regionális Parancsnoksága] (2012) 12 *Európai Jog* 37, which saw the Court of Justice's reasoning indicating two uses of proportionality as a precondition of objective sanctioning systems being compatible with EU law, namely, an objectivised use of proportionality and the use of proportionality as a benchmark of fairness.

[75] ibid, para 58.

The implementation of the judgment, because of the conflict between domestic and European principles, caused severe difficulties for the referring court. First, it was required to establish the illegality of the fine imposed by the public authority despite lacking jurisdiction under Hungarian law in this regard. From the perspective of domestic law, the public authority acted *intra vires* following the provisions of the applicable legislation, which in general were held to be compatible with EU law in the judgment, and it had no legal option other than to impose the exact fine determined in legislation. Although in such circumstances judicial interference with the administrative decision should be excluded under domestic doctrine, the referring court was required under EU law to declare the imposition of the fine on the basis of legislative provisions which allowed no discretion for public authorities as disproportionate.

Second, it followed from the Court of Justice's reasoning that, in principle, domestic courts are required to examine the proportionality of fines imposed under the scope of EU law on the basis of considerations which are not regulated explicitly in the relevant domestic legislation. The assessment of such external considerations in determining the legality of administrative decisions represents a departure from domestic doctrine which enables a similar judicial scrutiny only within the relevant legislative framework having regard, in particular, to the maximum and minimum amount of fines as relevant considerations. The ruling of the Court of Justice seems to overwrite domestic conceptions of *ultra vires* administrative action by suggesting that the Hungarian authority should have taken into account considerations outside those listed in the applicable domestic legislation.

Finally, the judgment left it unclear whether domestic courts are required, as a rule, to assess the proportionality of fines imposed under domestic law without having regard to the boundaries imposed on their jurisdiction by the relevant domestic legislative provisions. It was not spelt out particularly clearly that instead of the disproportionate application of the fine by domestic authorities the problem confronted in *Urbán* was that the EU requirement on proportionate penalties is far too limited as it is unable to distinguish between legitimately introduced national administrative sanctioning systems of different character.[76]

The suggestions by the judgment concerning the proportionality of fines also raised the fundamental dilemma of whether objective administrative sanctioning systems, which for legitimate reasons do not recognise the financial circumstances of individuals as a consideration relevant in the exercise of sanctioning powers, could satisfy the proportionality requirement in EU law. Objective fines will affect people with different financial means differently without offering a justification for different treatment, thus failing to take into an otherwise valid legal consideration

---

[76] It must be pointed out that the Court of Justice was indeed in a particular position. It had to respect Member States' autonomy in selecting the type of the administrative sanctioning system, but it also had to ensure that the applicable principle of EU law is observed. The compromise solution achieved may seem appropriate from the perspective of the EU level, but it caused grave doctrinal problems on the level of the Member States.

which may have an impact on the suitability of the sanction imposed. Arguably, the judgment in *Urbán* could be regarded as an indirect judicial indication that objective sanctioning systems applied in the Member States for the enforcement of EU law risk violating the proportionality requirement of EU law and that— despite the autonomy of the national level in regulating domestic administrative law—they should be 'softened' by the Member States by introducing elements which distinguish with sufficient clarity and preciseness between individuals in different circumstances. Again, the approach to be adopted by national courts is not particularly certain as they find themselves wedged between the uncertain obligations flowing from EU law and the legitimate choice for the Member States to maintain such coercive systems.

In the wake of judgments like *Urbán*, Hungarian law may consider the follow- ing options. First, it could overlook the adverse constitutional and legal implica- tions of the presence of competing legal doctrines before domestic administrative courts and allow their parallel application. Second, Hungarian courts could—as a convenient legal solution—draw upon the loyalty principle under Article 4(3) TEU to replace domestic legal doctrine, which would, however, allow an uncon- trolled and unstructured interference with domestic administrative law based on the interests of the Union.[77] Third, Hungarian courts could tease out the details of the required change with the help of preliminary references to the Court of Justice and negotiate any sensitive requirements from the perspective of domestic legal doctrine. Fourth, the applicable principles of EU administrative law could be implemented through general or sector specific legislation but that may not affect judicial doctrines of judicial review in domestic law. Fifth, adjustment in Hungary is carried out at a constitutional level but it is unclear how that would influence judicial behaviour (judicial deference, judicial activism) in relation to the administration. Finally, a comprehensive reform of legal accountability could be carried out in domestic administrative law in which the changes required by EU law could be implemented within a general reconsideration of the functions of judicial review in law and administration in the Hungarian state.

Because reinstating the complete influence of domestic legal doctrine is no longer possible, the dilemmas faced by Hungarian administrative law, especially if they are approached from the perspective of EU obligations, could lead to aug- menting the influence of European law in Hungary. With Europeanisation brought further, the coherence of domestic administrative law could be restored, confu- sion and inequality caused by the parallel application of competing legal doctrine could be avoided, and economy and simplicity in the application of the law could be restored. This, however, requires a voluntary accommodation in domestic law of European influences, beyond the actual legal obligations, and it necessitates a

---

[77] In the *UMTS* judgment, the court having realised this possibility made a decent effort to muffle the impact of the loyalty principle and, as we saw earlier, attempted to reconcile with each other the conflicting elements of the law.

commitment from domestic actors to integrate in bottom-up processes European requirements into domestic law. As noted earlier, a general overview of domestic administrative law and doctrine may be necessary as the accommodation of European legal principles, such as the principle of proportionality, is inconceivable without reconsidering the adjustment of the relevant constitutional doctrines of judicial review. Despite the visibility of the problems, Hungarian courts on their own seem unwilling to undertake this task without explicit constitutional and legislative authorisation.

In remedying the unjust and illegitimate fragmentation of domestic administrative law, it must be taken into account that allowing a complete reign to top-down interferences from EU obligations with domestic law may lead to further conflicts and unclear boundaries between domestic and European law and doctrine, as demonstrated in *Urbán*. Voluntary convergence and bottom-up adjustment, taking into account the needs of both EU and Hungarian administrative law, could produce more fitting legal outcomes. Voluntary convergence could be particularly important when the tension between the jurisdiction available for domestic courts to review the use of administrative discretion and the European requirement of proportionality is attempted to be resolved. The introduction of proportionality to replace unreasonableness as a general principle in determining the intensity of judicial review in Hungarian administrative law requires a departure from current doctrine and a reconsideration of the role of courts in the scrutiny of the administration. The more structured and nuanced assessment under proportionality of what constitutes a rational administrative decision is in stark contrast with the current constrained judicial attitude towards intervention with the conduct of public authorities. Using the principle of proportionality, national courts could require public authorities to provide more exacting justifications for their decisions and to defend the particular decisional route (and the choice between competing considerations) taken. This, however, presumes that a more defined position is carved out for administrative courts in the system of administrative accountability in Hungary.

VII. Conclusions

This chapter examined the uneasy position of Hungarian administrative judges as judges of Hungarian and European Union law. The doctrinal incompatibilities between EU and domestic legal requirements on the judicial review of administrative action present the Hungarian administrative court with the dilemma of choosing between their obligations as European and Hungarian judges, which impedes their complete integration into the multi-tiered judicial system of the European Union. This conflict of interest is not without genuine legal consequences for litigants. In case Hungarian administrative courts observe the restrictive doctrinal boundaries of the judicial review of administrative discretion in domestic law, it may be impossible for them to secure the effective judicial enforcement of EU law as required under the general jurisdictional rule of Article 19(1) TEU. Hungarian courts trying to navigate between their competing parallel obligations may fall between two stools putting the domestic system of administrative justice and the right of individuals to jeopardy.

Arguably, these issues are the consequences of the run of the mill legalistic approach of the pre- and post-accession reception of EU law in Hungary. While presenting the participation of national courts in the EU judicial system as a matter of meeting hierarchically produced legal obligations—and assessing their conduct from the perspective of observing or failing to observe those obligations—is technically appropriate, it may fail to appreciate the complexities and the genuine dimensions of integrating European requirements, which may be based on considerations intrinsic to the EU system, into the particular doctrinal framework of domestic laws. Since adjusting national law may be the only permitted option to escape the legal and doctrinal split caused by the parallel application of EU and national administrative law, a bottom-up, self-reflective and flexible reception of EU administrative law may be the only viable option. This should be framed within the fundamental dilemmas of administrative justice, such as the balance between effective administrative and judicial control, or the relationship between the legitimacy of the administration and the legitimacy of judicial intervention. For Hungarian administrative courts, this would entail an intensive, soul searching exercise in which they need to consider developing a novel doctrinal framework which explicitly recognises judicial deference and the constitutional bases of the judicial supervision of administrative discretion.

10

Changes in the Level of the National Judicial Protection Under the EU Influence on the Example of the Polish Legal System

NINA PÓŁTORAK

I. Preliminary Remarks

European Union law requires that the rights of individuals derived from the EU legal system must be effectively guaranteed and enforced. In order to ensure the effectiveness of EU law (*effet utile*) and effective legal protection of rights of individuals, EU law sets new standards of legal protection which are to be applied in domestic legal systems of the Member States. Those EU standards are shaped to a considerable degree by the rules of EU law, yet they are not detached from the law of the Member States. This is because the EU level of protection of rights is often based on or inspired by the laws of the Member States and the European Convention on Human Rights (ECHR). This is also because the EU system of legal protection must be complemented by national remedies.[1] The EU system of legal protection is incomplete in the sense that EU law does not provide for its own national enforcement in a complex way. There are, of course, some Union law provisions pertaining to the enforcement of EU law in the Member States, but they are either very general or fragmentary. The EU system of legal protection is therefore supplemented by legal provisions of the Member States. This process is

---

[1] J Schwarze, 'The Role of the European Court of Justice in Shaping Legal Standards for Administrative Action in the Member States. A Comparative Perspective' in D O'Keeffe and A Bavasso (eds), *Judicial Review in European Union Law: Liber Amicorum in Honour of Lord Slynn of Hadley* (The Hague, 2000) 413; J Schwarze, *European Administrative Law* (Sweet and Maxwell, 2006) 1437; JH Jans, R De Lange, S Prechal and R Widdershoven, *Europeanisation of Public Law* (Europa Law Publishing, 2007) 5.

part of the system of decentralised administration (enforcement), which means that EU law is enforced both by EU institutions and—to a greater measure—by Member States.[2]

The development of the European standard of legal protection has been required by the principle of effectiveness of EU law. This principle still lacks clear basis in the EU treaties, and is still not considered by the Court of Justice of the EU (CJEU) as a general principle of EU law. It is, however, crucial for the existence of the EU legal system and for the legal integration of the Member States. It has been given a more tangible form in the principle of effective legal protection, which is considered to be a general principle of EU law and which was incorporated into EU primary law by the Lisbon Treaty (Article 19 (1) TUE). The requirement of effective legal protection imposes certain requirements on national legal remedies whose objective is to ensure effective execution of rights derived from EU law. Respecting the procedural autonomy of Member States, EU law requires that national provisions serving the enforcement of rights derived from EU law should be applied in a non-discriminatory way and be effective. It means that the national procedures should be accessible under the same conditions as in the case of the realisation of rights resulting from national law, and also that they should not render enforcement of EU law impossible or excessively difficult in practice.[3] As a consequence, Member States are obliged not only to refrain from application of certain provisions of their national laws, but also to amend the remedies already existing in their legal systems (for example courts are obliged to apply interim

---

[2] The term *decentralised administration* is usually understood as enforcing EU law by national organs, including courts, M Dougan, *National Remedies before the Court of Justice, Issues of Harmonisation and Differentiation* (Hart Publishing, 2004) 2–3. This rule is also called *indirect implementation, delegated administration,* or *shared administration* see eg: Schwarze (n 1) 34, C Harding, 'Models of Enforcement: Direct and Delegated Enforcement and the Emergence of a "Joint Action" Model' in C Harding and B Swart (eds), *Enforcing European Community Rules. Criminal Proceedings, Administrative Procedures and Harmonization* (Dartmouth, 1996) 22; Jans et al (n 1) 7; H Hofmann and AH Türk, 'Introduction: Towards a Legal Framework for Europe's Integrated Administration' in H Hofmann and AH Türk (eds), *Legal Challenges In EU Administrative Law. Towards an Integrated Administration* (Edward Elgar, 2009) 1–4.

[3] The legal writing on the principle of effectiveness and the procedural autonomy is vast, inter alia D Curtin and K Mortelmans, 'Application and Enforcement of Community Law by the Member States: Actors in Search of a Third Generation Script' in D Curtin and T Heukles (eds), *Institutional Dynamics of European Integration, Essays in Honour of Henry G Schermers,* Volume II (Dordrecht, 1994) 446; R Caranta, 'Judicial Protection Against Member States: A New Jus Commune Takes Shape' (1995) 32 *CML Rev* 703–26; M Ruffert, 'Rights and Remedies in European Community Law: A Comparative View' (1997) 34 *CML Rev* 315, 307–36; S Prechal, 'Community Law in National Courts: The Lesson from Van Schijndel' (1998) 35 *CML Rev* 681, 681–706; W van Gerven, 'Of Rights, Remedies and Procedures' (2000) 37 *CML Rev* 502, 501–36; T Eilmansberger, 'The Relationship between Rights and Remedies in EC Law: In Search of the Missing Link' (2004) 41 *CML Rev* 1199–246; Dougan (n 2). For the critic of the concept of 'procedural autonomy of the Member States' see in particular C Kakouris, 'Do the Member States Possess Judicial Procedural "Autonomy"?' (1997) 34 *CML Rev* 1389–412; M Bobek, 'Why There is no Principle of "Procedural Autonomy" of the Member States' in H-W Micklitz and B De Witte (eds), *The European Court Of Justice And Autonomy Of The Member States* (Intersentia, 2011) 305; N Półtorak, *European Union Rights in National Courts* (Wolters Kluwer, 2015) 30.

relief unknown in the national legal system or to grant compensation in the cases of infringements of EU law).[4]

The aim and outcome of the process of Europeanisation of national remedies should be universal for the Member States of the EU. This aim is to ensure effectiveness of EU law and grant legal protection to EU rights. However, the course of this process will be different in each Member State as it will depend primarily on the system of legal protection already existing in a given State.[5] The majority of countries that acceded to the EU in 2004 and 2007 had their legal systems considerably modified in the post-communist era as part of the democratisation process and thus, those systems can hardly be seen as well established. Hence, the process of Europeanisation in these systems may prove to proceed faster and reach deeper than in the older States of the EU, in which the changes may not be welcomed with the same enthusiasm as in some new Member States.

Poland, as a country with a long constitutional tradition and, at the moment of accession to the EU, a Member State of the Council of Europe, generally respected the European standards of legal protection.[6] Therefore, the accession of Poland to the European Union has not resulted in fundamental changes in domestic legislation related to legal protection of individuals. However, as will be demonstrated, there are several Polish provisions that have been amended following the requirements of the principle of effective legal protection. Still, the influence of EU law is most significant in the case law of Polish courts.

The process of Europeanisation of Polish law has been in progress for a long time—the practice of referring to the Council of Europe's standards in the case law not only of the *Trybunał Konstytucyjny* (Constitutional Tribunal, hereinafter 'TK') but also of ordinary courts has a long tradition. Moreover, courts had frequently referred to the EU standards even before the accession of Poland to the European Union.[7] Currently, Polish courts often invoke the Charter of Fundamental Rights of the EU to support their argumentation based on domestic law even in cases in which the Charter could not be binding for the Member State according to its Article 51(1). For example, administrative courts refer to the Charter's right of good administration included in Article 41, but usually they do not analyse if the

---

[4] eg Case C-213/89, *The Queen v Secretary of State for Transport, ex parte Factortame* [1990] ECR I-2433; Case C-6/90, C-9/90, *Andrea Francovich and Danila Bonifaci v Italy* [1991] ECR I-5357; Case C-46/93 and C-48/93, *Brasserie du Pêcheur SA v Bundesrepublik Deutschland and The Queen v Secretary of State for Transport, ex parte: Factortame Ltd and others* [1996] ECR I-1029.

[5] On this process in national law see M Eliantonio, *Europeanisation of Administrative Justice? The Influence of the CJEU's Case Law in Italy, Germany and England* (Europa Law Publishing, 2009) 152.

[6] Some views in this chapter repeat the author's opinion expressed in N Półtorak, 'Europeanisation of public law as a consequence of the principle of effectiveness of European Union law' in K Wojtyczek (ed), *Public Law: Twenty Years After, The Public Law after 1989 from the Polish Perspective* (European Public Law Series, 2012) 199–244.

[7] See more S Biernat and P Wróbel, 'Stosowanie prawa Wspólnoty Europejskiej w polskim sądownictwie administracyjnym', Studia prawno-europejskie, Issue IX, 2007, p 7.

Charter might be at work in the given case or if the right to good administration might be addressed to the national administration.[8]

The aim of this chapter is to analyse how EU law influences domestic legal protection in Member States using the example of Polish law and to demonstrate that Europeanisation may result in improving the level of legal protection of the rights of individuals. In section II it would be argued that EU law granted Polish courts new competences which were used by the courts as useful tools for reconsidering and verifying the existing national measures of legal protection. Section III focuses on the outcomes of this verification. It gives examples of cases in which Polish courts applied the EU principle of effective legal protection.

II. Europeanisation of Competences of Polish Courts

EU law influences the competences of national courts that become part of the European Union's judiciary. As will be explained, the new competences granted to Polish courts by EU law made it possible for national courts to exert certain influence on the standard of legal protection of the EU rights of individuals.

Perhaps the most significant new competence granted to Polish courts is the possibility of 'dialogue' with the CJEU in the form of the preliminary rulings procedure. This competence has been quite often used. So far, Polish courts have made more than 60 requests for a preliminary ruling. Most of them have been asked by administrative courts, including *Naczelny Sąd Administracyjny* (Supreme Administrative Court, hereinafter 'NSA').[9] *Trybunał Konstytucyjny* has not submitted a request for a preliminary ruling yet. The TK deems the preliminary ruling procedure nonetheless to be an important tool for implementing the constitutional right to a lawful judge. It also disagreed with the argumentation claiming that the length of the preliminary ruling proceeding infringes the right to court.[10]

The preliminary rulings procedure may influence the level of judicial protection in two ways—by involving the CJEU in adjudicating a given case and by strengthening the position of lower courts towards domestic courts of higher instance. In this respect, it is worth noticing that *Sąd Najwyższy* (Supreme Court, hereinafter

---

[8] eg judgment of the NSA I FSK 1313/12 of 20.11.2013; judgment of Wojewódzki Sąd Administracyjny in Warsaw, II SA/Wa 1016/13 of 10.02.2014; these and all the further quoted decisions of the administrative courts can be found at: http://orzeczenia.nsa.gov.pl. The Polish courts have also asked questions regarding the Charter of Fundamental Rights, which has been declared inadmissible by the CJEU, see: Case C-28/14, *Ryszard Pańczyk* ECLI:EU:C:2014:2003; Case C-520/13, *Urszula Leśniak-Jaworska and Małgorzata Głuchowska-Szmulewicz* ECLI:EU:C:2014:263.

[9] As of April 2015, administrative courts had asked 48 questions, among them 30 have been initiated by the NSA (see www.nsa.gov.pl/index.php/pol/NSA/Prawo-Europejskie/Pytania-prejudycjalne-WSA-i-NSA).

[10] Judgment of TK of 18 February 2009, Kp 3/08. All the further quoted decisions of the TK may be located online at www.trybunal.gov.pl.

'SN') accepted the *Rheinmühlen* line of CJEU case law[11] confirming that the resolution of SN formally binding the court of lower instance cannot deprive this court of the possibility to ask a preliminary question.[12] Also the NSA decided to ask a preliminary question in a matter that had been previously decided in the binding resolution.[13] Thus, it indirectly confirmed that the domestic procedural requirements may not limit the competence of the court to request the preliminary ruling of the CJEU.

However, the most revolutionary new competence granted to Polish courts was the entitlement to evaluate national law. It was primarily the result of implementing the principles of direct effect and primacy of EU law.

In Polish law, the Constitution establishes a hierarchy of acts of law, including international law, yet neither the Constitution nor statutory provisions regulate the mode of operation which the courts should implement in the case of conflict between norms. This lack of clear legislation leads to a constitutional dispute pertaining to the competences of ordinary courts to supervise the hierarchy of acts of law. It is fairly universally accepted that in the process of law application, ordinary courts have the authority to disregard a provision of delegated acts (*rozporządzenie*) that has been deemed an infringement of a legislative act (*ustawa*). Nevertheless, such authority is rarely admitted—both in the case law and in the legal doctrine— in the case of legislative acts violating the Constitution. However, there is no doubt that a Polish judge has the authority to evaluate the compliance of a provision of the legislative act with EU law and the duty to abstain from application of such if it is not compliant with EU law.[14] Such authority is granted by EU law, but may also be derived from the constitutional provisions (Article 91), especially taking into account the principle of consistent interpretation. Article 91 of the Constitution provides that a ratified international agreement shall constitute part of the domestic legal order and shall be applied directly, unless its application depends on the enactment of a statute and that an international agreement ratified upon prior consent granted by statute shall have precedence over statutes. It states also, that if a ratified agreement establishing an international organisation so provides, the laws established by it shall be applied directly and have precedence in the event of a conflict of laws.

The entitlement of the Polish courts to apply the rule of the primacy of the EU law has been confirmed directly by *Trybunał Konstytucyjny* in its decision of 2006.[15] In this decision, the TK distinguished two spheres—the sphere of the binding force of law and the sphere of law application, and concluded that adjudicating

---

[11] Case 166/73 *Rheinmühlen-Düsseldorf v Einfuhr- und Vorratsstelle für Getreide und Futtermitt* [1974] ECR 33; Case 146/73 *Rheinmühlen-Düsseldorf v Einfuhr- und Vorratsstelle für Getreide und Futtermittel* [1974] ECR 139; Case C-173/09 *Georgi Ivanov Elchinov* [2010] ECR I-8889, para 32.

[12] Order of the SN of 28 April 2010, No III CZP 3/10, online at www.sn.pl.

[13] Resolution of the NSA, I GPS 1/12, and preliminary question C-349/13 *Oil Trading Poland*, ECLI:EU:C:2015:84.

[14] See also Półtorak (n 6) 215.

[15] Order of the TK of 19 December 2006, P 37/05.

specific cases by courts on the basis of EU law belongs to the sphere of application of law. In this respect the TK has no competence to adjudicate on questions
asked by courts pertaining to the compliance of Polish legal acts of law with EU
law. Such competence would contradict the principle of uniform interpretation
and application of EU law, since it is reserved for the CJEU. The TK confirmed
that Polish courts are bound by the rule of primacy of EU law so it is their role
to apply EU law in a given case, and the TK does not engage itself on the level of
law application. Admittedly, the TK did not quote the judgments of the CJEU of
the *Simmenthal* line of cases, but the main thesis of the decision is convergent
with the statement of the CJEU expressed in those judgments, in which the CJEU
ordered courts of law to leave out the competences of constitutional courts if such
competences would constitute an obstacle for the ordinary court in evaluating the
compliance of national law with EU law in the given case.[16]

However, TK consistently decides that EU law does not have primacy over
constitutional norms and, in consequence, it is the TK that has the competence
to adjudicate if there is a conflict between constitutional norms and EU law.[17]
TK held that it is competent to review the constitutionality of both primary and
secondary law of the EU. The TK even calls itself 'the court of the last word'.[18]
As regards EU secondary law, it seems that it shared the view of the German
Bundesverfassungsgericht that the review of the compatibility with the Constitution may be admissible only if one demonstrates that the level of protection
guaranteed in EU law does not comply with the standard of protection provided
for in the Constitution.[19] The TK restricted this competence of review of the secondary acts of EU law by special procedural requirements and directly pointed out
that in the course of such review, it should request the preliminary ruling of the
CJEU on the compatibility of such an act with the primary law of the EU.

It is also interesting that in its judgments the TK invokes the principles of effectiveness of EU law and effective legal protection. In the above mentioned ruling
regarding the review of EU secondary legislation, the TK analysed Article 47 of
the Charter and the effective judicial protection rule as formulated in EU law and
stated that in the sphere of the right to court, the Charter and Polish constitutional standards are convergent.[20] In another ruling, the TK decided that it was
unconstitutional to regulate the rights and obligations of the applicants for EU

---

[16] Case 106/77, *Amministrazione delle Finanze dello Stato v Simmenthal SpA* [1978] ECR 629,
para 24; Case C-348/89, *Mecanarte* [1991] ECR I-3277, paras 39–40; Case C-555/07, *Seda Kucukdeveci*
[2010] ECR I-365; Case C-188/10 and C-189/10, *Aziz Melki and Selim Abdeli* [2010] ECR I-5667,
paras 40–57; Case C-112/13, *A v B and Others*, *A B* ECLI:EU:C:2014:2195, para 46.

[17] Judgment of the TK of 11 May 2005, K 18/04.

[18] Judgment of the TK of 16 November 2011, SK 45/09.

[19] Judgment of the TK of 16 November 2011, SK 45/09, The arguments invoked by the TK as
supporting this view are also: the great significance of fundamental rights in the EU legal order; the
constitutional principle of favourable predisposition of the Republic of Poland towards the process
of European integration; and the Treaty's principle of sincere cooperation. See more S Dudzik and
N Półtorak, '"The Court of the Last Word": Competences of the Polish Constitutional Tribunal in the
Field of the Review of the European Union Law' (2012) 15 *Yearbook of Polish European Studies* 225.

[20] Judgment of the TK of 16 November 2011, SK 45/09.

funds as well as the appeal procedure in non-binding legal acts.[21] It was decided on the basis of the principles of the Polish Constitution, but the TK stated that such practice also jeopardised the principle of effectiveness of EU law by making it difficult for the applicants to enforce their rights.

With reference to the problem of the relation between the Constitution and the primacy principle, it should be noted that a Polish administrative court requested a preliminary ruling in which it asked about compliance with the principle of EU law primacy of procedural solutions provided for in the Polish Constitution (*Filipiak* case).[22] The provision in question was Article 190 (3) of the Constitution, which gives the TK the possibility to defer the date on which the provisions held to be unconstitutional would lose their binding force. In the opinion of the referring court, such competence of the TK may lead to making the principle of primacy impossible to respect. Under this provision as well as the established interpretation thereof, courts should apply unconstitutional provisions until the time when they lose their binding force.[23] In the situation when these provisions are not only unconstitutional but also inconsistent with EU law, acceptance of this rule would make it impossible for courts to disregard this provision in deciding a case. Consequently, the court asked a preliminary question whether the principle of primacy takes precedence over the provision of the Constitution allowing the TK to specify the date when an unconstitutional act is to lose its binding force.[24] It asked this question in spite of the fact that, as it pointed out itself, the TK does not recognise the principle of primacy of EU law over the Constitution of Poland.[25] The question was similar to the one asked by national courts in the *Simmenthal* line of cases, where, too, provisions of national procedural law prevented the full and independent realisation of the principle of primacy by a national court. The question of the Polish court was however peculiar since it referred directly to the potential infringement of EU law by the constitutional provisions. The CJEU answered that question repeating the phrases from its existing case law and stating that the primacy of EU law obliges the national court to apply EU norms and to refuse to apply the conflicting provisions of national law, irrespective of the judgment of the national constitutional court which has deferred the date on which those provisions, held to be unconstitutional, are to lose their binding force.[26]

---

[21] Judgment of the TK of 12 December 2011, P 1/11.

[22] Order of the Wojewódzki Sąd Administracyjny in Poznań, I SA/Po 1756/07 registered by the CJEU as case C-314/08 *Krzysztof Filipiak* [2009] ECR I-11049.

[23] There are however different views presented in the case law of Polish supreme courts as well as in the legal writings.

[24] The question asked by the Court was as follows: 'Must the principle of the primacy of Community law following from Article 10 EC and the first and second paragraphs of Article 43 EC be construed as taking precedence over the provisions of national law referred to in Article 91(2) and (3) and Article 190(1) and (3) of the Polish Constitution in so far as the entry into force of a judgment of the Polish Constitutional Court has been deferred on the basis of those provisions.'

[25] Judgment of the TK of 11 May 2005, K 18/04.

[26] Case C-314/08 *Krzysztof Filipiak* [2009] ECR I-11049. Those statements were repeated by the CJEU in Case C-409/06, *Winner Wetten* [2010] ECR I-8015. A similar view has been presented in Case C-188/10 and C-189/10, *Aziz Melki and Sélim Abdeli* [2010] ECR I-05667.

The *Filipiak* case presented in the preceding paragraphs is an example of the situation in which the constitutional rules were considered to be a potential obstacle in providing the judicial protection required by EU law. There are however examples of a situation where the constitutional principles were found to support the interpretation of EU law in a way compliant with the rules of effective legal protection. The case of the EU regulations which have not been published in Polish language in the Official Journal of the EU may be considered such an example. Polish courts refused to apply such provisions against the interests of individuals relying on the constitutional principles of the rule of law and legal certainty.[27] This practice has been later confirmed by the CJEU in the ruling issued in response to the question of a court of the Czech Republic.[28]

As can be seen in the light of the issues discussed above, national courts' competences are in the process of modification and certain unification in executing the principle of EU law primacy and direct effect. National courts, regardless of the lack of competence to decide on the constitutionality of domestic provisions, are authorised and obliged to evaluate national law as to its compliance with EU law and to refuse to apply those domestic provisions that are incompliant. They also have to apply the principle of consistent interpretation of domestic law. Those competences very often go far beyond the traditional understanding of the role of the court as an institution that applies the law, but does not evaluate or create it. Such is the understanding of the role of courts in the system of Polish law. In domestic situations, Polish courts cannot independently evaluate provisions of law as to their compliance with constitutional principles and refuse to apply a provision that is potentially unconstitutional. However, for the realisation of the principles of primacy and direct effect of EU law, they have acquired a new competence. This new competence has been then used also in order to improve the level of legal protection of the EU rights of individuals, which is discussed in the next section.

III. Polish Legal Remedies and Effective Legal Protection

In order to verify if domestic law respects the EU standard, the CJEU applies the conditions that are supposed to guarantee the principle of effective legal protection. Those conditions are: the principle of equivalence (non-discrimination), which says that national procedural provisions governing actions for safeguarding an individual's right granted by EU law must be no less favourable than those governing similar domestic actions, and the principle of effectiveness, which states that application of these procedural provisions cannot entail in practice that the

---

[27] Judgments of the Polish administrative courts, eg I SA/Bd 275/05; III SA/Gd 45/06.
[28] Case C-161/06 *Skoma-Lux* [2007] ECR I-10841.

enforcement of the rights resulting from Union law is 'virtually impossible' or 'excessively difficult'.[29] In this analysis the principle of effectiveness (*effet utile*) and the requirement of effectiveness are not treated as the same concept. The principle of *effet utile* refers to any actions undertaken with the purpose of enforcing EU law, whereas the requirement of effectiveness refers solely to national remedies and procedures applied to ensure enforcement and exercise of rights granted under EU law. The requirement of effectiveness (or as it is sometimes called effectiveness *sensu-stricto* or *Rewe-effectiveness*)[30] is thus one of the criteria for determination of whether national remedies and procedures observe the EU standard of effectiveness and effective legal protection. For this reason, it is merely a component of the much broader principle of Union law *effet utile* and of the principle of effective legal protection.[31]

The requirements of equivalence and effectiveness should be respected by the State authorities, including the national legislature. This does not mean that any special remedies should be provided for in the national law in order to enforce EU rights, but that the existing domestic remedies and procedures should be regulated in a way enabling effective enforcement of EU rights. In this respect, it should be noted that there indeed have been legislative amendments of some Polish provisions on remedies and procedure under the influence of the EU law. Those amendments were not directly required by EU law, but they were inspired by the standard of effective legal protection. One such amendment is a new basis to reopen tax proceedings introduced in the Tax Ordinance. Reopening of proceedings is now possible if a ruling of the CJEU has been issued which has influence on the final tax decision.[32] Other examples include a provision of the Tax Ordinance which obliges the Minister of Finance to take into account the case law of the CJEU when issuing general guidance on tax law[33] and a provision allowing taxpayers to claim overpaid tax if the overpayment is the result of the judgment of the CJEU.[34] There is also a new provision introduced in the Code of the Administrative Procedure on reopening of administrative proceedings, if there is a court ruling stating the infringement of the EU principle of equal treatment and the final administrative decision is affected by that ruling.[35] Also in the rules of court proceedings in administrative matters, certain legislative changes have been introduced with the

---

[29] See eg Case C-430/93 and C-431/93, *Jeroen van Schijndel and Johannes Nicolaas Cornells van Veen v Stichting Pensioenfonds voor Fysiotherapeuten* [1995] ECR I-4705, para 14; C-432/05, *Unibet (London) Ltd i Unibet (International) Ltd v Justitiekanslern* [2007] ECR I-2271, para 43.

[30] See eg K Lenaerts, I Maselis and K Gutman, *EU Procedural Law* (Oxford University Press, 2014) 110; S Prechal and R Widdershoven, 'Redefining the Relationship between "Rewe-effectiveness" and Effective Judicial Protection' (2011) 4 *Review of European Administrative Law* 31.

[31] See also Półtorak (n 3) 82.

[32] Art 240 § 1 point 11 of the Law of 29 August 1997 Tax Ordinance [Ordynacja podatkowa] (Dz U 2012, item 749—consolidated text).

[33] Art 14a § 1 of the Tax Ordinance.

[34] Art 74 of the Tax Ordinance.

[35] Art 145b of the Law of 14 July 1960 Code of Administrative Procedure [Kodeks postępowania administracyjnego] (Dz U 2013, item 267—consolidated text).

aim to reflect the EU standard. They provide for *ex officio* suspension of court proceedings if the court requested the preliminary ruling of the CJEU,[36] or a new procedure for declaring that the final judgment of the NSA manifestly infringes the EU law; this declaratory ruling is then the basis for claiming damages.[37]

Regardless of the measures adopted by the legislature, the obligation to provide effective legal protection of EU rights rests with the national courts. The courts are primarily responsible for such interpretation and application of national remedies so that they meet the EU standards. Polish courts are challenged to fulfil this task, which will be discussed in greater detail below.[38]

The competence of the Polish courts to rely on the EU rule of effective legal protection has been accepted by the Polish courts. This is visible in the cases in which they try to adapt the domestic procedural solutions to the requirements of the effective legal protection rule. For example, a judgment of the NSA stated that the non-application of the EU requirements of effectiveness and equivalence may be the ground of appeal against the judgment of a lower court.[39] It also explained the relationship between the requirement of equivalence and of effectiveness. The applicant in this case claimed a breach of the condition of equivalence in the situation where the time limit for the recovery of the VAT is longer for the tax authority and shorter for the taxpayer. The NSA correctly held that the claim should be based on the requirement of effectiveness, as equivalence concerns the same treatment of EU and national claims rather than the same treatment of the claims of the taxpayer and the tax authority.

The interesting examples of accepting the EU standard of the legal protection by the Polish courts can be observed in the cases relating to the right to court. This right has to be granted with respect to all 'rights and freedoms guaranteed by the law of the Union' (Article 47 of the Charter of Fundamental Rights) and constitutes an element of the rule of law.[40] The right to court is recognised in the Polish Constitution (Article 45 of the Constitution), and the TK adopts a very high standard of its interpretation.[41] It is also required by the ECHR, which was a model for the EU standard. Europeanisation of the national legal system in this respect will not involve accepting a new standard, but developing common detailed solutions as to how the right to court is to be understood in given cases. However, there still occur cases when the right to court will be denied, and the intervention of EU law will prove helpful. This can be illustrated by the provisions in which the Polish legislator deprived entities applying for structural funds and their beneficiaries of

---

[36] Art 124 of the Law of 30 August 2002 on proceedings before administrative courts [Prawo o postępowaniu przed sądami administracyjnymi] (Dz U 2012, 36 item 270—consolidated text).

[37] Art 285a § 3 on proceedings before administrative courts.

[38] On the relations between the principle of equivalence and the effectiveness in the Polish case-law see eg judgment of the NSA of 26 October 2011, I FSK 1606/10.

[39] Judgment of NSA of 26 October 2011, I FSK 1606/10.

[40] Explanation to the Charter (OJ L 2007 C 303, p 2, Art 47).

[41] eg judgment of the TK of 30 May 2007, SK 68/06.

access to court proceedings.[42] This measure has been questioned by administrative courts on the grounds of the constitutional right to court. It was however amended only after an application had been filed to the TK by the Ombudsman.[43]

The right to court in the aspect of the right to participate in the proceedings was the subject of the question referred by a Polish court of first instance to the CJEU in the *Alder* case.[44] It referred to the provision of the Code of Civil Procedure stating that judicial documents addressed to a party whose place of residence was abroad were to be placed in the case file and deemed to have been effectively served, if that party had failed to appoint a representative residing in Poland authorised to accept service.[45] In the preliminary ruling in this case, the CJEU decided that Polish procedural provisions deprived of all

> practical effect the right of the person to be served, whose place of residence or habitual abode is not in the Member State in which the proceedings take place, to benefit from actual and effective receipt of that document because it does not guarantee for that addressee, inter alia, either knowledge of the judicial act in sufficient time to prepare a defence or a translation of that document.[46]

Following this ruling, the relevant provisions of the Polish civil procedural code have been amended accordingly.[47]

The EU standard of the court proceeding has also been the subject of a request for a preliminary ruling in the *Iwona Szyrocka* case. The Polish court asked about the interpretation of the procedural requirements of the European order for payment provided for in Regulation 1896/2006 and the possibility of applying the national provisions governing the determination of the court fees.[48] Answering the questions, the CJEU invoked the procedural autonomy of the Member States and decided that the national court remains free to determine the amount of the court fees in accordance with the rules laid down by domestic law, provided that those rules are no less favourable than those governing similar domestic actions and do not make it in practice impossible or excessively difficult to exercise the rights conferred by EU law. The final decision as to whether those requirements are respected by the Polish procedural provisions has been left to the national court.

---

[42] Art 37 of the Act of 6 December 2006 on the principles of development policy [o zasadach prowadzenia polityki rozwoju] (Dz U 2009, No 84, item 712—consolidated text). It was amended only by the Act of 7.11.2008 on amendments of certain acts of law in connection with implementation of structural funds and the Cohesion Fund (Dz U of 2008 No 216, item 1370).

[43] See order of TK of 15 December 2008, K 32/07.

[44] Case C-325/11, *Krystyna Alder and Ewald Alder* ECLI:EU:C:2012:824. The ruling was based on the interpretation of Regulation (EC) No 1393/2007 of the European Parliament and of the Council of 13 November 2007 on the service in the Member States of judicial and extrajudicial documents in civil or commercial matters (service of documents), and repealing Council Regulation (EC) No 1348/2000 (OJ L 324 of 2007, p 79) and Art 47 of the Charter.

[45] Art 1135⁵ of the Law of 17 November 1964 Code of the Civil Procedure [Kodeks postępowania cywilnego] (Dz.U. 2014 No 101—consolidated text).

[46] ibid, para 41.

[47] The amendment was introduced by Law of 13 June 2013 (Dz U 2013, item 880).

[48] Case C-215/11, *Iwona Szyrocka* ECLI:EU:C:2012:794.

The EU standard of the right to court may influence national rules pertaining to *locus standi* of individuals in court proceedings. According to this standard, if a given EU norm grants any rights to certain entities, they should have the possibility to initiate court proceedings in order to protect these rights.[49] In the interpretation of the CJEU, the concept of a norm granting individual rights (protective norm) includes also a provision that serves the protection of general public interest and protects the rights of individuals only indirectly.[50] Therefore, in order to determine if a given provision imposing obligations on public authorities grants any rights to individuals, not only the wording of the provision should be analysed but also its objective. Even if protection of the individuals is not a direct aim of such provisions, they may be regarded as granting subjective rights.[51] In this respect, EU law might require modification of national, often very well established, laws governing the legal interest to initiate court proceedings. As has already been mentioned, the right to court is a constitutional principle in Poland. It is granted to everyone who has legal interest. It is an interest that has to arise from the provisions of law, although not necessarily from provisions aimed at protection of a specific individual group of entities. It may occur, however, that the notion of legal interest will have to be extended in some cases in order to comply with the CJEU's standpoint referred to above.

In this context, it is interesting to consider the judgment of the *Sąd Najwyższy*, which indicates the changes in understanding of *locus standi* in Polish law. In its judgment, the SN decided that the obligation, set by EU law, to grant the right of appeal against a decision to an entity affected by the decision, could not be defined by the Polish doctrine referring to the concept of a party to proceedings, but had to interpret in the context of the principles of EU law.[52] The case concerned a complaint lodged by a private entity against the decision of a regulatory authority in which the latter stated that there is no effective competition on the domestic telecommunication market. According to the courts of the first and second instances, the entity was not entitled to file a complaint against this decision, because it was not a party to the administrative proceedings leading to the issuance of the decision that was later challenged. The SN, however, based its ruling on the interpretation of the relevant telecommunications directive[53] and the EU requirement of the effective legal protection. It concluded that an interpretation of the procedural provisions that deprived the plaintiff of the legal standing to file a complaint, made the enforcement of the right to court virtually impossible. In consequence, the procedural measures as to the *locus standi* did not meet in this

---

[49] See eg Case C-87/90, *A Verholen and Others* [1991] ECR I-3757, paras 25–26.

[50] Case C-131/88, *Commission v Germany* [1991] ECR I-825, para 7; Case C-361/88, *Commission v Germany* [1991] ECR I-2567, para 16.

[51] See more eg Ruffert (n 3) 323; Półtorak (n 6) 225.

[52] Order of the SN of 20 February 2008, III SK 23/07.

[53] Directive 2002/21/EC of the European Parliament and of the Council of 7 March 2002 on a common regulatory framework for electronic communications networks and services (Framework Directive) (OJ 2002 L 108, p 33).

case the requirement of effectiveness. It is interesting that this interpretation of the Polish court has been indirectly confirmed by the CJEU in the preliminary ruling issued in response to the request of an Austrian court faced with a very similar problem.[54]

An example of considerable changes in Polish law under the influence of the EU requirement of effectiveness is the concept of prohibition of unjust enrichment in public law. According to the relevant tax provisions, any tax levied in violation of the applicable law must be repaid by the tax authority. The provisions of the Polish tax law do impose the return of unlawfully collected tax even if it leads to the tax payer's unjust enrichment. Polish law recognises a claim for repayment of sums constituting unjust enrichment as a private law claim. However, after the accession of Poland to the EU, the administrative courts began to issue decisions which quoted the EU principle prohibiting unjust enrichment[55] and on these grounds refused the right to tax recovery if it led to the unjust enrichment of the taxpayer. Because of the discrepancies in the case law, the NSA issued a resolution explaining that in Polish law unjust enrichment of a tax payer is not a prerequisite for refusal of tax return.[56] Afterwards, the judges of the NSA put forward a question to *Trybunał Konstytucyjny* as to the compliance of these provisions with the Constitution, but the TK refused to consider this question, mostly due to procedural reasons.[57] At the same time, however, the TK invoked the EU standard formulated by the CJEU in respect to the repayment of charges levied contrary to the EU law and stated that it should be respected by Polish courts. In a later resolution, the NSA decided that the repayment of taxes must be excluded if it would lead to unjustified enrichment on the side of the taxpayer.[58] Unjust enrichment as an obstacle to repayment was thus accepted in the tax law and justified by the arguments derived from the EU law. It was not based exclusively on the EU arguments as EU law recognises the prohibition, but does not require it in domestic law,[59] but the Union system was treated as important inspiration. It is also worth noticing that the NSA directly referred to the whole concept of the prohibition of the unjust enrichment as formulated in the case law of the CJEU also in respect to the procedural requirements such as burden of proof, evidentiary rules etc.[60]

EU law may require modification of national principles of court's actions undertaken *ex proprio motu*. Limitations of the ability of the court to consider *ex officio* arguments resulting from EU law will be admissible if they serve legitimate purposes, such as the principle of the certainty of law or proper course of proceedings. At the same time the limitation has to be proportional to its purpose,

---

[54] Case C-426/05, *Tele2 Telecommunication GmbH* [2008] ECR I-685.

[55] eg Case C-309/06, *Marks & Spencer plc* [2008] ECR I-02283.

[56] Resolution of NSA of 13 July 2009, I FPS 4/09.

[57] Order of NSA of 15 October 2009, I FSK 240/08; order of TK of 29 November 2010, P 45/09.

[58] Resolution of NSA of 22 June 2011, I GPS 1/11.

[59] See eg Case C-147/01, *Weber's Wine World Handels-GmbH and Others* [2003] ECR I-11365.

[60] See also Półtorak (n 6).

which should be assessed in the light of the analysis of the whole procedure, as well as of the results of this procedure in an individual case.[61]

An interesting line of jurisprudence has developed in the *Sąd Najwyższy* case law under the influence of these rules. First of all, the SN made use of the CJEU's case law referring to the obligation of the court to act *ex officio* as one of the arguments supporting the principle that a civil law court of the second instance adjudicating an appeal is not bound by the arguments of the appeal pertaining to infringement of substantive law. The SN argued that the adoption of the principle that the court should be bound by the arguments constituting grounds for the appeal 'would also violate the obligation to consider ex officio any infringements of Community law, especially when, according to the European Court of Justice case-law, it is indispensable'.[62] The SN went even further in its argumentation referring to the arguments constituting grounds for the cassational appeal. The cassational appeal provided for in civil procedure is a highly formalised measure, allowed in extraordinary circumstances, generally in order to protect public interest. The SN is of the opinion that in principle, while hearing a cassational appeal, it does not have to consider *ex officio* arguments stemming from EU law. However, the SN concluded that since, in its points for review, a party raises the argument that a particular provision of Polish law has been infringed, the court, while adjudicating if those Polish provisions can be applied in the case, has to consider if they are in compliance with the EU rules, as well as with their interpretation provided by the CJEU. The SN stated that the need to apply Union law *ex officio* emerges when it is obvious that the provisions of the EU law regulate the same subject as national law and there is a possibility of their direct application or a necessity to construe the national provisions in compliance with the EU provisions.[63]

The EU standard of legal protection includes also the requirement to challenge—in certain specific cases—a final administrative decision which is not compliant with EU law. The rules that govern challenging such decisions are left to national law, yet those rules must fulfil the requirements of equivalence and effectiveness. EU law imposes the obligation to challenge such decisions in certain extraordinary circumstances, which were formulated by CJEU for the first time in *Kühne & Heitz* case and then developed in further judgments.[64]

In order to reflect those EU principles in Polish law, there are suggestions put forward in the legal doctrine to make use of various extraordinary measures currently functioning in Polish procedure. Such measures are for example the possibility to amend or to revoke a decision which does not confer any rights on

---

[61] Case C-312/93, *Peterbroeck* [1995] ECR I-4599; Joined Cases C-430/93 and C-431/93, *Jeroen van Schijndel* [1995] ECR I-4705; Case C-225/05, *Van der Weerd and others* [2007] ECR I-4233, para 32.

[62] Resolution of SN of 31 January 2008, III CZP 49/07.

[63] Judgment of the SN of 18 December 2006, II PK 17/06, OSNP 2008, No 1–2, item 8.

[64] Case C-453/00, *Kühne & Heitz NV v Produktschap voor Pluimvee en Eieren* [2004] ECR I-837; Case C-2/06 *Willy Kempter KG v Hauptzollamt Hamburg-Jonas* [2008] ECR I-00411; Case C-392/04 and C-422/04, *i-21 Germany GmbH and Arcor AG & Co KG* [2006] ECR I-8559, para 51.

any of the parties, or the option to declare an administrative decision invalid.[65] The above measures require not only appropriate interpretation of the provisions in question, but also active involvement on the part of administrative organs in ensuring compliance of administrative acts with EU law. Additionally, a manifest breach of EU law should be the grounds for declaring an administrative decision invalid on the same conditions as a manifest breach of Polish law.[66] It refers also to a situation where a Polish provision applied by an administrative authority was manifestly contrary to EU law.[67]

Furthermore, as already stated, Polish legislation incorporated a pro-European measure providing for a direct possibility to re-open proceedings that ended with a decision contrary to EU law. These are provisions of the Code of the Administrative Procedure and the Tax Ordinance. The possibility to re-open administrative proceedings, as provided in the Code of the Administrative Procedure, is very limited. It has been introduced by the law implementing the EU directive on equal treatment and refers to situations where a court judgment states that the principle of equal treatment has been infringed and this infringement influenced the decision of the administrative authority.[68] The regulation of the Tax Ordinance is much wider as it refers to all tax decisions. The prerequisite necessary to re-open tax proceedings is a ruling of the CJEU that influences the content of the issued decision.[69] Administrative courts interpreting this provision often refer to the case law of the CJEU related to reopening administrative decisions based on the *Kühne & Heitz* judgment.[70] For example, the NSA decided that the above provision is not limited only to the preliminary ruling the CJEU issued in the given case, but also to other rulings regarding the same provision of law being the grounds for an administrative decision.[71]

None of the Polish court procedures, however, provided directly for the possibility to re-open court proceedings on the grounds of a decision of the CJEU or the non-compliance with EU law. As may be interpreted from the *Kapferer* judgment, national law is not obliged to introduce the provision enabling reopening of the court proceedings on the grounds of a CJEU's ruling provided however that the existing solutions fulfil the requirements of equivalence and effectiveness.[72]

---

[65] See eg S Biernat et al, *Consequences of Incompatibility with EC Law for Final Administrative Decisions and Final Judgments of Administrative Courts in the Member States* (Warszawa, 2008).

[66] Judgment of NSA of 13 January 2012, I FSK 409/11.

[67] Judgment of NSA of 11 June 2010, I FSK 449/09.

[68] Art 145b of the Law of 14 June 1960 Administrative Procedure Code [Kodeks postępowania administracyjnego] (Dz U 2013, item 267—consolidated text). The amendment was provided by the law of 3.12.2010 on implementation of EU law related to equal treatment [o wdrożeniu niektórych przepisów Unii Europejskiej w zakresie równego traktowania] (Dz U 2010 No 254, item 1700).

[69] Art 240 of the Law of 29 August 1997 Tax Ordinance [Ordynacja podatkowa] (Dz U 2012, item 749).

[70] *Kühne & Heitz* (n 64).

[71] eg judgment of NSA of 7 December 2011, I FSK 400/11.

[72] Case C-234/04, *Rosmarie Kapferer* [2006] ECR I-2585.

In the light of the above, it should be noticed that provisions on proceedings before administrative courts as amended in 2010 provide for a possibility to reopen proceedings before an administrative court if such need arises from a ruling issued by an international organ.[73] These provisions might constitute the grounds for re-instigation of administrative court proceedings after a judgment of the CJEU. However, the motives for this legislative amendment refer only to the need to reopen the court proceeding in connection with the judgment of the European Court of Human Rights, and not the CJEU. Therefore, it is obvious that EU law has not been a point of reference or inspiration for the new provisions. Nevertheless, for the sake of EU law effectiveness, administrative courts interpret this provision as referring also to judgments of the CJEU as the basis for reopening court proceedings.[74]

A very important aspect of the Europeanisation of the consequences of public organs unlawful activities is the harmonisation, in line with the *Francovich* judgment, of the principles regulating the liability of Member States for damages caused by those public organs.[75] Prerequisites for this type of liability for infringement of EU law are uniform and very often require fundamental modification of national law provisions and principles. In many Member States, the *Francovich* rule started a domestic doctrinal discussion on grounds of liability of the State in national law. In this respect, the EU legal system served as a point of reference for the legal doctrine and jurisprudence. Such discussions and the ensuing modification of the relevant legal measures have also taken place in Poland. It was directly required by the new Constitution of 1997, but was also inspired by EU law. The new rules on liability for legislative and judicial acts were introduced in 2004.[76] They adopt a monist approach, so the new rules apply both to EU and national cases. There is, however, one important exception—the liability for judgments of the supreme courts. Such liability as a rule is excluded in Polish law. However, to comply with the requirements derived from the *Köbler* judgment of the CJEU,[77] it has been permitted in one specific situation—where a ruling of the Supreme Administrative Court remains manifestly in breach of EU law.[78] Recently, this provision has been used to declare a judgment of the NSA manifestly breaching EU law, and the NSA explained that the violation of EU law by the Polish administrative court

---

[73] Law of 30.08.2002 on proceedings before administrative courts [Prawo o postępowaniu przed sądami administracyjnymi] (Dz. U. 2012, 36 item 270—consolidated text).

[74] eg judgment of Wojewódzki Sąd Administracyjny of 22 June 2011, I SA/Go 94/11.

[75] Case C-6/90, C-9/90, *Andrea Francovich and Danila Bonifaci* [1991] ECR I-5357; Cases C-46/93 and C-48/93, *Brasserie du Pêcheur SA v Bundesrepublik Deutschland and The Queen v Secretary of State for Transport, ex parte: Factortame Ltd and others* [1996] ECR I-1029, para 33; Case C-173/03, *Traghetti del Mediterraneo SpA* [2006] ECR I-05177.

[76] See more N Półtorak, 'State Liability for Violation of European Union Law—A Polish Perspective' (2012) 13 *ERA Forum* 185.

[77] Case C-224/01, *Gerhard Köbler* [2003] ECR I-10239.

[78] Art 285a § 3 of the Law of 30 August 2002 on proceedings before administrative courts [Prawo o postępowaniu przed sądami administracyjnymi] (Dz U 2012, 36 item 270—consolidated text).

may occur if the court has not applied directly effective provisions of Union law, or applied national law which was contrary to EU law, or applied national law in a way that is incompatible with EU law.[79]

There is also another interesting aspect of the Europeanisation of the State liability in Polish law. The provisions on State liability do not refer directly to any form of the qualified breach of law. However, the SN invoked the EU standards while interpreting the relevant provisions and stated that they should be applied only in cases of a manifest judicial breach (that is when the court has clearly and significantly exceeded the discretion available to it).[80] To justify this statement, the SN invoked among others the *Köbler* judgment. The same approach was used by the *Trybunał Konstytucyjny*, which in a judgment of 2012 stated that the rule allowing the State liability for a court's infringement of the law only in cases of a manifest breach of the law does not violate the Polish Constitution.[81] Of course, the decision was based on the analysis of the Polish constitutional law; however, the TK invoked the judgments of the CJEU about the manifest breach as the condition of the liability for courts decisions. Thus, the EU standard was treated as an additional justification of the Polish rule limiting the State liability.[82] This example illustrates a rather exceptional phenomenon of reverse harmonisation, in the sense that the standard of legal protection approved on the EU level is applied uniformly by the States even though it is lower than it could be in domestic law.

IV. Conclusions

The above analysis tried to demonstrate that there is an on-going process of improving the level of legal protection in Poland under the influence of EU law. This process is of course not specific to Poland only; it is a part of Europeanisation of remedies and improving the standard of protection of EU rights in many Member States.

As a rule, EU law does not require any specific measures to be introduced by national procedural rules (which corresponds to the principle of procedural autonomy of the Member States), but points to the standard of effective legal protection. In Polish law, however, this standard is also implemented with the use of legal measures inspired by the case law of the CJEU. This refers to the examples

---

[79] Judgment of 19 December 2013, II GNP 2/13.
[80] eg judgment of Supreme Court of 20 April 2011, I BU 5/11. See also Półtorak (n 76).
[81] Judgment of TK of 27 September 2012, SK 4/11.
[82] See also N Półtorak 'State Liability in EU Law—Have the Member States Learnt Anything in 20 Years after Francovich?' in J Iliopoulos-Strangas, S Biernat and M Potacs (eds), *Verantwortung, Haftung und Kontrolle des Verfassungsstaates und der Europäischen Union im Wandel der Zeit—Responsibility, Accountability and Control of the Constitutional State and the European Union in Changing Times—Responsabilités et Contrôle de l' État constitutionnel et de l'Union européenne au fil du temps* (SIPE, Band 9, 2014) 181–94.

presented above, such as re-opening of an administrative procedure in the case of infringement of the EU equal treatment rule; re-opening of a tax procedure after a judgment of the CJEU; the right to repayment of taxes after a judgment of the CJEU; re-opening of a procedure before an administrative court after a judgment of an international organ; a claim for declaring a ruling of the NSA to be against the law in the case of a manifest infringement of EU law.

Those important legislative changes are, however, not sufficient to safeguard the rights of individuals granted by EU law in every case. This task is left to national courts. In consequence, the national courts not only control the domestic legislature as to whether it implements the provisions of EU law properly, but also as to whether the national standard of legal protection complies with the Union's one. This process may imply redefinition of the role and competences of courts in national systems. As presented in the above analysis, Polish courts and the Polish system of legal protection are undergoing this process at present. This is, however, not an easy process, taking into account the position of courts towards the legislator and the absence of any competences of ordinary courts, under domestic law, to independently evaluate provisions of legislative acts. On the other hand, Poland, like the other Central and Eastern European new democracies, had to redefine concepts of legal protection of individuals vis-a-vis the State, which made it probably easier to absorb the new ideas and competences stemming from EU law. In order to achieve this goal, it was not enough to respect Union law. It was necessary to recognise that changing the standard of legal protection is desirable and justified in spite of the doubts as to the observance of the principles of legalism or division of powers. It was, and is, possible primarily in the situations where the court notices deficiencies of the national system of legal protection and where the Union standard gives it a chance to amend them.

11

When David Teaches EU Law to Goliath: A Generational Upheaval in the Making

ALEXANDER KORNEZOV

I. Introduction

If numbers could speak, they would probably tell a remarkable success story. After a short initial period of relative shyness, Bulgarian courts have become the champions of the preliminary reference mechanism in all of Central and Eastern Europe (CEE), deferring the biggest number of references from the twelve new Member States in the period from 2007 to 2013. Numbers aside, the quality of most Bulgarian references has also been impressive. Very few have been struck down as inadmissible or answered by reasoned order because the reply was clear or could be deduced from the case law. In most cases Bulgarian courts have successfully weeded out legislation incompatible with EU law, while manoeuvring with relative ease between the various EU tools at their disposal—primacy, direct effect, conform interpretation, procedural autonomy etc.

One of the root causes for the preliminary reference bonanza that seems to have befallen Bulgarian courts is to be found in the legislator's pro-active role. By 'transposing' the preliminary reference mechanism into national law, he transformed it overnight into a daily affair, which quickly entered the mouths, minds and files of lawyers, government agents, judges and the like. In particular, the legislator explicitly declared that the order for preliminary reference was not subject to appeal. This gave wings to lower courts. The stage was thus set for the triumphant arrival of the preliminary reference mechanism in Bulgaria.

But behind the scenes a different story has been unfolding. The vast majority of references came from lower courts, in particular administrative courts, with just a trickle from civil and criminal jurisdictions. By contrast, the Bulgarian supreme and appellate courts have played just a minor role in the process, while the *Konstitutsionen sad* (constitutional court, hereinafter the 'KS') has remained practically invisible in the European discourse. A peculiar phenomenon has been also taking place: Lower courts were using the preliminary reference to stand up to supreme courts and question their EU-competency. These might thus be the signs of an unusual upheaval of the lower courts against the system's inertia, a contemporary story of David standing up to Goliath. All of this would have been unthinkable before EU accession.

While the preliminary reference has probably become the strongest and the most efficient weapon of this commotion, behind it there are important generational and institutional undercurrents that shape the image of the system as a whole. The generational dimension goes far beyond the usual banality of juxtaposing the old against the young. It is rather a matter of different legal mentality, perceptions, style and culture. The application of EU law has served as litmus highlighting these differences between the generations. But there has also been a particularly interesting institutional experiment that tells a revealing story about the Bulgarian judiciary and its attitudes towards EU law. The experiment was carried out in the system of administrative justice, where the majority of judges in the lower courts came from outside the system. Incidentally or not, they have been the ones who have most actively pioneered the integration of EU law into Bulgaria's judicial landscape. These patterns are actually representative not only of the overall state of the Bulgarian judiciary but also of the post-accession judicial landscape in most of Central and Eastern Europe, where some of these phenomena have occurred in similar or different shapes, contexts and intensity.[1]

This chapter will unfold as follows. First, the numbers, the quality and the formal causes of the preliminary reference windfall that the Bulgarian judiciary has come to know, will be examined (section II). The chapter will then seek to unravel the mystery behind the numbers. It will look backstage in an attempt to identify the patterns that have so far characterised the Bulgarian preliminary reference experience, noting that its repercussions go far beyond the Article 267 TFEU (Treaty on the Functioning of the European Union) procedure. In particular, it will examine the roles played, on the one hand, by the KS, the supreme and the lower courts, and, on the other hand, by the administrative, civil and criminal jurisdictions (section III). The chapter will then set out to discuss the root causes of the patterns thus identified. This could help explain why some courts have remained on the side-lines of European discourse, while others have very actively sought to participate therein. It is at this point that the generational and the institutional dimension of these patterns will be examined (section IV). Finally, the chapter will discuss whether EU law has brought change in judicial style and reasoning (section V).

---

[1] See eg M Bobek, 'Landtová, Holubec, and the Problem of an Uncooperative Court: Implications for the Preliminary Rulings Procedure' (2014) 10 *European Constitutional Law Review* 54.

II. A Fairy Tale

The first seven years of the Bulgarian preliminary reference experience can be told as a fairy tale. Against a rather grim background of constant criticism and systemic weakness, which have justified the creation of the so-called 'cooperation and verification mechanism' in view of monitoring Bulgaria's and Romania's progress in the field of judicial reform,[2] no one was really expecting that Bulgarian courts would suddenly turn into a regular and competent interlocutor of the Court of Justice of the EU. And yet, Bulgarian judges entered the European preliminary reference arena with much aplomb. Their references were both numerous and most of the time competently written. Theirs is the golden medal of the most active preliminary reference judiciary in all of Central and Eastern Europe. These have been times of a true preliminary reference bonanza, as if Bulgarian courts sought redemption through the preliminary reference mechanism. This part of the chapter recounts the Bulgarian experience as a fairy tale, where numbers, quality and causes are all hard evidence of a remarkable success story.

A. Of Numbers

When numbers speak, even gods are silent. This old Bulgarian proverb still sounds valid in our today's statistic-addicted society. Statistics have been particularly flattering for the Bulgarian judiciary. Compared with the other Central and Eastern European Member States, the Bulgarian judiciary has performed particularly well in terms of (1) the absolute numbers of references since 1 January 2007; (2) the number of references per year; and (3) the number of references per capita.

In absolute numbers, Bulgarian courts have made an impressive lot of 69 preliminary references since Bulgaria's accession to the EU on 1 January 2007. This is more than any other Central and Eastern European Member State for the same period of time[3] and is on a par with Romania, noting however that the latter's numbers are somewhat inflated since many of its references have been either subsequently withdrawn or merged for joint examination.[4] This result is astonishing, given that the Central and Eastern European Member States which joined the Union on 1 May 2004 have had a longer period of adaptation and were therefore in a better starting position in the beginning of the reference period.

---

[2] The European Commission's latest reports can be found at <http://ec.europa.eu/cvm/index_en.htm>.

[3] The data have been extracted from the Court of Justice's database.

[4] Nine of Romania's 69 references have been withdrawn, as opposed to only 1 of Bulgaria's. Of the remaining 60 Romanian references, 10 have been merged into 5 joint cases.

Table 1

CEE Member State	Number of references (01/01/2007–01/04/2014)
Bulgaria	69
Romania	69
Hungary	61
Poland	52
Czech Republic	28
Latvia	24
Slovakia	20
Lithuania	13
Estonia	11
Slovenia	5

Interestingly, Bulgarian references also outnumber in absolute terms those originating from many of the old Member States of comparable size for the same period, for example Greece, Sweden, Portugal, Denmark or Finland.[5]

Bulgaria's prominence on the preliminary reference arena is even more evident, if the comparison is made on the basis of the number of preliminary references per year since May 2004. This comparison is actually fairer because it takes into account the initial period of post-accession adaption. Here Bulgaria also comes on top with roughly 10 references per year, much ahead, for instance, of Poland's six references per year and Slovakia's two.

The above classification obviously favours the bigger Member States, given that the volume in judicial activity (number of national courts, number of suits, etc) is bigger than in the smaller Member States. This factor could be neutralised by classifying the data on the basis of the number of preliminary references per capita.[6] According to this criterion, Bulgaria comes second only to Latvia.

All in all, and whichever way the available statistical data are classified, Bulgaria invariably comes up first or second. The statistics thus paint a bright picture of the Bulgarian judiciary as the vanguard of the preliminary ruling procedure in Central and Eastern Europe.

---

[5] The numbers are as follows: Greece—67; Sweden—49; Portugal—46; Denmark—42; Finland—41.

[6] While this sort of classification is certainly a ground-breaking contribution to the statistical science, I humbly note that the invention is not mine; it has indeed already been used elsewhere, see eg M Broberg and N Fenger, *Preliminary References to the European Court of Justice* (Oxford University Press, 2010) 38–39.

Table 2

CEE Member State	Number of references per year (01/05/2004–01/04/2014)
Bulgaria	9.5
Romania	9.5
Hungary	9
Poland	6.3
Czech Republic	3.5
Latvia	3.1
Lithuania	2.6
Slovakia	2.4
Estonia	1.5
Slovenia	0.5

Table 3

CEE Member State	Number of references per year/ per 1 million inhabitants (01/05/2004–01/04/2014)
Latvia	1.5
Bulgaria	1.4
Estonia	1.1
Hungary	0.9
Lithuania	0.9
Romania	0.5
Slovakia	0.4
Czech Republic	0.3
Slovenia	0.25
Poland	0.2

B. Of Quality

While numbers do matter, they do not necessarily tell the whole story. The fact that the jurisdictions of a given Member State have made the biggest number of preliminary references to the Court of Justice of the EU speaks little of the 'quality' of those references. While the 'quality' of a judicial act is immeasurable and highly subjective, one can nonetheless obtain a general idea on the basis of the number of orders—as opposed to judgments—delivered by the Court in reply to those references. It should be recalled that the Court replies by reasoned order in two sets of circumstances: (1) Where the reference is inadmissible or the Court manifestly lacks jurisdiction;[7] and (2) where the question has been already answered in the existing case law or where the answer is of no reasonable doubt.[8] Many of these cases—especially the first group—speak of a bad quality of the preliminary reference: It was either badly drafted, or lacked essential information, or concerned a matter alien to EU law. The quality of the second group of references is only marginally better, insofar as, albeit better drafted, these references could have been avoided, if only the national judge had taken the time to read the Court's case law or reflect a bit on the applicable Union law.

Therefore, the 'quality' of preliminary references can be measured indicatively by the ratio of reasoned orders against the total number of references. By this parameter, the quality of only about a tenth of Bulgaria's preliminary references can be considered as unsatisfactory.[9] Here Bulgaria ranks a joint third with Poland.

Table 4

CEE Member State	Orders/number of completed cases (01/05/2004–01/04/2014)[10]
Estonia	0%
Latvia	8%
Poland	12%
Bulgaria	12%
Czech Republic	13%
Lithuania	17%
Slovenia	25%
Hungary	28%
Slovakia	36%
Romania	61%

---

[7] Art 53(2) of the Court's Rules of Procedure.

[8] Art 99 of the Court's Rules of Procedure.

[9] This is lower than the EU average, see the Court's *Annual Report for 2013* (Office for Official Publications, 2014) 89.

[10] The cases where the reference has been withdrawn have been disregarded.

The 'quality' of preliminary references can also be measured by the level of importance of the legal issues they have raised. The relevant criterion in this regard is the percentage of judgments delivered by the Grand Chamber since it is this chamber that traditionally rules on the most difficult and/or most important questions of Union law.[11] Another relevant yardstick is the number of cases in which the Advocate General has given an opinion, since these cases usually raise a new point of law.[12] These criteria put Bulgarian references somewhere in the middle of Central and Eastern European Member States.

Table 5

CEE Member State	Grand Chamber judgments/ number of completed cases	AG Opinions/number of completed cases
Czech Republic	17%	67%
Slovakia	14%	50%
Hungary	10%	31%
Poland	4%	35%
Bulgaria	3.5%	22%
Romania	2%[13]	12%
Estonia	0%	33%
Lithuania	0%	31%
Slovenia	0%	25%
Latvia	0%	21%

The combined analysis of the above data shows that the quality of Bulgarian references has been relatively decent. Despite the low number of Bulgarian references which have attracted the attention of the Grand Chamber, few have been struck down for bad quality. Thus, without necessarily being on the cutting edge, Bulgarian references have been, as a whole, well written, rarely deficient and generally adequate. Therefore, the large number of references from Bulgarian courts has not had as a corollary the deterioration in their quality. To the contrary, the fact that Bulgarian jurisdictions have been the most active on the preliminary reference

---

[11] Art 60 of the Court's Rules of Procedure.

[12] Art 20 of the Statute of the Court of Justice of the EU.

[13] For the purpose of the analysis, the Grand Chamber order in Joint Cases C-97/13 and C-214/13 *Câmpean et Ciocoiu* EU:C:2014:229, was disregarded since, in this case, the attribution of the case to the Grand Chamber was not because of its difficulty or importance for the EU legal order but because of Romania's request to that effect on the basis of Art 16 of the Statute.

arena from all CEE Member States (section II.B), while at the same time maintaining the quality of these references at a decent level, shows that Bulgarian courts have successfully mastered the preliminary reference mechanism.

C. Of Causes

The causes of the preliminary reference bonanza that has befallen Bulgarian courts can be sought on several levels. On the formal level, the reasons for this singular achievement can be found, first and foremost, in the pro-active stance of the Bulgarian legislature.

Unlike other EU Member States, the Bulgarian legislature decided, in substance, to 'transpose' the preliminary reference mechanism into national law.[14] It added a whole new chapter dedicated exclusively to preliminary references to the Court of Justice of the EU in the 'Bible' of Bulgarian legal practitioners, the *Grajdanski protsesualen kodeks* (Code of Civil Procedure, hereinafter the 'GPK'),[15] thus 'translating' an otherwise unknown and exotic legal instrument into the most known piece of national judicial legislation. Admittedly, this had an immense practical effect in that it brought the preliminary reference mechanism into the mouths, minds and files of lawyers, government agents, judges and the like. It was shown around to everyone in broad daylight and judges were instructed to apply it. Its insertion in the GPK assisted enormously those practitioners unacquainted with the intricacies of EU law. It provided them with simple rules that are ready to use and easy to find. Judges and lawyers were thus spared the onerous task of going through thousands of pages of case law and other unfamiliar legal sources.

The 'transposition' into national law of the preliminary reference procedure was however far from flawless. In its effort to simplify and codify a legal mechanism which has evolved—and keeps evolving—mostly through case law, the Bulgarian legislature inevitably made mistakes.[16] These mistakes were however not of such a nature as to obstruct or misrepresent the preliminary reference procedure.

Most outstandingly however, this new chapter of the GPK contained one specific provision which set the stage for the triumphant arrival of the preliminary reference procedure in Bulgaria. Article 631(1) GPK stipulates that the order for preliminary reference is not subject to appeal. This provision is remarkable for several reasons. First, because it stands at odds with one of the basic rules of Bulgarian civil procedure, according to which all judicial decisions that bar, even

---

[14] The question of whether such a 'transposition' is permissible under EU law is beyond the scope of this ch.

[15] Ch 59, pt VII GPK. These provisions are also applicable in administrative judicial procedures (Art 144 Code of Administrative Procedure). For comparison, other CEE Member States, such as the Czech Republic and Slovakia, took a minimalist approach: M Bobek, 'Learning to Talk: Preliminary Rulings, the Courts of the New Member States and the Court of Justice' (2008) 45 *CML Rev* 1611, 1626.

[16] For a comment, see А Корнезов, *Преюдициалното запитване до Съда на Европейския съюз* [A Kornezov, *The Preliminary Reference to the Court of Justice of the EU*] 2nd edn (Сиби [Sibi], 2012) §§ 9, 19, 22–27, 55–57, 59, 62, 66, 75, 76.

temporarily, the further progress of the case, are subject to appeal.[17] Thus, court orders that stay the proceedings are, in principle, subject to appeal. The legislator however decided to derogate from this rule in a manifest move to encourage references to Luxembourg. Second, this provision was adopted in July 2007, that is at a time when there was no clear answer to the question of whether EU law precluded appeals against decisions of national courts making a reference to Luxembourg. Indeed, it was not until December 2008 that the Court of the Justice of the EU finally gave some valuable indications in *Cartesio*.[18] The matter was further clarified in March 2009 in *Nationale Loterij*.[19] Remarkably, the Court's subsequent case law proved the Bulgarian legislator right in that EU law does not permit an appellate court to vary the order for reference, set it aside or order the referring court to resume the domestic proceedings, if the latter remain pending before the referring court in their entirety.[20]

Thus, from the start, references to the Court of Justice have been enjoying a privileged status in Bulgarian procedural law. This has given wings to lower courts. It has empowered them in a way that no previous judicial reform ever has. It gave them the courage to seek an external opinion in Luxembourg without interference from the higher courts. This single provision thus sowed the seeds for a particularly abundant harvest.

In the meantime, the literature on the preliminary reference mechanism has flourished. The general[21] and often very detailed presentation of the preliminary reference procedure[22] was also sometimes coupled with practical tips, such as model preliminary references,[23] commentaries article-by-article of the Court's statute and rules of procedure,[24] as well as of the new chapter of the GPK.[25] Such practice-oriented manuals have usually proved useful to judges and other legal

---

[17] Art 274 GPK. Similar provisions apply in administrative and criminal procedures: Art 229 Code of Administrative Procedure; Arts 251 and 290 Code of Criminal Procedure.

[18] Case C-210/06, EU:C:2008:723.

[19] C-525/06, EU:C:2009:179.

[20] *Cartesio* (n 18), para 98.

[21] Ж Попова, *Право на Европейския съюз* [J Popova, *Law of the European Union*] 2nd edn (Сиела [Ciela], 2011); А Семов, Х Христев, З Грекова, Г Георгиев, *Съдебната система на Европейския съюз и САЩ* [A Semov, H Hristev, Z Grekova, G Georgiev, *The Judicial System of the EU and the USA*] (Институт по Европейско право [Institut po Evropeisko pravo], 2007); С Костов, *Актовете на Съда на Европейския съюз: правни последици* [S Kostov, *Acts of the Court of the Justice of the EU: Legal Effects*] (Сиби [Sibi], 2011); М Златарева, *Международен граждански процес* [M Zlatareva, *International Civil Procedure*] (Сиела [Ciela], 2010).

[22] Kornezov (n 16).

[23] ibid, § 75.

[24] А Корнезов, *Преюдициалното запитване до Съда на Европейските общности: Сборник нормативни актове и практически указания* [A Kornezov, *The Preliminary Reference to the Court of Justice of the EU: Statutory Acts and Practical Guidance*] (Сиби [Sibi], 2008).

[25] Р Иванова, Б Пунев, С Чернев, *Коментар на новия Граждански процесуален кодекс* [R Ivanova, B Punev, S Chernev, *Comments on the New Code of Civil Procedure*] (ИК 'Труд и право' [IK 'Trud i Pravo'], 2008); В Попова, *Актуални проблеми на Европейская граждански процес и част VII на ГПК* [V Popova, *Current Problems of European Civil Procedure and Part VII of the Code of Civil Procedure*] (Сиела [Ciela], 2012); Kornezov, above (n 24).

practitioners. The abundance of literature, together with the proliferation of all sorts of seminars focusing on Article 267 TFEU, have possibly also helped judges feel more at ease with preliminary references.

The first seven years of Bulgaria's experience with preliminary references might thus look like a fairy tale: A story of success and abundance, of competent judges helped by a competent legislature and a competent academic body.

But fairy tales are from a different world. The following section opens the curtains and looks behind the scenes for signs that could help obtain a fuller picture of the Bulgarian judiciary's first encounters with EU law.

III. Behind the Curtains

Scratching the surface of the statistical data discussed in the previous section reveals that behind the curtains a different story has been unfolding. Several additional indicators seem to point to a number of problem areas which have managed to remain unnoticed amidst the cheerful enthusiasm surrounding Bulgaria's performance on the preliminary reference stage. The following analysis looks closer at the referring courts that have so far been the most frequent interlocutor of the Court of Justice and at those that have remained on the side-lines.

It must be noted from the outset that the patterns underpinning the preliminary references made by Bulgarian courts are highly indicative of the general attitudes of Bulgarian courts towards EU law. It is certainly true that the number of references cannot be in itself conclusive. Indeed, the fact that a court has not made a reference does not necessarily mean that it has ignored EU law or that it has applied it incorrectly. Yet, in the aftermath of a Member State's accession, national courts are not yet fully versed in the complexities of EU law; rather, they are still learning, still coming to terms with EU law. It is therefore highly unlikely that a lack or a low number of references can be explained by the expert knowledge of EU law by national judges in a new Member State, enabling them to find the right solution to all EU-relevant matters that have ever come before them without seeking assistance from Luxembourg. A more plausible explanation is that either EU law was disregarded altogether or that national courts simply felt unprepared to make a reference because of a lack of experience, expertise or a mixture of both.

Therefore, the patterns of preliminary references remain a highly relevant indicator for the level of penetration of EU law in the domestic legal system, especially in the period following a Member State's accession. In addition, however, the subsequent analysis also takes account, as far as possible, of the EU-relevant case law of national courts in which no reference was made. These cases provide a precious insight of the workings of domestic courts and help identify some more general patterns of application of EU law in Bulgaria.

A. Oh Civil and Criminal Courts, Where Art Thou?

If someone should be given credit for the success story of Bulgarian preliminary references, it is the administrative courts. Indeed, the vast majority—nearly
90 per cent—of all preliminary references came from them, with just a trickle from
civil jurisdictions. Most frequently, the matters referred to Luxembourg concerned
VAT and customs classifications, but also, and ever more often, fundamental rights,
asylum and immigration matters, EU citizenship and free movement of persons,
social security, agriculture, antidumping, etc. Administrative courts have thus
been not only the frontrunners of the Bulgarian preliminary ruling experience,
but have also de facto monopolised the dialogue with Luxembourg. The overview
of parts of their case law also shows that in many cases where no reference was
made, EU law was nonetheless seriously taken into consideration.

By contrast, Bulgarian civil and criminal jurisdictions (which belong to one
and the same branch of the judiciary) have been practically absent—at least most
of the time—from the preliminary reference dialogue. Their interactions with
the Court of Justice are few, far between and of questionable quality. Out of the
eight references made so far by civil and criminal jurisdictions, two have been
struck down as inadmissible,[26] one was answered by order since the reply was
clear[27] and two were joined in a single case.[28] In informal discussions, civil and
criminal judges would normally state two reasons for their passiveness. First, they
would affirm that, unlike administrative law, civil and criminal law is not significantly affected by EU law. It does not really take much to rebut this illusion: It
suffices to mention, to name but a few, the various instruments of EU private
international law, labour law, family law, intellectual property law, discrimination
etc. The data on the subject matter of the preliminary references originating from
the other Member States clearly shows that such matters are often deferred to the
Court.[29] Second, criminal judges would argue that they are unable to refer questions to Luxembourg since Bulgaria has not accepted the jurisdiction of the Court
pursuant to the old Article 35 TEU (Treaty on European Union), which remains
applicable until 1 December 2014.[30] But this mantra has been used and abused
indiscriminately as a general disclaimer in all criminal proceedings, regardless of
whether the issue of EU law was or not covered by the old Article 35 TEU. After all,
various provisions of EU law which have *not* been adopted on the basis of the old
Title VI TEU can become relevant in a criminal proceeding. In such cases, a reference is admissible. But criminal judges have failed to comprehend this.[31] Third,

---

[26] Case C-181/09 *Canon* EU:C:2009:565; and Case C-32/10 *Semerdzhiev* EU:C:2011:288.
[27] Case C-449/09 *Canon* EU:C:2010:651.
[28] Joint cases C-250/09 et C-268/09 *Georgiev* EU:C:2010:699.
[29] Annual reports of the Court of Justice (eg 2010–2013).
[30] Art 10 of Protocol 36 TFEU.
[31] eg VKS judgment in case n° 101/2009.

the case law of civil and criminal courts shows numerous examples where EU law should have been applied but was disregarded altogether or was interpreted erroneously.[32]

The acclaim for the preliminary reference bonanza therefore goes exclusively to Bulgarian administrative courts. More importantly however, this shows that the much trumpeted success story is only partial. Indeed, civil and criminal courts seem to have failed to keep pace with modern-day European litigation. This observation does not only apply to the failure of these courts to partake in the preliminary reference mechanism but also to their general attitudes to EU law. This is worrying because it shows that a large chunk of the Bulgarian judiciary has been shunning the effective application of EU law.

B. Supreme Courts Hibernating?

Another peculiarity of Bulgarian preliminary references is that the overwhelming majority of them came from lower courts. Indeed, nearly 83 per cent of all references originated in lower courts, that is the courts of first instance.[33] By contrast, supreme and appellate courts have been either absent altogether from the preliminary reference dialogue or participated therein only marginally. The two Bulgarian supreme courts—*Varhoven kasatsionen sad* (Supreme Court of Cassation, hereinafter the 'VKS') and *Varhoven administrativen sad* (the Supreme Administrative Court, hereinafter the 'VAS')—have failed to lead the way to Luxembourg.

The VKS made only one preliminary reference back in 2010, which was rejected as manifestly inadmissible.[34] Since then the VKS has not dared reappear on stage. This is worrying news. First, there is evidence that the VKS has been rejecting requests for preliminary reference on questionable grounds.[35] Second, it is unimaginable that a court of that size—made, by last count, of 103 judges[36]—and of such a voluminous judicial activity[37] has never stumbled upon an issue of EU law worthy of discussion. The overview of its recent case law clearly shows that EU law was or should have been a relevant consideration in many cases and that the VKS has either failed to take account thereof or has erroneously done so.[38] Moreover, the VKS has lately attracted the criticism of the European Commission

---

[32] See below in this chapter, nn 75, 76, 77 and 78.

[33] This is much higher than the average of most of the other Member States, as evidenced by the Court's Annual Report for 2013 (n 9) 107–109.

[34] *Semerdzhiev* (n 26), where, despite the Court's request for clarifications, the VKS failed to justify the admissibility of its reference.

[35] А Корнезов, *Общностното право в българската съдебна практика (2007–2008)* [A Kornezov, *Community Law in the Case-Law of Bulgarian Courts (2007–2008)*] (Сиби [Sibi], 2009), pt III, ch II.

[36] <www.vks.bg/vks_p01_01.htm>

[37] The VKS delivers annually between 15,000 and 20,000 judgments (source: VKS annual reports 2007–2013).

[38] For some examples, see below, nn 75, 76 and 77 in this chapter.

which started the administrative phase of infringement proceedings because of the alleged inconsistency with EU law of that court's case-law. In a parallel development, a Dutch court deplored the VKS's manifestly wrong interpretation and application of EU law and asked the Court in a preliminary reference to authorise it not to recognise and execute VKS's vitiated judgments.[39] Third, there is also evidence that the VKS has not complied with its *obligation*, as a court of last instance, to refer matters of EU law to Luxembourg.[40] All of this shows that the VKS has been struggling to come to terms with EU law as a whole.

To this date, none of the six appellate courts, also of considerable size,[41] has made a single reference to the Court of Justice. More generally, EU law considerations appear only occasionally in their case law.[42]

The VAS, the Bulgarian supreme jurisdiction in administrative law, has been more visible in EU matters, but the overall picture is a mixed one, with some chambers taking a pro-active approach while others remain on the sidelines of EU discourse. It did use the preliminary reference mechanism several times, but it has been so far clearly overshadowed by lower administrative courts. Indeed, the VAS—which has 86 judges on its payroll[43]—has so far authored 11 references, which represent just about 18 per cent of the total number of references coming from Bulgarian administrative jurisdictions. Only one of these references justified an opinion of an Advocate General[44] and none attracted the attention of the Grand Chamber. VAS's references have thus been not only modest in number but also low in profile. The VAS has therefore only marginally—if at all—contributed to the development of EU law through the preliminary reference mechanism. More generally, the overview of a number of cases where EU law was pertinent but where no reference was made confirms the impression of an overall mixed picture: While in some of these cases a serious analysis of the relevant EU law was carried out, in others the VAS's reasoning was summary and dismissive.[45] The VAS has also quickly discovered the *CILFIT* exceptions, although their use remains sometimes questionable.[46]

As for the KS, the Bulgarian constitutional court, it has been invisible on the European level, even as many of its counterparts from the other Member States decide ever more often to actively participate in the judicial dialogue with the Court of Justice. The KS has indeed remained in the periphery of European discourse, even by local standards. There is no evidence in its case law that it has ever

---

[39] Case C-681/13 *Diageo Brands*, pending, case notice published in the OJ C 71/11 of 8 March 2014.

[40] eg VKS, judgment in case n° 101/2009.

[41] In 2013, 159 judges sat in the appellate courts in Sofia, Plovdiv, Bourgas, Varna and Veliko Turnovo, as well as in the specialised criminal appellate court (source: <www.vss.justice.bg/bg/start.htm>).

[42] The author has struggled (in vain!) to find good examples of correct application of EU law in their case law.

[43] VAS's annual report for 2012.

[44] Case C-374/12 *Valimar* EU:C:2014:2231.

[45] For some examples, see below in this chapter, nn 75, 77 and 80.

[46] Kornezov (n 35) pt II, ch I.

even considered making a reference to Luxembourg. There is no evidence either that it has ever discussed the question of whether it sees itself as a 'court or tribunal' in the meaning of Article 267 TFEU. More generally, the KS has not yet openly ruled on whether it considers itself to have jurisdiction to verify the compatibility of national laws with EU law.[47] While it does occasionally refer to EU law in its judgments, it does so briefly, in a sort of obiter, without conducting an in-depth examination of the relevant EU legal matter.[48]

In conclusion, the involvement of the Bulgarian constitutional, supreme and appellate courts in the European discourse has been either non-existent or marginal at best. This conclusion is confirmed not only by the lack of references from some of these jurisdictions but also by their overall failure to ensure an adequate level of consistency with EU law requirements in their case law.

C. Et la Province?

The Bulgarian judiciary is organised in a particularly dense local network: There are 113 district courts, 28 regional courts and 28 administrative courts, not to mention the appellate, supreme and martial courts.[49] But the huge majority—61 out of 69—of the preliminary references made so far came from jurisdictions located in Sofia and Varna. Their share is thus clearly disproportionate to the very large number of geographically dispersed courts and tribunals.

This might have slowly started to change over the past year or so, when the courts in Plovdiv, Burgas, Veliko Turnovo, Pleven and even Targovishte made their debut. For the time being however, references outside of Sofia and Varna remain few and far between. This indicator suggests that the preliminary reference mechanism—and more generally EU law—still remains terra incognita for the majority of Bulgarian courts.

D. A Personal Affair?

There is yet another curiosity about Bulgarian preliminary references. It is common knowledge that a considerable proportion of them have been drafted by the same few judges. There is no official statistical data in this respect but it could, nonetheless, be inferred from a number of sources[50] that the success story of Bulgaria's preliminary reference experience has indeed been due, at least partly,

---

[47] The case law might be interpreted as suggesting that the KS might have implicitly accepted jurisdiction in this respect—eg judgment n° 3/2012. For comparison, the Polish and the Slovak Constitutional Courts have explicitly accepted jurisdiction and acknowledged that they could make a reference to Luxembourg—see Bobek (n 15) 1633.

[48] eg judgments nos 2/2011; 11/2012; 3/2012; 7/2012; 12/2012.

[49] <www.adms-pv.bg/other/Struct.htm>.

[50] Most orders for reference have been published online, eg <www.admincourtsofia.bg/Дела/Преюдициалнизапитвания.aspx>.

to a handful of judges who regularly engage with EU law. This indicator, while speaking loads for the competence and EU drive of these magistrates, also shows that the preliminary reference mechanism—and hence EU law—has not really permeated the legal culture and practice of the Bulgarian judiciary as a whole. Rather, it seems to have emerged as an area 'reserved' for those few who have made the effort of acquainting themselves with the intricacies of EU law. This phenomenon thus casts doubt upon the assertion that the preliminary reference mechanism, and with it EU law as such, has indeed entered the heart and mind of the average Bulgarian judge.

This section has thus shown that behind Bulgaria's impressive numbers, there are serious signs of a particularly uneven level of engagement with EU law among municipal courts. Most worryingly of all, the supreme and appellate courts, as well as civil and criminal jurisdictions as a whole, have been particularly reluctant to get involved in EU law matters.

IV. David versus Goliath

The patterns of application of EU law identified in the previous section reveal a number of key phenomena and institutional problems in the Bulgarian judiciary. It is therefore important to examine the driving forces behind these phenomena, as well as the root causes of the systemic problems in certain jurisdictions with regard to the effective application of EU law.

A. Standing Up and Winning

There has been a clear tendency ever since Bulgaria's accession to the EU—noticeable, for that matter, in much of post-accession Central and Eastern Europe—of lower courts using the preliminary reference as a tool for standing up to the supreme courts and for questioning their EU-competency.[51] There is indeed strong evidence that lower courts have often sought, through the preliminary reference mechanism, to overcome the supreme courts' case law. This has caused unprecedented tectonic movements in a judiciary which has been traditionally structured on a hierarchical premise. The supreme courts have never been challenged by lower courts before. They used to enjoy a quasi-absolute authority over them. That authority was further conveyed through two specific mechanisms—the so-called 'interpretative judgments' and the so-called 'binding instructions' as to the interpretation of the law in a given case, both of which will be discussed in

---

[51] For comments on this trend in other parts of Central and Eastern Europe, see Bobek (n 1). This same trend might have played a marginal role in the older Member States, too, without however amounting to a general trend: Broberg and Fenger (n 6) 52–54.

more detail below. Post-accession, both of these instruments have come under heavy fire through the preliminary reference mechanism by disenchanted lower courts.

The first challenge came in 2009 with the reference in *Elchinov*, when a lower administrative court questioned the binding character of the instructions it had received from the VAS.[52] In Bulgarian procedural law (civil, administrative and criminal), when a supreme court quashes on appeal a lower court's judgment, it may send back the case to it, together with the so-called 'binding instructions' as to the interpretation of the law.[53] When the lower court resumes the case, it is obliged to apply the law as 'instructed' by the higher court without being permitted to deviate from these instructions. This rule has been for a very long time so entrenched in Bulgarian procedural law that it is often considered as a general principle or a judicial rule that is fundamental for the system. In *Elchinov*, a lower court had, in application of Regulation 1408/71,[54] ordered the authorities to reimburse Mr Elchinov for the medical expenses he had incurred in another Member State. On appeal, the VAS quashed the judgment and sent it back with binding instructions as to the interpretation of the Regulation. The lower court was however unconvinced. It doubted the correctness of the VAS's interpretation of the Regulation and was reluctant to follow it. It therefore decided to seek the intervention of the Court of Justice by asking it to rule whether the VAS had erred and whether, in such circumstances, it could disregard its instructions. The Grand Chamber of the Court replied with a resounding 'yes' on both counts: First, the VAS had indeed erred and, second, the lower court was not bound by the instructions of the VAS.

The judgment in *Elchinov* was revolutionary for the Bulgarian judicial mentality. It basically meant that lower courts could disregard the instructions given to them by the supreme courts, if they were contrary to EU law. That was a clear warning to the supreme courts: Lower courts would no longer follow blindly their instructions as they used to. It led to a fast and irreversible emancipation of lower courts which felt emboldened and encouraged to question the correctness of the supreme courts' judgments.

The second challenge came a few months later in *Canon*.[55] This time a lower civil court questioned the compatibility with EU law of a VKS's interpretative judgment. Interpretative judgments are a peculiarity of many Central and Eastern European judicial systems which was introduced in the Soviet bloc in the 1950s and which survives to this date.[56] These judgments are meant to interpret *in*

---

[52] Case C-173/09 *Elchinov* EU:C:2010:581.

[53] Art 224 Code of Administrative Procedure; Art 294(1) GPK; Art 355 Code of Criminal Procedure.

[54] Council Regulation (EC) No 1408/71 of 14 June 1971 on the application of social security schemes to employed persons, to self-employed persons and to members of their families moving within the Community (Consolidated version—OJ L 28/1 of 30 January 1997).

[55] *Canon* (n 27).

[56] Z Kühn, 'The Authoritarian Legal Culture at Work: The Passivity of Parties and the Interpretational Statements of Supreme Courts' (2006) 2 *Croatian Yearbook of European Law & Policy* 19, 23–25.

abstracto the applicable law, in the sense that they do not concern a specific dispute and, hence, there is no applicant and no defendant. In a way, they can be seen as an exercise of quasi-legislative functions by the supreme courts. In Bulgaria, only the VAS and the VKS can deliver interpretative judgments, if the case law on a point of law is either contradictory or considered wrong. When confronted with a question which has been the subject matter of an interpretative judgment, all courts are supposed to follow the adopted solution verbatim without further ado. Interpretative judgments are thus almost sacrosanct in Bulgaria. But in *Canon* a lower court thought that, in the light of the Court of Justice's case law, a VKS's recent interpretative judgment was erroneous and, in order to trump it, decided to raise the issue with the Court in Luxembourg. The latter not only agreed with the lower court but was particularly adamant, replying forcefully by reasoned order since the answer to the question followed clearly from the Court's case law. This was a humiliating blow for the VKS, who was practically told, by a lower court and by the Court of Justice, that it had manifestly breached EU law. The drama that subsequently unfolded surpassed however all expectations. The VKS decided to adopt a new interpretative judgment, in which it basically re-confirmed its previous interpretative judgment.[57] This time around, however, the European Commission intervened and started infringement proceedings against Bulgaria for the VKS's failure to bring its case law in line with EU law. The matter became even more dramatic when the Dutch Hoge Raad appeared reluctant to recognise and enforce a Bulgarian judgment which was based on the VKS's interpretative judgment since it was, according to the Hoge Raad, manifestly contrary to EU law.[58]

Canon was also revolutionary for the Bulgarian judicial mentality. It basically stripped the supreme courts' interpretative judgments of the status they used to enjoy. Any lower court could now question them and, more importantly, overturn them through the preliminary reference mechanism. The emancipation of lower courts thus became unstoppable.

Since then the challenges have become numerous. Another interpretative judgment of the VAS was put to the test in *Gaydarov*[59] and *Aladzhov*.[60] The question concerned the compatibility with EU law of an administrative ban on leaving the country imposed on recalcitrant debtors. Here the stand-off was a bit muted since the VAS had ruled that the bans were in any event disproportionate.[61] But a lower court wanted to know whether such bans could at all be justified on the grounds mentioned in Article 24(2) of the Citizenship Directive, since, if they could not be justified, the question of their proportionality became irrelevant.[62]

---

[57] VKS, commercial law department, interpretative judgment n° 1/2012. The president of the Court and five justices argued, in a dissenting opinion, that this interpretative judgment breaches EU law.

[58] *Diageo Brands* (n 39).

[59] Case C-430/10 *Gaydarov* EU:C:2011:749.

[60] Case C-434/10 *Aladzhov* EU:C:2011:750.

[61] VAS interpretative judgment n° 2/2011.

[62] Directive 2004/38/EC of the European Parliament and of the Council of 29 April 2004 on the right of citizens of the Union and their family members to move and reside freely within the territory of the Member States (OJ L 158/77 of 30 April 2004).

The KS was not spared either: In *Byankov* a lower court wanted to make sure that the case law of the former was compatible with EU law.[63] The case also concerned an administrative ban on leaving the country, but unlike in *Gaydarov* and *Aladzhov*, this time the ban was imposed because of a failure to pay a *private* debt. The KS had declared that such bans were justified by a legitimate objective but were disproportionate and, hence, unconstitutional.[64] The KS solved the case on the basis of the national Constitution, paying only lip service to EU law. The referring court in *Byankov* thought however that more consideration should have been given to EU law. In particular, it expressed doubts as to whether these bans could be justified at all, given that Article 27(1) of the Citizenship Directive prohibits restricting the right to free movement on economic grounds.

A lower court even tried to overhaul the system of allocation of cases among administrative courts. In *Agrokonsulting*,[65] the referring judge was manifestly unhappy with the way the territorial jurisdiction of Bulgarian administrative courts was determined. It sought to overturn the rule according to which the case must be brought before the court where the administrative body, the act of which is being challenged, is located. For agricultural aid schemes (but also in many other areas), that body is located in Sofia. That meant that a farmer living in the other corner of the country must go all the way to Sofia in order to have access to a court. The referring court argued that this made litigation inaccessible, costly and burdensome for individuals, since it was designed to favour the administration to the detriment of citizens and legal persons. This problem has been continuously raised by administrative courts in various fora and has been one of their most constant grievances. They complained not only that this rule infringed the right of effective judicial protection, but also that it put a disproportionate strain on the resources of the administrative court in Sofia, while the other 27 administrative courts located across the country were reportedly much less busy. At the time however, the legislator showed no interest in reviewing the system. Against that background, lower administrative courts had repeatedly taken the matter into their own hands by refusing jurisdiction in favour of the court which was located the closest to the applicant. But these endeavours were invariably quashed on appeal by the VAS. Amidst the lethargy of its superiors, a lower court decided to use its last weapon, the preliminary reference procedure, arguing that this system obstructed the right to effective judicial protection guaranteed by EU law. The Court's reply was nuanced but it did suggest that the applicant's right to effective judicial protection should be assessed on a case-by-case basis. This meant that the system was not invincible and that it could

---

[63] Case C-249/11 *Byankov* EU:C:2012:608. Compare with Case C-416/10 *Križan* EU:C:2013:8, where the Slovak Supreme Court sought to establish whether a judgment of the Slovak Constitutional Court was compatible with EU law.

[64] Judgment n° 2/2011.

[65] Case C-93/12 *Agrokonsulting* EU:C:2013:432.

be challenged according to the circumstances of each case. This outcome finally caused the legislator to budge and a proposal to amend the system has now been tabled.[66]

Other challenges to the supreme courts' case law kept tumbling down. In *Klub*, a lower court deplored the contradictory character of the case law of the VAS.[67] It overtly disagreed with part of this case law, arguing that it was contrary to EU law. The Court of Justice agreed. In *Kremikovtzi*,[68] a lower court was unimpressed by VAS's binding instructions and decided instead, in a replay of *Elchinov*, to defer the matter to Luxembourg. A similar situation occurred a year later in *Sani treyd*.[69] In *Stroy trans*, a lower court complained about the inconsistent case law of the VAS and sought, via the preliminary reference, to impose its view on the supreme judges.[70] In *Belov*, the Commission for Protection against Discrimination ('KZD') explicitly disagreed with the VAS's case law.[71] Although the Court did not reply to the question since it found that the KZD was not a jurisdiction within the meaning of Article 267 TFEU, the sigh of relief was short-lived since the same points of law were referred again to the Court of Justice some three years later by a first-tier administrative court in *CEZ Razpredelenie Bulgaria*.[72]

The foregoing examples highlight one of the root causes of the success of the preliminary reference mechanism in Bulgaria, namely the lower courts' new-found courage to stand up to their higher counterparts. The preliminary reference mechanism has thus become their strongest and, for the time being, their only weapon in this respect. They have used it skilfully and, most of the times, effectively. On the one hand, lower courts have succeeded, through the preliminary reference mechanism, in causing the supreme courts to reconsider their case law. On the other hand, they have used that mechanism as a tool allowing them to disregard the supreme courts' instructions in a given case. These are thus the sprouts of a true emancipation of lower courts. It also marks the end of the supreme courts' unquestionable authority. The potential of this upheaval could be thus far-reaching. It could indeed gradually lead to a more balanced and less hierarchical judicial system. This is good news for the Bulgarian judiciary. After all, the supreme courts need to convince through the strength of their arguments, not through hierarchical duress.

---

[66] А Адамова, 'Подсъдността по АПК срещу защитата на материални права, които произтичат от правото на ЕС' [A Adamova, 'Jurisdiction under the Code of Administrative Procedure and the Protection of Substantive Rights Stemming from EU Law] (2013) VII *Европейски правен преглед* [Evropeiski praven pregled] 203, 219.

[67] Case C-153/11 *Klub* EU:C:2012:163.

[68] Case C-262/11 *Kremikovtzi* EU:C:2012:760.

[69] Case C-153/12 *Sani treyd* EU:C:2013:201.

[70] Case C-642/11 *Stroy trans* EU:C:2013:54.

[71] Case C-394/11 *Belov* EU:C:2013:48

[72] Case C-83/14 *CEZ Razpredelenie Bulgaria*, pending.

B. The Clash of Generations?

Standing up to the higher courts is certainly not the normal course of doing business in a judicial system. It is a risky enterprise because it might hurt one's career perspectives. It might also be seen as pretentious or immature since, by definition, the higher courts are deemed to be right. Why then, against all odds, have Bulgarian lower courts so often dared challenge the EU-competency of the higher courts? One reason may be that, in a given case, lower courts opined that their higher counterparts got it wrong and simply tried to correct the error. But in many cases the challenge clearly surpassed the specificities of the particular case. As shown above, lower courts sought not only to achieve a different outcome in a given case, but also openly defied the mechanisms that the supreme courts have at their disposal for exerting influence on lower courts.

There must therefore be another reason for this upheaval. Most judges in the higher courts are 'old school' magistrates, who grew up in a different environment. During their studies in the 1960s, 1970s and 1980s, they had been trained to master confidently national law but attention was rarely paid to external legal sources, such as international law or human rights law, let alone EU law. Constitutional law was not high on the agenda either. Old school magistrates have thus been used to thinking and working in a single-layered legal order. This explains why, even though many of them are very competent magistrates when it comes to national law, they have been struggling to adjust to the post-accession legal reality. Actually, some did not even bother. They thought it was too late to start adjusting to something as odd as EU law. Career judges might have also found it disconcerting that younger lawyers versed in EU legal matters were telling *them* what to do. Those who did try to adjust, found it genuinely difficult. They have been trained to perceive judicial activity very much as an exercise of legal formalism and textualism. To them, EU law was an exotic creature which was difficult to understand, pin down, specify. The legal reality has in the meantime evolved into a new multi-layered coordinate system in which they felt lost. The numerous training sessions and programmes dedicated to EU law remedied part of the problem but only superficially. Talking EU law to old school magistrates still pushes them pretty much out of their comfort zone. It must however be borne in mind that their failure to apply correctly and regularly EU law has never really been a matter of opposition to or scepticism of the EU legal order. It has rather been a matter of generational fatigue, inertia and conformism.

By contrast, most judges in lower courts belong to a new generation of lawyers who have completed their studies on a post-communist curriculum. Constitutional law, human rights law and international law have been increasingly given more weight in their legal training. Many of them speak foreign languages, have a genuine interest in the EU and might have even studied EU law. Some will have followed some sort of training abroad. They are more adept and receptive to the evolving character of EU law and, more generally, to the constantly changing international legal order. Behaviourally, making a reference to Luxembourg has become a sign of sophistication, modernity, even conspicuousness. Against this background, it comes as no surprise that younger magistrates might have genuinely come to believe that they are more competent in EU law than their colleagues in the supreme courts. The clash of generations that has been unfolding behind the scenes is therefore not so much a clash of different ages but rather a clash of different backgrounds and mindsets.

However, the upsurge of the younger generation of Bulgarian magistrates has not been universal. The post-communist proliferation of law faculties of questionable reputation has produced an army of young lawyers with varying competence. Many have become judges, especially in provincial first- and second-tier courts. The experiment has produced mixed results: Some of those judges have coped decently with the job, while others have stumbled. It is an open secret that, as a consequence, the quality of judicial decisions in some of those courts has deteriorated significantly. This might explain, at least in part, why the vast majority of Bulgarian preliminary references have come from just a handful of lower courts. More generally however, this phenomenon implies that the evolution of the generational renewal of the judiciary should be watched with caution.

C. Insiders versus Outsiders

As shown above, the system of administrative justice has so far generated the bulk of preliminary references, while civil and criminal courts have been only marginally involved in the process, if at all. This observation also holds true for the application of EU law in general: While administrative courts now regularly discuss the applicable EU law in their judicial decisions, civil and criminal judges only rarely engage with EU legal matters. As demonstrated above, the reasons cited regularly by the latter as a justification for this state of affairs are unconvincing. There must therefore be another reason for the status quo.

The system of administrative justice was created almost entirely from scratch in 2007. A massive open competition for all of the newly created 28 first-tier administrative courts was conducted, where nearly 200 judicial vacancies were up for grabs. Critically, the competition was open to all legal practitioners: Previous judicial experience was not a relevant criterion. By all recounts, the experiment was a success: It was widely regarded as fair and standards were high given the fierce competition between candidates. The outcome however was astonishing: The overwhelming majority of the successful candidates had no previous judicial experience at all. They were solicitors, in-house legal counsel or public servants. Although there is no official data on this point, most recounts suggest that some administrative courts were almost entirely made up of 'outsiders' to the system. By one recount, for example, more than 80 per cent of all judges in the biggest administrative court—that of Sofia-grad—were 'outsiders'. At the time, this raised concerns that the newly created administrative courts would be unable to conduct their judicial duties due to a lack of experience. But such fears never materialised in practice. To the contrary, first-tier administrative courts have been a success. They have been functioning smoothly, efficiently and, as a whole, competently ever since. This has shown that judges recruited from outside of the system in an open competition are not only perfectly capable of doing well their job but also that they can change the system for the better. Most notably, 'outsiders' came unburdened with the pitfalls of judicial routine and the typical formalism and textualism of the Bulgarian judiciary. They were eager learners with open minds and no institutional backlog. This proved essential in the application of EU law which often requires engaging with numerous non-traditional legal sources and with wider considerations of teleological and comparative order. From an EU law perspective, as demonstrated above, first-tier administrative courts have authored the vast majority of preliminary references and have been amongst the most zealous advocates of EU law in Bulgaria.

By contrast, the creation of the highest administrative court, the Supreme Administrative Court, followed a different pattern. The old *Varhoven sad* (Supreme Court) was simply divided in two: Its administrative chambers became the Supreme Administrative Court in December 1996, while its civil and criminal chambers became the Supreme Court of Cassation. At that time therefore, no 'outsiders' to the system became supreme judges. It is true that over the years open competitions for certain vacancies were organised but these were, in any event, limited in number[73] and have not significantly changed the overall composition of the supreme courts. The latter have thus remained made up mostly of 'insiders' to the system and old school magistrates.

Civil and criminal courts were not (re)created from scratch either. They have remained a relatively closed system, much less exposed to 'external' influence than their administrative counterparts, in the sense that there has been no sudden influx of 'outsiders' capable of changing overnight the general perceptions of and within the system. Today, it is generally considered that civil and criminal courts are less efficient, more inveterate and probably less competent than administrative courts.

The institutional set-up of the judiciary has therefore played an important role in the way EU law has been perceived and applied in Bulgaria. It could be argued that judges coming from outside of the system are less prone to fall foul of the typical downsides of the traditional judicial mentality and are thus generally quicker to accept and adapt to the requirements and intricacies of EU law.

V. Judicial Style Post-Accession: A Missed Opportunity

Studying law in Bulgaria is still very much about memorising and reproducing a plethora of legal definitions, articles, paragraphs and subparagraphs. Over the years, this has created a culture of legal formalism and textualism, which has in

---

[73] Pursuant to Art 178 Judiciary Act (Закон за съдебната власт, обн, ДВ, бр 64 от 7.08.2007 г, последно изм и доп, бр 21 от 8.03.2014 г), 20% of all vacancies in the judiciary must be filled through a 'competition for initial appointment'.

turn significantly affected judicial style and reasoning. Against this background, EU law has offered the opportunity of a true revolution in judicial mentality. It gave lawyers the freedom to abandon their traditional ways and to embrace new horizons. There was a whole new world out there, full of unfamiliar legal sources, principles and concepts, coupled with new (or at least rarely used before) methods of interpretation. EU accession thus had the potential of bringing lasting change to judicial style and reasoning.

There has been no authoritative study on whether and how EU law has affected judicial reasoning, style and drafting techniques. In all fairness, it must be recognised that, given its sheer volume, it would be extremely challenging to compile an exhaustive study of the case law of the supreme courts. Indeed, each year the two supreme courts dispatch tens of thousands of judgments.[74] Such a heavy workload cannot but take its toll on the quality of the judicial reasoning. As a consequence, the supreme courts' case law rarely offers anything more than standardised reasoning, often copied from previous decisions.

It thus suffices to go through parts of the case law of the supreme courts in order to obtain a general idea about their judicial style and argumentation. As a whole, the legal reasoning remains painfully succinct, formal and uninspiring. Most judgments are only a couple of pages long, half of which are descriptive of the facts, the parties, their claims and the procedure. Legal argumentation is thus often cryptic and mostly textual. The relevant provisions and principles of EU law are either not mentioned at all[75] or only listed in a declaratory fashion. The latter trend has been surfacing lately ever more frequently as parties get the habit of invoking EU law in judicial proceedings, thus obliging the court to respond to their EU-related arguments. But the courts' response has often been sorely formal. They would sometimes declare, in a couple of sentences, that the conclusion they have reached on the basis of national law is in line with EU law.[76] Other times, they would state, in general terms, that their interpretation of national law is collaborated by EU law or is not opposed by it.[77] This would however be stated in a self-evident manner without really engaging with EU law.

This trend has been particularly dominant in the judgments of the KS. While its judgments are certainly more elaborated in terms of legal reasoning and engagement with general principles of law, as well as with international legal sources, its approach to EU law rarely surpasses a purely declaratory discourse. It does indeed mention EU law in its judgments more and more often. But it does not

---

[74] VKS's or VAS's annual reports (2007 to 2013).

[75] eg VKS judgment n° 194/2010; VKS judgment n° 350/2009; VKS judgment n° 526/2009; VKS judgment n° 321/2012; VKS judgment n° 517/2012; VKS judgment n° 191/2011; VAS judgment n° 13422/2010.

[76] eg VKS case n° 101/2009; VKS judgment n° 296/2013; KS judgments n°s 2/2011 and 12/2012. For more examples: Kornezov (n 35).

[77] eg VAS judgment n° 5699/2012; Regional Court Vratsa, judgment n° 26/2010, confirmed by VKS judgment n° 36/2011. For more examples: Kornezov (n 35).

seem to attach much weight to it.[78] The references to EU law made in its case law often leave the impression that their only purpose was of demonstrating the court's awareness of the EU legal order. Real engagement with EU law however remains rare. This might be due to the fact that the status of EU law in Bulgarian constitutional law remains ambiguous at best. Indeed, the KS has so far avoided the question of whether it considers itself competent to verify the compatibility of national laws with EU law.[79]

But there is the occasional ray of hope, too. One can indeed find some encouraging examples of purpose-oriented reasoning, supported with arguments and sources rarely used before, such as, for instance, the case law of international courts, most notably that of the European Court of Human Rights (ECtHR), but also of the EU Courts, the recitals of EU acts or their *travaux préparatoires*, even EU soft law instruments, etc.[80] There are also examples of genuine engagement with general principles of EU law, fundamental rights and broader considerations of equity, legitimacy and proportionality.[81]

Still, as a whole, and despite a number of promising examples that point to a positive change in judicial style and reasoning, the latter has remained heavily influenced by traditional formalism and textualism. Judges would often justify this by the excessive workload to which many of them have been subjected. While this is undoubtedly a valid—and regrettable—observation revealing the need for further structural reforms in the Bulgarian judiciary, there can be no excuse for failing to deliver well-reasoned and convincing judgments. The post-accession period has thus been, by and large, a missed opportunity for reinventing the way judicial arguments are conceived, conceptualised, shaped and presented.

VI. Conclusions

The first encounters of the Bulgarian judiciary with EU law have been a mixed experience. On the one hand, Bulgarian jurisdictions have very actively and effectively used the preliminary reference mechanism, deferring an impressive number of references with decent quality to the Court of Justice. A closer look at the system however shows that, while some courts have truly engaged with EU law, others have failed to do so. In particular, the supreme and the appellate courts, and, more generally, civil and criminal jurisdictions have only marginally participated in the

---

[78] eg judgments n°s 2/2011; 3/2012; 7/2012; 11/2012; 12/2012. Mentions of EU law are sometimes manifestly erroneous: eg judgment n° 3/2012, where it is stated that directives do not have direct effect.

[79] Some implicit signs that it might consider itself competent in this respect may be found in the case law—eg judgment n° 3/2012.

[80] eg VAS interpretative judgment n° 2/2011; VAS judgment n° 7776/2013; VAS judgment n° 11100/2011; VAS judgment n° 11056/2011; VAS judgment n° 15906/2010.

[81] eg the orders for reference in *Agrokonsulting* (n 65), *Byankov* (n 63), *Gaydarov* (n 59), *Aladzhov* (n 60).

European discourse. The KS has so far kept a very low profile, too. Lower courts have thus been the champions of EU law in Bulgaria. They often proved more willing, more adept and more forthcoming in the application and the interpretation of EU law.

Critically, they have used the preliminary reference mechanism in order to challenge the higher courts and force them to change their case law. The root causes of this astonishing upheaval are both generational and institutional. On the one hand, lower courts are generally younger and better acquainted with EU law. On the other hand, filling up the magistrate's vacancies through an open competition has proved a game changer, especially for administrative courts, which have become the vanguard of EU law in Bulgaria. The combination of these two factors has thus created a more EU law-friendly environment in lower jurisdictions, in particular in administrative courts.

Unfortunately, however, there is no place for enthusiasm. While it is true that over time some of these encouraging sprouts will move upstream in the appellate and supreme jurisdictions, the overall state of the art in lower courts is far from universally positive. Indeed, there is evidence that the general quality of the decisions of some of those courts has been deteriorating, possibly due to the low quality of the legal education in many law schools across the country. The risk that the application of EU law remains limited to a handful of judges, instead of being regularly and universally applied, thus looks real.

The first seven years of Bulgaria's accession to the EU have also been a missed opportunity for achieving a lasting change in judicial style and reasoning. The latter remain deeply rooted in legal formalism and textualism. While examples to the contrary can indeed be found, they remain isolated and unrepresentative. As a whole, Bulgarian courts are still struggling to engage with subtler but fundamental legal considerations which cannot be pinned down to a specific legal provision and which require resourcefulness, creativity and critical thinking. Only time will show whether Bulgarian magistrates will eventually be able to overcome a judicial mentality that has become almost institutionalised and often deeply entrenched in the legal profession.

12

Who are the Actors Mobilising Discourse among Courts?

ERHARD BLANKENBURG

I. Escaping into Formalism?

The membership of the European Union did not make the task of national judges easier. European law follows principles and policy goals which are not easily evaluated in a concrete case. It asks for weighing of sometimes competing norms in the light of the social context of a case and to test their decisions on their policy effects. Judges at national courts cannot stick in their argumentation to a purely formalistic 'style' of interpretation, but have to integrate in their 'judicial culture' the communication context with parties and their lawyers for whom the argumentation is formulated.

This might be called a 'system of two boxes'. In consequence, judges in the European member states have to follow the judge-made case law aggregated by rulings of the Court of Justice (ECJ) as well as the statutes of their respective national legislation. These rulings have in the course of the ECJ's history developed a jurisprudence of great detail and complexity.

Some authors[1] suggest that their reluctance to enter such discourse with policy principles may be a reaction to the swift political changes of post-communist law: The older generation had to master the turnover from socialist law and the introduction of constitutional courts in the 1990s as well as the integration of European law principles after 2004. Remaining within the first box of national law would resist political influence and stress judicial independence. It brought Kühn[2] to blame these judges for 'escaping into formalism'.

---

[1] Further above in ch 2 in this volume.

[2] Z Kühn, 'Worlds Apart: Western and Central European Culture at the Onset of the European Enlargement' (2004) 52 *American Journal of Comparative Law* 531.

II. Measuring Arguments in 'Motivations' of Judgements

Kühn together with Matczak and Bencze[3] tested this thesis by a linguistic analysis of the 'motivations', analysing of all published cases of the administrative law adjudication of law judges in Hungary, Poland and the Czech Republic. They categorised the style and topics of their argumentations in the period from 1999 to 2004 as to their references to domestic law or European law, constitutional or external values. Most of the arguments in the 'motivations' remained in the first box with purely textual references to their national law (approximately 82 per cent in Hungary, 61 per cent in Poland, but only 42 per cent in the Czech Republic).

A replication study over the following years of 2005 to 2011 (after the countries had joined the EU) shows a steady decrease of such legal formalism and a constant increase of references to European law as well as those to their respective constitutions. The administrative judges also started to refer more often to general values of the law such as the aims or the functions of laws. Even though Kühn et al admit that the linguistics of a 'judgement motivation' sometimes may be a form of semantic formalism—the 'motivation' of a judgement, does not declare the *motives* of judges, but their judicial *argumentation*—they see the overall change as an indication of more transparent weighing of the values underlying the interpretation of law.

III. Explicit References to European Law are Rare Events Even Among West European Judges

With their reluctance to (explicitly) refer to European law, Central European judges do not stand alone. Similar reasons for avoidance can also be heard from West European judges who have already gained many more years of experience with European law. In 2009 a survey study among Dutch and (West-)German civil (and labour) court judges[4] asked how far they had accepted European law. Most judges of the first and appeal instances said that they usually trusted that European directives are implemented in their national states. About half of the judges who were interviewed said that they once had a case where they had to explicitly apply European law. If so, they mostly simply cited the EU directives, seldom any case law. To do so, they would have needed more time to search for detailed references, because only 12 per cent felt themselves sufficiently secure in the European law

---

[3] Above, ch 3 in this volume.
[4] MT Nowak et al, *National Judges as European Union Judges. Knowledge, Experience and Attitudes of Lower Court Judges in Germany and the Netherlands* (Eleven International Publishing, 2011).

literature. We hear the same kind of excuses as those reported from Central European judges.

If necessary, however, Dutch judges can always ask an expert at their courts who is responsible for advice on European law. German judges more often report that they consult hand-commentaries: The literature in a big judicial culture is more detailed than in a small language such as Dutch. Judges need not constantly refer to European directives, as they may expect that these should be implemented into the national law of their Member States. Only if this is not the case, or if they deem the integration of European law values unclear or insufficient, they may ask for advice by requesting a preliminary ruling from the ECJ under Article 267 TFEU (Treaty on the Functioning of the European Union). Whether and when they would do that, they answered hesitantly.

IV. Requesting a Preliminary Ruling from the Court of Justice

The preliminary ruling procedure introduced in the Treaty of Rome was greeted enthusiastically in the literature as an 'empowerment of the judiciary' in Europe.[5] The preliminary ruling procedure enables judges at lower national courts to open a dialogue with the ECJ independent of the regular national judicial hierarchy. The ruling of the ECJ remains 'preliminary' in the sense that it does not take away the decision of the originating court, but it forces its judges to engage in a discourse about the arguments of their decision.

However, also Dutch and German civil judges, unless challenged by parties and their advocates, would not easily request a preliminary ruling Even though they entirely share European law values, they would avoid the time and the complexities of a procedure—unless the parties and their advocates would insist in asking for it. None of the judges who were interviewed expressed any resentment against the 'EU as a super authority'.[6] For their reluctance in asking the ECJ for a ruling they mainly give practical reasons, such as the time required for preparing the request and the delay for the parties which it would bring about.

Thus, if seen from the view of judges in lower courts, a request to the ECJ is a rather rare event. But the ECJ itself must look at its caseload of requests as an ever rising flood. It was not just the new members coming in 2004, but also the new and expanding domains of EU law. One might have expected Central and Eastern European (CEE) judges to immediately use this opportunity in order to get their

---

[5] JHH Weiler, 'A Quiet Revolution: The European Court of Justice and its Interlocutors' (1994) 26 *Comparative Political Studies* 510.

[6] AM Burley and W Mattli, 'Europe before the Court: A Political Theory of Legal Integration' (1993) 47 *International Organization* 41.

national codes in line with EU law while judges from earlier Member States of the EU had been able to use such discourse for a long time. But as with any integration of EU law, it took a few years until among some of the Central European judges the number of requests for preliminary rulings began rising. A considerable share of their requests came from lower courts. This, however, needs a specific explanation for each country, as can be illustrated by adding the respective figures for Germany and the Netherlands.

Table 1: Request for preliminary rulings to the ECJ by country

	Requests for preliminary ruling in total, 2004–2012	Requests submitted by lower courts
Bulgaria	55	80%
Czech Republic	27	48%
Hungary	64	91%
Poland	49	53%
Romania	46	48%
Slovakia	20	45%
Slovenia	4	75%
Germany	589	67%
Netherlands	251	36%

(Source: The European Commission for the Efficiency of Justice Evaluation Report 2014,[7] table 20, p113–15)

In the CEE countries, ECJ rulings are mostly requested by judges of lower courts.[8] Alter argues that the incentives and disincentives facing any national judge differs depending on her or his position in the national judicial hierarchy: 'The higher courts had the most to loose by the extension of the ECJ's ... authority over national legal issues' and the 'lower courts found few costs and numerous benefits in making their own referrals to the ECJ'.[9] The lower courts used referrals to enhance their own autonomy and to circumvent the authority of appellate courts above them.

---

[7] Online at <www.coe.int/t/dghl/cooperation/cepej/evaluation/default_en.asp>, last accessed 1 December 2014.

[8] See also above, ch 11 in this volume, observing the same phenomenon with respect to Bulgaria.

[9] K Alter, *The European Court's Political Power* (Oxford University Press, 2009) 264.

The judges in higher courts, however, 'tried to stop lower courts from making references to the ECJ' in order to maintain their status and to preserve the primacy of their own case law.[10] Such an argument may be true of some of the highest courts (as is the case with the *Solange*[11] decisions of the German *Bundesverfassungsgericht* but not of the Dutch highest courts (they have a number of highest courts but no judicial review and no constitutional court)). Both rank on top with respect to the amount of the requests for preliminary rulings made among Western European countries, and the Netherlands relative to its small size (17 million inhabitants) would rank even higher than Germany (with a population of 81 million). Comparative calculations show that the frequency of requests are not solely dependent on the size of population, but as Stone Sweet and Brunell[12] showed some other factors count even more, such as the intensity of cross border trade, the number of international corporations and the size of the legal profession in a country.

While these factors were paramount in the 1990s, other issues specific to one or the other country came up later. In the United Kingdom, for example, a strong feminist movement challenged the labour conditions of women, and in Italy the system of pension rights caused protest and consequently requests to the ECJ. We should not forget that requests are also motivated by some inconsistencies of the national legal system which could arise in any country independent of its size.

The literature which discussed the mobilisation of the ECJ in the 1990s therefore emphasised the role of private actors in activating European legal integration. Litigants and their interests were understood to be 'fuelling the machine of the European legal system'. Burley and Mattli[13] see the rulings of the ECJ in a 'self-sustaining logic socializing more and more actors—private litigants, judges, and politicians—into the system'.

V. Central European Actors Challenging Judges for Requests to the ECJ

Who are these actors in Central Europe, motivated by their own interests, who by their requests of ECJ preliminary rulings presumably generate the 'steady supply of litigation'? The previous chapters of this volume give only a few hints.

The breakthrough of references to preliminary rulings sometimes comes from a few protagonists among the judges of lower instances, as Kornezov reports in

---

[10] ibid, 268.

[11] Beschluss vom 22 Oktober 1986, Az: 2 BvR 197/83.

[12] A Stone Sweet and T Brunell, 'European Court and the National Courts: A Statistical Analysis of Preliminary References, 1961–95' (1998) 5 Journal of *European Public Policy* 66.

[13] Above (n 6).

Bulgaria.[14] The frequent requests for preliminary rulings from Bulgaria since 2009 may well indicate a 'generational upheaval' of Bulgarian judges, but they stem from a handful of courts in the capital. It adds a post-communist reason to the thesis of Alter[15] that after the turnovers of the 1990s in spite of the reform of the judiciaries and formation of constitutional courts, there was no immediate change of the personnel. In some countries—like Slovenia[16]—a 'remaining authoritarian mentality' is even entirely based on the account of the lack of a thorough purge of personnel after communism. They claim that by now the new generation of judges, trained in European law at their universities, feel more free to challenge the judgments of the older generation at the highest courts.

Other recruitment factors are reported from administrative courts in Hungary. When in the Hungarian judicial reform of 2013 administrative and labour courts were joined with the recruitment of judges from professions with practical experience, it resulted—apart from the obvious political intentions—in a much less formalistic style of argumentation in the judgments of the new courts.[17] Former practitioners could with more knowledge refer to the social context of their cases. Just as the lawyers they could challenge the court to adopt more discretionary principles of EU law.

Such hints at the interests of parties and the influence of their lawyers on the judgmental styles of the national courts were only occasional in the contributions to our meeting. Sometimes interest groups seem evident such as in claims for pension rights or in labour conflicts. Simply looking at the names of the plaintiffs in the original law suit often does not help, because they might have been test case individuals for an entire interest group. In the Central European countries Ombudsman institutions have standing before the courts, and they like plaintiffs with big lawyer offices behind them who can withstand a long fight through appeal instances and also to the ECJ. As a heritage from socialist times, these countries still have a rather high number of judges, but few lawyers and small law firms.[18] In some of them legal consultants still had to fight up to 2012 to become members of the advocacy.

VI. Discourse Between Civil Society, the National Courts and the ECJ

Most of the chapters presented in this volume discuss the communication between national courts and the ECJ; some also that with the European Court of Human

---

[14] Above, ch 11 in this volume.
[15] Alter (n 9).
[16] Above, ch 6 in this volume.
[17] Above, ch 3 in this volume.
[18] See 'The European Commission for the Efficiency of Justice Evaluation Report 2014' (n 7) 164.

Rights, others those between constitutional courts in Europe. All of these communications are restricted to judges. None of them talks about the communication which takes place in the original procedures with parties and their lawyers and possibly the 'parties behind the parties'. They, as well as the bigger law firms of multinational companies, want to make explicit some principles which are vital to their interests. Being professionals they would know how to challenge the national courts and take the time for suing or for requesting a ruling from the ECJ. Eventually, invoking the ECJ might also be a channel for circumventing legislative and party majorities by invoking the 'judges' rule'.

13

Transformation in the Eye of the Beholder

MATEJ AVBELJ

The aim of this volume was to identify the success of the transformation of the judiciary in the so-called new EU Member States 10 years after the big-bang enlargement. The question asked was to what extent the Central and Eastern European (CEE) judiciaries have been transformed due to their countries' full membership in the EU. In short, what was studied was the so-called transformative power of Europe. For that purpose several national perspectives on the role and functioning of the judiciary in the respective Member States were laid out and made subject to a critical analysis in comparative terms. As this volume attests, this method is certainly capable of producing illustrative and informative results, which are also conducive to a broader dynamic comparison between the legal systems of the countries under review.

However, this essay queries to what extent these results are reliable as they were narrated as well as to what extent these national narratives are, if not correctly, then at least accurately received and understood by their audience. In asking this question, the contribution proceeds from a starting point of a par excellence and inherently non-neutral pedigree or capacity of the narrators and of the audience. The narrators and the audience consist of individuals, who due to their intellectual and/or institutional status and corresponding engagement with public affairs in their respective countries or elsewhere, always harbour a particular normative (to say the least) *Weltanschauung*, which is not value free, but value-coloured and therefore biased. This bias, which ought not to be understood in a pejorative sense, functions as a lens through which they perceive and narrate about the world as well as receive and comprehend the said-narrations.

The lens is not neutral and always causes more or less numerous and extensive distortions between the narrating or receiving subjects and their object. These can consist of omissions, downplaying of certain facts or (over)-emphasising of others even in what is supposed to be objective descriptions and dry analytical treatments of national judicial (or broader legal) state of the art. Moreover, given that the discussed national perspectives are inevitably deeply situated in the relevant

comprehensive national societal contexts and could be most likely fully understood only from within these contexts, having the bigger national picture, the contribution also wonders to what extent the more specific national issues can be
decontextualised and meaningfully reported across the boundaries between the
several epistemic communities. In what follows, these theoretical points shall be
illustrated on a couple of examples taken from the national debates, concerning
notably Hungary and Slovenia.

I. The West–East or the Old–New Divide

Discussing the CEE countries and their transformation after 10 years of their
membership in the European Union must have assumed a specific status of these
countries that makes them worth analysing together as a singular, even if internally diverse, subject matter. This cannot be located in the temporal dimension,
for example in the fact that these countries, other than Romania, Bulgaria, let
alone Croatia that joined only recently, acceded to the EU simultaneously. Rather
it must be sought in some other shared feature, related to the past that is not yet
so distant to lack any influence on the present. I shall submit that this something
is these countries' shared communist or socialist past.[1] What makes CEE countries
worth studying together is their shared totalitarian past which needed to be overcome through the, by now protracted, process of transition to have them transformed into liberal democratic polities which can meet the criteria for the full
membership in the European Union.

    However, it is already at this stage—in identifying what the CEE countries share
as an object under research—that normative disagreements between different
observers apparently reign. The communist-socialist past of these countries is not
denied, but its actual totalitarian character, the latter's scope and content and even
more so its present legacy tend to be disputed. There are two extremes. On the
one hand, there are those who do not entertain a single doubt about the proper
totalitarian nature of the CEE communism and even 25 years after the fall of the
Berlin Wall relate the legal and democratic shortcomings of their countries almost
exclusively back to the communist legacy.[2] On the other hand, there are those who
see communism, or at least socialism as its closest ideological ally, wearing a more
human face, certainly distinct from the proper totalitarian regimes of fascism and
Nazism, one that might even be appealing as an idea, which was, however, badly
implemented and operationalised in practice. Naturally, within such a normative

---

[1] For the purpose of this chapter the concepts of communism and socialism are treated as syno-
nyms, even though they are not necessarily so.
[2] For the on-going legal impact of socialism in the CEE countries see R Manko, *Survival of the
Socialist Legal Tradition? A Polish Perspective* (2013) 4(2) *Comparative Law Review* 1.

framework communism is a vice in practice, but not as an idea and therefore could be or even should be tried again, this time even harder,[3] or perhaps better in a form of a so-called democratic socialism.[4] Consequently, the present legal and democratic digressions in the CEE countries cannot be blamed on the totalitarian communist past, rather they are a consequence of a deviation from the communism proper.[5]

Between these two extremes, of course, there are a number of more subtle approaches, which are nevertheless gravitating to one or another side. Those closer to the debunking of communism as an idea and practice subscribe or are proponents of the back-to-Europe narrative.[6] Those drifting closer to the opposite pole critique or even mock the back-to-Europe narrative as an apology of the overly-idealised West, as a protagonist of an equally (or even more) socially destructive neo-liberal agenda.[7] In practice, these views are closely connected to political beliefs, whereby those with more conservative or right-liberal views tend to emphasise the gravity of the (post)-communist legacy, and those belonging to the left-liberal or socialist camp, in contrast with the former, downplay it.

However, I shall submit, that this, in itself inevitable, political taking of sides as to the evaluation of CEE communism and its later transformation, fails to account for a fundamental overall contextual distinction between the East and the West. The normative beliefs and more concretely political beliefs in an individual always develop in and against the social context in which this individual is situated. As, in the best modernist tradition,[8] individuals always yearn for emancipation, to break the bond of oppression, the emancipatory societal and political narratives diverge depending on the dominant (hence oppressive) narrative in a given context. In this respect, due to fundamentally different models of economic and political development since 1945, a clear rupture between the West and the East exists in Europe, even if it often goes unnoticed. The dominant narrative, even ideology perhaps, of the West has been liberal capitalism. Its emancipatory language is

---

[3] The representatives of this view are A Badiou and S Žižek (eds), *L'idee du communisme* (Nouvelles Editions Lignes, 2010).

[4] In Slovenia this has given birth to a new civil society movement for a democratic socialism, which has grown into a now parliamentary political party the United Left, closely inspired by the Greek Siriza, see: <www.demokraticni-socializem.si/>, last accessed 10 November 2014.

[5] ibid.

[6] For a great analysis of the different narratives in this part of Europe, in particular after the fall of Communism, see S Kattago, *Memory and Representation in Contemporary Europe—the Persistence of the Past* (Ashgate, 2012).

[7] Most bluntly Victor Orban in his speech, available at: <http://budapestbeacon.com/public-policy/full-text-of-viktor-orbans-speech-at-baile-tusnad-tusnadfurdo-of-26-july-2014/>, last accessed 10 November 2014. For a comment see: G Halmai, *Illiberal Democracy and Beyond in Hungary* (VerfBlog, 28 August 2014) <www.verfassungsblog.de/en/illiberal-democracy-beyond-hungary-2>, last accessed 10 November 2014; for a critical take on a back to Europe narrative see also: J Komarek, 'Waiting for the Existential Revolution in Europe' (2014) 12 *International Journal of Constitutional Law* 190.

[8] Modernity is a contested concept. It might mean, at least, three things: A period of time, a state of mind and a specific concept. See S Douglas-Scott, *Law after Modernity* (Hart Publishing, 2013) 7. Here I allude to the mind set which is essentially wedded to the idea of progress.

therefore, naturally, some sort of left-liberalism or, more to the left: (Democratic) socialism. In contrast, the East has been reigned by communism, hence the liberating language is the right-liberalism, emphasising also economically (perhaps also socially) more conservative views that were trumped or even banned in the past.

In other words, what is socially progressive, liberating, leading to more (self-)fulfilment of the human potential in the West is not necessarily the same as in the East. For the consequences of the totalitarian communist past in the East simply cannot be eradicated or overcome by adding more socialism to it. In the same vein, and especially thanks to a unique metamorphosis of the political, economic and other, including intellectual, elites in the ex-communist East, those adhering to the left-liberal and social(ist) label there might often, other than the label itself, have very little in common, especially in terms of mindset, with their nominal counterparts in the West.[9] Looking with western eyes to the East (and vice versa) might paint a seeming, rather than a true, picture of certain phenomena, including the functioning of the rule of law and the role of the judiciary inside it.

This is then something that ought to be taken into account when analysing what makes the CEE countries special and particularly different from the West, as well as in evaluating to what extent these countries have actually transited, as expected from them, to the ideal of normalcy that the West lives up to much more closely than the East. The use of the language of normalcy is deliberate here, as I want to defend the hypothesis that the CEE countries are not 'normal countries.' Under the notion of a normal country I understand a constitutional democracy, resting on the values of political liberalism (left or right) contained in and concretised through human rights which are, as substantive standards, protected and ensured through the formal framework of the rule of law. To win the status of a normal country properly so-called requires the just outlined prerequisites of normalcy to exist not only in theory, but also in practice. As Hart has taught us, however, the fit (or the gap) between normative proclamations and their materialisation in practice depends on the practice of institutional actors of a legal system, most notably judges.[10] A veritable constitutional order will therefore exist only if a critical mass of institutional stakeholders develops an internal point of view: A genuine commitment to the values, principles and rules of that constitutional order. If that commitment is lacking the existing constitutional order will be only a half-built house. It will exist on paper, but not in practice.

And, it is precisely here: In the sociological, human dimension where the decisive difference between the European West and the East lurks. Despite the fact that since the end of the Cold War, both parts of the continent have, thanks to

---

[9] J Rupnik and J Zielonka, 'The State of Democracy 20 Years On: Domestic and External Factors' (2013) 27 *East European Politics & Societies* 3, 13: 'To add to the confusion, the cultural right in Hungary and Poland tends to be economically Left (statist), while the post-communist Left (allied with liberals) was economically on the right (pro-market)'. In Slovenia, however, it is again the other way around.

[10] HLA Hart, *The Concept of Law* (Oxford University Press, 1994).

the migration of constitutional ideas,[11] the success of the new constitutionalism[12] and, in particular, due to the incorporation of the *acquis*, featured very similar constitutional texts and legislative provisions, these constitutional systems, while formally harmonised, still function very differently in practice.[13] This is so because the social structures at large, including the professional classes building up the institutions of the respective state, due to their socialisation in profoundly different social systems: Liberal-democratic in the West and proto-soviet-titoist totalitarian in the East differ as to their knowledge, expertise, social skills, worldliness and indeed overall mindset. By the latter I mean the actual, not just pro forma, internalisation of the liberal democratic values such as: Human dignity, protection of the individual over the corporativist interests, respect for diversity and hence pluralism and the capacity to engage in a meaningful dialogue with everyone, not just your immediate ideological allies.

At the same time, however, this is not to argue that the West and the East are sealed, homogeneous blocks, the former mirroring a perfection and the latter a disarray.[14] The precise extent of the differences between the social structures and their elites in the West and in the East would, of course, need to be measured according to a rigorous sociological methodology and the findings would most likely demonstrate a great variety both inside the West as well as inside the East, and consequently, between the two. Irrespective of its actual scope, I shall proceed on a hypothesis that this difference is actually there, and that therefore a wholesale assumption that CEE countries are, by and large, liberal democracies too, just because they have on the books formally subscribed to these standards, might not be warranted. To confirm the assumption it would be necessary to pierce the epistemic veil and to penetrate through the socio-political membrane of these countries in order to establish, as objectively as possible, the real qualitative status: The prevailing public mindset in and of these countries. However, this is rarely done,[15] and certainly not among legal scholars who argue about the success or failure of the judicial transformation in the CEE countries, as in this volume.

Nevertheless, the assumptions with which one enters the analysis of a given social phenomenon do matter. They are hypotheses that shape and determine one's perception of a social concept under observation, its conceptualisation, which in turn also conditions the most advantageous remedies, of course pursuant

---

[11] S Choudhry, *The Migration of Constitutional Ideas* (Cambridge University Press, 2011).

[12] See, for example, R Hirschl, 'The Political Origins of the New Constitutionalism' (2004) 11 *Indiana Journal of Global Legal Studies* 71. For a more recent approach, see S Gill and CA Cutler, *New Constitutionalism and World Order* (Cambridge University Press, 2014).

[13] To focus only on the varying judicial performance throughout Europe, see The European Commission for the Efficiency of Justice at the Council of Europe Report: <www.coe.int/t/dghl/cooperation/cepej/evaluation/2012/Rapport_en.pdf>, last accessed 11 November 2014.

[14] Several countries in the West, most notably Greece, also Italy and to a certain extent Spain, expose systemic problems that undermine their status of a normal state. Other countries in the so-called PIIGS group, which has emerged in the EU economic crisis, might be listed here too.

[15] Rupnik and Zielonka (n 9) 5.

to the initial assumption, to be prescribed for the improvement or reform of that very same social phenomenon. In light of the above discussion of the historically generated difference in the overall societal character of the West and the East, whose extent is, as stressed, debatable and should be subject to a rigorous research, I submit that it would be more meaningful to approach the CEE countries with the opposite assumption. Instead of presuming that these countries are, more or less, normal liberal democracies, the argumentative starting point should perhaps better be that they are not. In this case the Slovenian judicial transformation, with which I am personally acquainted best, as well as the notorious Hungarian back-sliding, might be perceived and therefore approached differently as in the mainstream. I shall do so in turn, starting with the Hungarian example first.

II. The Hungarian Back-sliding

The story of the Hungarian so-called back-sliding in terms of rule of law and democracy is well known. It has been widely reported, not only in the scholarly circles, but also in the global media, very often through the mouth of the very same scholarly actors.[16] The story, however, has not remained on the level of media reports and academic debates, but it has echoed in various international expert, constitutional standards-setting bodies,[17] in the NGOs, at the ECtHR (European Court of Human Rights)[18] and, finally in the EU. Not only has the EU exerted political pressure on the Hungarian government, it has even successfully brought it before the Court of Justice.[19] According to the narrative, which will not be repeated here in great detail, it all started with a landslide victory of Viktor

---

[16] See, for example, JW Muller, 'The Hungarian Tragedy' (2011) 58(2) *Dissent* 5; G Halmai and K Lane Scheppele (eds), *Opinion on Hungary's New Constitutional Order: Amicus Brief for the Venice Commission on the Transitional Provisions of the Fundamental Law and the Key Cardinal Laws* (2012), available at: <http://lapa.princeton.edu/hosteddocs/hungary/Amicus_Cardinal_Laws_final.pdf> accessed 11 November 2014; K Lane Scheppele, 'The Unconstitutional Constitution' *New York Times* (2 January 2012), available at: <http://krugman.blogs.nytimes.com/2012/01/02/the-unconstitutional-constitution/> accessed 11 November 2014; see also a vibrant debate at Verfassungsblog: *Hungary—Taking Action* (Verfassungsblog on Matters Constitutional), available at: <www.verfassungsblog.de/en/category/focus/hungary-taking-action/> accessed 11 November 2014; M Dawson and E Muir, 'Hungary and the Indirect Protection of EU Fundamental Rights and the Rule of Law' (2013) 14 *German Law Journal* 1959; B Bugarič, 'Protecting Democracy and the Rule of Law in the European Union: The Hungarian Challenge' (2014) 79 *LSE 'Europe in Question' Discussion Paper Series*.

[17] European Commission for Democracy Through Law (The Venice Commission), Opinion 618/2011 on the Constitution of Hungary, June 2011, available at: <http://lapa.princeton.edu/hosteddocs/hungary/venice%20commission%20hungarian%20constitution.pdf>, last accessed 11 November 2014; European Commission for Democracy Through Law (The Venice Commission), Opinion on the Fourth Amendment of the Fundamental Law of Hungary, June 2013, available at: <www.venice.coe.int/webforms/documents/?pdf=CDL-AD(2013)012-e> accessed 11 November 2014.

[18] See *Baka v Hungary*, App no 20261/12 (ECtHR, 27 May 2014).

[19] See Case C-286/12, *Commission v Hungary* ECLI:EU:C:2012:687.

Orbán who in the 2010 election secured a constitutional majority for his party Fidesz. Such a strong electoral support enabled the party to initialise a constitutional revolution, as it was later called, which in the words of one commentator in only three years managed to transform Hungary 'from one of the success stories of the transition from socialism to democracy to a semi-authoritarian regime based on the illiberal order systematically dismantling checks and balances and thereby undermining the rule of law.'[20]

The Fidesz-run parliament, we were told, soon adopted an unconstitutional constitution.[21] Through the legislative hypertrophy it dismantled the main checks and balances in place. The existing state institutions were being filled by the ruling party loyalists.[22] On top of it new institutions were created, again to make room for party loyalists and to ensure the gradual irrelevance of the old institutions without interfering with them directly.[23] This has, however, happened to the judiciary whose independence, especially because of the sudden lowering of the retirement age, came under great strain.[24] The *Alkotmánybíróság* (Constitutional Court, hereinafter 'AB'), portrayed as the last defender of the rule of law in Hungary, has not been left intact either. Its composition was changed and competences restricted. All this has led several observers to conclude that Hungary has emerged as a politically distinctive case of authoritarianism.[25] Hungary has taken an illiberal turn, which is the course that has to be reversed both from the inside as well as from the outside.[26]

This narrative is, while in many ways, indeed by and large, descriptively accurate, nevertheless suffering from two shortcomings. It is simultaneously saying too much and too little. It says too little because it very often simply omits what existed in Hungary before Orbán's takeover.[27] Hungary was not really a consolidated liberal democracy. It was not a normal country. Like in other CEE countries, a state, while being liberated from a grip of a single party, has become a hostage of various informal groups, accessible only to selected social and family groups over which there is no public control.[28] As argued by Rupnik and Zielonka, in the countries such as Hungary, 'legal enforcement favours partisan political interests, whereas policy favours resource extraction for private ends.'[29] The same authors also insist

---

[20] Bugarič (n 16) 6, referring to Muller (n 16) 5.

[21] Lane Scheppele (n 16).

[22] M Bánkuti, G Halmai and K Lane Scheppele, 'Disabling the Constitution' (2012) 3 *Journal of Democracy* 138, 144.

[23] Bugarič (n 16) 11.

[24] See *Baka* (n 18) and *Commission* (n 19) cases.

[25] See, for example, EK Jenne and C Mudde, 'Hungary's Illiberal Turn: Can Outsiders Help?' (2012) 3 *Journal of Democracy* 147.

[26] ibid.

[27] As nicely explained by JW Muller in 'Eastern Europe Goes South—Disappearing Democracy in the EU Newest Member States' (2014) March/April *Foreign Affairs*: 'To be sure, Fidesz could not have done what it did on its own. It benefited from the way that left-wing post-communist elites discredited themselves in the 1990s, allowing corruption to flourish while failing to ease the social transition to liberal capitalism.'

[28] Rupnik and Zielonka (n 9) 13.

[29] ibid.

that the focus of scholarly observers has been, almost exclusively, on the formal institutions, while the de facto modus operandi of the system has escaped their attention.[30] In practice, however, the institutions have always tended to be filled by party loyalists,[31] media controlled, directly or indirectly, by political parties or their informal networks,[32] while the question of the actual independence of the judiciary and other state institutions largely depends on those who were occupying these positions. After all, Orbán's landslide victory was a reaction to a complete fiasco of the preceding socialist government which was enmeshed into corruption and clientelism to an unprecedented degree.[33]

Having said this, this is not to advance an apology for Orbán's government. It is only an attempt to sketch a more balanced and therefore accurate picture of Hungary. A picture which is too often distorted by what the conventional narrative contains too much: A normative, even political bias. The proponents of the Hungarian narrative make clear that 'the Western Left' has to do something with Hungary because 'a nationalist conservative' revolution is triumphing there.[34] They are concerned about the 'worrisome trends such as risings support for right-wing parties'[35] and stress that the strongest authoritarian challenges in the new EU Member States come from centre-right parties.[36] If this means that the political left is considered as more benign and its potential authoritarianism less perilous because of its more human, social face, such assumptions need to be dismissed out of hand. Authoritarianism is authoritarian irrespectively of its political leaning, right or left, and this has to be taken into account when describing, analysing and evaluating the transitions of the CEE countries, such as Hungary.

If we do that, we can see that Orbán's Hungary is only perpetuating the authoritarian practices that existed before due to the failed transition, since Hungary has never successfully done away with its authoritarian past. The modus operandi: Exclusivist, politically monist, illiberal, state-capturing, existed before Orbán, but mainly in the informal dimension. However, by gaining the constitutional majority, the gates were wide open to make this informal structure, revamped in the image of the new leading political party and its loyalists, formal, institutionalised, indeed constitutionalised. In that way, Orbán's Hungary, due to the formal and popularly legitimised means at its disposal, represents indeed a special case, but not one of back-sliding or of a dangerous conservative revolution, rather one of entrenching the dormant yet pervasive authoritarianism existing in the Hungarian public, but in particular political life. This authoritarianism is there and it is improbable that it will go away with Orbán's government out of power. It is not unlikely

---

[30] ibid, 5.

[31] ibid, 14, the authors speak of party clientelism within semi-state agencies of government.

[32] ibid: 'The media have proven to be among the most influential political forces, yet they are neither fully transparent not accountable.'

[33] Muller (n 27).

[34] Muller (n 16) 5.

[35] Jenne and Mudde (n 25) 148.

[36] ibid.

that Hungary after Orbán will witness a new authoritarian swing, this time to the left, repeating very similar patterns to the extent allowed by the received political majority. If that indeed occurs, the academia will need to respond with the same force as in Orbán's case and, even more importantly, devise the answer to the key question. This is not how to battle the conservative or right-wing authoritarian revolution, but how to break the vicious circle of authoritarianism, irrespective of its colour, inherent to the post-totalitarian countries with glaringly lacking liberal tradition and social elites required to set up a normal constitutional democracy.

III. The Missing Case of Slovenia

This is also the question that has always been present in Slovenia, but which has been accentuated in the last few years, following the outbreak of the economic crisis in 2008. The Slovenian case has, however, never reached the same kind of notoriety as its Hungarian counterpart. To the contrary, Slovenia has long managed to preserve its reputation of a good disciple, of a success story of transition and therefore of a role model among the CEE countries. Different than these countries, Slovenia opted for an economic model of gradual transition, with limited privatisation and a large degree of state ownership.[37] This economic model combined with appreciable starting economic advantages over the other CEE countries[38] ensured its citizens relatively high standards of living. In political terms, also in contrast with other CEE countries, Slovenia basically refused to carry out any lustration or, at least, to change its elites. The elite retention rate, the people who were in the key societal positions in the pre and post-communist times, was consequently exceptionally high.[39] The country did, however, adopt a western-style liberal constitution and adjusted its legal system to the requirements of the Council of Europe as well as later to the demands of the EU *acquis*. Formally Slovenia has certainly grown into a liberal constitutional democracy, but in practice this has failed to be the case.

The de facto emergence of a liberal democracy in Slovenia was prevented precisely by the kind of economic model that allegedly made the country a success story. Economic gradualism, closed to foreign investors, meant that half of the economy was state-owned and therefore run by the government in power; whereas the other half was privatised by insiders close to the very same government. As a

---

[37] See, for example, M Tomšič and L Prijon, *Ideological Profile and Crisis Discourse of the Slovenian Elites*, available at: <www.eisa-net.org>, last accessed 11 November 2014; also R Pezdir, *Slovenska tranzicija od Kardelja do Tajkunov* (Časnik Finance, 2008).

[38] Which has, however, almost disappeared in the last decade, see 'How "New Europe" has fared on its tenth birthday' *Economist* (1 May 2014) <www.economist.com/blogs/graphicdetail/2014/05/daily-chart?fsrc=scn/fb/wl/dc/growingupfast> accessed 11 November 2014.

[39] F Adam and M Tomšič, 'Transition Elites: Catalysts of Social Innovation or Rent Seekers' (2000) 32 *Družboslovne razprave* 138.

result, the economic power got concentrated in the hands of the post-socialist elite, now called liberal-democrats, which made the above mentioned elite retention possible and which gradually spilt into all other sectors of the society.[40] As succinctly explained by Bugarič:

> This elite managed to create better contacts with the business sector, media, academia, and most importantly, with a substantial part of the public sector, including the judiciary, civil service, state-owned companies etc… The [left-liberal control] and politicization was even more pervasive in the civil service, various state agencies, state-owned companies, banks, insurance companies, and even schools and hospitals.[41]

This elite's economic and political control over the media, however, proved decisive. For it was exactly the media with a strong left centre bias[42] which facilitated, justified and defended the conquering of the Slovenian public and private sphere by the leftist post-socialist elite. It has been the media which have been concealing rather than exposing the end result of the Slovenian success story in which 'cronyism'[43] and 'state capture' have become so widespread and 'internalised' that informal rules and habits are more important than formal rules.'[44]

In contrast to Hungary, Slovenia has been state-captured and its democracy diminished[45] in the absence of any constitutional change, in compliance with most of its laws, but frequently opposing their spirit.[46] The hijacking of the state has been committed not by the 'conservative national revolution', but by the left post-socialist elite. Due to the 'smooth-transition'[47] with a high elite retention, this elite, different than Orbán's government, neither needed to fill the institutions anew with their party loyalists nor had they to create new institutions for that purpose. As the members of this elite were already institutionalised, they only had to ensure that things stayed as they were. The defence of the status quo, under the guise of stability, predictability, order, was thus the main policy, combined with the subtle reproduction of this elite through the monopolised educational system and the all-encompassing welfare state. The latter, instead of alleviating the socio-economic hardship of the parts of society in need, has rather been used to benefit the existing ideological allies and to recruit new ones. All this resulted not

---

[40] F Adam and M Tomšič, 'The Dynamics of Elites and the Type of Capitalism: Slovenian Exceptionalism' (2012) 37(2) *Historical Social Research* 53, 63–64.

[41] ibid.

[42] For an overview of the state of the media in Slovenia see a comprehensive multifaceted analysis in (2007) 33–36 *Dignitas—Slovenian Journal of Human Rights*; also B Bugarič, 'Crisis of Constitutional Democracy in Post-Communist Europe: "Lands In-between" Democracy and Authoritarianism' (unpublished article, on-file with the author) 13.

[43] Tomšič and Prijon (n 37).

[44] Bugarič (n 42) 14.

[45] ibid, 17.

[46] ibid, 14.

[47] For a supportive view of Slovenian exceptionalism, see A Bebler, 'Slovenia's Smooth Transition' (2000) 13 *Journal of Democracy* 127; V Miheljak and N Toš, 'The Slovenian Way to Democracy and Sovereignty' in N Toš and KH Muller (eds), *Political Faces of Slovenia* (FDV, 2005).

just in what Friedman has described as the tyranny of the status quo,[48] a pervasive phenomenon whereby the newly elected governments with a clear popular mandate for reforms usually fail to implement them due to the powerful groups with vested interests, but in a captured state. In Slovenia the influence of the institutional and economic insiders actively working to preserve status quo is so strong that electing a government that could introduce any meaningful reforms has proven impossible.[49] These strong factions work hand in hand with the populace at large who is opposed to any relevant change too out of the deception that this 'welfare state', as it has been called, works in its favour. Eventually, but unsurprisingly, the outcome has been a deep financial, economic, political, institutional and finally social crisis from which Slovenia is still suffering as I write.[50]

This crisis has been facilitated further due to the Slovenian dysfunctional judiciary. The data gathered by the Council of Europe confirms that Slovenia, while boasting the highest number of judges per capita in Europe,[51] has the least efficient and the most expensive judiciary. As a result, the popular trust in the judiciary is among the lowest in Europe.[52] This finding cannot be dismissed as being established on the subjective grounds alone, since it, unfortunately, finds corroboration in the country's record before the European Court of Human Rights.[53] By the end of 2013 Slovenia had been convicted 275 times before the ECtHR, of which more than 240 cases concerned the violation of the right to a speedy trial and the right to an effective remedy.[54] In its landmark *Lukenda* pilot-judgment the ECtHR went as far as proclaiming that the Slovenia violation of the right to a trial within a reasonable time is

> a systemic problem that has resulted from inadequate legislation and inefficiency in the administration of justice. The problem continues to present a danger affecting every person seeking judicial protection of their rights.[55]

---

[48] M Friedman and R Friedman, *The Tyranny of the Status Quo*, 1st edn (Houghton Mifflin Harcourt, 1984).

[49] See Tomšič (n 40) 53, who has argued: 'However, the changes and events connected with financial crisis and economic crisis after 2008 may indicate that entire architecture of Slovenian social corporatism in the framework of state (national) type of capitalism generated a sort of immobilismo and inability to execute the necessary reforms.'

[50] See, for example, the set of recommendations by the European Commission, Recommendation for a Council Recommendation on Slovenia's 2014 national reform programme and delivering a Council opinion on Slovenia's 2014 stability programme, COM (2014) 425, Brussels, 2 June 2014.

[51] <www.coe.int/t/dghl/cooperation/cepej/evaluation/2012/Rapport_en.pdf> accessed 11 November 2014.

[52] See the report at: <www.europeansocialsurvey.org/docs/findings/ESS5_toplines_issue_1_trust_in_justice.pdf> accessed 11 November 2014, 9–10.

[53] See M Avbelj and JL Černič, 'Chapter on Slovenia' in L Hammer and F Emmert (eds), *The European Convention on Human Rights and Fundamental Freedoms in Central and Eastern Europe* (Eleven International Publishing, 2012).

[54] See the report: <www.echr.coe.int/Documents/Stats_violation_1959_2013_ENG.pdf> accessed 11 November 2014.

[55] See *Lukenda v Slovenia*, App no 23032/02 (ECtHR 6 October 2005).

Slovenia, despite its tiny population of 2 million, also belongs among the nine high case-count states, which are those with more than 1800 cases pending before the ECtHR,[56] and also falls into a group of those nine states with the highest number of applications per capita.[57] In the same vein, Slovenia's record before the Court of Justice of the European Union (CJEU) is equally poor. As nicely demonstrated by Kornezov's chapter in this volume, Slovenian courts rank last in the number of cases referred for a preliminary ruling and the quality of the references actually made is low too.[58]

Of course, it is no surprise to discover that countries have systemic problems with the judiciary and that their courts apply EU law poorly. However, it is certainly a surprise and a cause for concern when the judiciary in such a country adopts a complacent stance, refusing even to admit, let alone to address its systemic problems. This has been the modus operandi of Slovenian judiciary, which has either downplayed its own shortcomings, or, even more frequently, shifted the responsibility onto someone else's shoulders, be that on the legislative and/or the executive branch, on the allegedly too litigious population, on the opposition or even singular judges, who have publicly raised critiques about the system's malfunctioning.[59] While all the initially broadly conceived reform attempts, including those responding directly to the ECtHR rulings, have, as a rule, always been diluted in Slovenia, the judges have most determinately publicly stood for their salaries. They have thus confirmed the sobering finding of the pre-accession advisor to the Ministry of Justice, Judge Norman Manfred Doukoff, whose public statement that Slovenian judges had made no shift in their mindset and that they are occupied mainly by themselves and their salaries, stirred huge controversy and protests on behalf of the Slovenian judiciary.[60]

The complacent stance of the Slovenian judiciary has been exacerbated further by the fact that it has never been subject to lustration. While the legislation provided a narrowly circumscribed possibility not to re-appoint judges, who partook of the trials whose rulings had violated fundamental human rights and freedoms, this provision was little used and, according to the Constitutional Court (*Ustavno sodišče*—US), ought not to be regarded as an element of a 'real' lustration.[61]

---

[56] These are: Bulgaria, Romania, Georgia, UK, Russia, Italy, Serbia, Ukraine, Slovenia. <www.echr. coe.int/Documents/Stats_analysis_2013_ENG.pdf> accessed 11 November 2014, 7/60.

[57] These countries are: Bosnia and Herzegovina, Croatia, Republic of Moldova, Montenegro, Romania, Serbia, Slovenia, Macedonia, Ukraine.

[58] Above, ch 11 in this volume; see also *Court of Justice of the European Union*, Annual Report 2013, 105–06, available at: <http://curia.europa.eu/jcms/upload/docs/application/pdf/2014-06/qdag14001enc.pdf> accessed 11 November 2014.

[59] See M Avbelj, 'O sodnikih in vladavini prava' (2007) 20 *Pravna praksa* 26; M Avbelj, 'Odnos nosilcev oblasti do prava' (2009) 33 *Pravna praksa* 17.

[60] *Slovenia's Judges Appalled at Doukoff's Criticism* (STA, 2003), available at: <www.sta.si/vest. php?s=a&id=779193> accessed 11 November 2014.

[61] Decision of the US U-I-83/94: 'The disputed provision could represent a lustration element from the point of view of substantial demand, that the judges whose judicial office has been performed in violation of human rights as the result of submission of judicial office to politics shall not discharge judicial functions in a democratic system. But it does not imply lustration either in the sense of exclusion from an office or in the sense of exclusion from or access to any other public office, except judicial; neither does it imply lustration in the sense of its complete objectivity based on affiliation.'

This meant that, as in the country in general, the retention of the judicial elite was high too. Bugarič is therefore justified in claiming that Slovenian rule of law institutions, including the courts, 'have been deeply politicized by the cadre from the old political nomenclature.'[62]

The appointments of the President of Slovenian Supreme Court[63] (*Vrhovno sodišče*—VS) and the State Prosecutor General[64] are just two, but probably the most revealing example of this practice. The former's case is particularly instructive. The President of the Supreme Courts is appointed by the National Assembly on the proposal of the Minister of Justice after receiving a preliminary opinion of the Judicial Council and the Supreme Court *en banc*.[65] The current President has been appointed through this procedure despite the fact that he took part in a senate that rendered the last death-sentence verdict in the Socialist Republic of Slovenia and despite many indications that during the communist regime he participated at verifications of killings of renegades on the Yugoslav–Italian border.[66]

This is what has, inter alia, prompted a constitutional court Justice Jan Zobec to publicly raise his voice about the worrisome state of the Slovenian judiciary. In his article, which was very recently condemned by the said President of the Supreme Court for having opened the Pandora's box of discreditation of Slovenian judiciary,[67] he stressed:

> The paramount problem of the Slovenian judiciary is the judiciary itself. First of all, the politics residing inside it, which has been preserved as part of the heritage of the totalitarian era in form of obstinate mental patterns firmly rooted in the old regime, expressing itself in collectivist and corporativist mind-set. There, in the judiciary, this mind-set (as one form of the parallel, concealed, or deep state) thrives and feeds itself in terms of mode de pense, values and worldviews thanks to institutional closure and complacency. In a normal state with established democratic tradition and legal culture this would engender positive effects—it would foster what would already be there: internally, mentally independent judiciary. Unfortunately, in Slovenia it is also being fostered what there already is: anything but an intellectually autonomous and independent judiciary. 'Free riders', those who dare to think independently and critically (which ought to be inherent to each and every judge's intellect) are side-lined, isolated and stigmatized as conflicting, litigious and simply weird individuals.[68]

---

[62] Bugarič (n 42) 13.

[63] Branko Masleša, <www.sodisce.si/vsrs/predstavitev/2011021014160780/> accessed 11 November 2014.

[64] Dr Zvonko Fišer in 1977 prosecuted a local maid and two Catholic priests for having erected a cross commemorating extra-judicially killed 'national traitors' during WWII <www.rtvslo.si/slovenija/fiser-zrtve-komunisticnega-nasilja-oznacil-za-narodne-izdajalce/249361> accessed 11 November 2014.

[65] Courts Act, Official Journal of RS 94/07, Art 62.

[66] Mr Masleša has, however, repeatedly refuted these allegations as false and malicious.

[67] See, President of the Supreme Court, Branko Masleša, addressing the Slovenian judges at the annual event 'Days of Judiciary', official report available at: <www.sodisce.si/vsrs/objave/2014060616053789/> accessed 11 November 2014.

[68] J Zobec, 'Mehki trebuh slovenskega sodstva' *Delo* (8 December 2012) <www.delo.si/mnenja/gostujoce-pero/mehki-trebuh-slovenskega-sodstva.html>accessed11November2014(author's translation).

According to Judge Zobec it

> therefore comes as no surprise that such an 'independent' judiciary is presided by 'a secret favourite of judges'—like judiciary, like its President (who is autonomously chosen by the judges who, thus, also deserve him) ... [As a result ...]: The politics needs to do nothing, it needs not to impact on the judiciary in anything or with anything in order to submit it to itself and to put it under its influence for the time to be. This influence is already there, inside the judiciary, and it has, so to speak, been always there.[69]

Not only is thus, as a consequence, Slovenian judiciary still widely regarded as a strong ally of the post-communist retention elite,[70] the fact of the ideological capture of the judiciary has engendered a much more pernicious outcome. As it has been argued, these institutions have, unable to withstand the strong political pressure, through legal enforcement furthered not the rule of law but partisan political interests.[71]

A paradigmatic example of that is the notorious *Patria* case in which the leader of the centre-right opposition was first accused and then convicted with the force of *res judicata* exclusively on the basis of circumstantial evidence for having accepted a promise of an unknown award at an undetermined time, at an undetermined place and by an undetermined mode of communication to use his influence, then as a Prime Minister, to have a military contract awarded to a particular enterprise.[72] Despite harsh critique of the entire process, which has lasted for more than eight years now and directly impacted at least on three elections, on behalf of the part of Slovenian legal academia as well as foreign scholars,[73] the Constitutional Court refused to rule on the convict's constitutional complaint prior to the exhaustion of other remedies, effectively thus sending the leader of the opposition to a prison for at least a part of his two year sentence.[74]

If we add to this, merely as another highlight, that the President of the Ljubljana district court parties dressed up in communist symbols and flying the Yugoslav flag, while this behaviour receives only a lukewarm warning on behalf of the Slovenian Judicial Council,[75] an overall image of the Slovenian judiciary appears in a very different light from that expected in a normal, liberal constitutional democracy.

---

[69] ibid.

[70] Bugarič (n 42) 13.

[71] ibid.

[72] The *Patria* case Decision of the Local Court of Ljubljana II Kp 2457/2010 (5 June 2013), confirmed by Ljubljana Court of Appeals II Kp 2457/2010 (21 March 2014).

[73] See Opinion by Vlad Perju: <www.ijpucnik.si/media/Independent%20Legal%20Opinion%20Patria%20Case%20-%20Vlad%20Perju.pdf> accessed 11 November 2014.

[74] For an overview, see, M Avbelj, 'Failed Democracy: The Slovenian Patria Case—(Non)Law in Context', online at <http://papers.ssrn.com/sol3/papers.cfm?abstract_id=2462613> accessed 11 November 2014.

[75] The Judicial Council issued only a press release without adopting an official position: <http://m.delo.si/novice/slovenija/sodni-svet-brez-sklepa-o-pionirski-kapici.html> accessed 11 November 2014.

IV. Beyond Hungary and Slovenia: Undoing the Illiberal Past

Having said that, if we are to draw parallels between the Slovenian and Hungarian case, at the outset only the outcome appears to be the same: A frail democracy with huge gaps in the rule of law. The actors are different: Conservatives in Hungary, post-communist socialists and liberals in Slovenia. The means applied differ too: Hungary is an example of an overt constitutional capture brought into being by the continuing and widespread support of the electorate. Slovenia is an example of a covert, subtle state-capture by the post-communist elite occupying the public and private institutions and winning allegiance of interest groups, but also the support of the population at large by generously distributing taxpayers' money through the means of the all-encompassing Slovenian (welfare)-state and (semi)-state owned economy. The Hungarian constitutional revolution has been done through the adoption of new laws and creation of new institutions. The Slovenian case is different as this country's pathologies are caused by the communist revolution that has never been undone. After the formal fall of the communist regime, the existing communist social capital was not removed, but rather put under the protection of the new liberal constitutional order. The outcome was perverse. While in normal countries, the liberal constitutional framework is there to defend the liberal constitutional substance, in Slovenia, thanks to no substantive rupture with the previous totalitarian regime, the liberal constitutional form shields the (pre-)existing illiberal substance and even stands in the way of its gradual reform, let alone complete eradication.

However, both examples are not entirely unrelated. As stressed in the beginning, both countries have a shared historical experience with totalitarian communism and therefore come with a historically deeply seated illiberal pedigree. In Slovenia this past still, and overwhelmingly even if through subtle and informal means, governs the present. To convert the country in a liberal democracy properly so-called, the present should be freed from the past. This is what the Allies did to West Germany[76] and what the latter did to East Germany immediately following the fall of the Berlin Wall.[77] Purging the present of the totalitarian past ensures a sustainable and well-ordered liberal democracy in the future. The experiences both of West and East Germany thus prove that the illiberal regimes cannot be undone in a liberal way. On the other hand, the pursuit of the unrealised promises

---

[76] See, for example, JF Tent, *Mission on the Rhine: 'Reeducation' and Denazification in American-Occupied Germany* (Chicago University Press, 1982); N Frei, *Adenauer's Germany and the Nazi Past: The Politics of Amnesty and Integration* (Columbia University Press, 2002).

[77] See, for, example: HJ De Nike, *German Unification and the Jurists of East Germany: An Anthropology of Law, Nation and History* (Forum-Verlag Godesberg, 1997).

of 1989,[78] originally in the name of bringing about a liberal democracy, can, as Hungary under Orbán and Poland under the Kaczinski brothers prove, result in an illiberal revanchism.

The question therefore naturally arises as to how Slovenia could be success-fully de facto converted into a liberal democracy, which at present clearly it is not. Whose example should Slovenia follow, also to escape both the real threat of emer-gence of the revanchist illiberalism or a mere, but resounding charge, of its pres-ence. Whatever the exact answer, its source lies in the critical mass of institutional actors, in the elites, as well as in the population at large. If they do internalise the values and institutes of a liberal democracy and the rule of law, the country will be a well-ordered liberal society, otherwise not. This internalisation can happen through the imminent switch in the elites, where available, such as in Germany, or, more likely, through a gradual fostering of the liberal mindset, whose success, by no means definite, will be only detectable in the longer run.

V. In the Eye of the Beholder and Looking Ahead

Ten years after the enlargement of the European Union the effects of its trans-formative power on the new Member States is being evaluated. The results are mixed and ultimately very much dependent on the narrator. The success or failure of the CEE countries' transition is, not to a negligible extent, in the eye of the beholder. The mainstream narrative in the last 10 years tended to be quite opti-mistic. It painted the transformation of the CEE countries in too bright a light. The epistemic membrane separating the external observers from the insiders of these countries has never been truly pierced so as to discover their fuller and more accurate image. There was not much interest in doing that in the first place. The outsiders, institutional actors, scholars or journalists alike, satisfied themselves with these countries' by and large formal compliance with the standards of a nor-mal liberal democracy. What was *really* going on and the actual existing quality of the social capital on which the new liberal democratic frame was attached in these countries was of little concern, as long as the external interests were not threatened. This is understandable, for national, internal pathologies should be first cured by the robustness of the domestic democratic process. Stating the opposite would amount to the always resisted interference in the country's internal affairs.

Having said that, in assessing the CEE countries' progress or regress, one can-not overlook the strikingly uneven degree of attention different countries have received in the last years. Focusing merely on the academic world, it is quite clear that the critical fingers have been turned especially against those CEE countries

---

[78] See Jenne and Mudde (n 25) 142.

in which the centre-right parties have tried their reformative 'illiberal' attempts, such as Poland and nowadays Hungary, and much less against those countries, such as Slovenia, in which leftist parties and elites have been consolidating their informal deeply illiberal rule. It is therefore necessary to stress again that authoritarianism is authoritarian and deserves critique irrespective of its political orientation. At the same time, having set the normative bias as much as possible aside, for those writing from the West, they should be mindful of the specificity of the CEE countries before waging their charges of authoritarian or illiberal rule. These countries namely face specific challenges of pervasive illiberalism which, as at least the German historical examples discussed above prove, might not be effectively responded to by liberal means; especially in the upside-down political spaces whereby those wearing the liberal label are actually context-depending conservatives and vice versa.

Ten years on, my own assessment of the CEE countries and their progress amounts to a conclusion that all of them are still involved in the process of normalisation, of approaching, in theory and in practice, the liberal democratic and rule of law requirements. The degree of progress between the countries varies, but it seems that it very much depends on the extent of an actual break-up with the past and the decisiveness of this rupture precisely at the time when it ought to have occurred: In the late 1980s and the early 1990s. Those countries that have missed this opportunity, in particular Slovenia, have reproduced the old system with new means in a new dress and have for a long number of years, perhaps even in the longer run, made the achievement of the proper constitutional democracy impossible. Such countries run the risk of getting stuck in a permanent transition, which sooner or later becomes normalcy. They remain only partly consolidated democracies, which in due course, with the passage of time, remains of the concern of idealists only. But, as we all know, this world has not been built for them. So why bother?

Part III

Constitutional Courts

14

Invalidity of EU Law before the Polish Constitutional Tribunal: Court of Old Closure(s) or New Opening(s)?

TOMASZ TADEUSZ KONCEWICZ*

> Stop for a second in a rushing crowd. There is the Other next to you. Meeting Him is the greatest experience of all. Talking to the Other, feeling him out while at the same time knowing that he sees and understands the world differently, is crucial to building the atmosphere for positive dialogue.[1]

I. Polish *Trybunał Konstytucyjny* and European law. What Kind of Court?

Constitutional Courts have always been and will continue to be political actors with ambitions, self-understanding and preferences. It is no surprise then that on admission to the EU, the Constitutional Courts of Central and Eastern Europe (CEE) have established themselves as powerful activist players.[2] In Poland, the accession presented its *Trybunał Konstytucyjny* (Constitutional Tribunal, hereinafter TK) with a challenge of reconciling the Polish nation's regard for the EU integration project with the TK's existential desire to maintain its own constitutional authority and relevance. W Sadurski, in his comments on the TK's Accession Treaty judgment, observed that from the start the TK strove to establish a '*Solange*-like principle' for defining its guardianship of the relationship between

* I am grateful for comments on the earlier draft of this chapter to Professor Marek Safjan as well as to participants of the seminar *The Transformative Power of Europe Revisited on the 10th Anniversary of the Enlargement* held at the European University Institute in May 2014. Last but not least I am equally grateful to Michal Bobek for his editorial patience. Usual disclaimer applies. Comments are very welcome at www.tomasz-koncewicz.eu. I express gratitude to Ms Ina Lancman for making the English language more reader-friendly.
[1] R Kapuściński, *Ten Inny* [*The Other*] (Warszawa, 2010), translated by the author.
[2] W Sadurski, 'Judicial Review in Central and Eastern Europe: Rationales or Rationalizations?' (2010) 42 *Israel Law Review* 500 and his fundamental work *Rights Before Courts* (Springer, 2010).

national and European laws as part of the fundamental rights standards it had set forth in the national constitutional system.[3] However, to ensure the success of the integration project, it is crucial for all Member States to understand that today's constitutional struggle and power play are taking place on the European stage, and that it is of fundamental importance to shift the constitutional discourse from grand strategies and rhetoric to actual application. For in the post-national law era, the real world of EU constitutionalism is defined by the latter, and any constitutional dialogue must put a premium not on *what* the courts opine, but on what *they* do, *how* they play and argue their differences. For the present analysis of the scope of constitutional review of EU law by the TK to be meaningful, a consideration of both of these worlds is essential, since EU law is based on the premise that law never functions on its own but through its actors' actions.[4]

The TK marked its arrival on the European stage with a few strong judgments, in which it laid out its views on the EU law, its place in the Polish legal system and the relationship between the laws of Poland and the EU.[5] The TK's judgments are amply reflected in its case law, which is a classic manifesto of a defensive constitutionalism, marked by inward looking and disengagement. The TK presents itself as a guardian of the Polish Constitution, the court of 'last word', and its 'inalienable constitutional core' (the term introduced obiter dicta in the 'Lisbon judgment') expansively interpreted. While the judgments contain some conciliatory gestures towards the EU, in practice they function as a mere decorum whenever the TK feels that its roles are at stake. For the most part, the TK sees EU law as a source of its constitutional disempowerment. Hence, the primacy of EU law, in its view, applies only to the sub-constitutional law, and not to the Constitution itself, which as the supreme law of the land is unchallengeable both in the sphere of application (the TK speaks of 'precedence of application') and hierarchy of law (the TK speaks of 'precedence of binding force'). Supranationalism is a concept alien to the Polish Constitution; as a result, the TK flatly rejects any attempt to categorise EU institutions as supranationalist. In the eyes of the TK, the EU is just a classical

---

[3] W Sadurski, '"Solange Chapter 3": Constitutional Courts in Central Europe—Democracy—European Union', *EUI Working Paper* no 40/2006, 21.

[4] A Kozak, 'Niedoceniona wspólnota—prawnicy a integracja europejska' [Underestimated Community—Lawyers and European Integration] in J Kaczor (ed), *Teoria prawa europejskiego* [*Theory of European Law*] (Wydawnictwo Uniwersytetu Wrocławskiego, 2005).

[5] For general overview see B Banaszkiewicz, 'Prawo polskie a prawo Unii Europejskiej w orzecznictwie Trybunału Konstytucyjnego' [The Polish and European Law in the Case Law of the Constitutional Tribunal] *Europejski Przegląd Sądowy* 12/2005, at 49 and more recent monograph by K Wójtowicz, *Sądy konstytucyjne wobec prawa Unii Europejskiej* [*Constitutional Courts and EU Law*] (Wydawnictwo Trybunału Konstytucyjnego, 2012). A helpful recapitulation of the TK case law is provided by the Office of the TK in its *Summary of Selected Judgments of the Polish Constitutional Court on EU law* (Warsaw, 2006) and in the annual information on the case law published by the TK. See 'Informacja o istotnych problemach wynikających z działalności i orzecznictwa Trybunału Konstytucyjnego w 2006' [Information on the fundamental problems of the activities and case law of the Constitutional Court] (Warsaw, 2007) 48–51; 'Informacja o istotnych problemach wynikających z działalności i orzecznictwa Trybunału Konstytucyjnego w 2009 r' [Information on the fundamental problems of the activities and case law of the Constitutional Tribunal in 2007] (Warsaw, 2010) 80–81. Both documents are available online at <http://trybunal.gov.pl>.

international organisation and upon accession to the EU the Member States remain sovereign entities.[6] The Polish Constitution does not authorise delegation of competences to EU to such an extent as to render the Republic of Poland unable to function as a sovereign and democratic State. Sovereignty is the guarantor of democracy, and the TK considers itself the guardian of both.[7] Therefore, Poland doesn't delegate sovereignty, only its sovereign competences. It scoffs at the idea of the primacy of EU law, and sees it, at best, as a principle invented by the Court of Justice (ECJ), with no Treaty basis to back it up. The uneasiness of the TK with the EU law's claim of primacy is best demonstrated in the subtle interaction between *result* and *reasoning*.[8]

To alleviate its European partners' fears, the TK engages in constitutional rhetoric. It offers conciliatory gestures in its view on the European integration as a constitutional requirement; and it calls to the attention the friendliness of its law makers towards the EU law, their acceptance of the idea of a cosmopolitan and multi-centric character of the Polish law and its common axiology with EU law. Yet, all this cannot mask the fact that the TK abandons these blandishments whenever it perceives a threat to its role as the guardian of Polish sovereignty and the Constitution. For the TK, the spectre of normative conflict is, therefore, always present. And as long as it persists in its defensive posture, the argumentative approach to a conflict remains unavailable to it. The dominant supreme source of law approach translates then into the image and self-conception of the TK: Inflexibility and a clear-cut, once and for all definition of the relationships between the courts. This approach precludes an argumentative approach to the normative conflict as the interpreter is left with no choice but to give effect to the higher-ranking norm. The constitutional landscape is dominated by the domestic point of reference always provided by the constitutional text which, when all is said and done, reigns in supreme, notwithstanding all the nice words and gestures.

All this makes the TK a good constitutional court only when understood in traditional parlance that is keen on preserving constitutional features of its constitutional order. At the same time however it turns a blind eye to the ongoing

---

[6] For critical overview of the TK's understanding of EU law see TT Koncewicz, 'Trybunał Konstytucyjny wobec prawa europejskiego (część I)' [Polish Constitutional Court and European Law. Part One] *Przegląd Sejmowy* No 2/2012 and 'Part Two' in *Przegląd Sejmowy* No 3/2012, both available online at <http://orka.sejm.gov.pl>.

[7] For more in-depth analysis see D Piqani, 'Constitutional Courts in Central and Eastern Europe and Their Attitude towards European Integration' (2007) 2 *European Journal of Legal Studies* (online at <www.ejls.com>); W Sadurski, 'Judicial Review in Central and Eastern Europe: Rationales or Rationalizations?' *The Hebrew University of Jerusalem Faculty of Law Research Paper* 7/10; same author, 'Constitutional Courts in Transition Processes: Legitimacy and Democratization', *Sydney Law School Legal Studies Research Paper* 53/2011; same author, 'European Constitutional Identity?' *Sydney Law School Legal Studies Research Paper* 37/2006; K Kowalik-Banczyk, 'Should we Polish it up? The Polish Constitutional Court and the Idea of Supremacy of EU Law' (2005) 6 *German Law Journal* 1355; D Leczykiewicz, 'Case Note on the Judgment of 27 April 2005 of the Polish Constitutional Court' (2006) 43 *Common Market Law Review* 1187.

[8] Sadurski (n 3).

evolution of the constitutional courts. The TK's most recent rulings in particular on the Lisbon Treaty[9] and on the constitutional review of EU law,[10] show that it is fast becoming a constitutional 'Odd Man Out'. The latter decision captures perfectly the uneasiness of the TK vis-a-vis EU law and the Court of Justice, as well as hard choices the constitutional judges face.

II. Invalidity of EU Law before the TK

A. Case SK 45/09: The Judgment

In the SK 45/09 case, the TK heard a constitutional complaint that concerned the exclusion of a debtor from proceedings before the court of first instance; the complaint questioned the enforceability of the ruling issued by a court of another EU Member State as infringing on constitutional rights to court (Article 45 of the Constitution) and the principle of equality (Article 32 of the Constitution).

The TK held that Article 41 of the Council Regulation No 44/2001 of 22 December 2000 on jurisdiction, recognition and enforcement of judgments in civil and commercial matters was consistent with Article 45(1) as well as Article 32(1) (in conjunction with Article 45(1)) of the Constitution of the Republic of Poland. Pursuant to Article 39(1)(1)–(2) of the Constitutional TK Act of 1 August 1997, the TK decided to discontinue the proceedings as to the remainder.[11]

Due to the novel character of the legal act whose constitutionality was questioned, the TK began by examining Article 79(1) of the Constitution to see whether legal acts enacted by EU institutions may be challenged by way of a constitutional complaint.[12] It concluded that the scope, *ratione materiae*, of normative acts that might be subject to review as to their conformity with the Constitution had been set out in Article 79(1) of the Constitution, autonomously and independently of

---

[9] Case K 32/09 (English translation available at <http://trybunal.gov.pl>).

[10] Case SK 45/09 (English translation available at <http://trybunal.gov.pl>).

[11] Polish doctrine was itself divided on the issue. For useful recapitulation see A Wyrozumska, 'Prawo międzynarodowe oraz prawo Unii Europejskiej a konstytucyjny system źródeł prawa' [The International Law and the Law of the European Union in the constitutional system of sources of law'] in K Wójtowicz (ed), *Otwarcie Konstytucji RP na prawo międzynarodowe i procesy integracyjne* [*The openness of the Constitution of the Republic of Poland to International Law and integration processes*] (Wydawnictwo Sejmowe, 2006) 87. Having analysed the case law of the TK the author concluded (at 95) that 'the Court seems to be sending positive signal as to its jurisdiction to review EU secondary law'. In similar vein see B Banaszak, *Konstytucja Rzeczpospolitej Polskiej. Komentarz* [*The Constitution of the Republic of Poland. Commentary*] (CH Beck, 2009) 827.

[12] According to Art 79 of the Constitution, an individual can lodge with the TK a constitutional complaint questioning the compatibility with the Constitution of the statute or other normative act on the basis of which the court or administrative organ decided the case.

Article 188(1)–(3).[13] The examination of constitutional complaints constitutes a separate type of proceedings, which in the opinion of the TK is supported by two arguments. The first one stems from the system of the Constitution. Article 188 regulates the scope of the TK jurisdiction, and it stipulates in its point (5) that the TK shall adjudicate on constitutional complaints, as specified in Article 79(1). This provision is also referred to in Article 191(1)(6) of the Constitution, in the context of individuals or legal entities authorised to make application to the TK to instigate proceedings. It indicates that the constitution-maker regarded proceedings on the examination of a constitutional complaint as distinct from other proceedings before the TK. The second argument is well known and is concerned with the effectiveness of protection of constitutional rights and freedoms. However, it would be unjustified to narrow down its *ratione materiae* scope only to the normative acts of Article 188(1)–(3) of the Constitution. The latter manifests the division of the scope of jurisdiction over the examination of hierarchical conformity of normative acts between the TK and other courts.

Within the meaning of Article 79(1) of the Constitution, a constitutional complaint may concern a statute or a normative act. According to the TK, a normative act, within the meaning of Article 79(1) of the Constitution, may be issued by one of the organs of the Polish state, but also—provided it fulfils the necessary requirements—by an organ of an international organisation, such as the European Union, which the Republic of Poland belongs to. In fact, such legal acts do constitute part of the current Polish legal system. Pursuant to Article 288, second paragraph of the Treaty on the Functioning of the European Union (TFEU), regulations shall have general application, and be binding in their entirety in all Member States. The norms of a regulation are general and abstract in character. They apply to the Member States, their organs and their private entities, including the citizens. The TK also concluded that some of the provisions of EU regulations may serve as a basis for a final decision, by a court or an organ of public administration, on the freedoms, rights and obligations of individuals or legal entities, as specified in the Constitution. The regulations may constitute a legal basis of administrative decisions and court rulings in the Member States, including Poland. In the national courts' proceedings, individuals may rely on the norms of EU regulations and derive from them their rights.

---

[13] Art 188 of the Constitution sets out the competences making up the jurisdiction of the TK (no mention of European secondary law). In accordance with this provision:

The Constitutional TK shall adjudicate regarding the following matters: 1. The conformity of statutes and international agreements to the Constitution; 2. The conformity of a statute to ratified international agreements whose ratification required prior consent granted by statute; 3. The conformity of legal provisions issued by central State organs to the constitution, ratified international agreements and statutes; 4. The conformity to the Constitution of the purposes or activities of the political parties; 5. Complaints concerning constitutional infringements, as specified in Article 79, para 1.

In addition, Art 193 of Constitution deals with the legal questions posed to the TK by the ordinary judges on the compatibility of normative acts with the Constitution.

For these reasons, the TK found that an EU regulation may be subject to a constitutional complaint, specified in Article 79(1) of the Constitution. The fact that the object of the complaint is part of EU law, which is also part of the Polish legal system, affects the TK's judgment of its conformity to the Constitution.

The TK stated that EU regulations were legal acts whose position in the Polish constitutional system had been indicated in Article 91(3) of the Constitution.[14] One of the systemic principles of EU law is that of its primacy over the national law in cases of its nonconformity with EU law. By contrast, the Constitution retains its precedence, enshrined in Article 8(1)[15] and previously upheld by the TK, over all legal acts in the Polish legal system, including those of the EU law. Due to the position of the Constitution as the supreme law of the Republic of Poland, it is therefore admissible to subject the constitutionality of the norms of EU regulations to a review. According to the TK, it is crucial to recognise the distinction between the roles of the ECJ and those of the TK in matters of conformity of the two legal systems. The issues of conformity of the acts of the EU secondary legislation with the Treaties, that is the EU primary law, is the task of the former, while the matters of conformity of the EU acts with the Constitution falls to the latter. However, the ECJ sees things differently. It maintains that its jurisprudence has the sole jurisdiction in adjudicating the invalidity of the acts of the EU secondary legislation. Not so, as far as the TK is concerned. Its mission is to protect the Constitution, which, pursuant to Article 8(1), is the supreme law of the Republic of Poland. In addition, the Article endows the TK with 'the last word' in fundamental constitutional and systemic issues. The situation is ripe for potential conflict between the rulings issued by the TK and those delivered by the ECJ. With that in mind, the TK, while allowing for the possibility of examining the conformity of the acts of the EU secondary legislation with the Constitution, calls for caution and restraint.

All 28 Member States are bound by EU law. One of its systemic principles is that of sincere cooperation, spelled out in Article 4(3) of the TEU (Treaty on European Union). Allowing the Member States to declare norms of EU law as no longer binding would run counter to that principle. Article 4(2) TEU, however, states that the Union must respect the Member States' national identities, inherent in their fundamental political and constitutional structures. In the eyes of the TK, the national identity clause gives credence to its opinion that contradictions can be eliminated by applying interpretation based on the assumption of mutual loyalty and respect for autonomies of the respective laws of the EU and its Member States. The mutual loyalty notion requires the ECJ to be favourably inclined towards national legal systems, while the Member States are expected to approach EU norms with the utmost respect. Additionally, the TK's review of conformity of an EU regulation with the Constitution should be regarded as independent, and also subsidiary, in relation to the jurisdiction of the ECJ.

---

[14] Art 91(3) of the Constitution states that 'If an agreement, ratified by the Republic of Poland, establishing an international organization so provides, the laws established by it shall be applied directly and have precedence in the event of conflict of laws'.

[15] Art 8 (1): 'The Constitution shall be the Supreme law of the Republic of Poland'.

The TK stressed that on joining the EU, the Republic of Poland accepted the division of powers within the system of EU institutions. An element of that division is the jurisdiction of the ECJ to provide the final interpretation of EU law and ensure that it is observed consistently by all Member States. It also has an exclusive power to determine the conformity of the acts of EU secondary legislation to the Treaties and the general principles of the EU law. Finally, the TK considered the effects of its judgment on a possible adjudication of inconsistency of the EU secondary legislation norms with the Constitution. In the context of the Polish legal acts, non-conformity would result in declaring unconstitutional the no longer legally binding norms. With regard to the EU secondary legislation, such a result would be impossible to implement, as it is not up to the organs of the Polish state to decide whether such acts are legally binding or not. Therefore, the consequence of the TK's ruling would be to rule out the possibility that the acts of the EU secondary legislation would be applied by the organs of the Polish state and would have legal effects in Poland.[16] Undoubtedly, the ruling declaring the non-conformity of the EU law with the Constitution would take place only when other ways of solving a conflict between the norms of different legal systems have failed—and it would be final.

Due to the precedential character of the case, the TK carried out a thorough analysis of the conformity of the challenged EU regulation to the Constitution. However, the TK deemed it desirable—in the future—to indicate a way of examining the conformity of the norms of EU law (the Treaties and the EU secondary legislation) to the Constitution in the course of review proceedings commenced by way of a constitutional complaint. Accordingly, the TK made reference to the jurisprudence of the constitutional courts of other Member States, and concluded that a direct review of the conformity of the acts of the EU secondary legislation to the national constitutions had been conducted only in exceptional cases. This confirmed the thesis that a certain degree of caution is exercised in such cases. The German *Bundesverfassungsgericht* (Federal Constitutional Court—BVerfG) has stated that it wouldn't examine the conformity of the EU secondary legislation to the provisions of the Basic Law, the guarantor of fundamental rights, as long as the European Union ensures, notably by means of the jurisprudence of the ECJ, an effective protection of these rights, equal to that guaranteed by the Basic Law of the Federal Republic of Germany. Likewise, in the jurisprudence of the European Court of Human Rights ('ECtHR'), there is a presumption that both the EU law and the ECJ ensure the protection of human rights at a level on par with that required by

---

[16] In its Treaty of Accession judgment, the TK indicated three possible actions for the Republic of Poland if a conflict between the Constitution and the EU law arose: Amend the Constitution; take up measures aimed at amending EU provisions; and, ultimately, withdraw from the EU. Any of the three would have to be carried out by the Polish sovereign, ie the Polish Nation, or an organ of the state empowered by the Constitution to represent the Nation. The last solution would be reserved for the most serious and irreconcilable conflicts between the foundations of the constitutional order of the Republic of Poland and EU law, and only after the TK issued the ruling declaring the non-conformity of particular norms of the EU secondary legislation with the Constitution.

the European Convention for the Protection of Human Rights and Fundamental Freedoms. Therefore, the actions of the EU Member States are consistent with the European Convention as long as the EU protects human rights by applying—for that purpose—appropriate guarantees of protection as well as control mechanisms, which are at least equivalent to those guaranteed by the Convention.

The ECtHR found that it would be competent only in exceptional cases to assess whether actions, or lack thereof, on the part of the EU bodies and institutions are consistent with the Convention; namely, when the presumption of equivalent legal protection is undermined, and the protection of human rights at the EU level is 'manifestly deficient'.

In the opinion of the TK, the premises for adopting an analogical approach when examining the constitutionality of the EU law in Poland do exist. Prior to Poland's accession to the EU, legal acts adopted pursuant to the Treaty of Accession were introduced into the Polish legal system. The subsequent legal acts were issued when Poland was already a Member State of the EU, usually with the participation of the representatives of the competent organs of the Polish state. What justifies an approach analogical to that taken by other courts are the following arguments: The great significance of the fundamental rights in the EU legal order, the constitutional principle of favourable predisposition of the Republic of Poland towards the European integration, and the Treaty's principle of loyalty of the Member States towards the Union. The approach chosen has procedural consequences. A constitutional complaint that challenges the conformity of the EU law act with the Constitution should be required to make the probable claim that the challenged EU legal act undermines the level of protection of rights and freedoms guaranteed by the Constitution. This requirement arises from Article 79(1) of the Constitution. Providing the proof is not an additional requirement, but a more specific manifestation of the requirement to indicate in what manner given rights or freedoms have been infringed. The requirement to make probable that the level of protection of rights and freedoms has been undermined in comparison with the level of protection guaranteed by the Constitution follows from the allocation of the burden of proof in the review proceedings commenced by way of a constitutional complaint. This is not tantamount to a proof that there has been an infringement of the Constitution, which is solely the task of the TK. If the requirement is not fulfilled, the TK may conclude that the constitutional and statutory conditions of the constitutional complaint have not been met and, consequently, it may discontinue the proceedings or altogether decline to proceed on the complaint.

B. Unpacking the Premises

The public discourse in Poland about the judgment in SK 45/09 was rather superficial and given to oversimplification. At its core was the commentators' insistence on the TK's mission to protect Poland's sovereignty and the Constitution's status as the supreme law of the land. In the process, the discourse missed the complex and multifaceted nature of the decision and its call to rise above the drumbeat of sovereignty.[17] To truly understand the message of the TK, one has to take a long view and see it in a wider context. It is worthwhile noting that the ruling coincided with a renewal of the debate on the extent of EU law validity in Poland. The proponents (right wing, politically) of the extensive reading of the powers of the TK, playing on the nationalistic anxieties of their electorate, claimed that survival of Poland (as a democracy) hinges on the TK's ability to question the EU law validity and retain the proverbial 'last word'.

As it happens, the TK's case-law did not provide an unambiguous answer to this constitutional problem. However, in the Accession judgment, some hints could be discerned that the TK might be in favour of claiming such competence. The Polish doctrine too was divided. Some claimed the jurisdiction to review the EU acts' conformity with the Constitution, others strongly opposed it.[18] The advocates pointed to the supremacy of the Polish Constitution and the effectiveness of constitutional review by the TK. According to them, the term 'normative act' should be interpreted broadly and should encompass EU secondary law. That would bring the regulations and directives binding in Poland within the scope of 'normative acts'. The dissenters argued that unless the Constitution expressly spelled out such competence, any attempt to grant it to the TK would represent a wide interpretation of the constitutional text, which they regarded as inadmissible. They argued that EU law does not lie within the TK's competences clearly and exhaustively enumerated in Article 188 of the Constitution. Claiming such competence would, moreover, constitute a grave disregard for the well-established case law of the ECJ. As a result, they believed that the review functions within EU law must be centralised,[19] leaving only the constitutional review of the primary EU law as subject to the TK's constitutional jurisdiction. This was the result of a conscious choice of the Polish Constitutional law maker when it had drafted the Constitution. Any attempt to grant itself such power would call on the TK to engage in more than the interpretation of the Constitution, and require it to consider factors other than its text. In the view of the dissenters, judicial politics would in the end determine the issue. And that is exactly what has happened in the case under consideration.

---

[17] See daily press coverage by M Graczyk, 'Czy polski Trybunał ma czuwać nad prawem UE' [Should Polish TK Supervise European Law] *Dziennik Gazeta Prawna* (10 and 11 November 2009); E Siedlecka, 'Spór Trybunałów może się przydać' [Dispute of the courts might be a good thing] *Gazeta Wyborcza* (13 November 2009).

[18] See the discussion part of the book edited by M Granat, *Stosowanie prawa międzynarodowego i wspólnotowego w wewnętrznym porządku prawnym Francji i Polski: L'application du droit international et dans l' ordre juridique interne en France et en Pologne* (Wydawnictwo Sejmowe, 2007) and contributions therein by L Garlicki (at 103) and by M Masternak-Kubiak (at 101, 103).

[19] The importance of the '*Foto–Frost* precedent' was not lost on Polish legal doctrine. See TT Koncewicz, 'Sędziowska kreatywność w obronie integralności i jednolitości prawa wspólnotowego. Uwagi na marginesie wyroku Trybunału Sprawiedliwości w sprawie 314/85, Foto-Frost' [Judicial creativity in the defence of the integrity and uniformity of European Law] *Palestra* 9–10/2007.

i. *Question of* Judicial Style

At the outset it must be pointed out that the internal structure of the TK's reasoning in the SK 45/09 judgment is inconsistent and marred by repetitions. It is as if the TK were anxious that the reasons informing its decision, such as, for example, the necessity of a safety net against the future intrusions of EU law, would not be lost on anybody. Inevitably, these structural shortcomings of the judgment impact negatively on its overall presentation. In its analysis, for the sake of clarity, the TK divides its motives into three main parts (I–III), subdivided further into numbered sections. In part I, the TK sets out the factual background of the case that originated in the constitutional complaint,[20] and arguments of the interveners (Public Prosecutor General, Parliament and Minister of Foreign Affairs). In part II, the TK summarises the parties' arguments at the hearing. Part III contains *in meritii* considerations of the TK.

Of special interest for present discussion are parts that deal with admissibility (III.1); the EU secondary legislation as the subject of constitutional review; and the required level of proof in cases that challenge EU law. The reading of the statement of reasons is nonetheless impeded by the TK's inexplicable decision to split admissibility considerations into two parts (III.1–2 and III.8), which resulted in confusing overlaps and repetitions. For better readability and overall presentation of the judgment, the TK would have done well to include the admissibility considerations in the opening part, and then proceeded, on the basis of these considerations, to the constitutional review of EU regulation. Moreover, the review would have fared much better had it been placed in the final part of the judgment instead of in the middle section of part III (III.3–III.7).

ii. *Question of* Substance

What is so striking about the SK 45/09 judgment is the TK's notable shift in emphasis, when compared to the decidedly anti-EU 'Lisbon judgment'.[21] The latter was highly traditional, cautious and conservative. It cited at every turn the sovereignistic rationale, and the constitutional limits to Polish membership in the EU and it postured as the genuine (unique?) guardian of the Polish constitutional integrity. All the while, it treated EU law as a mere afterthought. However, the judgment under consideration here, SK 45/09, has confirmed that the jurisprudence of constitutional compromise between being faithful to its own Constitution on the one hand and the opening up to the rigours of European constitutionalism on the other posed a conceptual challenge for the TK and its judges.

---

[20] The complaint had alleged that regulation 44/2001 infringes certain fundamental rights guaranteed in the Polish Constitution. They included the right to fair trial (Art 45 of the Constitution), right to appeal against a first-instance decision (Art 78 and Art 176 of the Constitution), and equality (Art 32 of the Constitution).

[21] Judgment of 24 November 2010 in case K 32/09.

Reading SK 45/09, one cannot help but feel that the TK decided to hand down such a strong judgment out of fear of the threat to its position and stature posed by the European integration. It is, therefore, just a matter of time before the TK starts to build on this judgment. Wishing to be heard, the TK barged into the arena of high constitutional politics. It has firmly established its emergency jurisdiction, (calling it 'subsidiary') vis-a-vis EU acts by invoking procedural and substantive conditions for triggering it. In that, it was clearly influenced by the *Bosphorus* jurisprudence of the ECtHR,[22] where a declaration of invalidity of an EU act becomes an *ultima ratio* and can be resorted to only when all other means of resolving the conflict fail. In addition, *ultima ratio* can be invoked only in 'the most serious and irreconcilable conflicts'[23] between the foundations[24] of the constitutional order of the Republic of Poland and the EU law. This language suggests ('leaving aside the last solution') that the TK feels fairly confident in its ability to avoid withdrawing from the EU by managing potential frictions through interpretation and application of the Constitution as well as measures of political nature. Furthermore, the TK believes that emergency jurisdiction should be exercised in accordance with the principle of the Constitution's openness towards the EU law, and with due regard to the respective autonomies of national and EU laws. After all, both legal orders have to co-exist on the basis of mutually acceptable interpretation and cooperative application. Mutual loyalty means that the ECJ is expected to 'be favourably inclined towards national legal systems,' and the Member States are expected to approach EU law 'with utmost respect'.

Having set down the ground rules for triggering subsidiary jurisdiction, the TK proceeded to the review benchmarks, or, in the words of the TK, to the question of the 'kind of non-conformity between EU secondary legislation and the Constitution that can be subjected to review, commenced by way of constitutional complaint'. This part of the judgment is bitter-sweet, and only a scrutiny of the combination of pros and cons can reveal the true meaning of the TK's message. One subtle obiter dicta might be worthwhile pondering here: The exceptional nature of the conflict 'between the bases of constitutional orders of Poland and the EU' that could trigger the subsidiary jurisdiction of the TK. The dictum can

---

[22] See point 2.6 of the TK's judgment, referring to the ECtHR *Bosphorus* judgment of 30 June 2005 (App No 45036/98). For a further analysis see F Benoit-Rohmer, 'À propos de l'arrêt Bosphorus Air Lines du 30 juin 2005: L'Adhésion contrainte de l'Union à la Convention' (2005) 64 *Revue trimestrielle des droits de l'homme* 827; case note by S Douglas-Scott in (2006) 43 *Common Market Law Review* 243; AH Parga, '*Bosphorus v Ireland* and the Protection of Fundamental Rights in Europe' (2006) 31 *European Law Review* 251; I Cabral-Barreto, 'La Cour Européenne des droits de l'homme et le droit communautaire. Quelques réflexions à propos de l'arrêt Bosphorus' in MG Kohen (ed), *Promoting Justice, Human Rights and Conflict Resolution Through International Law: Liber Amicorum Lucius Caflisch* (Brill, 2007); C Eckes, 'Does the European Court of Human Rights Provide Protection from the European Community? The Case of Bosphorus Airways' (2007) 13 *European Law Journal* 47.

[23] In Polish original 'wyjątkowe przypadki najcięższego i nieusuwalnego konfliktu'.

[24] It is to be noted that the translation of this part of the judgment uses wrongly the term 'bases of the constitutional order'. The term should rather be 'the foundations of the constitutional order of the Republic of Poland' ('podstawy porządku konstytucyjnego RP').

be read as meaning that only a conflict of fundamental[25] aspects of constitutional orders would justify the TK's resort to its subsidiary jurisdiction. This would fit nicely with the emerging ECJ case law on the interpretation and legal significance of the constitutional identities of the Member States and the EU obligation to respect them.

In reality, a measure of caution is in order when drawing definite conclusions as to the position of the TK on this issue, since the appeasing language in part III.2.7 is later qualified, rather unexpectedly, in the final part of the judgment, in point 8. This is where the splitting of considerations of constitutional review and its conditions into two distant parts of the analysis makes the construction of the TK's message unwieldy, and its meaning elusive since considerations in part III 2.9 and in point 8 of the judgment overlap to a great extent. The TK failed to explain its understanding of the Polish constitutional tradition as a possible benchmark for the review. For the TK, the constitutional rights and freedoms of the individual, in particular those outlined in Chapter II of the Polish Constitution, set the minimal threshold which cannot be lowered by an EU act. The contours are nonetheless far from clear since the TK also speaks of the contradiction with the explicit wording of constitutional norms, thus expanding almost limitlessly the potential for conflict and its jurisdiction. It also renders questionable its earlier declarations of cooperation in good faith, and the allegedly subsidiary character of its constitutional review. The TK's term for 'constitutional norms' is much wider in scope than the constitutional catalogue of fundamental rights and may encompass any provision of the Constitution.[26]

Overlooking these obvious implications betrays the TK's lack of rigour.[27] As a result, the TK presents a vague, ill-defined picture that allows it considerable latitude for manoeuvre, while leaving everybody else in a state of uncertainty. The question whether the TK would be willing to nuance its case law remains as yet

---

[25] At one point the judgment uses the term 'systemic' for activating its subsidiary jurisdiction and says the following: 'it should be stated that, also due to the content of Article 8(1) of the Constitution, the TK is obliged to perceive its position in such a way that—as regards fundamental matters concerning systemic issues—it is 'the court which will have the last word' with regard to the Polish Constitution' (point 2.4 of the reasons). I revert to 'the last word' rhetoric below.

[26] At point 2.9 of the judgment we read '... the lower level of protection of the individual's rights that arises from the EU law, in comparison with the level of protection guaranteed by the Constitution, would be unconstitutional. The constitutional norms from the realm of the rights and freedoms of the individual set a threshold which may not be lowered or challenged as a result of the introduction of EU regulation. Interpretation "consistent with the EU law" has its limits. It may not lead to results which contradict the explicit wording of the constitutional norms and which are incompatible with the minimum of the guarantees provide by the Constitution'.

[27] Again it would be pertinent here to point out slight differences between the TK's English translation of the judgment and the original. For the limits of pro-European interpretation the Polish original says: 'Wykładnia przyjazna dla prawa europejskiego ma swoje granice. Nie może prowadzić do rezultatów sprzecznych z wyraźnym brzmieniem norm konstytucyjnych i *niemożliwych do uzgodnienia z* minimum funkcji gwarancyjnych, realizowanych przez Konstytucję'. It means that the incompatibility must be preceded by the interpretation aimed at ruling out such incompatible results and will kick in only when the TK is not able to reconcile (Polish 'uzgodnić') the result with the minimal guarantees of the Constitution.

unanswered. The TK considers all fundamental rights[28] included in Chapter II of the Constitution as part and parcel of the constitutional identity—an umbrella under which it can carry out a review. There is no indication to date that the constitutional identity provides a separate benchmark for review, with its own dynamics and admissibility criteria. The latter option would mean that the TK would be willing to follow its German counterpart and contextualise its review. This is a crucial point since the '*Solange* approach' has made the constitutional review practically dormant, while the future of the relationship between the ECJ and the national courts remains to be shaped by the dialogue on the meaning of Article 4(3) TEU. As a result, the picture of the constitutional review is far from being complete.

Despite its pre-emptively laid out strict conditions for the admissibility of constitutional complaints against the acts of the EU, the TK might not readily rush into exercising this competence. The beauty of judicial politics lies both in the detail and the possibilities it creates for the TK. In its judgment in SK 45/09, the TK did not rule out anything. Rather, it kept all options open, even the dormant ones. Thus, the current question is no longer *if* but *when*, and this is the most important message of the judgment. This change of emphasis in the doctrinal debate cannot be lost on the outside world. With its significant nod to the '*Bosphorus* jurisprudence', the TK has accepted that

> the scope of the powers of an international organization that includes Poland as its member should ensure protection of human rights commensurate with that guaranteed by the Polish Constitution. The comparability concerns the catalogue of the rights on the one hand, and the scope of admissible interference with the rights on the other. The requirement of appropriate protection of human rights pertains to their general standard, and does not imply the necessity to guarantee identical protection of each of the rights analysed separately.[29]

The 'pluralist movement' has had an intellectual impact on the TK's judges because the coexistence of the autonomous legal orders and their simultaneous claims to being operative is one of the underpinnings of the justices' approach. However, the plurality strain of the TK's reasoning would have been complete had the TK recognised its role in the common project, with no jurisdictional strings attached. On the question of legality, the cosmopolitan system of law rejects the hierarchical position of courts. Be it as it may, the TK makes it clear in the judgment's final part that in case of a conflict between EU and national constitutional norms, it is the latter that prevails. Thus the Euro-friendly statements in the opening part of the judgment are hedged in its concluding part. Despite all this, there is no doubt that

---

[28] I already pointed out that the TK speaks also of 'systemic issues' as triggering the subsidiary jurisdiction of the TK. It is not clear however if the 'systemic issues' are equivalent to the fundamental rights as minimum threshold of protection or maybe they stand for something novel and encompassing more than the catalogue of constitutional rights.

[29] Point 2.9 of the SK 45/09 judgment. Furthermore, *Bosphorus* is unnecessarily repeated and restated again at point 8.3 of the judgment.

Poland's accession to the EU is for the TK an asset worth protecting. EU law enjoys a special status (short of supranational, though) and any attempt to question it constitutionally requires a burden of proof. The mere claim of infringement does not suffice. The applicant is required to prove a prima facie claim of unconstitutionality (in a qualified manner) by showing not only that the decision is based on an act that contravenes constitutional rights (and freedoms, basic admissibility condition under Article 79 of the Constitution) but that it causes a considerable decline in the standard of protection of rights and freedoms in comparison with the standard of protection guaranteed by the Constitution.

The above considerations would be nothing out of the ordinary, were it not for the obiter dictum, which changes completely the internal dynamics of the ruling. The TK went beyond the problem at hand (the constitutionality of EU secondary law) and extended its findings to the entire EU law![30] The future complainants thus may claim by way of constitutional complaint that not only EU secondary norms, but also the Treaties, violate the Constitution. Such a conclusion would be far-reaching and dangerous. It would call into question the TK's avowed desire to keep its review functions to a minimum and would go against the long-established doctrine of claiming such competence vis-a-vis the Treaties only at the stage of Accession. Within the meaning of Article 79 of the Constitution, the Treaties are not normative acts, so the reason for the TK's constitutional jolt at the end of the ruling is puzzling, to say the least. The special place accorded to the Treaties in the Polish law (see point 8.4 of the judgment) rings hollow if one can question their constitutionality via constitutional complaints.

In consequence of the TK's judgment, Poland has gotten a 'chequerboard Constitution'. Internal diversification of the Constitution ensues—divergent *locus standi*, depending on the legal basis, even though the normative act questioned can be identical when coupled with some imaginative interpretation of admissibility conditions *rationae personae* of constitutional complaints verging on *contra legem*. The constitutionality of EU secondary law cannot be questioned on the basis of Article 188 point 1 to 3 of the Constitution since it is not mentioned there. On the other hand, Article 79 of the Constitution is a separate head of jurisdiction and, therefore, subject to autonomous interpretation. And that means that 'a normative act' within the meaning of Article 79(1) of the Constitution may not only be a normative act issued by one of the organs of the Polish state, but also—if the additional requirements are met—a legal act issued by an organ of an international organisation, provided that the Republic of Poland is a member thereof. This primarily concerns the acts of EU law enacted by EU institutions.

---

[30] The relevant excerpt is to be found in the opening part of point 8.2 of the judgment: 'The TK notes that there is a need to determine, for the future, the manner of reviewing the constitutionality of the norms of EU law (the Treaties and secondary legislation) in the course of review proceedings commenced by way of constitutional complaint' and identically in Polish original 'Trybunał Konstytucyjny dostrzega potrzebę wyznaczenia na przyszłość sposobu kontroli zgodności z Konstytucją norm prawa unijnego (traktatowego i prawa pochodnego) w trybie skargi konstytucyjnej'.

They constitute part of the legal system which is binding in Poland and they shape the legal situation of the individual. It is not, however, the end of the story. Following the same logic of interpretation as adopted with regard to Article 79 of the Constitution makes it possible for the issue of constitutionality of EU law to be brought before the TK also via Article 193 of the Constitution. The article empowers each ordinary court to ask the TK questions of the constitutionality of 'normative acts' with the Constitution. Asking questions based on Article 193 of the Constitution constitutes a competence of the TK that is autonomous and independent from Article 188 (1–3), similar to that in the case of Article 79 of the Constitution. If the TK wants to remain consistent, it must adopt analogous interpretation of 'normative acts'. The judgment, while not dealing with this issue directly, contains enough in it to indicate that the scope of both provisions of the Constitution (Article 79 and Article 193) can be interpreted along the same lines. In consequence, all of EU secondary law might be called into question either directly, by the individual constitutional complaint, or indirectly, by the ordinary court's questioning its constitutionality.

As already outlined above, the TK found that EU regulations have all the characteristics of a normative act within the meaning of Article 79(1) of the Constitution. It was able to concede, though, that their special nature as acts coming from the legal order of the EU law, does impact the review carried out by the TK when faced with a (constitutional) complaint about the constitutionality of EU secondary act. A jurisdictional distinction is made between a review by the ECJ and that by the TK. The former is responsible for carrying out the 'ultimate' review of the EU acts' conformity with the Treaties, the latter deals with the conformity of EU regulations with the Constitution. It seems that the existing analysis of this distinction by the TK is perfunctory and pays no more than a lip service to the constitutional role of the ECJ. The attitude of restraint is perfectly understandable in light of the European jurisprudence of the TK which sees the ECJ as a classic international court and rejects any constitutional mooring for the supranationalism talk.[31] What is worrisome about this is that the TK sees the EU as no more than just another international organisation. Such short-sightedness is regrettable. It exposes a paucity of constitutional imagination and a vocabulary that doesn't venture beyond the assertion of the Constitution as the supreme law of the land. While it is incumbent upon EU law to be ready to make concessions to national laws, the national law too must show appreciation for the claims made by EU law. The acceptance of limitations and mutual regard are the things that should define this emerging community.

---

[31] It is of note that M Safjan—former President of the TK—observed after his term of office that dialogue is taking place between constitutional and supranational courts: 'Politics and Constitutional Courts. A Judge's Personal Perspective', *EUI Working Papers* 10/2008 available at <http://cadmus.eui.eu>.

It is important to remember, however, that in the case at hand the TK has distinguished itself with its earlier order in U 6/08 case, in which it held inadmissible the motion for constitutionality of EU law review lodged by the members of Parliament. In stark contrast to the interpretation that prevails in the SK 45/09, in the U 6/08 case, the TK has chosen literal and restrictive interpretation of Article 188, point 1 to 3 of the Constitution. According to the TK, this Article lays down exhaustively the jurisdiction of the TK, and since there is no mention there of EU law as an object of constitutionality review, the TK lacks the requisite power of review. As a result, the TK found inadmissible the motion that draws on the alleged non-constitutionality of the EU act. In case SK 45/09, however, the TK made clear that this dictum does not apply to Article 79 of the Constitution, as it constitutes an autonomous head of jurisdiction, independent from Article 188 point 1 to 3 of the Constitution. As a result, the term 'normative act' has to be given autonomous interpretation for the purpose of Article 79.

It is regrettable that the TK has never explained how it understands the crucial term 'dysfunctionality' as applied to the relations between 'the EU legal order and the Polish one' (point III.2.4 of the judgment). It appears that 'dysfunctionality' might be understood to encompass more than incompatibility, which in the future could give the TK wide latitude for manoeuvre. What stands out here is the strong language used to characterise its function and vocation vis-a-vis the ECJ, stating that when it comes to fundamental matters concerning systemic issues, 'the Court is obligated' (in original '*jest zobowiązany*') to see its position as the court of the last resort. This represents a largely outdated language, and its antagonistic tone is out of place and should have been avoided. It falls to the European constitutionalism to redirect the ongoing discussion away from 'the last resort' logic of those flexing constitutional muscle and towards the constitutional conciliation. Critically constructive and engaging, it should put a premium on constitutional players with courage to 'have and put forward the first word'. The TK wants to have a cake and eat it too, to be a pro-European and open, and maintain the stance of a defensively-minded guardian of the national constitution. This is not a recipe for building a coherent message; cracks and inconsistencies soon become all too obvious. In view of the strong 'sovereignistic fixation' of the TK, that permeates its European jurisprudence, the 'last-word court' language should come as no surprise. Both the Accession judgment of 2005 and the 'Lisbon Treaty' ruling of 2010 are premised on extremely traditional view of the European integration. Poland is sovereign and a Master of the Treaty; Polish Constitution recognises transfer of competences only for the benefit of international organisations, and the EU is seen through the prism of the classic international law. Hierarchy is the order of the day, and only a constitutional court can claim the ultimate power to defend it. In this vision, there is no place for supranationalism and any claim on the part of the ECJ to the original character of EC/EU law is seen as a dangerous aberration, with no basis in the Polish Constitution. The TK acts as a repository of centralised sovereignty and has the single authority for resolving legal questions. It is in the light of such reasoning that references to a multilevel system and plural legal orders should be read. When stakes are high, argument from the sovereignty cancels and trumps all those seen as no more than constitutional hot talk. There is room for one player only: The TK, not the ECJ.

However, it is of some importance that the TK went to great lengths to make it known that it sees its rediscovered subsidiary power of constitutional review of EU law in a wider constitutional context, and that is why it evokes the notions of mutual loyalty and the consequent 'obligation to approach the EU norms with the utmost respect' (point 2.6 of the judgment). This jurisdiction is the *ultimate ratio* reserved by the TK for exceptional cases of serious and irreconcilable conflicts between the constitutional orders of the Republic of Poland and the EU. It is to be resorted to only when all other options to resolve the conflict fail. The pluralist vision of EU law imposes a mutually acceptable interpretation and cooperative application as well as relative autonomies of EU and national laws. It also dictates that contradictions should be eliminated by an interpretation respectful of such autonomy. In this, the TK deftly combines rhetoric of constitutional caution with assurances of friendliness towards Europe, and takes on the task of counterbalancing one against the other. The former is demonstrated by underlining the independent character of its constitutional review of EU acts, the latter by the subsidiary nature of this review in relation to the ECJ. This counterbalancing is a crucial part of the TK's reasoning as it provides important constraints on its power to examine EU law.

The recognition of the division of the jurisdiction with regard to the review of legal acts is of great importance. The TK does not, though, stop there, and it characterises as exclusive its power to determine the conformity of the EU acts with the Treaty and with the general principles of law.[32] Bearing in mind the egos and ambitions of constitutional courts, these concessions, at least in the sphere of language, are considerable and worthy of appreciation. The language will surely find attentive ears on Kirchberg as it clearly echoes the cherished rhetoric of the EU rule of law, and alludes to the ECJ's mandate of ensuring that in the interpretation and application of the Treaty the law is respected (Article 19 TEU). It also stands for express acceptance of the '*Foto-Frost*' doctrine of the ECJ, and this augurs well for the future. The fact that the TK takes seriously the exclusive jurisdiction of the ECJ and accepts it as a building block of the EU legal edifice, must not be underestimated. Remembering how dear '*Foto-Frost*' is to the ECJ, such recognition on the part of the TK is a small but significant sign that it is ready to play European game in a loyal fashion, and that, indeed, it may be prepared to match its actions with its rhetoric. To prove it, the TK crosses the 'jurisdictional Rubicon' and breaks silence on the question of its willing to refer preliminary rulings

---

[32] We should bear in mind that the TK has already accepted that ruling on collisions between domestic law and EU law lies within exclusive jurisdiction of ordinary courts. It is thus inadmissible for the ordinary courts to refer to the TK questions on the compatibility of national law with EU law— TK's Order of 19 December 2006 in case P 37/05.

questions to the ECJ.[33] In a gesture of good will that seems ground-breaking, the TK now accepts that prior to adjudicating on non-conformity with the Constitution of an act of EU secondary legislation, the content of its norms subject to review should be clarified. According to the TK

> this may be achieved by referring questions to the ECJ for a preliminary ruling in accordance with Art 267 TFEU, which deals with the interpretation and validity of provisions that raise doubts.[34]

It is therefore a good sign that the TK finally accepts the possibility of referral since it is here that these conciliatory gestures will be given a practical test. Should, in the future, the TK proceed to declare the EU act invalid, without giving the ECJ chance to address the issue pre-emptively, the gestures would be nothing more than constitutional rhetoric devoid of substance. Should it, on the other hand, be willing to consult the ECJ and to ask for guidance, that would then be a sign that the TK is serious about Europe as a common project managed by different, mutually respecting courts, deferring when necessary to one another.

In the SK 45/09, however, the TK applies the *acte claire* doctrine and argues, rather laconically, that there is no reason to refer the case to the ECJ in the present case (conclusion at point 8.1). It remains to be seen what approach to the preliminary ruling procedure the TK would ultimately choose. Would it act to forestall a conflict and give the ECJ an opportunity to address constitutional doubts before they turn out into an all-out war, or would it be inclined to use its subsidiary jurisdiction to the full, signalling its independence of the *ex-ante* referral under Article 267 TFEU? The SK 45/09 case does not provide a clear answer. Only once does the TK mention Article 267 of the TFEU, and does it in a succinct obiter dictum.[35]

The TK's willingness to cooperate with the ECJ must be now put to the test. Will it do as it says, within the context of real disputes? Will it show its readiness to become one of the players in the cosmopolitan world? Interestingly enough, the

---

[33] For the importance of the preliminary rulings see also internal study commissioned by the TK with its Office of Case Law and Studies—'Relacje między prawem konstytucyjnym a prawem wspólnotowym w orzecznictwie sądów konstytucyjnych państw Unii Europejskiej' [Relationship between Constitutional and Community Law in the case law of the Constitutional Courts of the European Union]. Text available online at <www.trybunal.gov.pl>.

[34] Point 2.6 of the judgment. In this way the TK joins the growing list of the constitutional courts willing to refer cases to the ECJ. For the Italian Constitutional Court see order of 12 February 2008 (Case 102/2008 and 103/2008) with commentary by L Serena Rossi in (2008) 46 *Common Market Law Review* 319; for the Austrian Court see judgment of the *Verfassungsgerichtshof* of 13 December 2001 (case B 2251/97) as recapitulated at the TK's study cited in preceding note, at 17; for Belgian referral see Case C-303/05, *Advocaten voor de Wereld* [2007] ECR I-3633; for Lithuanian example see Case C-239/07, *Julius Sabatauskas* [2008] ECR I-7523.

[35] In the case law predating the case SK 45/09, the preliminary ruling mechanism was regarded by the TK as an important component of the EU system of legal protection. See the order of 19 December 2006 in case P 37/05 and more recently judgment (Full Court) of 18 February 2009 in Kp 3/08. Preliminary ruling is defined by the TK in P 37/05 as 'an *essential* mechanism for judicial cooperation between the courts of member states and the ECJ which is based on the *subtle* distinction between interpretation and application of law, the former being also the province of the ECJ, whereas the latter belonging to the national judge' (my emphasis).

TK made an obiter dicta regarding the granting of powers to particular Member States to declare the norms of the EU law (invalid). Such powers should no longer be legally binding since they run counter to the principle of sincere cooperation which, according to the TK, is one of the systemic principles of EU law. Yet, this is exactly what the TK has done in the judgment, and no amount of its rhetorical nods to the pro-European interpretation—(the recognition of the ECJ and the importance of cooperation with it, or the emphasis on the jurisdictional due caution and restraint, when exercising the jurisdiction to examine EU law)—can change that. What counts in the end is the constitutional message, and it clearly remains that of 'I am the guardian of the Polish legal system'. And that's the crux of the matter. We are not dealing with a normative question, but rather with the lack of trust on the part of constitutional judges in the performance of the ECJ. For them, the question comes down to: Can the ECJ be trusted with the task of reviewing EU acts?

With the TK's high praise for the judicial dialogue between the ECJ and the ordinary courts of Member States, and its acceptance of the preliminary rulings as the driving force of integration through law, the time has come for a more fundamental and universal assessment of the judgment under consideration. Namely, what is the TK's view of its national mandate vis-a-vis its European counterpart? The TK takes a fairly liberal stance on its relationship with the ECJ. The English translation of the judgment talks of excluding the 'juxtaposition of both Courts as competing with each other' (point 2.4 of the judgment). The translation doesn't quite do justice to the original, which speaks unequivocally of the unacceptability of a competitive relationship between the two courts. It is also of note that the Polish original of the judgment uses the term 'two-track adjudication' (original has it literally as '*dwutorowość orzekania*'), and the English version renders it, inaccurately, as 'concurrent'. The TK wishes to exclude from case law two divergent lines that could be developed by both courts, but not necessarily simultaneously, as the word 'concurrent' suggests. Therefore, it is the discrepancy which is of concern to the TK, and not the concurrence. The TK's aim clearly is to eliminate overlapping and incompatible judgments. The positioning of both courts on this issue, as projected by the TK, is nothing short of commendable. Yet, it has not had any bearing on the state of affairs, since the very idea of subsidiary jurisdiction, which the SK 45/09 judgment upholds, creates a potential for overlap and divergence. It might be more appropriate and, certainly, more realistic to agree that both courts would compete, via dialogue, for the best possible interpretation, and the interpretation would be the focal point for both. Such a conclusion is inevitably prompted by the principled language on the hierarchy between orders, which in the end would play a decisive role in solving conflicts.

The point of departure and the assumptions made at the beginning of one's road define one's choices on the road. And that is exactly the case with the TK. Its rhetoric aside, the SK 45/09 judgment leaves no doubt that the TK is ready to resort to its emergency competence, should the circumstances arise. One should not be misled by its nice gestures and words; it is the constitutional substance that count(s). The certainty flows unambiguously from the European jurisprudence the TK has built so far. Its assurances of good will, sympathetic interpretation and common axiology notwithstanding, the TK is overwhelmingly devoted to a highly traditional conception of the Polish constitution and its role, enhanced by the language of fear and suspicion, as the guardian of the Polish legal system. Here, the sting is in the tail, for the TK's guardianship of the Polish Constitution is, most crucially, not framed as simply an option, but conveyed in a strong language of an 'obligation' to act in accordance with the status of the 'court of last word'. This pronouncedly antagonistic and bellicose stance was already reflected in obiter dictum in the P 37/05[36] case which stressed the role of ordinary courts as the European courts of first contact for solving conflicts between statutes and EU law. It was furthermore reiterated with confidence in the SK 35/09 case where it formed the heart of the TK's reasoning. Whereas in this last case the TK eventually stepped back, in the SK 45/09 case it regained attention and a rebel stage.

These vacillations corroborate the image of the TK in flux, still searching for its place and voice. The combination of the pro-European elements with some circumspect and guarded statements seems to indicate that the arguments which shape the emerging European jurisprudence of the TK are far from homogenous. As noted correctly by W Sadurski, these arguments do not point firmly towards a single direction. Rather, they reflect the constitutional judges' uncertainty, hesitations and a genuine lack of confidence in coping with the new reality.[37] This affliction is common to the new Member States: Hybrid judgments that combine the pro-European elements (accession importance and the compliance pull of new obligations), with tentative red lights for the future of the integration project.

C. Searching for the Right Constitutional Fit

With the SK 45/09 judgment the TK sends an unambiguous message to the ECJ. Its traditional mission is to remain as it has been, and should be taken seriously by the EU. It is submitted here that the TK chose the wrong path for asserting its authority vis-a-vis the ECJ. Once the national constitutional supremacy ceases to be a matter solely of national legal practice and national constitutions lose their attribute of exclusivity, then the supremacy of EU law will increasingly become an element of national legal practice. And the TK, now an actor and a player, will become competent to modify accordingly the rules of the game and the constitutional practice. With this in mind, it should be quite reasonable to expect the TK to cease its claim on competence within the sphere of conferral since such conferral presupposes the EU mechanism taking over and owning the field. Within this sphere, the issue of national supremacy is moot. The states have conferred on the

---

[36] Order of 19 December 2006, case No P 37/05.

[37] W Sadurski, *Constitutionalism and the Enlargement of Europe* (Oxford University Press, 2010) 132.

EU certain competences, among them the power of the ECJ to police these competences as a matter of EU law. Poland's acceptance of the *acquis* and *Foto-Frost* is beyond doubt and was never questioned during the accession talks.[38] The TK's judgment confirms, in no uncertain terms, its rejection of inclusive inter-systemic interactions, and its insistence on exclusiveness (between law and territory and state-centred thinking).

In order to put forward an alternative model for the TK that would enable it to make a reasonable compromise between its notion of traditional guardianship of the state constitution on the one hand, and the fidelity to the European constitutional text on the other, one is invited to venture *beyond* the case at hand. The TK's inflexible *conclusion* s (positive assertion of jurisdiction) as opposed to the flexible *reasons* do not sit easily with the constitutional reading of the European system of governance through the courts, none of which enjoys the power of the last word in conflicts arising from the divergent interpretations of rights. In this system, the legitimisation is found in a discourse of many. They compete for a judicial protection and, along the way, through a judicial dialogue marked by cooperation and competition, change, develop and accommodate.[39] The TK does not seem to be ready to embrace the fact that EU law imposes change on the constitutional courts and relegates them to the status of courts of local law. These courts lack the competence to review the constitutionality of EU acts, save for one occasion—the accession.[40] Following accession, the EU law becomes a de facto subsystem of national law, excluded from the jurisdiction of the national constitutional court. The constitutional review cannot function as a substitute for control at the EU level. It does not, of course, mean that a constitutional court is condemned to being a passive spectator. Quite the contrary, its function is to minimise the dangers of discrepancy and fractiousness by moulding the pro-European interpretation of the Constitution and paying due regard to the principles established in the case law of the ECJ. The interpretation of the Polish Constitution should now be supplemented by the European axiology, for it stands to enrich the meaning of terms such as proportionality, freedom of commerce, abuse or discrimination. The TK's approach must be pragmatic and flexible, focused on

[38] It might be interesting to inform the foreign audience that the reporting judge on the case (Professor S Biernat) wrote extra-judicially (long before he became a judge of the TK) that EU secondary law should not be the subject of constitutionality review exercised by the TK. See his 'Miejsce prawa pochodnego Wspólnoty Europejskiej w systemie konstucyjnym Rzeczpospolitej Polskiej' [Place of EC secondary law in the Polish legal system] in C Mik (ed), *Konstytucja Rzeczpospolitej Polskiej z 1997 roku a członkostwo Polski w Unii Europejskiej* [*Polish Constitution of 1997 and Poland's EU membership*] (ToNIK, 1999) 185–86.

[39] A Stone Sweet, 'A Cosmopolitan Legal Order: Constitutional Pluralism and Rights Adjudication in Europe' (2012) 1 *Journal of Global Constitutionalism* 53.

[40] See E Łętowska, 'Le droit Européen face aux Cours constitutionnelles des Etats members: la possibilité d'une revision implicite de la Constitution' in M Granat (ed), *Stosowanie prawa międzynarodowego i wspólnotowego w wewnętrznym porządku prawnym Francji, Polski: L'application du droit international et communautaire dans l'ordre juridique interne en France et en Pologne* (Wydawnictwo Sejmowe, 2007) 143–46.

avoiding an outright dispute. The EU law doesn't make demands on explicit revision of the Polish Constitution; its interest is in its implicit revision, via new axiology addition, nuanced constitutional interpretation, and discovery of ways to strike a reasonable compromise between the 'constitutional' and the 'European'. It is a mental process, no less important than a change in legal text. Polish lawyers suffer from a textual disease—text must at all times reflect the change, otherwise it lacks legal relevance. Their focus should instead be on acquiring skills needed for reflections on change through wise and anticipatory interpretation that builds on general principles and common sense.

On its face, case SK 45/09 marks a considerable step forward for the TK in reasoning, when compared with the '*Lisbon* decision'. The latter was replete with inconsistencies, repetitions and self-contradictions that bordered on arbitrariness. The message the TK sends in SK 45/09 is phrased in a much more disciplined way. Its focus is on balancing the effectiveness of its jurisdictional mandate with assuring that the integrity of EU law and the powers of the ECJ are not hastily undermined. The TK seems to understand the catastrophic consequences that the declaration of the invalidity of the EU law in Poland would have for its future relationship with the Luxembourg Court. There is no doubt that sooner rather than later the TK would be called on to clarify standards for constitutional review of EU acts. That would be the moment for putting its assurances of good will and loyalty to a critical test. The open question, however, would be how a disagreement would be construed.

For now, the TK's judgment still remains firmly rooted in the traditional conception of state constitutionalism. In SK 45/06, the TK remained faithful to the constitutional narrative, though it did show signs of being ready to shape and adapt it in response to the demands of the external pluralist world. These two perspectives are unlikely to be reconciled unless the TK does the unthinkable and renounces the Constitution as the ultimate source of constitutional empowerment. At present, the TK's focus is elsewhere, on laying down foundations for defensively minded structural judicial review. A cosmopolitan legal order, highly nuanced and ambitious, demands constitutional engagement and problematisation. The system strives to move beyond the dilemma of hierarchy and a single court with the universal power of the last word on the question of legal validity. It faces the world of 'disorder of normative orders'[41] that impinge on and penetrate each other in ways more intensive and complex than those in the TK's version of a multi-centric world. Seen from this perspective, the TK follows in the footsteps of its European jurisprudence. Decision to give up powers of review of EU acts was for the TK in theory conceivable, and legally defensible, but not realistic in view of its present understanding of its role in the EU. Rather, the TK did what it should

---

[41] N Walker, 'Beyond Boundary Disputes and Basic Grids. Mapping the Global Disorder of Normative Orders' (2008) 6 *International Journal of Constitutional Law* 373.

have done. Its positive assertion of the jurisdiction undermines all subsequent gestures of good will towards EU law. For the TK it is the crunch time of asserting the competence of constitutional review of EU acts that really matters. At crunch time the TK's reasoning was dominated by the defence of democratic statism connecting constitutionalism with the tradition of statehood and sovereignty.[42] A more pragmatic and less dogmatic approach would show the TK a route of escape from the simplicity of argument that conferral of competences must be equivalent to upholding the states' right to police the borders of the conferral. It would put forward the proposition that conferral of the competences leads to an internal change in the Constitution and the role of the TK.[43] National anchoring of the integration into the Constitution does not ineluctably lead to the conclusion that the competence stays with the TK. Bearing in mind the fact that fundamental rights protected at the level of the EU find their source, among others, in the constitutional traditions of the member states, the risk of conflict is hypothetical and overblown. As a result the TK has made a wrong choice of instruments to ensure that its voice is heard. Altogether, equally plausible was the TK's assertion that faced with the possibility of a conflict between the EU legal acts and Polish Constitution, it had to be ready to refer questions to the ECJ straight away without triggering its own control mechanism and engaging in substantive review.

III. Polish *Trybunał Konstytucyjny: Still* Court of Old Closures or of *Already* New Openings?

With regard to the TK, it is yet unknown how it will build on its jurisprudence in order to exert a formative influence on how things will be done at the EU level. When analysed separately, the 'European judgments' of the TK open up promising new vistas. Yet doubts linger as to the possible bumps and U-turns. The Polish case law shows varying degrees of judicial self-confidence and different forms of institutional self-conception, combining trust with distrust. Going forward, the TK must realise that it is the courtroom that is fast becoming a forum for a difficult dialogue with the outside world, a dialogue in which every participant is ready to defer to the other. By sticking to the language of 'Member States as Masters of the Treaty' and the inflexible interpretation of the outdated concepts, such as sovereignty and inviolable constitutional core, it falls short of explaining the reality of the constitutional maze replete with various and credible claims to respect and

---

[42] M Kumm, 'The Best of Times and the Worst of Times. Between Constitutional Triumphalism and Nostalgia' in P Dobner and M Loughlin (eds), *The Twilight of Constitutionalism* (Oxford University Press, 2010) 203.

[43] For critical commentary on the judgment see the case note by P Bogdanowicz and P Marcisz, 'Szukając granic kontroli' [Searching for the limits of constitutional review] *Europejski Przegląd Sądowy* no 9/2012.

validity. The problem with the TK is that it is not sure if it can play at 'European constitutionalism', managing its constitutional ego and ambitions while simultaneously becoming a serious voice in the European legal space.

The challenge lies in breaking the paradigmatic self-vision of the TK as a defensive guardian of the Polish Constitution, slavishly followed by the Polish legal doctrine. As long as this vision persists, the TK will be unable to rethink the outdated axioms and take the discourse to the next conceptual level. Without postulated *shift* from the internal (the inward perspective of the Constitution) towards the external, the TK risks marginalisation and loss of influence on the way European law enters and penetrates the Polish constitutional order. The shift would encompass opening to and absorbing of the European constitution; *changing the language* (finding common ground and linking the network nodes instead of separating and underlining divergences); adapting to a new logic (not only the ever-present 'either … or' but also 'both … and') and learning to problematise reality. To harness the change, the TK must recognise the value of balancing on a case-by-case basis constitutional arguments against European integration, avoid general and abstract principles which might tie its hands in the future and deprive it of breathing room in its interactions with the ECJ as well as problematise and contextualise its European case law and review functions.

The true role of the TK in exercising these review functions is that of monitoring European integration and the ECJ by way of reasonable and foreseeable constitutional constraints placed on the integration project. The parameters of the game should be set down clearly by the TK, and all actors should know in advance how far they can take their respective case law and systemic claims without breaking down the fragile equilibrium of European constitutional space in *statu nascendi*. The constitutional interpretation should be set within the limits set by the European context. Such interpretation should build an acceptable compromise between a reasonable *deference* towards the ECJ and EU law on the one hand, and a legitimising, constructive and acceptable *defiance* on the other. Of special significance for Poland would be to focus the constitutional debate on the comity of the courts, transcending the established and universally recognised 'community of courts'.[44] Such comity acts as a decentralised sovereign within a new kind of polity—a cosmopolitan legal order characterised by legal pluralism, where no system, no single organ possesses the 'final word' in a conflict between divergent interpretations. Instead, the system would develop through inter-court dialogue, both cooperative and competitive. The Constitutional pluralism teaches us that there is a necessary overlap of legal sources without *ex ante* hierarchy and 'it is the individual who has a choice which source to plead and the judges who have a choice of the Right to enforce'.[45]

---

[44] A D'Alterio, 'From Judicial Comity to Legal Comity: A Judicial Solution to Global Disorder?' *Jean Monnet Working Paper* no 13/10.

[45] Stone Sweet (n 39) 53 (capital R in the original).

At present, there is yet little in terms of case law to make any definitive statements on the shape the TK's jurisdiction would take, and the direction it would go. Uncertainty, hesitation and genuine lack of confidence are still palpable all over its case law, which makes it hard to distinguish the emerging tendencies from the mere incidents.[46] For the genuine cooperative constitutionalism[47] to materialise, and be worthy of its name, what really counts is not *what* the court says but *how* it plays and *what* it does. The TK must speak, argue and break new grounds. When its voice is heard, the ECJ would act accordingly and shape its case law with the TK's concerns in mind. In the end, the concerns might be either upheld (nod to diversity) or discarded (nod to uniformity), but never ignored. This is no zero-sum game: Every actor, be it a constitutional one or the ECJ, would be positioned to win in these never-ending constitutional disagreements.

As the process moves forward, the TK is going to be confronted with a formidable challenge of making sure that divergent strands of its case law fit the overarching principle of European friendliness. It must come to terms with the fact that the European integration has made it a political actor, and put a premium on its actions. To meet the challenges of the integration, the TK has to become a court that calculates, anticipates, plans ahead, makes choices, speaks to various audiences all at the same time (both Euro-enthusiasts and Euro-sceptics) and manoeuvres deftly between the pro-European result and the Euro-sceptic reasoning. It is also crucial for the TK to absorb the legal change around it and accommodate its case law accordingly. It must speak up and make its understanding of European law known to all the parties concerned. Being Euro-friendly calls for more than a simple 'pro-European interpretation' alternative (role of courts) or explicit revision of constitution (role of the political process). In between there is a grey area where more problematisation is called for, going beyond a simple revision of the constitutional text to an engaging revision of axiology or constitutional interpretation,[48] and linking courts with parliaments.[49] A 'grey area' calls for broadening the constitutional perspective, for more action and for conflict pre-emption and not a mere ex post reaction, for adaptation, not subjugation, for learning, not imposing,

---

[46] Sadurski (n 37) 132, 140.

[47] Term from O Pollicino, 'The New Relationship between National and the European Courts after the Enlargement of Europe: Towards a Unitary Theory of Jurisprudential Supranational Law?' (2010) 29 *Yearbook of European Law* 65.

[48] Wonderful example of a more nuanced approach is provided in judgment of 21 April 2004 (case K 33/03—bio-components in gasoline and diesel) and in a dictum contained therein: 'while reconstructing the constitutional benchmark for review, regard must be had not only to the statutory provision which refers to terminology, concepts and principles of European law, but also the meaning given to these concepts and principles in the acquis communautaire of the united Europe' and that 'rules and principles of the Community law have an impact on the freedom of economic activity of the actors on the domestic market' (para 10 of the judgment, translated by the author). For English excerpts see *Summaries of selected judgments of the Polish Constitutional Court concerning EU law* (Polish Constitutional Court, 2006) 250–55.

[49] D Piqani, 'Arguments for a Holistic Approach in European Constitutionalism: What Role for National Institutions in Avoiding Constitutional Conflicts between National Constitutions and EU Law' (2012) 8 *European Constitutional Law Review* 493.

for discursive incorporation, rather than a one-way traffic.[50] When the TK plays a strategic game, it should act accordingly, be cautious in its choice of words used, circumspect in solving issues necessary for the disposal of the case at hand, and always leave some issues open for future litigations. The message at the level of words might be strongly anti-European, with warnings and red lights, yet it would be equally important what actions the TK would be ready to take in conjunction with these words, and how far it would go. The sphere of actions opens up a new world of possibilities and interpretations, and that is exactly where the true power of words is tested. Every European decision of the TK has been characterised as either EU-friendly or EU-critical, as activist or restrained, sovereignty-centred or integration-conducive. In the real world of constitutional politics, things are seldom that clear-cut and unambiguous. The TK can never satisfy everybody, and it must play to each audience and pick and choose judiciously among plausible interpretations of the constitutional text.

The key issues shaping current debates in the West are diversity, deference, postnational perspective and accommodation. The concepts of sovereignty, constitutional absolutism and classic supranationalism have been steadily losing ground in its discourse. These concepts remain, however, of great import for the Polish constitutional doctrine. Insistence on constitutional uniqueness, hierarchy and sovereignty robs the TK of the resolve and tools to tackle important emerging problems. The TK shows no interest in breaking new ground, or, at the very least, in ditching hollow presuppositions or contemplating their alternatives. It has thus condemned itself to passivity and the interpretation of the Constitution from the inside, rather than from the outside. The TK finds itself today at a crossroads and critical juncture.[51] Should it lead the way as a constructive interlocutor or play a constant game of catch-up as a backward trouble-maker which is not sufficiently pro-European? A good constitutional court must understand that being faithful to its own Constitution is no longer a decisive factor in the overall assessment of its mandate and performance. Such a court must absorb the legal change around it and adapt its case law accordingly. It should be ready to recognize its political function and build on its *'political jurisprudence'* to find compromise solutions going beyond simply declaring one party the winner.[52] The ensuing constitutional

---

[50] As rightly remarked by E Łętowska (n 40) 149, 'constitutional courts' virtues of flexibility and creativity are a challenge to their professional efficiency'.

[51] Understood 'as rupture in norms and practices that starts a social system down a new but unpredictable path'—A Stone Sweet, 'The Juridical Coup d'État and the Problem of Authority' (2007) 8 *German Law Journal* 915, 927.

[52] I argue here that the concept of *'political jurisprudence'* as elaborated by M Shapiro could help TK better understand, and come to terms with, its role as a political player which both shapes the contours of European constitutionalism and keeps it under constitutional check. Of special explanatory relevance here would be M Shapiro's understanding of courts as institutions engaged in a process of incremental policy change that is in His own words 'lines of precedent that do not reflect fluctuations around a locus of principle, but *as the record of series of marginal adjustments designed to meet changing circumstances'* (emphasis added). This is exactly what we should expect of Polish TK moving forward.

bargaining should not be just about the result. It should be more process- and argument-oriented. The European constitutionalism should not be seen as an enemy of the national constitutionalism but rather as its constructive and critical interlocutor and any disagreements should take place in the spirit of judicial comity. Any conclusive statements on the contours of this comity must be preceded by one crucial caveat. The comity brings together two perspectives which sometimes make the whole rather blurry and in danger of failing apart. One perspective reflects the TK's perception of itself looking from within, the other is its interpretation from the outside. The meeting of the two can result in the inspirational potential, provided, however, that the internal is ready to be tested critically from the outside and change accordingly. It is this kind of opening as opposed to a defensive closure that we should expect of the TK in a near future.

The TK and Polish doctrine of constitutional law must put constitutional case law and that of EU in the context of the European-wide debate. For the moment, Polish constitutionalists choose to remain in the comfortable zone of their Constitution. This hampers their ability to feed off its doctrine. A pro-European interpretation of national law is as far as they are willing to go. What is desperately needed in Poland is a legal interpretation that imbues European dialogue with a constitutional imagination understood as a 'bundle of impression and images, which can be found, not merely in statutes and cases, but in a myriad of texts and treatises'.[53] Constitutional imagination is not about solving cases *here and now* but about anticipating the next step, building strategies for the future and accommodating itself within the broader community. Constitutional imagination is not constructed by a single decision. It takes many decisions to shape it. The future 'essential jurisprudence'[54] of the TK should be defined by its willingness to balance its constitution against European claims in the spirit of constitutional imagination. Constitutional imagination calls on the constitutional courts to practise the art of anticipation, reconciliation of divergent interests and true constitutional synthesis *in the days to come*. Only such constitutional reconstruction can respond to the exigencies of today's world.

Both the opening and the closure function as two levels of the judicial message. As the case law grows, the 'what you say' level circumscribes to an ever-growing extent the TK's discretion at the 'what you do' level. The TK could aspire to be a court of old closures at the level of rhetoric, while at the same time be a court of new openings at the level of actions, although the latter is much more difficult when the constitutional lines are carefully drawn. More closure means less room

---

See M Shapiro, *Stability and change in Judicial Decision-Making: Incrementalism or Stare Decisis?* (1965) 2 *Law in Transition Quarterly* 134 at 142 and his ground-breaking *Politics in the Supreme Court: New Approaches to Political Jurisprudence*, (New York, 1964).

[53] I Ward, 'A Charmed Spectacle: England and its Constitutional Imagination' (2000) 22 *Liverpool Law Review* 235.

[54] I borrow the term from JHH Weiler, 'The Essential (and Would-be Essential) Jurisprudence of the European Court of Justice: Lights and Shadows too' in I Pernice, J Kokott and C Saunders (eds), *The Future of the European Judicial System in a Comparative Perspective* (Nomos, 2005).

for opening. So far, in the 'invalidity case' examined in this chapter, when it really mattered, the TK acted as a court of old closures at the level of rhetoric. It remains to be seen if it will also be a court of new openings at the level of 'what you do' when confronted with the inevitable challenges to EU law. Ideally, a court should strive to be one of new openings at both the rhetoric ('what') and the action ('do') levels. It may prove to be too high of an expectation for a constitutional court. But adopting a 'new opening approach', at least at one of the levels is something that can be built on moving forward. Therefore, our logic should not be 'old closures *or* new openings' but rather 'old closures *and* new openings'. The time for moving decisively toward opening and only opening has not yet come and possibly, in view of the elusiveness and incrementalism of constitutional politics, it might never come!

There is no doubt that the TK is torn and hesitant right now as it searches for the right equilibrium, voice and place. It is facing a crucial institutional question of self-conception: What it *should* become as opposed to what *it is* now. This question becomes even more imperative with the advent of a novel kind of constitutional litigation centred not so much on fundamental rights but rather on a vague concept of constitutional features of domestic legal systems.[55] Today, the EU and the domestic laws, interconnected more than ever, set themselves on the road towards a new version of *Van Gend en Loos 2*, this time bringing together vigilant constitutional courts. Taking its cue from the opening citation of Ryszard Kapuściński, the emerging comity of courts must work on the assumption that courts should learn from each other's decisions, in addition to serving as sources of inspiration. The perspective of 'The Other' should help the courts contributing to the ongoing constitutional debate, change their ways and methods of thinking and, in the end, help them open up. Only then will we have a chance of finally embracing 'The Other'. Looking from this perspective, the genuine constitutional synthesis worthy of the name still awaits the TK. For the time being, it remains a court of old closures, seeing its vocation as a protector of the home turf against the Other, with only occasional and hesitant opening(s) towards 'The Other'. The stakes of the challenge to re-imagine itself could not be higher for the TK: Rediscover itself or sink into oblivion. By way of a tentatively (hopeful!) conclusion then: 'Polish constitutional chain novel is to be continued...'

---

[55] G van der Schyff, 'The Constitutional Relationship between the European Union and its Member States: The Role of National Identity in Article 4(2) TEU' (2013) 37 *European Law Review* 563.

15

Constitutional Sovereignty in Post-Sovereign Jurisprudence of the Czech Constitutional Court: From the Lisbon Judgments to the Landtová Ultra Vires Controversy

JIŘÍ PŘIBÁŇ[*]

I. Introduction

In this chapter, I discuss the persistence of the semantics of sovereignty in the EU and use recent constitutional developments and conflicts in the Czech Republic as its example. After a brief description of the sovereignty's persistence and resurgence in Member States of the EU, I focus on recent constitutional conflicts between different branches of constitutional power in the Czech Republic and eventually between the *Ústavní soud* (Czech Constitutional Court, hereinafter ÚS) and the Court of Justice (hereinafter ECJ). I analyse various uses of the concept of sovereignty employed in the Lisbon Treaty case by the Treaty's critics and the ÚS itself. These conceptualisations have their external context and define the ÚS's relationship to the EU and its institutions, most notably the ECJ.

Furthermore, I describe how the ÚS gradually moved from basic conceptualisations of sovereignty, such as in the *Sugar Quota III* judgment, to more complex and theoretically challenging definitions in the Lisbon Treaty judgments. Comparatively analysing the ÚS's *Lisbon I* and *Lisbon II* judgments and the *Bundesverfassungsgericht*'s (German Federal Constitutional Court, hereinafter BVerfG) *Lisbon* judgment, I argue that the ÚS actually addresses profound questions of constitutional sovereignty in global society typical of legal and political systems evolving beyond the organisational framework of the sovereign constitutional state.

[*] Some sections of this chapter use material previously published in the article 'The Semantics of Constitutional Sovereignty in Post-Sovereign "New" Europe: A Case Study of the Czech Constitutional Court's Jurisprudence' published in (2015) 13(1) *International Journal of Constitutional Theory* 180–99.

The ÚS perceives sovereignty as part of political and legal globalisation and considers it an instrument of achieving the post-national rule of law and constitutional accountability beyond classical notions of power politics and state organisation. Nevertheless, the ÚS does not shy away from using the constitutional sovereignty argument in the most robust ways, as proved by the *Holubec* case, and thus reasserting its powers against both the EU and national judicial bodies. While criticised as incoherent in terms of reasoning and inconsistent with the ÚS's previous reasoning, this case persuasively demonstrates that the *Kompetenz der Kompetenz* question replicates the paradox of sovereignty having the exclusive form and legal force of a constitution, yet exceeding the logic of legal reasoning and positive laws by the ultimate decision making power.

Instead of tracking the logic of constitutional reasoning and its possible incoherence and contradictions in the context of the ÚS's history of decision making, I pursue the goal of demonstrating that this complex practice and engagement of the ÚS in debates regarding the concept of sovereignty and its changing meaning in legal and political globalisation and supranationalism, of which the EU is a prime example, has its intrinsic jurisprudential context and belongs to the ÚS's tradition of fundamental value judgements and interventions.

II. A Sort of European Prelude: On Sovereign Nations, Constitutional Nationalisms and the Nation States of the EU

The Euro-crisis of 2010 revealed the vulnerability of the EU's common currency, this most striking example of supranational limitation of state sovereignty by economic means, and prompted a series of vitriolic media attacks and a revival of extremely strong nationalist resentments among Greeks, Germans and other EU nations.[1] The system of European economy and its administrative supranational governance thus became responsible for an avalanche of modern nationalist prejudices, once again proving that modernity evolves as a parallel growth of instrumental rationality and what Max Weber referred to as a 'new polytheism' and 'the coming wars of the gods'.

The acrimonious Belgian constitutional crisis, devolution politics and persisting ethno-nationalisms in parts of the United Kingdom, traditional nationalism and recent ethno-terrorist campaigns in the Basque country and Corsica also show that the typically modern claim to national sovereignty has not disappeared

---

[1] For the German media's stereotypical portrayal of 'the lazy and corrupt Greeks' contrasted to the hardworking German citizens, see, for instance, H Bickes, T Otten and L Chelsea Weymann, 'The *Financial Crisis* in the German and English Press: Metaphorical Structures in the Media Coverage on Greece, Spain and Italy' (2014) 25(4) *Discourse & Society* 424.

but often reinvented itself as a politics of ethnic identity, self-determination and self-government in the post-national and post-sovereign EU constellation.

The self-limitation of nation-state sovereignty within the EU does not necessarily weaken collective aspirations for some level of, if not full, sovereignty over historically and ethnically defined territory. The weakening of state sovereignty is accompanied by a reclamation and redefinition of sovereignty beyond the nation state. Sovereignty and identity politics continues to be an important vehicle of formulating new sets of goals, interests and public demands but also different forms of social and political inclusion and exclusion.

Traditional ethnic and national divisions acquire new importance, force and political or constitutional settlements. For instance, the Act of Autonomy granted significant autonomy, especially in taxation and judicial matters, to Catalonia within the Spanish state in 2006. Following this constitutional reform and the subsequent judgment of the Spanish Constitutional Court in June 2010, which declared a number of the Act's articles unconstitutional and ruled that there was no legal basis to recognise the Catalans as a nation and no reason for the Catalan language to take precedence over Spanish,[2] a million-strong crowd protested in Barcelona in July 2010 calling for even greater autonomy, if not independence for Catalonia. The Euro crisis and its devastating effect on the Spanish economy subsequently increased tensions between the Catalonian and central governments and the tide of both economically and culturally driven nationalism has been translated into the most serious constitutional crisis of the Spanish democratic statehood.[3]

More examples of the persistence of nationalism and sovereignty politics are easy to find in other parts of the EU. For instance, following a crushing victory in the Hungarian parliamentary election of April 2010, a new conservative nationalist government led by Prime Minister Viktor Orbán, whose Fidesz party won a constitutional supermajority of seats in Parliament (while a right-wing extremist and openly anti-Semitic and anti-Roma party Jobbik managed to attract 17 per cent of the national vote), announced a constitutional revolution and immediately enacted two laws. Surprisingly, these laws did not deal with the colossal economic problems of the country. One act was aimed at strengthening bonds with ethnic Hungarians living abroad by giving them a chance to acquire Hungarian citizenship. The other act declared June 4—the day in 1920 when the post-war Treaty of Trianon, which ended Hungarian political domination in many parts of the former Habsburg monarchy and decreed that millions of ethnic Hungarians would henceforth live outside the post-1918 Hungarian state, was signed—a 'day of national remembrance'.

---

[2] Constitutional Court of Spain, *Sentencia* STC 031/2010, de 28 de junio de 2010 (BOE núm 172, de 16 de julio de 2010) para 7.
[3] For a more general overview, SL Greer, *Nationalism and Self-Government: Politics of Autonomy in Scotland and Catalonia* (SUNY Press, 2008); for more specific information on the Spanish economic crisis and political mobilisation in Catalonia, see G Rico, 'The 2010 Regional Election in Catalonia: A Multilevel Account in an Age of Economic Crisis' (2012) 17(2) *South European Society and Politics* 217.

More significantly, this nationalist imagination was a driving force behind the constitution making project of the Orbán government resulting in the new Constitution of Hungary which was enacted by Parliament in April 2011 and went into force on 1 January 2012 despite fundamental protests by the Hungarian political opposition parties and European political representations and expert bodies.[4] The new Hungarian Constitution has effectively dismantled republican and liberal achievements of the post-1989 democratic constitutionalism and replaced them with nationalist intuitions and settlement promoting the clientelist authoritarian state.[5] Nevertheless, this settlement was approved by the electorate in the 2014 parliamentary election in which Prime Minister Orbán, following the election law change and Parliament's reconstruction, managed to secure the constitutional majority while the extremist Jobbik party emerged even stronger with 21 per cent of the national vote.

These national identity politics, old and new, show the paradox of both the inadequacy and persistence of national statehood and sovereignty. Traditional control and the solidarity of a state's inhabitants are being questioned in the globalised world of which Europeanisation is just one of many manifestations. However, one does not need examples of stateless forms of ethnic nationalisms in the EU, the rhetorical and legal excesses of contemporary Hungarian nationalists, corrupt Greek elites, the German media and angry crowds on European streets and squares to see that political propaganda and economic or legal reasoning based on the notion of state and national sovereignty remain strong. Despite the ongoing transformation of international law and statehood in European and global society,[6] the semantics of sovereignty persists in both political and legal communication[7] and even thrives within the discourse of emerging European post-sovereign constitutionalism.[8]

III. Sovereignty as Part of European Political and Constitutional Semantics

Apart from democracy and constitutionalism, the semantics of sovereignty continues to shape the systems of positive law and politics and remains one of the formative concepts of both national and post-national political and constitutional

---

[4] See especially 'Opinion on the New Constitution of Hungary: European Commission for Democracy Through Law (Venice Commission)' in GA Tóth (ed), *Constitution for a Disunited Nation: On Hungary's 2011 Fundamental Law* (CEU Press, 2012) 491.

[5] See especially J Kis, 'From the 1989 Constitution to the 2011 Fundamental Law' in Tóth (n 4) 1.

[6] M Koskenniemi, 'The Future of Statehood' (1991) 32 *Harvard International Law Journal* 397.

[7] JL Cohen, *Globalization and Sovereignty. Rethinking Legality, Legitimacy and Constitutionalism* (Cambridge University Press, 2012).

[8] C Schreuer, 'The Waning of the Sovereign State: Towards a New Paradigm of International Law?' (1993) 4 *European Journal of International Law* 447.

constellations. Sovereignty signifies the permanent tension between *de iure* authority and *de facto* power and the paradoxical relationship between the normativity of a legal constitution and the unrestrained political will. It marks the boundary between politics and law and thus highlights the legal context of politics and the political context of law which is not limited by the nation state organisation and stretches to the supranational legal and political institutions of the EU.[9]

Due to its paradoxical and ambivalent nature and close associations with political modernity and constitutional statehood, sovereignty becomes regularly questioned in contemporary theories of globalised politics and law typical of supranational and transnational networks and regimes.[10] Nevertheless, political and legal conflicts and debates in the EU, especially those following post-Maastricht Treaty and post-Amsterdam Treaty integration and enlargement,[11] the process of constitution making and eventually the ratification of the Lisbon Treaty,[12] show that the concept of state and constitutional sovereignty remains highly relevant and no less popular[13] among citizens, peoples, politicians, civil servants and judges living and working in the European post-national and post-sovereign constellation.[14]

In the 1990s, fully committed supporters of European political integration, such as former Prime Minister of Belgium and MEP Leo Tindemans, were already sceptical regarding the federalist state-like EU.[15] More recently, politicians and top judges are also increasingly concerned and even openly speak out against the idea of a supranational EU progressively limiting sovereignty of its Member States in some kind of federal or other state-like constitutional settlement.[16] Through these conflicts and contested decisions, processes and visions, the EU has been evolving

---

[9] N Walker, 'Late Sovereignty in the European Union' in N Walker (ed), *Sovereignty in Transition* (Hart Publishing, 2003) 3–32, 20.

[10] See, for instance, a classic critique by SD Krasner, *Sovereignty, Organized Hypocrisy* (Princeton University Press, 1999).

[11] I Pernice, 'Multilevel Constitutionalism and the Treaty of Amsterdam, European Constitution Making Revisited' (1999) 36 *CML Rev* 703.

[12] A Biondi, P Eeckhout and S Ripley (eds), *EU Law after Lisbon* (Oxford University Press, 2012).

[13] J Hayward and R Wurzel (eds), *European Disunion: Between Sovereignty and Solidarity* (Palgrave, 2012).

[14] J Habermas, *Postnational Constellation: Political Essays* (Polity, 2001); W Wallace, 'Europe after the Cold War: Interstate Order or Postsovereign Regional System?' [1999] 25(5) *Review of International Studies* 201, 217–18.

[15] L Tindemans, 'Dreams Come True, Gradually: The Tindemans Report a Quarter of a Century on' in M Westlake (ed), *The European Union beyond Amsterdam: New Concepts of European Integration* (Routledge, 1998) 130, 139.

[16] See, for instance, Roman Herzog, Germany's former federal President, and Lüder Gerken, *Stop the European Court of Justice* manifesto, EU Observer, 10 September 2008; the UK's problematic relationship with the EU in general and the ECJ in particular is reflected, for instance, in the House of Commons' European Scrutiny Committee and its Forty-Third Report, 2013–14, HC979 'The Application of the EU Charter of Fundamental Rights in the UK: A State of Confusion'; for general comments, see G Conway, *The Limits of Legal Reasoning and the European Court of Justice* (Cambridge University Press, 2012) 83.

into a hybrid pluralistic model contradicting the monistic conception of one exclusive basic norm behind federal statehood but equally stretching far beyond the framework of dualistic theories of international law.[17]

For instance, the notion of a 'transnational constitution' was paradoxically coined by Eric Stein to signify the increasing juridification of the EU and its hierarchical 'federal-type' political structure.[18] However, the current state of the Union, its transnational governance and 'constitutionalism without a Constitution'[19] are far away from the monistic supranational federalist vision of European statehood and the persisting semantics of sovereignty of Member States requires adopting a much more pluralistic and differentiated perspective.

In the current state of the EU, the tirelessly discussed democratic deficit[20] of the Union and potential risks attached to the erosion of the democratic legitimacy and sovereignty of Member States cannot easily be countered by ideas of the governance-based post-sovereign and post-constituent supranational European polity. As regards the EU's Member States and their state sovereignty, in the United Kingdom, for instance, it is not only the tabloids blaming Brussels for all the ills of the British Isles that invoke the special need to defend state sovereignty against the supranational power of the EU. In parliamentary debates, the issue of parliamentary sovereignty is increasingly raised whenever it comes to matters of European integration, foreign policy, immigration, defence, judicial independence and other topics associated with the territorial nation state.[21] Sovereignty, its exercise and democratic constitution are major issues of electoral campaigns, often internally dividing both government and opposition.[22]

In German constitutional debates reflecting on the process of European integration, the *Bundesverfassungsgericht* has famously and repeatedly ruled that constitutional sovereignty and the rights of German citizens take precedence

---

[17] See, for instance, M Borowski, 'Legal Pluralism in the European Union' in AJ Menendez and JE Fossum (eds), *Law and Democracy in Neil MacCormick's Legal and Political Theory: The Post-Sovereign Constellation* (Springer, 2011) 185, 189.

[18] E Stein, 'Lawyers, Judges, and the Making of a Transnational Constitution' (1981) 75 *American Journal of International Law* 1.

[19] A Cohen, 'Constitutionalism Without Constitution: Transnational Élites Between Political Mobilization and Legal Expertise in the Making of a Constitution for Europe (1940s–1960s)' (2007) 32 *Law & Social Inquiry* 109, 113.

[20] See, for instance, B Kohler-Koch and B Rittberger (eds), *Debating the Democratic Legitimacy of the European Union* (Rowman & Littlefield, 2007).

[21] M Elliott, 'United Kingdom: Parliamentary Sovereignty under Pressure' (2004) 2(3) *International Journal of Constitutional Law* 545.

[22] Pre-2010 election discussions and programmes revealed growing Euroscepticism across the whole political spectrum pushing even the traditionally pro-European Liberal Democratic Party to make huge programme concessions as a junior partner of the coalition government. This government subsequently legislated for the European Union Act 2011 which was heavily inspired by the national sovereignty oriented politics. The Act is available at <www.legislation.gov.uk/ukpga/2011/12/contents/enacted/data.htm> [last accessed on 1 December 2014].

over European law. In its classic and endlessly discussed *Maastricht* judgment,[23] the BVerfG controversially stated:

> If the peoples of the individual States (as is true at present) convey democratic legitima-tion via the national parliaments, then limits are imposed, by the principle of democracy, on an extension of the functions and powers of the European Communities. State power in each of the States emanates from the people of that State. The States require sufficient areas of significant responsibility of their own, areas in which the people of the State con-cerned may develop and express itself within a process of forming political will which it legitimates and controls, in order to give legal expression to those matters which concern that people on a relatively homogenous basis spiritually, socially, and politically.[24]

Despite the fact that the judgment echoed Hermann Heller's idea of constitutional democracy and popular sovereignty emanating from social homogeneity,[25] the BVerfG was criticised for promoting the pre-political notion of a nation.[26] How-ever, the BVerfG did not treat the sovereign nation state as an absolute organisation and an existential reservoir of political values and principles. It, rather, considered it an organisation and instrument and guarantee of the democratic selfhood, self-rule, welfare generated by social solidarity and popular government[27]—something the BVerfG summarised in its recent *Lisbon* judgement in the following words:

> Within the order of the Basic Law, the structural principles of the state laid down in Article 20 of the Basic Law, ie democracy, the rule of law, the principle of the social state, the republic, the federal state, as well as the substance of elementary fundamental rights indispensable for the respect of human dignity are, in any case, not amenable to any amendment because of their fundamental quality.[28]

In the German context, the constitutional sovereignty argument was a response to the progressive political and legal integration of the EU in the 1990s.[29] The *Lisbon Judgment* of the BVerfG refers to the state as a democratic primary space and, in the classical dualist view of international law applied to the EU,[30] states that 'the Member States are the constituted primary political area of their respective

[23] See, for instance, M Herdegen, 'Maastricht and the German Constitutional Court: Constitutional Restraints for an "Ever Closer Union"' (1994) 31 *CML Rev* 235; TC Hartley, *European Union Law in a Global Context: Text, Cases and Materials* (Cambridge University Press, 2004) 159–60.

[24] The BVerfG's judgment of 12 October 1993, BVerfGE 89, 155; *Brunner v European Union Treaty* [1994] CMLR 57, s C/I/2/b2.

[25] The Court's reference was: H Heller, *Politische Demokratie und soziale Homogenität, Gesammelte Schriften*, Band II (Leiden, 1971).

[26] JHH Weiler, 'Does Europe Need a Constitution? Demos, Telos and the German Maastricht Deci-sion' (1995) 1(3) *European Law Journal* 219.

[27] For recent theory of the constitutional subject and its identity, see M Rosenfeld, *The Identity of the Constitutional Subject: Selfhood, Citizenship, Culture, and Community* (Routledge, 2009).

[28] The BVerfG's judgment of 30 June 2009, BVerfG, 2 BvE 2/08, para 217. Available at: <www.bverfg. de/entscheidungen/es20090630_2bve000208en.html> [last accessed on 24 January 2014].

[29] DP Kommers and RA Miller, *The Constitutional Jurisprudence of the Federal Republic of Germany*, 3rd edn, revised and expanded (Duke University Press, 2012) 331–42.

[30] ibid, 345.

polities, the European Union has secondary, ie delegated, responsibility for the tasks conferred on it.'[31]

This reasoning shows that popular sovereignty hardly can be substituted for by judicial sovereignty[32] of the ECJ shared with other top judges in Member States through channels of 'constitutional cooperation' or 'judicial dialogue'.[33] Reflecting on the growing tension between the democratically legitimate and representative bodies of Member States and the primarily technocratic and expert-driven legitimacy of the administration and justice of the EU,[34] the drafters of the Lisbon Treaty explicitly recognised different forms of constitutional settlement, national identities and state sovereignty in Article 4(2). The Article protects the constitutional identity of Member States and thus legally confirms what legal theorists have been describing as a state of constitutional, legal and political pluralism and the end of the EU law's absolute primacy doctrine.[35]

Though the concept of constitutional pluralism originally evolved as a specific theoretical reflection and positive assessment of the process of European Constitution making,[36] it also turned out to be a useful model explaining the failure of the Union's Constitution making and more recent legal and constitutional conflicts within the EU. It is able to critically reassess the major principles and operations of EU law and its relationship with the legal systems of Member States, a relationship full of structural and semantic collisions, cooperation and contestations.

The paradoxical concept of coevally shared and divided sovereignty is a hallmark of the EU's legal and constitutional pluralism. It is not just a theoretical construct haunting the logic of legal reasoning and jurisprudence. As this chapter seeks to demonstrate, the concept of divided sovereignty has been explored, adopted and used in different ways by constitutional judges and lawyers in different Member States of the EU.

The semantics of divided and constitutional sovereignty in the EU, its political context and pragmatic uses remains a primary focus of the following analysis. In the next sections of this chapter, I, therefore, pursue the goal of both demonstrating this semantic persistence of constitutional sovereignty in the post-sovereign EU constellation and analysing its theoretical and practical conceptualisations and uses by the ÚS and other constitutional bodies of the Czech Republic as one of

---

[31] Above (n 28) para 301.

[32] For the concept of judicial sovereignty, its general jurisprudential meaning and contextualisation in other countries, such as India, see PB Mehta, 'The Rise of Judicial Sovereignty' (2007) 18(2) *Journal of Democracy* 70.

[33] F Jacobs, 'Judicial Dialogue and the Cross-Fertilization of Legal Systems: The European Court of Justice' (2003) 38 *Texas International Law Journal* 550, 547–56.

[34] See, for instance, JA Caporaso, 'The European Union and the Forms of State: Westphalian, Regulatory or Post-modern' (1996) 34 *Journal of Common Market Studies* 29.

[35] A von Bogdandy and S Schill, 'Overcoming Absolute Primacy: Respect for National Identity under the Lisbon Treaty' (2011) 48 *CML Rev* 1417, 1432–54.

[36] See especially N Walker, 'The Idea of Constitutional Pluralism' (2002) 65 *MLR* 317. The publication of Walker's article 'The Idea of Constitutional Pluralism' coincides with deliberations of the European Convention and includes a particularly detailed analysis of EU law and politics.

the EU's Member States. I argue that the ÚS's complex doctrine of self-limited constitutional sovereignty is an example of arguments evolving within the post-sovereign EU that actually facilitate the legal and political operations and communication emerging at both EU and Member State levels. Even the ÚS's most controversial *Holubec*[37] judgment, which declared the ECJ's *Landtová* judgment[38] ultra vires, belongs to this supranational jurisprudential communication. Discussing the variety of uses of the concept of sovereignty in different judgments, I argue that the ÚS considers sovereignty an instrument of promoting the rule of law values, political legitimacy and constitutional accountability both within and beyond the sovereign state.

IV. A Brief History of the *Ústavní soud*'s Doctrine of Constitutional Sovereignty and the Delegation of Powers on the European Union

Since the communist regime's fall in 1989, constitutional developments in the Czech Republic and other post-communist countries may be summarised as a gradual shift from simple interpretations to more complex doctrines and jurisprudence of constitutional sovereignty and statehood in the post-sovereign EU constellations. Early constitutional and political transformations were typical of regaining, rebuilding and legitimising the sovereign constitutional and democratic state, yet the same process was instrumental for one of the most fundamental goals, namely accession to the EU.[39] These parallel processes of constitution making reconstituting state sovereignty and EU integration limiting exactly this reconstituted sovereignty and using it as a primary vehicle of entering the exclusive club of EU Member States have been extensively analysed by legal and political scholars in the past two decades.[40]

Similarly, early constitutional arguments and deliberations on the supremacy of EU law and their effect on pre-accession candidate states of Central and Eastern Europe were the subject of numerous studies in constitutional theory and EU

---

[37] The ÚS's judgment of 31 January 2012, Pl ÚS 5/12 (*Slovak Pensions XVII* Case). Available at: <www.usoud.cz> [last accessed on 1 December 2014].

[38] Case C-399/09 *Landtová* [2011] ECR I-5573.

[39] See, for instance, A Albi, *EU Enlargement and the Constitutions of Central and Eastern Europe* (Cambridge University Press, 2005) 9–13; AHE Morawa and K Topidi (eds), *Constitutional Evolution in Central and Eastern Europe: Expansion and Integration into the EU* (Ashgate, 2011). For more general comments of the EU enlargement process, see M Cremona (ed), *The Enlargement of the European Union* (Oxford University Press, 2003) and Ch Hillion (ed), *EU Enlargement: A Legal Approach* (Hart Publishing, 2004).

[40] A Czarnota, M Krygier and W Sadurski (eds), *Spreading Democracy and the Rule of Law: The Impact of EU Enlargement on the Rule of Law, Democracy and Constitutionalism in Post-Communist Legal Orders* (Springer, 2006); AE Kellermen et al (eds), *The Impact of EU Accession on the Legal Orders of New Member States and (Pre-)Candidate Countries* (TMC Asser Press, 2006).

law.[41] Technical uses of constitutional sovereignty generally facilitated the accession of post-communist states to the EU, yet they also highlighted a more general
problem of democratic legitimacy and accountability vis-a-vis these supranational
integration processes. Constitutional bodies of different countries, especially constitutional courts, thus gradually adopted the post-accession doctrine of divided
sovereignty and *Kompetenz der Kompetenz* reflecting on the supremacy of democratically legitimised national legal systems.[42]

A good example of such early semantics of sovereignty in the post-sovereign
EU legal and political structures is the ÚS's *Sugar Quota III* judgment[43] from
March 2006. In their complaint, the conservative opposition MPs argued that the
EU regulation of the sugar market amounted to the violation of the right to free
commerce activities. The ÚS declared the national regulation void on procedural
grounds and basically reiterated the BVerfG's position regarding the delegation of
powers and the relationship between Member State Constitutions and EU law in
the following words:

> the conditional nature of the delegation of these powers is manifested on two planes: the
> formal and the substantive plane. The first of these planes concerns the power attributes
> of state sovereignty itself, the second plane concerns the substantive component of the
> exercise of state power. In other words, the delegation of a part of the powers of national
> organs may persist only so long as these powers are exercised in a manner that is compat-
> ible with the preservation of the foundations of state sovereignty of the Czech Republic,
> and in a manner which does not threaten the very essence of the substantive law-based
> state.[44]

The ÚS also acknowledged 'a definite principle of constitutional self-restraint'[45]
regarding economic measures flowing from the EU policies and the case law of
the ECJ. Due to this self-restraint in economic matters, the ÚS refused to review
the EU law-based sugar quota regulations.[46] Repeating the BVerfG's *so long as*
(*Solange*) formula in the Czech context,[47] the ÚS, nevertheless, specifically recalled
Article 9(2) of the Czech Constitution protecting the substantive core of the democratic state which is considered unchangeable by any constitutional amendments
and laws. Any transfer of national competences to the EU must comply with the
very essence of the democratic republic and its laws founded on the rights and

---

[41] See especially W Sadurski, *Constitutionalism and the Enlargement of Europe* (Oxford University Press, 2012) 66–79.

[42] W Sadurski, 'Solange, chapter 3': Constitutional Courts in Central Europe—Democracy—European Union' (2008) 14(1) *European Law Journal* 1, 6–23.

[43] The ÚS's judgment of 8 March 2006, Pl. ÚS 50/04 (the Sugar Quota III Case). Available at: <www.usoud.cz> [last accessed on 1 December 2014].

[44] ibid, part VI. B.

[45] ibid, part VI.A-3.

[46] This position was criticised by some scholars for reasons such as its potential for weakening the protection of constitutional rights of citizens in the new Member States of the EU after its enlargement in 2004. See A Albi, 'Ironies in Human Rights Protection in the EU: Pre-Accession Conditionality and Post-Accession Conundrums' (2009) 15(1) *European Law Journal* 46.

[47] Sadurski (n 42) 6–9.

freedoms of citizens. These foundations protected by Article 9(2) of the Constitution are unalterable and therefore impossible to transfer to another political and juridical entity, such as the supranational EU.

Despite these principled limitations of the delegation of national constitutional powers to the supranational EU, the ÚS further stretched its commitment to the EU friendly interpretation of constitutional provisions in its judgment rejecting the petition of the conservative opposition MPs to annul the national implementation of the *European Arrest Warrant*.[48] Apart from emphasising the necessity of EU cooperation in criminal law matters,[49] the ÚS's reasoning highlighted the close relationship between rights and responsibilities related to the legal status of EU citizenship. Recalling the importance of effective international extradition procedures, The ÚS took the view that

> [T]he contemporary standard for the protection of fundamental rights within the European Union does not ... give rise to any presumption that this standard for the protection of fundamental rights, through invoking the principles arising therefrom, is of a lesser quality than the level of protection provided in the Czech Republic.[50]

Following these early reflections on the relationship between the Czech constitutional order and EU law, the ÚS's adopted doctrine of divided sovereignty and general commitment to the pro-EU interpretation of the Czech Constitution, nevertheless, needed to be substantially refined during the process of the Lisbon Treaty ratification.

V. The Lisbon Treaty Ratification and its Political Context in the Czech Republic

Before analysing the landmark *Lisbon I*[51] and *Lisbon II*[52] judgments of the ÚS, a brief description of political developments and different players is vital for understanding the constitutional context of the Lisbon Treaty's ratification in the Czech Republic.[53]

---

[48] The ÚS's judgment of 3 May 2006, Pl ÚS 66/04 (The *European Arrest Warrant* Case), No 434/2006 Coll. Available at: <www.usoud.cz> [last accessed on 1 December 2014].

[49] H van der Wilt, 'On the Hierarchy between Extradition and Human Rights' in E De Wet and J Vidmar (eds), *Hierarchy in International Law: The Place of Human Rights* (Oxford University Press, 2012) 148, 163.

[50] Above (n 48) para 71.

[51] The ÚS's judgment of 26 November 2008, Pl ÚS 19/08 (The *Treaty of Lisbon I* Case) Available at: <www.usoud.cz> [last accessed on 1 December 2014].

[52] The ÚS's judgment of 3 November 2009, Pl ÚS 26/06 (The *Treaty of Lisbon II* Case). Available at: <www.usoud.cz> [last accessed on 1 December 2014].

[53] G Pridham, 'European Party Cooperation and Post-Communist Politics' in A Szczerbiak and P Taggart (eds), *Opposing Europe?: The Comparative Party Politics of Euroscepticism: Volume 2* (Oxford University Press, 2008) 76, 89.

Václav Klaus, President of the Czech Republic between 2003 and 2013, was one of the most radical critics of the EU. Nevertheless, he did not have enough constitutional power and political force to block the country's accession to the EU in 2004 and its participation in the process of European constitution making. Using the public authority of his office, Klaus often voiced his fundamental opposition to the Constitutional Treaty of the EU. While not having any direct constitutional power to sideline its ratification, he relied on traditionally sceptical and hostile views of the Czech public and heavily supported the ratification referendum to undermine the pro-European and pro-Treaty politics in the Czech Republic.

Following the collapse of the Constitutional Treaty's ratification in the French and Dutch referenda and the formation of the centrist conservative coalition government in the Czech Republic in 2006, President Klaus attempted at exercising more pressure and influence in the Government's executive powers. The Civic Democratic Party, of which Václav Klaus was one of the most important founding fathers,[54] was the strongest party of the coalition and its Eurosceptic faction supported the President's anti-EU position. The period between 2007 and 2009 was thus typical of President Klaus's conflicts with Karel Schwarzenberg, Minister of Foreign Affairs, who then was nominated by the pro-European Green Party as a junior coalition partner in Government. After the coalition Government of the Civic Democratic Party, the Christian Democratic Party and the Green Party lost the vote of confidence in March 2009, a new caretaking 'government of experts' headed by a former director of the National Statistics Office Jan Fischer was appointed by President Klaus to lead the country to the early parliamentary election in 2010.

The Lisbon Treaty was a product of the failed EU constitution making process drafted at the time when the conservative coalition government came to power in the Czech Republic in January 2007.[55] While the initial manoeuvring space of these Eurosceptics in Parliament and Government was limited and contained by the coalition manifesto and negotiated agreements, it gathered pace after the first Irish referendum rejecting the Lisbon Treaty on 12 June 2008.[56] In this respect, President Klaus repeatedly remarked that the ratification process should not be hurried and stated that he would not ratify the Lisbon Treaty until Ireland's ratification pending on the repeated referendum.

The Treaty and its potential clash with the constitutional order of the Czech Republic was discussed especially by a strong faction of the Eurosceptic Civic Democratic members of the Senate—the upper chamber of Parliament—and this faction eventually submitted a petition of the Senate to the ÚS seeking review of whether the Lisbon Treaty is consistent with the constitutional order of the

---

[54] S Hanley, *The New Right in the New Europe: Czech Transformation and Right-Wing Politics, 1989–2006* (Routledge, 2007).

[55] P Craig, *The Lisbon Treaty: Law, Politics, and Treaty Reform* (Oxford University Press, 2010) 20–31.

[56] J-C Piris, *The Lisbon Treaty: A Legal and Political Analysis* (Cambridge University Press, 2010) 51–60.

Czech Republic. The ÚS's landmark judgment of 26 November 2008—known as the *Lisbon I* judgment—therefore was directly responding both to the specific legal challenges of the anti-Lisbon Treaty senators and more general political conflicts and tensions emerging within the executive branch between President and the coalition Government and between different parties of this Government.[57]

It was only after the *Lisbon I* judgment of the ÚS that the Chamber of Deputies—the lower chamber of Parliament with primary legislative power—ratified the Lisbon Treaty by the constitutional majority of 125 MPs (the motion was supported by the opposition Social Democratic Party while rejected by a number of Eurosceptic MPs from the Civic Democratic Party as a major party in government) on 18 February 2009. The Senate subsequently ratified the Treaty by a sound majority of 54 votes on 6 May 2009, yet the critical minority of senators, closely coordinating their motion with President Klaus and explicitly using his own criticisms, submitted another petition to the ÚS on 29 September 2009. This motion effectively put the ratification process on hold because the Czech Constitution states that such a treaty cannot be ratified until a judgment of the ÚS is delivered.

Meanwhile, President Klaus responded to the second Irish referendum, which approved the Lisbon Treaty on 2 October 2009, by raising yet another objection to the Treaty. This time, he asked for an opt-out from the Charter of Fundamental Rights of the European Union arguing that the Charter could lead to the annulment of the post-World War II Presidential Decrees. Issued by President of Czechoslovakia Edvard Beneš, these decrees had been a legal basis of expelling and confiscating the property of those ethnic Germans and Hungarians who could not prove that they had actively resisted the Nazi occupation during the war.[58] While being dead-letter laws for decades, the so called *Beneš decrees* technically continue to be part of the legal order of the Czech Republic and, more importantly, form a very important symbol in the Czech post-war collective memory and recent national history. The President's argument thus belonged to the arsenal of political populism without any legal substance, especially after the European Parliament's *Frowein Report* in 2002 clearly stated that EU laws do not have retrospective effects and the 1945 Beneš decrees' status is unaffected and constituted no obstacle for the Czech Republic's accession to the EU.[59]

While short of legal reasons and certainly ultra vires in terms of powers granted to the President of the Czech Republic, President Klaus's move was politically powerful due to its historical reminiscences and political symbolism. The weak

[57] For further description and details, see, for instance, P Bříza, 'The Czech Republic: The Constitutional Court on the Lisbon Treaty Decision of 26 November 2008' (2009) 5 *European Constitutional Law Review* 143.

[58] For further discussion, see R Uitz, *Constitutions, Courts, and History: Historical Narratives in Constitutional Adjudication* (CEU Press, 2005) 123–25.

[59] See the European Parliament's document *Legal Opinion on the Beneš Decrees and the Accession of the Czech Republic to the European Union* prepared by Prof Dr Dres h.c Jochen A Frowein, Prof Dr Ulf Bernitz, The Rt Hon Lord Kingsland QC, October 2002. Available at: <www.europarl.europa.eu> [last accessed on 1 December 2014].

caretaking government, therefore, agreed to adopt the President's position and, despite the successful ratification of the Lisbon Treaty by the Parliament of the Czech Republic and the ÚS's *Lisbon I* judgement, asked the European Council for an opt-out. On 29 October 2009, Member States of the EU in the European Council agreed on a political promise to grant the same opt-out already granted to Poland and the UK if it is demanded by the Czech government during the next round of opt-out negotiations.

During this time, the ÚS considered the second petition of the senators and eventually rejected it in a strongly worded judgment on 3 November 2009— known as the *Lisbon II* judgement—thus firmly closing the door for any further constitutional review of the Lisbon Treaty and removing the final obstacle in the ratification process.[60] On the same day, the Lisbon Treaty acquired the Presidential Assent and its ratification could be completed in the Czech Republic.[61]

VI. From Adopted Doctrines to the Complex Jurisprudence of Constitutional Sovereignty: The *Ústavní soud*'s Reflections on Globalisation and Sovereignty

In these circumstances, the ÚS dealt with most of the challenges well and success-fully insulated its constitutional arguments from ongoing constitutional confron-tations, party politics and ideological conflicts. In principle, the Court ruled that the Lisbon Treaty does not alter the EU's status of an international organisation with attributed powers and therefore without the capacity to change its powers at its will.

The most remarkable outcome of the ÚS's ruling is its rejection of what may be described as an absolutist notion of sovereignty in the current globalised and Europeanised political societies. Using the Czech constitutional order as their point of reference,[62] the judges stated that 'today sovereignty can no longer be understood absolutely; sovereignty is more a practical matter.'[63] It is not an exis-tential matter of the *either, or* choice. Sovereignty, rather, can be pooled, shared and divided and, therefore, exercised by participating in supranational, interna-tional and transnational global legal and political settings.

---

[60] See J Komárek, 'The Czech Constitutional Court's Second Decision on the Lisbon Treaty of 3 November 2009' (2009) 5(3) *European Constitutional Law Review* 345.

[61] J Ziller, 'The Treaty of Lisbon: Constitutional Treaty, Episode II' in F Laursen (ed), *Designing the European Union: From Paris to Lisbon* (Palgrave, 2012) 244, 264.

[62] For further details see, for instance, E Ruffer, 'The Quest of the Lisbon Treaty in the Czech Repub-lic and Some of the Changes It Introduces in EU Primary Law' (2010) 1 *Czech Yearbook of International Law* 23, 32.

[63] Above (n 51) para 4 of the introductory reasoning summary.

In paragraph 104 of the *Lisbon I* judgment, the ÚS comments on the paradoxical semantics of state sovereignty in the post-sovereign EU constellation by stating:

> The European Union has advanced by far the furthest in the concept of pooled sovereignty, and today is creating an entity sui generis, which is difficult to classify in classical political science categories. It is more a linguistic question whether to describe the integration process as a 'loss' of part of sovereignty, or competences, or, somewhat more fittingly, as, eg, 'lending, ceding' of part of the competence of a sovereign. It may seem paradoxical that the key expression of state sovereignty is the ability to dispose of one's sovereignty (or part of it), or to temporarily or even permanently cede certain competences.[64]

According to the ÚS, these arrangements are agreed by the sovereign state in advance and may be reviewed and therefore actually strengthen the state's sovereignty by its joint actions at supranational levels, such as the EU institutional framework. As long as review of the scope and the exercise of the transferred powers is guaranteed and the possibility of future changes to it guaranteed, the state's sovereignty is not weakened.

The ÚS 'can review whether an act by bodies of the Union exceeds the powers that the Czech Republic transferred to the European Union under Article 10a of the Constitution, although only in wholly exceptional cases.'[65] According to the ÚS, this review represents another important safeguard within the sovereign constitutional and democratic state against encroachment of supranational political and legal institutions. Furthermore, the ability of Member States to withdraw from the EU guaranteed by Article 50 of the Treaty on EU confirms, according to the ÚS, the principle 'States are the Masters of the Treaty' which reiterates the persisting and continuing sovereignty of Member States.[66]

The ÚS summarises:

> these deliberations that the transfer of certain state competences, that arises from the free will of the sovereign, and will continue to be exercised with the sovereign's participation in a manner that is agreed on in advance and that is reviewable, is not a conceptual weakening of the sovereignty of a state, but, on the contrary, can lead to strengthening it within the joint actions of an integrated whole. The EU's integration process is not taking place in a radical manner that would generally mean the 'loss' of national sovereignty; rather, it is an evolutionary process and, among other things, a reaction to the increasing globalization in the world.[67]

Sovereignty signifies the state's dynamic legal status defined by European law which, nevertheless, is an outcome of close collaboration and participation of Member States of the EU including the Czech Republic. This collaboration evolves and the very meaning of state sovereignty, therefore, is subject of historical change.

---

[64] ibid, para 104.
[65] ibid, para 5 of the introductory reasoning summary.
[66] ibid, para 106.
[67] ibid, para 108.

The ÚS subsequently makes a lengthy comment on state sovereignty and globalisation in its judgments when it states:

> The global scene can no longer be seen only as a world of isolated states. It is generally accepted that the state and its sovereignty are undergoing change, and that no state is such a unitary, separate organization as classical theories assumed in the past. An international political system is being created in the global scale that lacks institutionalized rules of its own self-government, such as the international system created by sovereign states had until now. It is an existential interest of the integrating European civilization to appear in global competition as an important and respected force. These processes quite clearly demonstrate that the sovereign legitimate state power must necessarily observe the ongoing developmental trends and attempt to approach them, understand them, and gradually subject this spontaneous globalization process, lacking hierarchical organization, to the order of democratic legitimacy.[68]

This conclusion and emphasis on efficient and principled governance beyond the nation state in global society[69] is different from, for instance, the BVerfG's *Lisbon* judgment which mainly highlights the precondition of sovereign statehood[70] and reiterates the old task of the EU to keep peace in Europe and to strengthen the possibilities of policy making by joint coordinated action.[71]

Regarding the specific arrangements of the Lisbon Treaty, the ÚS adopted the general post-war international law doctrine that sovereign equality of states does not mean that all states are equal in terms of their power and international influence, yet the equality of all states as subjects of international law means that these states are equally constrained in their freedom of action and required to fulfil their legal obligations.[72] The ÚS even makes a strongly worded reference to this principle in the *Lisbon II* judgment when it states:

> [S]overeignty does not mean arbitrariness, or an opportunity to freely violate obligations from international treaties, such as the treaties on the basis of which the Czech Republic is a member of the European Union. Based on these treaties, the Czech Republic has not only rights, but also obligations vis-à-vis the other Member states. It would contravene the principle of pacta sunt servanda, codified in Article 26 of the Vienna Convention, if the Czech Republic could at any time begin to ignore these obligations, claiming that it is again assuming its powers. If it were to withdraw from the European Union, even in the present state of the law, the Czech Republic would have to observe the requirements imposed by international law on withdrawal from the treaty with other Member

---

[68] ibid, para 105.

[69] M Koskenniemi and P Leino, 'Fragmentation of International Law? Postmodern Anxieties' (2002) 15 *Leiden Journal of International Law* 553.

[70] D Thym, 'In the Name of Sovereign Statehood: A Critical Introduction to the Lisbon Judgement of the German Constitutional Court' (2009) 46 *CML Rev* 1795; see also D Grimm, 'Defending Sovereign Statehood Against Transforming the European Union into a State' (2009) 5 *European Constitutional Law Review* 353.

[71] Above (n 28) paras 220 and 222.

[72] For further insights and comments, see B Fassbender, 'Sovereignty and Constitutionalism in International Law' in N Walker (ed), *Sovereignty in Transition* (Hart Publishing, 2003) 115–43 at 128–29.

States. This follows from Article 1(2) of the Constitution, pursuant to which 'The Czech Republic shall observe its obligations resulting from international law'. Thus, it is fully in accordance with this constitutional law requirement that the Czech Republic would have to, if withdrawing from the European Union, observe the pre-determined procedures.[73]

Furthermore, the hypothetical situation raised by the Senate's initial petition of using the Lisbon Treaty's regime if the Czech Republic seriously violates the values defined in the Treaty's Article 2 is tackled by the ÚS by stating that such a violation would be considered violation of the fundamental constitutional values of the Czech Republic itself. The ÚS, therefore, would have to protect these values against any violation in the first place.[74]

However, the most important conclusion of the ÚS is that these *values* and their protection cannot be compromised even by the concept of *the people* as a source of all state. Because these rights and values are protected at both the national and EU level, suspending the rights because of membership in the EU does not come into consideration and the ÚS concluded that this parallel protection of the rights and values at the EU and national level was evidence that reinforced 'the arguments that the two systems, domestic and Union, are mutually compatible and support each other in the most important area, concerning the very essence of law and justice'.[75]

The ÚS thus adopts the view of the EU as an avant-garde organisation reformulating the notion of sovereignty as both substantive value and formal legal constraints on the freedom of state actions beyond the common framework of international law. This institutional and conceptual layout is summarised as follows:

[I]n a modern, democratic state, governed by the rule of law, state sovereignty is not an aim in and of itself, in isolation, but is a means for fulfilling the fundamental values on which the construction of a constitutional state governed by the rule of law, stands.[76]

According to this view, the fundamental values of democracy and the rule of law take precedence over state sovereignty.[77]

VII. Sovereignty as a Post-Sovereign Technique

According to the ÚS, the concept of sovereignty as independent exercise of the state power both internally and externally is obsolete in global society in which states

---

[73] Above (n 52) para 168.
[74] Above (n 51) para 209.
[75] ibid.
[76] ibid, para 14 of the introductory reasoning summary.
[77] For another example of this normative interpretation, see, for instance, M Kumm, 'The Cosmopolitan Turn in Constitutionalism: On the Relationship between Constitutionalism in and Beyond the State' in JL Dunoff and JP Trachtman (eds), *Ruling the World? Constitutionalism, International Law and Global Governance* (Cambridge University Press, 2009) 258.

enter multiple relationships and legal obligations or political commitments.[78] Strictly speaking, any state obligation would mean deprivation of its sovereignty if it is narrowly perceived as mere ability to exercise political will independently and without internal or external constraints. Citing the classic work of Georg Jellinek, the ÚS ruled that the ability to restrict itself by the rule of law or international obligations and thus to regulate its competences is a sign of sovereignty and not its inadequacy.[79] The Czech Republic's EU membership, therefore, can even enhance and strengthen its sovereignty in the global world and its new geopolitical and economic constellations.[80]

Instead of theorising sovereignty as a rigid legal or political concept, the ÚS considers sovereignty a practical concept opening the possibility for states to be active players and negotiators at an international and global level of political and legal interdependence and networking.[81] This is a profound shift from political and constitutional essentialism to the pragmatist concept of sovereignty as a technique enhancing operative power of states in global legal and political settings and making them more flexible and adaptable to the emergence of supranational and transnational legal and political networks.[82]

To understand this general and theoretical position of the ÚS, one has to remember that the judges were forced to respond to the President's general questions regarding state sovereignty summarised in the initial petition and repeated in the second petition regarding the Lisbon Treaty. The President asked in his initial brief of June 2008 sovereignty test questions, such as whether the Czech Republic will remain a sovereign state and full subject in the international community after it ratifies the Treaty of Lisbon. Furthermore, the President's second brief, submitted to the ÚS on 16 October 2009, stated that the ÚS 'avoided answering directly, and raised a new theory of sovereignty shared jointly by the European Union and the Czech Republic (and other Member States).' According to the President, the concept of shared competence 'is a contradiction in terms'[83] because 'the essence of sovereignty is the unrestricted exercise of power. Sovereignty rejects the sharing of power.'[84]

---

[78] Compare this view, for instance, with M Koskenniemi, 'The Fate of Public International Law; Between Technique and Politics' (2007) 70 *MLR* 1.

[79] Above (n 51) para 100.

[80] For an academic reflection on the same topic, see, for instance, A von Bogdandy, 'Globalization and Europe: How to Square Democracy, Globalization, and International Law' (2004) 15 *European Journal of International Law* 885.

[81] Above (n 51) para 107; the Court quotes from DP Calleo, *Rethinking Europe's Future* (Princeton University Press, 2001) 141.

[82] JL Cohen, 'Sovereignty in the Context of Globalisation: A Constitutional Pluralist Perspective' in S Besson and J Tasioulas (eds), *The Philosophy of International Law* (Oxford University Press, 2010) 261.

[83] Above (n 52) para 61.

[84] ibid, para 62.

Responding to the President's essentialist view of sovereignty, the ÚS's *Lisbon II* judgment includes a quote from the memorandum attached to the Czech Republic's application to join the EU which read:

> The Czech nation has only recently reacquired full state sovereignty. However, the government of the Czech Republic has irrevocably reached the same conclusion as that reached in the past by today's Member states, that in modern European evolution, the exchange of part of one's own state sovereignty for a share in a supra-state sovereignty and shared responsibility is unavoidable, both for the prosperity of one's own country, and for all of Europe.[85]

It is a deep irony that this memorandum, dated 13 December 1995, was authorised by the then Prime Minister Václav Klaus himself. As the text clearly shows, the concept of shared sovereignty and competence had been familiar to the Czech and European political representatives including Václav Klaus as early as the mid-1990s.[86]

Another essentialist question submitted by the President to the ÚS in his brief was targeting the European Union itself when he asked whether the post-Lisbon EU will remain 'an international organization, or institution, to which Article 10a of the Constitution permits transferring the powers of the authorities of the Czech Republic.'[87]

Responding to this challenge, the ÚS, once again, repeated its argument summarised in the *Lisbon I* judgment, paragraph 104, and stated in the *Lisbon II* judgment that

> the European Union has advanced by far the furthest in the concept of shared— 'pooled'—sovereignty, and today already forms an entity sui generis, which is difficult to classify in classical political science categories. A key manifestation of a state's sovereignty is the ability to continue to manage its sovereignty (or part of it), or to cede certain powers temporarily or permanently.[88]

Again, replacing the essentialist concept of sovereignty by the pragmatic one the ÚS reiterated its views and position defined in the *Lisbon I* judgment that state sovereignty is not an aim in and of itself but 'a means for fulfilling the fundamental values on which the construction of a democratic state governed by the rule of law stands.'[89] The transfer of specific state competences therefore can be considered continuation of the exercise of sovereignty if it is agreed upon in advance and remains subject to review. The ÚS's emphasis on consistency of the EU objectives and the fundamental values of the constitutional order of the Czech Republic explains why general interests of the Union actually materialise state interests of the Czech Republic.

---

[85] ibid, para 148.
[86] ibid, para 149.
[87] ibid, para 65.
[88] ibid, para 147.
[89] ibid.

For the ÚS, the transfer of sovereign powers is not principally unlimited. However, it is extremely important that the ÚS rules itself out of specifying these limits and states that they should be left primarily to the legislature as an a priori political question.[90] The ÚS considers possible interference with the legislator as *ultima ratio* only in a situation where the legislator clearly exceeds political discretion and the most important constitutional principles stated in Article 1(1) of the Czech Constitution are affected due to the excessive transfer of powers beyond the scope of Article 10a of the Constitution.

VIII. Beyond the Dualistic View of the EU and its Member State: Comparative Remarks on the ÚS and BVerfGs' *Lisbon* Judgments

The ÚS engaged in the pragmatic and strategic conceptualisation of state sovereignty and criticised the essentialist notion of sovereignty, yet it did not state that sovereignty is just a formalist concept drawing on constitutional power operations. Consistent with its previous case law, the ÚS adopted the semantics of the substantive values and foundations of the sovereign constitutional state. In this sense, the Lisbon Treaty judgments were argumentatively close to one of the most robust and landmark cases decided by the ÚS in its 20 years' existence—the *Melčák* judgement of 2009 in which the ÚS declared the Constitutional Act on Shortening the Term of Office of the Chamber of Deputies of Parliament unconstitutional and ruled itself to be the guardian of the substantive core of the democratic state legislated for by Article 9(2) of the Constitution.[91]

In the Lisbon Treaty judgments, the ÚS emphasised the coeval basis of the EU and the Czech constitutional democratic state as organisations sharing fundamental values, rights and principles which apply across the board and are common to all Member States. This emphasis on political and legal mutuality between the EU and its Member State may even be contrasted to the BVerfG's *Lisbon* judgment as drawing on a view separating European and German national political and constitutional developments.

Indeed, the BVerfG referred to the *Lisbon I* judgment of the ÚS[92] and its reserved power to review whether legal instruments of the EU institutions remain within the limits of the sovereign powers conferred on them. However, this reference would be hard to take as evidence of judicial cross-fertilisation or even the emergence of transnational epistemological community of senior judges because the

---

[90] Above (n 51) para 109.

[91] The ÚS's judgment of 10 September 2009, Pl ÚS 27/09 (The *Melčák* Case). Available at: <www.usoud.cz>, [last accessed 1 December 2014].

[92] Above (n 28) para 338.

BVerfG actually recursively refers to its *so long as (Solange)* doctrine formulated several decades ago. This act of self-referential reasoning, therefore, is mainly an evidence of doctrinal narcissism without any theoretical impact or innovation.

Invoking 'the obligation under European law to respect the constituent power of the Member States as the masters of the Treaties',[93] the BVerfG effectively reiterated the impossibility of the ECJ to claim the *Kompetenz der Kompetenz* to unilaterally determine whether the principle of enumerated powers has been respected. Unlike the BVerfG's *Lisbon* judgment,[94] the ÚS engaged in more profound consideration of European and national legal and political developments as coeval and mutually intertwined processes. In this context, the reader certainly should not be distracted by the ÚS's references to classic theories of the modern nation state, such as Georg Jellinek's statist monism. Unlike the BVerfG's dualistic view, which makes a clear distinction between European and national institutions and can be summarised as 'what happens in Europe is for Europe to decide and remains subject of the ultimate constitutional review by this Court', the ÚS's view invokes the commonly shared values and principles of the democratic constitutional state and the rule of law as pluralistically applicable across the EU and within its institutional settings.

The BVerfG's justification of the EU on the basis of its peacekeeping mission in the continent is entrenched in classic doctrines of international law completely missing out on problems of supranational and multilevel governance and regulatory practices drawing on legitimacy through efficiency instead of democratic representation, participation and deliberation. In this respect, it is significant that the ÚS re-enters the problem of legitimation by the fundamental democratic and rule of law values to the EU level by stating that these are commonly shared and constitute the legitimation foundation of both European integration and constitutional democracy of the EU Member States.

Where the BVerfG separates European integration and national democracy,[95] the ÚS highlights the legitimation issues and deficits of both national democracies and EU regulatory and governance networks and practices. Instead of simply contrasting national representative democracy to the supranational organisation of the EU, it calls for scrutinising all forms and techniques of governing, whether local, national or supranational, in terms of their consistency with the democratic values which obviously cannot be limited by forms and techniques of political representation exclusively facilitated at the nation state level.[96]

---

[93] Above (n 28) para 235.

[94] See, for instance, D Chalmers, 'European Restatements of Sovereignty' in R Rawlings, P Leyland and A Young (eds), *Sovereignty and the Law: Domestic, European and International Perspectives* (Oxford University Press, 2013) 186, 205–06.

[95] D Halberstam and Ch Möllers, 'The German Constitutional Court says "Ja zu Deutschland"' (2009) 10 *German Law Journal* 1241.

[96] For further details regarding the difference between the Czech and German Constitutional Courts' Lisbon judgments, see M Wendel, 'Comparative Reasoning and the Making of a Common Constitutional Law: EU-related Decisions of National Constitutional Courts in a Transnational Perspective' (2013) 11(4) *International Journal of Constitutional Law* 981, 987–90.

IX. … and now for Something Completely Different: The ÚS Reasserting its *Kompetenz der Kompetenz*

Comparisons contrasting the arguments of the Czech ÚS and the German BVerfG could provide for a clear-cut conclusion of this chapter had it not been for the ÚS's response to the ECJ's *Landtová* judgment. On 31 January 2012, the ÚS ruled in its *Holubec* case[97] that the ECJ's judgment in the *Landtová* case[98] from 22 June 2011 was ultra vires because the ECJ wrongly applied an EU regulation.[99] Another contrast, therefore, may be drawn between the BVerfG and the ÚS: If the German BVerfG is described as 'the Dog that Barks but does not Bite',[100] The Czech ÚS, after the *Holubec* ruling, may be described as the dog simultaneously biting and wagging its tail.

The dispute matter may be briefly summarised as follows: After the split of Czechoslovakia in 1992, the Czech Republic and Slovakia came to a special agreement according to which the employer's residence at the time of the split of Czechoslovakia would determine the pension scheme of its employees. This, however, resulted in a series of disputes[101] due to the fact that Slovak pensions were substantially lower and some people, while never working in the Slovak part of the federation, ended up with significantly lower financial support merely because their employer's residence was in Slovakia. These disputes eventually reached the ÚS which declared this impact of the agreement between the Czech and Slovak Republics unconstitutional and ordered to pay those pensioners a special increment.[102] However, the *Nejvyšší správní soud* (Supreme Administrative Court, hereinafter NSS) did not accept the ÚS's judgments granting the increment to Czech citizens and, by means of a preliminary question, seized the opportunity and referred the *Landtová* case to the ECJ in 2009.

The conflict between the ECJ and the ÚS was thus initiated by the NSS[103] asking the ECJ a preliminary question and arguing that the ÚS's judgments were incompatible with EU law. The confrontation between the ÚS and the ECJ, therefore, is a direct consequence of another confrontation between the two top judicial bodies

---

[97] Above (n 37).

[98] Above (n 38).

[99] Council Regulation (EEC) No 1408/71 of 14 June 1971 on the application of social security schemes to employed persons, to self-employed persons and to members of their families moving within the Community.

[100] JHH Weiler, 'The Lisbon Urteil and the Fast Food Culture: Editorial' (2009) 20 *European Journal of International Law* 505.

[101] The judgment of the Court stating that the ECJ's decision was ultra vires is No XVII.

[102] Judgment of 3 June 2003, 405/02 II. US, Slovak Pensions I.

[103] For general information regarding the structure and administration of the Czech system of justice, see M Bobek, 'The Administration of Courts in the Czech Republic—In Search of a Constitutional Balance' (2010) 16 *European Public Law* 251.

of the Czech Republic which had been going on for several years. The whole situation was further complicated by the fact that the Czech Government submitted observations to the ECJ which openly stated that it believed the ÚS's case law contradicted EU law. The Government's financial interest to avoid extra funding of pension increments pushed it into the most unusual position of undermining the ÚS's position vis-a-vis the EU's legal system—a position criticised by the Advocate General as 'unprecedented.'[104]

The ECJ was clearly aware of the *Landtová* case's complexities and the potentially damaging consequences of its judgment. A Spanish jurist and one of the ECJ's Advocates General Cruz Villalón explicitly remarked that the case 'has arisen in an institutional context which is as controversial as it is delicate.'[105] Though ruling that the ÚS's judgment discriminated both directly (requirement of citizenship) and indirectly (requirement of residence), the ECJ attempted at softening its judgment by stating that the increment could be maintained if extended to all EU nationals. It also ruled that 'there is no provision of EU law which requires that a category of persons who already benefit from supplementary social protection ... should be deprived of it.'[106]

According to the ECJ, the Czech Republic, therefore, would be able to find a practical solution satisfying both the EU law requirements and the Czech ÚS's interpretation of the relevant constitutional rights.[107] However, the Czech response to the ECJ's ruling in the *Landtová* case was anything but conciliatory because Parliament, referring to the ECJ's decision, passed an act banning prospective payments of the increment to everybody.[108] As regards the NSS's response, its position was described by some commentators as amounting to the provocation of the ÚS[109] because it stated that the ÚS's case law violating EU law could not be binding on the NSS. The general question of the European mandate of ordinary courts and its impact on the jurisdiction of constitutional courts of Member States[110] thus became part of the most specific power struggle within the Czech system of justice.[111]

---

[104] J Komárek, 'Playing with Matches: The Czech Constitutional Court Declares a Judgement of the Court of Justice of the EU *Ultra Vires*; Judgment of 31 January 2012, Pl ÚS 5/12, *Slovak Pensions XVII*' [2012] 8 *European Constitutional Law Review* 323, 327.

[105] Opinion of AG Cruz Villalón of 3 March 2011, in Case C-399/09, para 5.

[106] Above (n 38) para 53.

[107] R Zbíral, 'Czech Constitutional Court, Judgment of 31 January 2012, Pl US 5/12. A Legal Revolution or Negligible Episode? Court of Justice Decision Proclaimed *Ultra Vires*' (2012) 49 *CML Rev* 1475, 1480.

[108] S 106a of the Act of Parliament No 155/1995Coll, amended by the Act of Parliament No 428/2001 Coll. That came to force on 28 December 2011. It is noteworthy that the Chamber of Deputies specifically referred to the ECJ judgment.

[109] Komárek (n 104) 328.

[110] M Bobek, 'The Impact of the European Mandate of Ordinary Courts on the Position of Constitutional Courts' in M Claes et al (eds), *Constitutional Conversations in Europe* (Intersentia, 2013) 287.

[111] On 9 May 2012, the NSS, responding to the ÚS's *Slovak Pensions XVII* judgment, actually raised the stakes by sending the ECJ another set of preliminary questions related to the Slovak pensions dispute. The question was, however, later withdrawn.

Without sending a preliminary question, the ÚS eventually responded to the ECJ's judgment in *Landtová* by another ruling in the ongoing dispute regarding the increment of Slovak pensions. In the *Holubec* case, the ÚS summarised its previous case law establishing the pro-EU interpretation of the Czech Constitution. It reasserted its commitment to the cooperation between Member States and EU institutions and the principle of Euro-conformity as intrinsic part of its decision making. Nevertheless, it also stated that the EU could not violate the basic principles of the Czech Constitution and transgress the competences transferred to it by the Czech state. It has thus established itself as the ultimate judicial body exercising the sovereign *Kompetenz der Kompetenz* even against its EU partner court. In other words, the ÚS firmly reserved the right of *ultima ratio* actor to review the constitutionality of EU legal acts.

The ÚS did not bother engaging in substantial arguments, for instance by invoking the TEU (Treaty on European Union)'s constitutional identity clause.[112] While referring to the German BVerfG's jurisprudence regarding the possibility of its *Kompetenz der Kompetenz*, the ÚS, nevertheless, ignored the subtleties of the BVerfG's position.[113] These are mentioned, for instance, in the *Honeywell* case[114] principally responding to the ECJ's landmark and controversial *Mangold* case,[115] yet stating that an ultra vires act would have to be 'drastic … manifest, consistent and grievous'. Furthermore, the BVerfG's position[116] assumes sending a preliminary question to the ECJ before declaring its judgment ultra vires and grants the ECJ's right 'to a tolerance of error'—something ruled out by the ÚS's 'zero tolerance' policy towards the ECJ.[117]

X. Conclusion

The Czech ÚS's response to the ECJ's *Landtová* case was praised, for instance, by President of the German BVerfG as following the German example and reinvigorating the nation state's sovereignty vis-a-vis the process of European integration.[118] At the same time, other commentators described the Czech ÚS's position in the

---

[112] Art 4(2) TEU. For an academic assessment of the clause, see Von Bogdandy and Schill (n 35).

[113] For general comments, see A Dyevre, 'The German Federal Constitutional Court and European Judicial Politics' (2011) 34 *West European Politics* 346–61.

[114] The German Federal Constitutional Court's judgment of 6 July 2010, BVerfG, 2BvR 2661/06 (the *Honeywell* Case). Available at: <www.bundesverfassungsgericht.de/en/>.

[115] Case C-144/04 *Mangold v Helm* [2005] ECR I-9981; the case was heavily criticised as ultra vires by constitutionalists and legal scholars in Germany.

[116] Ch Möllers, 'German Federal Constitutional Court: Constitutional Ultra Vires Review of European Acts Only Under Exceptional Circumstances; Decision of 6 July 2010, 2 BvR 2661/06, Honeywell' (2011) 7(1) *European Constitutional Law Review* 161.

[117] For comparisons, see Zbíral (n 107) 1485.

[118] Andreas Vosskuhle's lecture 'Bewahrung und Erneuerung des Nationalstaats im Lichte der Europäischen Einigung', the Hessen Regional Parliament, Wiesbaden, 1 March 2012.

Slovak Pensions case law as 'the aggressive application' of ultra vires argument against the ECJ.[119]

Indeed, the interpretation is controversial and challenging for all parties of the conflict. The ultra vires review of the ECJ rulings challenges the settlement between the ECJ and the constitutional courts of Member States which, according to Weiler, has resembled the Cold War MAD (Mutually Assured Destruction) strategy drawing on the assumption that no party can secure any gains and benefits by pushing the red button of the ultimate confrontation and war.[120]

Some scholars have described the *Holubec* case as 'an odd case about judicial weariness and judicial ego.'[121] However, the ÚS's position in the *Slovak Pensions* cases is not just bellicose and hardly can be criticised as merely an excessive arbitrary measure. It equally is not just an outcome of deliberations of the judges falling victim to the growing anti-EU sentiments among the political and judicial elites of the EU's Member States. The reasoning of the *Holubec* case actually reads like a summary of the divided sovereignty doctrine and the Euro-conformity principle of the Czech Constitution's interpretation adopted by the ÚS. Like any conceptualisation of sovereignty, the *Kompetenz der Kompetenz* question, however, is impossible to entirely reduce to the normative structure of either the Member State's Constitution, or the supranational system of EU law. This intrinsic tension between the normative and volitional aspects of constitutional sovereignty, which was briefly discussed in the third part of this chapter, thus explains the diversity of decisions, conceptualisations and arguments employed by the ÚS as regards the *Kompetenz der Kompetenz* question in the last two decades.

While reaffirming its commitment to the pro-EU interpretation of the Czech Constitution, the ÚS resorted to the most general argument of the basic constitutional principles and values to confront the ECJ in the *Holubec* case and thus strictly confirmed its position as the guardian of the Czech Constitution. Despite its different practical and jurisprudential consequences in the realm of EU law and divided sovereignty, the Slovak pensions case law of the ÚS, therefore, may be described as belonging to the robust cases defining the foundations of the rule of law and constitutional democracy in the Czech Republic since 1993, part of which are both the *Lisbon I* and *Lisbon II* judgments.

Criticising formalist notions of legality and legitimising the rule of law by the substantive values of the democratic state and human rights, the *Lisbon I* and *Lisbon II* judgments in particular define the very concept and conditions of legitimacy of the sovereign constitutional and democratic state in the post-sovereign political and social constellation. These judgments fundamentally contributed

---

[119] G Anagnostaras, 'Activation of the *Ultra Vires* Review: *The Slovak Pensions* Judgment of the Czech Constitutional Court' (2013) 14(7) *German Law Journal* 959, 965.

[120] JHH Weiler, 'The Reformation of European Constitutionalism' (1997) 35(1) *Journal of Common Market Studies* 97, 125.

[121] M Bobek, 'Landtová, Holubec, and the Problem of an Uncooperative Court: Implications for the Preliminary Rulings Procedure' (2014) 10 *European Constitutional Law Review* 54, 71.

to the formulation of the substantive core of the Czech Constitution. They also promulgated the ÚS's determination to protect it against both internal and external threats and risks. Recent jurisprudence of the ÚS is thus a persuasive example of a general process in which constitutional courts adopt post-sovereign perspectives of the constitutional democratic state while keeping the semantics of constitutional sovereignty as their persisting point of reference and empowerment.

16

'Keeping the Faith': The Trials and Tribulations of the Hungarian Constitutional Court in Following its European Vocation

ALLAN F TATHAM[*]

I. Introduction

The 2010 elections[1] brought a conservative-led coalition Government into power in Hungary with the necessary two-thirds parliamentary majority to amend and/ or replace the then Constitution, basically a product of the settlement between the (former) communist and democratic opposition forces which had led to a smooth transition from totalitarianism in 1989/1990.[2] The new conservative Government initiated the most sweeping constitutional changes to the system since the transition, culminating in the passing by Parliament of a new 2011 Fundamental Law which entered into effect on 1 January 2012.[3] As part of this new constitutional settlement, the powers of the *Alkotmánybíróság* (Hungarian Constitutional Court, hereinafter 'AB') under the 1989 Constitutional Court Act[4] were also significantly revised and included in a new Act in 2011.[5]

[*] The present author would like hereby gratefully to acknowledge the assistance and advice given in the preparation of this chapter by Dr András Jakab, Director of the Institute for Legal Studies, Tenured Research Chair (*tudományostanácsadó*), Hungarian Academy of Sciences, Budapest. This work was initially completed on 23 April 2014, and revised on 28 June 2014, 4 November 2014 and 26 April 2015. The usual disclaimer applies.
  [1] This result was repeated in the general election of 6 April 2014 when the conservative-led coalition Government again won a two-thirds majority. This majority was subsequently lost after a by-election in February 2015.
  [2] AF Tatham, *Central European Constitutional Courts in the Face of EU Membership: The Influence of the German Model of Integration in Hungary and Poland* (Martinus Nijhoff, 2013) 135–37.
  [3] For an extensive and topical discussion on this, see P Sonnevend, A Jakab and L Csink, 'The Constitution as an Instrument of Everyday Party Politics—The Basic Law of Hungary' in A von Bogdandy and P Sonnevend (eds), *Constitutional Crisis in the European Constitutional Area: Theory, Law and Politics in Hungary and Romania* (Hart Publishing, 2014).
  [4] Act XXXII of 1989 on the Constitutional Court: MK 1989/77.
  [5] Act CLI of 2011 on the Constitutional Court: MK 2011/136.

Yet despite these profound alterations to the surrounding political and constitutional environment and the serious challenges which these developments have had on the AB—whether in terms of jurisdiction, personnel or leadership—its decision making on EU law matters has exhibited more continuity than change. The cumulative impact on the AB of the many changes brought about by the Government since 2010 have been the subject of much analysis.[6] Intriguingly, though, the trials and tribulations arising from jurisdictional limitations and court-packing by the Government have not, so far, had any profound (perceptible) influence on the AB's approach to EU law. In this sense, the AB appears to have kept its faith in ensuring that its understanding of the position of EU law in the domestic legal order is not compromised. This may however be put down instead to the AB's rather tepid or understated European vocation displayed over the last 10 years or more and is in marked contrast to the somewhat more robust decision making of the German *Bundesverfassungsgericht* ('BVerfG'), the Polish *Trybunał Konstytucyjny* ('TK') and the Czech *Ústavní soud* ('ÚS').

The three Central European constitutional courts clearly emulate the BVerfG model's approach to deepening European integration and, through their own decision making, form a natural part of the continuing transjudicial communication between the Court of Justice ('ECJ') and national constitutional courts.[7] This contribution is intended to address the evident reticence of the AB in taking part in this dialogue, by focusing on its own responses to issues dealt with in recent times by her sister courts—for example the TK in the *2003 Accession Treaty* case,[8] *Lisbon*[9] and *EU Regulation*;[10] the ÚS in *Sugar Quotas III* and *Slovak Pensions*;[11] and the BVerfG in *Lisbon*[12] and the Euro crisis[13] cases.[14]

---

[6] For example, Tatham (n 2) 135–203.

[7] A-M Slaughter, 'A Typology of Transjudicial Communication' (1994) 29 *University of Richmond Law Review* 99.

[8] *Decision K 18/04*, 11 May 2005: OTK ZU 2005/5A, Item 49.

[9] *Decision K 32/09*, 24 November 2010: OTK ZU 2010/9A, Item 108.

[10] *Decision SK 45/09*, 16 November 2011: OTK ZU 2011/9A, Item 97.

[11] ÚS, 8 March 2006, Case No Pl ÚS 50/04, *Sugar Quotas III* (application of ultra vires review and following the BVerfG especially in *Maastricht*, BVerfG 12 October 1993: BVerfGE 89, 155; [1994] 1 *CMLR* 57); and ÚS, 31 January 2012, Case No Pl ÚS 5/12 *Slovak Pensions* (ignoring a ECJ ruling and following to its logical conclusion the BVerfG in *Honeywell*, 6 July 2010, 2 BvR 2661/06: BVerfGE 126, 286; [2011] 1 *CMLR* 33, 1067). For ÚS Decisions <www.usoud.cz/en/decisions/>. See R Zbíral, 'Czech Constitutional Court, Judgment of 31 January 2012, Pl ÚS 5/12: A Legal Revolution or Negligible Episode? Court of Justice Decision Proclaimed *Ultra Vires*' (2012) 49 *CML Rev* 1475. Nevertheless, the ÚS has subsequently sought to distinguish itself from its ruling in *Slovak Pensions* and this decision might be regarded as the revolution that never was. For a detailed explanation of the case and its aftermath, see M Bobek, '*Landtova, Holubec*, and the Problem of an Uncooperative Court: Implications for the Preliminary Rulings Procedure' (2014) 10 *European Constitutional Law Review* 54.

[12] *Lisbon*, 30 June 2009, 2 BvE 2/08 and 5/08, and 2 BvR 1010/08, 1022/08, 1259/08 and 182/09: BVerfGE 123, 267; [2010] 3 *CMLR* 13, 276.

[13] For example, *Greek Bail-Out and Euro Rescue Package*, 2 BvR 987/10, 1485/10 and 1099/10, 7 September 2011: BVerfGE 129, 124; and *ESM Treaty and Fiscal Compact*, 2 BvR 1390/12, 1421/12, 1438/12, 1439/12, 1440/12 and 2 BvE 6/12, 12 September 2012: BVerfGE 132, 195. The ESM Treaty and Fiscal Pact were finally ruled as constitutional by the BVerfG on 18 March 2014 <www.bundesverfassungsgericht.de/entscheidungen/rs20140318_2bvr139012.html> accessed 9 April 2014.

[14] For reasons of space and the present lack of comparative case-law from Hungary, the BVerfG in its ground-breaking Article 267 TFEU reference to the ECJ in *OMT Decision* will not be discussed

Through including EU law and European integration into its deliberations and decision making, the AB (like all other constitutional courts in the EU Member States) acts not only as guardian of its Constitution but also as arbiter of the reception of EU norms into its legal system. The cross-fertilisation or migration of constitutional ideas, mediated especially though not fully exclusively through the German model,[15] has allowed it to approach the issue of European integration in a measured and deliberative manner, as befits the nature of 'deliberative institutions.'[16] The AB has acknowledged the German model but has tempered its decision making in a clear attempt to distance itself from being regarded as forwarding a more rigorous, combative style in defence of constitutional identity and the use of ultra vires review, as expounded by the BVerfG, for example in *Lisbon*.

Before looking at the AB case law in some detail, the next sections will briefly consider the changes that the 2011 Fundamental Law and the 2011 Constitutional Court Act have wrought which could potentially have impacted on the AB's own understanding of the constitutional position of EU law in the domestic legal order. This will then be followed by a discussion first of the cases which indicate the AB's understanding of the primacy and nature of EU law and then the ways in which it has interpreted its role as guardian of the Constitution (or the Fundamental Law) by reference to the German model and those in Central Europe. The conclusion attempts to consider how and why the AB has tended to avoid a clear and unequivocal articulation of its position with respect to EU law, as well as the likelihood as to whether the Court's softly-softly approach will continue to be adhered to in the coming years.

II. Constitutional Change and its Impact on the Europe Clause

In order to understand the role of the AB and its approach to EU law since accession, it is necessary to consider the constitutional context provided by the Europe clause in both the 1989/1990 Constitution ('the Constitution') and the 2011 Fundamental Law ('the Fundamental Law').

---

here. For the case, see *OMT Decision*, 2 BvR 1390/12, 1421/12, 1438/12, 1439/12, 1440/12 and 2 BvE 6/12, 17 December 2013 and 14 January 2014: <www.bundesverfassungsgericht.de/entscheidungen/rs20140114_2bvr272813en.html> accessed 9 April 2014.

[15] See GA Tóth, *Túl a szövegen: Értekezés a Magyar alkotmányról* [Beyond the text: Treatise on the Hungarian Constitution] (Osiris, 2009) 273–77.

[16] J Ferejohn and P Pasquino, 'Constitutional Courts as Deliberative Institutions: Towards an Institutional Theory of Constitutional Justice' in W Sadurski (ed), *Constitutional Justice, East and West. Democratic Legitimacy and Constitutional Courts in Post-Communist European a Comparative Perspective* (Kluwer Law International, 2002) ch 1, 21.

A. Constitution Article 2/A

The first integration clause under the Constitution was inserted by a constitutional amendment in the lead up to EU accession. Constitution Article 2/A(1) provided:

> By virtue of treaty, the Republic of Hungary, in its capacity as a Member State of the European Union, may exercise certain constitutional powers jointly with other Member States to the extent necessary in connection with the rights and obligations conferred by the treaties on the foundation of the European Union and the European Communities (hereinafter referred to as 'European Union'); these powers may be exercised independently and by way of the institutions of the European Union.

The AB itself addressed the effect of Constitution Article 2/A in *Decision 61/B/2005 AB*[17] in which it noted that the aim of that provision was to define the premises and framework of Hungary's participation in the EU. It identified how the authorisation in that Article operated together with its limitations:

> The above mentioned provision of the Constitution provides authorisation for the Republic of Hungary on the one hand to conclude international treaties under which it would exercise certain powers jointly with other Member States, and on the other to exercise joint powers through the European Union's institutions. There are, however two limitations: (1) The joint exercise of powers should only take place as far as it is necessary in order to exercise rights and fulfil duties laid down by the European Union's founding treaties; (2) Only certain specific powers that are authorised by the Constitution may be exercised jointly, in other words the scope of powers that can be exercised jointly are limited.[18]

The Constitution (through Article 2/A) accordingly provided not only a clear, constitutional conferral of powers on the EU (as also determined by the BVerfG in *Maastricht* and later confirmed and expanded on in *Lisbon*) but also a limitation to such conferral and common exercise of powers, that is, the recognition by the AB of an ultra vires limit similar to that of the BVerfG in *Maastricht* and more strongly articulated as basis for the BVerfG's constitutional review in *Lisbon*. Thus no competence could be transferred from Hungary, unilaterally and without its consent.[19] With the limits referred to in Article 2/A, it was understood that the common exercise of competences could not be made beyond the areas established in the founding treaties. Consequently, through incorporating the ultra vires limit, Article 2/A rendered it a domestic constitutional question as to whether or not such competences had been exceeded.

---

[17] ABH 2008, 2201.

[18] ibid, 2206–07.

[19] P Csuhány and P Sonnevend, '2/A. § [Európai Unió]' [European Union] in A Jakab (ed), *Az alkotmány kommentárja* [Commentary on the Constitution], Vol I, *Általános rendelkezések* [Fundamental provisions] 2nd edn (Századvég Kiadó, 2009) 238, 257.

B. Fundamental Law Article E

With the entry into force of the 2011 Fundamental Law on 1 January 2012, a new Europe clause[20]—based largely on Constitution Article 2/A was introduced in Article E. The paragraphs relevant to this work state:

(2) With a view to participating in the European Union as a Member State, Hungary may exercise some of its competences arising from the Fundamental Law jointly with other Member States through the institutions of the European Union under an international agreement, to the extent required for the exercise of the rights and the fulfilment of the obligations arising from the Founding Treaties.

(3) The law of the European Union may stipulate a generally binding rule of conduct subject to the conditions set out in paragraph (2).

(4) The authorisation to recognise the binding nature of an international agreement referred to in paragraph (2) shall require a two-thirds majority of the votes of the Members of Parliament.

Writing in the aftermath of the entry into force of the Fundamental Law, the present author argued[21] that if the views in the above paragraph were to prove to be correct, then the differences between the two Europe clauses would appear to be slight. From this conclusion, it would then follow that the pre-2012 AB case law on EU law would remain applicable without any change. In fact, the AB confirmed this view in *Decision 22/2012 (V.11) AB* in which it noted:

The Constitutional Court's interpretation of certain institutions, principles and provisions can be found in its decisions. The Constitutional Court's statements made on the fundamental values, human rights and freedoms and on the constitutional institutions that have not been changed fundamentally by the Fundamental Law remain valid. The principal statements expressed in the Constitutional Court's decisions based on the previous Constitution shall remain applicable as appropriate also in the decisions interpreting the Fundamental Law. However, the statements made in the decisions based on the previous Constitution cannot be taken over automatically without any examination; the provisions of the previous Constitution and of the Fundamental Law have to be compared and carefully weighed. If the comparison results in establishing that the constitutional regulation has not been changed or it is essentially similar to the previous one, then the interpretation can be transposed.[22]

The only true difference that the AB noted[23] between both texts was that under the Fundamental Law the vote of the two-thirds of the MPs was now necessary for the authorisation given to acknowledging the mandatory force of the treaty and not, as under the previous Constitution, for the ratification and the promulgation of it. That said, the similarity between the texts and the maintenance of the same

---

[20] For a full discussion of this clause and other EU aspects of the 2011 Fundamental Law, see the analysis of A Bragyova, 'No New(s), Good News? The Fundamental Law and the European Law' in GA Tóth (ed), *Constitution for a Disunited Nation. On Hungary's 2011 Fundamental Law* (CEU Press, 2012) 335–58.

[21] Tatham (n 2) 158.

[22] *Decision 22/2012 (V.11) AB*: ABH 2012, 10, 15–16.

[23] ibid, 16–17.

regulatory environment allowed the AB to conclude that the provisions of the previous Constitution and of the Fundamental Law concerned in this case had identical content with regard to the question to be judged upon, and that therefore it was possible to apply the principles elaborated in pre-Fundamental Law decisions of the AB.[24]

However, for political reasons, the conservative coalition Government did not wish to maintain the previous constitutional principles in place, simply by allowing the AB to incorporate them by reference through the backdoor and transplant them by judicial fiat into the new order of the 2011 Fundamental Law. Moreover, a series of AB decisions had seriously impacted on the Government's legislative policy-making.[25] As a response, then, the ruling majority in Parliament passed a series of changes in the Fourth Amendment to the Fundamental Law in March 2013[26] that overruled these decisions as well as clarified the position and role of the AB in the coming future.[27]

As a result, Fundamental Law, Closing and Miscellaneous Provisions, point 5[28] now reads that AB rulings 'given prior to the entry into force of the Fundamental Law are hereby repealed. This provision is without prejudice to the legal effect produced by those rulings.'[29] This would seem to constitute an effective and irrevocable break with the past, undermining legal certainty and transparency, and incidentally calling into question the AB's already well-established approach to the Union. Despite the intention of both Government and Parliament, however,

---

[24] In this case, the AB made express reference to its judgment of the Lisbon Treaty, *Decision 143/2010 (VII.14) AB*: ABH 2010, 698. This ruling is discussed below.

[25] The AB struck down a number of laws regarded as of importance by the present Government, including in 2012 and 2013 those on the Transitional Provisions of the Fundamental Law (on the grounds that they were clearly not 'transitional' in nature): *Decision 45/2012 (XII.29) AB*: ABH 2012, 347; on the legal status and remuneration of judges, *Decision 33/2012 (VII.17) AB*: ABH 2012, 99; on criminalising vagrancy, *Decision 38/2012 (XI.14) AB*: ABH 2012, 185; on disability benefits, *Decision 40/2012 (XII.6) AB*: ABH 2012, 229; on legal aid, *Decision 42/2012 (XII.20) AB*: ABH 2012, 279; on the protection of the family, *Decision 43/2012 (XII.20) AB*: ABH 2012, 296; on compulsory voter registration, *Decision 1/2013 (I.7) AB*: ABK 2013, 50; on the prohibition of symbols of totalitarianism, *Decision 4/2013 (II.21) AB*: ABK 2013, 188; and on church registration, *Decision 6/2013 (III.1) AB*: ABK 2013, 334.

[26] Fourth Amendment to the Fundamental Law (25 March 2013): MK 2013/49. For a consideration of the implications of this Fourth Amendment, see Venice Commission, *Opinion on the Fourth Amendment to the Fundamental Law*, Opinion no 720/2013, adopted by the Venice Commission at its 95th Plenary Session (Venice, 14–15 June 2013), Venice Commission/Council of Europe, Strasbourg (17 June 2013) <www.venice.coe.int> accessed 30 November 2013.

[27] Human Rights Watch, *Wrong Direction on Rights. Assessing the Impact of Hungary's New Constitution and Laws*, May 2013, 14–17 <www.hrw.org> accessed 30 November 2013; Hungarian Helsinki Committee, Eötvös Károly Policy Institute and Hungarian Civil Liberties Union, Joint Opinion, *Main Concerns regarding the Fourth Amendment to the Fundamental Law of Hungary*, 26 February 2013 <helsinki.hu> accessed 30 November 2013. Not all opinions have been unfavourable, for which see the report commissioned from three European constitutional experts for Dr János Martonyi, the then Hungarian Minister of Foreign Affairs: F Delpérée, P Devolvé and E Smith, *Opinion on the Fourth Amendment of the Constitution of Hungary*, 1 May 2013 <www.kormany.hu> accessed 30 November 2013.

[28] As inserted by s 20(2) of the Fourth Amendment.

[29] Venice Commission, *Opinion on the Fourth Amendment to the Fundamental Law* (n 26) paras 88–99, 20–23.

the AB deftly handled the situation in *Decision 12/2013 (V.24) AB*[30] when it noted that in the exercise of its powers, as the principal organ for the protection of the Fundamental Law, it would continue to interpret and apply the Fundamental Law as a coherent system[31] and would consider and measure against one another, every provision of the Fundamental Law relevant to the decision of the given matter. The AB added, it would take into consideration the obligations Hungary had assumed under international treaties or those that followed from EU membership, together with the generally recognised rules of international law, and the basic principles and values reflected in them. According to the AB, such rules constituted a unified system of values which were not to be disregarded in the course of framing the Fundamental Law or legislation or in the course of constitutional review.[32] While these statements seem to anchor the Fundamental Law within the broader international and more regional European firmament, it remained to be seen how the AB will actually be able to apply effectively this policy formulation in practice.

The point was consequently settled broadly in favour of the approach suggested in *Decision 22/2012 (V.11) AB*.[33] Thus in *Decision 13/2013 (VI.17) AB*,[34] the AB—having expressly mentioned its pre-Fourth Amendment ruling—noted that, in determining newer cases under the Fundamental Law, it could use arguments developed in its earlier decisions, constitutional principles and their respective constitutional contexts provided that the content of the provision of the previous Constitution was consistent with that of the Fundamental Law.

In employing its previous reasoning, the AB was required—on the grounds of legal certainty and transparency—to indicate them clearly and with sufficient detail within the reasoning of a new decision so that the public would know from where the arguments had been derived. The ability to employ the reasoning in its earlier decisions was always to be achieved on a case-by-case basis, in the context of specific proceedings before the AB. This also meant that it was possible to ignore the principles from the previous decisions even if the content of certain

---

[30] *Decision 12/2013 (V.24) AB*: ABK 2013, 542.

[31] P Paczolay, 'The New Hungarian Constitutional State: Challenges and Perspectives' in A Dick Howard (ed), *Constitution Making in Eastern Europe* (Woodrow Wilson Center Press, 1993) ch 2, 21, 36. This approach echoes that of the BVerfG which, in its first major decision (*Southwest State*, 2 BvG 1/51, 23 Oktober 1951: BVerfGE 1, 14), underlined the internal coherence and structural unity of the German Constitution as a whole, stating:

No single constitutional provision may be taken out of its context and interpreted by itself … Every constitutional provision must always be interpreted in such a way as to render it compatible with the fundamental principles of the Constitution and the intentions of its authors.

[32] This wording of the AB here is reminiscent of its previous ruling in *Decision 53/1993 (X.13) AB*: ABH 193, 323, 326–27. In that case, the AB had to interpret its jurisdiction to consider questions of international law when ruling on the constitutionality of a voted on but not yet promulgated statute. The AB claimed the right to review the statute's conformity with international law because the AB was required under Constitution, Article 7(1) to ensure harmony between domestic law and obligations assumed under international law (whether treaty or customary) when evaluating a statute's constitutionality.

[33] *Decision 22/2012 (V.11) AB*: ABH 2012, 10.

[34] *Decision 13/2013 (VI.17) AB*: ABK 2013, 618. The case concerned the constitutional review of Act CLXI of 2011 on the Organisation and Administration of the Courts and the Act CLXII of 2011 on the Legal Status and Remuneration of the Judges.

provisions of the previous Constitution and the Fundamental Law were to be the same or very similar.

In such a way, the Court's approach remains within the letter of the Fundamental Law while hopefully maintaining its well-established practice of referring and using previous judgments in its decision making, for example on EU law. However, this is probably as far as the AB has felt safe in going, in order to reassert the utility of its earlier decisions, in the face of the strong reaction from the governing coalition, as epitomised by the express wording of the Fourth Amendment.

III. Constitutional Court Acts 1989 and 2011

Under the 2011 Act, the functions and nature of constitutional review have been greatly altered compared to those under the 1989 Act. A priori review of statutes on the proposal of MPs made a return in the 2011 Act while a true constitutional complaint was initiated, which latter brought the AB procedurally closer to the BVerfG. This latter procedure was, at least, *some* compensation for the abolition of the *actio popularis*;[35] the omission to legislate procedure was also removed.[36] The actual result of removing the *actio popularis* and of instituting a true constitutional complaint is clear evidence of the AB being changed from a potential veto-player[37] and potential (extra-parliamentary) opposition to the Fidesz-led government's policies into a human rights court subject to the supremacy of parliament. Clearly the shift from control of abstract general rules (as evinced with the *actio popularis*) to that of the application of laws in particular cases (as shown by use of the revamped, 'true' constitutional complaint) leads the AB away from being part of the governance landscape linked to the legislature to that of part of the judiciary, thus having repercussions for the latter in its work.[38]

Intriguingly, a priori examination has been retained or reintroduced under the 2011 Act for statutes passed but still to be promulgated (as well as international treaties) for certain political actors. Thus for pre-promulgated statutes, such prior review can now be commenced by Parliament, that is the majority of MPs (on the motion of the proponent(s) of the bill, the Government or the Speaker of the House) or by the President of the Republic.[39] This then potentially returns the

---

[35] On these changes generally, see F Gárdos-Orosz, 'The Hungarian Constitutional Court in Transition—from Actio Popularis to Constitutional Complaint' (2012) 53(4) *Acta Juridica Hungarica* 302–15.

[36] Whether the AB will be minded to follow the examples of its counterparts throughout Europe and re-develop this competence under the cover of and as part of a different review jurisdiction remains to be seen.

[37] An actor whose agreement is required for a policy decision: See G Tsebelis, 'Decision Making in Political Systems: Veto Players in Presidentialism, Parliamentarism, Multicameralism and Multiparty-ism' (1995) 25 *British Journal of Political Science* 289, 293.

[38] L Csink and B Schanda, 'The Constitutional Court' in L Csink, B Schanda and A Zs Varga (eds), *The Basic Law of Hungary: A First Commentary* (Clarus Press, 2012) ch 9, 293, 301–04.

[39] Fundamental Law, Arts 6(2) and (4) and 24(2) (a), together with 2011 Act, s 23.

AB back into the political decision making sphere, from which it had voluntarily withdrawn in 1991 (and which move had subsequently been confirmed by legal changes to its jurisdiction in 1998).[40] Moreover, given the government parties' continuing majority in Parliament (even after losing its two-thirds parliamentary majority in February 2015 with the Veszprém by-election victory of the independent candidate, Zoltán Kész), opposition MPs have effectively been denied use of this action since 1 January 2012 when the Fundamental Law came into force.

IV. Principle of Primacy of EU Law

Compared to both the BVerfG and the TK, as well as to some extent, the ÚS,[41] there has been a relative paucity of decisions dealing with EU law from the AB since accession in 2004.[42] In fact, the AB seems to have gone out of its way on many occasions in order to avoid making any definitive and clear statement on the issue. Moreover, even in its own Lisbon Treaty case, *Decision 143/2010 (VII.14) AB*,[43] the AB—while referring to the three courts mentioned above, was at pains to avoid any confrontation with the Union.

The AB recognised the autonomous character of the EU legal order and its laws in *Decision 1053/E/2005*[44] in which it indicated (Bihari, P, dissenting) that—despite their treaty origins—the founding and amending Treaties of the EU were not to be treated as international treaties,[45] an implicit acceptance of their *sui generis*

---

[40] *Decision 16/1991 (IV.20) AB*: ABH 1991, 58; and legislated for in Act I of 1998: MK 1998/10. Granted the jurisdiction exists in some other CEEs and in the Western Balkans but the Venice Commission had expressly warned the Hungarian Government against re-enacting this type of provision *Opinion on Act CLI of 2011 on the Constitutional Court of Hungary*, Opinion no 665/2012, adopted by the Venice Commission at its 91st Plenary Session (Venice, 15–16 June 2012), Venice Commission/Council of Europe, Strasbourg (19 June 2012) para 24, 7 <www.venice.coe.int/WebForms/documents/?pdf=CDL-AD(2012)009-e> accessed 24 June 2014.

[41] N Chronowski and Z Nemessányi, 'Európai Bíróság—Alkotmánybíróság: felületi feszültség' [European Court of Justice—Constitutional Court: Preliminary tensions] 2004/3 *Európai Jog* 19, 25–28.

[42] M Varju, 'On the Constitutional Issues of EU Membership and the Interplay between the ECHR and Domestic Constitutional Law Concerning the Right of Assembly and Freedom of Expression' (2009) 15 *European Public Law* 295, 297–301; L Blutman and N Chronowski, 'Az Alkotmánybíróság és a közösségi jog: alkotmányjogi paradoxon csapdájában (I.) és (II.)' [The Constitutional Court and Community law: in the snare of constitutional paradox, parts (I) and (II)] 2007 (2) *Európai Jog* 3 and 2007 (4) *Európai Jog* 14, respectively; and M Varju and F Fazekas, 'The Reception of European Union Law in Hungary: The Constitutional Court and the Hungarian Judiciary' (2011) 48 *CML Rev* 1945, 1946–63.

[43] *Decision 143/2010 (VII.14) AB*: ABH 2010, 698.

[44] *Decision 1053/E/2005 AB*: ABH 2006, 1824. See E Várnay, 'Az Alkotmánybíróság és az Európai Unió joga' [The Constitutional Court and EU law] (2007) LXII *Jogtudományi Közlöny* 423, 434; E Várnay and AF Tatham, 'A New Step on the Long Way—How to Find the Proper Place for Community Law in the Hungarian Legal Order?' (2006) 3 *Miskolc Journal of International Law* 76, 80–84; and F Fazekas, 'A közösségi jog elsőbbségét érintő Magyar alkotmánybírósági határozatok' [The primacy of Community law in the decisions of the Hungarian Constitutional Court] (2007) XI *Collega* 207, 210–12.

[45] That EU law is not international law was further confirmed in *Decision 87/2008 (VI.18) AB*: ABH 2008, 707.

nature. Moreover, since the 2003 Accession Treaty was an amending treaty, it was itself unlikely to be the subject of constitutional review. In Kovács, J's concurring Opinion,[46] he noted that:

Also taking into account the *sui generis* nature of European law, the founding and amending European Treaties ('[primary or] original law') and the Regulations, Directives, other norms and acts ('secondary or derived law') form part of the uniform (therefore to be treated in a uniform manner) European law. Despite their treaty origins, the norms of European law are much closer to domestic law than to international law; this can be demonstrated especially as regards their enforcement based on primacy and direct effect.[47]

Kovács, J's words read like a textbook reiteration of ECJ constitutional thinking and practice over the past 50 years. The position of the AB in *Decision 1053/E/2005 AB* was expressly repeated and built on by the AB in *Decision 72/2006 (XII.15) AB*[48] when it additionally stated:

The Constitutional Court has established in *Decision 1053/E/2005AB* that the founding and amending treaties of the European [Union] are not considered treaties under international law in respect of establishing the competence of the Constitutional Court (ABK 2006, 498, 500), and these treaties—being primary sources of the law—and the Directive—being a secondary source of the law—are as European law part of internal law, as Hungary has been a Member State of the European Union since 1 May 2004. With regard to the competence of the Constitutional Court, European law is not considered international law as specified in Article 7(1) of the Constitution.[49]

Nevertheless, the AB did not go (and has never gone) so far as to endorse Kovács, J's points on EU law primacy and direct effect. As regards the position of EU law in Hungary, the AB also ruled in *Decision 1053/E/2005 AB* that:[50] 'the so-called accession clause in Article 2/A of the Constitution determines the conditions and the framework of the Republic of Hungary participating in the European Union as a Member State, as well as the structural position of EU law in the Hungarian hierarchy of the sources of law.' In his concurring Opinion[51] to *Decision 72/2006 (XII.15) AB*, Kovács, J noted that the context of the case in hand reflected the complexity of the interrelation between the Hungarian and European legal systems and showed the reasonable practical consequences primarily for Hungarian courts as they formed an integral part of the judicial system applying EU law.[52]

---

[46] L Trócsányi and L Csink, 'Alkotmány v közösségi jog: az Alkotmánybíróság helye az Európai Unióban' [Constitution v Community law: the place of the Constitutional Court in the European Union] (2008) LXIII *Jogtudományi Közlöny* 63, 65.

[47] *Decision 1053/E/2005 AB*: ABH 2006, 1824, 1828. Bagi, J concurred in the Opinion written by Kovács, J.

[48] *Decision 72/2006 (XII.15) AB*: ABH 2006, 819. Várnay, 'Az Alkotmánybíróság' (n 44) 434–36; Fazekas (n 44) 210–12; and A Raisz, 'Confronted with Direct Applicability of a Directive: The Hungarian Constitutional Court before Challenges' (2007) 4 *Miskolc Journal of International Law* 113.

[49] ABH 2006, 819, 861.

[50] *Decision 1053/E/2005 AB*: ABH 2006, 1824, 1829.

[51] Trócsányi and Csink (n 46) 65.

[52] *Decision 72/2006 (XII.15) AB*: ABH 2006, 819, 863. Kiss, J concurred in the Opinion written by Kovács, J.

Kovács, J subsequently appeared to adhere to the priority of application thesis as expounded by the BVerfG[53] and endorsed by the TK.[54] Referring back to *Decision 1053/E/2005 AB*, he observed that the AB interpreted the 'structural position in the hierarchy of sources of law' concretising it in respect of the given EU norm and stated:[55] 'A Directive—when it falls into the exceptional category of direct effect—enjoys finally the same position as a decree directly applicable *ex lege*, ie it is a source of law of statutory level under the level of the Constitution, but as *lex specialis* it has primacy over domestic law in case of conflicts.' Recognition of the priority of application, it can be strongly argued, has accordingly been afforded by Kovács, J but never endorsed by the full AB.

V. Limitations to the Primacy of EU Law

The AB—unlike its German, Polish and Czech counterparts—has also been less than forthcoming in explaining its understanding of the vital national limits to further constitutionalisation of the European legal order by the ECJ. The sparse case law on the subject nevertheless indicates the existence of powers to supervise the process of continuing integration so as not to permit a surrender of sovereignty (at any stage) to the Union, at least without compliance with the necessary constitutional procedures. The absence of an unalterable core of sovereignty—as provided for under the German Constitution[56]—or the establishment in the Constitution that it is the supreme law of the State—as in Poland[57]—may explain in some way why the AB has not taken such an active role in the pursuit of setting the acceptable constitutional limits to integration.

A. Exercise of Constitutional Review

Since accession, the AB as a bench has tended to evade any confrontation on the point:[58] In *Decision 17/2004 (V.25) AB*, it avoided any attempt at goading it into constitutional review of a Regulation.[59] Nevertheless it would appear that it

---

[53] Tatham (n 2) 85–88.

[54] ibid, 227–30.

[55] ABH 2006, 819, 865–66.

[56] 1949 German Constitution, Art 79(3) together with Arts 1 and 20.

[57] 1997 Polish Constitution, Art 9.

[58] F Fazekas, 'La Cour constitutionnelle et la Cour suprême hongroise face au principe de la primauté du droit de l'Union européenne' *Actes du VIIIe Séminaire Doctoral International et Européen*, Université de Nice-Sophia Antipolis (2008) 139, 141–46.

[59] *Decision 17/2004 (V.25) AB*: ABH 2004, 291. Várnay (n 44) 430. Moreover, by a judicial sleight of hand, it also passed up the opportunity of clarifying the situation through making an Article 267 TEFU reference to the ECJ: A Sajó, 'Learning Co-operative Constitutionalism the Hard Way: the Hungarian Constitutional Court Shying Away from EU Supremacy?' 2004 3 *Zeitschrift für Staats- und Europawissenschaften* 351.

continued to be mindful of the remaining constitutional jurisdiction it enjoyed, as expressly voiced by Kovács, J in *Decision 1053/E/2005 AB*. He noted, in that case, the serious constitutional and EU law debates of previous decades[60] as to 'whether constitutional courts ... could exercise their constitutional protectionist function.' Through a 'significant metamorphosis of European law,' based partly on the relationship of cooperation between the ECJ and national courts, Kovács, J stated:

> Following all this, the European constitutional courts adopted a very similar approach, and out of them the practice of the German constitutional court and the French constitutional council are the most referred to. As regards the present request, we might come to the same conclusion by using another path already followed by many other European constitutional courts. This means that the very narrow scope of application—in which the theoretical possibility of a constitutional court decision regarding European law matters exists—is determined theoretically and in the spirit of self-restraint.[61]

It was apparent then that the AB retained a limited but vital jurisdiction—which in practice it would almost always refuse to exercise—that continued to protect the essential core of Hungarian sovereignty and put the power to decide upon the rate of integration into its hands.

This is in fact what occurred: In *Decision 57/2004 (XII.14) AB*[62] and *Decision 58/2004 (XII.14) AB*,[63] the AB regarded the 2004 EU Constitutional Treaty as an international treaty which was subject to its a priori (pre-ratification) review. Similarly in *Decision 61/2008 (IV.29) AB*,[64] the AB also regarded the 2007 Lisbon Treaty as an international treaty before ratification by Hungary. It stated[65] that 'as long as the required conditions included in the treaty—which are needed to enter into force—are not fulfilled, the Constitutional Court can only appraise the founding and amending [EU] treaties as sources of international law.'

In all three cases, then, the AB clearly viewed treaties amending the basic EU Treaties as susceptible to review because they amounted to international treaties, decided on by the Member States unanimously. This exercise of its a priori jurisdiction might be regarded as a more acceptable form of review power to be exercised in relation to amending the Treaties, thereby allowing the AB some residual control, if called upon, to examine whether or not an amending Treaty were constitutional.

In view of the foregoing, it would accordingly come as no surprise that the AB decided that it was competent to rule in *Decision 32/2008 (III.12) AB*[66] on the

---

[60] *Decision 1053/E/2005 AB*: ABH 2006, 1824, 1829–30. Bagi, J concurred in the Opinion written by Kovács, J.

[61] ibid, 1830.

[62] ABH 2004, 809.

[63] ABH 2004, 822.

[64] ABH 2008, 546.

[65] ibid, 550.

[66] ABH 2008, 334. N Chronowski, 'Nullum crimen sine EU?' 2008/4 *Rendészeti Szemle* 39; and P Kovács, 'Az EUIN-megállapodás és az alkotmányosság' [The EU-Iceland and Norway Agreement and the Constitutional Court] (2008) LV *Magyar Jog* 409.

constitutionality of certain provisions of the Act transposing into Hungarian law the Agreement between the EU and Iceland and Norway on the surrender procedure between the parties[67] which effectively extended the European Arrest Warrant procedure to these two Scandinavian States.

Moreover, in the later *Lisbon* case to be examined below, *Decision 143/2010 (VII.14) AB*,[68] the AB exhorted the relevant political institutions with standing to use the a priori review in respect of treaties, like the 2007 Lisbon Treaty, which enjoyed such a high level of constitutional importance.[69] It repeated this call in *Decision 22/2012 (V.11) AB*[70] within the new legal environment which came about after the entry into force of the 2011 Fundamental Law and 2011 Constitutional Court Act.

B. Lisbon Treaty Case: Constitutional Identity Review and Ultra Vires Review

Following in the footsteps of the BVerfG, the TK and the ÚS, the AB was further able to explain its understanding of the limits to the transfer of the exercise of sovereignty in its own *Lisbon* case, *Decision 143/2010 (VII.14) AB*.[71] In that case, a petitioner, using the then *actio popularis* procedure for a posteriori review, sought review of Act CLXVII of 2007[72] which had promulgated the Lisbon Treaty. His petition underlined the fact that various new rules and mechanisms of the Treaty jeopardised the existence of the Republic of Hungary as an independent, sovereign state governed by the rule of law as provided for under Constitution Article 2 which at that time provided:[73]

(1) The Republic of Hungary shall be an independent, democratic state under the rule of law.

(2) All power is vested in the people who exercise their sovereignty through elected representatives and directly.

At the outset of its ruling, the AB indicated that the reasoning and the examples of the petition were more or less similar to those examined by other constitutional

---

[67] Agreement between the European Union and the Republic of Iceland and the Kingdom of Norway on the surrender procedure between the Member States of the European Union and Iceland and Norway [2006] OJ L292/2.

[68] *Decision 143/2010 (VII.14) AB*: ABH 2010, 698.

[69] However, in *Decision 143/2010 (VII.14) AB*, the AB clearly did not, by implication, exclude an *a posteriori* review using the *actio popularis*. Although the requirement of legal certainty and the exclusion of the AB from participating in foreign policy areas reserved for the executive and legislature, post ratification, would have tended to militate against any potential consequential disruption in external relations through review of the Hungarian statute promulgating the relevant European treaty, this is indeed what happened in that case.

[70] *Decision 22/2012 (V.11) AB*: ABH 2012, 10, 20.

[71] *Decision 143/2010 (VII.14) AB*: ABH 2010, 698. See, eg Á Mohay, 'Decision 143/2010 of the Constitutional Court of the Republic of Hungary Regarding the Constitutionality of Act CLXVIII of 2007 Promulgating the Lisbon Treaty' (2012) 6 *Vienna Journal on International Constitutional Law* 301.

[72] Act CLXVIII of 2007: MK 2007/182.

[73] Now Fundamental Law Art B.

courts in the framework of their a priori review of the Lisbon Treaty where they had concluded either that that Treaty was compatible with their Constitution or that its ratification could be achieved with a constitutional amendment. Of particular interest for the present study was the following statement by the AB:

> Several constitutional court decisions [on the Lisbon Treaty] (BVerfG: 2 BvE 2/08, delivered on 30.06.2009; the Czech Constitutional Court: Pl ÚS 19/08, delivered on 28.11.2008; and Pl ÚS 29/09, delivered on 03.11.2009) referred to the importance of protecting state 'constitutional identity' in the European Union, even after the Lisbon Treaty had entered into force. The Constitutional Court studied these decisions ... The Constitutional Court notes that a posteriori constitutional review was also initiated before the Polish Constitutional Tribunal (Case Nos K 32/09 and K 37/09) but no decision has yet been made.[74]

From the outset of the decision, then, the AB had acknowledged that it had taken into account the deliberations of the BVerfG and the ÚS on the issue of constitutional identity as well as the arguments raised before the TK. This theme is pursued implicitly by the AB in its reasoning as it discusses, at some length, the relationship between Constitution Articles 2 and 2/A. It noted[75] that Article 2/A contained the constitutional power—'transfer of sovereignty' or 'transfer of power'—through which the Constitution established a clear constitutional basis and framework to enable Hungary to accede to the EU. Under Article 2/A(1), 'international treaty' was to be interpreted not only as being the so-called 2003 Accession Treaty[76] but it logically included a new international treaty according to which, through the development of the EU, further powers of the Constitution would need to be exercised 'jointly' or 'through the institutions of the EU', with the transfer of these powers being to the 'extent necessary.' Were the AB to be seized of a petition from the Government or the President for an a priori review of such international treaty:

> In this case the Constitutional Court—with other domestic or EU bodies— independently determines whether or not the proposed reform goes beyond Constitution Article 2/A(1) regarding the common exercise of competences (coming from the founding Treaties) with other Member States or through the institutions of the EU and if it is considered as a 'necessary measure.' Therefore, in such far-reaching reforms, it is desirable for a priori norm control when a treaty is supposed to be signed.

> The Constitutional Court—taking the general role of protection of the Constitution into account—points out that in respect of the Act promulgating the Lisbon Treaty the reconsideration of constitutional issues raised a posteriori happened without an initiative of a priori norm control.[77]

The AB clearly called on the Government and/or the President to use their powers under the 1989 Act, section 1(a) so that it might conduct a constitutional identity

[74] *Decision 143/2010 (VII.14) AB*: ABH 2010, 698, 700.
[75] ibid, 705–08.
[76] ibid, 705.
[77] ibid.

review of a further proposed European treaty before promulgation.[78] The AB continued by re-examining its previous case law on state sovereignty and the limitations on it,[79] in *Decision 36/1999 (XI.26) AB*,[80] *Decision 5/2001 (II.28) AB*,[81] *Decision 1154/B/1995 AB*[82] and *Decision 30/1998 (VI.25) AB*.[83] In respect of the latter case, the AB noted that it had already examined the relationship between EU law and state sovereignty under Constitution Article 2(1) and (2) before EU accession: This previous case law on sovereignty was to be followed in the *Lisbon* case. The AB accordingly noted in *Lisbon*:

> The requirement of the traceability of popular sovereignty, according to this Decision, was complied with in the preparation for EU accession by placing [this requirement] into Constitution Article 2/A ... *The prevalence of Article 2/A may not however deprive Article 2(1)–(2) of its substance.* (emphasis added)[84]

Consequently, although Constitution Article 2/A was the domestic constitutional basis for continuing EU membership and amendments to the founding Treaties (now the TEU and TFEU), Constitution Article 2(1) and (2) on sovereignty and the rule of law arguably constituted the 'constitutional identity' of Hungary and thus the transfer of competences to the EU could not exceed the extent necessary to exercise the rights and perform the obligations under EU law. To this mix must be added Constitution Article 6(4) according to which participation in European integration was a state goal. As the AB pointed out: 'Participation is not a goal in itself but has to serve human rights, prosperity and security.' An EU law which did not serve these aims either could be regarded as infringing the constitutional identity of Hungary.

In fact, in the case itself, the concurring Opinion of Trócsányi, J[85] suggested that principles which comprised the constitutional identity or essential core of Hungarian sovereignty and were thus protected from restriction by the EU included the rules on the election of MPs, the dissolution of Parliament or the appointment of members of the Government or of the judiciary.

To this nucleus of constitutional identity, it had already been argued that the protection of fundamental rights belonged[86] and this appears to have been confirmed in *Decision 61/2011 (VII.13) AB*[87] in which the AB rejected the constitutional

---

[78] As noted earlier, the AB repeated this call under the new constitutional situation existing after the coming into force of the 2011 Fundamental Law and the 2011 Constitutional Court Act in *Decision 22/2012 (V.11) AB*: ABH 2012, 10, 20.

[79] Tatham (n 2) 153–56.

[80] ABH 1999, 320, 322.

[81] ABH 2001, 86, 89.

[82] ABH 2001, 823, 826 and 828.

[83] ABH 1998, 220.

[84] *Decision 143/2010 (VII.14) AB*: ABH 2010, 698, 707–08.

[85] ibid, 713–14.

[86] A Bragyova, 'Vannak-e megváltoztathatatlan normák az Alkotmányban?' [Are there unamendable norms in the Constitution?] in A Bragyova (ed), *Ünnepi tanulmányok Holló András hatvanadik születésnapjára* [Festschrift for the 60th birthday of András Holló] (Bíbor Kiadó, 2003) 65–88.

[87] *Decision 61/2011 (VII.13) AB*: ABH 2011, 290, 320–21.

challenge to certain amendments to the Constitution introduced to alter the AB's jurisdiction. The AB indicated, *inter alia*, that *ius cogens* in international law—which covered fundamental rights under international treaties—might form part of the inalienable principles of Hungarian constitutional law.

If these are taken together, then it would appear that the AB is moving towards the direction that indicates an essential core of sovereignty which forms the EU-immune constitutional identity of Hungary.

In conclusion, post Lisbon, the AB considered that Hungary remained an independent state and the EU's gaining legal personality had not altered that fact. It observed that the necessary two-thirds majority in the Hungarian Parliament had been garnered to ratify the Lisbon Treaty according to the 1990 Constitution:[88] Such exercise of power was still done jointly with other Member States or through EU institutions. Having earlier referred to Article 50 TEU (Treaty on European Union) on withdrawal from the EU as underlining the continuing independence of the state in European integration,[89] thereby following the example of the BVerfG in respect of the same TEU Article in its *Lisbon* ruling,[90] the AB found the petition unfounded since the independence, the rule of law and the existence of a separate state had not disappeared.

While certainly more compact than the ruling on the Lisbon Treaty by the BVerfG, the AB enunciated its own understanding of constitutional identity, possibly laying down the foundation stones for the development of an essential core of sovereignty which could not be limited or touched by deepening European integration. The plea to the Government and/or President to petition the AB *before* a treaty as highly important as the Lisbon Treaty was promulgated, was directly linked to its understanding of a Hungarian constitutional identity review as well as a possible ultra vires review. By rendering its decision at a time before promulgation, the AB would be able to avoid much of the negative implication of the same types of review proposed by the BVerfG in its *Lisbon* ruling[91] and so considerably reduce the political tensions that would surround the threat of an a posteriori review of the same treaty.

C. Fiscal Compact Case: Lisbon Confirmed

This suggested approach to a priori review was in fact fully complied with when the AB was petitioned on behalf of the Government by the Minister of Public

---

[88] The Hungarian Government had considered that neither the proposed EU Constitutional Treaty or nor the Lisbon Treaty would require a national referendum to enter into force. Consequently it ratified both instruments with the necessary two-thirds majority of MPs: (1) the EU Constitutional Treaty on 20 December 2004, with 323 votes in favour and 12 against (with 8 abstentions); and (2) the Lisbon Treaty on 17 December 2007, with 325 votes in favour and only 5 against (with 14 abstentions).

[89] See on Article 50 TEU, AF Tatham, "'Don't Mention Divorce at the Wedding, Darling!': EU Accession and Withdrawal after Lisbon' in A Biondi, P Eeckhout and S Ripley (eds), *EU Law after Lisbon* (Oxford University Press, 2012) 128, 148–54.

[90] *Lisbon*, 30 June 2009, 2 BvE 2/08 and 5/08, and 2 BvR 1010/08, 1022/08, 1259/08 and 182/09: BVerfGE 123, 267, 349–50 and 395–96; [2010] 3 *CMLR* 13, 276, 335 and 367–69.

[91] ibid, 351–55; ibid, 336–38.

Administration and Justice in *Decision 22/2012 (V.11) AB*[92] to rule on the constitutionality of one of the measures adopted by EU governments as a result of the 2008 financial crisis. This was the intergovernmental Treaty on Stability, Co-ordination and Governance in the Economic and Monetary Union ('Fiscal Compact')[93] which, basically, requires signatories to enact laws requiring national budgets to be balanced or in surplus according to the Fiscal Compact's terms. The BVerfG had previously considered[94] the constitutionality of this international treaty between the majority of EU Member States (since March 2014, the UK has been the only State which has refused to sign).

With the elimination of the *actio popularis*, the Government and/or Parliament accordingly needed to avoid the possibility of an a posteriori review and the severe constitutional and EU implications that would mean. Thus, in order to head off any such political consequences, the Government followed the advice of the AB in *Decision 143/2010 (VII.14) AB*[95] and petitioned the Court on the constitutionality of the Treaty. Needless to say, the AB was most accommodating with the Government's request: Having affirmed the applicability of its reasoning in that case to the present one, it then outlined in effect the requirements for an ultra vires review jurisdiction using Fundamental Law Article E:

> Accordingly, the Constitutional Court reaffirms that an authorisation given by two-thirds of MPs is necessary for every treaty that leads to transferring further competences of Hungary, specified in the Fundamental Law, through the joint exercising of competences by way of the institutions of the European Union. It means that Article E(2) and (4) apply not only to the accession treaty and to the founding treaties and their amendments but to all treaties—the reform of the European Union—in the preparation of which Hungary has participated as a Member State. In the present case it is not necessary to take a stand about the extent of the transfer of sovereignty, as the petition for the interpretation of the Fundamental Law does not cover it; Article E(4) of the Fundamental Law shall be applicable in the case of *any treaty that leads even to the slightest transfer of competence*. (emphasis added)[96]

From this it would appear that the AB has attempted to formulate an ultra vires review jurisdiction, akin to that of the BVerfG in *Maastricht* and *Lisbon*. In order to offer further guidance as to this possible ultra vires review, the AB underlined the fact that the essential content of Article E(2) and (4) of the Fundamental Law guaranteed the transfer of sovereignty and of competence to the Union and set out the preconditions for its use:

> What treaties are to be considered as such a treaty shall be established case by case on the basis of the object and the subjects of the Treaty as well as the rights and obligations

---

[92] *Decision 22/2012 (V.11) AB*: ABH 2012, 10.

[93] For the text, consult the European Council website <www.consilium.europa.eu/media/1478399/07_-_tscg.en12.pdf> accessed 5 April 2014.

[94] *ESM Treaty and Fiscal Compact*, 2 BvR 1390/12, 1421/12, 1438/12, 1439/12, 1440/12 and 2 BvE 6/12, 12 September 2012: BVerfGE, 132, 195.

[95] *Decision 143/2010 (VII.14) AB*: ABH 2010, 698.

[96] *Decision 22/2012 (V.11) AB*: ABH 2012, 10, 17–18.

deriving from the Treaty. It is a necessary condition that Hungary, as the Member State of the European Union, should be a party to the treaty together with other Member States. It is a precondition that the treaty should cause the joint exercise of further competences, or their exercise through the institutions of the European Union. At the same time, it should not necessarily take place already at the time of putting the treaty into force; it would enough if it were an obligation depending on a condition. Provided that it is based on an international treaty, the requirement of qualified majority is also applicable to the implementation of the founding treaties and their supervision: it means that the implementing measures based on the founding treaties (adoption of secondary legal acts) are not sufficient any more, and therefore the implementation tools need to be amended, or new tools are needed. It is not a condition, however, that the treaty specify itself as the European Union's law, and neither is it a requirement that it should belong to the founding treaties of the EU.[97]

As a consequence, the votes of two-thirds of MPs would not be required, if the treaty were not to result in exercising, jointly with the institutions of the EU or with other Member States, new competences originating from the Fundamental Law. Yet despite the guidance, the AB in the new constitutional order under the 2011 Fundamental Law and the 2011 Constitutional Court Act clearly reflects the changes whereby, with the abolition of the *actio popularis* the executive and the legislature have regained the initiative in the EU policy making arena. It thus recognised that it was the primary obligation of the Government, as the presenter of the draft, and of the Parliament, as the legislator of the Act promulgating the international treaty, to form an opinion as to whether or not an international treaty fell within the scope of Article E(2) and (4) of the Fundamental Law. Only if they decide that the treaty affects sovereignty or goes beyond the competences already transferred might the AB be seized of a petition to examine the adopted but not promulgated Act of Parliament with regard to its compatibility with the Fundamental Law.[98]

This appears to be the final triumph in the field of EU matters of the executive and legislative powers over the constitutional judiciary and emphasises the AB's loss of position or subordination to them as guardian of national sovereignty in the face of deepening EU integration.

VI. Conclusion

The AB's relationship with EU law in its decision making has proved to be both hesitant and cautious.[99] Even the elucidating Opinions of Kovács, J (sometimes with another judge concurring) cannot be said to have made up for this shortfall. The researcher is therefore left having to provide an interpretation somewhat

---

[97] ibid, 18.
[98] Art 24(1)(a) of the Fundamental Law.
[99] Such opinion is confirmed, eg by Varju and Fazekas (n 42) 1983–84.

more dependent on hints and suggestions than unambiguous judicial guidance and thought, an exercise in textual exegesis of rather Biblical proportions.

Such reticence might indeed have initially resulted from the reaction of a court in a recently-acceded Member State encountering, for the first time, the brave new world of EU multilevel judicial governance; and linked to the way in which the AB then regarded itself as the guarantor of the 1989/1990 constitutional settlement. The BVerfG enjoys a much longer perspective in this respect and took many years to come to terms with the full implications of Union membership. Its process of 'dialogue' or 'co-operation' is still ongoing (*cf Maastricht* and *Lisbon* with the ECJ reference case, *OMT Decision*) and, without doubt, the AB is seeking to find its own way to its relationship with EU law, guided by the German model. The impact of this model on the AB has indeed been profound, dating from before the actual operation of the AB and throughout the development of its transition case law; it has even extended to the development of the AB's approach to the EU both before and after accession.[100]

The AB's general approach to the issue of EU law after accession remains—to some extent—an incongruous interplay of shadows and mirrors, a sense of pale images and even paler reflections amounting to tricks of the light through opaque glass. Indeed, it was not helped by the wording of the initial Europe clause, Constitution Article 2/A, a matter which has been repeated in Fundamental Law Article E. This lack of substance and clarification has had a negative impact on the perception of the AB. Granted the Hungarian constitutional jurisdiction might not have been designed to allow for the submission of the types of cases on EU law as had happened before its German and Polish counterparts, but in those cases which came before it, the AB has eschewed addressing such principles as priority of application of EU law, direct effect and ECJ references.

In fact, in its decision making, the AB has underlined its wish generally to 'deconstitutionalise' the issue of EU law[101] thereby leaving the ordinary courts free to follow it (including the ECJ's interpretations).[102] It has also turned towards the practice of the BVerfG (and the TK) with its acceptance in *Decision 6/2011 (II.3) AB*[103] of the need for a Euro-friendly interpretation of domestic law (and, of course, implicit recognition of *Marleasing*):[104] Bragyova argued[105] that the case itself raises this principle of interpretation to the level of a constitutional value, carrying with it the necessary requirement to interpret sub-constitutional national legal rules in a Euro-conform manner but also the Constitution itself. The AB in fact conceded this latter point in *Decision 32/2012 (VII.4) AB*[106] on the constitutionality of students contracts when it observed that it 'must not ignore the

---

[100] Tatham (n 2) 135–203.
[101] Thereby following the ECJ in Case 106/77 *Simmenthal* [1978] ECR 629.
[102] Varju and Fazekas (n 42) 1963–76.
[103] *Decision 6/2011 (II.3) AB*: ABH 2011, 31.
[104] Case C-106/89 *Marleasing* [1990] ECR I-4135.
[105] Bragyova (n 20) 342–43.
[106] *Decision 32/2012 (VII.4) AB*: ABH 2012, 71.

applicable EU rules and relevant ECJ case-law during the interpretation of the right to freely choose one's work or profession.'[107]

Moreover, in its *Lisbon* ruling in *Decision 143/2010 (VII.14) AB*,[108] itself clearly inspired by the BVerfG in *Lisbon*, the AB signalled an intention to concentrate only on the sensitive cases of a priori review of amending European treaties. This is evidenced by its strong invocation to the President or the Government to use their powers under the 1989 Constitutional Court Act, section 1(a)[109] and petition the AB for an a priori review of important amendments to the founding European treaties (a point confirmed when the relevant minister made such a petition on behalf of the Government in relation to the Fiscal Pact in *Decision 22/2012 (V.11) AB*).[110] By advocating this type of review, the AB would avoid entering the maelstrom of national politics which situation would ensue if a party were to use its standing to challenge the amending EU treaty a posterior. In advancing a priori review, the ball would rather be in the Government's court which could either seek to revise the amending EU treaty or, alternatively, to change the Fundamental Law in order to comply with such amending treaty.

It therefore appears clear that the AB has recognised its jurisdiction to conduct not only an ultra vires review with respect to the protection of the limits of the powers conferred on the Union by Hungary (which has its original foundation in the BVerfG ruling in *Maastricht* and recently reaffirmed in *Lisbon*), but also a constitutional identity review (though again less well articulated than that made by the BVerfG in *Lisbon*). The preservation of the constitutional identity of the state stems from its own understanding of the relationship between Article 2(1) and (2) and Article 2/A of the Constitution, namely that the former cannot be emptied of their content vis-a-vis the latter. The AB in more recent cases intends to maintain this interplay under the Fundamental Law (Articles B and E) and this would seem to suggest an essential core of sovereignty that cannot be touched by European integration without leading to the infringement of the principles of the democratic state under the rule of law and popular sovereignty.

Despite the acknowledged influence of the BVerfG, the AB's ruling in *Lisbon* was diminutive in comparison although its relative size compares favourably with that of the Austrian Constitutional Court, rejecting a petition (on technical grounds) seeking to challenge the constitutionality of the Lisbon Treaty.[111] As with the BVerfG and the *Honeywell*[112] and Euro-crisis cases,[113] *Decision 22/2012 (V.11) AB* put this reasoning of the AB into practice within the context of the Fundamental

---

[107] ibid, 80.
[108] *Decision 143/2010 (VII.14) AB*: ABH 2010, 698.
[109] Now 2011 Constitutional Court Act, s 23.
[110] *Decision 22/2012 (V.11) AB*: ABH 2012, 10.
[111] VfGH, *SV 1/10*, 12 June 2010: (2010) 37 *EuGRZ* 493.
[112] *Honeywell*, 6 July 2010, 2 BvR 2661/06: BVerfGE 126, 286; [2011] 1 *CMLR* 33, 1067.
[113] For example, *Greek Bail-Out and Euro Rescue Package*, 2 BvR 987/10, 1485/10 and 1099/10, 7 September 2011: BVerfGE 129, 124; and *ESM Treaty and Fiscal Compact*, 2 BvR 1390/12, 1421/12, 1438/12, 1439/12, 1440/12 and 2 BvE 6/12, 12 September 2012: BVerfGE 132, 195.

Law. The similarity in wording between the relevant Europe clauses in the Constitution and in the Fundamental Law have therefore not so far led to any radical change in the AB's approach to EU law.

To what extent may the amended jurisdiction of the AB and the appointment—since 2010—of nearly all of the 15-member Court by the conservative-led coalition Government be said to have impacted on the Court's approach to EU law since 2004?

In answer to the first point, the amended jurisdiction could be said to have two particular impacts. On the one hand, the withdrawal of the *actio popularis* may have had the effect of reinforcing legal certainty in EU matters: It means that Hungarian citizens are no longer in a position to second-guess their own Government and Parliament constitutionally by challenging ex post new and amending treaties in this abstract review. Nevertheless, this leaves the right to decide if and when such treaties are constitutional, at least initially, in the hands of the Government and Parliament through an a priori review. While this has distinct echoes of the pre-2008 position in France with the *Conseil Constitutionnel*'s then largely a priori constitutional review in EU treaty matters being in the hands of the executive and legislature or members of them,[114] the Hungarian alternative at this present time does not allow for opposition MPs to initiate such an a priori review as a majority of MPs needs to vote in favour.[115] Moreover, although the current rules provide inter alia that only one quarter of MPs are needed to commence an ex post review,[116] the reality is that, post-2010 and post-2014 elections—the parliamentary opposition has split between the left/liberal parties and the far-right Jobbik party. They would therefore be extremely improbable bedfellows even to consider initiating any review of the conservative coalition Government's law making: the opposition's victories in by-elections in early 2015, while depriving the Government of its two-thirds parliamentary majority, will thus not lead to any change in their present objections to working together in order to initiate an ex post review.

On the other, the AB might consider developing the constitutional complaint like the BVerfG in order to get around the absence of the *actio popularis*. For example, the creative use of democracy and the right to vote to give individuals the standing to seek BVerfG review of economic and financial decision making of the German Government (ostensibly in favour, generally, of the *Bundestag*) in the Euro-crisis cases might have the effect of emboldening the AB to use its own interpretative capacities in order to circumvent the constitutional restrictions put

---

[114] Under Art 61 of the 1958 Constitution. In 2008, a constitutional amendment was introduced and Art 61-1 provides: 'If, during proceedings in progress before a court of law, it is claimed that a legislative provision infringes the rights and freedoms guaranteed by the Constitution, the matter may be referred by the Conseil d'État or by the Cour de Cassation to the Conseil Constitutionnel which shall rule within a determined period.'

[115] Fundamental Law, Arts 6(2) and (4) and 24(2)(a), together with 2011 Act, s 23.

[116] Fundamental Law, Art 24(2)(e), together with 2011 Act, s 24 and s 24/A.

on its review control, vis-a-vis financial and economic matters,[117] through a similar creative use of the right to human dignity under Article II of the Fundamental
Law and in the Avowal on National Faith. Nevertheless, given its circumscribed
position in the constitutional governance system, there may be little optimism in
promoting this possibility.

What then of the second point on judicial packing of the Court? Under the
former Constitution, the judges of the Court (the original 15-member AB was
reduced in 1994[118] to 11 members by a two-thirds majority constitutional amendment agreed to by the government and opposition parties) were elected by Parliament but retained the right to choose from their own number the President of the
Court. In contrast, Article 24(8) of the Fundamental Law returned the number
of judges back to the 15 originally proposed under the Constitution. Moreover
Parliament, rather than the members of the AB, was given the power to elect the
President of the Court. According to the practice, pre-2010 election, the Government and opposition needed to work together to obtain the necessary two-thirds
majority to have their own candidate elected: Thus compromise and a biparti-
san agreement was required. However, with the advent of a two-thirds majority
Fidesz-led Government in 2010 and 2014, the opinion of the opposition has effectively been side-lined: This has allowed the conservative coalition first to dilute the
influence of the left/liberal-appointed judges in the new 15-member Court and
then, following the 2014 elections, to complete the job by being able to appoint
further judges with the result that (by spring 2015) only three judges, appointed
before 2010, still sit on the bench. The position of Fidesz has also been strengthened by the extension of the judge's term of office to 12 years thereby packing the
bench with its own appointees who will thus still be able to exercise control over
possible future left/liberal governments, their parliamentary majorities and policies well into the next decade.

Interestingly, there has in fact been broad agreement in most cases on EU law
since 2004 and, even where judges made their dissent, there were no discernible

---

[117] Under Article N of the Fundamental Law, in the course of performing its duties, the AB (together
with other state organs) is bound to respect the principle of balanced, transparent and budgetary management. This notion is reinforced by Fundamental Law Article 37(4), which—as long as the level of
state debt exceeds one half of GDP—only permits the AB the possibility of exercising constitutional
review (on the basis of Fundamental Law Article 24(2)(b)–(e)) over statutes concerning the state
budget and taxes in respect of infringements of the right to life and human dignity, of the protection
of personal data, of the freedom of thought, conscience and religion, or of rights related to Hungarian
citizenship. By avoiding the right to property as a basis for infringement, the Fundamental Law effectively protects the Government from AB interference with economic and financial policy which had
occurred under the pre-2012 rules, eg against the 'Bokros package' of austerity measures of the mid-
1990s, named after the then finance minister, when the AB ruled (eg *Decision 43/1995 (VI.30) AB*: ABH
1995, 188) unconstitutional a series of statutes which contained serious reductions in social benefits
on the grounds that the Government's failure to maintain at least a nominal level of social support violated fundamental rights and that the speed with which these programmes had been amended violated
the principle of legal certainty: see further the analysis of K Lane Scheppele, 'A Realpolitik Defense of
Social Rights' (2004) 82 *Texas Law Review* 1921.
[118] Act LXXIV of 1994: MK 1994/117.

'left-right' axis or 'integrationist-étatist' axis which determined voting prefer-ences (as evidenced by the concurring and dissenting opinions). Further evidence of a non-partisan approach to EU law which does not as yet exhibit a profound nationalist, sovereignty-protective bias in this field may be seen from a series of recent cases concerning the AB's reminding the *Kúria* (the former Supreme Court, renamed by the Fundamental Law) that it was to follow and apply the relevant ECJ rulings when deciding cases before it. In *Decision 3126/2013 (VI.24) AB*,[119] a five-member chamber of the AB[120] ruled that while the *Kúria* had failed to follow the relevant ECJ case law in coming to its decision, such failure was not fatal to that judgment. This was followed the following month in *Decision 3144/2013 (VII.16) AB*[121] when a differently composed five-member chamber[122] found the *Kúria* had failed to observe and follow the relevant ECJ case law and struck down its judg-ment. More recently, yet another differently constituted chamber[123] ruled in *Deci-sion 3041/2014 (III.13) AB*[124] that, in tax cases, the *Kúria* should follow ECJ case law in practice otherwise this would amount to a breach of Article E Fundamental Law. Thus the AB has expressly indicated to the *Kúria* that non-observance of the pertinent rulings from the ECJ would give it the opportunity of overruling *Kúria* decisions. In this way, the AB has given priority to ECJ rulings and emphasised the constitutional requirement to use them in cases before the Hungarian courts.

Further, in its decision making, while the AB has avoided making grand state-ments on the relationship between national (constitutional) law and EU law, it has given rein to Kovács, J in his concurring Opinions to formulate and express the traditional viewpoint on this relationship and the nature of EU law as proffered by the ECJ. This undoubtedly reflects his position as a public international law pro-fessor[125] who developed a specialisation in the field.[126] Other pre-2011 appointed AB judges have written in their non-judicial capacities on EU law, for example Bragyova, J.[127] However, both these judges retired from the AB in autumn 2014 when their mandates came to an end.

How then to explain the approach of the AB? It could be founded on its desire to adhere strictly to the rules governing its competences or that, by declining

---

[119] *Decision 3126/2013 (VI.24) AB*: ABK 2013, 677.

[120] Balogh, J, Paczolay, P, Pokol (rapporteur), Stumpf and Szívós, JJ.

[121] *Decision 3144/2013 (VII.16) AB*: ABK 2013, 774.

[122] Lenkovics, Dienes-Oehm, Lévay, Salamon (rapporteur) and Szalay, JJ.

[123] Balsai, Bragyova, Juhász, Kiss and Kovács (rapporteur), JJ.

[124] *Decision 3041/2014 (III.13) AB*: ABK 2014, 278.

[125] He has been professor in this subject at the University of Miskolc (1983–2005) from where in 2004 he launched (as editor-in-chief) the online journal, *Miskolc Journal of International Law*: <www.mjil.hu> and the Péter Pázmány Catholic University, Budapest (1997–2005), where the present author was one of his colleagues.

[126] For example, P Kovács, 'Vol (communautaire) au-dessus d'un nid de coucou (ou le calcul du temps de travail des médecins et la jurisprudence de la Cour constitutionnelle de Hongrie)' 2007/3 *Revue française de droit constitutionnel* 667.

[127] For example, Bragyova (n 20); and judicially his detailed dissenting Opinion in the *Lisbon Treaty* case, *Decision 143/2010 (VII.14) AB*: ABH 2010, 698, 714–22.

competence over EU law, it is much better able to control the growth of its work-load. The AB may even have been driven by the practical consideration that, in its decision making, if it were not required to engage in fundamental theoretical issues, 'it is not necessary to produce a coherent system of theoretical and norma-tive reasons regarding the legal status of EU norms in the Hungarian legal order.'[128] These reasons all tend to underline the fact that, after the coming to an end of the era under László Sólyom in 1998 (who is widely regarded as having presided over an activist AB that helped lay the foundations for a democratic state under the rule of law) and the complete replacement (on grounds of the end of their mandate, whether or not due to retirement) of the 11 judges in the first Court by June 1999, the Court seemed to settle down to a less activist role.[129] The next President, János Németh (1998–2003), adopted a more conservative, formalistic approach, being averse to the role played by the previous incumbent on the political scene and was more deferential to the executive and legislative branches.[130] The subsequent presidencies of András Holló (2003–2005), Mihály Bihari (2005–2008) and even, to some extent, Péter Paczolay (2008–2015) followed this change in approach and continued to steer a less interventionist role in national constitutional life. The new President, Barnabás Lenkovics (February 2015–present), has already indi-cated in the Hungarian press a continuing deference to national political institu-tions in the AB's approach to the exercise of its jurisdiction.

This background may give the lie to the hitherto 'quiescence' of the conserva-tive-appointed judges on the AB vis-a-vis EU law. In fact, it can arguably be traced back to *Decision 30/1998 (VI.25) AB*[131] that concerned a petition challenging the application of Article 62 of the EC–Hungary Europe Agreement on the prohibi-tion of anti-competitive practices and the related domestic rules implementing the relevant Association Council Decision on the grounds that such application limited Hungary's national sovereignty and those provisions were accordingly unconstitutional.[132] The AB asserted that: 'It is, therefore, a general principle to be followed on the basis of Article 2(1) and (2) of the Constitution [democratic state under the rule of law and popular sovereignty, now Article B of the Fundamental Law] that all legal norms of a public law nature to be applied in the domestic law to Hungarian subjects of law must be based on democratic legitimacy allowing [them] to be traced back to popular sovereignty.'[133] Essentially, the AB made clear

---

[128] F Fazekas, 'EU Law and the Hungarian Constitutional Court' in M Varju and V Ernő (eds), *The Law of the European Union in Hungary: Institutions, Processes and the Law* (HVG-ORAC, 2014), 32, 44.

[129] The different emphases in style of the AB under various presidents are set out in G Halmai, 'The Transformation of Hungarian Constitutional Law from 1985 to 2005' in P Takács, A Jakab and AF Tatham (eds), *The Transformation of the Hungarian Legal Order 1985–2005* (Kluwer Law International, 2007) 1, 5–18.

[130] ibid 9–12.

[131] *Decision 30/1998 (VI.25) AB*: ABH 1998, 220.

[132] AF Tatham, 'Constitutional Judiciary in Central Europe and the Europe Agreement: Decision 30/1998 (VI.25) AB of the Hungarian Constitutional Court' (1999) 48 *International and Comparative Law Quarterly* 913.

[133] *Decision 30/1998 (VI.25) AB*: ABH 1998, 220, 234.

that the Constitution could not authorise the conclusion of an international treaty whose content would conflict with the most fundamental constitutional values and principles, without a prior amendment of the Constitution. *Decision 30/1998 (VI.25) AB* thus, in itself, represents a strong 'étatist/sovereigntist' approach that has exerted a profound influence on succeeding generations of AB judges, irrespective of the political basis of their nomination: None of them have yet seen fit to disturb this settlement. Indeed, its influence has remained consistently strong, even in the post-accession period, and its quotation and approval in the Lisbon case, *Decision 143/2010 (VII.14) AB*, which latter ruling was itself used extensively in the Fiscal Compact case, *Decision 22/2012 (V.11) AB*, signal the 1998 decision's continuing importance to the interpretation of the Fundamental Law.

Given this 'implicit' understanding on EU law, long established within the AB, may it be subject to challenge now that the Fidesz-dominated coalition Government has effectively 'packed' the AB with its appointees? While the jury is still out on this matter, it may be worth considering the professional and academic background of two judges, appointed by the present Government in 2011 and who have certain experiences in domestic and European constitutional matters.

The first is Dienes-Oehm, J. He was the former State Secretary (and post 2003, Deputy Under-State Secretary) for Integration Issues at the Ministry of Foreign Affairs, originally appointed to that position under the first Fidesz Government (1998–2002) and subsequently appointed by the ensuing socialist-liberal Government as deputy Permanent Representative at the Permanent Representation of Hungary to the European Union in Brussels (2003–2007). In these roles, he has had first-hand experience in defending Hungary's national interests in the EU accession negotiations and subsequently in Brussels. Although a recognised EU law professor and academic colleague of Kovács, J,[134] his political experiences *may* influence him into taking a more determined position with respect to protecting Hungarian national sovereignty and interests in the face of further European integration, leading the AB into a deepening protection of constitutional identity as already exhibited by its sister courts in Germany, Poland and the Czech Republic. It should however be stressed that, at this time, there has been no indication in his Opinions at the AB as to any propensity to develop such a position.

The second is Pokol, J who has already written extra judicially of the dangers inherent in the emergence of the much-vaunted global constitutional oligarchy and its threat to national sovereignty.[135] Arguing for stronger use of constitutional identity and ultra vires review—along the lines suggested by the BVerfG in *Honeywell* but taken to an extreme conclusion by the ÚS in the *Slovak Pensions*

---

[134] Guest lecturer, József Attila University, Szeged (1987–1998); lecturer, University of Miskolc (1993–1998); and lecturer and honorary senior lecturer, Pázmány Péter Catholic University, Budapest (1997–date).

[135] B Pokol, 'Globális uralmi rend és állami szuverenitás' [Global oligarchy and state sovereignty] 2014/13 *MTA Law Working Papers*, Magyar Tudományos Akadémia (Hungarian Academy of Sciences), Budapest (2014) <jog.tk.mta.hu/mtalwp> accessed 23 April 2014.

case—he appears to be signalling the need for a more robust line by the AB, especially in respect of the judicial decision making of the European Court on Human Rights as well as the ECJ. In outlining his more 'étatist' approach, he seems to draw inspiration from US Supreme Court's reluctance to accept comparative constitutional law arguments into its reasoning and decision making. Pokol, J thus contends that the AB, in the absence of any action by the Hungarian Government or Parliament, remains the last bastion to defend the Hungarian State against encroachment from the EU.

Moreover, a further limit to the AB's ability to interpret provisions of the Fundamental Law is the fact that—under Article R(3)—such interpretation is required to be conducted in accordance with their purposes, the Avowal of National Faith contained in it and with the achievements of the historical Constitution. If this were to be used by the (almost exclusively) conservative-appointed AB in order to determine that, for example Christianity formed an essential part of Hungarian constitutional identity (this argument, in view of the wording of the Avowal,[136] may not be beyond the realms of possibility), then the AB could use it as a yardstick in review proceedings. In such a case, the Government and Parliament as presently constituted might wish to allow the AB much more room to manoeuvre, in order to allow them to develop a more profound 'étatist/sovereigntist' agenda vis-a-vis EU law than that previously set out in *Decision 30/1998 (VI.25) AB* but more in tune with the thinking of Fidesz–KDNP coalition. Such room might even lead to a change in the AB's jurisdiction under the Fundamental Law or Constitutional Court Act. The potential certainly exists for the AB to adopt a different faith and pursue an alternative European vocation—especially since the expiry of the term of office of AB President Péter Paczolay in February 2015 when Fidesz finally managed to complete an almost total change to the pre-2011 composition of the AB.[137] The lack of alternative or dissenting voices within the AB's deliberative process may subsequently lead the Court to reconsider the constitutional position and role of EU law in Hungary.

---

[136] The Avowal of National Faith states: 'We recognize the role Christianity has played in preserving our nation. We value our country's different religious traditions.'

[137] The new President, Barnabás Lenkovics, was elected AB judge in 2007 as was Lévay, J while Kiss, J was first elected in 1998 (and re-elected in 2007) and is now the longest serving member of the bench.

17

Central and Eastern European Constitutional Courts Facing New Challenges: Ten Years of Experience

MAREK SAFJAN

I. The Context

The complexity of relations between CEE (Central and Eastern Europe) constitutional courts and the European Union courts does not allow us to subordinate their evaluation to one simple 'key explanatory' formula which is sometimes proposed in the legal scholarship. It is undebatable that ambiguity and tensions between different goals and purposes after the collapse of the communist system were at that time inevitable and even inscribed into the nature of the process of transformation in our part of Europe. They consisted, on the one hand, of a clear imperative to rebuild the constitutional ethos, as well as to restore the concept and the values of the State ruled by law and democratic axiology, on the other hand of an imperative to create a stable and strong fundament for the future European integration, for which the new relations with Western Europe were very important.

This process required the recreation of the constitutional culture and constitutional awareness among the people. It constituted an enormous effort and challenge after almost 50 years of authoritarian experience in this part of Europe. First of all, at the beginning of the 1990s, it was absolutely necessary to convince the society that the constitutional culture based on the rule of law and democracy merits considerable respect and that it can guarantee the rights and interests of the individuals in their relations with the State and public authorities. In fact, it required the rejection of a paradigm which up until then determined the status of a citizen in a communist State, in which vertical relations were totally deformed and the individuals were deprived of their rights, and in which the interest of the communist authorities was to preserve their status, including their uncontrolled power.

For these reasons the post-communist environment was a perfect ground for creation (recreation) of the constitutional ethos. In some CEE States, the constitutional courts became the main actors of the transformation process and the constitutional case law strongly stimulated the complex process of rebuilding the democratic State ruled by law. Just after the collapse of the communist system, when the old constitutional provisions originating from the communist period were still in force, the constitutional case law allowed to fill the vacuum left by the previous regime in the field of democratic axiology, imposing by its very creative judgments the respect for democratic standards and particularly for the fundamental rights which had vanished for almost 50 years from the public sphere. In some States (as, for example, in Poland) it was a special time when the Constitution as the ideal 'model' or a perfect sublimation of the will of the nation had a significant place in the system and became 'a real body' only through the constitutional case law. The reason for this specificity was the fact that the written Constitution remained for a long time (in Poland until 1997) not adapted to the aspirations of a democratic society. When waiting for a new written Constitution, which would constitute an adequate answer to the requirements of the democratic State, the effort of creating the new constitutional architecture, and especially the constitutional framework for the transformation process, was made by the *Trybunał Konstytucyjny* (Constitutional Tribunal, hereinafter 'TK'). The TK reintroduced (or at least has revived) to the legal system such basic principles as for example protection against discrimination, protection of private ownership against the State, protection of privacy, protection of acquired rights (sometimes further specified as 'justly acquired'), the citizen's confidence in the democratic State ruled by law, interdiction of retroactivity of legal acts, interdiction to change tax rules during a current year and the principle of the so called decent legislation.[1] The constitutional case law has become a clear and manifest expression of constitutional sovereignty. For the first time this part of Europe has sent a significant message concerning the limits which must be respected even by a democratically elected parliament, underlining also the crucial place which has to be attributed to the fundamental rights in the constitutional architecture of a democratic State.[2]

Such trends were observed in all post-communist States.[3] This phenomenon of a very creative jurisprudence and judicial activism was present at that time in Hungary, during the presidency of Mr Sólyom,[4] achieving open and creative interpretation of

---

[1] The principle of the so called decent legislation is featured by characteristics such as transparency and accessibility to legal acts, respect for hierarchy of normative rules, division of competencies between the parliament and the executive power, comprehensibility and non-contradiction between legal rules, respect for the requirement of *vacatio legis* before the normative act enters into force, etc. One can observe that most of these requirements in some sense coincide with the LL Fuller's theory on the minimal and necessary features of every legal act described in the book *Morality of Law* (Yale University Press, 2003).

[2] This reasoning was often difficult to accept and therefore widely discussed.

[3] Of course, nothing was absolutely perfect and at that time some negative phenomena were also established as for example the politicisation of constitutional *iustitia* or excessive judicial activism, see: W Sadurski, *Rights before Courts: A Study of Constitutional Courts in Post-communist States of Central and Eastern Europe* (Springer, 2005).

[4] See L Sólyom, 'Constitutional Justice—Some Comparative Remarks' in Venice Commission, Conference on 'Constitutional Justice and the Rule of Law' on the occasion of the 10th anniversary of the Constitutional Court of Lithuania (Vilnius, 4–5 September 2003), online at <www.venice.coe.int>, last accessed 1 December 2014.

the Hungarian Constitution. The essence of his idea has been formulated in the so called theory of the 'living Constitution'. Most manifestly such a wide and flexible approach towards the interpretation of the Constitution was applied in the judgment of the Lithuanian Constitutional Court related to the impeachment procedure against the President of the Republic, in which the Court decided to complete some insufficient constitutional rules in that matter by making reference to the idea of the 'spirit of the Constitution'.[5] No doubt, at that time the development of the constitutional concepts and ideas was largely borrowed from constitutional courts of older Member States and ECtHR (European Court of Human Rights) case law. However, these borrowings did not deprive the CEE constitutional courts from seeing sense and necessity in searching for their own concepts, better adapted to the specific requirements of the transformation process. No simple answers were given in this complex political and social environment and CEE constitutional courts had to search for completely new solutions, not having at their disposal any precedent in the case law of the old European constitutional courts.

Allow me to mention a few examples of the cases that never before occurred in the constitutional case law in Europe. One of them was an exceptionally hard question related to the so called 'lustration process',[6] which required the constitutional courts to answer extremely ethically, politically and legally complex questions about the impact of the past of numerous collaborators of the communist secret services on the evaluation of their accountability in the democratic environment, especially with regard to civil servants, judges, prosecutors or members of different governmental bodies.

Other examples relate to the present constitutional evaluation of the consequences stemming from the former decisions taken by the communist authorities, with regard to nationalisation of private property,[7] criminal responsibility for the crimes committed by the communist officials against their political opponents,[8] legality of martial law introduced in Poland in 1981,[9] or compensation for the loss of property by the Polish citizens relocated after the Second World War from the eastern territories (now outside the borders) to the western part of Poland.[10] These questions required an entirely new approach to the constitutional standards and above all an interminable confrontation of the basic principles which were in clear and sharp opposition to one another almost in every case. These were for example legal security versus protection of private property (with regard to nationalisation), *nullum crimen sine lege* versus criminal

---

[5] Concept formulated in the judgment of the Lithuanian Constitutional Court of 25 May 2004, No 24/04 published in Valstybės žinios, 2004, No 85-3094, further developed in the judgment of 13 December 2004, No 51/01-26/02-19/03-22/03-26/03-27/03, published in Valstybės žinios, 2004, No 181-6708.

[6] See the judgment of TK K 39/97 on lustration proceedings of 10 November 1998, OTK ZU 1998/6/99 and the judgment of TK K 7/01 on procedures applied by the Institute of National Remembrance of 25 March 2003, OTK ZU 2003/3A/19.

[7] See the judgment of TK SK 22/01 of 24 October 2001 on decree of PKWN, OTK ZU 2001/7/216.

[8] See the judgment of TK P 2/99 of 6 July 1999, OTK ZU 1999/5/103.

[9] See the judgment of TK K 35/08 of 16 March 2011 on martial law, OTK ZU 2011/2A/11.

[10] See the judgment of TK K 33/02 of 19 December 2002 on mienie zabużańskie, OTK ZU 2002/7A/97.

responsibility (in cases on the responsibility of the former officials of the communist State, including judges), privacy versus public interest (with regard to lustration), acquired rights versus the principle of social justice and equal treatment (when the system of privileges acquired by the former servants and officials of the communist State as for example special high pensions were analysed).

My experience as a former constitutional judge allows me to say that the first stage after the collapse of the communist system was particularly marked by a large and very serious interpretation by the constitutional jurisdictions of the constitutional guarantees of fundamental rights which, at that time, created a strong fundament of the constitutional culture in CEE Member States. I have the impression (shared by a part of the doctrine) that in my country the protection of fundamental rights has become in some fields stronger and more effective than the one guaranteed by the international courts and in the European case law. There is a groundswell of opinion that the 'constitutional protectionism' of individual rights includes the use of the principles of decent legislation (requiring a certain quality of legal acts, including transparency and clarity of laws), protection against retroactivity of laws, stability of the tax system as a necessary component of the legal security and a wide protection of the right to fair trial. The level of sensitivity to some potential violation of the fundamental rights was perhaps stronger than in the old Member States' systems, in particular because of the still vivid memory of the communist time, when the abuse of power by the public authorities was part of everyday life.

Of course, it is not my intention to describe the historical role and the achievements of CEE constitutional courts in the chapter devoted to the constitutional case law in the new Member States, and especially to their relations with the European legal space. However, it must be stressed that without this historical perspective we are not able to understand either the role of these courts in the process of transformation, or the construction of the 'constitutional building'. Even this very superficial description allows us to identify two main features which characterised the case law at that time. First, the replacement of the purely positivist or dogmatic interpretation of constitutional provisions in favour of a functional, teleological interpretation[11] was carried out, with the latter being strongly determined by the clear axiological choices made by the judges.[12] Second, the attachment to the specific 'constitutional sovereignty' which was at that time an inalienable part of

---

[11] For that reason I am not convinced by the evaluation of the Constitutional case law made by T Koncewicz above in ch 14 of this volume, where he present an opinion that 'the case law is analysed in an extremely dogmatic fashion'.

[12] This aspect sometimes provoked fundamental criticism stressing that choices made by the judges were politically motivated and therefore they disregarded the limits of the competencies attributed to judicial power and in fact entered into the field of legislative power. In this regard, see my article 'The Constitutional Court as a Positive Legislator' in *Rapport polonaise, XVIII Congrès International de droit comparé. Washington 2010* (Wydawnictwo Uniwersytetu Łódzkiego, 2010). See also for example the commentaries of P Radziewicz, K Skotnicki, A Szmyt, of the TK judgment on lustration, case K 2/07 of 11 May 2007, (2007) *Przegląd Sejmowy* 6 (83).

the process of transformation permitting, on the one hand, to boost the process of transformation and, on the other hand, to limit seriously the discretion of the lawmaker[13] in favour of the standards featuring the State ruled by law. Of course, one can say that, at least sometimes, it took the form of a very naïve 'constitutional patriotism' and created illusions and unjustified expectations in the society towards the constitutional power, seen as being able to ensure an absolute justice and perfect equilibrium between the different fundamental rights.[14] However, even later, when the constitutional culture acquired a more mature form, these two features (judicial activism and a trend towards the protection of the 'constitutional sovereignty') persisted and they are substantive factors to better understand the complicated 'story' concerning the relations between the CEE constitutional courts and the European justice.

At the end of this section, it is worth adding that if we look at the public opinion survey at that time, we can see (and it is not a great surprise) that constitutional courts enjoyed the greatest degree of public confidence and respect among all State authorities. It was a typical phenomenon not only in Poland but also in almost all post-communist States. We can thus come to a conclusion that this 'constitutional patriotism' was an indispensable factor to push forward the process of transformation and to get a large part of the society attached to this new ideology of the democratic space.

II. The Ambiguities

Without understanding the complexity of the process during the post-communist transformation and the enormous effort to recreate social and political space in these countries where the rule of law and democracy were absent for almost 50 years, we will not be able to evaluate the discrepancy and tensions between the growing sentiment for 'constitutional sovereignty' on the one hand, and the will to join the European Union on the other hand. The latter requires partial resignation from sovereignty and the replacement (at least in the light of the popular narration dominant among the general public) of one 'Big Brother' that is the Soviet Union with a new one—the European Union.

For these reasons, the accession to the European Union was a greater and probably more complex challenge for the CEE Member States than it was in the past for the long-established democracies. We should remember that the accession

---

[13] See for example the famous decision of the TK overriding, before entry into force of the new Constitution, the requirement that the constitutional ruling should be confirmed by the parliament. It was a kind of a real revolt against the remainders of the previous regime, see TK resolution W 6/93 of 20 October 1993, OTK ZU 1993/51; OTK ZU 1986-1995/t4/1993/cz2/51; OTK ZU 1993 part II p 482–94.

[14] In Poland this was visible in particular just after the adoption of the new constitution (1997), which set up an individual constitutional complaint. The disappointments became inevitable.

was for the new Member States a kind of 'shock therapy', completely incomparable with the process which the old Member States underwent many years earlier. The former had no possibility to adapt their legal systems in a peaceful, slow and multi-stage process. They were obliged to introduce all the revolutionary changes until the 'Big Bang' momentum, meaning the accession.

Some ambiguities and even contradictions were inevitable in these conditions. The imperative to protect the Constitution as a supreme normative act in the legal order does not offer a very clear answer to the problems related to the primacy of the European law. Interpretation in favour of integration and compatibility of the Accession Treaty with the constitutional norms, especially with the rule which stresses the superior status of the Constitution over all norms being in force in the national legal order,[15] requires a very subtle interpretation and resembles 'a dance on a tightrope'. If we take the TK's judgment on the Accession Treaty as an example, on the one hand, the judgment stressed the importance of the internationalisation of law and its openness to the external standards set up by the international rules, case law and the customary law. On the other hand, it underlined the value of sovereignty and unquestionable supremacy of the Constitution.[16] The Polish political scene, for instance, was not free from very aggressive statements against the integration process. Even the constitutional review before the TK related to the Accession Treaty was initiated by the members of the Polish Parliament who argued that the Treaty flagrantly violated basic constitutional principles, in particular the principle that the ultimate sovereign power is attributed to the Polish nation. The political and social context of the debate was not insignificant for the final message sent by the TK in particular to this party which saw the Constitution as the ultimate guarantor of the sovereignty.[17]

I believe that during this initial stage of the integration process, the constitutional jurisdictions in CEE passed their exam with relatively good notes, shaping and adapting the constitutional framework to the integration process, and at the same time preserving the very ethos of the constitutional supremacy and their status as supreme guarantors of the fundamental rights and freedoms. In my view, the position of the constitutional courts of CEE was rather flexible and open

---

[15] See for example the Art 8 (1) of the Polish Constitution.

[16] See the judgment of TK K/18/04 on the Accession Treaty of 11 May 2005, OTK ZU 2005/49/5A and especially para 13 of the English version (corresponding to para 6.4. of the Polish version): 'such a collision between regulations of Community law and the Constitution may in no event be resolved by assuming the supremacy of a Community norm over a constitutional norm. Furthermore, it may not lead to the situation whereby a constitutional norm loses its binding force and is substituted by a Community norm, nor may it lead to an application of the constitutional norm restricted to areas beyond the scope of Community law regulation.'

[17] See the judgment of TK K/18/04 on the Accession Treaty of 11 May 2005, OTK ZU 2005/49/5A and especially para 8 of the English version (para 4.5 Polish version) in which the role of the Constitution as the supreme source of law is clearly stressed: 'neither Article 90(1) nor Article 91(3) authorise delegation to an international organisation of the competence to issue legal acts or take decisions contrary to the Constitution, being the 'supreme law of the Republic of Poland' (Article 8(1)). Concomitantly, these provisions do not authorise the delegation of competences to such an extent that it would signify the inability of the Republic of Poland to continue functioning as a sovereign and democratic State.'

towards the integration and eventually not very different from the constitutional case law in old Member States.[18]

The process of the opening towards European law started many years before the accession. It began with the constitutional jurisprudence which introduced the principle of an EU favourable interpretation of domestic laws,[19] followed by the references to EU law made in the constitutional case law, in particular in the field of consumer protection.[20] By the way, even the idea of the favourable interpretation raised a lot of criticism in some political milieus, because for them it was an evident symptom of the resignation from the constitutional sovereignty. References to EU law and the adopted interpretation were not in themselves—as some believe—a clear manifestation of 'asymmetric relations' between EU and national legal systems and a logical consequence of the 'centre–periphery' scheme pretending to describe the constitutional reality in Europe before and just after the accession. In my view, there is no justification for the assumption that at that time the case law of the CEE constitutional courts indicated the defiance of autonomy in constitutional thinking. I would rather suggest that it was a fully controlled process permitting an approach to the European legal system step by step, but always respecting the boundaries designed by the concept of the constitutional sovereignty.

In my view, an excellent illustration of this ambiguity or rather flexibility—but in the first place a well nuanced judgment—was the European Arrest Warrant (EAW) decision of the TK.[21] In this judgment, an ideal balance between, on the one hand, the requirements stemming from the clear constitutional rule which forbade extradition of Polish citizens and, on the other hand, the requirements of the European framework decision on EAW, was struck. Two goals were achieved at the same time: Supremacy of the inviolable constitutional norm, on the one hand, and the effectiveness of the European provisions, on the other. The TK, adjudicating on the incompatibility with the Constitution of the provisions of

---

[18] See for instance the decisions taken by the Courts of Denmark, Germany, Spain or France; see: M Wyrzykowski, 'When Sovereignty Means so Much: The Concept(s) of Sovereignty, European Union Membership and the Interpretation of the Constitution of the Republic of Poland' in *The Court of Justice and the Construction of Europe/La Cour de Justice et la Construction de l'Europe* (Springer, 2013) 229–55.

[19] In fact, this interpretative directive was also addressed to the constitutional rules. See, eg, the judgment of TK on Biofuels K 33/03 of 21 April 2004, OTK ZU 2004/4A/31 or judgment of TK on alcohol advertising K 2/02 of 28 January 2003, OTK ZU 2003/1A/4, see also my article 'Niezależność Trybunału Konstytucyjnego i suwerenność konstytucyjna RP' ['The Independence of the Polish Constitutional Tribunal and the Constitutional Sovereignty of the Republic of Poland'] (2006) LXI(6) *Państwo i Prawo* R 3–17 on the Constitution and European Law. See D Kiedrowska, '"Proeuropejska" wykładnia prawa polskiego w okresie przedakcesyjnym—analiza wyroku Trybunału Konstytucyjnego z dnia 28 stycznia 2003 r' in L Leszczynski (ed), *Wykładnia prawa odrębności w wybranych gałęziach prawa* (Lublin, 2006) 177–87.

[20] In the context of constitutional prohibition of reverse discrimination see judgment of TK K 33/03 of 21 April 2004, on biofuels, OTK ZU 2004/4A/31.

[21] See the judgment of TK P 1/05 of 27 April 2005, on the European Arrest Warrant, OTK ZU 2005/4A/42.

the national code of criminal procedure necessary to implement EAW, decided at the same time on the suspension of the legal effects of that judgment for 18 months, in order to give the Parliament a real possibility to adopt the necessary constitutional amendments.[22]

III. Field of Confrontation

Taking into account this background, it seems evident that the most serious battles between the constitutional courts and the Court of Justice (ECJ) take place in the field related to the fundamental rights and freedoms. One can consider that this situation is inherently inscribed into the nature of the relationships between these supreme jurisdictions—at the European and at the national level. Recent years were marked by the trend towards the 'constitutionalisation' of the European legal system. The entry into force of the Lisbon Treaty and the Charter of Fundamental Rights (the Charter), only accelerated this trend, foreseeable already more than 30 years ago. Fundamental rights protection is the central activity of all constitutional jurisdictions, not only those of the CEE Member States. However, differences between the new members and the old members persist. In my opinion, one difference is the fact that the former jurisdictions are more attached to their constitutional ethos because of various historical and political reasons mentioned above.

In this post-accession context, the approach based on the 'constitutional ideology' had to clash with a strong, relatively recent trend towards the functional protection of fundamental rights granted by the Charter, which widely opened the doors of the national legal systems for reintroduction of the Charter protection standards, in situations when the European provisions are implemented through domestic laws.[23] The interpretation of Article 51 of the Charter given by the ECJ in *Åkerberg Fransson*[24] is a very clear confirmation of this tendency. Hence, the potential clash

---

[22] The EAW judgment is not the only example of the openness towards the integration represented by the case law. This tendency was also present in the TK judgment K15/04 of 31 May 2004, on the electoral rights in local elections, OTK ZU 2004/5A/47 where TK underlined the constitutionality of law which provided the electoral rights also in favour of EU citizens being residents in Poland. A relatively recent judgment of TK K 33/12 of 26 June 2013, on European Stability Mechanism (decision of European Council 2011/199/EU), OTK ZU 2013/5A/63 can be also placed in the same line of case law.

[23] See eg A Rosas, 'The Applicability of the EU Charter of Fundamental Rights at National Level' (2013) *European Yearbook on Human Rights* 97; K Lenaerts and JA Guitierrez-Fons, 'The Place of the Charter in the EU Constitutional Edifice' in S Peers et al (eds), *The EU Charter of Fundamental Rights— A Commentary* (Hart Publishing, 2014) 1559–93; M Safjan, 'Fields of A pplication of the Charter of Fundamental Rights and Constitutional Dialogues in the European Union' (EUI Distinguished lectures series, CJC DL 2014/02, Florence 2014), online at <http://cadmus.eui.eu>, last accessed 1 December 2014.

[24] Case C-617/10 *Åkerberg Fransson*, ECLI:EU:C:2013:105. See also other judgments which represent that line in jurisprudence C-411/10 *NS*, ECLI:EU:C:2011:865; Case C-279/09 *DEB*, ECLI:EU:C:2010:811; Case C-168/13 *Jeremy F.* ECLI:EU:C:2013:358.

between the European and national constitutional ethos becomes in some sense inevitable. However, the tensions between them are not the particularity of the relations between CEE constitutional courts and the ECJ but, simultaneously, create a crucial challenge for the constitutional courts from the 'old' Europe as well. The German *Bundesverfassungsgericht* formulated many reservations and objections[25] against the approach developed in *Mangold*[26] and *Kücükdeveci*[27] and also in its message sent in the post *Åkerberg Fransson* case—the *Counter Terrorist Database* judgment.[28] This position is very well known and has been vastly developed in the literature. Nevertheless, also other constitutional courts are not free from serious dilemmas raised by the possible tensions between the constitutional guarantees and the Charter standards. Some recent judgments of the ECJ initiated by the constitutional courts or supreme courts expressly featured at least the possibility of clashes between different standards of fundamental rights protection at the European and national level. As an example we can refer to ECJ judgments: *Melki and Abdeli*[29] and *Jeremy F*[30]—in the French context; *Melloni*[31]—in the Spanish context; *Chartry*[32]— in the Belgian context; and *Åkerberg Fransson*[33]—in the Swedish context.

We should also note that the dialogue between the ECJ and the constitutional courts is neither easy nor evident. This observation relates to the constitutional courts from all the Member States. The first preliminary references of the constitutional courts of Spain, Italy, Germany and of the French *Conseil Constitutionnel* have been introduced in recent years—after decades of membership of the respective States in the European Union.[34] The only rational explanation for this phenomenon is that the constitutional ethos related to the fundamental rights protection plays an essential role as the main motive and even the very identification of the constitutional jurisdictional activity, both in the new and old Member States.

I believe that we have to be careful in our evaluations related to the constitutional case law. For the same reason, we should avoid overgeneralised opinions about the evolution of the dialogue between the constitutional courts of the CEE states and the ECJ. Some single judicial decisions, even those which relate to crucial issues, as for instance the TK's judgment on the Brussels I Regulation,[35] could, from my perspective, not create a sufficient basis for a definite prognosis for the further relationship between the ECJ and the TK. I have the impression that two

---

[25] Case 2 BvR 2661/06 *Honeywell*, judgment of BVerfG 6 July 2010.

[26] Case C-144/04 *Mangold*, ECLI:EU:C:2005:709.

[27] Case C-555/07 *Kücükdeveci*, ECLI:EU:C:2010:21.

[28] Case 1 BvR 1215 /07 *Counter—terrorist Database*, judgment of BVerfG of 24 April 2014.

[29] Case C-188/10, C-189/10 *Aziz Melki and Sélim Abdeli*, ECLI:EU:C:2010:363.

[30] Case C-168/13 *Jeremy F* (n 24).

[31] Case C-399/11 *Melloni*, ECLI:EU:C:2013:107.

[32] Case C-457/09 *Claude Chartry*, ECLI:EU:C:2011:101.

[33] Above (n 24).

[34] See D Ritleng, 'Cours constitutionnelles nationales et renvoi préjudiciel' in *Mélanges en l'honneur du Professeur Joël Moliner* (LGDJ, 2012) 583.

[35] See the judgment of TK SK 45/09 of 16 November 2011 on the Brussels I Regulation 44/2001, OTK ZU 2011/98A/97.

different narratives concerning this judgment are not excluded. The message may be read as being either in favour of the traditional constitutional ethos, seen as a possibility of constitutional review of the European provisions or, on the contrary, in favour of the coherent legal protection of fundamental rights in the European Union because the conditions of the potential challenge of the European provisions are rather purely hypothetical and almost impossible to be fulfilled. Of course, the judgment itself is not coherent because the judges wanted to reach a completely different goal by their statement expressed in the reasoning. The statement given in this judgment about the possibility of constitutional review of the European provisions was, I believe, only a simple pretext for the TK to express its own theoretical 'constitutional ideology' with regard to the tendency of the European case law concerning an intensified protection of fundamental rights.

In my opinion, the judgment is not a manifestation of a real will to object to the established position of the ECJ's case law and the principle that the review of European provisions constitutes an exclusive competence of the ECJ. For the above mentioned reasons, to say that the TK has broken—through this judgment—a delicate and fragile balance in the relations between the European and national orders would be, in my view, a great simplification, especially if we take into consideration the existence of many other judgments of the TK which adopt a favourable approach towards strengthening the idea of the common European legal space and towards the dialogue.[36] We should necessarily distinguish between, on the one hand, specific constitutional language used in the case law addressed not only to the academia and specialised lawyers but also (and first of all) to the general public and, on the other hand, the message expressed by a certain decision taken in a particular case. The discrepancy between, on the one hand, the arguments which, being purely theoretical figures, operate among some hypothetical premises and try to define and to test potential consequences stemming from different and/or alternative approaches and, on the other hand, the real outcomes which are most often very moderated or equilibrated, and usually perfectly harmonised with the great lines established in the European case law, become sometimes very large (or even too large).[37]

This kind of specific, constitutional language adopting 'a strong sovereign perspective' applied by the TK in such cases as related to the Accession Treaty,[38] Lisbon Treaty,[39] or, in particular, the Brussels I Regulation[40] could be found—as mentioned above—either in numerous constitutional decisions taken by the

---

[36] See for example the judgment of TK already quoted above (n 21) on EAW, P 1/05 of 27 April 2005, OTK ZU 2005/4A/42; the judgment of TK P 37/05 of 19 December 2006, OTK ZU 2006/11A/176; the judgment of TK K 33/12 of 26 June 2013 on the European Stability Mechanism (decision of European Council 2011/199/EU), OTK ZU 2013/5A/63.

[37] Unfortunately it is not the case of the judgment of the Czech Constitutional Tribunal on Slovak Pensions (Pl ÚS 5/12 of 31 January 2012) which instead of being a pure 'warning' goes further and clearly opposes the ECJ's judgment.

[38] See the judgment of TK K/18/04 of 11 May 2005 on the Accession Treaty, OTK ZU 2005/49/5A.

[39] See the judgment of TK K 32/09 of 24 November 2010 on the Lisbon Treaty, OTK ZU 2010/9A/108.

[40] See the judgment of TK SK 45/09 of 16 November 2011 on the Brussels I Regulation 44/2001, OTK ZU 2011/98A/97.

constitutional courts of the old Member States[41] and especially by the German *Bundesverfassungsgericht* (including the recent case law).[42] The reasons for such case law expressing this specific 'constitutional warning' are not necessarily dictated by 'purely egoistic, dogmatic constitutional absolutism', that is by the will of the constitutional courts to preserve their own exclusive prerogatives over the national legal systems. My personal experience allows me to say that paradoxically one of the motives for applying such language can be the intention to prevent potential collisions with EU law, that could be caused by clearer determination of the boundaries of the field subordinated exclusively to the national constitutional provisions and to ensure better cooperation between the ECJ and national jurisdictions. Of course, such an approach is probably naïve because it does not sufficiently take into account the dynamic nature of the integration process and the mutual permeation between the European and national law, however it expresses a rather natural tendency, typical for national constitutional courts, not only in our part of Europe. In my view, it would be very risky to postulate the model of constitutionalism called 'vigilant', as it urges the Court to move away from the traditional notion of constitutional court as a guardian of Constitution only towards a court that is more engaged in a constructive dialogue on the European stage and reads its mandate through the prism of European constitutionalism.[43]

We cannot deny that constitutional courts are by their nature the guardians of the Constitution and this role is their basic mission in each national system where constitutional justice exists. Constitutional judges who would like to refrain from their main task which is to guarantee the respect of the constitutional rules would betray their duties. For this reason, we should not require that they become judges with 'divided loyalty' between their own Constitutions and the European constitutionalism, and recognise the two systems as an entirely equivalent fundament of their judicial activity. The real challenge for a constitutional judge consists in such an execution of his or her tasks that—being the main and most important guardian of the Constitution—he or she is able, if possible, to apply the Constitution taking into account the European legal environment and to ensure the perfect complementarity of the two systems. Is this suggestion purely 'wishful thinking'?

---

[41] See for example the judgments of the French Constitutional Council 2008-560 DC of 20 December 2007; the judgment of the Belgian Constitutional Court 58/2009 of 19 March 2009; the Spanish Constitutional Tribunal's decision on the Constitution for Europe, Declaration 12/2004, DTC 1/2004 of 13 December 2004; Danish Supreme Court's decision on the constitutionality of Maastricht Treaty, I 361/1997 of 6 April 1998.

[42] See the judgments of the *Bundesverfassungsgericht* 2 BvR 197/83, Solange (II) of 22 October 1986; 2 BvR 2661/06 of 6 July 2010 or Case 1 BvR 1215/07 Counter-terrorist Database, judgment of *Bundesverfassungsgericht* of 24 April 2014 in which it warned the ECJ not to overstretch the competencies attributed by EU law and to respect a no ultra vires principle.

[43] Above, ch 14 in this volume.

IV. Is the Very Dialogue Possible?

I hope that the space for dialogue has been cast wide open through the recent ECJ judgments in *Melloni* and *Åkerberg Fransson*. It is beyond any doubt that for the first time the ECJ clearly stated that the application of national constitutional standards of protection of fundamental rights could coexist with the application of the Charter. In my view, these judgments created a new platform for the dialogue between the ECJ and constitutional courts. I may express my hope that national and EU courts have now been given a useful tool which can be used in their mutual relations and which can, at the same time, diminish the level of asymmetries in these relationships. Through this platform, the constitutional traditions of the Member States could also permeate more effectively into the European case law. The essential question is whether the national constitutional courts will take advantage of this new approach of the ECJ[44] and, above all, whether they will be able to initiate a good and fruitful dialogue with the ECJ. Personally, I believe that through a rational and convincing argumentation national courts may significantly contribute to shaping the standards of protection of the fundamental rights in the EU.

For the constitutional justice in the CEE, such a new platform of dialogue raises ironically a new dilemma of a socio-politico-psychological nature because it requires a more intensive participation in this dialogue through the preliminary references addressed to the ECJ. However, two potential difficulties may arise. First, the constitutional judges have to accept the idea that the initiation of a dialogue by means of preliminary reference does not express any hierarchical dependency between the jurisdictional structures. Second, the approach towards the constitutional identity should be rethought in the future because presently there are many misinterpretations of this idea.

---

[44] This new approach has been expressed in the recent, already cited cases of *Åkerberg Fransson* (above n 24) and *Melloni* (above n 31), in which the Court opened the door to the simultaneous application of the standards of protection of the fundamental rights steaming from the Charter and those originating from the national constitutions. See in this regard [29] of *Åkerberg Fransson*: 'where a court of a Member State is called upon to review whether fundamental rights are complied with by a national provision or measure which, in a situation where action of the Member States is not entirely determined by European Union law, implements the latter for the purposes of Article 51(1) of the Charter, national authorities and courts remain free to apply national standards of protection of fundamental rights, provided that the level of protection provided for by the Charter, as interpreted by the Court, and the primacy, unity and effectiveness of European Union law are not thereby compromised.' In relation to the latter aspect, see [60] of *Melloni*: 'It is true that Article 53 of the Charter confirms that, where an EU legal act calls for national implementing measures, national authorities and courts remain free to apply national standards of protection of fundamental rights, provided that the level of protection provided for by the Charter, as interpreted by the Court, and the primacy, unity and effectiveness of EU law are not thereby compromised.'

V. Constitutional Identity

One can say that in constitutional case law, constitutional identity[45] represents the 'last bastion' of defence against the 'constitutional imperialism' of the ECJ. The spectrum of the idea of constitutional identity is very broad. The definition given by the TK in the Lisbon Treaty Judgment[46] can serve as an example in this regard. It includes not only the essential features of the constitutional structures of the State but also the constitutional standards of the guarantees of fundamental rights and freedoms. There are two possible scenarios of the future developments in this field.

First, the idea of constitutional identity becomes a permanent source of clashes between national jurisdictions and the ECJ. This implies a broad, literal interpretation of this concept (adopted for instance by the TK)[47] with all possible consequences, as for instance the fact that even small differences of the standard of protection between the Charter and a national Constitution could create a conflict and justify a refusal to apply the standard adopted by the ECJ. It is a pessimistic scenario. I personally do not believe in it.

Fortunately, there is also a second possibility which provides for a more constructive use of the idea of constitutional identity. The concept of constitutional identity could in fact serve as a point of departure for a dialogue with the ECJ and could constitute heavy ammunition in this exchange of arguments.[48] However, this requires from both parties of the dialogue, that is the ECJ and constitutional

---

[45] See B Guastaferro, 'Beyond the "Exceptionalism" of Constitutional Conflicts: the "Ordinary" Functions of the Identity Clause' (2012) 31 *Yearbook of European Law* 263; V Constantinesco, 'La confrontation entre identité constitutionnelle européenne et identités constitutionnelles nationales: convergence ou contradiction? Contrepoint ou hiérarchie?' in *L'Union Européenne, Union de droit, Union des droits, Mélanges en l'honneur de Philippe Manin* (Pedone, 2010) 79–94; A von Bogdandy and S Schill, 'Overcoming Absolute Primacy: Respect for National Identity under the Lisbon Treaty' (2011) 48 *Common Market Law Review* 1417; V Belling, 'Supranational Fundamental Rights or Primacy of Sovereignty? Legal Aspects of the So-called Opt-out from the EU Charter' (2012) 18 *European Law Journal* 254.

[46] See the judgment of TK K 32/09 of 24 November 2010 on Lisbon Treaty, OTK ZU 2010/9A/108.

[47] This broad concept was expressed in the reasoning of the judgment of TK on the Treaty of Lisbon (n 39). This approach covers also constitutional standards of the guarantees of fundamental rights. Such a wide approach poses an obvious risk of confrontation, especially because it leaves out the fact that EU law has a certain constitutional consensus (eg standards of protection of certain fundamental rights as interpreted by the ECJ) which should be treated as a relevant point of reference when assessing the compliance of national solutions with EU law. However, such a broad understanding of the notion of constitutional identity is present for example also in the German constitutional case law, see judgment of BVerfG, 2 BvE 2, 5/08, 2 BvR 1010, 1022, 1259/08, 182/09274 of 30 June 2009, and judgment of BVerfG, 2 BvR 2661/06 of 6 July 2010.

[48] See K Lenaerts, 'Wartości Unii Europejskiej a pluralizm konstytucyjny' (2014) 9 *Europejski Przegląd Sądowy* 4–16 and also A Alen et al, 'Human Rights Protection through Judicial Dialogue between National Courts and the European Court of Justice' in A Alen et al (eds), *Liberae Cogitationes: Liber Amicorum Marc Bossuyt* (Intersentia, 2013) 367–77; N Walker, 'The Idea of Constitutional Pluralism' (2002) 65 *Modern Law Review* 317.

courts, a necessary degree of flexibility and openness towards the opposite side. From constitutional judges, it requires the recognition of the fact that the scope of application of constitutional identity concept in a given case—if applied in the context of European law—is finally decided by the ECJ in the scope of its competencies. From the ECJ it demands a greater openness to the constitutional traditions of the Member States and more flexibility allowing some evolution of the standard of protection of fundamental rights. Sometimes, the effectiveness of EU law could give way to more intensive guarantees of the fundamental rights, according to the model adopted in the national constitutional case law.

VI. European Federalism and Constitutional Pluralism—Conditions Necessary for a New Dimension of the Dialogue

Constitutional pluralism is one of the important myths of the theoretical (academic) narrative relating to the modern description of the European legal space in the present stage of the integration process. I intentionally use the expression 'myth' because of the very broad and imprecise meaning of the notion of constitutional pluralism. Sometimes, I have the impression that the concept is used in a meaning resulting from a purely subjective vision and expectations of a concrete narrator. Personally, I am not convinced whether this notion is an adequate theoretical explanation of the present stage of integration and whether it properly identifies the nature of the relations between diverse legal orders creating legal space of the EU. In my view, neither 'constitutional pluralism' nor 'constitutional uniformity' (as an alternative) is a correct description of the complexity of the relations between the legal orders. In fact, we are confronted with these two different approaches at the same time—pluralism and uniformity—and we should avoid reducing all issues simply to these theoretical concepts. It could be also argued that the constitutional relations between legal orders in the EU are built according to an asymmetric scheme. This is due to the fact that, in principle, the fields in which priority is given to the concept of the constitutional pluralism do not fall within the competence of EU law. By contrast, in the fields that actually fall within the area of EU competence, the dominant feature is a trend towards primacy, uniformity and effectiveness of EU law. However, these relations are becoming more and more fragile and dynamic and it is getting more challenging to strike the balance between the idea of pluralism and uniformity.

There is a general problem that should attract our attention. With the progress of 'constitutionalisation' of the EU legal order, we can observe an increasing number of the fields of law where the demarcation line between the national orders and EU law becomes very unclear and hard to draw. Moreover, in these fields, the tendency towards uniformity is directly confronted with the tendency towards respect of the constitutional autonomy (or sovereignty). This confrontation is particularly visible in the domain of protection of fundamental rights.

It would be naïve to think that by using the axiology and the basic values universally shared by all participants of the dialogue, a solution could be easily found. Theoretically, a clear and precise solution is not possible because the constitutional sovereignty concept and the European legal ideology are based on a completely different logic. However, what all participants share is the view that each of them is more important than the others. In the framework of the existing concept of EU integration, the potential conflict is inscribed into the nature of the relations between sovereign Member States and the EU. Only a strategic idea of federalism could bring the ultimate solution in the future. Nevertheless, I am optimistic because the growing awareness of the risk of tensions and in particular of a destructive effect of this possible conflict has prevented us effectively for the last 60 years from the realisation of the most pessimistic scenario. At the end of the day, it has always been the very risk of jeopardising the European unity that in fact strengthened the European cohesion.

18

Conclusions: Of Form and Substance in Central European Judicial Transitions

MICHAL BOBEK[*]

I. Introduction

Legal transition is over. Long live the legal reform! This might be, in a nutshell, the gist of a number of chapters contained in this volume. Legal transition in terms of a large scale, deep-reaching transformation of judicial and legal institutions in Central Europe[1] is now no doubt over. There is no more political or social momentum for radical, far-reaching structural changes. The fact that a number of key changes have not been carried out or even attempted, or that they have failed, makes little difference in this assessment. The sub-optimal status quo, deficient as it may be, becomes the normal state of affairs. There still remains perhaps some hope for further change in the future. This may come, however, only in the form of individual legal reforms, hard to push through, since maintaining the status quo is the default guiding principle of any community, not to speak of by definition rather conservative judiciaries. In sum, what can be hoped for are individual snowflakes, but hardly any more avalanches.

Drawing on the rich discussions contained in preceding chapters, this concluding chapter critically revisits some of the common themes recurring throughout the volume. Section II adds three more caveats to those already listed in the introduction.[2] First, the blurry notion of Central and Eastern Europe is examined. Second, an overall change in attitude towards the 'West' in the 'East' is noted. Third, it is suggested

---

[*] I am indebted to Matej Avbelj, Pavlína Hubková, Alexander Kornezov and David Kosař for their comments on the draft of this chapter. The usual disclaimer, however, fully applies.
[1] In this chapter, the notion of 'Central Europe' refers to Poland, the Czech Republic, Slovakia, Hungary and Slovenia. 'Central and Eastern Europe' includes all the post-communist countries that joined the EU in 2004 and also Romania, Bulgaria, Croatia. On the geographical delimitation, see also above, ch 1, s III.C and also below, s II.A of this ch.
[2] Above, ch 1, s III.

that in the post-2004 European Union, it has not been just the Union that has been changing the new Member States, but also that the new Member States have been transforming the Union.

Section III focuses on judicial reasoning. The notions of 'formalism' and 'textualism' are examined. It is suggested that since the notion of 'formalism' is hopelessly overbroad and vague, with little or no consensus on what it is in fact supposed to mean (with the exception of serving as the universal insult for whatever type of judicial vices reproached), the problematic element in the reasoning style of some CE (Central European) judges might be better referred to as 'textualism'. On this basis, section III further explains, historically and sociologically, why CE judges have been more inclined to stick to the letter of the law, hesitating to project too much of their individual value choices in the form of purposive or contextual reasoning into the process of legal interpretation. The section concludes with the reflection on whether or not excessive textualism is in fact a problem for correct national application of EU law.

Section IV examines the quantitative as well as qualitative elements of the transformation of CE judicial institutions, structures and procedures under the European lead. To what degree have the new Member States been 'Europeanised'? It is demonstrated why a 'quantitative' study of the degree of 'Europeanisation' cannot but serve, at its best, as an approximate indicator for this phenomenon that needs to be verified by in-depth qualitative studies. Furthermore, an attempt at capturing the 'qualitative' side of the Europeanisation process and its externalities in Central Europe is made.

Section V zooms in on the CE constitutional courts and, in particular, on one unsettling question: How is it possible that constitutional courts, that served before 2004 as the pro-active champions of 'Europeanisation' in the CE countries, taking EU law on board in their decision making, instructing the lower courts to proceed in the same way, seeking inspiration in 'Europe', invoking 'European standards' ever so often, arrived just several years later after the 2004 enlargement to directly reviewing EU secondary law as to its compatibility with EU law or even declaring an act of EU law as ultra vires? Finally, section VI concludes by pondering on the process of legal transition as such. When is a transition in fact over? How can its success or failure be measured or evaluated?

II. Preliminary Points

A. Is there a 'Central and Eastern Europe'?

A well-known point that keeps nonetheless being forgotten in heated discussions about Central and Eastern Europe is the fact that these countries do not form a monolithic block. They never did. It was the pre-1989 geopolitical division of Europe and then the pre-2004 enlargement vantage point that put quite a diverse mix of countries into one bag, following the logic of a 'left-over' definition: The four Visegrad countries (Poland, Czech Republic, Slovakia and Hungary), came together with the three Baltic States (Estonia, Lithuania and Latvia), to be joined by Slovenia, and later by Bulgaria, Romania, and eventually by Croatia. Moreover, if a finer stress were to be put on the 'Eastern' element in the notion of 'Central and Eastern Europe', then a number of post-Soviet countries might start being included as well, such as Ukraine, Belarus, Moldova, as well as perhaps the Caucasus countries, and also the countries of the Western Balkans.

Certainly, if compared with Ghana, Venezuela or Japan, and viewed on the global scale, then the CEE countries will appear from outside of Europe as one block. At such a level of generality and abstraction, the commonalities among them are likely to outweigh the differences. On a closer look, however, in particular if compared only within Europe, the amount of difference rises considerably. Different pasts lead to different presents: It is not only different heritage from the times before 1918,[3] but also differentiated versions of 'living' or 'real' socialism[4] account for differences in structures, mentality and approaches today.

For these reasons, it is difficult to refer to one 'Central and Eastern European' judicial style, judicial ideology or institutions. As individual chapters in this volume demonstrate, the discussions and concerns in the various CEE countries of today are different, or at least representatives of the different legal systems choose to focus on different issues. Perhaps the greatest surprise to a continuous observer of this area and its evolution over the past 10 or 20 years might be how, in contrast to the 1990s, the roles have changed. Countries that, at the onset of the legal, social and economic transformation in the early 1990s, were generally believed to be the forerunners, the 'poster boys' for successful transformation, such as Slovenia or Hungary, are today being referred to as 'failed democracies'.[5] The depicted 'oligarchisation' of judiciaries and the absence of any further positive reforms in these countries for the last decade or more are everything but encouraging.[6] Yet again,

---

[3] Legal and administrative cultures are strikingly resilient. Thus, even in the early 21st century, it might still matter if and what kind of foundations, what kind of legal culture a state built in this regard in the course of the 19th and early 20th century. It would be most intriguing if a time traveller from late 19th century Austria could be sent for example to a lower administrative authority in the Czech countryside today in order to observe how much had really changed, in particular in terms of administrative culture: How is a file assembled; how does it circulate; how is an administrative decision supposed to look; and so on.

[4] Although typically perceived as one block from the outside, there was quite some internal differentiation within the Eastern block, especially in the 1970s and 1980s. The difference with regard to Central Europe was between, on the one hand, the more 'liberal' Poland and Hungary and, on the other hand, the 'hard-line' Czechoslovakia and the DDR, with former Yugoslavia being a completely different story altogether. For a case study on universities, see eg J Connelly, *Captive University: The Sovietization of East Germany, Czech, and Polish Higher Education, 1945–1956* (University of North Carolina Press, 2000). For a more personal comparative account of the different atmosphere and openness in each of the CE countries in late 1980s, see T Gordon Ash, *The Uses of Adversity: Essays on the Fate of Central Europe* (Penguin, 1999).

[5] Above, ch 13 in this volume.

[6] Above, ch 6 and to some extent also ch 5.

the old wisdom suggesting that a good starting position guarantees no victory in a race appears to be confirmed.

Stressing the internal difference among the CEE countries is not to suggest that a comparison among the CEE countries would not be advised: Quite to the contrary. But it should indeed be a comparison, in which similarities and differences are examined and objectively evaluated. '*Preasumptio similitudinis*'[7] should not be pushed too far, if it ought to be employed at all. A common problem in the discussions on 'Central and Eastern Europe' is that authors coming from just one country in the region quickly transform propositions that are based on the experience and situation in their system to the predicament of all CEE countries, which might not always be entirely appropriate.

B. *Die Entzauberung des Westens*

In his 'Science as Vocation', Max Weber referred to the 'Entzauberung der Welt' (Disenchantment of the World) as being one of the consequences of progress in sciences.[8] With the advancement in science, the outside world loses its magic. The principles of functioning of even the most complex mechanism and machines can be captured and understood.

Observing the discussions in this volume as well as more broadly the current debates in the CEE, one could speak of certain '*Entzauberung des Westens*' creeping into such debates. The European West is (no longer) seen as offering guaranteed solutions, flawless institutional blueprints, and the assembled wisdom and know-how for a successful reform. The authors, perhaps in particular the younger generation coming from the CEE region, who often studied in the West and have a personal experience of living in the West, do see more shades of grey when talking about the West, not just light.[9] In a way, some twenty years later, the 'promised' land of the early 1990s gradually became 'just another' land.[10] Or better to say, it started being recognised as a number of different lands. With the logic of the Cold War slowly dissipating, the 'East' might no longer be referred to as 'Central and Eastern Europe', and there is no single 'West', but a bulk of very different countries that just found themselves before 1989 in an apparent monolith called the 'West'.

---

[7] Already K Zweigert and H Kotz, *Introduction to Comparative Law*, translation T Weir, 3rd edn (Clarendon Press, 1998) 40. Critically see eg R Michaels, 'The Functional Method of Comparative Law' in M Reimann and R Zimmermann (eds), *Oxford Handbook of Comparative Law* (Oxford University Press, 2006).

[8] M Weber, 'Wissenschaft als Beruf' in Max Weber, *Schriften 1894–1922* (Kröner, 2002) 474, 488.

[9] For a rather sharp example of such a challenge, see J Komárek, 'The Struggle for Legal Reform after Communism. A review of Zdeněk Kühn, The Judiciary in Central and Eastern Europe: Mechanical Jurisprudence in Transformation?' *LSE Law, Society and Economy Working Paper No 10/2014*, 10–11 and 13–17.

[10] Although there certainly is again some internal differentiation, with (perhaps a bit surprisingly for a civil law country) the 'promised land' becoming the common law systems—see above, ch 6, s IV.

This is certainly not to suggest that similar 'disenchantment' with the West would question the legal and political orientation of Central and Eastern Europe, which would now be tempted to turn (again) to the East. Those few who might wish just for that have in fact never been enchanted by the West in the first place. One could therefore hardly speak of a change in orientation. If viewed in an optimistic light, a certain degree of disenchantment is a healthy development. A mutual relationship based on more of a sober, rational knowledge of one's partner is likely to last longer than the initial enchantment and magic that evaporates with the light of the day. At the same time, the nature of the relationship changes: From a rather asymmetrical, pupil-master relationship to a more horizontal, if perhaps not entirely equal, kind of relationship. In a way, the 'East' started growing up.

C. The Transformative Power of Europe or (Another) Transformation of Europe?

The primary focus of this volume has been on how 'Europe', be it the European Union, but also the Council of Europe (in particular the European Convention and the European Court of Human Rights), has (not) been transforming the formerly 'new' Member States. The rather straight-forward, top-down 'Europeanisation' of the new Member States under the influence of Europe has been examined. However, in some contributions, another issue kept surfacing: If we were to assume that there is a distinct CE or even CEE judicial style, legal thinking, and, on the whole, 'way of doing things', have they not made their way into Europe, that is into the EU institutions as such? Have the new Member States not had an impact on some of the decision making of the EU institutions?

A positive answer to such a question would have at least two important consequences. First, it would remind us yet again that 'Europeanisation' can hardly be conceived of as a 'one-way' street, as mutual exchange limited to top-down imposition of solutions. Second, it might indirectly confirm that there is indeed something different, something distinct about CEE law or legal culture, a discussion that kept recurring in a number of chapters of this volume.[11]

Certainly, much more research is needed before any suggestions can be attempted as to how the 'big bang' enlargement in 2004, together with is 'sequels' in 2007 and 2013, altered the Union. It is also true that the enlargement of any institution, community or society is initially marked by the new members just learning their way around, being perhaps more silent and more on the 'recipient side' than directly contributing to the running of the institution. Moreover, it should be also borne in mind that the increase in the number of Member States did not immediately translate into a corresponding increase of the nationals of the new Member States, certainly not at the higher positions within the EU institutions.

---

[11] Above, ch 2, but also 6, 7, 13 and 17.

If one looks at the courts, however, in particular the Court of Justice, in 2004, 10 new judges from CEE (including Malta and Cyprus) came in, with a further two in 2007 and another one in 2013. Thus, within less than 10 years, the size of the institution almost doubled, at least with regard to the members of the Court of Justice. However, the absence of dissenting opinions in the Court of Justice makes the tracking of individual judicial views, reasoning styles and approaches, and their impact on the decision making in the Court of Justice after 2004 very difficult.

A glance at the European Court of Human Rights (ECtHR) and its case law following its 'Eastern Enlargement' that took place already in the 1990s may nonetheless support the suggestion that at least to some extent, the East transforms the European level, which is then translated into the West. In contrast to the more horizontal and direct West-East transfers, the East-West transfers tend to be indirect and diagonal. Examples might be provided by judicial or legal institutions that since the Eastern enlargement of the Council of Europe are viewed with a more demanding eye as far as their external appearance and solid institutional safeguards are concerned. What might have been previously accepted with regard to the West is no longer permissible once encountered in the East.[12] However, once the more stringent requirements with regard to institutional separation and the external appearance of institutions are imposed on the East, they are likely to backfire on the West.[13] They make it politically and diplomatically difficult to explain why certain institutions are 'allowed' in the West but are 'not allowed' in the East.[14] It is in this way that the incoming East first modifies the European level and later the West.

With regard to the EU, on the level of a hypothesis, it could be suggested that 'something has changed' also within the European institutions following their Eastern enlargement. Fascinating avenues for further research would be to find out what precisely and to what extent. What if, for example, to push the point to

---

[12] See for example *Gurov v Moldova*, judgment of 11 July 2006, App no 36455/02 (concerning the automatic renewal of judges whose term of office expired) or *Volkov v Ukraine*, judgment of 9 January 2013, App no 21722/11 (on institutional 'flexibility' in terms of composition and the internal structure of the High Council of the Judiciary). One might only speculate whether similar structural issues would pose a problem if emerging within cases coming from within more established democracies. See in this regard also para 3 in the concurring opinion of Judge Garlicki and Judge Pellonpää in *Gurov v Moldova*.

[13] Another example in this regard might the uncompromising quest of the ECtHR against 'non-judicial members' of high courts representing public interest, such as advocates general or public procurators, which was launched in the 1990s. Further see M Bobek, 'A Fourth in the Court: Why Are There Advocates-General in the Court of Justice?' (2012) 14 *Cambridge Yearbook of European Legal Studies* 529, 546–47, or generally D Kosař, 'Policing Separation of Powers: A New Role for the European Court of Human Rights?' (2012) 8 *European Constitutional Law Review* 33.

[14] See in this regard the concurring opinion of Judge Myjer in *Sanoma Uitgevers BV v the Netherlands*, judgment of the Grand Chamber of 14 September 2010, App no 38224/03, where he explicitly acknowledges this by stating that [at para 5]:

What would your answer have been if a similar case, with a comparable show of force by the police and the prosecution service, had been brought before us from one of the new democracies? … Would you still have allowed yourself to be satisfied by the involvement, at the eleventh hour, of a judge who has no legal competence in the matter? … That was ultimately the push I needed to be persuaded to cross the line and espouse an opinion opposite to that which I held earlier.

the hypothetical extreme, following the 2004 enlargement, the new Member States did not change themselves much internally but instead 'infected' the European courts with more of positivistic self-restraint and even 'formalism', whatever that notion might actually entail?

III. Judicial Reasoning: Formalism, Textualism and other Insults

A lot has been written with regard to 'formalism' of and in the CEE courts. Chapters two to seven in the first part of this volume add valuable insights into this debate. All the chapters offer illuminating, but also very different views on CEE formalism. This section will, in lieu of some tentative conclusions, look into three issues: The notion of CEE formalism itself; what were its roots; and, finally, perhaps the most important issue for a volume dealing with the impact the EU membership has had on the new Member States—is formalism in fact a problem for the national application of EU law?

A. What is the Problem? 'Formalism' versus Textualism

What is meant by judicial 'formalism'? Perhaps the only common denominator to this notion is that it tends to be invariably used as an insult. Apart from that, even the elucidating chapters in the first part of this volume[15] have not brought us much closer to pinning down exactly what the CEE judges are not supposed to do if they do not wish to be 'formalists'. If we do not know what formalism precisely is, and/or we adopt a sufficiently broad notion of 'formalism', then of course we are bound to conclude that CEE countries 'are not alone' in showing some or all of the previous outlined nine potential types of 'formalism'.[16]

Because of the jellyfish-like notion of formalism, when seeking to describe what might be occasionally wrong with judicial reasoning in Central Europe, the notion of textualism might be preferable.[17] 'Textualism' means excessive (or even exclusive) reliance on literal, linguistic arguments, while leaving the broader (legislative as well as social) context, as well as the aim and purpose of the rule, unaddressed. In its external appearance, that is when transcribed onto paper into a judicial decision, the reasoning structure for such 'textualist' approach is an apparent[18] judicial syllogism: Because the provision of law X says Y, and now there is an X, the result will be Y. Any alternatives or deeper choices are withheld. Only the result is

---

[15] See in particular the different visions of the notion in chs 2, 3, 4, as well as partially in chs 5 and 6.
[16] Above, ch 2, s III.
[17] Further M Bobek, *Comparative Reasoning in European Supreme Courts* (Oxford University Press, 2013) 260–63.
[18] 'Apparent' since the reasoning disclosed does certainly not account for all the considerations that guided the judicial mind in making the decision in question.

announced, often with little or no further reasoning displayed going beyond the mere restatement of the applicable legislation.

It is for describing such narrower vision of the problematic elements in judicial reasoning that the notion of 'textualism' is preferred to the too broad notion of 'formalism'. The use of the former notion also better captures the key reproach that such reasoning style attracts: It pushes out of judicial consideration the broader context and purpose of the rule and relies excessively or exclusively on the text of the provision to be interpreted.

The choice between the merely textual and the more contextual/purposive approach in interpreting legal rules matters. One example might illustrate such difference in outcome, in the particular context of national application of EU and international law. The case concerned Czech administrative procedures for town and country planning. Prague airport wished to construct a third runway. The decision authorising its construction was challenged by a number of individuals and smaller municipalities owning properties in the vicinity of the projected runway. The applicants challenged the planning decision in a special procedure before the *Nejvyšší správní soud* (Supreme Administrative Court, 'NSS'). Since this was the first case of its kind, the preliminary issue that arose was jurisdictional: Was the NSS in fact entitled to review such planning decisions?

In this particular case, the choice of judicial approach or 'ideology' clearly determined the outcome of the dispute. This becomes obvious by comparing the way in which the same legal problem was dealt with by four different judicial formations it was brought to. First, the first chamber of the NSS asserted jurisdiction.[19] In doing so, it relied extensively upon the indirect effect of the Åarhus Convention[20] and that of the related EU directives implementing the Åarhus Convention in the Union legal order.[21] The reasoning of the chamber was clearly purposive, taking on board the fact that the very aim of the Åarhus Convention as well as the accompanying EU legislation was to allow individual access to courts and judicial review of planning decisions in environmental matters. In order to do so, the first chamber of the NSS tweaked the meaning of the relevant national legislation somewhat, in order to protect the individual rights of the land owners and the concerned municipalities.

---

[19] NSS judgment of 18 July 2006, 1 Ao 1/2006, published as no 968/2006 Coll NSS.

[20] (United Nations) Convention on Access to Information, Public Participation in Decision-Making and Access to Justice in Environmental Matters, done at Åarhus, Denmark, on 25 June 1998, which is a 'mixed' treaty, as the EU and the Member States are parties to it—see Council Decision 2005/370/EC of 17 February 2005 on the conclusion, on behalf of the European Community, of the Convention on access to information, public participation in decision-making and access to justice in environmental matters [2005] OJ L 124/1.

[21] Directive 2001/42/EC of 27 June 2001 on the assessment of the effects of certain plans and programmes on the environment [2001] OJ L 197/30; Directive 2003/4/EC of 28 January 2003 on public access to environmental information [2003] OJ L 41/26; Directive 2003/35/EC of 26 May 2003 providing for public participation in respect of the drawing up of certain plans and programmes relating to the environment [2003] OJ L 156/17.

However, since another chamber of the NSS faced with a similar case held different views as to its admissibility, but, in the meantime, the first chamber already announced its decision, the legal issue was referred to the Grand Chamber of the NSS. The Grand Chamber is called to arbitrate in cases of conflicts in legal opinions between the chambers. The Grand Chamber was of the opinion that the NSS had no jurisdiction to hear similar type of cases.[22] Its reasoning was more textual in its approach: Since the applicable Czech national legislation at the material time in question did not expressly vest the administrative courts with the power to review the particular type of planning decisions, the NSS had no jurisdiction to do so. The 'aims and purposes' of the Åarhus Convention as well as EU law was, in the view of the Grand Chamber, not pertinent, as neither of them expressly provided for the review of such specific planning decisions. Going beyond the clear formal definition of a reviewable administrative act provided for in the law would violate the principle of separation of powers and legal certainty.

The decision of the Grand Chamber was eventually challenged before the *Ústavní soud* (Constitutional Court, hereinafter 'ÚS').[23] The ÚS annulled the decision of the Grand Chamber, while approvingly quoting and identifying itself with the position originally taken by the first chamber of the NSS. The ÚS stressed that a purely formal approach to defining what administrative acts might be reviewed is incorrect. The approach ought to be substantive and take into account precisely the broader requirements and the purpose of the Åarhus Convention as well as EU law in question.

The outlined case neatly demonstrates the importance of the ideological choice guiding judicial interpretation of the law. More textually-oriented judges, such as the majority of the members of the Grand Chamber of the NSS, wish to rely more on the letter of the law. As they clearly indicated in the case at hand, they do not feel comfortable making their own projections of aims, purposes and values into the law, if that was not made clear by the legislature itself. Conversely, the more active vision of judicial function, represented in the present example by the first chamber of the NSS and the ÚS, is ready to draw more on the context and purpose of the law(s) in order to achieve a value compatible result in the particular case.

This is what is meant by 'textualism' here. As already explained, it is preferred to the notion of 'formalism', since the former captures better what the choice is really about: How much weight the letter of the law should have in the judicial reasoning. Finally, it should be stressed, however, that the example chosen for demonstrating the ideological difference in this section is quite an advanced, elaborate example of 'civilised textualism'. It is hardly representative of its more limited variety that may be encountered and is more likely to be reproached with regard to some CE judges. The latter one is a not a matter of nuanced ideological choice, but rather the example of senseless textualism, where sticking to the letter of the law and

---

[22] NSS (Grand Chamber) judgment of 13 March 2007, 3 Ao 1/2007, published as No 1276/2007 Coll NSS.

[23] ÚS (plenary) judgment of 19 November 2008, Pl ÚS 14/07, published as N 198/51 SbNU 409.

the refusal to take other arguments onboard leads to clearly absurd and/or unjust results. Moreover, as also mentioned, this problematic variety of textualism tends to be accompanied by the absence of any practical and discernable reasoning being offered by the judge, with the mere listing of legal provisions seen as sufficient for arriving at a result in a particular case.

B. Textualism in Central European Judiciaries: The Historical Roots

If we accept the working description of 'textualism' as offered in the previous section, where are its roots in the Central European judicial minds? It should be stressed from the outset that nobody would seriously claim that textualism, or even 'formalism', whatever the precise content of the latter notion, is a feature *unique* to Central Europe. The claim is rather different: There appears to be, at least at first sight and in comparison to other civilian continental countries, an excessive amount of it. Thus, it is not a difference *in kind*, but a difference *in degree*.

Certainly, the proposition that for example Polish, Hungarian or say Slovenian judges are more textual in their reasoning than their Austrian, German or for example Swiss counterparts, to remain within the broadly speaking Germanic legal family to which all of these arguably belong, is an empirical claim that would need to be verified. Internal comparisons among the individual Central European countries, such as the valuable and telling studies carried out by M Matczak, M Bencze, and Z Kühn,[24] are only able to depict the internal differentiation within the Visegrad countries. They cannot confirm whether or not the judges in these countries use formalist arguments more often than their Western counterparts.

To discard, however, the extensive and long-standing debate on formalism in Central Europe as a largely misguided ideological fight between the pro-Western 'naïve reformers' and the pro-Eastern 'nationalistic conservatives' fails to convince. It certainly does not fail to excite, at least those who might identify themselves as being depicted as the representatives of either of the two 'ideal types of narrative' as presented by P Cserne.[25] True, there certainly is a thick layer of ideology and value conflicts present and being translated into a debate on 'formalism' and 'proper methodology'. It is also true that in the debate, empirical and historical claims tend to be mixed with normative ones. However, to discard the entire issue as just an ideological fight between two extreme, 'ideal' narratives, with the (not so) subliminal proposition that both ideological camps just 'subordinate the accuracy of historical or present factual details to practical desiderata' may appear as sweeping too far.

---

[24] Above, ch 3 in this volume and its 'prequel' in M Matczak, M Bencze and Z Kühn, 'Constitutions, EU Law and Judicial Strategies in the Czech Republic, Hungary and Poland' (2010) 30 *Journal of Public Policy* 81.
[25] Above, ch 2, in particular s II.

If one nonetheless moves beyond the rather uncompromising and bi-polar stance of Cserne and perceives the argument not as an exhaustive and all-encompassing meta-narrative for the entire CE legal discourse on formalism, but just a thought-provoking introduction into the debate, then the chapter certainly provides a number of intriguing insights. There is no doubt, however, that a number of further categories between the two categorical extremes of Cserne's 'formalism-as-bad-heritage' and 'formalism-as-noble heritage' might be added. In particular, as the author himself cautioned, historical claims ought to be kept separately from normative claims. Hence, the historical explanation of *why* textualism emerged and why Central European judges might be somewhat ideologically reserved towards excessive purposive reasoning does not necessarily mean that the same approach is being normatively defended, or that it is being turned into an issue of national tradition, identity and advantage.[26]

Thus, remaining on the side of historical explanations: Where did the tendency, assuming there is one, of Central European judges to 'sail close to the text of the law', come from? There might be a dual explanation: *cultural* and *functional*. On the side of legal culture, to some extent, textualism has always formed part of the CE judicial self portrait. CE judiciaries are built on a myth: The myth that judging is a clear-cut analytical exercise of mechanical matching of facts with the applicable law. It is almost 'legal arithmetic'. Judges do not pass any ethical or moral judgements. They just find (never create) the applicable (that is, already extant) law strictly within the laws passed by the legislature. The judicial authority is derived from such technical legal knowledge, acquired and tested in a mandarin-like entrance examination and further fostered in a similar style of promotion and advancement. Such expertise-derived authority restrains and protects judges at the same time. Judges are not called to judge the others because they would be better in moral or ethical terms. Judges are called to judge the others because *they know the law*, meaning that they have the technical knowledge of the codes, the acts of the Parliament, the case law of the higher courts and the respective procedures to be followed. The text of the binding law is what decides. Judges are presented as invisible, grey mice, devoid of any personal values, choices and personality.

Apart from this cultural judicial self-portrait, in itself not too dissimilar to other civilian continental countries,[27] there is arguably another, *functional* reason for the inclination towards textualism in Central Europe. In a nutshell, textualism serves as a tool of judicial self-preservation in instable political environments, within which legal values that normally ought to guide the contextual and purposive reasoning of judges change a bit too often. To understand this functional reason, one has to look into the

---

[26] At least that was the attempt made in M Bobek, 'On the Application of European Law in (Not Only) the Courts of the New Member States: "Don't Do as I Say"?' (2007–2008) 10 *Cambridge Yearbook of European Legal Studies* 1, 23–25.

[27] Further eg JP Dawson, *The Oracles of the Law* (The University of Michigan Law School, 1968), ch 1 or J Krynen, *L'Etat de justice France, XIIIe–XXe siècle. Tome II: L'emprise contemporaine des juges* (Gallimard, 2012) 21 ff. For the jurisprudential account of such positivist interpretive ideology, see eg B Frydman, *Le sens des lois: histoire de l'interprétation et de la raison juridique* 3rd edn (Bruylant, 2011).

logic of revolutions, which has been the same in fascist Italy,[28] Nazi Germany[29] as well as Stalinist Central Europe.[30] All of these examples have one thing in common: As a number of other revolutions in modern history, they were based on *value discontinuity* with the previous regime *and continuity in the body of positive law*.[31] A revolution typically happens overnight. Very soon thereafter, a new constitution or a sort of basic law is passed, thus changing the value foundation of the legal regime. However, the entire system of positive law, for some time, lags behind. No new regime is able to replace within days or weeks the entire system of positive laws including codifications like the criminal, civil, commercial and other codes.[32] This takes years.

It is precisely in this period immediately after the revolution but before the system adopts its own laws, that is laws that correspond with the new values of the society, that adjudicators are asked to 'remedy' the deficient old laws via interpretation. Marxist law required, at least in its early (Stalinist) phase, that judges disregard the remnants of the old bourgeois legal system in the interest of the victory of the working class and the communist revolution. Judges were supposed to apply the law in a teleological way, always directing its purpose towards the victory of the working class and the dialectic approach.[33] Open-ended clauses, typically of a constitutional or even political nature, took precedence over a textual interpretation of the existing written law. In a way, the 'faulty' old laws were, for some time, replaced by a direct application of principles and slogans.[34]

This accent on anti-textualism (or, in the period lingo, dialectical materialism) disappears once the new political system established itself and replaced the corpus of positive law and the codes with its own codifications. From that moment on the requirements of the system vis-a-vis its officials, including the judges, change. They are no longer required to be activist, anti-textualists and question the correctness

---

[28] G Calabresi, 'Two Functions of Formalism' (2000) 67 *University of Chicago Law Review* 479.

[29] B Rüthers, *Die unbegrenzte Auslegung: Zum Wandel der Privatrechtsordnung im Nationalsozialismus* (Mohr Siebeck, 1968) or B Rüthers, 'Recht als Waffe des Unrechts—Juristische Instrumente im Dienst des NS Rassenwahns' [1988] *Neue juristische Wochenschrift* 2825, 2833–35.

[30] Z Kühn, *The Judiciary in Central and Eastern Europe: Mechanical Jurisprudence in Transformation?* (Martinus Nijhoff, 2011).

[31] Together with other examples, such as Vichy France—see the collected essays in 'Juger sous Vichy', *Le genre human*, No 28, November 1994. With regard to the administrative judiciary, see P Fabre, *Le Conseil d'Etat et Vichy: Le contentieux de l'antisémitisme* (Publications de la Sorbonne, 2001) or J Massot, 'Le Conseil d'Etat et le régime de Vichy' (1998) 58 *Vingtième Siècle—Revue d'histoire* 83.

[32] The French Revolution in 1789 and the Bolshevik Revolution in 1917 came as close as possible to a complete legal discontinuity, discarding most of the earlier laws. On a closer inspection, however, also they were just gradual revolutions with longer or shorter interim periods, in which the previous laws were still in force. Further see HJ Berman, *Law and Revolution* (Harvard University Press, 1983) 28ff.

[33] See generally: O Ulč, *Malá doznání okresního soudce* [Small Confessions of a District Court Judge] (68 Publishers 1974) 39–58. Otto Ulč is an émigré Czech lawyer who worked as a judge in a District Court (court of first instance) in Western Bohemia in 1950s. See also the excellent 'ground-level' account in I Markovits, *Justice in Lüritz: Experiencing Socialist Law in East Germany* (Princeton University Press, 2010).

[34] See, eg F Boura, 'K otázce výkladu zákonů' (On the Question of Interpretation of Laws) (1949) 88 *Právník* 292, 297 who, shortly after the Communist takeover in the former Czechoslovakia, argued that 'the fundamental canon of interpretation is that the interpretation of any legal provision must be in conformity with the nature and aims of the peoples' democratic order'.

and the applicability of the legal norms. Now they are just asked to (textually) follow, as the new legal order is already in line with the new political system.

Textualism played an intriguing dual role in the developments described above. In the anti-textual (Stalinist) period, recourse to a strict textual interpretation of the existing (old) law became a line of defence against the anti-formalistic teleological style of judicial reasoning officially required by Party policy. In the early period therefore, textualism helped to defeat the new system: If a judge textually followed the still liberal pre-Communist laws,[35] which would have guaranteed basic procedural rights for every accused, it could for instance lead to an acquittal of an enemy of the new regime. This vision changed, however, in the later period of Communist law, when there were already new codifications. Then textualism became the way to stay in line and not to expose oneself by making any personal value judgements. Textualism thus turned from the way of challenging the new regime into a philosophy of hiding and capitulation.

It is with this ideological and cultural heritage that Central European judiciaries enter the era of transformation after 1989. The 1989 changes are, in a way, nothing less than yet another legal revolution in this region, with respect to the Czech Republic or Slovakia already a *fourth one* within the twentieth century. This time around, there is again formal legal continuity (positive law and legal relationships stand as before), but (certainly politically proclaimed) value discontinuity with the previous regime. The same patterns developed again: There is a new constitution, a charter of fundamental rights and a new political order which now claims to be based on democracy and the rule of law. However, the entire mass of positive law is composed of decades-old Communist codifications mostly from the early 1960s, with the provisions naturally bearing a deep ideological imprint of the era in which they were adopted. The newly established CE constitutional courts therefore command all the institutions (in particular judicial and administrative, but also legislative) to bring the old laws as well as the new ones in line with the new constitution and its values by the fiat of interpretation.[36]

---

[35] Insofar as this was 'allowed' by the Party in less significant cases perhaps. There is, however, a widespread belief that judges could use 'formalism' or 'textualism' as a line of defence against the Party directives and manipulation with their cases, thus retaining some degree of 'integrity' even within a Communist state. This 'narrative', however, somewhat downplays the fact that within a totalitarian Communist state, the ideology and the ideological application of the law was omnipresent, certainly in the early Stalinist period. Thus, in a system of 'class-conscious' judging, it mattered also by whom a normal civil or administrative claim was brought. For example, a divorce and/or a child care dispute would be resolved differently if the opposing parties were in one case two members of the Communist Party or, in another, a Party member and, by whatever game of chance, a dissident. For case examples, see Ulč or Markovits (n 33).

[36] *cf* the early decision of the constitutional courts in the CE region, proclaiming the duty of all other bodies in the state, including the ordinary courts, to (re)interpret old Communist laws in line with the new constitutional values. See the decision of the Czech *Ústavní soud* of 21 December 1993, Pl ÚS 19/93 ('on the lawlessness of the Communist regime'), No 14/1994 Coll, or the decision of the Hungarian *Alkotmánybíróság* of 15 March 1992, 11/1992 ('on retroactive criminal legislation'), AB (ABH 1992, 77), in an English translation in L Sólyom and G Brunner, *Constitutional Judiciary in a New Democracy: The Hungarian Constitutional Court* (The University of Michigan Press, 1999) 214–28. See also above, ch 17 in this volume.

Against such settings, if textualism is revived once again, it becomes a tool for defying the new system. This is the tension which lies at the heart of judicial conflicts in some of the CE countries in the 1990s, especially between the newly established and newly staffed constitutional courts and the ordinary supreme courts. The constitutional courts, guardians of the new constitutional settlement in the new democracies, demand for the judges to do (on the level of judicial method) essentially the same as what the Communist Party asked them to do before in the Stalinist period: To interpret the old Communist laws and codes in the light of new values, disregarding their text. The more seasoned judges may be reluctant if not outright hostile to do so. Some of them might indeed be using textualism as a tool for rejecting the new system and its values. Others, however, might not be hostile towards the system at all. Their historical experience, accumulated within the behavioural patterns and a sort of a 'collective memory' of the judiciary, nonetheless advises them to be very careful.

It is the learned wisdom of the CE judiciaries that those who were seduced by the luring of transcendental values of whatever origin and stepped outside of the textual box are likely to be quickly dismissed once the nature of the political transcendental changes again. Textual interpretation thus helps to survive in any regime. It saves judges from making any visible value judgements and passes on the responsibility for any legal change to the legislator.

For such reasons, cultural and functional combined, CE judges might be more reserved towards broader contextual and purposive arguments in adjudication. This does certainly not mean that CE judges would not be able to understand and employ similar types of arguments, should they wish to. What impact such judicial mindset might have, however, for the national application of EU law, will be examined in the following section.

C. Is Textualism a Problem for the National Application of EU Law?

As was demonstrated above with regard to the Czech case concerning the judicial review of planning decisions,[37] the choice of interpretative method has a decisive impact in individual cases. However, beyond the fate of individual cases, on the more general, structural level, is there a problem if, in one or more Member States of the Union, some judges might be more 'textually-inclined'? At the onset of the 2004 enlargement, Z Kühn voiced concerns in this regard, suggesting that the prevailing CE judicial ideology is at odds with many requirements EU law sets for the national judicial function.[38] Later on, it has been (counter-) suggested

---

[37] Above, text to nn 19–23.

[38] See in particular Z Kühn, 'Worlds Apart: Western and Central European Judicial Culture at the Onset of the European Enlargement' (2004) 52 *American Journal of Comparative Law* 531 and Z Kühn, 'The Application of European Law in the New Member States: Several (Early) Predictions' (2005) 3 *German Law Journal* 565. See also T Ćapeta, 'Courts, Legal Culture and EU Enlargement' (2005) 1 *Croatian Yearbook of European Law and Policy* 23.

that perhaps this incongruity might not be the problem of only Central European judiciaries, but also of the Court of Justice itself, which keeps requiring Member States' courts to interpret and apply EU law in a way which might be somewhat far-fetched from the normal national judicial potential, be it in the new or in the old Member States.[39]

Empirically speaking, the reality of the application of EU law in the new Member States in the course of the first 10 years might not turn out to be as gloomy as sometimes predicted, as the individual chapters in this volume bear witness to, together with the research emerging in recent years on judicial application of EU law in the new Member States.[40] This does not mean that all has been great and flawless, but there were not many tragedies either.

Normatively speaking, is it a problem if national judges are more textual in their application of EU law? The answer to this question depends on our vision of the role attributed to national judges in the European judicial architecture. The more pro-active, perhaps idealist, answer would be 'yes', it is of course a problem if national judges do not proactively apply the broader purposes and aims of EU law. They ought to be the active interlocutors of the Court of Justice, seeking and weeding out incompatibilities on the national level and addressing mature, reasoned and advised requests for preliminary rulings to the Court of Justice.

Conversely, the more pragmatic answer, bordering slightly on the cynical one, might present an opposing vision. The fact that national judges might not be that pro-active in the application of EU law in pulling aims, purposes and deep level context into the game is not such a problem if and as long as they duly apply the 'formal' EU law, including the established case law of the Court of Justice. The hidden and sometimes underestimated advantage of textualists is that they follow, they obey. It might not always be with happiness and enthusiasm, but they are unlikely to challenge what is clearly stated. On the other hand, judicial anti-textualism and activity is a double-edged sword: It all depends on the values, on the particular *telos* that will be used for the interpretation of the relevant legislation. It is perhaps no surprise that sometimes, national courts and in particular national constitutional or supreme courts might have quite different *telos* in mind than the Court of Justice has.

In sum, whether or not a (naturally reasonable) degree of textualism in Central European courts is a problem for the correct application of EU law on the national level is an open question, dependent on the structural vision of the EU legal order one has. Instead of advocating that the national courts ought to be the active powerhouses of EU law, a more self-restrained view might suggest that

---

[39] M Bobek, 'On the Application of European Law in (Not Only) the Courts of the New Member States: "Don't Do as I Say"?' (2007–08) 10 *Cambridge Yearbook of European Legal Studies* 1.

[40] In English, see eg T Evas, *Judicial Application of European Union Law in Post-Communist Countries: The Cases of Estonia and Latvia* (Ashgate, 2012) or U Jaremba, *National Judges as EU Law Judges: The Polish Civil Law System* (Martinus Nijhoff Publishers, 2014). See also the individual chs in A Łazowski (ed), *The Application of EU Law in the New Member States—Brave New World* (TMC Asser Press, 2010).

extensive, purpose-based judicial creativity is best left to the Court of Justice. This is the only way to ensure that it is ultimately the same aim and purpose across the Union guiding the interpretation of the same piece of EU legislation.

IV. Institutions and Structures: How Much Europe is Europe Enough?

The proverbial *fil rouge* weaved into the chapters in part one and two of this volume is the change in judicial thinking, style, procedures and institutions in the new Member States under the European lead. The views of individual authors clearly differ: From moderate institutional optimism to quite gloomy statements of no change at all or entirely failed transformations. The common assumption is, however, that there has been some sort of engagement between the national and the European judicial structures and that this engagement has induced some sort of reaction on the national level. This section examines both elements of this assumption in turn: First, it will critically look at the issue of 'quantity' of exchange and, second, at its 'quality', more precisely the kind of changes which have occurred.

A. Quantity

There are typically two unspoken assumptions about the national exchanges with 'Europe'. First, such engagement induces change. If national courts want to/are obliged to engage with European law, they will not only take it on board as far as the substance of their reasoning is concerned when applying EU law domestically. The incoming European inspiration will also make them think more critically about what they do and why they do it, ignite critical reflection, induce change, generate spillovers and so on. Second, the more engagement there is, the more change there is likely to be. Thus, quantity is supposed to matter.

In some of the chapters of this volume, the engagement quantity has been measured in two ways. First, A Kornezov looked at the number of preliminary references submitted by Bulgarian courts in comparison with other CEE courts.[41] Second, M Matczak, M Bencze, and Z Kühn quantified the amount of references made by the Polish, Czech and Hungarian administrative courts to EU law.[42] Both chapters clearly show significant increases in the respective categories observed. Thus, one might be tempted to conclude that there must now be more 'Europeanisation' in all of the countries observed.

---

[41] Above, ch 11 in this volume.
[42] Above, ch 3 in this volume.

If looked at more critically, however, as the authors do themselves when interpreting their results, it is clear that mere numbers say rather little. Moreover, their interpretation is very precarious.[43] For example, the numbers of preliminary rulings submitted from the new Member States serve as a confirmation that the courts in the new Member States have started engaging with the Court of Justice, in their own way and at their own pace. However, the numbers say nothing of reasons, causes, tensions or strategies behind those aggregated numbers. Five following points will illustrate some of the question marks in this regard.

First, when looking at the tables presented,[44] in comparison to most of the old Member States, it could be said that the amount of references from the new ones remains relatively low, even 10 years after the accession. For example, in previous years, an average of nine requests for a preliminary ruling each year have been brought by Polish courts[45] (with Poland being the largest new Member State), with about 12 requests originating from Bulgaria, Romania or Hungary. This is a relatively low number, certainly if measured against the 'middle-sized' old Member States that have traditionally been on the active side in terms of the amount of the preliminary rulings sent, such as Belgium (approximately 30); Netherlands (approximately 30) or Austria (approximately 20); not to mention the larger countries like Germany (approximately 80) or Italy (approximately 60).[46] However, it is fair to admit that there is a considerable disparity in the 'input' coming from the older Member States as well, with larger jurisdictions like Spain, France or the UK generating fewer requests for preliminary rulings.[47] On the whole, it could be perhaps suggested that in the first 10 years of their membership, the new Member States' courts did not disproportionately burden the Luxembourg Court.

Second, when looking at which particular courts in the new Member States have made the submissions, a pattern familiar from the old Member States starts unfolding: Most of the references originated from the same courts within a given Member State or even from the same judges within a given court. For example, the vast majority of Bulgarian references to date were submitted by the first instance administrative courts in just two cities, Sofia and Varna.[48] A considerable bulk of Slovak references came from either the Prešov District Court or the Prešov Regional Court and all concern consumer protection. Over half of the preliminary references from the Czech Republic originate from one jurisdiction only, the Czech Supreme Administrative Court. A closer look at the institutional and the geographical origins of the references therefore does not warrant overly optimistic

---

[43] As pointed out in the discussions in chs 7 and 12.

[44] Above, ch 11, s II. See also Court of Justice of the European Union, *Annual Report 2013* (EU Office for Official Publications, 2014) 106.

[45] For a review of their qualitative side, see also above, ch 10.

[46] *Annual Report 2013* (n 44) 106.

[47] For further discussion, see for example, M Broberg and N Fenger, *Preliminary Reference to the European Court of Justice* (Oxford University Press, 2010) 37–58.

[48] Above, ch 11, s III.

conclusions concerning the genuine and far-reaching 'penetration' of EU law and EU law thinking beyond several selected 'usual suspects'.

Third, interestingly, in most of the new Member States (in particular in the Czech Republic, Estonia, Cyprus, Latvia, Lithuania and Poland), references from the respective supreme courts account for half or more than half of all the requests submitted from within these countries. Conversely, in Bulgaria, Romania and Hungary, a clear majority of requests was submitted by lower courts.[49] Such institutional repartition of requests for a preliminary ruling may be seen as either challenging the often held belief that the most important (or the quantitatively strongest) 'fuel' for the development of the EU legal order comes from the lower national courts, or indirectly bearing testimony to the significance of judicial hierarchy in the Member States in question, or to the rather differentiated vision of judicial hierarchy within the individual CEE countries.

Fourth, the issue of generational tensions and conflict within the judiciaries of the new Member States is partially connected to the previous point concerning the institutional hierarchy. It is often assumed that younger judges in the new Member States use EU law and requests to the Court of Justice as a tool for their internal emancipation and challenge vis-a-vis the older national judicial elites. The younger judges, who are more recent law school graduates, are believed to be better versed in foreign languages. They studied EU law at the university and often completed a foreign study somewhere abroad. As a result, they are believed to be more open to EU law reasoning and, consequently, to the preliminary rulings procedure.[50]

This narrative may be largely true. It has, however, no universal validity. Incidentally, the institutional repartition of the requests for preliminary rulings made and outlined in the previous point already suggests some caution in this regard. In a number of the new Member States, a majority of the requests for the preliminary ruling was in fact made by the highest national courts. Even if in some of the systems, the composition of these highest courts might have been considerably renewed since 1989, it is unlikely that they would be predominantly staffed with junior judges. Thus, the motives for and the likelihood of submitting a request for a preliminary ruling cannot be reduced merely to the question of age and 'generational readiness' to engage with EU law, although the latter one certainly remains a factor.

Fifth and finally, even a closer look at the aggregated numbers is not capable of providing much information about the actual 'quality' of the questions submitted by the courts of the new Member States. Have they been using the preliminary ruling procedure 'responsibly' and 'effectively'? Or have they 'wasted' the Court of Justice's time with questions that have already been addressed and which have become established case law? Have all of the submitting courts grasped that the European judicial potential should preferably be used for addressing broader,

---

[49] *Annual Report 2013* (n 44) 107–09.
[50] Above, ch 11, s IV.

structural, pan-European issues, important for maintaining the unity and further development of the EU legal order, and not just for 'self-serving' local or marginal issues and interests?

It is notoriously difficult to evaluate a request for a preliminary ruling as to its 'quality'. How should it be measured? Perhaps the fact that the question submitted was not answered by a mere reasoned order pursuant to Article 99 of the Rules of Procedure might provide the first indicator. However, to be entirely fair, it is open to argument whether the Court of Justice has always used this procedural tool exclusively for questions that can be 'clearly deduced from existing case law or where the answer to the question referred for a preliminary ruling admits of no reasonable doubt'. Or are 'quality questions' those that make it to the Grand Chamber? There is certainly some correlation, but not necessarily an exclusive link.

In sum, the numbers of requests of preliminary rulings made by the courts of a Member State provide in themselves little evidence for any genuine 'transformation' or 'Europeanisation' of national judiciaries on the ground, unless they are complemented by an in-depth study of their genuine repartition within the national judicial hierarchy, motives and causes lying beneath. If such a contextual and 'qualitative' corrective is carried out, the result might be in fact much more nuanced or even the opposite one to the number-induced optimism.[51]

In a similar vein, the analysis offered by Matczak, Bencze and Kühn also demonstrate, in quantitative terms, a steady growth in 'EU law values' or 'EU law topics', as the authors call arguments with and out of EU law sources.[52] When looked at diachronically, the increase in the amount of EU law related reasoning in the period after the 2004 accession in Polish, Czech and Hungarian administrative courts is stunning: From 'just' an increase of 300 per cent in the case of the Czech Republic to a breath-taking increase of 1,000 per cent in the case of Hungary.[53] Again, however, context matters a lot. Leaving aside the issue of methodology and the limits in quantifying legal reasoning in such a way,[54] a problem of which the authors themselves are well aware, it should be perhaps added that the increase of 1,000 per cent was in relation to the pre-2004 figures, where the use of 'EU law topics' in the reasoning of Hungarian administrative courts was 0.8 per cent only. Thus, a 'jump' to 9.1 per cent for the period after 2004 is bound to appear gigantesque, in spite of perhaps being itself deeply below the EU average.[55]

More importantly, even an increased number of certain sources or certain types of arguments being invoked in judicial decisions may not ultimately mean much for a genuine transformation of judicial thinking and reasoning. To push

---

[51] As in fact carried out above in ch 11.

[52] Above, ch 3.

[53] ibid, s III (table 1).

[54] See also the critical remarks on this account above in ch 7, s IV.

[55] The figure for which is certainly very far from clear. On the issue of 'how many national cases are EU law cases' see M Bobek, 'Of Feasibility and Silent Elephants: The Legitimacy of the Court of Justice through the Eyes of National Courts' in M Adams et al (eds), *Judging Europe's Judges: The Legitimacy of the Case Law of the European Court of Justice* (Hart Publishing, 2013) 208–13.

this point to an extreme: Judges might be invoking EU law more often, thus statistically 'increasing' the frequency of the use of a certain argument, while safely remaining the same 'textualists' or 'formalists' as before. Only the formal authority has changed. The style and approach have not.

B. Quality

The heretical and somewhat cynical point just made is *not* suggested as an overall conclusion to this volume. Still, it is fair to admit that the majority of the contributions presented in this volume can hardly be labelled as excessively institutionally optimistic in this regard. Most of them concur in stressing that the *internal* or mental change within the CEE judiciaries has been somewhat lagging behind the *external* façade. The extreme proposition contrasting external appearance with an internal change was rather aimed at helping to clearly disentangle the two claims that normally come connected: Greater quantitative engagement with 'Europe' is bound to bring about an internal change in style and thinking as well. Such a proposition is certainly plausible and likely in terms of a hypothesis. It needs to be, however, rigorously tested, on the basis of both quantitative and qualitative elements.

With regard to the *qualitative* side of the Europe-induced change, there are five points that may be offered for wrapping up at least some elements discussed in this volume. They cannot represent but few selected and subjective impressions. First, there is no doubt that the engagement with Europe has been growing steadily since 2004 in the new Member States. That is hardly surprising, since judges as well as all other public authorities are obliged to apply and work with EU law qua full members of the Union. However, such engagement has been mostly limited to the implementation of individual legal instruments or policies. Safe for some isolated 'late-comers', there has been not much further structural, ideological change in the world of CE judiciaries since 2004. With the pre-2004 pre-accession conditionality and pressure removed, a number of reform steps have been even halted or reversed, with the problem of backsliding and illiberal tendencies becoming plainly visible. A less candid observer might suggest that with the pre-accession carrots and sticks removed, the masks fell as well. In sum, since 2004, quantitatively greater and in some way 'consolidated' engagement with the EU may be observed, defined by the amount of the incoming EU policies, laws, case law in the various areas, but not much further reaching, deeper structural, institutional and mental change.

Second, although this volume focuses on the judicial transformation in the new Member States under the lead of the European Union, the real patterns of influence tend to be much more multi-polar and varied. They include a number of other European actors, such as the ECtHR and its case law, other institutions and bodies of the Council of Europe, the Venice Commission, other international actors, but also a number of NGOs, judicial and other networks. Moreover, it ought not to be forgotten that there is also a significant 'traffic in ideas' going on horizontally in Europe, with the Central European countries being under a distinct German influence in terms of law importation.[56] It might be therefore sometimes difficult to clearly attribute from where exactly the decisive influence originated. The above discussed example of the Europe-induced spread of judicial councils into CEE[57] provides an illuminating example in this regard. The original model came from the national level, notably from Italy and other Latin countries. It then became 'Europeanised' through the various Council of Europe bodies, later on pushed towards the CEE countries as a part of the EU pre-accession conditionality and EU membership preparation package, while being still actively promoted on the horizontal level by its countries of origin. Another example is the gradual change in judicial style in some of the CE courts. Is it attributable to the EU? Or rather to a sort of joint influence of the ECtHR, national constitutional courts and horizontal inspiration coming from judges in say Hungary or the Czech Republic closely following the *Bundesverfassungsgericht*?[58]

Third, examining the results of the massive societal change before and at the moment of the 2004 enlargement puts into focus the limits of the 'absorption capacity' of any legal order or society. If the influx of new rules, new procedures and new institutions becomes too numerous and too frequent, the novelty no longer stimulates excitement and curiosity, but leads to disregard and norm scepticism. Europeanisation in terms of the incorporation of all the *acquis communautaire* in the few years before the 2004 accession meant the obligation to incorporate some 80,000 pages of EU secondary law,[59] together with primary law, the case law of the Court of Justice and soft law. In practical terms, this meant that before and around the accession, in the candidate countries or by then already new Member States, all the key laws or codes have been amended several times a year, sometimes even more. In the opinion of the former vice-president of the Czech *Ústavní soud*, P Holländer, the speed and frequency of the new legislation and amendments to the new legislation amounted to a 'deconstruction' of the legal order and information suffocation.[60]

Fourth, in view of the previous point, it will not come as a surprise that such 'fast-track Europeanisation' yields only limited and rather superficial results, with the new rules often remaining on paper only. As the reality in some CEE countries vividly reminds us, adopting laws and regulations is something rather different, sometimes even worlds apart, from embracing their spirit, culture and

---

[56] Further Bobek (n 17), in particular 255–57 and 269–72.

[57] Above, ch 8 in this volume.

[58] See for a discussion with regard to the change in reasoning style in the Czech Republic as opposed to Slovakia Bobek (n 17) 189–91 and 230–33.

[59] This is the lowest estimate, generated by the European Commission itself. Other sources have indicated even greater, even double the amount of pages—in the House of Commons Library Research Paper 10/62 'How Much Legislation Comes from Europe' of 13 October 2010, online at <www.parliament.uk>, last accessed 15 August 2014, at p 8.

[60] P Holländer, *Ústavněprávní argumentace* [Constitutional Legal Reasoning] (Linde, 2003) 11–12, refers to an example of the key procedural norm, the Czech Code of Civil Procedure, being amended, directly or indirectly, 18 times in the span of one year between 2001 and 2002.

true meaning. Thus, EU rules on, for example gender equality and equal pay for equal work, or public participation in environmental matters, may have been formally transposed and the appropriate transposition box ticked off following the submission of the relevant concordance or transposition tables to the European Commission. This says, however, little about the enforcement of such rules on the ground. The same phenomenon is even more clearly visible when nominally 'Europeanised' institutions that look like the European blueprint on paper are to be assessed as to their genuine operation. The real internal culture of such institutions might be, however, quite different from the original model, ranging from varieties of amusing but still rather harmless 'cargo cults'[61] to outright hijacking and misuse of the new institution.[62] Yet again, the fate of the newly established judicial councils in CEE offers a sad case study in this regard.[63]

All this leads, finally, to an extreme and acute variety of rule cynicism, and an instrumental understanding of the law, still prevailing in a number of CE countries. This becomes translated onto the most basic ontological level. With similar cultural and historical 'luggage', CE lawyers or judges are bound to have a rather different vision of even basic notions like 'law', 'statute' or even 'justice' than their West European counterparts. Furthermore, within the judiciary, such scepticism often leads to apathy and resignation, especially with CE judges who perceive themselves as specialised experts, who are supposed to perfectly master the specific area of law they are assigned to adjudicate upon. The picture used for the cover of this volume, incidentally shot by a senior CE judge, neatly visualises the feeling: A piece of old wood being washed up at the shore, remaining outside the stream of new developments and trends and not really able or willing to jump in again.

V. Constitutional Courts and EU Law: Uneasy Bedfellows?

Constitutional courts have always been rather special creatures. In the German model of specialised and concentrated constitutional review, a constitutional court is, for all practical purposes, the court above all courts, or rather the court placed above the entire constitutional system. Since the German inspiration in the

---

[61] Cargo cult is a known metaphor of natives, who do not understand much of the content of an activity they have seen before being carried out by the more advanced societies, but keep mimicking it in the hope it might produce the desired effects. It was used metaphorically for describing some areas of (social) science, which allegedly instead of producing real science just play at it (see famously RF Feynman, 'Cargo Cult Science' (1974) 37 (7) *Engineering and Science* 10, 11).

[62] Sceptically see above, ch 13 in this volume.

[63] Above, ch 8 in this volume.

area of constitutional justice,[64] in both institutional design as well as substance, has been since 1989 the strongest one in Central Europe, the CE constitutional courts evolved into quite powerful institutions.[65] If we, however, continue with the powerful-creature-metaphor, then the 2004 accession meant that the creature was caged. Parts of its former habitat were declared out of bounds. Furthermore, with the 2009 entry into force of the Treaty of Lisbon and the EU Charter of Fundamental Rights being binding primary law, the already caged creature was told that now it has to share its already restricted habitat with other animals as well. How will such a restrained creature react? Defy the reality, suggesting that it is still free as a bird? Sit grumpily and silently in the corner of the cage, uninterested in what is going on? Bark and growl, but in fact accept its fate? Fall dangerously silent, which might be mistaken for acquiescence, but is in fact tactical waiting for the new warden to become reckless and make a mistake?

The contributions offered in the third part of this volume with respect to Poland, the Czech Republic and Hungary, show that different approaches are indeed possible. They range from a bit of 'wait and see' tactics, also due to considerable internal upheaval, such as is the case of Hungary[66] to the re-assertion of its own habitat, in the milder form in Poland,[67] or in the rather explicit and belligerent tone as in the Czech Republic.[68] Other approaches might include breaking the silence and referring requests for a preliminary ruling,[69] or instead of submitting requests for a preliminary rulings, start issuing rather 'preliminary ultimata'.[70]

It is of course true that the CE constitutional courts are experiencing nothing else than their counterparts in Western Europe and also, to some degree, national supreme jurisdictions, have been exposed to before. However, the CE 'sample' provides an intriguing case study not because it would be that different, but because it is so *condensed*. The process that in the West and also in the South of Europe has been spread over several decades happened in Central Europe in just one decade.

What is the problem the constitutional courts face within the European judicial structure? What is the position of constitutional courts under EU law? On the one hand, there is the formal, legalistic answer, formulated from the point of view

---

[64] For an overview, see eg JA Frowein and T Marauhn (eds), *Grundfragen der Verfassungsgerichtsbarkeit in Mittel- und Osteuropa* (Springer, 1998). A qualitative in-depth study of the process provides eg C Dupré, *Importing Law in Post-Communist Transitions: The Hungarian Constitutional Court and the Right to Human Dignity* (Hart Publishing, 2003).

[65] For a pre-2004 review, see eg R Procházka, *Mission Accomplished: On Founding Constitutional Adjudication in Central Europe* (Central European University Press, 2002) or W Sadurski, *Rights before Courts: A Study of Constitutional Courts in Post-Communist States of Central and Eastern Europe* (Springer, 2005).

[66] Above, ch 16.

[67] Above, ch 14. But see the more nuanced interpretation of the Polish approach offered in ch 17.

[68] Above, ch 15.

[69] *cf* eg the order of the Slovenian *Ustavno sodišče* of 6 November 2014, U-I-295/13-132, Uradni list RS, št 82/2014.

[70] *cf* the tone of the first request for a preliminary ruling submitted by the German *Bundesverfassungsgericht* in BVerfG of 14 Jan 2014, 2 BvR 2728/13, online at <www.bverfg.de>.

of EU law orthodoxy: Constitutional courts are 'courts or tribunals' within the meaning of Article 267 TFEU. They are an institution of the Member State. They are therefore equally obliged, as any other body of a Member State, to apply EU law fully and effectively within the scope of their competence. They may submit a request for a preliminary ruling as any other national court. In fact, as they are functionally courts of last instance, they are even under an obligation to do so.

On the other hand, however, such a simple and rather doctrinal answer fails to satisfy perhaps on both the normative level, concerning the question what the role of constitutional courts ought to be, as well as on the empirical level, that is in recognising what their role in reality is. Ever since the Nicomachean Ethics,[71] it has been considered unequal and hence unjust not only to treat the same cases differently, but also treating objectively and evidently different cases the same. Most of the national constitutional courts, especially those of German institutional design, which are entitled to carry out not only an abstract but also a concrete review of constitutionality, consider themselves to be special. They are not 'a court or tribunal'. They are 'a court of courts' or a 'court beyond mere courts'.

Therein lies, in a nutshell, the heart of the institutional dimension of the problem. A number of constitutional courts might feel that they have been left out of the EU project. Or, more precisely, EU law brought them only losses in terms of institutional and procedural uniqueness without providing much gain in return. Accordingly, a number of these courts have driven themselves, wisely or not, into a sort of 'splendid isolation'. They insist, sometimes on rather shaky grounds, that they are not concerned with EU law.[72]

This antagonistic relationship EU law and the case law of the Court of Justice might generate in the minds of national constitutional courts is neatly visible in the rapid evolution some of constitutional courts in the new Member States went through in the last decade. Before the 2004 enlargement, a number of constitutional courts in Central Europe, in particular the Polish *Trybunał Konstytucyjny* or the Czech *Ústavní soud*, were the pro-active champions of 'Europeanisation'. They even insisted on legal approximation and interpretative use of EU law in the periods before the accession.[73] Around or after the accession, these courts issued strongly pro-European decisions.[74] However, only seven or eight years later, the same courts started assertively reviewing the compatibility of an EU regulation with the national constitution,[75] or even declared an EU act to be ultra vires.[76]

---

[71] Aristotle, *Nicomachean Ethics*, book V.

[72] In detail see M Bobek, 'The Impact of the European Mandate of Ordinary Courts on the Position of Constitutional Courts' in M Claes et al (eds), *Constitutional Conversations in Europe* (Intersentia, 2012).

[73] See above, ch 17.

[74] By the way of illustration, the ÚS judgment of 3 May 2006, Pl ÚS 66/04, might be recalled. In this decision, the Czech ÚS showed an extremely pro-European stance, pushing the doctrine of consistent interpretation to its limits in order to conclude that Article 14 (4) of the Czech Constitution that states 'No citizen may be forced to leave his homeland' does not preclude the surrendering of Czech nationals to other Member States within the European Arrest Warrant Framework Decision.

[75] The *Supronowicz* case (Polish TK of 16 Nov 2011, SK 45/09) discussed in detail above, ch 14.

[76] For the discussion of the *Holubec* decision (Czech ÚS of 31 January 2012, Pl ÚS 5/12), see above, ch 15.

This is a radical U-turn. It is still in need of deeper conceptualisation beyond the narratives of individual 'hurt judicial egos' or 'EU law ignorant national judges from the new Europe'. In realist, functional terms, the already offered hypothesis might of course be the effective 'demotion' of constitutional courts following the EU accession. Such a hypothesis might be further supported by contrasting the EU law approach towards constitutional courts with the standing of constitutional courts under the European Convention. The ECHR (European Convention on Human Rights) enables the review of national decisions, including the decisions of national constitutional courts. However, even if some decisions coming from Strasbourg might not be received with enthusiasm as far as their substance is concerned, in its institutional dimension, the Strasbourg mechanism leaves the internal standing of constitutional courts and the internal hierarchies intact. The European Convention allows the national constitutional courts to keep control over the national legal system. In systems with an individual constitutional complaints procedure, all cases before coming to Strasbourg must effectively go through the national constitutional court so that the remedies exhaustion rule is satisfied. Thus, the powers of constitutional courts remain intact, with the national constitutional courts being given the additional role of the Strasbourg national gatekeeper and later 'translator' of the Strasbourg case law back on the national level. Conversely, EU law empowers only national ordinary courts; for constitutional courts, it only means the loss of uniqueness and open gates for their circumvention via the preliminary rulings procedure.

Did the coming into force of the EU Charter of Fundamental Rights as binding primary law provide a good opportunity to try to bring national constitutional courts back into the EU game? (Normative) views differ.[77] What is clear, however, is that since its entry into force, the EU Charter has been exercising similar centripetal effects onto the legal discourse in EU law as national bills of rights have had on national law since the Second World War. More and more cases coming to the Court of Justice are argued in terms of human rights protection and EU Charter application.[78] Moreover, since, similar to the national discourses, there is in fact no clear limit between 'mere legality' and 'constitutionality', virtually any legal dispute can be rephrased in terms of fundamental rights protection. Thus,

---

[77] See eg J Komárek, 'The Place of Constitutional Courts in the EU' (2013) 9 *European Constitutional Law Review* 420, 443–46 and 449–50 or J Komárek, 'National Constitutional Courts in the European Constitutional Democracy' (2014) 12 *International Journal of Constitutional Law* 525. Further see more recently eg the various contributions in P Popelier et al (eds), *The Role of Constitutional Courts in Multilevel Governance* (Intersentia, 2012) or V Ferreres Comella, *Constitutional Courts and Democratic Values: A European Perspective* (Yale University Press, 2009).

[78] For a quantitative illustration, see eg European Commission, *2012 Report on the Application of the EU Charter of Fundamental Rights* (Publications Office of the European Union, 2013) 22. For a review of some of the post-Lisbon fundamentals rights case law, see eg S Iglesias Sánchez, 'The Court and the Charter: The Impact of the Entry into Force of the Lisbon Treaty on the ECJ's Approach to Fundamental Rights' (2012) 49 *CML Rev* 1565 or D Sarmiento, 'Who is Afraid of the Charter? The Court of Justice, National Courts and the New Framework of Fundamental Rights Protection in Europe' (2013) 50 *CML Rev* 1267.

with the boundaries of the national applicability of EU law (or the scope of EU law) being somewhat blurry, a number of disputes can be potentially brought to the Court of Justice, thus completely bypassing national constitutional courts.

In sum, the position of national constitutional courts remains far from settled. The study of the reaction and approaches of CE constitutional courts towards the EU is most rewarding not only because it has been, due to its already discussed condensed nature, a genuine roller coaster. Perhaps more importantly, with the 2004, 2007 and 2013 enlargements, the model of concentrated constitutional review exercised by one specialised constitutional court within the national system ceased to be *a* model within the EU. It became *the* model. If, before the 2004, 2007 and the 2013 enlargements, there was a fair portion of Member States without a specialised constitutional court, the last enlargements clearly tipped the balance. With the exception of Cyprus and Estonia,[79] all the new Member States which joined the EU in the last three enlargement waves brought with them into the Union their constitutional courts. Thus, in 2014, 18 out of 28 Member States possess a constitutional court in the form of a specialised institution.[80] Accommodating constitutional courts and national constitutional concerns within the EU judicial structures thus becomes an imperative.

VI. Conclusion: The Success and the End of a Transition

When does a transition end? In its narrow sense, a transition may just mean the shift from one regime to another, a change in the formal constitutional and state structure. In the broader sense, it means much more: Not just a constitutional shift, but also a change in the values of a society, their enforcement and the real life of the new institutions.[81] In its latter, broader sense, a transition ought to be ideally over once a country becomes a stable democracy governed by the rule of law, with functional and genuinely independent and impartial judiciary.

Ten years after the accession of the 10 new Member States to the EU and some 25 years since the fall of the Iron Curtain, this volume revisited the process of legal

---

[79] Although Estonia has no institutionally separate constitutional court, constitutional review is being carried out by a special chamber (constitutional chamber) of the Estonian Supreme Court.

[80] The countries without a (institutionally separate) constitutional court are Denmark, Finland, Greece, Ireland, Luxemburg, the Netherlands, Sweden, the United Kingdom and the already-mentioned Cyprus and Estonia. However, it is obvious that the fact that no specialised constitutional court has been established in these countries does not mean that there would be no constitutional review in functional terms.

[81] See eg C Varga, *Transition to Rule of Law: On the Democratic Transformation in Hungary* (Loránd Eötvös University, 1995) 74. Varga quotes the former president of the Hungarian Constitutional Court, L Sólyom, who claimed that for him, the 'transition' was, from the legal point of view, finished in October 1989. From then on, Hungary has been a law-governed state and there is no further stage to transit to.

transition in Central European countries. Most of the contributions in this volume appeared to implicitly assume that legal transition is still going on in Central Europe. Since we are apparently 'not there yet', we have arguably not yet reached the desired ideal, we must still be on the road.

In realist terms, however, the transition, if understood as an on-going, large scale structural reform in CE countries, is now over. Regrettably perhaps, the transition in the broader sense is not over once 'we get there', but rather when larger scale, often painful legal and other reforms become unfeasible. The transformation reformist momentum is lost. Arguably, in Central Europe, this moment came at or soon after the accession to the EU in 2004. At the latest, any remnants of further reformist zeal were effectively terminated with the advent of the economic crisis in 2007/2008. Since then, remaining system deficiencies, including those within the CE judiciaries, simply became the normalcy. They turned into permanent features of a system.[82] This does not preclude the possibility of remedying one or more of the outstanding deficiencies. These would be, however, individual legal reforms arduously piercing the overall inertia of any system, but no more large scale systemic change driven by the force of the momentum.

Moreover, the problem of backsliding on the achieved degree of transformation or 'Europeanisation' in a number of the new Member States, not just Hungary, raises a number of significant questions about the entire process. Was it indeed wise to rush the process, achieving certain political momentum for Europe, but at the price of embracing a rather raw 'Europeanised semi-product' at its best? Hungary's sliding toward authoritarianism has been identified and widely discussed from various angles.[83] Within the ado created around Hungary, however, it might be less apparent that the state Slovenia finds itself in might be qualified as a 'failed democracy';[84] that Bulgaria and Romania, the countries that arguably joined a bit too early, are not really improving in terms of institution and rule of law building;[85]

---

[82] In a similar vein, nobody would be referring to eg Greece or to some of the other 'old' EU Member States, as to 'countries in transition' today, even though they might be still plagued by recognised problems in terms of legal protection. *cf* for example in this regard *MSS v Belgium and Greece*, ECtHR judgment of 21 January 2011, App No 30696/09, or Joined Cases C-411/10 and C-493/10, *NS (C) and ME and others*, ECLI:EU:C:2011:865.

[83] For a review of the constitutional changes, see eg A Jakab, 'On the Legitimacy of a New Constitution. Remarks on the Occasion of the New Hungarian Basic Law of 2011' in MA Jovanović and Đ Pavićević (eds), *Crisis and Quality of Democracy in Eastern Europe* (Eleven Publishers, 2012) or L Salamon, 'Debates Surrounding the Concepts of the New Constitution' (2011) 3 *Hungarian Review* 1522.

[84] Above, ch 13 in this volume.

[85] The reports issued by the European Commission over the past eight years under the 2006 established Cooperation and Verification Mechanism (a diplomatic euphemism for a rather unprecedented step within the Union which means on-going monitoring of an EU Member State as to its compliance with the rule of law) are certainly not too optimistic in this regard. The latest two reports of 28 January 2015—'Report from the Commission to the European Parliament and the Council on Progress in Bulgaria under the Co-operation and Verification Mechanism' [COM (2015) 36 final] and 'Report from the Commission to the European Parliament and the Council on Progress in Romania under the Co-operation and Verification Mechanism [COM (2015) 35 final]—can be located, together with the previous reports, online at < http://ec.europa.eu/cvm>, last accessed 15 February 2015.

and that across the region generally, including the Czech Republic and Slovakia, a questionable sort of populism is gaining ground, often involving challenges or outright rejections of the EU and any 'Europeanisation'. Can the EU and the 'West' now play at being surprised about the state of the state in some of these countries, complaining that they expected more after a few years of often superficial pre-accession reforms, or even hasty repaint? Can one be really that surprised that a paint put over a half corroded fence in a hurry starts peeling off soon? On the more positive side, the backsliding of some of its members nonetheless at least forces the entire club to think anew about the rules of the club. What are the minimal standards for membership? How can they be enforced?[86]

In the end, however, and perhaps in contrast to some of the gloomy outlooks presented throughout this volume, as well as to the critical remarks of this conclusion, it would be mistaken to sign off the CE judicial transformation as a failure. In a way, 10 or 25 years is a short period of time. True, in some cases with some detours, but on the whole, the CE Member States might be on the right track. Perhaps we wished for too much in such a short period of time, provided that we actually really knew what we were wishing for in the first place.[87] There is an English proverb suggesting that 'it takes three generations to make a gentleman'. Why should the Central European judiciaries be any different in this regard?

---

[86] Recently see notably A Von Bogdandy et al, 'Reverse Solange—Protecting the Essence of Fundamental Rights against EU Member States' (2012) 49 *Common Market Law Review* 489 and A von Bogdandy and M Ioannidis, 'Systemic Deficiency in the Rule of Law: What it is, What has Been Done, What can be Done' (2014) 51 *Common Market Law Review* 59.

[87] Above, ch 1, s II.

SELECT BIBLIOGRAPHY

Aautheman, V and Eelena, S, 'Global Best Practices-Judicial Councils: Lessons Learned from Europe and Latin America' (2004) 2 *International Foundation for Electoral Systems Rule of Law White Paper Series*

Adam, F and Tomšič, M, 'The Dynamics of Elites and the Type of Capitalism: Slovenian Exceptionalism' (2012) 37(2) *Historical Social Research* 53

——— and ———, 'Transition Elites: Catalysts of Social Innovation or Rent Seekers' (2000) 32 *Družboslovne razprave* 138

Ajani, G, 'By Chance and Prestige: Legal Transplants in Russia and Eastern Europe' (1995) 43 *American Journal of Comparative Law* 93

Alberstein, M, 'Measuring Legal Formalism: Reading Hard Cases with Soft Frames' (2012) 57 *Studies in Law, Politics, and Society* 161

Albi, A, *EU Enlargement and the Constitutions of Central and Eastern Europe* (Cambridge University Press, 2005)

———, 'Ironies in Human Rights Protection in the EU: Pre-Accession Conditionality and Post-Accession Conundrums' (2009) 15(1) *European Law Journal* 46

Albrecht, PA and Thomas, J, *Strengthen the Judiciary's Independence in Europe! International Recommendations for an Independent Judicial Power* (Intersentia, 2009)

Alen, A et al, 'Human Rights Protection through Judicial Dialogue between National Courts and the European Court of Justice' in A Alen et al (eds), *Liberae Cogitationes: Liber Amicorum Marc Bossuyt* (Intersentia, 2013)

Alexy, R, *A Theory of Constitutional Rights* (Oxford University Press, 2007)

Alter, KJ, 'Explaining National Court Acceptance of European Court Jurisprudence: A Critical Evaluation of Theories of Legal Integration' in AM Slaughter, A Stone Sweet and JHH Weiler (eds), *The European Court and National Courts—Doctrine and Jurisprudence* (Hart Publishing, 1998)

———, 'The European Legal System and Domestic Policy. Spillover or Backlash?' (2000) 54 *International Organization* 489

———, 'The European Court's Political Power: Across Time and Space' and 'Law and Politics in Europe and Beyond' in KJ Alter (ed), *The European Court's Political Power* (Oxford University Press, 2009)

Anagnostaras, G, 'Activation of the Ultra Vires Review: The Slovak Pensions Judgment of the Czech Constitutional Court' (2013) 14(7) *German Law Journal* 959

Andrews, N, *English Civil Procedure, Fundaments of the New Civil Justice System* (Oxford University Press, 2003)

Arendt, H, *The Origins of Totalitarianism* (Schocken Books, 2004)

Arnull, A, *The European Union and its Court of Justice* (Oxford University Press, 2006)

Avbelj, M, 'Failed Democracy: The Slovenian Patria Case—(Non)Law in Context' (2014) originally published in Slovenian, 26 *Pravna praksa*

—— and Černič, JL, 'Chapter on Slovenia' in L Hammer and F Emmert (eds), *The European Convention on Human Rights and Fundamental Freedoms in Central and Eastern Europe* (Eleven International Publishing, 2012)

Badiou, A, and Žižek, S (eds), *L'idée du communisme* (Nouvelles Editions Lignes, 2010)

Bánkuti, M, Halmai, G and Lane Scheppele, K, 'Disabling the Constitution' (2012) 3 *Journal of Democracy* 138

Bakardijeva-Engelbrekt, A, 'The Impact of EU Enlargement on Private Law Governance in Central and Eastern Europe: The Case of Consumer Protection' in F Cafaggi and H Muir-Watt (eds), *Making European Private Law: Governance Design* (Edward Elgar, 2009)

Bebler, A, 'Slovenia's Smooth Transition' (2000) 13 *Journal of Democracy* 127

Bell, J, 'Mechanisms for Cross-fertilization of Administrative Law in Europe' in J Beatson and T Tridimas (eds), *New Directions in European Public Law* (Hart Publishing, 2000)

Belling, V, 'Supranational Fundamental Rights or Primacy of Sovereignty? Legal Aspects of the So-called Opt-out from the EU Charter' (2012) 18 *European Law Journal* 254

Benoit-Rohmer, F, 'À propos de l'arrêt Bosphorus Air Lines du 30 juin 2005: L'Adhésion contrainte de l'Union à la Convention' (2005) 64 *Revue trimestrielle des droits de l'homme* 827

Berman, HJ, *Law and Revolution* (Harvard University Press, 1983)

Bibó, I, *The Art of Peacemaking. Selected Political Essays, trans P Pásztor, ed with and intro IZ Dénes* (Yale University Press, 2015)

Biernat, S and Wróbel, P, 'Stosowanie prawa Wspólnoty Europejskiej w polskim sądownictwie administracyjnym' (2007) *Studia prawno-europejskie* No IX 7

Biondi, A, Eeckhout, P and Ripley, S (eds), *EU Law after Lisbon* (Oxford University Press, 2012)

Bix, B, 'Form and Formalism: The View from Legal Theory' (2007) 20 *Ratio Iuris* 45

Bobek, M, 'On the Application of European Law in (Not Only) the Courts of the New Member States: "Don't Do as I Say"?' (2007–08) 10 *Cambridge Yearbook of European Legal Studies* 1

——, 'Learning to Talk: Preliminary Rulings, the Courts of the New Member States and the Court of Justice' (2008) 45 *Common Market Law Review* 1611

——, 'The Fortress of Judicial Independence and the Mental Transitions of the Central European Judiciaries' (2008) 14 *European Public Law* 1

——, 'Quantity or Quality? Reassessing the Role of Supreme Jurisdictions in Central Europe' (2009) 57(1) *American Journal of Comparative Law* 33

——, 'Reasonableness in Administrative Law: A Comparable Reflection on Functional Equivalence' in G Sartor et al (eds), *Reasonableness and Law* (Springer, 2009)

——, 'The Administration of Courts in the Czech Republic: In Search of a Constitutional Balance' (2010) 16 *European Public Law* 251

——, 'Why There is no Principle of "Procedural Autonomy" of the Member States' in HW Micklitz and B De Witte (eds), *The European Court Of Justice And Autonomy Of The Member States* (Intersentia, 2011)

——, *Comparative Reasoning in European Supreme Courts* (Oxford University Press, 2013)

——, 'Of Feasibility and Silent Elephants: The Legitimacy of the Court of Justice through the Eyes of National Courts' in M Adams et al (eds), *Judging Europe's Judges: The Legitimacy of the Case Law of the European Court of Justice* (Hart Publishing, 2013)

——, 'The Impact of the European Mandate of Ordinary Courts on the Position of Constitutional Courts' in M Claes et al (eds), *Constitutional Conversations in Europe* (Intersentia, 2013)

——, 'Landtová, Holubec, and the Problem of an Uncooperative Court: Implications for the Preliminary Rulings Procedure' (2014) 10 *European Constitutional Law Review* 54

Bodnar, A, and Bojarski, L, 'Judicial Independence in Poland' in A Seibert-Fohr (ed), *Judicial Independence in Transition* (Springer, 2012)

Bojarski, L and Köster, WS, *The Slovak Judiciary: Its Current State and Challenges* (Open Society Foundation, 2011)

Bomhoff, J, *Judicial Discretion in European Law on Conflicts of Jurisdiction* (Sdu Publishers, 2005)

Borowski, M, 'Legal Pluralism in the European Union' in AJ Menendez and JE Fossum (eds), *Law and Democracy in Neil MacCormick's Legal and Political Theory: The Post-Sovereign Constellation* (Springer, 2011)

Bozhilova, D, 'Measuring Success and Failure of EU-Europeanization in the Eastern Enlargement: Judicial Reform in Bulgaria' (2007) 9 *European Journal of Legal Reform* 285

Bragyova, A, 'No New(s), Good News? The Fundamental Law and the European Law' in GA Tóth (ed), *Constitution for a Disunited Nation. On Hungary's 2011 Fundamental Law* (Central European University Press, 2012)

Bříza, P, 'The Czech Republic: The Constitutional Court on the Lisbon Treaty Decision of 26 November 2008' (2009) 5 *European Constitutional Law Review* 143

Broberg, M and Fenger, N, *Preliminary References to the European Court of Justice* (Oxford University Press, 2010)

Brodecki, Z, *Prawo integracji: Konstytucja dla Europy* (Lexis Nexis, 2011)

Bučar, F, 'Pravnik v današnjem času' (2004) 36 *Pravna praksa* 6

Bugarič, B, 'Protecting Democracy and the Rule of Law in the European Union: The Hungarian Challenge' (2014) 79 *London School of Economics 'Europe in Question' Discussion Paper* Series 1

Burley, AM and Mattli, W, 'Europe before the Court: A Political Theory of Legal Integration' (1993) 47 *International Organization* 41

Cabral-Barreto, I, 'La Cour Européenne des droits de l'homme et le droit communautaire. Quelques réflexions à propos de l'arrêt Bosphorus' in MG Kohen (ed), *Promoting Justice, Human Rights and Conflict Resolution Through International Law: Liber Amicorum Lucius Caflisch* (Brill, 2006)

Cafaggi, F, Cherednychenko, OO, Cremona, M, et al, 'Europeanization of Private Law in Central and Eastern Europe Countries (CEECS): Preliminary Findings and Research Agenda' (2010) 15 *European University Institute Working Papers Law* 1

Calabresi, G, 'Two Functions of Formalism' (2000) 67 *University of Chicago Law Review* 479

Calleo, DP, *Rethinking Europe's Future* (Princeton University Press, 2001)

Caporaso, JA, 'The European Union and the Forms of State: Westphalian, Regulatory or Post-modern' (1996) 34 *Journal of Common Market Studies* 29

Cappelletti, M and Jolowicz, JA, *Public Interest Parties and the Active Role of the Judge in Civil Litigation* (Giuffrè/Oceana, 1975)

Cappelletti, M, 'Who Watches the Watchmen? A Comparative Study on Judicial Responsibility' (1983) 31 *American Journal of Comparative Law* 1

Caranta, R, 'Judicial Protection Against Member States: A New Jus Commune Takes Shape' (1995) 32 *Common Market Law Review* 703

Chalmers, D, 'European Restatements of Sovereignty' in R Rawlings, P Leyland and A Young (eds), *Sovereignty and the Law: Domestic, European and International Perspectives* (Oxford University Press, 2013)

Choudhry, S, *The Migration of Constitutional Ideas* (Cambridge University Press, 2011)

Chronowski, N, 'Nullum crimen sine EU?' (2008) 4 *Rendészeti Szemle* 39

Claes, M and De Visser, M, 'Are You Networked Yet? On Dialogues in European Judicial Networks' (2012) 8 *Utrecht Law Review* 100

Closa, C, Kochenov, D and Weiler, JHH, 'Reinforcing Rule of Law Oversight in the European Union' (2014) 25 *Robert Schuman Center of Advanced Studies Working Paper* 7

Cohen, A, 'Constitutionalism Without Constitution: Transnational Élites Between Political Mobilization and Legal Expertise in the Making of a Constitution for Europe (1940s–1960s)' (2007) 32 *Law & Social Inquiry* 109

Cohen, JL, *Globalization and Sovereignty. Rethinking Legality, Legitimacy and Constitutionalism* (Cambridge University Press, 2012)

——, 'Sovereignty in the Context of Globalisation: A Constitutional Pluralist Perspective' in S Besson and J Tasioulas (eds), *The Philosophy of International Law* (Oxford University Press, 2010)

Coman, R and Dallara, C, 'Judicial Independence in Romania' in A Seibert-Fohr (ed), *Judicial Independence in Transition* (Springer, 2012).

Comandé, G, 'The Fifth European Union Freedom, Aggregating Citizenship Around Private Law' in H-W Micklitz (ed), *Constitutionalisation of European Private Law* (Oxford University Press, 2014)

Constantinesco, V, 'La confrontation entre identité constitutionnelle européenne et identités constitutionnelles nationales: convergence ou contradiction? Contrepoint ou hiérarchie?' in JC Masclet, H Ruiz Fabri, C Boutayeb et al (eds), *L'Union Européenne, Union de droit, Union des droits, Mélanges en l'honneur de Philippe Manin* (Pedone, 2010)

Conway, G, *The Limits of Legal Reasoning and the European Court of Justice* (Cambridge University Press, 2012)

Couso, JJ, 'Judicial Independence in Latin America: The Lessons of History in the Search for an Always Elusive Ideal' in T Ginsburg and RA Kagan (eds), *Institutions & Public Law: Comparative Approaches* (Peter Lang, 2005)

Craig, P, *The Lisbon Treaty: Law, Politics, and Treaty Reform* (Oxford University Press 2010)

——, 'Pringle: Legal Reasoning, Text, Purpose and Teleology' (2013) 20 *Maastricht Journal of European and Comparative Law* 1

—— and de Búrca, G, *EU Law: Text, Cases and Materials* (Oxford University Press, 2011)

Cremona, M (ed), *The Enlargement of the European Union* (Oxford University Press, 2003)

Cruz Villalón, P, 'Rights in Europe: The Crowded House' (2012) 1 *King's College London Working Papers in European Law* 1

Csink, L and Schanda, B, 'The Constitutional Court' in L Csink, B Schanda and A Zs Varga (eds), *The Basic Law of Hungary: A First Commentary* (Clarus Press, 2012)

Curtin, D and Mortelmans, K, 'Application and Enforcement of Community Law by the Member States: Actors in Search of a Third Generation Script' in D Curtin and T Heukles (eds), *Institutional Dynamics of European Integration, Essays in Honour of Henry G Schermers. Volume II* (Dordrecht, 1994)

Cserne, P, 'The Recodification of Private Law in Central and Eastern Europe' in P Larouche and P Cserne (eds), *National Legal Systems and Globalization: New Role, Continuing Relevance* (TMC Asser, 2013)

Czarnota, A, Krygier, M and Sadurski, W (eds), *Spreading Democracy and the Rule of Law: The Impact of EU Enlargement on the Rule of Law, Democracy and Constitutionalism in Post-Communist Legal Orders* (Springer, 2006)

D'Alterio, E, 'From Judicial Comity to Legal Comity: A Judicial Solution to Global Disorder?' (2010) 13 *Jean Monnet Working Paper* 1

Dawson, JP, *The Oracles of the Law* (The University of Michigan Law School, 1968)

Dawson, M and Muir, E, 'Hungary and the Indirect Protection of EU Fundamental Rights and the Rule of Law' (2013) 14 *German Law Journal* 1959

de Búrca, G, 'After the EU Charter of Fundamental Rights: The Court of Justice as a Human Rights Adjudicator?' (2013) 51 *New York University School of Law, Public Law & Legal Theory Research Paper Series* 16

De Nike, HJ, *German Unification and the Jurists of East Germany: An Anthropology of Law, Nation and History* (Forum-Verlag Godesberg, 1997)

De Visser, M and Claes, M, 'Judicial Networks' in P Larouche and P Cserne (eds), *National Legal Systems and Globalization: New Role, Continuing Relevance* (TMC Asser Press & Springer, 2013)

Dénes, IZ, 'Adopting the European Model versus National Egoism: The Task of Surpassing Political Hysteria' (2012) 20 *European Review* 514

Dezalay, Y and Garth, BG, *Dealing in Virtue: International Commercial Arbitration and the Construction of a Transnational Legal Order* (University of Chicago Press, 1996)

Dežman, J, 'Communist Repression and Transitional Justice in Slovenia' in P Jambrek (ed), *Crimes Committed by Totalitarian Regimes* (Slovenian Presidency of the Council of the European Union, 2008)

Dika, M and Uzelac, A, 'Zum Problem des richterlichen Aktivismus in Jugoslawien' (1990) *Zbornik Pravnog fakulteta u Zagrebu* 391

Dougan, M, *National remedies before the Court of Justice, Issues of Harmonisation and Differentiation* (Hart Publishing, 2004)

Douglas-Scott, S, 'Bosphorus Hava Yollari Turizm Ve Ticaret Anonim Sirketi v Ireland, Application No 45036/98, Judgment of the European Court of Human Rights (Grand Chamber) of 30 June 2005, (2006) 42 EHRR' (2006) 43 *Common Market Law Review* 243

——, *Law after Modernity* (Hart Publishing, 2013)

Dudzik, S and Półtorak, N, '"The Court of the Last Word"—Competences of the Polish Constitutional Tribunal in the field of the review of the European Union Law' (2012) 15 *Yearbook of Polish European Studies* 225

Duve, TH, 'Von der Europäischen Rechtsgeschichte zu einer Rechtsgeschichte Europas in globalhistorischer Perspektive' (2012) 1 *Max Planck Institute for European Legal History Research Paper Series* 1

Dyevre, A, 'Unifying the Field of Comparative Judicial Politics: Towards a General Theory of Judicial Behaviour' (2010) 2 *European Political Science Review* 304

——, 'The German Federal Constitutional Court and European Judicial Politics' (2011) 34 *West European Politics* 346

Eckes, C, 'Does the European Court of Human Rights Provide Protection from the European Community? The Case of Bosphorus Airways' (2007) 13 *European Law Journal* 47

Eilmansberger, T, 'The Relationship between Rights and Remedies in EC Law: In Search of the Missing Link' (2004) 41 *Common Market Law Review* 1199

Eliantonio, M, *Europeanization of Administrative Justice? The Influence of the CJEU's Case Law in Italy, Germany and England* (Europa Law Publishing, 2009)

Elster, J, *Nuts and Bolts in the Social Sciences* (Cambridge University Press, 1989)

Emmert, F, 'Administrative and Court Reform in Central and Eastern Europe' (2003) 3 *European Law Journal* 295

Epstein, L and Jacobi, T, 'The Strategic Analysis of Judicial Decisions' (2010) 6 *Annual Review of Law and Social Sciences* 341

Evas, T, *Judicial Application of European Union Law in Post-Communist Countries: The Cases of Estonia and Latvia* (Ashgate, 2012)

Fabre, P, *Le Conseil d'Etat et Vichy: Le contentieux de l'antisémitisme* (Publications de la Sorbonne, 2001)

Fassbender, B, 'Sovereignty and Constitutionalism in International Law' in N Walker (ed), *Sovereignty in Transition* (Hart Publishing, 2003)

Fazekas, F, 'La Cour constitutionnelle et la Cour supreme hongroise face au principe de la primauté du droit de l'Union européenne' (2008) *Actes du VIIIe Séminaire Doctoral International et Européen, Université de Nice-Sophia Antipolis* 139

——, 'EU Law and the Hungarian Constitutional Court' in M Varju and V Ernő (eds), *The Law of the European Union in Hungary: Institutions, Processes and the Law* (HVG-ORAC, 2014)

Ferejohn, J, 'Independent Judges, Dependent Judiciary: Explaining Judicial Independence' (1999) 72 *Southern California Review* 353

—— and Pasquino, P, 'Constitutional Courts as Deliberative Institutions: Towards an Institutional Theory of Constitutional Justice' in W Sadurski (ed), *Constitutional Justice, East and West. Democratic Legitimacy and Constitutional Courts in Post-Communist European a Comparative Perspective* (Kluwer Law International, 2002)

Fernandez Esteban, ML, 'National Judges and Community Law: The Paradox of the Two Paradigms of Law' (1997) 4 *Maastricht Journal of European and Comparative Law* 143

Ferrand, F, 'The Respective Role of the Judge and the Parties in the Preparation of the Case in France' in N Trocker and V Varano (eds), *The Reforms of Civil Procedure in Comparative Perspective* (Giappichelli Editore, 2005)

Fitzmaurice, J, 'National Parliamentary Control of EU Policy in the Three New Member States' (1996) 19 *West European Politics* 88

Fleck, Z, 'Judicial Independence in Its Environment in Hungary' in J Přibáň, PI Roberts and J Young (eds), *Systems of Justice in Transition. Central European Experiences since 1989* (Ashgate, 2003)

Fogelklou, A, 'East European Legal Thinking' (2002) 4 *Riga Graduate School of Law Working Papers* 8

Frei, N, *Adenauer's Germany and the Nazi Past: The Politics of Amnesty and Integration* (Columbia University Press, 2002)

Friedman, M and Friedman, R, *The Tyranny of the Status Quo* (Houghton Mifflin Harcourt, 1984)

Frydman, B, *Le sens des lois: histoire de l'interprétation et de la raison juridique* 3rd edn (Bruylant, 2011)

Fuller, LL, 'Positivism and Fidelity to Law—a Reply to Professor Hart' (1957) 71 *Harvard Law Review* 633

——, *Morality of Law* (Revised Edition, Yale University Press, 2003)

Galič, A, 'A Judge's Power to Disregard Late Facts and Evidence and the Goals of Civil Justice' in *Recent Trends in Economy and Efficiency of Civil Procedure, Materials of International Conference* (Vilnius University Press, 2013)

——, 'Does a Decision of the Supreme Court Leave to Appeal Need to Contain reasons?' in J Adolphsen et al (eds), *Festschrift für Peter Gottwald zum 70. Geburtstag* (CH Beck, 2014)

Galligan, D and Matczak, M, 'Formalism in Post-Communist Courts. Empirical Study on Judicial Discretion in Polish Administrative Courts Deciding Business Cases' in R Coman and J-M De Waele (eds), *Judicial Reforms in Central and Eastern European Countries* (Vanden Broele, 2007)

Gárdos-Orosz, F, 'The Hungarian Constitutional Court in Transition—from Actio Popularis to Constitutional Complaint' (2012) 53(4) *Acta Juridica Hungarica* 302

Garoupa, N and Ginsburg, T, 'Guarding the Guardians: Judicial Councils and Judicial Independence' (2009) 57 *American Journal of Comparative Law* 103

Gill, S and Cutler, CA, *New Constitutionalism and World Order* (Cambridge University Press, 2014)

Ginsburg, T, 'Pitfalls of Measuring the Rule of Law' (2011) 3 *Hague Journal on the Rule of Law* 269

Goldstein, S, 'The Rule of Law vs The Rule of Judges: A Brandeisian Solution' in S Shetreet and C Forsyth (eds), *The Culture of Judicial Independence* (Martinus Nijhoff Publishers, 2012)

Goowdwin-Gill, GS and Lambert, H, *The Limits of Transnational Law: Refugee Law, Policy Harmonization and Judicial Dialogue in the European Union* (Cambridge University Press, 2010)

Gray, TC, 'Judicial Review and Legal Pragmatism' (2003) 38 *Wake Forest Law Review* 473

Greer, SL, *Nationalism and Self-Government: Politics of Autonomy in Scotland and Catalonia* (SUNY Press, 2008)

Grimm, D, 'Defending Sovereign Statehood Against Transforming the European Union into a State' (2009) 5 *European Constitutional Law Review* 353

Grimmel, A, 'Judicial Interpretation or Judicial Activism?: The Legacy of Rationalism in the Studies of the European Court of Justice' (2010) 176 *Center for European Studies Working Paper Series, Harvard University* 26

Guarnieri, C and Pederzoli, P, *The Power of Judges: A Comparative Study of Courts and Democracy* (Oxford University Press, 2002)

Guarnieri, C and Piana, D, 'Judicial Independence and the Rule of Law: Exploring the European Experience' in S Setreet and C Forsyth (eds), *The Culture of Judicial Independence* (Martinus Nijhoff Publishers, 2012)

Guastaferro, B, 'Beyond the "Exceptionalism" of Constitutional Conflicts: The "Ordinary" Functions of the Identity Clause' (2012) 31(1) *Yearbook of European Law* 263

Habermas, J, *Postnational Constellation: Political Essays* (Polity, 2001)

Halberstam, D and Möllers, C, 'The German Constitutional Court says "Ja zu Deutschland"' (2009) 10 *German Law Journal* 1241

Halmai, G, 'The Transformation of Hungarian Constitutional Law from 1985 to 2005' in P Takács, A Jakab and AF Tatham (eds), *The Transformation of the Hungarian Legal Order 1985–2005* (Kluwer Law International, 2007)

Hammergren, L, 'Do Judicial Councils Further Judicial Reform? Lessons from Latin America', (2002) 28 *Working-Paper Series Democracy and Rule of Law Project*

——, *Envisioning Reform: Improving Judicial Performance in Latin America* (Penn State University Press, 2007)

Hanley, S, *The New Right in the New Europe: Czech Transformation and Right-Wing Politics, 1989–2006* (Routledge, 2007)

Harding, C, 'Models of Enforcement: Direct and Delegated Enforcement and the Emergence of a "Joint Action" Model' in C Harding and B Swart (eds), *Enforcing European Community Rules. Criminal Proceedings, Administrative Procedures and Harmonization* (Dartmouth, 1996)

Hart, HLA, *The Concept of Law* (2nd edn, Oxford University Press, 1994)

Hartley, TC, *European Union Law in a Global Context: Text, Cases and Materials* (Cambridge University Press, 2004)

Hayward, J and Wurzel, R (eds), *European Disunion: Between Sovereignty and Solidarity* (Palgrave, 2012)

He, X, 'Black Hole of Responsibility: The Adjudication Committee's Role in a Chinese Court' (2012) 46 *Law & Society Review* 681

Heller, H, 'Politische Demokratie und soziale Homogenität' in M Drath, C Müller and H Heller (eds), *Gesammelte Schriften, Band II* (Sijthoff, 1971)

Herdegen, M, 'Maastricht and the German Constitutional Court: Constitutional Restraints for an "Ever Closer Union"' (1994) 31 *Common Market Law Review* 235

Hess, B, 'Juridical Discretion—General Report; Part I' in M Storme and B Hess (eds), *The Discretionary Power of the Judge: Limits and Control* (Kluwer Law International, 2003)

Hesselink, MW, *The New European Legal Culture* (Kluwer Law International, 2001)

Hillion, C (ed), *EU Enlargement: A Legal Approach* (Hart Publishing, 2004)

Hilson, C, 'The Europeanization of English Administrative Law: Judicial Review and Convergence' (2003) 9(1) *European Public Law* 125

Hirschl, R, 'The Political Origins of the New Constitutionalism' (2004) 11 *Indiana Journal of Global Legal Studies* 71

Hofmann, H and Türk, AH, 'Introduction: Towards a Legal Framework for Europe's Integrated Administration' in H Hofmann and AH Türk (eds), *Legal Challenges In EU Administrative Law. Towards an Integrated Administration* (Edward Elgar, 2009)

Inglis, K, 'EU Enlargement: Membership Conditions Applied to Future and Potential Member States' in S Blockmans and A Lazowski (eds), *The European Union and its Neighbours: Legal Appraisal of the EU's Policies of Stabilisation, Partnership and Integration* (TMC Asser Press, 2006)

Jacob, JM, *Civil Justice in the Age of Human Rights* (Ashgate, 2007)

Jacobs, F, 'Judicial Dialogue and the Cross-Fertilization of Legal Systems: The European Court of Justice' (2003) 38 *Texas International Law Journal* 547

Jakab, A, 'On the Legitimacy of a New Constitution. Remarks on the Occasion of the New Hungarian Basic Law of 2011' in MA Jovanović and Đ Pavićević (eds), *Crisis and Quality of Democracy in Eastern Europe* (Eleven Law, 2012)

Jans, JH, De Lange, R, Prechal, S, et al, *Europeanisation of Public Law* (Europa Law Publishing, 2007)

Jaremba, U, *National Judges as EU Law Judges: The Polish Civil Law System* (Martinus Nijhoff, 2014)

Jenne, EK and Mudde, C, 'Hungary's Illiberal Turn: Can Outsiders Help?' (2012) 3 *Journal of Democracy* 147

Joerges, C and Ghaleigh, NS, *Darker Legacies of Law in Europe: The Shadow of National Socialism and Fascism over Europe and its Legal Traditions* (Hart Publishing, 2003)

Josselin, JM and Marciano, A, 'How the Court Made a Federation of the EU' (2007) 2 *Review of International Organizations* 59

Jowell, J and Lester, A, 'Beyond Wednesbury: Substantive Principles of Administrative Law' (1988) 14(2) *Commonwealth Law Bulletin* 858

—— and ——, 'Proportionality: Neither Novel Nor Dangerous' in J Jowell and D Oliver (eds), *New Directions in Judicial Review* (Stevens, 1988)

Kakouris, C, 'Do the Member States Possess Judicial Procedural "Autonomy"?' (1997) 34 *Common Market Law Review* 1389

Karanikic, M, Micklitz, HW and Reich, N, *Modernising Consumer Law—The Experience of the Western Balkan* (Nomos, 2012)

Karolczyk, B, 'Pretrial as a Part of Judicial Case Management in Poland in Comparative Perspective' (2013) 15 *Comparative Law Review* 151

Kas, B, 'A Socio-legal Study on the Operation of Hybrid Collective Remedies in the Area of European Social Regulation' in H-W Micklitz, Y Svetiev and G Comparato (eds),

'European Regulatory Private Law—The Paradigm Tested' (2014) 4 *European University Institute Paper Law* 19

Kattago, S, *Memory and Representation in Contemporary Europe—The Persistence of the Past* (Ashgate, 2012)

Kellermen, AE, et al (eds), *The Impact of EU Accession on the Legal Orders of New Member States and (Pre-)Candidate Countries* (TMC Asser Press, 2006)

Kengyel, M, 'Veränderungen des Inhalts der Dispositions- und Verhandlungsmaxime im ungarischen Zivilprozess' (1997) 2 *Zeitschrift für Zivilprozess International* 270

Kenney, SJ, 'Beyond Principles and Agents: Seeing Courts as Organizations by Comparing Référendaires at the European Court of Justice and Law Clerks at the US Supreme Court' (2000) 33 *Comparative Political Studies* 593

Kessier, G and Finkelstein, LJ, 'The Evolution of a Multi-Door Courthouse' (1988) 37 *The Catholic University Law Review* 577

Kis, J, 'From the 1989 Constitution to the 2011 Fundamental Law' in GA Tóth (ed), *Constitution for a Disunited Nation: On Hungary's 2011 Fundamental Law* (Central European University Press, 2012)

Klamert, M, *The Principle of Loyalty in EU Law* (Oxford University Press, 2013)

Knieper, R, 'Möglichkeiten und Grenzen der Verpflanzbarkeit von Recht' (2008) *Rabels Zeitschrift* 88

Kochenov, D, *EU Enlargement and the Failure of Conditionality* (Kluwer Law International, 2008)

Kohler-Koch, B and Rittberger, B, (eds), *Debating the Democratic Legitimacy of the European Union* (Rowman & Littlefield, 2007)

Komárek, J, '"In the Court(s) We Trust?" On the Need for Hierarchy and Differentiation in the Preliminary Ruling Procedure' (2007) 32 *European Law Review* 467

——, 'The Czech Constitutional Court's Second Decision on the Lisbon Treaty of 3 November 2009' (2009) 5(3) *European Constitutional Law Review* 345

——, 'Playing with Matches: The Czech Constitutional Court Declares a Judgement of the Court of Justice of the EU Ultra Vires; Judgment of 31 January 2012, Pl ÚS 5/12, Slovak Pensions XVII' (2012) 8 *European Constitutional Law Review* 323

——, 'The Struggle for Legal Reform after Communism' (2014) 10 *London School of Economics Law, Society and Economy Working Papers* 1

——, 'Waiting for the Existential Revolution in Europe' (2014) 12 *International Journal of Constitutional Law* 190

Kommers, DP and Miller, RA, *The Constitutional Jurisprudence of the Federal Republic of Germany* (Duke University Press, 2012)

Kosař, D, 'The Least Accountable Branch' (2013) 11 *International Journal of Constitutional Law* 234

Koskenniemi, M, 'The Future of Statehood' (1991) 32 *Harvard International Law Journal* 397

——, 'The Fate of Public International Law; Between Technique and Politics' (2007) 70 *Modern Law Review* 1

—— and Leino, P, 'Fragmentation of International Law? Postmodern Anxieties' (2002) 15 *Leiden Journal of International Law* 553

Kovács, P, 'Vol (communautaire) au-dessus d'un nid de coucou (ou le calcul du temps de travail des médecins et la jurisprudence de la Cour constitutionnelle de Hongrie)' (2007) 3 *Revue Française de Droit Constitutionnel* 667

Kowalik-Banczyk, K, 'Should we Polish it up? The Polish Constitutional Court and the Idea of Supremacy of EU Law' (2005) 6 *German Law Journal* 1355

Krasner, SD, *Sovereignty, Organized Hypocrisy* (Princeton University Press, 1999)

Krynen, J, *L'Etat de justice France, XIIIe–XXe siècle. Tome II: L'emprise contemporaine des juges* (Gallimard, 2012)

Kühn, Z, 'Worlds Apart: Western and Central European Judicial Culture at the Onset of the European Enlargement' (2004) 52 *American Journal of Comparative Law* 531

——, 'The Authoritarian Legal Culture at Work: The Passivity of Parties and the Interpretational Statements of Supreme Courts' (2006) 2 *Croatian Yearbook of European Law and Policy* 19

——, 'The Democratization and Modernization of Post-communist Judiciaries' in A Febbrajo and W Sadurski (eds), *Central and Eastern Europe After Transition* (Ashgate, 2010)

——, *The Judiciary in Central and Eastern Europe: Mechanical Jurisprudence in Transformation?* (Martinus Nijhoff, 2011)

——, 'Formalism and Anti-Formalism in Judicial Reasoning' in B Melkevik (ed), *Standing Tall. Hommages à Csaba Varga* (Pázmány Press, 2012)

Kumm, M, 'The Cosmopolitan Turn in Constitutionalism: On the Relationship between Constitutionalism in and Beyond the State' in JL Dunoff and JP Trachtman (eds), *Ruling the World? Constitutionalism, International Law and Global Governance* (Cambridge University Press, 2009)

——, 'The Best of Times and the Worst of Times. Between Constitutional Triumphalism and Nostalgia' in P Dobner and M Loughlin (eds), *The Twilight of Constitutionalism* (Oxford University Press, 2010)

Lane Scheppele, K, 'A Realpolitik Defense of Social Rights' (2004) 82 *Texas Law Review* 1921

Larouche, P, 'Legal Emulation Between Regulatory Competition and Comparative Law' in P Larouche and P Cserne (eds), *National Legal Systems and Globalization: New Role, Continuing Relevance* (TMC Asser Press & Springer, 2013)

Łazowski, A (ed), *The Application of EU Law in the New Member States—Brave New World* (TMC Asser Press, 2010)

——, 'Half Full and Half Empty Glass: The Application of EU Law in Poland (2004–2010)' (2011) 48 *Common Market Law Review* 503

Le Quinio, A, *Recherche sur la circulation des solutions juridiques: le recours au droit comparé par les juridictions constitutionnelles* (Fondation Varenne, 2011)

Leczykiewicz, D, 'Case Note on the Judgment of 27 April 2005 of the Polish Constitutional Court' (2006) 43 *Common Market Law Review* 1187

Legrand, P, 'European Legal Systems are not Converging' (1996) 45 *International and Comparative Law Quarterly* 52

Leigh, I, 'Taking Rights Proportionately: Judicial Review, the Human Rights Act and Strasbourg' (2002) *Public Law* 265

Leiter, B, 'Positivism, Formalism, Realism: Review of Legal Positivism in American Jurisprudence, by Anthony Sebok' (1999) 99 *Columbia Law Review* 1138

Lenaerts, K and Gutierrez-Fons, JA, 'The Place of the Charter in the EU Constitutional Edifice' in S Peers et al (eds), *The EU Charter of Fundamental Rights—A Commentary* (Hart Publishing, 2014)

——, Maselis, I and Gutman, K, *EU Procedural Law* (Oxford University Press, 2014)

Letnar Černič, J, 'Responding to Crimes against Humanity Committed in Slovenia after the Second World War' in D Svoboda, C O'Connor and J Liška (eds), *Crimes of the Communist Regimes: International Conference: An Assessment by Historians and Legal Experts: Proceedings* (Ústav pro studium totalitních režimů, 2011)

Łętowska, E, 'The Barriers of Polish Legal Thinking in the Perspective of European Integration' (1997) 1 *Yearbook of Polish Legal Studies* 55

Li, L, 'The "Production" of Corruption in China's Courts: Judicial Politics and Decision Making in a One-Party State' (2012) 37 *Law & Social Inquiry* 848

Ligi, T, 'Judicial Independence in Estonia' in A Seibert-Fohr (ed), *Judicial Independence in Transition* (Springer, 2012)

Lucy, WNR, 'Criticizing and Constructing Accounts of Legal Reasoning' (1994) 14 *Oxford Journal of Legal Studies* 303

MacCormick, DN and Summers, RS (eds), *Interpreting Statutes. A Comparative Study* (Dartmouth Publishing, 1991)

Magalhaes, PC, 'The Politics of Judicial Reform in Eastern Europe' (1999) 32 *Comparative Politics* 1

Mańko, R, 'The Culture of Private Law in Central Europe after Enlargement: A Polish Perspective' (2005) 11 *European Law Journal* 527

——, 'Quality of Legislation Following a Transition from Really Existing Socialism to Capitalism: A Case Study of General Clauses in Polish Private Law' in J Rozenfelds et al (eds), *The Quality of Legal Acts and Its Importance in Contemporary Legal Space* (University of Latvia Press, 2012)

——, 'Resistance towards the Unfair Terms Directive in Poland: The Interaction between the Consumer Acquis and a Post-Socialist Legal Culture' in J Devenney and M Kenny (eds), *European Consumer Protection: Theory and Practice* (Cambridge University Press, 2012)

——, 'The Institutional Implications of the Unfair Terms Directive in Poland' in J Rutgers (ed), *European Contract Law and the Welfare State* (Europa Law Publishers, 2012)

——, 'Survival of the Socialist Legal Tradition? A Polish Perspective' (2013) 4(2) *Comparative Law Review* 1

——, 'Weeds in the Gardens of Justice? The Survival of Hyperpositivism in Polish Legal Culture as a Symptom/Sinthome' (2013) 7 *Pólemos* 223

——, '"War of Courts" as a Clash of Legal Cultures: Rethinking the Conflict Between the Polish Constitutional Tribunal and Supreme Court over "Interpretive Judgments"' in M Hein et al (eds), *Law, Politics and the Constitution: New Perspectives from Legal and Political Theory* (Peter Lang, 2014)

Massot, J, 'Le Conseil d'Etat et le régime de Vichy' (1998) 58 *Vingtième Siècle—Revue d'histoire* 83

Markovits, I, *Gerechtigkeit in Lüritz, Eine Ostdeutsche Rechtsgeschichte* (CH Beck, 2006)

——, *Justice in Lüritz: Experiencing Socialist Law in East Germany* (Princeton University Press, 2010)

Matczak, M, Bencze, M and Kühn, Z, 'Constitutions, EU Law and Judicial Strategies in the Czech Republic, Hungary and Poland' (2010) 30 *Journal of Public Policy* 81

Maurer, A and Wessels, W (eds), *National Parliaments on their Ways to Europe: Losers or Latecomers?* (Nomos Verlag, 2001)

Mehta, PB, 'The Rise of Judicial Sovereignty' (2007) 18(2) *Journal of Democracy* 70

Meij, AWH, 'Circles of Coherence: On Unity of Case-Law in the Context of Globalisation' (2010) 6 *European Constitutional Law Review* 84

Michaels, R, 'Dreaming Law without a State: Scholarship on Autonomous International Arbitration as Utopian Literature' (2013) 1 *London Review of International Law* 35

Micklitz, HW, 'Divergente Ausgangsbedingungen des Verbraucherrechts in West und Ost' in H-W Micklitz (ed), *Rechtseinheit oder Rechtsvielfalt in Europa?* (Nomos, 1996)

——, 'Verbraucherschutz West versus Ost—Kompatibilisierungsmöglichkeiten in der Europäischen Gemeinschaft—Einige Vorüberlegungen' in H Heiss (ed), *Brückenschlag zwischen den Rechtskulturen des Ostseeraums* (Mohr Siebeck, 2001)

——, 'The Expulsion of the Concept of Protection from the Consumer Law and the Return of Social Elements in the Civil Law—A Bittersweet Polemic' (2012) 35(3) *Journal of Consumer Policy* 283

——, 'A Common Approach to the Enforcement of Unfair Commercial Practices and Unfair Con-tract Terms' in M v Boom, O Akseli and A Garde (eds), *Experiencing Unfair Commercial Practices: Impact, Enforcement Strategies and National Legal Systems. Markets and the Law* (Ashgate, 2014)

——, 'The (Un)-Systematics of (private) Law as an Element of European Legal Culture' in G Helleringer, K Purnhagen (eds), *Towards a European Legal Culture* (Hart Publishing/ Nomos, 2014)

—— and Roethe, TH, *Produktsicherheit und Marktüberwachung im Ostseeraum— Rechtsrahmen und Vollzugspraxis* (Nomos, 2008)

Miheljak, V and Toš, N, 'The Slovenian Way to Democracy and Sovereignty' in N Toš and KH Muller (eds), *Political Faces of Slovenia* (FDV, 2005)

Milardović, A, 'Elite Groups in the Waves of the Democratization and Lustrations' in V Dvořáková and A Milardović (ed), *Lustration and Consolidation of Democracy and the Rule of Law in Central and Eastern Europe* (Political Science Research Centre Zagreb, 2007)

Mohay, A, 'Decision 143/2010 of the Constitutional Court of the Republic of Hungary regarding the Constitutionality of Act CLXVIII of 2007 Promulgating the Lisbon Treaty' (2012) 6 *Vienna Journal of International Constitutional Law* 301

Möllers, C, 'German Federal Constitutional Court: Constitutional Ultra Vires Review of European Acts Only Under Exceptional Circumstances; Decision of 6 July 2010, 2 BvR 2661/06, Honeywell' (2011) 7(1) *European Constitutional Law Review* 161

Morawa, AHE and Topidi, K (eds), *Constitutional Evolution in Central and Eastern Europe: Expansion and Integration into the EU* (Ashgate, 2011)

Morgan, GG, *Soviet Administrative Legality: The Role of Attorney General's Office* (Stanford University Press, 1962)

Muller, JW, The Hungarian Tragedy (2011) 58(2) *Dissent* 5

Neudorf, L, 'Promoting Independent Justice in a Changing World' (2012) 12 *Human Rights Law Review* 107

Nicolaidis, K, 'The Idea of European Democracy' in J Dickson and P Eleftheriadis (eds), *The Philosophical Foundations of European Union Law* (Oxford University Press, 2012)

Nowak, MT et al, *National Judges as European Union Judges. Knowledge, Experience and Attitudes of Lower Court Judges in Germany and the Netherlands* (Eleven International Publishing, 2011)

O'Keeffe, D and Bavasso, A, *Judicial Review in European Union Law: Liber Amicorum in Honour of Lord Slynn of Hadley* (Kluwer Law International, 2000)

Paczolay, P, 'The New Hungarian Constitutional State: Challenges and Perspectives' in A Dick Howard (ed), *Constitution Making in Eastern Europe* (Woodrow Wilson Center Press, 1993)

Parau, C, 'The Drive for Judicial Supremacy' in A Seibert-Fohr (ed), *Judicial Independence in Transition* (Springer, 2012)

Parga, AH, 'Bosphorus v Ireland and the Protection of Fundamental Rights in Europe' (2006) 31 *European Law Review* 251

Perju, V, 'Constitutional Transplants, Borrowing and Migration' in M Rosenfeld, A Sajó (eds), *The Oxford Handbook of Comparative Constitutional Law* (Oxford University Press, 2013)

Pernice, I, 'Multilevel Constitutionalism and the Treaty of Amsterdam, European Constitution Making Revisited' (1999) 36 *Common Market Law Review* 703

Piana, D, 'The Power Knocks at the Courts' Back Door: Two Waves of Postcommunist Judicial Reforms' (2006) 42(6) *Comparative Political Studies* 816

——, *Judicial Accountabilities in New Europe: From Rule of Law to Quality of Justice* (Ashgate, 2010)

Picardi, N, 'La Ministère de la Justice et les autres modèles d'administration de la justice en Europe' in P Abravanel et al (eds), *L'indipendenza della giustizia, Oggi Judicial— Independence today: Liber Amicorum In Onore di Giovanni E Longo* (Guiffrè, 1999)

Piqani, D, 'Constitutional Courts in Central and Eastern Europe and Their Attitude towards European Integration' (2007) 2 *European Journal of Legal Studies* 1

——, 'Arguments for a Holistic Approach in European Constitutionalism: What Role for National Institutions in Avoiding Constitutional Conflicts between National Constitutions and EU Law' (2012) 8 *European Constitutional Law Review* 493

Piris, JC, *The Lisbon Treaty: A Legal and Political Analysis* (Cambridge University Press, 2010)

Pokol, B, 'Judicial Power and Democratization in Eastern Europe' in *Europeanization and Democratisation: The Southern European Experience and the Perspective for the New Member States of the Enlarged Europe* (European Press Academic Publishing, 2005)

Pollicino, O, 'The New Relationship between National and the European Courts after the Enlargement of Europe: Towards a Unitary Theory of Jurisprudential Supranational Law?' (2010) 29 *Yearbook of European Law* 65

Półtorak, N, 'Europeanisation of Public Law as a Consequence of the Principle of Effectiveness of European Union Law' in K Wojtyczek (eds), *Public Law: Twenty Years After, The Public Law After 1989 from the Polish Perspective* (European Public Law Series, 2012)

——, 'State Liability for Violation of European Union Law—a Polish Perspective' (2012) 13 *ERA Forum* 185

Posner, R, 'Pragmatic Adjudication' (1996) 18 *Cardozo Law Review* 1

——, *How Judges Think* (Harvard University Press, 2008)

Prechal, S, 'Community Law in National Courts: The Lesson from Van Schijndel' (1998) 35 *Common Market Law Review* 681

—— and Widdershoven, R, 'Redefining the Relationship between "Rewe-effectiveness" and Effective Judicial Protection' (2011) 4 *Review of European Administrative Law* 31

Pridham, G, 'European Party Cooperation and Post-Communist Politics' in A Szczerbiak and P Taggart (eds), *Opposing Europe?: The Comparative Party Politics of Euroscepticism: Volume 2* (Oxford University Press, 2008)

Procházka, R, *Mission Accomplished: On Founding Constitutional Adjudication in Central Europe* (Central European University Press, 2002)

Raisz, A, 'Confronted with Direct Applicability of a Directive: The Hungarian Constitutional Court before Challenges' (2007) 4 *Miskolc Journal of International Law* 113

Reich, N, 'Transformation of Contract Law and Civil Justice in the New EU Member Countries: The Example of the Baltic States, Hungary and Poland' in F Cafaggi (ed), *The Institutional Framework of European Private Law* (Oxford University Press, 2006)

Rico, G, 'The 2010 Regional Election in Catalonia: A Multilevel Account in an Age of Economic Crisis' (2012) 17(2) *South European Society and Politics* 217

Ritleng, D, 'Cours constitutionnelles nationales et renvoi préjudiciel' in *Mélanges en l'honneur du Professeur Joël Moliner* (LGDJ, 2012)

Rodin, S, 'Discourse and Authority in European and Post-Communist Legal Culture' (2005) 1 *Croatian Yearbook of European Law* 12

Roethe, TH, *Arbeiten wie bei Honecker, Leben wie bei Kohl* (Eichborn, 1994)

Rosas, A, 'The Applicability of the EU Charter of Fundamental Rights at National Level' (2013) *European Yearbook on Human Rights* 97

Rosenfeld, M, *The Identity of the Constitutional Subject: Selfhood, Citizenship, Culture, and Community* (Routledge, 2009)

Rüthers, B, *Die unbegrenzte Auslegung: Zum Wandel der Privatrechtsordnung im Nationalsozialismus* (Mohr Siebeck, 1968)

——, 'Recht als Waffe des Unrechts - Juristische Instrumente im Dienst des NS Rassenwahns' [1988] *Neue juristische Wochenschrift* 2825

Ruffer, E, 'The Quest of the Lisbon Treaty in the Czech Republic and Some of the Changes It Introduces in EU Primary Law' (2010) 1 *Czech Yearbook of International Law* 23

Ruffert, M, 'Rights and Remedies in European Community Law: A Comparative View' (1997) 34 *Common Market Law Review* 307

Rupnik, J and Zielonka, J, 'The State of Democracy 20 Years On: Domestic and External Factors' (2013) 27 *East European Politics & Societies* 3

Sadurski, W, *Rights before Courts: A Study of Constitutional Courts in Post-communist States of Central and Eastern Europe* (Springer, 2005)

——, 'European Constitutional Identity?' (2006) 37 *Sydney Law School Legal Studies Research Paper* 1

——, '"So Lange Chapter 3": Constitutional Courts in Central Europe—Democracy—European Union' (2006) 40 *European University Institute Working Papers* 1

——, 'Partnering with Strasbourg: Constitutionalisation of the European Court of Human Rights, the Accession of Central and East European States to the Council of Europe, and the Idea of Pilot Judgements' (2009) 3 *Human Rights Law Review* 409

——, *Constitutionalism and the Enlargement of Europe* (Oxford University Press, 2010)

——, 'Judicial Review in Central and Eastern Europe: Rationales or Rationalizations?' (2010) 42 *Israel Law Review* 500

——, 'Constitutional Courts in Transition Processes: Legitimacy and Democratization' (2011) 53 *Sydney Law School Legal Studies Research Paper*

Safjan, M, 'Politics and Constitutional Courts. A Judge's Personal Perspective' (2008) 10 *European University Institute Working Papers* 1

——, 'Fields of Application of the Charter of Fundamental Rights and Constitutional Dialogues in the European Union' (2014) 2 *European University Institute Center for Judicial Cooperation DL* 1

Sajó, A, 'Learning Co-operative Constitutionalism the Hard Way: the Hungarian Constitutional Court Shying Away from EU Supremacy?' (2004) (3) *Zeitschrift für Staats- und Europawissenschaften* 351

—— and Losonci, V, 'Rule by Law in the East Central Europe: Is the Emperor's New Suit a Straightjacket?' in D Greenberg et al (eds), *Constitutionalism and Democracy—Transitions in the Contemporary World* (Oxford University Press, 1993)

Salamon, L, 'Debates Surrounding the Concepts of the New Constitution' (2011) 3 *Hungarian Review* 1522

Scharpf, FW, *Governing in Europe: Effective or Democratic* (Oxford University Press, 1999)

——, 'The Joint-Decision Trap Revisited' (2006) 44 *Journal of Common Market Studies* 548

——, 'Legitimacy in the Multilevel European Polity' (2009) 1 *European Political Science Review* 173

Schauer, F, 'Formalism' (1988) 97 *Yale Law Journal* 509

——, *Profiles, Probabilities, and Stereotypes* (Harvard University Press, 2006)

——, 'Formalism: Legal, Constitutional, Judicial' in GA Caldeira, RD Kelemen and KE Whittington (eds), *The Oxford Handbook of Law and Politics* (Oxford University Press, 2008)

Schönfelder, B, 'Judicial Independence in Bulgaria: A Tale of Splendour and Misery' (2005) 57 *Europe-Asia Studies* 1

Schreuer, C, 'The Waning of the Sovereign State: Towards a New Paradigm of International Law?' (1993) 4 *European Journal of International Law* 447

Schwarze, J, 'The Role of the European Court of Justice in Shaping Legal Standards for Administrative Action in the Member States. A Comparative Perspective' in D O'Keeffe and A Bavasso (eds), *Judicial Review in European Union Law* (Kluwer Law International, 2000)

——, *European Administrative Law* (Sweet and Maxwell, 2006)

Seibert-Fohr, A, 'Judicial Independence in European Union Accessions: The Emergence of a European Basic Principle' (2009) 52 *German Yearbook of International Law* 405

——, 'European Perspective on the Rule of Law and Independent Courts' (2012) 20 *Journal für Rechtspolitik* 161

Segal, JA, 'Judicial Behaviour' in KE Whittington, RD Kelemen and GA Caldeira (eds), *The Oxford Handbook of Law and Politics* (Oxford University Press, 2008)

Serena Rossi, L, 'Corte costituzionale (Italian Constitutional Court): Decisions 348 and 349/2007 of 22 October 2007, and 102 and 103/2008, of 12 February 2008' (2009) 46 *Common Market Law Review* 319

Shetreet, S, 'The Discretionary Power of the Judge—General Report; Part II' in M Storme and B Hess (eds), *The Discretionary Power of the Judge: Limits and Control* (Kluwer Law International, 2003)

Siltala, R, *A Theory of Precedent. From Analytical Positivism to a Post-Analytical Philosophy of Law* (Hart Publishing, 2000)

Slaughter, AM, 'A Typology of Transjudicial Communication' (1994) 29 *University of Richmond Law Review* 99

——, 'The Real New World Order' (1997) *Foreign Affairs* 183

Smilov, D, 'EU Enlargement and the Constitutional Principle of Judicial Independence' in A Czarnota, M Krygier and W Sadurski (eds), *Spreading Democracy and the Rule of Law: The Impact of EU Enlargement on the Rule of Law, Democracy, and Constitutionalism in Post-communist Legal Orders* (Springer, 2006)

Smith, GB, 'The Soviet Procuracy and the Supervision of Administration' (1980) 28(4) *The American Journal of Comparative Law* 700

Soininen, N, 'Easy Cases and Objective Interpretation' in J Husa and M van Hoecke (eds), *Objectivity in Law and Legal Reasoning* (Hart Publishing, 2013)

Solomon, PH, 'Courts and Judges in Authoritarian Regimes' (2007) 60 *World Politics* 122

——, 'Authoritarian Legality and Informal Practices: Judges, Lawyers and the State in Russia and China' (2010) 43 *Communist and Post-communist Studies* 351

Sonnevend, P, Jakab, A and Csink, L, 'The Constitution as an Instrument of Everyday Party Politics—The Basic Law of Hungary' in A von Bogdandy and P Sonnevend (eds), *Constitutional Crisis in the European Constitutional Area: Theory, Law and Politics in Hungary and Romania* (Hart Publishing, 2014)

Spiller, PT and Gely, R, 'Strategic Judicial Decision-making' in KE Whittington, RD Kelemen and GA Caldeira (eds), *The Oxford Handbook of Law and Politics* (Oxford University Press, 2008)

Stein, E, 'Lawyers, Judges, and the Making of a Transnational Constitution' (1981) 75 *American Journal of International Law* 1

Stone Sweet, A, 'The Juridical Coup d'État and the Problem of Authority' (2007) 8 *German Law Journal* 915

——, 'A Cosmopolitan Legal Order: Constitutional Pluralism and Rights Adjudication in Europe' (2012) 1 *Journal of Global Constitutionalism* 53

Stone Sweet, A and Brunell, T, 'European Court and the National Courts: A Statistical Analysis of Preliminary References, 1961–95' (1998) 5 *Journal of European Public Policy* 66

Stone, M, 'Formalism' in J Coleman and S Shapiro (eds), *The Oxford Handbook of Jurisprudence and Philosophy of Law* (Oxford University Press, 2002)

Storskrubb, E, 'What Changes Will European Harmonization Bring' in J Walker and O Chase (eds), *Common Law, Civil Law and Future of Categories* (Lexis Nexis Canada, 2010)

Summers, RS, 'The Formal Character of Law' (1992) 51 *Cambridge Law Journal* 242

——, *Form and Function in a Legal System: A General Study* (Cambridge University Press, 2006)

Szabó, M, 'Change of Legal Thought in Hungary 1990–2005' in A Jakab, P Takács and AF Tatham (eds), *The Transformation of the Hungarian Legal Order 1985–2005* (Kluwer Law International, 2007)

Taruffo, M and La Torre, M, 'Precedent in Italy' in DN MacCormick and RS Summers (eds), *Interpreting Precedents* (Ashgate, 1997)

Tatham, AF, 'Constitutional Judiciary in Central Europe and the Europe Agreement: Decision 30/1998 (VI.25) AB of the Hungarian Constitutional Court' (1999) 48 *International and Comparative Law Quarterly* 913

——, '"Don't Mention Divorce at the Wedding, Darling!": EU Accession and Withdrawal after Lisbon' in A Biondi, P Eeckhout and S Ripley (eds), *EU Law after Lisbon* (Oxford University Press, 2012)

——, 'The Impact of Training and Language Competence on Judicial Application of EU Law in Hungary' (2012) 18 *European Law Journal* 577

——, *Central European Constitutional Courts in the Face of EU Membership: The Influence of the German Model of Integration in Hungary and Poland* (Martinus Nijhoff, 2013)

——, '"The Taming of the Judicial Shrew": Changes to the Constitutional Court's Role and Powers under the Fundamental Law' in M Dani and R Toniatti (eds), *The Partisan Constitution. The Fundamental Law of Hungary and European Constitutional Culture* (Wolf Legal Publishers, 2014)

Tent, JF, *Mission on the Rhine: 'Reeducation' and Denazification in American-Occupied Germany* (Chicago University Press, 1982)

Thym, D, 'In the Name of Sovereign Statehood: A Critical Introduction to the Lisbon Judgement of the German Constitutional Court' (2009) 46 *Common Market Law Review* 1795

Tindemans, L, 'Dreams Come True, Gradually: The Tindemans Report a Quarter of a Century on' in M Westlake (ed), *The European Union beyond Amsterdam: New Concepts of European Integration* (Routledge, 1998)

Tóth, GA (ed), *Constitution for a Disunited Nation: on Hungary's 2011 Fundamental Law* (Central European University Press, 2012)

Tridimas, T, *The General Principles of EU Law* (Oxford University Press, 2006)

Trocker, N and Varano, V, 'Concluding Remarks' in N Trocker and V Varano (eds), *The Reforms of Civil Procedure in Comparative Perspective* (Giappichelli Editore, 2005)

Tsebelis, G, 'Decision Making in Political Systems: Veto Players in Presidentialism, Parliamentarism, Multicameralism and Multipartyism' (1995) 25 *British Journal of Political Science* 289

Tuori, K, *Lawyers and Savages: Ancient History and Legal Realism in the Making of Legal Anthropology* (Routledge, 2014)

Uitz, R, *Constitutions, Courts, and History: Historical Narratives in Constitutional Adjudication* (Central European University Press, 2005)

Ulč, O, *Malá doznání okresního soudce* (68 Publishers, 1974)

Unger, R, *What Should Legal Analysis Become* (Verso, 1996)

Uzelac, A, 'Accelerating Civil Proceedings in Croatia—A History of Attempts to Improve the Efficiency of Civil Litigation' in RCH van Rhee (ed), *The Law's Delay—Essays on Undue Delay in Civil Litigation* (Intersentia, 2004)

——, 'Survival of the Third Legal Tradition?' (2010) 49 *Supreme Court Law Review* 377

Van der Schyff, E, 'The Constitutional Relationship between the European Union and its Member States: The Role of National Identity in Article 4(2) TEU' (2013) 37 *European Law Review* 563

Van der Wilt, H, 'On the Hierarchy between Extradition and Human Rights' in E De Wet and J Vidmar (eds), *Hierarchy in International Law: The Place of Human Rights* (Oxford University Press, 2012)

Van Gerven, W, 'Of Rights, Remedies and Procedures' (2000) 37 *Common Market Law Review* 501

Varga, I, 'Foreign Influences on Hungarian Civil Procedure' in M Deguchi and M Storme (eds), *The Reception and Transmission of Civil Procedural Law in the Global Society* (Maklu, 2008)

Varga, C, *Transition to Rule of Law: On the Democratic Transformation in Hungary* (Faculty of Law of Loránd Eötvös University and of the Institute for Legal Studies of the Hungarian Academy of Sciences, 1995)

Varju, M, 'On the Constitutional Issues of EU Membership and the Interplay between the ECHR and Domestic Constitutional Law Concerning the Right of Assembly and Freedom of Expression' (2009) 15 *European Public Law* 295

——, 'The Judicial Reception of EU Law' in M Varju and E Varnay (eds), *The Law of the European Union in Hungary* (HVG-Orac, 2014)

—— and Fazekas, F, 'The Reception of European Union Law in Hungary: The Constitutional Court and the Hungarian Judiciary' (2011) 48 *Common Market Law Review* 1945

Várnay, E and Tatham, AF, 'A New Step on the Long Way—How to Find the Proper Place for Community Law in the Hungarian Legal Order?' (2006) 3 *Miskolc Journal of International Law* 76

Vashkevich, A, 'Judicial Independence in the Republic of Belarus' in A Seibert-Fohr (ed), *Judicial Independence in Transition* (Springer, 2012)

Vékás, L, 'Models in Central-Eastern European Codes' in S Grundmann and M Schauer (eds), *The Architecture of European Codes and Contract law* (Kluwer Law International, 2006)

Vermeule, A, *Judging Under Uncertainty: An Institutional Theory of Legal Interpretation* (Harvard University Press, 2006)

——, 'The Judiciary Is A They, Not An It: Interpretive Theory and the Fallacy Of Division' (2009) 14 *Journal of Contemporary Legal Issues* 549

Voermans, W and Albers, P, *Councils for the Judiciary in EU Countries* (European Commission for the Efficiency of Justice, Council of Europe 2003)

Volcansek, MML, 'Judicial Selection in Italy: A Civil Service Model with Partisan Results' in K Malleson and PR Russell (eds), *Appointing Judges in an Age of Judicial Power: Critical Perspectives from around the World* (University of Toronto Press, 2006)

Von Bogdandy, A, 'Globalization and Europe: How to Square Democracy, Globalization, and International Law' (2004) 15 *European Journal of International Law* 885

—— and Schill, S, 'Overcoming Absolute Primacy: Respect for National Identity under the Lisbon Treaty' (2011) 48 *Common Market Law Review* 1417

——, et al, 'Reverse Solange—Protecting the Essence of Fundamental Rights against EU Member States' (2012) 49 *Common Market Law Review* 489

—— and Ioannidis, M, 'Systemic Deficiency in the Rule of Law: What it is, What has been done, What can be done' (2014) 51 *Common Market Law Review* 59

Waldron, J, 'Dirty Little Secret' (1998) 98 *Columbia Law Review* 510

——, 'Is the Rule of Law an Essentially Contested Concept?' (2002) 21 *Law and Philosophy* 137

Walker, N, 'The Idea of Constitutional Pluralism' (2002) 65 *Modern Law Review* 317

——, 'Late Sovereignty in the European Union' in N Walker (ed), *Sovereignty in Transition* (Hart Publishing, 2003)

——, 'Beyond Boundary Disputes and Basic Grids. Mapping the Global Disorder of Normative Orders' (2008) 6 *International Journal of Constitutional Law* 373

Wallace, W, 'Europe after the Cold War: Interstate Order or Post Sovereign Regional System?' (1999) 25(5) *Review of International Studies* 201

Ward, I, 'A Charmed Spectacle: England and its Constitutional Imagination' (2000) 22 *Liverpool Law Review* 235

Weber, M, *Max Weber on Law in Economy and Society* (Harvard University Press, 1969)

Weiler, JHH, 'A Quiet Revolution: The European Court of Justice and its Interlocutors' (1994) 26 *Comparative Political Studies* 510

——, 'Does Europe Need a Constitution? Demos, Telos and the German Maastricht Decision' (1995) 1(3) *European Law Journal* 219

——, 'The Reformation of European Constitutionalism' (1997) 35(1) *Journal of Common Market Studies* 97

——, 'The Essential (and would-be Essential) Jurisprudence of the European Court of Justice: Lights and Shadows too' in I Pernice, J Kokott and C Saunders (eds), *The Future of the European Judicial System in a Comparative Perspective* (Nomos, 2005)

——, 'The Lisbon Urteil and the Fast Food Culture: Editorial' (2009) 20 *European Journal of International Law* 505

Weinrib, EJ, *The Idea of Private Law* (Oxford University Press, 2012)

Weitz, K, 'Die Bedeutung der Rezeption für die Entwicklung des polnischen Zivilprozessrechts' (2010) 27 *Ritsumeikan Law Review* 141

Wendel, M, 'Comparative Reasoning and the Making of a Common Constitutional Law: EU-related Decisions of National Constitutional Courts in a Transnational Perspective' (2013) 11(4) *International Journal of Constitutional Law* 981

White, BT, 'Rotten to the Core: Project Capture and the Failure of Judicial Reform in Mongolia' (2009) 4 *East Asia Law Reform* 209

Wieacker, F, 'Foundations of European Legal Culture' (1990) 38 *The American Journal of Comparative Law* 1

Wójtowicz, K, *Sądy konstytucyjne wobec prawa Unii Europejskiej* (Wydawnictwo Trybunału Konstytucyjnego, 2012)

Wróbel, A, 'Zasady ogólne (podstawowe) prawa Unii Europejskiej' in A Wróbel (ed), *Stosowanie prawa Unii Europejskiej przez sądy* (Zakamycze, 2005)

Wróblewski, J, *The Judicial Application of Law* (Kluwer Law International, 1992)

Wyrzykowski, M, 'When Sovereignty Means so Much: The Concept(s) of Sovereignty, European Union Membership and the Interpretation of the Constitution of the Republic of Poland' in Court of Justice of the European Union (ed), *The Court of Justice and the construction of Europe/La Cour de Justice et la construction de l'Europe* (Springer, 2013)

Yagou, A, 'Metamorphoses of Formalism: National Identity as a Recurrent Theme of Design in Greece' (2007) 20 *Journal of Design History* 145

Zalar, B, 'Administrative Workload for Judges: A Dangerous Approach to Case-Flow Management' in B Zalar (ed), *Five Challenges for European Courts: The Experiences of German and Slovenian Courts* (Supreme Court of the Republic of Slovenia, Slovenian Association of Judges, 2004)

——, 'Basic Values, Judicial Dialogues and the Rule of Law in the Light of the Charter of Fundamental Rights of the European Union: Judges Playing by the Rules of the Game' (2013) 14 *ERA Forum* 319

Zbíral, R, 'Czech Constitutional Court, judgment of 31 January 2012, Pl. US 5/12. A Legal Revolution or Negligible Episode? Court of Justice Decision Proclaimed Ultra Vires' (2012) 49 *Common Market Law Review* 1475

Ziller, J, 'The Treaty of Lisbon: Constitutional Treaty, Episode II' in F Laursen (ed), *Designing the European Union: From Paris to Lisbon* (Palgrave, 2012)

Zirk-Sadowski, M, 'Transformation and Integration of Legal Cultures and Discourses—Poland' in W Sadurski et al (eds), *Spreading Democracy and the Rule of Law? The Impact of EU Enlargement on the Rule of Law, Democracy and Constitutionalism in Post-Communist Legal Orders* (Springer, 2006)

Zuckerman, A, 'Court Control and Party Compliance—The Quest for Effective Litigation Management' in N Trocker and V Varano (eds), *The Reforms of Civil Procedure in Comparative Perspective* (Giappichelli Editore, 2005)

Zweigert, K and Kötz, H, *Introduction to Comparative Law* (Oxford University Press, 1998)

INDEX

*Page references in **bold** indicate information in tables.*